D1560971

Praise for *Indo-European Language and Culture*

"Ben Fortson's book is the best existing introduction to Indo-European linguistics: up-to-date and comprehensive, accessible without being oversimplified. Students and interested laypersons will find it indispensable."
Don Ringe, University of Pennsylvania

"Fortson's *Introduction* continues to be the textbook of choice for introductory Indo-European. In its presentation of both fact and theory, it is a marvel of accuracy, completeness, and sound judgment."
Brent Vine, UCLA

Praise for the Previous Edition:

"Superb . . . [Fortson's] short general discussions of the histories and ecologies of the individual languages are the best I have ever read."
Recensiones – Salesianum, 2008

"I would like to conclude by stressing that this is an excellent textbook. I have taught from it, and the students in my class not only learned a great deal from it, they also seemed to enjoy the book almost as much as I did."
Bryn Mawr Classical Review

"Finally, there is a reliable, engaging and accessible presentation of the communis opinio. And there are even exercises! . . . Fortson has produced an excellent book that fulfills its goals admirably. I hope it will inspire a renaissance of Indo-European linguistics in English speaking countries."
Journal of the American Oriental Society

Blackwell Textbooks in Linguistics

The books included in this series provide comprehensive accounts of some of the most central and most rapidly developing areas of research in linguistics. Intended primarily for introductory and post-introductory students, they include exercises, discussion points and suggestions for further reading.

1	Liliane Haegeman	*Introduction to Government and Binding Theory* (Second Edition)
2	Andrew Spencer	*Morphological Theory*
3	Helen Goodluck	*Language Acquisition*
4	Ronald Wardhaugh	*An Introduction to Sociolinguistics* (Fifth Edition)
5	Martin Atkinson	*Children's Syntax*
6	Diane Blakemore	*Understanding Utterances*
7	Michael Kenstowicz	*Phonology in Generative Grammar*
8	Deborah Schiffrin	*Approaches to Discourse*
9	John Clark and Colin Yallop and Janet Fletcher	*An Introduction to Phonetics and Phonology* (Third Edition)
10	Natsuko Tsujimura	*An Introduction to Japanese Linguistics* (Second Edition)
11	Robert D. Borsley	*Modern Phrase Structure Grammar*
12	Nigel Fabb	*Linguistics and Literature*
13	Irene Heim and Angelika Kratzer	*Semantics in Generative Grammar*
14	Liliane Haegeman and Jacqueline Guéron	*English Grammar: A Generative Perspective*
15	Stephen Crain and Diane Lillo-Martin	*An Introduction to Linguistic Theory and Language Acquisition*
16	Joan Bresnan	*Lexical-Functional Syntax*
17	Barbara A. Fennell	*A History of English: A Sociolinguistic Approach*
18	Henry Rogers	*Writing Systems: A Linguistic Approach*
19	Benjamin W. Fortson IV	*Indo-European Language and Culture: An Introduction* (Second Edition)
20	Liliane Haegeman	*Thinking Syntactically: A guide to Argumentation and Analysis*
21	Mark Hale	*Historical Linguistics: Theory and Method*
22	Henning Reetz and Allard Jongman	*Phonetics: Transcription, Production, Acoustics and Perception*
23	Bruce Hayes	*Introductory Phonology*

Indo-European Language and Culture

An Introduction

Second edition

Benjamin W. Fortson IV

WILEY-BLACKWELL
A John Wiley & Sons, Ltd., Publication

This second edition first published 2010
© 2010 Benjamin W. Fortson IV

Edition history: Blackwell Publishing Ltd (1, 2004)

Blackwell Publishing was acquired by John Wiley & Sons in February 2007. Blackwell's publishing program has been merged with Wiley's global Scientific, Technical, and Medical business to form Wiley-Blackwell.

Registered Office
John Wiley & Sons Ltd, The Atrium, Southern Gate, Chichester, West Sussex, PO19 8SQ, United Kingdom

Editorial Offices
350 Main Street, Malden, MA 02148-5020, USA
9600 Garsington Road, Oxford, OX4 2DQ, UK
The Atrium, Southern Gate, Chichester, West Sussex, PO19 8SQ, UK

For details of our global editorial offices, for customer services, and for information about how to apply for permission to reuse the copyright material in this book please see our website at www.wiley.com/wiley-blackwell.

The right of Benjamin W. Fortson IV to be identified as the author of this work has been asserted in accordance with the Copyright, Designs and Patents Act 1988.

All rights reserved. No part of this publication may be reproduced, stored in a retrieval system, or transmitted, in any form or by any means, electronic, mechanical, photocopying, recording or otherwise, except as permitted by the UK Copyright, Designs and Patents Act 1988, without the prior permission of the publisher.

Wiley also publishes its books in a variety of electronic formats. Some content that appears in print may not be available in electronic books.

Designations used by companies to distinguish their products are often claimed as trademarks. All brand names and product names used in this book are trade names, service marks, trademarks or registered trademarks of their respective owners. The publisher is not associated with any product or vendor mentioned in this book. This publication is designed to provide accurate and authoritative information in regard to the subject matter covered. It is sold on the understanding that the publisher is not engaged in rendering professional services. If professional advice or other expert assistance is required, the services of a competent professional should be sought.

Library of Congress Cataloging-in-Publication Data

Fortson, Benjamin W.
Indo-european language and culture : an introduction / Benjamin W. Fortson. — 2nd ed.
p. cm. — (Blackwell textbooks in linguistics ; 19)
Includes bibliographical references and index.
ISBN 978-1-4051-8895-1 (hardcover : alk. paper) — ISBN 978-1-4051-8896-8 (pbk. : alk. paper) 1. Indo-European languages. 2. Indo-Europeans. I. Title.
P561.F67 2009
410—dc22

2008051179

A catalogue record for this book is available from the British Library.

Set in 10/12pt Sabon by Graphicraft Limited, Hong Kong
Printed and bound by CPI Group (UK) Ltd, Croydon, CR0 4YY

C9781405188951_060924

Contents

List of Illustrations

Preface

In spite of its venerable status as one of the oldest and most successful disciplines in linguistics, the comparative study of the Indo-European family has hitherto lacked an introductory textbook, or an introductory book of any kind appropriate for classroom use or for an intelligent layperson with linguistic interests but without specialized training. The few introductory books on the market do have virtues, but in all cases known to me these virtues are compromised, sometimes severely, as by idiosyncratic or minority views masquerading as *communes opiniones*, by uneven coverage or omission of important topics, by out-of-date views or erroneous material, or by excessively technical information. None is a textbook.

Some of the features an Indo-European textbook should have are rather obvious. It should be up-to-date and, to the extent possible, present non-controversial views. It should not overwhelm the reader with detail, but also be comprehensive enough to satisfy the serious student at the beginning of his or her scholarly career. It should have copious exercises. Some other features an Indo-European textbook should have are less obvious (at least for some), but are in my view as essential as the preceding. It should not only cover phonology and morphology, but syntax as well, and incorporate relevant findings from generative linguistics where they are not limited to (or by) a particular (and quite likely evanescent) theoretical framework. Data should not be oversimplified or skewed by leaving out diacritics and other funny-looking symbols. There should be annotated text samples in all the ancient languages, and of a sufficient size to impart a real feel for the languages and to introduce readers to the practice and importance of philology. Basic information should be provided on the archaeological, cultural, and literary history of each branch. The modern languages should not be omitted from discussion. Finally, it should outline what we know about Proto-Indo-European culture and society.

These are the goals of the present work. If it falls short of any of them, hopefully it at least improves over other books currently available. It is designed for use with an instructor or for private consumption. It is assumed that the reader is interested in language and linguistic history, but no prior knowledge of linguistics or any older Indo-European language is necessary. Technical terminology is explained as needed, with a glossary appended for good measure.

Layout

Chapter 1 presents the tools of the trade and an overview of various basic issues that confront the researcher in the field. This is followed by a chapter on the reconstructed culture of the Proto-Indo-Europeans, which attempts an organized and comprehensive introductory synthesis of a kind that I do not believe I have seen elsewhere. As interest in the matters discussed here usually runs high, this chapter has been put toward the beginning of the book rather than at the end.

Chapters 3–8 provide a reasonably complete introduction to reconstructed Proto-Indo-European that serves not only as background for the subsequent chapters, but also as a solid basic reference grammar in its own right. Not all the material included here will be needed in an introductory class; it is modular enough that individual instructors (and readers) can choose to omit whatever sections they please.

Each of the remaining twelve chapters treats a particular branch of the family, proceeding in chronological order of attestation from oldest to most recent and concluding with a chapter on the fragmentarily attested languages of uncertain filiation. Indo-Iranian is split over two chapters. All the branches and languages are treated as equally as possible, and in essentially the same format; but no attempt was made to make each chapter slavishly conform to identical specifications. In a book of this kind, no branch's history can or should be treated exhaustively. The developments discussed are selective; the chapters are tailored to what is interesting and important for each branch or language. Unlike the chapters on reconstructed Proto-Indo-European grammar, these are intended more to get one's feet wet than to give an overview that covers everything equally. The material can be supplemented at will by instructors, and again the modular structure of these chapters allows easy skipping of unneeded information.

Importantly, no language was deemed too trivial for coverage. The reader's interest should be engaged, and his or her curiosity piqued, with regard to *all* the Indo-European languages. The notion that certain languages are not particularly useful for Indo-European linguistics is both counterproductive and sadly perpetuated by books that only grant passing mention to those languages. Albanian may not, it is true, provide us with as much information about the proto-language as Sanskrit, but it does tell us some useful things, and in any event has a maddeningly fascinating (or fascinatingly maddening) history that merits careful attention. It bears repeating that Indo-European comparative linguistics is not just concerned with reconstructing Proto-Indo-European; it also must account for the histories of all the languages of the family.

In addition to the requisite basic sound laws, etc., short discussions of topics are included that are intended to appeal to readers with some experience in the languages, or to interested readers without any such background. The Greek chapter, for example, has a section on Homeric philology. A few topics that might seem a bit off the beaten path are scattered throughout. For instance, a student of first-year Russian, while in the throes of wrestling with the syntax of the cardinal numerals, may have become curious about how this unusual system came to be; a short discussion of this in the section on Slavic is therefore included.

The Sample Texts and Other Features

The text samples are meant to give an idea of what the languages look like, and to impress the student with the importance of philology, whose methods and purpose are outlined in chapter 1. The texts are about a paragraph in length on average. It is to be hoped that exposure to good-sized text samples with philological commentary will inspire an interest not only in the languages themselves, but also in close textual and etymological analysis. Where possible I have chosen texts having literary and cultural interest; many are connected to discussions in chapter 2. The commentary is geared especially to the reader interested in learning a bit more: it provides word histories and comparanda, points out examples of developments covered in the chapter, and also adds notes on developments not met with in the chapter. Unless indicated otherwise, all translations are my own.

I decided to eschew the usual interlinear word-by-word analytical glosses that are otherwise standard in the linguistic literature; the commentary stands partly in lieu of them. The reason for doing this is perhaps unorthodox, but I believe sound: interlinear glosses distort one's perception of the aesthetics of a written language, which is not a trivial concern for a book such as this. The look of a language should never be underestimated as a tool for engaging a student's interest. The commentary at any rate usually makes it possible for students who seriously want to match each word of the original up with its translation to do so. (For some longer passages, however, and in some longer chapters, commentary could only be given selectively, due to limitations of space.)

This leads to one further point. Some who have written introductory materials on Indo-European have left out phonetic details, such as long marks and accents. Such simplification of the data renders all students a great disservice by selling the languages short. Someone likely to pick up a book such as this or to take an introductory Indo-European course will not be put off by unusual marks and symbols. Quite the opposite – they are likely to be *intrigued* by the peculiar look of the strange forms, and will discover in them an inviting mystery and beauty. The decision to ignore "details" such as accents should at any rate be left to the reader's discretion.

Each chapter closes with several additional sections. The "For Further Reading" sections provide brief commentary on the most important or prominent secondary literature; the full references (together with a few extra that are not discussed) are listed in the Bibliography preceding the Index. Devoting space to such commentary rather than to long bibliographical lists is more useful for this kind of book. The "For Review" sections list the main terms and concepts, and the "Exercises" that follow are designed both for review and for going beyond the material discussed in each chapter. Finally, starting in chapter 9, a short list of reconstructed roots or words in Proto-Indo-European is given, arranged by semantic category. How instructors choose to integrate these in with their course is left up to them.

Since few of the localities mentioned in the text will be familiar to most readers, illustrative maps are provided in each chapter on the branches as well as chapters 1 and 2. These were deemed to be the most important visual component of the book.

Chapter 1 also contains a diagram of the Indo-European family tree. Regrettably, cost and space limitations prohibited the inclusion of other planned illustrations, as of artifacts and ancient scripts; it is hoped that these can appear in a future edition.

Ann Arbor, May 2004

Preface to the Second Edition

The response to this book has been gratifyingly positive, and the appearance of over half a dozen published reviews, together with my own marginalia, has generated enough material for a revised edition. All errors that have come to my attention have been corrected; a significant number of extended sections have been reworked or added; and many smaller changes to style and content have been made throughout. In addition, sufficient funds were available this time to include the reproductions of inscriptions and scripts that could not appear the first time around. Do note, however, that since the space of only a few years separates this revision from the first edition, I did not undertake a complete and systematic overhaul of the entire book; as a result, many chapters have only been lightly touched and must still await a thorough updating.

For reference's sake I shall briefly highlight some of the more substantial changes to the content. Newly added are discussions of the "trimoraic" long vowels in Germanic and Balto-Slavic; a Hieroglyphic Luvian text sample in chapter 9; and coverage of the Balto-Slavic accentual system and a description of the nominal accent classes. I have heavily revised the discussion of the PIE accent-ablaut classes, especially with regard to root nouns; expanded the discussion of the middle; greatly expanded the material on Middle and Modern Armenian; and added several pages of new and revised material to the Iranian, Balto-Slavic, and especially the Albanian chapters. Thirty new numbered sections have been added in all.

The first decade of the new millennium has seen a surprising bumper crop of introductory books on Indo-European in English. Aside from my own book and Michael Meier-Brügger's *Indo-European Linguistics* (translated from German), there have now also appeared J. P. Mallory and D. Q. Adams's *The Oxford Introduction to Proto-Indo-European and the Proto-Indo-European World* (Oxford University Press, 2006), Eva Tichy's *A Survey of Proto-Indo-European* (Hempen, 2006; translated from German), and James Clackson's *Indo-European Linguistics: An Introduction* (Cambridge University Press, 2007). The appearance of all these works is a testament to the vitality of the field, as is the fact that their aims and approaches are quite different from my own in many respects. Students using this book should be encouraged to browse around in these others; when they discover a difference in opinion, their curiosity will be piqued, and their intellectual journey can then begin in earnest.

Ann Arbor, May 2008

Acknowledgments

I have received the invaluable assistance of many colleagues, students, and friends since I conceived the idea of writing this textbook half a decade ago. Jay Jasanoff and Brent Vine used earlier drafts in their introductory Indo-European courses at Harvard and UCLA and provided extraordinarily helpful and detailed comments, corrections, and suggestions on the entire manuscript. I deeply appreciate the time and effort they both gave so generously to making this a better book.

I have been extremely fortunate to benefit from many others' interest and input as well. Raimo Anttila, Lisi Oliver, and Timothy Pulju also used earlier drafts in their courses at UCLA, LSU, and Dartmouth, respectively. Tim read through the whole manuscript and saved me from quite a few mistakes. Lisi engaged her students in writing reviews of the book, which generated much useful input at an early stage and guided me to a better presentation of the material. My own students over several years of teaching, especially in my Indo-European course at the Harvard Extension School, caught errors, made important suggestions, and – perhaps most importantly – convinced me that the project was both workable and worthwhile, and that my organizational and presentational decisions were on the whole satisfactory. I would like to single out in particular Valerie Goodspeed, Matthew Harrington, William Heess, Ilya Lapshin, Robert Maher, Keith Plaster, and William Waters for their helpful comments and criticisms.

Many other colleagues and friends improved the book by their careful reading and valuable input, and provided very helpful critiques of individual chapters or larger portions of the work: Kelly Askew, Don Cameron, Steve Dworkin, Simon Eckley, Joseph Eska, Michael Flier, Mark Hale, Joseph Harris, Richard Janko, Robert Kyes, J. P. Mallory, H. Craig Melchert, Alan Nussbaum, Hugh Olmsted, Marc Pierce, P. Oktor Skjærvø, Bert Vaux, Aurelijus Vijūnas, Rex Wallace, and Calvert Watkins. To Cal I also owe some innovative organizational suggestions that I believe have enhanced the book's readability and interest. All of the people above not only provided material contributions in the form of corrections and so forth, but were unflagging in their encouragement and enthusiasm for this project. Writing this textbook has mostly been its own reward, but it has meant a great deal that so many people that I look up to have been so supportive and positive in their assessment. At the University of Michigan I was lucky enough to have a recently graduated Senior, Dan Brooks, volunteer to read the whole manuscript, work through all the exercises, and assist me in proofreading and fact-checking; his keen attention caught all manner of infelicities that had escaped others. I was able to pay Dan for his services with a generous subvention from the Block Funding Initiative of the College of Literature, Science, and the Arts at the University of Michigan.

Had I not been initially contacted by Tami Kaplan (then at Blackwell) and encouraged to submit a very rough-and-ready chapter of the manuscript, I am sure the book would still lie unfinished and unpublished to this day. I have Tami to thank for seeing it through the approval process, and Sarah Coleman, my editor at Blackwell, receives my gratitude for so ably overseeing the book's progression from submitted manuscript to published volume. In a day when computerized typesetting has too often fallen short of the exacting aesthetic requirements of good Indo-European publications, I wish to shine a most grateful spotlight on the superb typographical skills of Graphicraft Limited, whose eye-winning work graces every page. To Chartwell Illustrators and their careful attention to cartographic detail I owe the conversion of even my most involved instructions into all the highly readable maps in the book. And without the careful copy-editing by Margaret Aherne, numerous errors and inconsistencies would still remain in every chapter; to her I am deeply indebted for her diligence, eagle eyes, and patience.

My family has given me great encouragement throughout this long process. I thank my mother for her unflagging support and positive remarks on the manuscript, and my father for his enthusiasm and infectious eagerness to see the finished product. For all the happiness and support that Kelly and Christopher have brought me at every stage of this work, and for so much else besides, I am more grateful than words can express.

As often as I could, I took the advice of all these good people I have mentioned, and am alone responsible for whatever errors and infelicities remain.

Additional Acknowledgments for the Second Edition

Most of the improvements in this edition I owe to the careful and critical reading by those whose reviews came to my attention: Gary Holland, Brian Joseph, Jared Klein, Manfred Mayrhofer, Lisi Oliver, Donald Reindl, Zsolt Simon, Eva Tichy, and Michael Weiss. I am additionally indebted to several of them for passing on to me other suggestions and corrections beyond what appeared in print, and for patiently enduring a host of follow-up questions and email exchanges. Only a vanishingly few of their suggestions could not be adequately encompassed within the scope of my revisions. Above all, I hope that the revised product does the job as satisfactorily as its predecessor.

This revision would not have seen the light of day without the efforts of Danielle Descoteaux at Blackwell, who originally approached me about writing it, and my faithful copy-editor Margaret Aherne, with whom I was lucky to be able to work once more. For advice about various miscellaneous items I wish to thank again Michael Flier, Joe Harris, Stephanie Jamison, Jay Jasanoff, Craig Melchert, Marc Pierce, Oktor Skjærvø, Bert Vaux, Brent Vine, and Rex Wallace, as well as Brian Joseph and Gernot Windfuhr. For their valuable comments and suggestions on Chapter 19 I am indebted to Eric Hamp and Joachim Matzinger.

Guide to the Reader

A. Abbreviations

abl.	ablative	masc.	masculine
accus., acc.	accusative	ME	Middle English
act.	active	Mod.	Modern
adj.	adjective	neut.	neuter
Alb.	Albanian	nomin., nom.	nominative
Anat.	Anatolian	Norw.	Norwegian
aor.	aorist	OAv.	Old Avestan
Arm.	Armenian	OCS	Old Church Slavonic
Av.	Avestan	OE	Old English
B.-Sl.	Balto-Slavic	OFr.	Old French
Celt.	Celtic	OHG	Old High German
Class.	Classical	OHitt.	Old Hittite
Cz.	Czech	OIcel.	Old Icelandic
dat.	dative	OIr.	Old Irish
dial.	dialectal	OLith.	Old Lithuanian
du.	dual	ON	Old Norse
Du.	Dutch	OPers.	Old Persian
Eng.	English	OPruss.	Old Prussian
fem.	feminine	OS	Old Saxon
Fr.	French	Osc.	Oscan
fut.	future	OSp.	Old Spanish
Gaul.	Gaulish	pass.	passive
genit., gen.	genitive	PIE	Proto-Indo-European
Gk.	Greek	pl.	plural
Gmc.	Germanic	Pol.	Polish
Goth.	Gothic	pres.	present
Hitt.	Hittite	Russ.	Russian
Icel.	Icelandic	S.-Cr.	Serbo-Croatian
IE	Indo-European	sing., sg.	singular
imperf.	imperfect	Skt.	Sanskrit
Indo-Ir.	Indo-Iranian	Slav.	Slavic
instr.	instrumental	Sp.	Spanish
It.	Italian	Toch.	Tocharian
Lat.	Latin	Umbr.	Umbrian
Latv.	Latvian	Ved.	Vedic
Lith.	Lithuanian	voc.	vocative
loc.	locative	W.	Welsh
Luv.	Luvian	YAv.	Young Avestan

B. Symbols

*	denotes a reconstructed form, not preserved in any written documents
<	"comes from" or "is derived from"
>	"turns into" or "becomes"
–	indicates morpheme boundary, or separates off that part of a word that the reader should focus on
( )	encloses part of a word that is not relevant to the discussion, or that is an optional part
~	separates pairs of examples or forms

C. Spelling Conventions

All linguistic forms are written in *italics*. The only exceptions are inscriptional forms in Italic dialects (such as Oscan and Umbrian) that are not written in the Latin alphabet; these, following standard convention, are given in **boldface**. See chapter 13. For Latin, *i* and *u* are used for both the vowels and the glides (instead of *j* and *v*).

D. International Phonetic Alphabet (IPA)

Phonetic transcriptions using the IPA are enclosed in square brackets. The symbols used for American English sounds are:

Consonants				**Vowels**	
b	bell	p	pat	a	father
d	dim	r	roof	æ	hat
ð	this	s	silver	e	care
f	fail	ʃ	shelf	ɛ	pet
g	go	t	tin	ə	about
h	heal	θ	thin	i	beat
j	yarn	v	vat	ɪ	bit
k	coal	w	well	o	bore
l	light	z	zero	ɔ	bought
m	magic	ʒ	measure	u	boot
n	near			ʊ	book
ŋ	sing			ʌ	but

1 Introduction: The Comparative Method and the Indo-European Family

The Study of Language Relationships and the Comparative Method

1.1. All languages are similar in certain ways, but some similarities are more striking and interesting than others. Consonants, vowels, words, phrases, sentences, and their ilk are fundamental structural units common to all forms of human speech; by contrast, identical or near-identical words for the same concept are not, and when two or more languages share such words, it attracts notice. This kind of resemblance can have several sources, which must be clearly distinguished from one another in order to investigate similarities between languages scientifically.

The first source for such resemblance is **chance**. There are only so many sounds that the human vocal tract can produce, and their possible combinations are also limited. These facts conspire to create a certain number of words that coincidentally resemble one another in any two languages picked at random. The Greek and Latin words for 'god', *theós* and *deus*, are of this kind; they have no historical relationship with one another.

A second source of such similarity is **borrowing**. People speaking different languages are often in contact with one another, and this contact typically leads to mutual borrowing (adoption) of both cultural and linguistic material. English, for example, has borrowed the Inuit (Eskimo) word *iglu* 'house' for a type of shelter (*igloo*).

A third source of similarity is a sundry collection of **language universals**; these are basic characteristics of human linguistic creativity that are found the world over. Two common examples are onomatopoeia or sound-symbolism (whereby words sound like what they mean, such as English *cuckoo* and German *Kuckuck*, names based on imitation of the bird's cry), and nursery or baby-talk words for kinship terms, which typically contain syllables like *ma*, *ba*, *da*, and *ta* (compare English *Ma* with Mandarin Chinese *mā* 'mother').

1.2. Sometimes, however, languages present similarities in their vocabulary that cannot be attributed to any of these sources. To take a concrete example, consider the words for the numerals 1–10 in Spanish, Italian, French, and Portuguese:

	Spanish	Italian	French	Portuguese
1	uno	uno	un	um
2	dos	due	deux	dois
3	tres	tre	trois	três
4	cuatro	quattro	quatre	quatro
5	cinco	cinque	cinq	cinco
6	seis	sei	six	seis
7	siete	sette	sept	sete
8	ocho	otto	huit	oito
9	nueve	nove	neuf	nove
10	diez	dieci	dix	dez

The striking similarities in each row attract immediate attention and demand an explanation. Chance seems well-nigh impossible. There is also no connection between the sounds of these words and their meanings, which rules out onomatopoeia; nor are other linguistic universals such as baby-talk relevant. A third possibility is that one or more of the languages borrowed its numerals from one of the other languages, or that they all borrowed them from some outside source. It is true that there are languages that have borrowed the names of some or all numbers from other languages, as Japanese did from Chinese. But if we look a bit further afield, we notice that the numerals are not the only words evincing such strong mutual resemblance:

		Spanish	Italian	French	Portuguese
(1)	'two'	dos	due	deux	dois
	'ten'	diez	dieci	dix	dez
	'tooth'	diente	dente	dent	dente
	'of'	de	di	de	de
	'they sleep'	duermen	dormono	dorment	dormem
(2)	'am'	soy	sono	suis	sou
	'you (sing.) are'	eres	sei	es	és
	'is'	es	è	est	é
	'we are'	somos	siamo	sommes	somos
	'you (pl.) are'	sois	siete	êtes	sois
	'they are'	son	sono	sont	são

We see that not just the words for 'two' and 'ten', but all the other words in group (1) above agree in beginning with *d-* in each language. It is rather uncommon for basic terms like 'tooth', 'of', and 'sleep' to be borrowed, and even more uncommon for three languages to have borrowed them from a fourth, or for all four of them to have borrowed these words from a fifth language. The forms in (2) show that the whole present tense of the verb 'to be' is similar across all four languages, and in very specific ways. It is extremely unlikely that a language (to say nothing of four languages) would borrow wholesale a complete verbal paradigm from another language, especially one as basic as this one – and one that, as it happens, is highly irregular in nearly the same way in each language.

1.3. If two or more languages share similarities that are so numerous and systematic that they cannot be ascribed to chance, borrowing, or linguistic universals, then the only hypothesis that provides a satisfactory explanation for those similarities is that they are descended from the same parent language. This is the essential statement of what is known as the **comparative method**. And in the case of Spanish, Italian, French, and Portuguese this hypothesis would be right: we know from other evidence that these languages are all descended from a variety of Latin.

Languages like these that are descended from a common ancestor are said to be **genetically related**. This technical term has nothing to do with biology; it makes no claims about the race or ancestry of the *speakers* of the languages in question, who may belong to many ethnicities. (Just think of all the different ethnic backgrounds of people speaking English as their native language within any large English-speaking city.)

Comparative reconstruction

1.4. So far we have shown how genetic relationship can be demonstrated, and in one sense our task – of explaining the similarities between Spanish, Italian, French and Portuguese – is done. But historical and comparative linguists typically do not stop there; they are also interested in figuring out what a putative ancestral language was like – in other words, to **reconstruct** it. Reconstruction is accomplished through systematic comparison of the forms in the descendant languages. Here we must content ourselves with one brief illustration. Let us take another look at the words for 'tooth' in our four languages above:

Spanish	Italian	French	Portuguese
diente	dente	dent	dente

All these words begin with *d-*, meaning their ancestor surely began with *d-* as well. The four words also agree in having the consonant cluster *nt* (ignore for the moment the fact that the *nt* in the French form is not pronounced as *nt*; in older French it was pronounced as written). The ancestral word thus probably had the "skeleton" *d . . . nt . . .* Italian, French, and Portuguese agree in having *e* before the consonant cluster, but Spanish has a diphthong *ie.* Since only Spanish is deviant here, the simplest thing (barring evidence to the contrary) is to suppose that it changed an earlier *e* to *ie*, rather than that the other three each changed an earlier *ie* to *e*. In fact, if we were to look at other examples, we would find that this was a regular sound change in the history of Spanish. Finally, all the languages except French agree in having the word end with the vowel *e*; since in the general course of language change sounds are not added to words willy-nilly, we may suppose that French lost an original final vowel here that is still preserved in the other three languages. Final-vowel loss of this kind is in fact extremely common cross-linguistically.

Putting all this information together, we may surmise that the ancestral word for 'tooth' had the shape *dente*. As a final but crucial touch we must add an asterisk before this reconstruction (**dente*), which is the conventional marker in historical linguistics for a hypothetical form – one that is not actually attested (preserved in documents) but is thought to have once existed. (As some readers may know, asterisks have other uses in other branches of linguistics, such as to denote ungrammatical sentences; the historical linguistic usage should not be confused with those.)

1.5. Each of the groups of words that we have been comparing with one another are called **correspondence sets**, and the words in each correspondence set are termed **cognates**. Thus the Spanish cognate of French *dent* is *diente*, the Italian cognate of French *dix* is *dieci*, etc. While we based an example of reconstruction on a sole correspondence set, in actual practice many correspondence sets must be examined for reconstructions to have much weight. Sound correspondences across one set of cognates must recur in other sets to be of any scientific worth. This principle is known as the **regularity of sound correspondences**; without it, comparative linguistics would be impossible. (Again, in setting up correspondence sets we must exclude instances where a symbolic relationship obtains between the sounds in a word and its meaning, as in onomatopoetic words (§1.1). But such cases are very rare, because in the vast majority of words the relationship between sound and meaning is purely arbitrary. This important fact, technically referred to as the *arbitrariness of the linguistic sign*, undergirds the whole science of comparative linguistics and lends regular sound correspondences their significance for reconstructing history.)

1.6. An ancestral language is called a **proto-language**, and its descendants are termed its **daughter languages**. In this book, the phrase "the proto-language" will refer to Proto-Indo-European (see below). The prefix *proto-* is attached to the name of a language or group of languages to designate the immediate ancestor of that language or group; one therefore speaks of *Proto-Greek*, *Proto-Germanic*, *Proto-Chinese*, etc. The word for 'tooth' that we reconstructed above is in a language we can call Proto-Romance, the common ancestor of the Romance languages. (Note in passing that Proto-Romance was not the same as standard Classical Latin, where the word for 'tooth' was *dēns* [stem *dent-*].)

Importantly, observe that terms like *proto-language* and *Proto-Romance* do not designate a "prototype" language that still needed some time in the shop before it could be billed a "real" language. A central finding of linguistics has been that all languages, both ancient and modern, spoken by both "primitive" and "advanced" societies, are equally complex in their structure. We have no reason to believe that reconstructed, unattested languages were qualitatively any different from attested ones: the ability to speak complex language is common to all members of the species *Homo sapiens*, and that species has changed little if at all over the past 100,000 years.

Language change

1.7. The fact that a single language (such as Latin) can develop into two or more different languages (such as Spanish or French) is due to language change. We cannot here present a detailed discussion of the causes of language change, but will outline just a few basic points, a bit simplified for brevity. Linguists view language as a cognitive faculty whose core structures mostly develop during the first few years of childhood. A child's native language is acquired from scratch. Contrary to popular wisdom, no one teaches children their native language; they must analyze the speech of people around them and construct their own individual **grammar** of the language. A grammar, in linguistic parlance, is a body of knowledge consisting of unconscious rules and principles; it may be conceived as the invisible underlying machinery used to produce and comprehend linguistic utterances in a particular language. No one has direct access to anyone else's grammar, only to speech – the output of a grammar; because of this, the new grammar that the child constructs may well turn out to be subtly different from the grammars of his or her parents and other people in the child's environment. These differences, which can be considered linguistic *changes*, may be reflected by differences in the child's speech from that of others in the speech community; any of them can be picked up by other speakers and spread through part or all of the community.

Over successive generations, these differences multiply; as some of them diffuse throughout a community, the speech of the community evolves differently from that of other communities. We may then talk of communities that have developed their own *dialects*; and given enough time these dialects can develop into what eventually may be labelled different *languages*. (These terms are not scientific, but useful for general descriptive purposes.)

1.8. Language change, whatever its precise mechanism, is an entirely natural phenomenon, part and parcel of every living language. A number of popularly held misconceptions may cloud appreciation of this point. It is often claimed that languages change to become easier or simpler. But as was said above, all human languages, past and present, exhibit the same level of complexity; they are also learned by children at the same rate, with equal ease, and in the same well-defined developmental stages. Linguistic difficulty is a purely subjective valuation, and has no basis in scientific fact. Another common belief is that languages change through laziness, ignorance, stupidity, or some benighted combination thereof. This view is typically taken by those for whom a particular linguistic stage or style is perfect and sublime, and all subsequent deviations from it are a product of decay. But this "sublime" form of the language is itself always a "decayed" development of an earlier stage. The changes happening today that are so often decried are in fact no different from the changes that languages have always undergone.

1.9. When the sounds of a language change, one speaks of *sound change*. Sound changes, importantly, are *regular* and *exceptionless* – that is, they affect all the relevant examples of the particular sound(s) in the language. This claim about sound change is called the **Neogrammarian hypothesis**, named after the Neogrammarians, an influential group of nineteenth-century linguists. A sound change in a language that turns a *p* between vowels into *b*, say, will change every intervocalic *p* in the language to *b*. The regularity of sound change accounts for the regularity of sound correspondences between related languages that we discussed above. Tracing sound change is often easier than tracing other kinds of change, and for this reason a listing of sound changes makes up a large and detailed portion of the historical sketches in this book. A fairly extensive terminology has been developed to label the various results of sound change; these and other technical terms will be defined as they arise and are also listed in the Glossary.

All other components of language change as well. The smallest linguistic units that have meaning are **morphemes** (whole words such as *foot*, *oyster*, *devil*, or prefixes and suffixes like *un-* or *-ing*); the rules for using and combining morphemes constitute the **morphology** of a language, and any change to these rules is called *morphological change*. A common type of this is change in the *productivity* of a morpheme – that is, in how freely it can be used to form new words or grammatical forms. The *-th* in words like *sloth*, *breadth*, and *filth* was once a productive suffix for forming nouns from adjectives (*slow*, *broad*, and *foul*, respectively), but is no longer (its function has been taken over by *-ness* and other suffixes); a reverse development is illustrated by the English plural suffix *-s*, now limitlessly productive but once used only with certain classes of nouns. Words and morphemes are stored in the **lexicon**, one's mental dictionary; changes to individual words (rather than to whole classes of words at once, as when a morphological rule has changed) constitute *lexical change*. The replacement of the old plural *kine* by *cows*, and of the old past tense *holp* by *helped*, are examples of a lexical change; in cases such as these, an old irregular form (containing morphemes or morphological processes that are no longer productive) is replaced by a regular form, by a process called *analogy*. The words stored in the lexicon are combined into larger units (phrases, clauses, sentences) by rules encoded in a language's **syntax**. Change to these rules is *syntactic change*, as when a language that used to put verbs at the ends of clauses now puts them at the beginning. Finally, the meanings of words, also stored in the lexicon, constitute the words' **semantics**; changes to word meanings constitute *semantic change*. This is really a subtype of lexical change, since only individual words are affected; but sometimes there are far-reaching ramifications of semantic change, as when a noun like French *pas* 'step' gets specialized as a grammatical marker (in this case the negator, 'not'), by a process called *grammaticalization*.

Determining the pronunciation of dead languages

1.10. The ability to compare ancient languages rests upon knowledge of the sounds and grammatical structures of those languages. How do we figure out such facts about languages that are no longer spoken? The basic answer is that we use everything that is at our disposal: contemporary descriptions, the testimony of descendant languages, orthographic practice (including spelling errors), the rendering of loanwords from known source languages, and metrical evidence from poetry.

Sometimes, as in the case of Sanskrit, we are fortunate in having detailed descriptions of the language's pronunciation and structure by ancient grammarians. If a language has living descendants, as in the case of Latin, we can apply the comparative method to the descendants to establish the pronunciation of their ancestor. When we lack thorough contemporary descriptions or the testimony of living descendants, we must look to texts as they were written by speakers of the language.

Misspellings are valuable for revealing the effects of changes in pronunciation. We know, for example, that in the late pre-Christian era, the Latin diphthong spelled *ae* came to be pronounced as a monophthong (single vowel) *e*. A Roman in the first century AD who spelled the word *aetate* 'age' improperly as *etate* shows the effects of this change. Standard spelling conventions, not just misspellings, can also elucidate facts about pronunciation. In Hittite, like English, words were written with spaces between them; but various short function words like *ma* 'but' were joined to a preceding word without a space, indicating that they and the preceding word were pronounced together as a unit. (Compare the *-n't* of English *didn't* for a similar situation.) Such spelling conventions will be discussed further in §8.33.

We can glean further information from the way words are spelled when borrowed from another language. Educated Romans of the first century BC regularly rendered the Greek letter phi (Φ) as *ph* in words that they borrowed from that language (as in *philosophia* 'philosophy'). The sequence *ph* was not used in writing native Latin words, so the Romans must have been trying to represent a sound that they did not have in their own language – an aspirated stop consonant, as it happens, different from the native Latin unaspirated *p* and also from the native Latin fricative *f*. A few centuries later, however, we find the Gothic bishop Wulfila using *f* (as in the name *Filippus*), showing that the pronunciation of the letter in Greek had changed.

Poetry is often a useful source of information on how a language is pronounced. Much ancient poetry is structured according to particular sequences of heavy and light syllables. In the Archaic Latin poetry of Plautus, a word like *patre* 'by the father' scans as two light syllables. Light syllables end by definition in a short vowel, so the word was pronounced *pa-tre* with the consonant cluster *tr* not split between the two syllables. Metrical practice has thus revealed a fact about Latin syllabification.

1.11. With regards to larger levels of linguistic structure such as morphology and syntax, and with regards to word-usage and meaning, we must always look to the original texts. Linguistic analysis of texts is the domain of **philology** – an enterprise that has been neatly summarized as "the art of reading slowly." It is a multifaceted discipline with many uses, including the determination of the original wording of texts by comparing and dating extant manuscripts, as well as the determination of grammatical facts by examining how forms are used in context and paying attention to relative ages of particular usages. ("Philology" is also a somewhat old-fashioned term for what we now call comparative historical linguistics, hence the phrase "comparative philology".)

Both these and other aspects of philology are crucial for writing an accurate history of a language's development. When texts are copied and recopied by hand and original source manuscripts (called *archetypes*) are lost, errors and modernizations inevitably creep in. If the language of the text is particularly archaic compared with the language of the copyist, errors can become legion. Careful comparison of different versions of the same text usually allows one to reconstruct chains of transmission and to determine the relative ages of manuscripts, which in turn helps us determine which linguistic forms are older and which more recent.

1.12. Using philology to figure out how words and grammatical forms are used has allowed countless puzzling details about ancient languages to be clarified. Dictionaries, being essentially lists of words, do not give a whole picture of a language, much less its history, and the forms they contain cannot always be taken at face value. Two examples from ancient Greek and Sanskrit will make this point clear.

The first example concerns the Greek word *prophḗtēs* 'prophet'. This word etymologically consists of the combination form *-phḗtēs* 'sayer', derived from the verb *phēmí* 'I say', preceded by the prefix *pro-*, which can mean either 'before' or 'forth'. Does the word mean 'one who says beforehand, one who foretells' or 'one who speaks forth, one who announces'? There is a verb *próphēmi* 'I speak before', and so we might jump to the conclusion that *prophḗtēs* comes from this verb and means 'one who speaks beforehand'. But a look at the actual textual occurrences of these words shows that *prophḗtēs* first appears a good 700 years *before* the earliest attestations of *próphēmi*. Clearly the noun cannot be derived from a verb that did not yet exist. Additionally, an investigation of the other compounds beginning with *pro-* reveals that the meaning 'before' is not the prefix's oldest meaning, and does not appear until later than the first occurrences of *prophḗtēs*. We conclude that a 'prophet' was originally one who 'spoke forth' or 'announced' the will of the gods rather than one who foretold the future.

The second example concerns the Sanskrit word *náveda-* 'knowledgeable'. This word is clearly related to the word *véda-* 'knowledge', but the first element, *na-*, is not a known prefix elsewhere in the language, and it seems to have little effect on the overall sense. An examination of the earliest passages in which the word occurs, in the Rig Veda (the oldest Sanskrit text), suggests an explanation for this form. Frequently, *náveda-* is part of a phrase meaning 'be knowledgeable (of)'. One version of this phrase is *bhūta návedāḥ* 'be ye knowledgeable', where the word *bhūta* is the plural imperative of the second person of the verb 'to be'. A glance at a Vedic grammar-book will show that there is a common alternate version of this form, namely *bhūtana*, with an element *-na* that can optionally be added to the second plural. We can thus reasonably surmise that someone, in the course of the transmission of the text, misanalyzed this particle as a prefix on the following word, thereby creating the form *náveda-* which then spread to other versions of this phrase. (A similar sort of false division has happened many times in English, as when the older phrase *an ekename* 'a supplementary name' was reanalyzed as *a nekename*, the source of our word *nickname.*)

Indo-European Historical Linguistics

1.13. Already in classical antiquity, it was noticed that Greek and Latin bore some striking similarities to one another like those that we saw among the Romance languages. Ancient writers pointed out, for example, that Greek *héks* 'six' and *heptá* 'seven' bore a similarity to Latin *sex* and *septem*, even pointing out the regular correspondence of initial *h-* in Greek to initial *s-* in Latin. The ancients explained such facts by viewing Latin as a descendant of Greek. During and after the Renaissance, as the vernacular languages of Europe came to be known to scholars, it slowly became understood that certain groups of languages were related, such as Icelandic and English, and that the Romance languages were derived from Latin. But no consistent scientific approach to language relationships had been developed.

1.14. Following the British colonial expansion into India, a language came to the attention of Western scholars knowledgeable in Greek and Latin that ushered in a new way of thinking about such matters. An orientalist and jurist named Sir William Jones was the first to state this way of thinking, in a lecture to the Asiatick Society on February 2, 1786, and published two years later in *Asiatick Researches* 1:

> The *Sanscrit* language, whatever be its antiquity, is of a wonderful structure; more perfect than the *Greek*, more copious than the *Latin*, and more exquisitely refined than either, yet bearing to both of them a stronger affinity, both in the roots of verbs and in the forms of grammar, than could possibly have been produced by accident; so strong indeed, that no philologer could examine them all three, without believing them to have sprung from some common source, which, perhaps, no longer exists: there is a similar reason, though not quite so forcible, for supposing that both the *Gothick* and the *Celtick*, though blended with a very different idiom, had the same origin with the *Sanscrit*; and the old *Persian* might be added to the same family, if this were the place for discussing any question concerning the antiquities of *Persia*.

This was a turning point in the history of science. For the first time the idea was put forth that Latin was not derived from Greek, but that they were both "sisters" (as we would now call them) of each other, derived from a common ancestor no longer spoken. The idea was inspired by the critical discovery of the third member of the comparison (the *tertium comparationis* in technical jargon), namely Sanskrit – a language geographically far removed from the other two. Also, this passage contains the first clear formulation of the central principle of the comparative method.

The IE family: branches, subgrouping, models

1.15. Jones's insight marks the beginning of the scientific study of the language family now called **Indo-European,** or IE for short. The field is variously known as Indo-European historical linguistics, Indo-European comparative linguistics, or Indo-European comparative philology. Jones's brief statement already enumerates fully half the branches now recognized for the family: **Indo-Iranian** (containing Sanskrit and the Iranian languages), **Greek, Italic** (containing Latin and related languages of Italy), **Celtic,** and **Germanic** (containing Jones's "Gothick" and its relatives of northern Europe, including English).

After Jones's pronouncement, nearly three decades passed before any activity that could be called Indo-European linguistics arrived on the scene. Once it did arise it came rather fast and furious, with three seminal works published within a half-dozen years in Denmark and Germany, including one by Jacob Grimm, one of the two Grimm brothers of fairy-tale-collecting fame. These pioneers and the scholars who followed them realized that not only the languages in Sir William's account were "sprung from some common source," but also the Baltic and Slavic languages (now grouped together as **Balto-Slavic**), **Armenian,** and **Albanian.** In the twentieth century two more branches, **Anatolian** and **Tocharian,** were added to the family, containing extinct languages only discovered in the early 1900s. Anatolian, it turned out, was the most ancient of them all, with texts in Hittite dating to the early or mid-second millennium BC. A few other languages with only meager remains are also clearly Indo-European, such as Phrygian, Thracian, and Messapic; whether

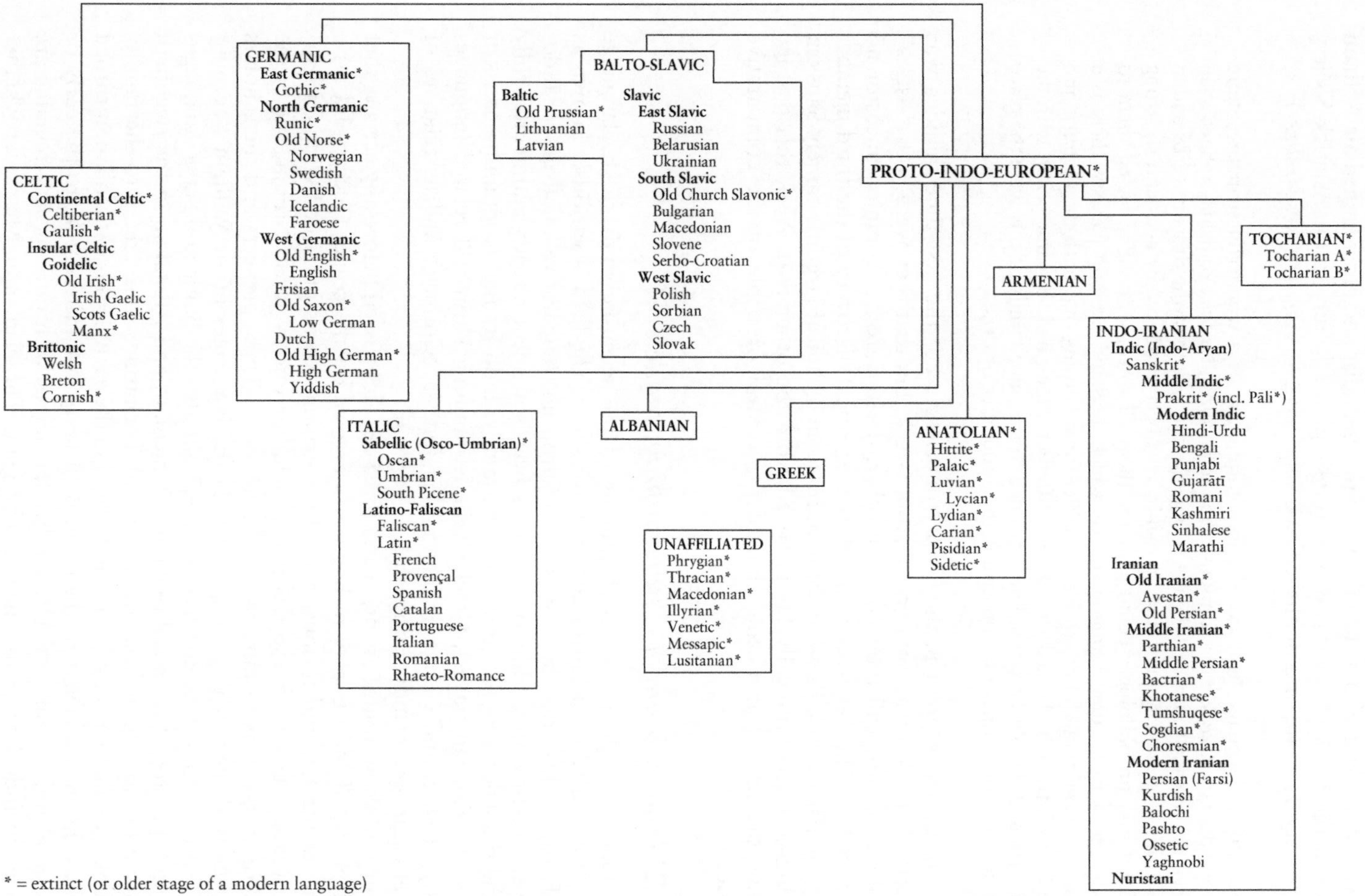

* = extinct (or older stage of a modern language)

Figure 1.1 The Indo-European family tree, showing the approximate geographical distribution of the branches and the principal ancient, medieval, and modern languages of each. The names of branches and subbranches are in boldface. Not all languages or language stages are represented.

they belong to any of the ten recognized branches, or constitute separate branches of their own, is not clear.

The nineteenth century also saw the creation of a name for the family, Indo-European or, in German-speaking lands, usually *Indogermanisch* 'Indo-Germanic'. The ancestor of all the IE languages is called *Proto-Indo-European*, or PIE for short. During the course of the nineteenth century, the methods of comparative linguistics and linguistic reconstruction were developed; a prodigious number of important discoveries in the watershed decade of the 1870s was responsible for significant refinement of the method and for firmly establishing historical linguistics as a science unto its own. By the dawn of the twentieth century, a picture of reconstructed PIE had emerged that was quite similar to the one that is presented in this textbook.

All standard diagrams of the IE family tree, such as the one in figure 1.1, represent it as a starburst: PIE is placed at the top or center, with the ten branches radiating out therefrom. Implicit in the traditional diagrams is the notion of a more or less simultaneous "breakup" of the proto-language into ten or more dialect areas (the future branches). This notion has often come under attack. For one thing, the trees of most other language families tend to have a binary branching structure. In addition, it has been speculated for a long time that certain branches of IE are to be grouped together into what are known as *subgroups*. For example, it has been proposed that Indo-Iranian, Greek, and Armenian all descend from one common dialect area of late PIE; and the same has been forwarded for Italic and Celtic, for which an "Italo-Celtic" subgroup has been suggested.

1.16. The discovery of Anatolian and Tocharian in the twentieth century has further fueled the debate over the internal structure of the PIE family tree. Anatolian in particular is significantly different from the picture of PIE that scholars had developed by the close of the nineteenth century on the basis of the other branches, even though Anatolian is the oldest attested branch. In the 1930s, the American linguist Edgar Sturtevant proposed that PIE was not the ancestor of Anatolian, but a sister of it, and that both PIE and Anatolian were descended from a language he called **Indo-Hittite.** Sturtevant's theory was not widely followed, and the term "Indo-Hittite" has largely been abandoned. But the hypothesis that Anatolian, and then Tocharian, split off from the family first, and that the remainder of PIE underwent further common development before the other branches emerged has found increasing support in recent years and is in many ways little different from Sturtevant's original claim. We will discuss these matters further in chapter 9.

Although many pieces of evidence have been marshalled over the years in defense of one or another subgrouping model, unfortunately the evidence is of varying quality and open to multiple interpretations. For example, it is often impossible to judge whether a linguistic feature shared by geographically contiguous branches is inherited from an earlier stage ancestral to them in which the feature was innovated (in which case it would be diagnostic of a genuine subgroup), or rather represents an innovation of one branch that spread by diffusion to the neighboring ones (in which case it has nothing to say about subgrouping). This is true, for example, of many of the similarities among the so-called Balkan Indo-European branches (Greek, Armenian, Phrygian, and Albanian), which are often thought to constitute a subgroup (see §16.5 for more discussion).

Another difficulty with trying to determine the inner subgrouping of the family tree is the fact that the earliest documentation of IE languages (from the mid-second millennium BC) is, by current estimates, still over two millennia later than the date of PIE itself. The branches therefore had considerable time to undergo changes before their first attestation, changes that could have obscured earlier developments that would help identify any subgroups. Also, some branches (such as Anatolian and Indo-Iranian) enter into recorded history much earlier than others (such as Baltic and Albanian, nearly three thousand years later), meaning they are not all at a comparable stage of development when we get our first glimpses of them.

1.17. The fact that there are so many gaps in our knowledge about the prehistory of the branches of PIE has also provided ample room for speculation about the causes of the more significant structural innovations undergone by particular branches. Many scholars have been attracted to the notion that some of these innovations are due not to the usual processes of language-internal change, but to influence from languages spoken by the original non-IE-speaking populations of the territories into which IE speakers migrated. These languages are called *substrate languages.*

When dealing with vocabulary, this claim is normally uncontroversial: all would agree, for instance, that terms for local flora and fauna were borrowed from indigenous non-IE languages. In some cases, if enough such words can be plausibly identified we can dimly espy elements of phonology and morphology of the substrate language; for an example, see §12.1. (Of course, this does not mean that we can attribute willy-nilly any word without a decent IE etymology to a substrate language.) But matters are not so straightforward with regard to structural changes to the grammatical system. It is certainly possible that substrate influence might be the source of some of them. But with very few exceptions, we know nothing about the pre-IE languages in the relevant regions, and so the claim of substrate influence, being untestable, is not very useful – it simply replaces one unknown with another.

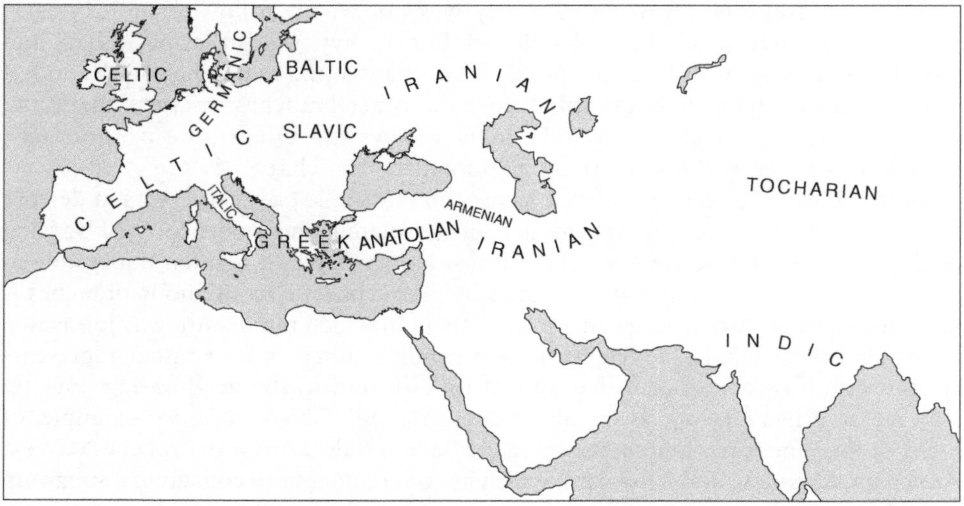

Map 1.1 Geographical distribution of the major Indo-European peoples around 500 BC

(For one of the few exceptions, see §17.4.) On methodological grounds, too, there is rarely any compelling reason to externalize the causes of the structural innovations in question, as they can normally be explained through familiar language-internal processes of change.

Indo-European and other language families

1.18. Indo-European is merely one of hundreds of known language families, and PIE was merely one of hundreds of languages (or more) spoken during the late Neolithic. PIE is therefore not the primeval ancestor of all languages now spoken, nor even of a majority of them (although there are more speakers of IE languages than of the languages of any other family). At the present time, we do not know whether any other language families share a common ancestor with PIE. The comparative method can give us solid results for a time depth of perhaps eight thousand years; most estimates of the age of PIE are in the neighborhood of six thousand years. (The age of PIE will be treated in detail in the next chapter.) Sporadic, irregular, and unpredictable linguistic changes such as analogy, paradigm leveling, borrowing, and semantic change all make reconstruction more difficult the farther back in time one goes since they add "background noise": borrowings become indistinguishable from native words, semantic changes make it difficult to reconstruct word meanings, and morphological analogies and leveling processes erase evidence of earlier inflectional patterns.

1.19. These problems have not prevented some adventurous souls from positing relationships between IE and other language families, or from coming up with classifications of huge numbers of language families into a handful of super-families. Chief among the former claims – the latter do not concern us – is the so-called *Nostratic* hypothesis (from Latin *nostrās* 'one of us', from *noster* 'our'): this is the name of a putative language family that includes such groups as Indo-European, Uralic (Finnish, Estonian, Hungarian, etc.), Semitic (Arabic, Hebrew, Ethiopic, etc.), Dravidian (Tamil, Telugu, Kannaḍa, and other languages of southern India), and Kartvelian (Georgian and its relatives in the Caucasus). Supporters of the Nostratic hypothesis claim that Proto-Nostratic reconstructions help to elucidate the prehistory of PIE. But most Indo-Europeanists are not persuaded by it, and find that the Nostraticists' methods lack the required rigor; at best the Nostratic hypothesis is premature.

This is not to say that the Nostratic hypothesis (or others like it) is necessarily wrong, or might not yield interesting results in the future if the methods are improved. One cannot disprove the claim that two languages or language families are related; but the more distant and obscure the relationship, the more vacuous the claim. Past a certain point, attempts at classification become uninteresting for scientific or historical purposes. The language relationships that have the most to tell us are those whose histories can be traced in some detail and with reasonable certainty. The comparative method seeks to explain why certain languages have systematic similarities too regular and too numerous to be due to chance. Indo-European does indeed share similarities with other language families, but to most eyes these similarities are too scattered and occasional to warrant application of the comparative method.

Conclusion

The limits of – and on – our knowledge

1.20. How complete is our picture of PIE? We know there are gaps in our knowledge that come not only from the inevitable loss and replacement of a percentage of words and grammatical forms over time, but also from the nature of our preserved texts. Both the representative genres and external features such as writing systems impose limits on what we can ascertain about the linguistic systems of both PIE and the ancient IE languages. As regards the first, our corpus of ancient IE texts is marked by a preponderance of poetic or literary works. These were often the ones that were deemed the most sacred or important, and were therefore carefully preserved. This means that specimens of ordinary language are rarer overall, which affects the nature and completeness of our picture of PIE in ways that we cannot always be aware of.

As regards the second point, the ancient (and of course also the modern) IE languages are written in a diverse assortment of writing systems, not all of which are equally well-suited for representing the finer details of pronunciation. Alongside the very serviceable alphabets and clear spelling systems used, for example, by the ancient Greeks and Romans are the syllabaries that the Hittites and some other peoples used. Syllabaries, as will be discussed further in chapters 9 and 12, tend to be poorly suited for unambiguously representing certain combinations of speech sounds, and do not always encode all the sounds present in a language to begin with (as is the case with Linear B, used to write Mycenaean Greek). This often puts the modern researcher at a considerable disadvantage.

1.21. While these hindrances are very real, they do not impede progress in the field outright. As of this writing, we approach the threshold of the third century of Indo-European studies (or, dating from Sir William Jones, we have long since crossed it), and our picture of PIE and the histories of its daughters has constantly undergone revision since the field's inception. We can rest assured that that picture will continue to grow and change. For this reason, the account of linguistic prehistory given in this book is not an immutable truth. Some of the most basic and long-held assumptions about PIE grammar have been challenged and even overturned in recent decades. In the 1950s and 1960s, Noam Chomsky of MIT founded the field of generative linguistics, which has revolutionized the study of language and made a whole host of new insights and theoretical apparatus available. The marriage of the traditional methods of comparison and philology with the findings of generative linguistics has in some cases led to the solution of long-intractable problems in Indo-European, and will without doubt yield great advances to come.

Since no documents in reconstructed PIE are preserved or can reasonably hope to be found, the structure of this hypothesized language will always be somewhat controversial. Of necessity, then, this book contains views on problems that still await final resolution; but most of the historical accounts presented here are subscribed to by a majority of researchers in the field, and care has been taken to flag any views for which this is not the case.

In spite of all the scholarly disagreements that enliven the pages of technical books and journals, all specialists would concur that enormous progress has been made since the earliest pioneering work in this field, with consensus having been reached on many substantial issues. The Proto-Indo-Europeans lived before the dawn of recorded human history, and it is a testament to the power of the comparative method that we know as much about them as we do.

The goals of Indo-European linguistics

1.22. Much of the preceding discussion has focused on the reconstruction of Proto-Indo-European, which is often imagined to be the field's main goal. Yet this is only one of the activities in which Indo-Europeanists are engaged. Reconstruction in many ways is important not as an end in itself, but because it provides a necessary means for elucidating the histories and properties of the attested daughter languages. This includes the modern languages, which – it should not be forgotten – are later and altered forms of the same ancient tongue that Latin and Greek are altered forms of. Regardless whether one is more interested in reconstruction of PIE or in developing historical linguistic theories to explain post-PIE linguistic developments, the exegesis of our ancient texts using philological principles is of fundamental importance, and much research in IE studies has always been devoted to that endeavor. In no other way can we refine our understanding of the primary evidence from the languages upon which we base our comparisons, reconstructions, and historical accounts.

A further goal of many Indo-Europeanists is not a linguistic one: the reconstruction of PIE culture, and tracking the cultural developments of the descendant IE lineages. Much can be said about these matters purely on the basis of comparative linguistic evidence. As a prelude to outlining the structure of the language of the Proto-Indo-Europeans, in the next chapter we will explore what we know about their culture, and follow some of the attempts to locate them in time and space.

For Further Reading

(The works referred to in this and the other "For Further Reading" sections are listed in the Bibliography at the end of the book, together with a few additional titles that are not commented on; these are labeled with an asterisk. Emphasis is placed on works written in English, but any serious student intending to do Indo-European linguistics over the long term must learn to read German and French, and preferably also Italian, Spanish, and Russian. Important works in these languages are also noted.)

The classic treatment of the comparative method is Meillet 1925. A good introduction to historical linguistics for non-specialists is Sihler 2000; a bit more specialized is Campbell 1999. From the literature on the Nostratic hypothesis, a useful recent survey is Salmons and Joseph 1998; see therein the articles by Brent Vine and Lyle Campbell. A superb description of the evolution of historical linguistics and Indo-European studies into the beginning of the twentieth century is still Pedersen 1959, to which may also be added chapter 7 of Robins 1997.

As for general overviews of Indo-European linguistics, still the only complete treatments are the nearly century-old work of Brugmann 1897–1916 and the slightly later and smaller Hirt 1927–37, which in spite of their age have useful collections of data. Single-volume introductions to the field include Meillet 1937 (a celebrated classic), Beekes 1995 (readable but idiosyncratic), Szemerényi 1996 (quite idiosyncratic but filled with useful bibliographies after each section), Meier-Brügger 2003 (a revision and unfortunately not terribly good English translation of a German original; has an extensive bibliography but is difficult to use for a beginner), Tichy 2006 (another English translation of a German original; much shorter than other overviews but very informative), Mallory and Adams 2006 (taken up almost entirely with vocabulary and culture rather than grammar), and Clackson 2007, which by the author's admission is not intended to be a general handbook but an introductory discussion of selected controversial topics in the field. Bader 1997 and Ramat and Ramat 1998 are both collections of essays by different authors that treat the individual branches; many of the articles are excellent.

The most prominent scholarly journals devoted to Indo-European are generally published in Europe: *Bulletin de la Société de Linguistique de Paris*, Paris; *Glotta*, Göttingen; *Historische Sprachforschung* (formerly *Zeitschrift für Vergleichende Sprachforschung* or *KZ* for short, since it was once *Kuhns Zeitschrift für Vergleichende Sprachforschung*), Göttingen; *Indogermanische Forschungen*, Berlin; *Journal of Indo-European Studies*, Washington; *Kratylos*, Wiesbaden; *Münchener Studien zur Sprachwissenschaft*, Munich; *Die Sprache*, Vienna. Note also now the *(Friends and Alumni of) Indo-European Studies Bulletin* (UCLA). There is also a growing list of online resources. First is the TITUS project (short for Thesaurus Indogermanischer Text- und Sprachmaterialien, or Thesaurus of Indo-European Text and Language Materials) led by Jost Gippert at the University of Frankfurt (titus.uni-frankfurt.de), which will, if it is completed, have electronic versions of all the ancient and medieval Indo-European texts in searchable form; quite a few of them are already available, as well as other related information. The homepage of the Indo-European Institute at the Free University of Berlin (www.fu-berlin.de/indogermanistik) keeps up-to-date links to the major European and American research centers in Indo-European, and to announcements, bulletins, and many other sources of information.

For Review

Know the meaning or significance of the following:

comparative method	cognate	daughter language	Sir William Jones
genetically related	regularity of sound correspondences	Neogrammarian hypothesis	Indo-Hittite
reconstruction	proto-language	philology	Nostratic
correspondence set			

Exercises

1 Memorize the names of all the branches of the IE family, and the names and filiations of all the extinct languages in figure 1.1.

2 Below are given the names of the cardinal numerals 1–10 in nine languages. Based on this information only, do you think all the languages are genetically related? If not, which one(s) do you think is/are not related to the rest? Give evidence for your answer in a short paragraph. Ignore diacritic marks over and under the letters.

	A	B	C	D	E	F	G	H	I
1	heis	ipū̃n	yksi	yek	un	ains	mi	sas	kahi
2	dúō	lū̃	kaksi	do	dau	twai	erku	wu	lua
3	treĩs	čī	kolme	se	tri	threis	erekʿ	tre	kolu
4	téttares	čpū	neljä	cahār	pedwar	fidwōr	čorkʿ	śtwar	hā
5	pénte	wuču	viisi	panj	pump	fimf	hing	päñ	lima
6	héks	wuṣu	kuusi	šeš	chwech	saihs	vecʿ	ṣäk	ono
7	heptá	sɛtɛ	seitsemän	haft	saith	sibun	evtʿn	ṣpät	hiku
8	oktṓ	āstë	kahdeksan	hašt	wyth	ahtau	owtʿ	okät	walu
9	ennéa	nū	yhdeksän	noh	naw	niun	inn	ñu	iwa
10	déka	lez	kymmenen	dah	deg	taihun	tasn	śäk	ʻumi

3 It is not infrequently claimed that the tools developed for comparative reconstruction of Proto-Indo-European do not work outside the Indo-European family – as, for example, when working with the indigenous languages of Papua New Guinea, which have been stated to be very different from one another and spoken by a great variety of different ethnicities. Based on the discussion of the comparative method in this chapter, analyze this claim critically. What might be another explanation for the failure of the comparative method as applied to these Papuan languages?

4 Remains of a previously unknown ancient language are unearthed in western Asia. How could one determine whether it is Indo-European?

2 Proto-Indo-European Culture and Archaeology

Introduction

2.1. In the previous chapter, we saw how the comparative method is used to reconstruct extinct languages, and in the next few chapters we will see specifically what it has accomplished in reconstructing the structure of Proto-Indo-European (PIE). But the comparative method has other applications, too. In its ability to reconstruct a prehistoric people's vocabulary, it opens up a valuable window onto their culture. A language does not exist apart from a people, and it always mirrors their culture to some extent. Furthermore, we can broaden the scope of comparison to include not only individual words but also their use in context, which reveals the semantic and cultural associations that attend different concepts. Thus comparative linguistic study allows us to reconstruct a *proto-culture* alongside the proto-language. (As with the term *proto-language*, there is nothing more "primitive" or "unformed" about a proto-culture; the term simply refers to a prehistoric culture which we know about by virtue of having reconstructed its language.)

Besides comparing linguistic forms, much effort has been devoted to the comparison of myths, laws, and all manner of social institutions. Here a methodological point is in order. There is considerable difference of opinion regarding the degree to which linguistic reconstructions are necessary for cultural reconstruction, with some scholars insisting that they are always required and others comfortable with comparing categories, mythic motifs, gods, and social institutions without in all cases their being anchored in (or by) cognate linguistic expressions. Certainly the attribution of a myth, custom, or the like to the proto-culture is more secure if it is buttressed by a linguistic equation; without it, it can be harder to dismiss the possibility of independent innovation or borrowing on the part of the daughter traditions. On the other hand, it does not follow that linguistic evidence is indispensable in all cases. For example, Hittite and Old Irish legal texts describe a duty of sick-maintenance on the part of a man who has severely injured another: the offender must hire help for the injured man, see to it that he is nursed back to health, and pay him recompense; in the Hittite version he pays also for the doctor, and in the Irish version for the man's retinue. This set of requirements is not otherwise known in the ancient world and cannot have diffused from the one tradition to the other; it is generally agreed to be inherited from a PIE law of sick-maintenance, in spite of the fact that there are no cognate "smoking-gun" linguistic terms for the institution.

Below we will sketch some of what has been proposed about PIE culture and society based on the reconstructed vocabulary of PIE and the cognate cultural traditions of the daughter branches. We will follow this with a discussion of the great (and notorious) question of the location of the PIE homeland and the allied question of the date of the breakup of PIE. Because space is limited, and because we have not yet introduced the notational conventions used for spelling reconstructed PIE forms, specific reconstructions and lists of descendant forms will be almost entirely eschewed. Note also that in most cases, comparanda for any given cultural institution, myth, etc. are only given selectively; where an illustrative example of a particular item is given from only one or two branches of the family, it should not be assumed that that item is represented only in those branches.

2.2. Before embarking on these discussions, it should be noted that an important question is begged by such endeavors as reconstructing PIE culture, locating the PIE homeland, and dating the end of PIE linguistic unity. These pursuits all assume that there was at one time a fully homogeneous and reifiable PIE language and culture that suddenly ceased to exist as such. In fact, we know quite well that this is not true of any speech community or culture, and that linguistic "breakups" are gradual processes. Science often finds it necessary, however, to distance itself from the messiness of the real world and to deal in idealizations; and that is what must be done here. The true heterogeneity of the PIE speech community is not something we can possibly recover; but what we can recover is a picture of what PIE speakers had in common, both linguistically and culturally. It is not the business of comparative linguistics to reconstruct a panoply of individual variation or even to worry about it, for that would strip the whole notion of a "common ancestor" of any meaning. The temporal side of all of this is that we cannot hope to know, except maybe in a few important cases to be discussed below, which reconstructed words belong to which chronological layer of the proto-language. Suffice it to say that the words discussed in this chapter are ascribed to PIE by a majority of specialists, rather than just to some later dialect area that postdated the common period (that is, the period of PIE linguistic unity); on some of these, however, individual opinions do differ.

Society

Social stratification and organization

Classes of society

2.3. It is universally agreed that PIE society was hierarchical. First, there was a general distinction between free persons and slaves; the latter, as in many non-IE societies, were typically captives taken in war or debtors unable to repay a debt. (Words meaning 'man, warrior' came secondarily to mean 'slave' in some traditions.) The free segment of society was further subdivided into an elite class of kings, warriors, and priests (and probably poets; cf. §§2.37–38) on the one hand, and into a class of common people on the other. These distinctions had legal repercussions: in Old Irish law, for example, an injury to a person of high rank demanded a greater penalty than the same injury to one of low rank. Additionally, men outranked women; the society was patriarchal, patrilineal, and patrilocal (with brides going to live with the family of their husbands, on which more in §2.6 below).

2.4. One of the most influential structural approaches to analyzing PIE society is that propounded by the twentieth-century French Indo-Europeanist Georges **Dumézil**. In his view, PIE society, especially in the form of its free males, was divided into three basic aspects or "functions." The first function encompassed both sovereignty and religion, and was embodied in priests and kings that kept religious and legal order. The second function was that of martial force and was represented by the warrior class. The third function was that of fertility, embodied in pastoralists and in other producers of goods (artisans, for example).

Dumézil saw evidence for this especially in the societies of ancient India and Iran. The traditional caste system in India, which divides society into priestly, warrior, and herder-cultivator classes (plus a fourth into which were originally relegated the subjugated non-Indic peoples), is already mentioned in the Rig Veda, the oldest Sanskrit (Old Indic) text, and in Dumézil's view is a direct continuation of the three functions. But elsewhere in the IE world such clear threefold divisions are difficult to come by. The ancient Celtic society of the Gauls, as described by Julius Caesar, consisted of priests, knights, and a nearly slavelike commonfolk; and descriptions of certain Ionic and Doric Greek tribal divisions agree with the general model, but seem to have been rather marginal.

As Dumézil developed his theory, he grew to envision these functions less as actual divisions of society, and more as composing a (not always clearly defined) kind of cognitive framework, an "ideology" (*idéologie*), which he claimed was reflected in the structure of the pantheons of different IE religions, in myths, in religious practices, and in other cultural arenas across the Indo-European-speaking world. We will have occasion to examine and evaluate this application of his framework in §§2.35–36 below.

Kinship and the family

2.5. The kinship system of the Indo-Europeans is fairly well understood. The PIE words for father, mother, brother, sister, son, and daughter have descendants in almost every branch; also reconstructible are words for grandfather, mother's brother, and nephew and niece. The terms for 'nephew' and 'niece' also meant 'grandson' and 'granddaughter'; all of these are agnates at least a generation younger and two relations removed from the person of reference. Words for several more complex relationships can also be reconstructed, including daughter-in-law, husband's father, husband's mother, husband's brother, and brother's wife. A few others are a bit more uncertain: Indic and Slavic have cognate words for wife's brother, though a third cognate, in Armenian, means 'son-in-law'; and two languages, Old Norse and Greek, apparently preserve an inherited term for wife's sister's husband.

As the evidence above shows, more kinship terms for males or relatives of male kin can be reconstructed than for females. Anthropologists have classified the kinship systems of the world into several basic types; the PIE system fits none of these exactly (and they are ideal constructs anyway), but the closest match is the one known as the Omaha system. This system is found in patrilineal exogamous societies, that is, those where descent is reckoned through the father's line and spouses are taken from outside the kin group.

2.6. No single term for 'marriage' can be reconstructed; different legal kinds of marriage were recognized, including marriage by abduction. Specific procedures had to be followed for each of them. In the daughter languages, 'to marry' (a woman) is usually expressed by a verb meaning 'lead away' or 'take' (as Latin *uxōrem dūcere* 'lead a wife, marry'), and this can be confidently projected back onto the proto-language; the relevant roots are used also of cattle or water, and their use here indicates exogamous and virilocal marriage where the bride was 'taken' or 'led' from her father's family to her husband's. (For this reason, the PIE word for daughter-in-law came to mean 'bride' in Albanian; from the husband's family's point of view, the daughter-in-law was the new bride in the family.) In PIE society the husband's family had to pay bridewealth (also called bride price), the word for which has descendants in several branches. Several daughter cultures also attest a practice of "free" marriage in which no bridewealth was paid and the wife remained legally part of her father's family.

2.7. Fosterage was surely practiced in PIE times, just as it was in many of the daughter cultures. In several cases, the relationship to one's foster-father was closer than to one's natural father. Thus in Old Irish the inherited words for 'mother' and 'father' (*máthair*, *athair*) refer to one's biological mother and father, whereas the more affectionate baby-talk words *muimme* and *aite* refer to one's foster-mother and -father. Foster-parents were chosen preferentially from the mother's kin; the maternal uncle was particularly common in the role of foster-father.

Social units

2.8. Aside from having class divisions, PIE society also consisted of small units organized into larger ones. Here, though, there is no agreement among scholars on the specifics, since about a half-dozen words for social units from the household on up can be reconstructed, but their precise meanings are uncertain. None seems to have referred to anything more extensive than the clan, except perhaps the word **teutā-*, meaning 'people, tribe', which has descendants in Italic, Celtic, Germanic, and Baltic, and is probably also found in personal names in Thracian, Illyrian, and Messapic. But as this word is confined to European languages, its status as a PIE inheritance is uncertain. Nonetheless, it has recently been proposed that the **teutā-* was the central unit of PIE social organization, with a division between those outside and those inside the tribe. According to this theory, proposed by the Celticist Kim McCone, certain adolescent males would join a warrior-band (or, as it is frequently called, a *Männerbund*, the German term) that engaged in various acts of violence (including raiding and pillaging), for which they were identified symbolically with wolves. Under this view, society was partially structured around the organization of warfare.

2.9. We can reconstruct words for leaders of at least three ranks, up to what is usually translated as 'king' (the source of Latin *rēx* and Gaulish *rīx*), who was at the head of the **teutā* in those languages which knew the term. No self-designation of the Proto-Indo-Europeans has survived (there may have been no special term); it was formerly thought that the Indo-Iranian tribal self-designation, **ărya-* (Aryan), was the continuation of such a term in PIE, but this theory is no longer generally accepted. We will discuss this term in more detail in §10.28.

Economics and reciprocity

Types of property

2.10. The older IE languages typically distinguish between movable and immovable wealth, and in the former category between two-footed and four-footed chattels, with humans being the two-footed kind. Movable wealth *par excellence* in a pastoral society was livestock. The most prominent PIE term in this regard was **peḱu*, but scholars differ over whether it referred to livestock (the meaning of such descendants as Sanskrit *páśu*, Latin *pecū*, and Old High German *fihu*) or more generally to 'movable wealth' (the English descendant is *fee*).

Property was probably divided into hierarchical categories that had legal relevance. Ancient Roman law classifies small livestock, large livestock, men, and rights to land in a separate category from other types of property; and within this category these types of property form a hierarchy where small livestock is at the bottom and land is at the top. This exact same hierarchy occurs in Indo-Iranian legal tradition, and is likely inherited.

Exchange and reciprocity

2.11. Various roots having to do with transaction, buying and selling, payment, and recompense have been reconstructed. They attest to a well-developed economic exchange system, one of the aspects of IE society that revolved around reciprocity. A gift always entailed a countergift, an exchange always involved a mutual transaction; this simple principle was manifest in the meanings of the central terms of exchange, which – it has been argued – did not mean simply 'give' or 'take' but referred to the whole act involving both parties of the exchange. For this reason, such roots have descendants that refer to one side of the exchange in one set of daughter languages and to the other side in other daughters: Greek *németai* 'allots' is cognate with German *nehmen* 'take'; Tocharian B *ai-* 'give' is cognate with Greek *aínumai* 'I take'; and so forth.

Reciprocity was manifest in virtually every corner of PIE society – in the relationship between the two parties in a contractual agreement, between guest and host (see the next paragraph), poet and patron (§2.38 below), and gods and humans (§2.37 below). These may seem like fundamentally different interactions, but not from the PIE point of view: each party to these relationships was mutually bound to the other, and the relationship was cemented (and only made possible) by trust. Derivatives of the PIE root for 'trust' are widespread, and include words referring to that concept (such as Latin *fidēs*) as well as to particular types of mutual agreements bound by trust (everything from Latin *foedus* 'treaty' to Albanian *besë* 'truce in a blood feud'). These trust-based institutions transcended the boundaries between economics, law, and religion.

2.12. The institution of **hospitality**, the guest–host relationship, is a case in point. As far as we can tell, PIE did not have words distinguishing 'guest' from 'host'; rather, there was a single term meaning something like 'a stranger with whom one has reciprocal duties of hospitality'. The giving and receiving of hospitality was accompanied by a set of ritual actions, including gift-giving, that indebted the guest to show hospitality to his host at any time in the future. The obligation was even heritable, making guest-friendship practically a kind of kinship. A famous passage in the *Iliad* describes an encounter between the Lycian warrior Glaukos (fighting for the Trojans) and the Greek warrior Diomedes that nicely illustrates this principle. In the encounter, Glaukos and Diomedes tell each other the story of their lineages, whereupon they discover that Glaukos's grandfather had once been a guest at the house of Diomedes's grandfather. Upon discovering this, the two decide not to fight each other, and instead exchange armor and renew the vow of guest-friendship inherited from their grandfathers. The exchange of armor repays the old debt: Glaukos's armor is much more valuable than Diomedes's. (The narrator of the tale, interestingly, seems not to understand the proceedings and claims that Glaukos's wits were addled.)

Violations of the guest–host obligation were illegal, immoral, and unholy. In Irish law, refusing to give hospitality was a crime that demanded payment of the offended person's full honor-price, the same penalty exacted for serious injury and murder. The killing of a guest in IE societies was greeted with singular revulsion, and is the fertile subject of many legends. In the *Odyssey*, what made the killing and eating of some of Odysseus's men by the Cyclops so revolting was that they were the Cyclops's guests. Hospitality could be abused too; the Trojan prince Paris, by abducting Helen, the wife of his host Menelaos, was perhaps the ultimate bad guest, and the *Odyssey* spends considerable time developing the motif of the suitors, "anti-guests" who camped out in Odysseus's home in his absence while suing for the hand of his wife, Penelope.

Law

2.13. The study of legal vocabulary is important for IE linguistics because the archaic nature of traditional legal phraseology preserves old forms and meanings of words that are often not preserved elsewhere. As with religious formulations, legal formulations must be uttered precisely the same way each time to be binding; the Roman jurist Gaius (fl. second century AD) gives an example of a lengthy legal formula in its legally binding version and in a minimally different version that, he tells us, is legally worthless.

Relatively little work has been done on the comparative reconstruction of PIE law and legal vocabulary. This is not for want of material, which is abundant and includes (among other things) the Hittite Law Code, the Code of Manu in Vedic India (the *Mānavadharmaśāstra*), the Gortynian Code from Crete, the Laws of the Twelve Tables of ancient Rome, numerous Old Irish legal texts, northern Albanian customary law (the Code of Lekë Dukagjini), and various medieval Germanic and Slavic law codes. Rather, there are certain problems inherent in the texts themselves. One is that outside influence must always be reckoned with; for example, the Hittite Laws contain elements that are common to other (and non-IE) ancient Near Eastern societies. Another is that laws that have been codified and written down represent, at least in part, legal reform rather than untouched ancient practice.

2.14. These problems can be easily overemphasized, however. Careful comparative linguistic study of legal phraseology in cognate traditions can uncover, and has uncovered, inherited legal vocabulary and idioms – and with it, PIE legal practice. In Hittite and Roman law, restitution for damages done by one's son or slave to another party was achieved by the father or master paying for the damages himself or surrendering the perpetrator to the offended party. This act of compensation is expressed in Latin by the verb *sarcīre* and in Hittite by its cognate, *šarnik-* (the *-ni-* is not part of the root). Since the two traditions agree precisely in both legal and linguistic content, it is safe to assume that the PIE root **sark-* that underlay *sarcīre* and *šarnik-* had a technical legal usage in referring to this particular type of recompense.

2.15. Future studies will surely uncover many more technical IE legal terms of this kind; in the meantime, there is not much that we can say about this corner of the PIE lexicon. We are not even sure what the general term or terms for 'law' were. A word probably meaning 'law' or 'religious law', originally in the sense of 'legal or ritual statement that must be pronounced' or the like, has been reconstructed on the basis of Indo-Iranian and Italic; it is the source of Latin *iūs* 'law' (whence English *justice*). The verb meaning 'place, put' apparently had legal overtones; it furnishes such derivatives as *dhā́ma* 'law' in Vedic Sanskrit and *thémis* 'law' in Greek. The notion was that of something 'placed' or established. English *law*, a borrowing from Old Norse, comes from a root meaning 'lay' and is therefore 'that which is laid down'; it is possible that Latin *lex* comes from the same root, though this is debated. We cannot reconstruct a word for the central concept of the 'oath', the swearing of which was both a religious and a legal act (as it is today when one swears by the Bible to tell the truth in a court of law); each branch has a different term.

2.16. In PIE society, there was no public enforcement of justice. In order for contractual obligations to be met, private individuals probably acted as sureties (that is, they pledged to be responsible for payments of debts incurred by someone else in case the latter defaulted). The fact that there were no higher officials that enforced justice meant that individuals had to take matters into their own hands sometimes; in Irish law and the Roman Laws of the Twelve Tables, one could formally bar someone from access to their property to compel payment. PIE society probably knew no formal court as we know it today, but suits could be brought by one party against another, and cases were argued before judges (perhaps kings) that featured witnesses. Irish and Gothic preserve what might be an inherited term for 'witness' that is a derivative of the verbal root meaning 'see' or 'know'. Italic has famously innovated a term meaning 'third person standing by' (*testis*, from earlier **tri-stis or *trito-stis*), for which there is a near-equivalent in Hittite: a compound verb meaning 'stand over' (*šēr ar-*) had an extended technical meaning 'bear witness'.

Religion, Ritual, and Myth

Indo-European deities

2.17. All the older IE religions are polytheistic, as was that of the Proto-Indo-Europeans. Nothing like a complete picture of PIE religious beliefs and practices is possible; in what follows, we can only give a sampling of the major divine figures, myths, and a few elements of religious ritual. On the whole, few divine names can be confidently reconstructed. Most of the familiar Greek and Roman gods, for example, have names of unknown etymology, and some (like Aphrodite) are known to be of Semitic provenance. Others, like Venus and the Germanic god Woden, have names that derive from Indo-European roots, but there are no deities in other branches with cognate names. Clearly the daughter traditions have undergone considerable change and evolution.

2.18. Some idea of how the Proto-Indo-Europeans conceived of their relationship to the gods can be seen in the etymology of their term for 'human being', whose descendants include Latin *homō* and Old English *guma* (the latter preserved in altered form in the compound *bride-groom*): the PIE form was derived from the word for 'earth' or 'land', attesting to a conception of humans as 'earthlings' as contrasted with the divine residents of the heavens. Another paired contrast is evident in the widespread use of the word for 'mortal' as a synonym for 'human', as opposed to the immortal gods.

Given that gods were in the first instance celestial beings in the IE view of the cosmos, it is not surprising that the most securely reconstructible members of the PIE pantheon had to do with the sky and meteorological phenomena; they were also mostly male (but see below). The general word for 'god' is a derivative of a root meaning 'shine', as of the bright sky; its descendants include such words as Vedic *devás*, Latin *deus*, Old Irish *día*, and Lithuanian *diẽvas* (but not Greek *theós* 'god', which is from a different root).

2.19. The same root for 'shine' furnished the name of the head of the PIE pantheon, a god called **Father Sky**, whose name is securely reconstructible from the exact equation of Vedic Sanskrit *dyàuṣ pítar* '(o) Father Sky', Greek *Zeũ páter* '(o) Father Zeus', and Latin *Iū-piter* 'Jupiter' (literally 'father Jove', also originally a vocative or form of direct address like the previous two). Compare also Luvian *tatiš Tiwaz* 'father Tiwaz', where the deity has been transformed into a sun-god, and Old Irish *In Dagdae oll-athir* 'the Good God, super-father'. In Germanic, the head god became the god of war: Old Norse *Týr*, Old English *Tīg*, whence our *Tues-day*. The appearance of the word for 'father' as part of the IE Sky-god's title probably referred to his hierarchical position at the head of the pantheon, and not necessarily to any role as progenitor. It would then be like the same use of Latin *pater* 'father' in the ancient phrase *pater familiās* 'head of the household'.

2.20. Alongside Father Sky was another male deity, the **Sun**. His daily course across the sky is envisioned in many IE traditions as a horse-drawn chariot ride; though probably inherited, this motif cannot be more ancient than the invention of wheeled vehicles, which were a late addition to PIE culture (see §2.58 below). In the western IE branches, the Sun and associated deities rested on an island in the western sea after their daily journey, an island frequently described as having an apple-orchard and sometimes associated with the realm of the dead. Whether this is an inherited motif is uncertain.

2.21. The Indo-Europeans had a **god of thunder and lightning**, probably represented as holding a hammer or similar weapon; this is how the Baltic thunder-god Perkunas and the Old Norse god Thor are depicted (the name of the latter's hammer, Mjǫllnir, is cognate with words in Celtic and Balto-Slavic for 'lightning'), and also in some representations the Anatolian Stormgod. Thunder and lightning have both destructive and regenerative associations; a lightning bolt can cleave stone and tree, but is accompanied by fructifying rain. This gives rise to the folk-motif of the lightning bolt that impregnates rocks and trees (especially the oak), and explains the strong associations between the Balto-Slavic god of thunder (Lithuanian *Perkū́nas*, Old Russian *Perunŭ* or Perun) and the oak. It is interesting to note in this connection that the PIE word for 'stone' secondarily refers to 'heaven' in Indo-Iranian and Germanic; while we are not entirely certain of the underlying association, it may rest on a conception of the heaven as a stony vault, from which fragments might fall in the form of meteorites; or it may be connected with the stony missiles thought to be hurled by the god of thunder.

2.22. Alongside these male sky and weather gods, we know of at least one goddess in PIE mythology, the **Dawn**, whose Indo-European name becomes *Uṣā́s* in Vedic myth, *Ḗṓs* in Greek, and *Aurōra* in Latin. In three traditions (Indic, Greek, and Baltic) she is also called the 'daughter of heaven', perhaps an inherited epithet; and in these three branches plus a fourth (Italic) there is a story of the reluctant dawn-goddess who is chased or beaten from the scene for tarrying. The Indo-Europeans oriented themselves by facing east, toward the dawn, as shown by the fact that 'south' in PIE was expressed by the word for 'right'. ('East' itself was expressed by the word for 'dawn' or a derivative of it, and similarly 'west' was expressed by the word for 'evening'.)

Other goddesses have been proposed for PIE as well, but they are less certain. Most daughter branches have a 'Mother Earth', a figure ubiquitous around the world and not specifically Indo-European, but within the IE family itself there is no reason why her name could not be inherited.

2.23. An important pair of figures in IE myth are the **divine twins** (their names cannot be recovered), whose most familiar representatives are Castor and Pollux in Greco-Roman myth (the Dioskouroi, 'sons of Zeus'). They are also continued by the Nāsatyas or Aśvins in Vedic India and as the Dieva dēli or 'sons of heaven' in Latvian folklore. From the considerable mass of often quite varied legends that surround these figures, it appears that the PIE divine twins were offspring of Sky, were youthful, and were connected with (or even took the form of) horses, especially the horses that drew the chariot of the Sun. More distant echoes of the horse-twins are arguably found in the Irish legend of Macha, who gave birth to twins after winning a footrace against horses, and in the Germanic figures Hengist and Horsa, legendary or semi-legendary leaders of the Anglo-Saxon invaders of England and founders of the kingdom of Kent (their names mean 'stallion' and 'horseman', respectively).

2.24. The opposing elements of fire and water are intimately associated in the divine Indo-Iranian figure called the '**grandson** (or **nephew**) **of the waters**' (Vedic

Apā́m Nápāt, Avestan *Apąm Napå*), depicted as a fiery god residing in the water, giving off light, and needing to be propitiated for the proper use of bodies of water. An Irish mythical figure, Nechtan, is the subject of a myth with similar elements; etymologically, his name can be reconstructed as **neptonos*, formed from **nept-*, one of the stems of the PIE word for 'grandson' or 'nephew' that gives *napāt* in Indo-Iranian. This same stem **nept-* recurs in the name of the Roman god of waters, *Neptūnus* (Neptune); in Roman myth there is no longer any overt connection between him and fire, although there are tantalizing traces of an old Neptune cult with elements recalling those found in the cults of Apām Napāt and Nechtan. The Armenian tale known as the Birth of Vahagn (see §16.46) is analogous to these in featuring fire born of a water-dwelling plant.

Ritual and cultic practice

Fire-worship

2.25. An interesting fact of the reconstructed PIE lexicon is that 'fire' and 'water' could each be expressed by different terms, one of animate gender and one of inanimate gender; this has been taken to reflect two conceptions of fire and water, as animate beings and as substances. The most dramatic reflection of the former is in the deification of fire that is seen in various IE traditions. The evidence for fire-worship as part of PIE cultic practice is scanty, but compelling in its details. Vedic India worshiped the fire-god Agni (literally 'Fire'), and the ancient Iranian Zoroastrians were famous fire-worshipers, though their fire-god had a different name, Ātar (also literally 'Fire'). The Romans divinized the domestic hearth and its fire in the form of the goddess Vesta. Though the names of these deities are all different, the temple of Vesta that housed her sacred fire, uniquely among Roman temples, was circular rather than square; and the domestic fire in ancient India was accorded a round altar, rather than the square one used for public worship.

Kingship ritual and the horse sacrifice

2.26. Indic, Roman, and Irish traditions, and indirectly also Anatolian, attest to an important ritual held to consecrate kingship whose central act was horse sacrifice. We know far more details about the Indic ritual, called the *aśvamedha*, than the others; its core elements were the sacrifice of a stallion (specifically, one that excels on the right-hand side of the yoke), ritual copulation with the dead stallion by the queen, and the cutting up and distributing of the horse's parts. We have traces of an ancient Roman ritual called the October Equus, which involved the sacrifice (to Mars) of the right-hand horse of the victorious team in a chariot race, the cutting off of its head to be fought over by two groups of people, and the affixing of its tail to the wall of the Regia (the ancient royal palace from when Rome was ruled by kings). In the twelfth century, a Welshman named Giraldus Cambrensis described in his *Topography of Ireland* a ritual among the Irish that involved the copulation of a king with a mare that is then killed and boiled and cut into parts, which are subsequently distributed to everybody to eat.

On the basis of these comparanda, one can conjecture that the Proto-Indo-Europeans had a ritual for the renewal of kingship involving the ritual copulation of a king or queen with a horse, which was then sacrificed and cut up for distribution to the other participants in the ritual. Some details may be of a later date, such as the Indic and Roman specification that the horse excel on the right side of the yoke: paired draft-horses do not appear in the archaeological record before the mid-third millennium BC – a date that (as we will discuss in greater detail later) is well after the breakup of PIE. In Anatolia, we have some traces of ritual royal copulation, but without horses. The Hittite laws demand the death penalty for copulation with any animal except the horse or mule; this has attracted notice in light of the preceding, but the laws go on to state that copulation with a horse or mule still renders the person ritually impure.

The afterlife

2.27. Several daughter traditions believed that the soul journeyed after death across a body of water to an afterlife. The journey undertaken could be arduous, and required prayers and offerings of food on the part of the soul's living kin, at least for a period of time. (It also required burying various goods along with the deceased that would be needed on the journey; see §2.65 below.) A Hittite ritual calls for pouring honey and oil onto the ground to "smooth out" the path for the soul. The journey on land culminated in reaching a body of water across which the soul had to be ferried, probably by an old man; the Greek myth of Charon and the river Styx is the most familiar descendant of this, but comparable myths are found in Celtic, Old Norse, and – with some modification – Indic and Slavic. There is no particular agreement across the different daughter traditions on what the underworld was like (according to one theory, it was originally conceived as a meadow, but this is disputed). In Greek, Germanic, and Celtic myth, a dog guards the entrance to the underworld (the 'hellhound'), and dogs are choosers of the dead in Indic and Celtic. In several traditions, underworld bodies of water are associated with memory, either taking it away (as the river Lethe in the Greek underworld) or imparting great wisdom (as the wellspring of Mímir in Old Norse myth).

Magic

2.28. We know comparatively little about magic in PIE times, although there is no doubt that it was practiced. Several branches attest the use of magical charms, spells, and curses. The Hittites used sympathetic magic involving the ritual manipulation of dolls and other objects or substances representing various evils; of central importance was the utterance of a spell, typically consisting of an extended simile (such as, "Just as this wax melts, and just as the mutton fat dissolves, let whoever breaks these oaths melt like wax [and] dissolve like mutton fat," from a text known as the Soldier's Oath). The Greeks, Italic peoples, and ancient Gauls left behind many prayer and curse tablets; the practice of writing curse tablets probably diffused from the ancient Near East, but the verbal artistry found in some of these spells has an Indo-European flavor and may continue an inherited tradition. Some charms, such as certain ones against worms, are woven out of the same verbal fabric used in the telling of the dragon-slaying myth described below.

The use of spells and incantations was one of three categories of medical treatment in the ancient IE world, the others being the use of a knife or surgical instrument and the use of herbs or drugs. Texts in Vedic, Greek, and Celtic agree on this threefold division of medicine, and the use of incantations, according to the Vedic poet, is the best – a testament to the power of the word, on which more presently.

Myths

2.29. Certain aspects of religion are remarkably resistant to change. Religious formulae used in ritual, like legal formulae, must be worded just right to have the desired effect, and fixed religious phrases usually preserve archaic language. Also, the basic wording of myth narration is often exceptionally stable, even in the face of significant changes to or substitutions in the characters and events portrayed. A number of recent studies have shown that the specific words used in telling the kernel of a mythic tale are part and parcel of the myth itself. These words constitute the *basic formula*, the verbal vehicle encapsulating the myth. Thus, when two Indo-European cultures share not only a particular story but also particular formulaic words and expressions in telling that story, it can be shown that the story is inherited. A prominent example is the dragon-slaying myth.

The dragon-slaying myth

2.30. Dragon-slaying myths are told the world over; thanks to research by the American Indo-Europeanist Calvert Watkins, the verbal and cultural elements that are specific to the IE version have now been detailed. The IE myth is directly continued, for example, in the Vedic Indic story of the god Indra (the head of the ancient Hindu pantheon) smiting the serpent Vr̥tra to free the waters that the latter has trapped in his mountain lair. The story is simple on its face, but has deep significance: the waters are necessary for the health of the community; by hoarding them, the serpent has upset the natural order whereby wealth and nourishment are allowed to circulate, and Indra must thus do battle to restore order. The serpent as hoarder finds a close analogue in the well-known portrayal of dragons in Germanic legend (and in Tolkienesque derivatives thereof) as hoarders of treasure; their treasure-hoarding upsets the societal order by keeping wealth from circulating. In longer versions of the Hindu myth, Indra is in fact first defeated by the serpent; he must then get help from other deities who provide him with the intoxicating drink called soma to give him strength. This expansion is also an inherited motif: in the cognate Hittite legend, the storm-god Tarḫunnaš is at first defeated by the serpent, and only succeeds the second time around after drinking an intoxicant.

2.31. In PIE, this myth was encapsulated in the alliterative formulaic phrase **(e-)g^{w}hen-t og^{w}him* '(he) killed the serpent'. (The sound *g^{w}h* will be explained in the next chapter.) The root **g^{w}hen-* was one of several reconstructible roots for 'smite, kill', but a close study of the use of its descendants shows that it was reserved for acts of killing that involve a monstrous adversary, or acts of killing that are themselves monstrous and upset the natural order of things. (It was, in fact, quite comparable in usage to Modern English *slay*.) The formulaic language of the dragon-slaying myth could thus be extended to a number of heroic exploits that did not involve dragons or serpents per se. In Greek literature, the same words are used of heroic slayings such as Bellerophon's of the Chimaera, and of slayings that upset the societal order such as Herakles's murder of his guest Iphitos, and Clytemnestra's slaying of her husband Agamemnon (where she in fact is overtly compared to a snake). Furthermore, Watkins was able to show that the formula was connected with another one that translates as 'overcome death' (compare §2.37 below), which has a whole host of other associations. Thus the words used as a vehicle for the serpent-slaying myth encapsulate not only that myth, but also a whole complex of cultural notions pertaining to the slaying of (or by) a monstrous opponent, the struggle of order against chaos, and rebirth.

Creation and foundation myths

2.32. At least three traditions – Indic, Italic, and Germanic – have interrelated creation and foundation myths that involve the sacrifice of a primeval being named 'Twin' by a primeval man, and the carving up of a primeval man into the parts that make up the physical or social world. Norse myth tells of Ymir ('twin'), whose carcass was carved up by the gods to create the world. The motif of creating the world from the body of a primordial figure is quasi-universal, but the fact that the figure is named 'twin' is not. In Indic mythology, the primeval twin, Yama, was the first man to die, and his brother, Manu, was the founder of religious law. Manu means 'man', and another Germanic myth, reported by the Roman historian Tacitus, tells of the creation of three ancient Germanic tribes that represented the three classes of society by Mannus ('man') and his father Tuisto ('twin'). Resembling a combination of the Ymir and Mannus myths are two legends from ancient India and Iran. The first is the story of the creation of the four castes of Hindu society from the body parts of the primeval man Puruṣa (Purusha): his upper body parts became the upper castes, and his lower parts became the commoners (see the excerpt in §10.51). The second is the Iranian myth of Yima Xšaēta, who, as a consequence of sinning, had his triple halo taken away and distributed to the heads of the social classes, and was later cut in two by his brother.

The legends of the founding of cities or the origins of a people are often based on cosmogonic myths; if we turn to ancient Italy, we encounter another analogue, the myth of the founding of Rome by Romulus and his twin brother Remus and the latter's murder at the hands of the former (interpreted by some modern scholars as a primordial sacrifice that was necessary for the act of societal creation).

Theft of fire

2.33. PIE mythology evidently had a myth of the theft of fire. In Greek mythology, the titan Prometheus stole fire from the gods and gave it to the humans that he had just created. We usually read that the titan's name meant 'forethought', but that is simply a folk etymology on the part of the Greeks, who had long before forgotten the true meaning of his name. *Promētheús* originally meant 'the one who steals'; it has an exact cognate, including the prefix, in the Vedic verb *pra math-*, which means 'to steal' and is used in the Vedic myth of the theft of fire. We cannot reconstruct the details of the PIE myth, but can assume that this particular compound verb was at the core of telling it.

Animals in PIE myth and folklore

2.34. Several animals had mythological and folkloric associations. Goats draw the chariot of the god Thor in Norse mythology and the chariot of the Indic god Puṣan (Pushan), and they are associated with the Baltic god Perkunas. The wolf's name underwent *taboo deformation* (as we would say *gosh* for *God*) in several branches, suggesting it was feared; we also know it was associated in PIE culture with outlaws (cp. §2.8 above). In Hittite law, calling a person a wolf was a speech-act that legally branded the person an outcast. The wolf was also a symbol of death; seeing a wolf was a metaphor for being struck dumb, itself metaphorical for losing vitality and dying. (This is found in non-IE folk beliefs in Europe, too.) Probably owing to a hunters' superstition whereby uttering the name of one's quarry was forbidden for fear the animal might hear his name and make himself scarce, the bear's name was taboo in the northern European branches and was replaced by circumlocutions like 'the brown one' (Germanic), 'honey-eater' (Slavic), 'licker' (of honey, Baltic; the inherited word may survive in a term meaning 'bear's den'), 'honey-desirer' or 'good calf' (Irish; the inherited word survives as the personal name *Art*). Several daughter branches preserve a legend, perhaps inherited, of a mythical crane that devours an enemy people. The crow and raven were associated with prophetic knowledge in IE legend; both the Celtic god Lug and the Norse god Odin had two ravens that supplied them with information.

Dumézilian trifunctionalism and the interpretation of PIE religion

2.35. As discussed earlier, the trifunctional ideology proposed by Georges Dumézil (cf. §2.4 above) is said to be reflected in the structure of many aspects of IE religion. In early Roman religion, for example, a central trio of gods was formed by Jupiter the sovereign god (first function), Mars the god of war (second function), and Quirinus the patron of the common people (third function). An Old Persian inscription of Darius the Great contains a prayer asking for protection from enemy onslaught (second function), poor crops (third function), and the Lie, the evil antithesis of religious Truth in the Persian Zoroastrian religion (first function). Similarly, an archaic Roman prayer (given in §13.53) contains an entreaty for warding off diseases (first function; medicine was part of the religious realm, since diseases were treated by spells, prayers, and the like), devastation caused by war (second function), and devastation caused by nature (third function).

2.36. The recognition of recurring structural similarities across such disparate material is arguably Dumézil's most notable achievement, and the tripartite ideology that he used to explain it has become standard doctrine among many specialists in comparative IE myth and culture. But many of Dumézil's most prized examples have been seriously questioned or refuted, and there are good reasons to be very cautious with his framework. In the first place, the ideology does not match very well much of the material that scholars try to apply it to. The many deviations from expected trifunctionality have been explained away by the ad hoc postulation of various historical distorting influences. This introduces considerable interpretive flexibility that robs the theory of methodological rigor, and there is also a dangerous circularity in applying a theory to a set of myths and analyzing those myths in such a way as to make them fit the theory. This flexibility extends to the definitions of the three functions themselves, which, over the course of Dumézil's scholarly lifetime, came to encompass many overlapping and sometimes contradictory characters, leading numerous detractors to reject the three functions outright as simply nonexistent. Most of the divinities in the various daughter cultures are complex figures that have facets belonging to two or even all three of Dumézil's functions; it is unclear how much understanding, or interest, is gained by reducing such rich cultural material to a framework that is ultimately rather bare. Even if the trifunctionalism of PIE is real, it may turn out to be a cognitive quasi-universal, as it has been documented for some non-IE cultures as well.

Poetics

Poets, patrons, and fame

2.37. The Indo-European poet was the society's highest-paid professional, specially trained in the art of the word. Not only was he a repository and transmitter of inherited cultural knowledge, but was also entrusted with singing the praises of heroes, kings, and the gods. Composing hymns in praise of the gods ensured that the gods would in turn bestow wealth and beneficence on the community, and singing kings' or warriors' praises ensured that the kings would live on in the memory of later generations. Fame lives on after death, and the concept had central importance in PIE society, especially for the warrior class. A phrase for '**imperishable fame**' can be reconstructed for PIE on the basis of an exact equation between Sanskrit (*śrávas ákṣitam*, Rig Veda 1.9.7) and Greek (*kléos áphthiton*, appearing in the excerpt from the *Iliad* in §12.65); in altered form the phrase appears also in several other branches. A warrior went into battle seeking fame because fame brought immortality, a way of overcoming death; a phrase for 'to overcome death' can be reconstructed for PIE, and survives ultimately in the Greek word *néktar*, the drink that bestowed immortality to the gods. (It is not inconceivable that the more militaristic aspects of the Indo-Europeans' successful spread owed something to this desire for achieving fame.)

2.38. The value placed on fame, and by extension on the poets that insured the immortality of a person's fame, is reflected in the generous largesse that poets received from their patrons in older IE societies. The relationship between poet and patron was mutually beneficial, one of reciprocal gift-giving: a king's or hero's livelihood in a very real sense depended on the preservation of his fame and on his reputation as surely as the poet's livelihood depended on being rewarded. A 'king without a poet' was proverbial in ancient Ireland for a poor king; and satire – the opposite of praise

– was much feared and could have fatal consequences for the one at whom it was directed. The poet–patron relationship is neatly summed up in a Medieval Welsh account of a poet, Llywarch Hen, who, retreating from battle while carrying his slain patron's body, said, "I carry the head that carried mine." (In his artistic roles and his relationship to his patron, the IE poet is closely paralleled by the griots, poets and transmitters of traditional knowledge in western Africa.)

2.39. IE poetic tradition belongs to the type of poetry known as **oral-formulaic poetry**. Fundamental to this is the use of *formulaic* language, fixed words or groups of words that often had the function of filling out a verse-line. For example, in the *Iliad* Achilles is described as *pódas ōkús* ('swift-footed'), a phrase that has a convenient metrical shape; and the Homeric bards inserted it when the construction of a line needed a phrase of that shape, even in a passage where (for example) Achilles was sitting down. Having a storehouse of such formulae also makes it easier to compose and retell poems; although it is often stated that poems like the *Iliad* were memorized, in fact such poems are never the same each time they are retold because of on-the-spot improvisations and substitutions of one formula for another.

It is in the manipulation of formulae that IE poets showed their art, for IE poems are always a mixture of the old and the new; one hymn in the Rig Veda (3.31) has a passage that reads, "I make an anciently-born song new," while another (8.40) says, "Thus a new (poem) was spoken for Indra and Agni in the manner of the ancestors." Novelty was achieved first and foremost through the use of various grammatical, phonetic, and stylistic figures, some of which are described in the discussion to follow; in addition, an essential part of the aesthetic of much IE poetry was the use of obscure or difficult language. Skilled poets would often resist the temptation of using familiar formulae outright, but would distort them in certain ways, or allude to them obliquely with related notions or concepts. Examples of this are legion in the Rig Veda, the Old Avestan Gathas, the Homeric epics, and the odes of Pindar.

2.40. Formulae were more than just place-fillers; they had considerable cultural weight attached to them. Essential to the poet's ability both to use obscure language and to be understood was the manipulation of knowledge shared by his audience. This knowledge consisted in the associative semantic networks by which words and concepts were interconnected. Many of the major themes of IE poetry – religious truth, combat, heroic deeds, immortality, fame, reciprocity, fertility – found expression in certain words that had complex cultural and linguistic links to other words and concepts. Thus a poet could use one highly charged word or phrase as an allusion to a whole semantic complex, and by combining it with another word that brought to mind a different semantic complex could generate a new and often profound connection or equation, a cultural truth. The technique is not unlike the quotation of part of the melody of another work during a jazz improvisation: the brief quotation brings to mind the other piece and whatever associations that piece might have, and gives it new meaning in the context of the improvisation. Since part of the study of IE poetics necessitates figuring out these associative semantic networks, comparative IE poetics is crucially important for uncovering this most subtle component of PIE culture and world-view.

In the hands of a skilled poet, the density of culturally loaded verbiage can be staggering. To illustrate, consider the following excerpt from one verse in the Rig Veda (1.152.2):

> satyó mántraḥ kaviśastá ŕ̥ghāvān
> "True (is) the powerful formula pronounced by the poet." (trans. C. Watkins)

This snippet is only four words long, but each is packed with associations to important Vedic themes and formulas, many of IE antiquity, and their particular combination draws all those themes together in interesting ways. Let us begin with the final word, *ŕ̥ghāvān* 'powerful', literally 'possessing reproductive power'. It is very similar to another word, *r̥tā́vān* 'possessing religious truth', which normally occupies the same position in a line; in the world of IE poetry, by its metrical position and phonetic similarity *ŕ̥ghāvān* calls *r̥tā́vān* and the latter's associations to mind. Religious truth (*r̥tá-*) is a central concept in Vedic India, and a primary vehicle of its expression was the poet's 'true formula' (*satyó mántraḥ*, the first two words of our line), which was conceived as bringing order to the universe. This formula is further described in our excerpt as ***kaviśastá*** 'pronounced (*śastá-*) by the poet (***kaví-***)'. The word *śastá-* 'pronounced, solemnly stated' is derived from a verb which has important connections of its own to the art of the poet. In particular, one of its derivatives, the noun *śáṁsa-* 'praise', occurs in the famous compound word *nárāśáṁsa-* 'praise of men', establishing an associative link between ***kaviśastá-*** and *nárāśáṁsa-* and a sort of equivalency of ***kaví-*** 'poet' and *nár-* 'man, hero'. We know from elsewhere that this connection is real, and not a modern-day scholarly construct; compare the phrase *mántram nár yā átakṣan* '(poets who) crafted the formula in a manly (*náryā*) way' (Rig Veda 7.7.6; n.b. *mántra-* 'formula' here also!). And this brings us back to *ŕ̥ghāvān*, whose literal meaning 'possessing reproductive power' quite directly identifies the poet as virile; it, too, is a formulaic word in Vedic poetry and (together with closely related forms) is a traditional epithet of the warrior-god Indra, the head of the Vedic pantheon. Using *ŕ̥ghāvān* here to describe the praise-poem instead of the god being praised echoes the reciprocal relationship between gods and humans; this relationship was primarily expressed on the part of humans with a hymn of praise.

Metrics

2.41. A comparison of the metrics of the older IE poetic traditions reveals several different practices that, according to the most recent research, probably point to two distinct PIE poetic forms. The first, which has been recognized for a good century, had verse-lines of a fixed number of syllables and a rhythm that was quantitative, that is, based on a regular alternation of heavy and light syllables. (Light syllables are those ending in a short vowel; all others are heavy.) Lines came in longer versions of ten to twelve syllables and shorter versions of seven or eight syllables, and were grouped into strophes (stanzas) of three or four lines each. The longer lines had an obligatory caesura (break) neighboring the fifth syllable; both types were fairly free at the beginning but ended in a rhythmically fixed cadence (typical of many poetic systems around the world). The last syllable could be either long or short.

The following two strophes from the Rig Veda will illustrate these principles of long- and short-line construction. The symbol – represents a heavy syllable and ⏑ a light; the caesura is marked ‖, and the last syllable is marked × because it was indifferent to quantity (could be filled with either a light or a heavy syllable). The cadence is boldfaced; note that it is unchanging. The macrons indicate long vowels; *o* is also a long vowel; *r̥̄* is a long syllabic *r* that counts as a long vowel; and *th* and *bh* are single consonants.

índrasya nú vīríyāṇi prá vocam	– – ⏑ ⏑ ‖ – ⏑ – – ⏑ – ×	
yā́ni cakā́ra prathamā́ni vajrī́	– ⏑ ⏑ – – ‖ ⏑ ⏑ – ⏑ – ×	
áhann áhim ánu ápas tatarda	⏑ – ⏑ ⏑ ‖ ⏑ ⏑ ⏑ – ⏑ – ×	
prá vakṣáṇā abhinat párvatānām	⏑ – ⏑ – ‖ ⏑ ⏑ – – ⏑ – ×	(1.32.1)

"I will now relate the manly deeds of Indra which he first did, wielding a cudgel: He slew the serpent, drilled through to the waters, (and) split the belly of the mountains."

mó ṣu varuṇa mr̥nmáyaṃ	– ⏑ ⏑ ⏑ ⏑ – ⏑ ×	
gr̥háṃ rājann aháṃ gamam	⏑ – – – ⏑ – ⏑ ×	
mr̥̄ḷā́ sukṣatra mr̥̄ḷáya	– – – – ⏑ – ⏑ ×	(7.89.1)

"Let me not go to the grave right soon, o Varuna, o king. Have mercy, o gracious ruler, have pity."

It should be kept in mind that these were composed orally, long before writing came to India.

2.42. A second, potentially more archaic, poetic form has been argued for by Calvert Watkins and is termed the **strophic style**. Poetry in this form consists of strophes of relatively short lines whose structure is determined by grammatical and phonetic parallelism; there is no fixed line length or syllable count. It has also been termed, a bit misleadingly, as "rhythmic prose" (it is neither rhythmic nor prose). The strophic style is especially characteristic of archaic liturgical and legal texts, and certain mythological narratives. Some examples from several traditions follow:

(Hittite, Soldier's Dirge)

Nešaš wašpeš Nešaš wašpeš	Shrouds of Nesa, shrouds of Nesa,
tiya-mmu tiya	bind me, bind.
nu-mu annaš-maš katta arnut	Bring me down for burial with my mother,
tiya-mmu tiya	bind me, bind.
nu-mu uwaš-maš katta arnut	Bring me down for burial with my forefather,
tiya-mmu tiya	bind me, bind.

(Avestan, Yasna Haptaŋhāiti 35.4)

rāmācā vāstrəmcā dazdiiāi	(. . .) peace and pasture to be provided (by)
surunuuatascā asurunuuatascā	those who hear and those who do not hear,
xšaiiaṇtascā axšaiiaṇtascā	those who rule and those who do not rule.

(Umbrian, Iguvine Tables VIa)

nerf arsmo	(. . .) magistrates (and) formulations,
ueiro pequo	men (and) cattle,
castruo fri	heads of grain (and) fruits,
salua seritu	keep safe.
futu fos pace pase tua	Be favorable (and) propitious in your peace.

(Classical Armenian, The Birth of Vahagn)

erknēr erkin	Heaven was in labor,
erknēr erkir	Earth was in labor,
erknēr ew covn cirani	the purple sea also was in labor.

(Old Irish, "Cauldron of Poesy" §16)

Fó topar tomseo	Good is the source of measuring
fó atrab n-insce	good is the acquisition of speech
fó comar coimseo	good is the confluence of power
con-utaing firse.	which builds up strength.

2.43. These examples exhibit most of the strophic style's characteristic features. Grammatical parallelism and repetition is very frequent ('bring me down for burial with my mother' ~ 'bring me down for burial with my forefather'; 'those who hear and those who do not hear' ~ 'those who rule and those who do not rule'; 'Heaven was in labor' ~ 'Earth was in labor'; 'Good is the acquisition of speech' ~ 'good is the confluence of power'). Bipartite alliterative phrases are also common (*salua seritu, futu fos*, *erknēr erkir*, *covn cirani*, *topar tomseo*, *comar coimseo*). Also characteristic of the strophic style are bipartite phrases of various kinds that express a totality. One widespread type, called a **merism**, is represented by the Umbrian phrase *ueiro pequo* 'men (and) cattle', standing for the totality of movable wealth. The Avestan phrase *surunuuatascā asurunuuatascā* 'those who hear and those who do not hear' represents a second type; compare, from the Latin prayer in §13.53, *morbōs uīsōs inuīsōsque* 'diseases seen and unseen'. Yet other types are represented by Old Persian *hašiyam naiy duruxtam* 'true and not false' and Greek *litás t' epaoidás* 'prayers and incantations' (two synonyms or near-synonyms).

2.44. Many IE poetic forms seem to combine fundamental features of the strophic style (such as alliterating word-pairs and freedom in the number of syllables) with some structural rigidity reminiscent of the rhythmic/quantitative forms (a fixed rhythm at line-end preceded by a caesura, or a fixed number of syllables for the whole line). This is perhaps clearest in poetry like the following South Picene epitaph (see §13.76):

postin viam videtas	Along the road you see
tetis tokam alies	the toga (?) of Titus Alius (?)
esmen vepses vepeten	buried (?) in this tomb.

It can be divided either into bipartite alliterating phrases (excluding the first word) or into three seven-syllable units ending in a trisyllable. Such seven-syllable lines with internal alliteration and a final trisyllable are found also in Luvian and Irish, and a similar eight-syllable line ending in a trisyllabic cadence (but without alliteration) is characteristic of traditional Slavic historical ballads. Lines ending in a trisyllabic cadence and with a variable number of syllables before are characteristic of archaic Irish verse and of archaic Roman Saturnian verse. In traditional Germanic heroic verse, a line is divided into two half-lines, the first of which has two words that alliterate and that further alliterate with one word in the second half-line; there is some freedom in the number of syllables, but the first half-line in particular tends to be weighted toward the end (but without a fixed cadence).

Repetition of sounds (including alliteration, assonance, and, less frequently, end-rhyme) is characteristic of IE poetry even outside the strophic style. A line like the following, from the Roman comic playwright Plautus (*Miles Gloriosus* 603), is quite typical of the technique:

> sī minus cum cūrā aut cautēlā locus loquendī lēctus est
> "If your place of conference is chosen with insufficient care or caution . . ."
> (trans. P. Nixon)

We have the alliterating *k* sounds (spelled *c*) of *cum cura aut cautela* followed by *l*'s in ***locus loquendi lectus***, all of which also have *k* sounds in their interior (*locus loquendi lectus*). The two words ***cum cura*** both have *u*'s, and the following two words ***aut cautela*** share the sequence *aut*; and note the repeated *oc oc ec* of ***locus loquendi lectus***. In Plautus, the repetition of these sounds is partly for comic effect; in a line like the following, from a different tradition (*Iliad* 11.547), the phonetic figures underscore the sense and add gravity:

> entropalizómenos olígon gónu gounòs ameíbōn
> "continually turning his head (and) shifting one knee past the other a little"

At this moment in the story, the Greek warrior Ajax is being struck with fear, and the repeated *gon gon goun* is iconic of his jittery demeanor. (The earlier form of *gounos* was *gonwos*, which was probably the form used when the line was composed; so originally the line contained a perfectly repeating *gon gon gon*!)

Behaghel's Law

2.45. Among the many other poetic techniques that IE poets availed themselves of, mention may be made of a tendency to give more verbal flair to the last thing enumerated in a series, a practice called Behaghel's Law of Increasing Members, after the Germanicist Otto Behaghel. Typical examples include, from Sanskrit, *Damaṃ Dāntaṃ <u>Damanaṃ</u> ca <u>suvarcasam</u>* 'Dama, Dānta, and <u>Damana who has good life</u>' (*Mahābhārata* III 50.9); from Old English, *Heorogār ond Hrōðgār ond Hālga til* 'Heorogar, Hrothgar, and Halga (the) good' (*Beowulf* 61); and a double instance from Greek, from the Catalogue of Ships in the *Iliad* (2.532–3), *Bē̃ssán te Skárphēn te kaì <u>Augeiàs erateinàs</u> Tárphēn te Thrónión te <u>Boagríou</u> amphì <u>rhéethra</u>* '(who lived in) Bessa and Skarphe and <u>beautiful Augeiai</u>, and Tarphe and Thronion and along the <u>waters of Boagrios</u>'.

Personal Names

2.46. In a society where the spoken word was of such importance, it is no surprise that bestowing a name upon a newborn was the subject of a ritual. We can reconstruct the phrase for the act itself, literally 'make a name', on the basis of such cognate phrases as Hittite *lāman dāi-*, Vedic Sanskrit *nā́ma dhā-*, Greek *ónoma títhesthai*, Lat. *nōmen in-dere*, and Tocharian A *ñom tā-*. In Vedic India, the name is given as part of the *nāmadheya-* ('name-placing') festival on the tenth day after the mother has left the childbed and been bathed; in Greece the name was given on the tenth day also. In Rome, the name was given nine days after the birth of a boy, eight days after the birth of a girl. Among Germanic peoples, according to Alemannic and Frankish legal texts the name was given on the ninth or tenth day after birth, accompanied by a ritual; here too the mother was first bathed. These facts would indicate that in PIE society, the mother recovered for nine (?) days after childbirth, rose, was bathed, and the child was then named.

2.47. The importance attached to names is due partly to the connection between one's name and one's reputation, especially among the ruling or warrior classes. In several IE traditions, the inherited words for 'name' and 'fame' are collocated (e.g., Greek *onomáklutos* 'famous in name', Tocharian A *ñom-klyu* 'name-fame', Vedic Sanskrit *śrútyam nā́ma* 'famous in name'). In Old Irish, an everlasting name was synonymous with everlasting fame.

2.48. We have a large dossier of ancient Indo-European names, many of which furnish information about naming practices in PIE times, especially (again) within the warrior class. One very common type of name, found in most branches and securely reconstructible for PIE, is a bipartite compound X-Y where one or both compound members are concepts, virtues, or animals that were important in Indo-European society, such as fame, guest, god, and strength. A sampling will illustrate their character:

'fame'	Old Russian *Bole-slavŭ* 'having greater fame/glory'
	Illyrian *Ves-cleves* 'having good fame'
	Greek *Themisto-klē̃s* 'law-fame'
'guest'	Lepontic *Uvamo-kozis* 'having supreme guests'
	Runic *Hlewa-gastiz* 'fame-guest'
'protection'	Luvian *Tarḫunta-zalmaš* 'having the Stormgod as protection'
	Old High German *Ans-elm* 'having god as helmet'
	Gaulish *Anextlo-mārus* 'great in protection'
'god'	Vedic *Devá-śravās* 'having divine fame'
	Czech *Bohu-slav* 'having the fame of god'
	Greek *Dio-génēs* 'born of god, born of Zeus'
	German *Gott-fried* 'having the peace of god'
'battle'	Gaulish *Catu-rīx* 'battle king'
	Old Welsh *Cat-mōr* 'great in battle'
	Old High German *Hlūd-wīg* 'loud in battle' (*Ludwig*)

'people'	Greek *Agé-lāos* 'leader of the people'
	Old High German *Liut-pold* 'brave among the people' (*Leopold*)
	Gothic (Latinized) *Theode-rīcus* 'people's king'
'man, hero'	Irish *Fer-gus* 'having a hero's strength'
	Old Persian *Xšay-āršā* 'ruling over men' (*Xerxes*)
	Greek *Aléks-andros* 'warding off heroes' (*Alexander*)
animals	Vedic *R̥jí-śvā* 'having swift dogs'
	Old Norse *Ráð-ulfr* 'counsel wolf' (*Ralph*)
	Gaulish *Mori-tasgus* 'sea badger'
	Ogam Irish *Cuno-rix* 'dog king'

2.49. In several IE societies, names of sons were picked (or created) so as to resemble the names of their fathers in specific ways. This was often done by recycling one of the compound members: Greek *Dīno-krátēs* 'having fearful strength', son of *Dīno-klē̃s* 'having fearful fame'; *Eu-krátēs* 'having good strength', son of *Euru-krátēs* 'having broad strength'; Old High German *Walt-bert* 'bright in power', son of *Wald-ram* 'power raven'; *Hilti-brant* son of *Haðu-brant*, both meaning 'battle sword'. Such practices are partly behind the appearance of nonsensical compound names like Old High German *Fridu-gundis* 'peace-battle' or Greek *Rhód-ippos* 'rose-horse', where one of the compound members was copied over from the name of one's father without regard for what the new compound would mean.

Nicknames are widely attested and were likely also part of PIE onomastic practice. As today, nicknames in the older languages were typically formed by truncation and other modifications: Sanskrit *Kuntis* for *Kuntibhojas*; Greek *Hupsō* for *Hupsipúlē* and *Kléomis* for *Kleoménēs*; Old Irish *Chúcan* or *Chúcuc* for *Cú Chulainn*; and Old English *Bugga* for *Eadburh*.

Archaeology and the PIE Homeland Question

2.50. No issue in Indo-European studies has aroused more controversy or popular interest than determining the place the Proto-Indo-Europeans called home. The variety of different suggestions put forth – some of them quite outlandish – is enormous. As J. P. Mallory writes in his book *In Search of the Indo-Europeans* (p. 143),

> We begin our search for the homeland of the Indo-Europeans with the deceptively optimistic claim that it has already been located. For who would look further north than [L]ok[a]manya Tilak and Georg Biedenkapp who traced the earliest Aryans to the North Pole? Or who would venture a homeland further south than North Africa, further west than the Atlantic or further east than the shores of the Pacific, all of which have been seriously proposed as cradles of the Indo-Europeans? This quest for the origins of the Indo-Europeans has all the fascination of an electric light in the open air on a summer night: it tends to attract every species of scholar or would-be savant who can take pen to hand. It also shows a remarkable ability to mesmerize even scholars of outstanding ability to wander far beyond the realms of reasonable speculation to provide yet another example of academic lunacy.

Allied with the purely geographical question of where the Proto-Indo-Europeans lived is the temporal question of when they lived there. The insurmountable difficulty with answering both these questions is the simple fact that no material artifact of a preliterate people, nor their mortal remains, can tell us what language they spoke. Much of the time, we cannot even assuredly identify a type of artifact with a particular people: styles of pottery, for example, can diffuse from culture to culture, just as computer technology has spread globally today. While we can reconstruct a number of helpful terms relating to PIE material culture (see the next section), none of them is specific enough for matching particular archaeological finds with speakers of PIE. For example, we can reconstruct a word for 'fortification', but we are in the dark about whether there was an "IE type" or style of fortification that could be identified with particular prehistoric fortifications of Eurasia. As Mallory rather sardonically puts it (p. 126), "Indeed, it is bizarre recompense to the scholar struggling to determine whether the Proto-Indo-Europeans were acquainted with some extremely diagnostic item of material culture only to find that they were far more obliging in passing on to us no less than two words for 'breaking wind'."

Some scholars, in fact, consider these problems to be overwhelming, and reject the notion that any inferences about the physical world of the Proto-Indo-Europeans can be drawn from reconstructed vocabulary whose real-world referents are unknowable. This is technically true. On the other hand, if taken to its logical conclusion, this argument would result in the whole enterprise of linguistic reconstruction grinding to a halt. All of our reconstructions are hypotheses; we do not *know* that they ever existed, yet we posit them in order to explain certain facts. So we explain the fact that almost every branch of the family has a related word for 'dog' by reconstructing a word for PIE with that meaning. Meanings do not exist in a vacuum; a word for 'dog', even if silent on the exact type of dog or how the animal was viewed and so forth, has certain implications for the nature of the world in which the people having that word lived.

The following picture, therefore, like the preceding one on PIE non-material culture, is presented with all due caution, and it should be kept in mind that controversy hovers over practically every claim. Let us first consider the question of when PIE was spoken, for which we must review what we know about the Indo-Europeans' material culture and technology.

Material culture and technology

Wheels and tools

2.51. The Proto-Indo-Europeans knew the wheel, for which they had at least two words, one of which (the family of English *wheel*, Greek *kúklos*, and Sanskrit *cakrám*) is found in most of the branches (see further §2.58 below). We can also reconstruct words for wheel hub (nave) and axle, and a specific verb referring to the act of conveyance in a vehicle; from this verb the noun for 'wheeled vehicle, wagon' was derived. The use of draft animals for pulling the wheeled vehicles required yokes and thills (yoke poles); terms for both in PIE have been reconstructed.

Some prominent members of the inherited wheel vocabulary are not represented in Anatolian, an absence that has engendered vigorous debate. As noted in the previous chapter (§1.16), many view the Anatolian branch as having split off from the family first, and some who follow this view believe that the absence of these words from Anatolian means the Proto-Indo-Europeans did not yet know the wheel. Under this approach, only after Anatolian left the family did the remaining Indo-European population come into contact with wheels and develop a vocabulary for them. But while it lacks the words for 'wheel', 'axle', 'nave', and 'wagon', Anatolian does have the words for 'yoke', 'thill', and 'transport in a vehicle', though some scholars claim that these words could have originally referred to non-wheeled transport. Under current knowledge the issue cannot be conclusively decided.

Pastoralism

2.52. The Proto-Indo-Europeans practiced agriculture and made use of various farming implements. A verb meaning 'to plow' is securely reconstructed, and several branches have similar words for 'plow' (the implement) that are probably inherited. We also know the words for some other farming tools, such as the harrow and sickle. Although words for grain, for threshing and grinding grain, and for some specific grains can be reconstructed (wheat, barley, and probably emmer and spelt), it is uncertain whether grains were cultivated by the Proto-Indo-Europeans; however, such cultivation is strongly suggested by the fact that grains have a prominent role in the mythology, folklore, and ritual practices of many IE traditions that can be projected back onto the proto-culture and that point to the importance of cereals for their livelihood. The PIE word for 'field' has descendants in most branches, and was a derivative of an equally widely represented verbal root referring to leading or driving cattle, which points to the use of draft-oxen in plowing. Slavic, Germanic, and Celtic have cognate words for 'fallow', indicating that their ancestors may have engaged in shifting cultivation; but we do not know if this is an inheritance from PIE, as it may also be a later, locally innovated term of these three geographically contiguous branches.

2.53. As we have seen, an important part of the Indo-Europeans' material culture consisted in stockbreeding, and we are well informed about the IE words for various domesticated animals. Among bovines, the PIE lexicon distinguished cow, steer, ox, and bull. The Indo-Europeans were familiar with dairy products (whether from cows, goats, or mares): we know their words for coagulated or sour milk, butter, and curds. Interestingly, while we can reconstruct a verb for the act of milking, we cannot reconstruct a word for the liquid itself: the terms in the daughter languages are apparently related (e.g. Gk. *gálakt-*, *glak-*, Lat. *lact-*, Eng. *milk*), but differ too much from one another to allow precise reconstruction.

2.54. To these may be added words for sheep (and its wool), ram, lamb, goat, horse, and dog, the last of these domesticated earlier than any of the others. We do not know if ducks and geese were domesticated, but we can reconstruct the words for them. There were separate roots for piglet and fully-grown pig, suggesting that swine were domesticated. The horse is often thought of as the IE animal par excellence; it was important in PIE myth and ritual (see §§2.23 and 2.26 above), and is thought to have played a critical role in the rapid expansion of the early IE tribes, on which more presently.

Dwellings

2.55. Some terms pertaining to houses and house-construction have survived. The general PIE word for house has descendants in most branches, as does the word for door (usually attested in the dual or plural; presumably doors came in pairs). We can also reconstruct a word for doorjamb. Doors were probably kept shut with pegs of some kind, referred to by a word whose descendants variously mean 'key', 'peg', or 'nail' and that is derived from the verb meaning 'to close'. Roofs were thatched; words for 'roof' in some IE languages are cognate with words for 'thatch' in others, all of them derived from a verbal root meaning 'to cover'. Inside a dwelling was the hearth, which had great symbolic and even religious significance (recall §2.25 above) and for which a PIE word can be reconstructed.

Food preparation

2.56. At least four branches – Indo-Iranian, Greek, Italic, and Germanic – have cognate words for oven. Cooking, baking, and boiling are all terms we can reconstruct, as is a term for broth. Grinding grain could be done in a hand-mill or *quern* (the direct descendant of the PIE term for this implement). Also part of the PIE culinary dossier was fermentation: the Indo-Europeans drank mead, their word for which has descendants in most of the daughter branches. Whether wine was known is a contentious issue. Viticulture is at least as old as the sixth millennium BC in the Caucasus, and the word for 'wine' is the same in the IE family (Eng. *wine*, Lat. *uīnum*, Gk. *(w)oînos*, Russ. *vino*, etc.), Semitic (**wayn-*), and the Kartvelian languages of the Caucasus (e.g. Georgian *ghvino*). Though some believe the word is native PIE, the arguments for this are speculative, and most researchers believe rather that it diffused into the IE languages at a post-PIE date.

Textiles and clothing

2.57. The well-represented word for sheep's wool stood alongside a word for linen (or flax); these, together with reconstructed roots for sewing, spinning, weaving, and plaiting, and nouns for needle and thread, show that the Proto-Indo-Europeans produced textiles. A verbal root meaning to clothe has descendants in most of the branches; we can also reconstruct the verb for girding, which formed a derivative noun for belt. The Proto-Indo-Europeans were also familiar with combs, and with ointments or salves. Aside from this, though, we know little about their dress or bodily adornments.

2.58. This represents the bulk of the linguistic evidence for the Indo-Europeans' material culture. There are various additional terms, of course, as for other tools and weapons, but the latter are archaeologically widespread and go back much further than most dates entertained for PIE. A prehistoric society somewhere in Eurasia that practiced agriculture and stockbreeding, had the plow and other specialized agricultural implements, and had developed secondary products from milk and wool would most likely have belonged to the late Neolithic (fifth and fourth millennia BC). Based on the available archaeological evidence, the addition of wheeled vehicles to this picture allows us to narrow the range to the mid- or late fourth millennium. Evidence in the archaeological record for wheeled vehicles appears simultaneously at several sites in Europe, the Caucasus, Anatolia, and Mesopotamia around 3500–3400 BC; wherever wheel technology was invented, it clearly spread very rapidly over a wide area and the Proto-Indo-Europeans would not have been long in adopting it. That means the latest stage of pre-breakup PIE cannot have been earlier than about that time. The wheel- and wagon-related terms are particularly telling linguistically: all of them save 'thill' are transparently secondary, that is, derived from known roots. One of the words for wheel, the ancestor of Sanskrit *cakrám*, Gk. *kúklos*, and Eng. *wheel*, is derived from the verb 'to turn' and has the look of a colloquial neologism, as we will discuss in §6.63. The other word, represented e.g. by Latin *rota*, is from the verb 'to run'. 'Nave' is identical to, or related to, the word for 'navel', and 'axle' is also the word for 'shoulder joint'. 'Yoke' is derived from the verb 'to join'. Thus the whole complex of terms looks like a set of new metaphorical extensions of already existing terms to denote novel technologies. (Compare the use of *mouse* to denote a computer input device.)

2.59. We may add to this the IE lexical facts concerning metals. Iron and tin do not appear in the archaeological record until after the fourth millennium, while copper is found already by the early sixth millennium, and silver in the late fourth millennium. Aside from a general word for 'metal' (which may, for all we know, have referred to copper), the only specific metal term that has any chance of being of common PIE date is 'silver' (represented e.g. in Avestan *ərəzatəm*, Latin *argentum*, and Gaulish *arganto-*). Although it is a transparent derivative of an adjectival root meaning 'shiny, white', in five of the six branches where it appears it has the same unusual morphology, making common descent from PIE more likely than not. This is consistent with a breakup of PIE in the late fourth millennium.

Linguists would not be comfortable with a date much later than this; by common consent a later date would have left insufficient time for Anatolian and Indo-Iranian to diverge as much as they had diverged by the time their first written traces appear in the early and mid-second millennium. Note, though, that there is no generally accepted method for determining average rates of language change, and it is far from assured that such rates even exist. But there are other reasons to think that PIE had broken up by the end of the fourth millennium, which we will look at shortly.

Location of the homeland

2.60. Several methods of approach have been used for locating the homeland of the Proto-Indo-Europeans. Most famously, perhaps, are investigations of IE words for the natural world – the physical environment, fauna, and flora, in the hope that one of these terms would refer to something with a very limited geographical distribution. The reconstructed terms for topographic features are too basic to be helpful: mountain, river, lake or sea, and marshy land. These do no more than rule out a desert home for the Indo-Europeans (as does the reconstructed word for 'boat'!).

The terms for animals and plants, however, are more varied and have aroused greater interest.

Fauna

2.61. We can reconstruct the names for the bear, fox, wolf, beaver, otter, hedgehog, and elk (or deer), as well as words for quite a few birds, including the sparrow, quail, thrush, crane, vulture, blackbird, crow, raven, eagle, falcon (or hawk), jay, kite, pheasant, stork, and probably owl. (Some specialists dispute one or another of these.) As for reptiles and aquatic animals, we only know terms for the turtle, frog, and snake, plus two general words for fish and terms for a few specific fish species, especially the trout and salmon or a related species (see further below), and a word for some large fish that later came to be applied to cetaceans. Celtic and Indo-Iranian have words for leech that are probably cognate, and two rhyming words for worm are widely represented. As for insects, we know the name of the bee, together with words for its honey and wax, as well as the PIE words for wasp and hornet. The Indo-Europeans were also well acquainted with those perennial unwanted companions of humans and their dwellings, the mouse and louse (a rhyming pair then as now); reconstructible alongside the latter is the word for its egg, the nit, and a word for flea.

2.62. Almost all these animals are ubiquitous throughout Europe and large parts of Asia, with the possible exception of the beaver, which is not found in Greece or Anatolia, locations that are doubtful for the PIE homeland for many other reasons (though see §2.71 below). But these terms do suggest that the Indo-Europeans lived in regions that were at least partly forested. The bear and elk are forest-dwelling animals, as are honeybees, and the otter and beaver dwell specifically in riverine forests. Some excitement was generated at one point by a theory that one of the reconstructed fish-names, **lok̂sos* (the ancestor of English *lox*), referred specifically to the Atlantic salmon (*Salmo salar*), whose distribution in Eurasia is limited to rivers flowing into the Baltic. But it is now believed that the word referred to the salmon trout (*Salmo trutta*), which is found over a much wider area. (Whatever the **lok̂sos* was, it seems to have been viewed as pre-eminent, to judge by the fact that it became the general word for 'fish' for the Tocharians. On the other hand, this may not mean anything, given that the PIE word for 'louse' became the general Tocharian word for 'animal'!)

Flora

2.63. The reconstruction of names for plants is more problematic than for animals. Very few plant names in the western IE languages have cognates in the eastern languages, a fact that has occasioned much debate over how many terms to reconstruct for PIE. The most clear-cut is the birch, whose name is found in six branches; after it come the willow and ash (the latter the preferential wood for making spears), and it is possible though more controversial to include the pine and yew. The oak was known, since the word for 'acorn' is securely reconstructible for PIE (though the most widespread word for 'oak' is only found in the European branches). These trees occur pretty much all over Europe and Asia. Hittite and Irish preserve a cognate word for 'hawthorn', and also attest to magical uses of it that may be inherited from PIE. Five branches attest a word that sometimes means 'beech' (e.g. *beech* in English), sometimes 'elder' (e.g. Russian *buzina*), and 'oak' in Greek *phēgós*. For a while, attempts were made to show that the word meant 'beech' originally, because it used to be thought that the beech was found only west of Russia. However, we now know the range of the beech extended much farther east in the recent past, so the whole issue is moot for determining the location of the PIE homeland.

2.64. The European languages allow the reconstruction of words for such trees as the oak, elm, juniper, alder, apple, hazel, and cherry. These may have been PIE, or specifically European terms that arose later; complicating our analysis is the fact that several of these words, such as 'apple' (**abel-*), have an un-Indo-European look to them that suggests borrowing (although the borrowing could itself be of PIE date). See further §4.11 on this. Greek, Latin, Germanic, and Slavic share a word variously referring to mistletoe, black cherry, or birdlime; birdlime can be obtained from both mistletoe and black cherries, but which plant was designated by the term in PIE is uncertain. We also know the PIE words for berry and bean. All of these flora are quite widespread, but some of them are not found very far south, suggesting (together with the presence of a PIE word for 'snow') a temperate rather than a tropical or subtropical region.

Burials and the kurgan cultures

2.65. Bridging the gap between material and non-material culture, and of particular importance in archaeology, are burials. While a culture might well adopt technological innovations from other cultures, burial practices are considerably more resistant to outside influence. Ancient IE texts describing burials, especially of kings or warriors, are known from several branches, and although they do not agree with one another in every detail, they allow us to piece together a reasonably good picture of PIE burial practices. A dead person was buried in his own individual tomb that was like a mortuary house and heaped over with earth (a tumulus or burial mound). The corpse was sometimes cremated; this was the norm in the Indo-Iranian world and a special honor for heroes in ancient Scandinavia. Buried with the deceased were various grave goods, including ornaments, food, clothing, weapons, tools, and often wheeled vehicles, sacrificed animals, and even people. All these things would be needed in the afterlife.

2.66. Various Copper and Bronze Age cultures in the steppeland of southern Russia, around the Black Sea and middle Volga, are associated with characteristic tumuli called **kurgans** (from the Russian term). The kurgans and the burials they contain are consistent with the early IE burial practices outlined above, and the late Lithuanian archaeologist Marija Gimbutas proposed that the kurgan peoples were in fact early Indo-Europeans. The archaeological excavations, in Gimbutas's view, indicate that the kurgan cultures had a pastoral economy, hierarchical social structure, patriarchy, aggressive warfare, animal sacrifice, worship and/or use of the horse, wheeled vehicles, and worship of a solar deity. All these are Indo-European cultural characteristics.

Gimbutas emphasized the differences between kurgan burials and the indigenous "Old European" burials that predate the intrusion of the Indo-Europeans into Europe. The "Old European" burials were in oval or egg-shaped tombs, without the sorts of grave goods seen in kurgan burials. Gimbutas viewed this "Old European" culture as matrifocal (that is, having a ritual focus on women and goddesses), peaceful, and goddess-worshiping – strongly contrasting with the patriarchal, aggressive, skygod-worshiping Indo-Europeans. These views, however, have not stood the test of time, and there are too many differences among the various cultures that Gimbutas lumped together under the rubric of "kurgan cultures" for the term to be meaningful.

2.67. Nonetheless, among Indo-Europeanists her basic notion of an incursion of early Indo-Europeans westward into Europe from the steppe region has become the most widely followed theory of IE expansion. If we start to look at some more specific cultural entities within the general area of the Pontic-Caspian steppes (the vast grasslands north of the Black and Caspian Seas), a coherent historical picture emerges of considerable interest. Recall from the previous discussion that a date of c. 3500–3400 BC – the invention of wheeled vehicles – was the earliest possible date for the breakup of common PIE. A date of about 3500 BC corresponds with the first large-scale occupation of the Pontic-Caspian steppes, by a people known as the **Yamna culture** (or Yamnaya culture). This culture originated in the borderland between the Pontic-Caspian steppes and the neighboring forest regions between the Dnieper and Volga Rivers. From as early as 3700 BC comes the first possible (though very controversial) evidence of horseback riding in the archaeological record, in the form of microscopic abrasions on horses' teeth from clamping down on a bit. This evidence of bit microwear, as it is called, is primarily associated with the related **Botai culture**, as well as probably with the Yamna. The discovery was made by the archaeologists David Anthony and Dorcas Brown, and if their interpretation is correct, it pushes horseback riding much further back than previously thought. (The oldest pictorial representations of horseback riding date only to about 2000 BC.)

2.68. This has enormous consequences for the whole question of the IE homeland and expansions. Anthony and his colleagues have emphasized that the advantages lent by horseback riding are far more than just military, especially for a people who had previously been confined to riverine forested regions for their livelihood. Horseback riding would have allowed the population to scout far and wide for new pastures, transport goods quickly, undertake large-scale livestock breeding and herding, sustain a mobile and flexible pastoral economy, and engage efficiently in long-distance trading (as well as raiding and warfare). There is archaeological evidence for all of these activities on the part of the Yamna, and they were the first people in the Pontic-Caspian area to spread into the deep steppe and exploit it.

2.69. Importantly, the Yamna can be linked rather clearly with a later cultural complex that we are reasonably sure was Indo-European – specifically, Indo-Iranian: the **Andronovo culture**, the earliest archaeological complex that can be identified with a particular IE linguistic group. The Andronovo culture evinces numerous features explicitly described in early Indo-Iranian texts, especially aspects of tomb-construction and burial ritual. Their kurgan burials, some of them spectacular, contain wheeled vehicles, livestock (horses, sheep, goats, cattle), weapons, ornaments (including cheek-pieces for horses), and scatterings of sacred straw (called *barhís* in

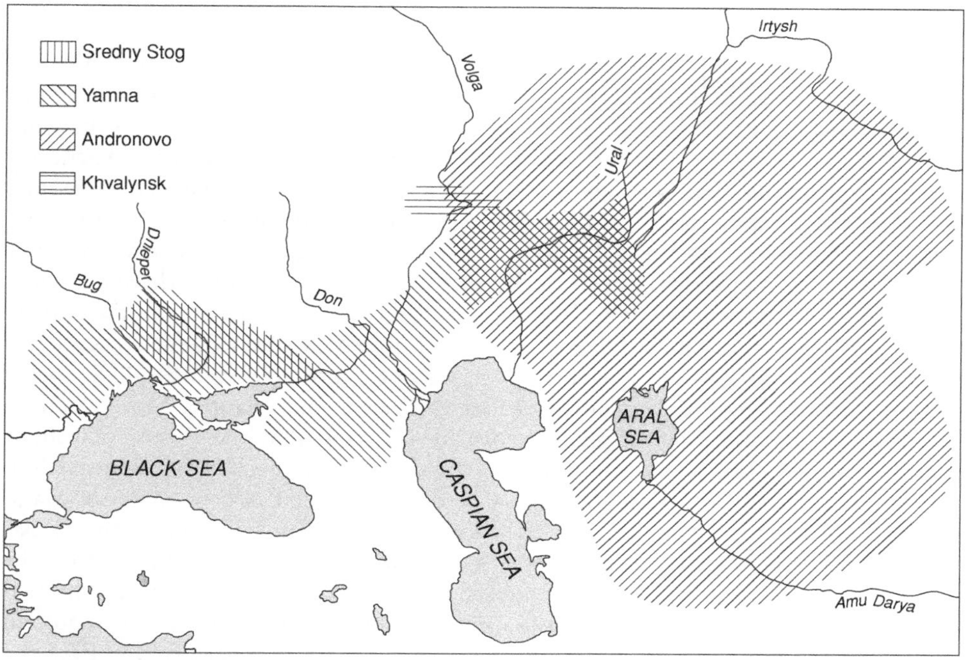

Map 2.1 Selected Late Neolithic and Chalcolithic (Bronze Age) cultures north of the Black and Caspian Seas

the Rig Veda). The Andronovo appeared around 2200 BC in northern Kazakhstan between the Ural and Irtysh Rivers, and is generally agreed to have ultimately developed from an early third-millennium eastern outgrowth of the Yamna.

2.70. We can therefore follow a direct line back from early Indo-Iranians to a cultural complex of the Pontic-Caspian steppes of the mid-fourth millennium BC. Does this mean the Yamna culture was in fact the early Indo-Europeans? Some see the Yamna as merely ancestral to the Indo-Iranians. But given that we have already established a date of c. 3400 BC as the earliest possible end of PIE linguistic unity, it seems quite unlikely that anything specific enough to be identified as Indo-Iranian or pre-Indo-Iranian was already on the scene at that time. The Yamna culture, in fact, certainly fits the bill of being the late Proto-Indo-Europeans: rapid expansion from an original area that comprised a temperate forest; the recent adoption (or invention) of wheel technologies; widespread stockbreeding; and use of the domesticated horse, including in ritual.

2.71. However convincing this scenario just outlined may be, its tentative and controversial nature cannot be too strongly emphasized. Part of it hinges crucially on the date of the domestication of the horse, and of horseback riding in particular. Both of these are hotly debated issues, although more and more scholars agree that the horse was at least domesticated by the time of the Yamna. We do not have any written texts to prove or disprove the late fifth- and early fourth-millennium-BC

Pontic-Caspian steppes as the IE homeland, and will likely never have any. There is thus ample room for other views.

Probably the most prominent alternative hypothesis is that the homeland was in eastern Anatolia and neighboring regions in the Caucasus, as propounded most famously by the English archaeologist Lord Colin Renfrew and, in a somewhat different version, by the then-Soviet team of Tamaz V. Gamkrelidze and Vyacheslav V. Ivanov. It is true that archaeologists have identified an early dispersal of peoples out of Anatolia that is associated with the spread of farming into Europe. However, most Indo-Europeanists reject the notion that this dispersal can represent any early Indo-European migrations. The critical difficulty is that it was a full three millennia before the earliest known wheeled vehicles, and we have seen that the wheel-technology vocabulary must have already been present before PIE-speakers started spreading too far and wide. This theory can only be maintained by willfully ignoring the comparative linguistic evidence discussed earlier in this chapter. More recently, Renfrew has modified his original theory by claiming that the Proto-Anatolians remained in Anatolia while the ancestors of the rest of the family migrated into Europe, settling and remaining around Greece for the next two or three thousand years before coming into contact with wheel technology and dispersing both westward and eastward. This scenario is also problematic; though it may avoid the wheel-vocabulary problem (or not, depending on one's view of the Anatolian evidence; recall §2.51), few if any linguists would countenance the notion that Anatolian split off from the family so many thousand years before the rest. By the time the Anatolian languages are attested (four or five thousand years later!) they are not a strongly differentiated family, which is well-nigh impossible if they had been developing on their own for so long. The historical record on the side of Anatolia additionally suggests strongly that the Indo-European-speaking ancestors of the Anatolians were latecomers in the region, not original inhabitants.

2.72. By contrast, several considerations, both archaeological and linguistic, point independently to the Yamna of the Pontic-Caspian steppe as the Indo-Europeans in their early expansionist phase. The Yamna itself is usually agreed to have developed partly out of the **Sredny Stog culture**, which stretched over an area north of the Black Sea with a western boundary around the Dnieper River, and out of the **Khvalynsk culture**, which was located east of the Sredny Stog. The area inhabited by the Sredny Stog has been seen by some as the "real" PIE homeland. The Sredny Stog flourished c. 4500–3500 BC, until the appearance of the Yamna. There is no conclusive evidence for horseback riding from this period; horses were apparently mainly used for hunting and for food, and settlements were permanent rather than nomadic.

Europe and the Indo-Europeans

2.73. It is more difficult to connect the various European cultures with the Pontic-Caspian; in fact, the archaeological prehistory of all the European IE groups is quite murky. Many archaeologists in fact use this as evidence for rejecting the kurgan theory. But in the period 3100–2900 BC came a clear and dramatic infusion of Yamna cultural practice, including burials, into eastern Hungary and along the lower Danube. With this we seem able to witness the beginnings of the Indo-Europeanization of Europe. By this point, the members of the Yamna culture had spread out over a very large area and their speech had surely become dialectally strongly differentiated; a common PIE must no longer have existed. A number of archaeologists, however, dispute the conclusion that any archaeological connection can be ascertained between the Yamna spread and the subsequent IE expansions in Europe. This is, to be sure, an unsolved problem, but there are different ways in which peoples and languages can spread that are not always so clearly reflected in the archaeological record: a given language in particular is not associated with one single kind of artifact or other material remains.

However exactly it proceeded, the Indo-Europeanization of Europe was all but complete by the dawn of the Christian era. The only surviving descendant of a pre-Indo-European language of Europe is **Basque**, spoken in the Pyrenees in northern Spain and southern France. Basque is descended from **Aquitanian**, which is known from about 400 personal names and several dozen divine names preserved in Latin texts from Spain. The best-attested ancient language having a claim to being an indigenous pre-IE language of Europe (though this is controversial) is **Etruscan**, spoken in Italy; see §13.2. Inscriptions in several other presumably pre-IE languages have been found, but are difficult or impossible to interpret, such as Tartessian and Iberian in Spain, North Picene in Italy, and the pre-Greek Minoan language written in the Linear A script. Indirect traces of pre-IE languages in the form of borrowings (recall the discussion in §1.17) have not yielded much hard information. In more recent years, DNA tests of skeletal remains have begun to be carried out in an effort to map the origins and migrations of ancient populations. Their results are rarely uncontroversial, given, for example, the ease with which these items can be contaminated with modern DNA; and in spite of much wishful thinking along these lines, genes cannot be matched with languages.

So the search for the Indo-Europeans goes on. Whether we are closer to finding them now, or whether we are just as far from the truth as ever, is perhaps not knowable. As with the reconstruction of the Indo-European proto-language that will occupy our attention in the next several chapters, and as is true in the sciences in general, we can only deal in probabilities – what explanations have the best and most convincing evidence and arguments to back them up. Yet this is no mere academic exercise. The Indo-Europeans have been a uniquely successful people, whose impact on human history has been as great as, if not greater than, that of any other. We will not be able to understand the historical fact of their spread and success without first illuminating their origins.

For Further Reading

The classic ethnolinguistic investigation of PIE vocabulary is Benveniste 1969, a collection of over fifty studies covering livestock and wealth, economic obligations, kinship, social status, law, and religion. It is a unique work, summing up a lifetime of research into IE culture by one of the twentieth century's foremost Indo-Europeanists. The standard dictionary of PIE is Pokorny 1959–69, in German; the only English work of similar scope is Mann 1984–7, which however is substandard. Smaller but very useful, especially for English-speaking non-specialists, is Watkins 2000, which contains all the Indo-European roots (over 1300) that have descendants in English, with entries detailing the intermediate prehistoric stages. The volume begins with an excellent overview of PIE culture and vocabulary. Also of high use-fulness is Buck 1949, which lists groups of terms in most IE branches by category, with etymological commentary on each group.

A recent reference work on IE vocabulary, culture, and archaeology is Mallory and Adams 1997, which contains hundreds of articles, some fairly extensive, by numerous contributors. See now also their handbook, Mallory and Adams 2006 (reference given in the Bibliography to the previous chapter). The quality and coverage of the articles are uneven, but it is still a welcome volume and particularly useful for the archaeological information it provides, however controversial and incomplete some of it is. Also recommended are the technical articles contained in the second volume of Watkins 1994 and the second volume of Gamkrelidze and Ivanov 1984; the latter contains an extensive collection and discussion of cultural and folkloric material.

Good introductions to the theories of Georges Dumézil are Dumézil 1958 and the slightly earlier Dumézil 1952. Contemporary studies in the Dumézilian mold frequently grace the pages of the semiannual *Journal of Indo-European Studies*, which also publishes many articles on IE archaeology and mythology. Schlerath 1995–6 is an important critical assessment of Dumézilian trifunctionalism. Puhvel 1987 is a lively and useful comparative collection of various IE myths.

For IE poetics, global reference may be made to Watkins 1995, which is an exhaustive study of the IE dragon-slaying myth and of IE poetic practice, though not uncontroversial in its broad view of what constitutes a formula. Readers of German and Italian should also consult Schmitt 1967 and the writings of Enrico Campanile, such as Campanile 1977.

The best recent overview of IE archaeology and the attempts to locate the PIE homeland and reconstruct PIE culture is Mallory 1989, with copious maps and illustrations; it is very accessible to a general audience. Mallory's command of the linguistic issues is better than most archaeologists'. A useful collection of articles by Marija Gimbutas on these and related subjects is her collection Gimbutas 1997. Renfrew's alternate theory discussed in §2.71 is presented in Renfrew 1987. David Anthony's view of the spread of the Indo-Europeans has now been given book-length treatment in Anthony 2008.

For Review

Georges Dumézil	hospitality	'imperishable fame'	strophic style
trifunctionalism	Father Sky	oral-formulaic poetry	merism
Omaha kinship system	divine twins	formula	Behaghel's Law
	aśvamedha	quantitative verse	kurgan
Männerbund	taboo deformation		Marija Gimbutas

Exercises

1 Write a sentence or two describing or exemplifying each of the following aspects of PIE culture:

a social stratification
b patrilineal exogamy
c movable wealth
d gift and countergift
e guest-friendship
f enforcement of justice
g gods and humans
h consecration of kingship
i medical treatment
j dragon-slaying myth
k outlaws
l poets
m fame
n burial customs

2 Briefly explain the significance of each of the following items for attempts to locate the homeland of the Proto-Indo-Europeans:

a salmon **b** burial customs **c** beaver **d** beech

3 Briefly explain the significance of each of the following items for establishing the approximate date that PIE was spoken:

a wheeled vehicles **b** milk products **c** silver **d** plow

4 Briefly describe or explain the following and, where relevant, comment on their significance:

a the PIE phrase _*(e-)g^{w}hen-t og^{w}him_
b the journey of the soul to the afterlife
c the relationship between poet and patron
d to 'lead away' a woman in marriage
e assonance
f name and fame
g horseback riding

5 Below is an excerpt from Homer's *Odyssey* (19.106–118). Odysseus has made it home to Ithaca but has not revealed himself to his wife Penelope yet. Here is his first encounter with her, while he is still in disguise as a beggar. The Greek (slightly simplified) is given first, followed by an English translation; the various boldfacings, italicizings, etc. are designed to help you match the Greek words with the words in the translation.

Tēn d' **apameibomenos** *prosephē* polumētis Odusseus:
"ō gunai, **ouk** *an* **tis** se **brotōn** ep' apeirona gaian
neikeoi; ē gar seu kleos ouranon eurun hikānei,
hōs te **teu** ē **basilēos amūmonos**, *hos* te theoudēs
andrasin en **polloisi** kai iphthīmoisin *anassōn*
eudikiās **anekhēisi**, pherēisi de gaia melaina
pūrous kai krīthas, *brithēisi* de dendrea karpōi,
tiktēi d' empeda **mēla**, thalassa de parekhēi ikhthūs
ex **euēgesiēs**, aretōsi de *lāoi* hup' autou.
tōi eme nūn ta men alla **metalla** sōi *eni* oikōi,
mēd' emon *exereeine* genos kai patrida gaian,
mē moi mallon *thūmon* eniplēsēis odunāōn
mnēsamenōi: . . .

Answering her, wily Odysseus *said*:
"O lady, **no mortal** on the boundless earth *would reproach*
you, for indeed your fame reaches wide heaven,
like that **of some blameless king** *who*, reverencing the gods,
reigning among men **great in number** and powerful,
upholds good justice, so that the black earth bears
wheat and barley, and the trees *are heavy* with fruit,
and **the flocks** *produce young* without cease, and the sea provides fish
due to his **good rule**, and *the people* prosper under him.
Now **ask** me other things *in* your house
– **don't** *inquire* of my race and native land,
lest you fill my *heart* even more with sufferings
as I am reminded: . . .

a Discuss the poetic artistry of this passage (concentrating on the Greek, not the English translation!). You do not need to know Greek to do this. Give examples of phonetic repetition, merisms, or anything else worth noting. For example, the beginning of line 109 (*hōs te teu*) is phonetically mirrored by *hos te theou(dēs)* at the end. The vowel letters *a e i o u* are pronounced as in most European languages (Italian, Spanish, German, Latin, etc.); *ā*, *ē*, etc. are long *a*, *e*, etc.; the sequences *ai*, *ei*, *oi*, *au*, *eu*, *ou*, *āi*, *ēi* are diphthongs and count as single syllables; all other vowel combinations (e.g. *oo*, *ee*) make up two separate syllables; *x* represents *ks*; and the combinations *ph*, *th*, *kh* represent *p*, *t*, *k* with a puff of breath after them (as in the first sound of Eng. *pit*, *tip*, *kit*).

b A common feature of IE poetry is *ring composition*, in which a poet uses a word or words toward the beginning of a section and repeats them or phonetically similar words toward the end, forming a "ring" that binds the section together. This section has a double ring that begins with the words *Odusseus* and *gaian* ('land') at the end of lines 106 and 107. Identify the two forms, and their location, that close this ring. One of these may not be immediately obvious.

6 Write a paragraph comparing the content of the middle of the above excerpt from the *Odyssey*, where Odysseus talks about a just ruler, with the following excerpt from the Old Irish *Audacht Morainn* (*Testament of Morann*), a set of instructions for princes (§§17–21, translated by Fergus Kelly; for the original, see §14.50): "It is through the justice of the ruler that abundances of great tree-fruit of the great wood are tasted. It is through the justice of the ruler that milk-yields of great cattle are maintained. It is through the justice of the ruler that there is abundance of every high, tall corn. It is through the justice of the ruler that abundance of fish swim in streams. It is through the justice of the ruler that fair children are well begotten . . ."

3 Proto-Indo-European Phonology

Introduction

3.1. The science of linguistic reconstruction goes back to work of the German philologist August Schleicher in the 1860s. He imputed only three vowels to Proto-Indo-European (*a i u*) and a total of fifteen consonants. A rush of discoveries in the later 1860s and 1870s revealed that this reconstruction was inadequate. By the close of the nineteenth century, the model of PIE phonology that is presented in this chapter, with 25 consonants and 10 vowels, was mostly in place.

The notation of the reconstructed sounds of PIE has its own history. Readers familiar with the International Phonetic Alphabet (IPA), a universal phonetic transcription system devised in the late nineteenth century, need to be aware that the notation of PIE sounds is similar to, but not identical with, that of the IPA. As is standard, whenever recourse is made to IPA symbols, they will be enclosed in square brackets.

Consonants

3.2. Consonants are speech sounds produced by partially or completely blocking the flow of air through the vocal tract. They are classified according to where in the vocal tract this obstruction occurs (the *place* of articulation), how the obstruction is produced (the *manner* of articulation), and whether there is accompanying vibration of the vocal cords (*voicing*).

Stops

3.3. Stop consonants (or plosives) are produced by completely blocking, then releasing, the flow of air through the mouth. From the comparative evidence afforded by the most ancient IE daughter languages, we know that PIE was rich in stop consonants. Over the next couple of pages, we will examine the evidence and briefly show the reasoning behind the standard reconstruction of the PIE stop inventory. (Space will not allow similar treatment of the sounds discussed in the rest of this chapter; the reader may bear in mind that similar reasoning was employed for all of the other reconstructions.)

3.4. Let us begin with the following sound correspondences from a selection of IE daughter languages, a bit simplified for our present purposes:

Sanskrit	Avestan	Greek	Latin	Welsh	English	Armenian	Lithuanian
p	p	p	p	–	f	h	p
t	t	t	t	t	th	tʿ	t
b	b	b	b	b	p	p	b
d	d	d	d	d	t	t	d

(The symbol *tʿ* in Armenian represents a *t* with aspiration, a following puff of breath.) All of these are *reflexes*, that is, descendant outcomes, of ancestral PIE sounds. This table is a shorthand for saying that, for any Sanskrit word containing *p*, its Avestan, Greek, Latin, and Lithuanian cognates will also contain a *p* in the same position, while the English cognate will have *f*, the Armenian cognate will have *h*, and the Welsh cognate will have no sound. (We will provide actual word equations illustrating these sound correspondences below in §3.7.) The same is true, *mutatis mutandis*, for the other sounds listed above, where all the languages agree across the board except English and Armenian. Cross-linguistic research has shown that it is more natural for the English and Armenian inventories to have developed from *p t b d* than the other way around; furthermore, if we hypothesize that only English and Armenian have changed the original state of affairs (and Welsh in the case of *p*), we are not forced to claim that all the other branches underwent major independent but parallel (and cross-linguistically unnatural) change.

For these and other reasons, on the basis of these comparanda Indo-Europeanists reconstruct the voiceless stops **p* and **t* and the corresponding voiced stops **b* and **d* for PIE; they were pronounced as in English. **p* and **b* are both labial stops, and **t* and **d* are dentals. (Precisely what kind of dental stop **t* and **d* were is not certain, as "dental" is a cover term for a variety of sounds produced by the tip of the tongue touching the upper teeth; but this level of phonetic detail is not likely to be recoverable for PIE.)

3.5. A second set of correspondences is more complicated, and caused early Indo-Europeanists considerable trouble:

Sanskrit	Avestan	Greek	Latin	Welsh	English	Armenian	Lithuanian
k	k	k	k[1]	c	h	kʿ	k
ś	s	k	k[1]	c	h	s	š
k	k	p	qu	p	wh	kʿ	k
g	g	g	g	g	k[2]	k	g
j	z	g	g	g	k[2]	c	ž
g	g	b	u[3]	b	qu	k	g

[1] Spelled *c*. [2] Often spelled *c*. [3] Or *v*; pronounced *w*.

These sets all involve *velar* sounds of various kinds – *k*'s and *g*'s – produced with the back of the tongue raised to touch the soft palate (velum). The big issue was how many velars to reconstruct for PIE. It turns out that the only satisfactory solution is to reconstruct a separate sound for each of these correspondence sets. For the first and fourth rows, all the languages except English and Armenian (where *k*ʿ stands for a *k* with aspiration) agree on having ordinary *k* and *g* (Welsh *c* represents *k*). We therefore reconstruct **k* and **g* for these two correspondence sets. (This **g* is the "hard" *g* as in English *garden.*)

The second and fifth rows include plain velars in some languages but a palatal fricative (written *ś*) in Sanskrit, an alveopalatal affricate (*j*, as in English) in Sanskrit, a collection of sibilants (*s*, *z*, *š*, *ž*, the last two like English *sh* and *zh*), and an alveolar affricate (*c* in Armenian, pronounced *ts*). All these sounds commonly develop out of palatal or palatalized sounds in the histories of many of the world's languages. It is therefore believed that these sounds go back to *palatal* stops in PIE, written **k̂* and **ĝ*, pronounced like ordinary *k* and *g* but farther forward in the mouth (as in *Tokyo* and *argue*). In some languages, such as Greek, Latin, and English, the palatal velars fell together with the ordinary velars, more on which later.

This leaves the third and sixth sets above, both of which distinguish themselves by having a labial element of some kind in several of the branches: labial stops (*p b*) in Greek and Welsh, and a labiovelar sound in Latin and English (*qu, wh*) – that is, a velar sound with rounding of the lips. There is essentially only one kind of sound that could have had such diverse developments (as either plain velar, labial, or labiovelar): a *labiovelar stop*. We therefore reconstruct two PIE labiovelars, *k^w (voiceless; also written *$k^{u̯}$) and *g^w (voiced; also written *$g^{u̯}$). These were single speech sounds, velars pronounced with rounding of the lips; they were not sequences of velar plus *w*. (We know this because such sequences have different outcomes from the labiovelars in some languages. In Sanskrit and Lithuanian, the PIE labiovelar *k^w became *k*, but the consonant cluster **ku̯* (= *kw*) became *kv*.)

Although the term *velar* normally refers specifically to *k* or *g*, all the six sounds we have just reconstructed – **k* **g* **k̂* **ĝ* *k^w *g^w – are collectively referred to as "velars" in Indo-European studies (or "gutturals" in older literature; occasionally they are also called *dorsals* or *tectals*). To avoid confusion, **k* and **g* are often called the *plain velars* to distinguish them from the others (which, as we have seen, are called palatal velars and labiovelars).

3.6. There is one final set of correspondences involving stop consonants:

Sanskrit	Avestan	Greek	Latin	Welsh	English	Armenian	Lithuanian
bh	b	ph	f	b	b	b	b
dh	d	th	f	d	d	d	d
h	z	kh	h	g	g	j	ž
gh	g	kh	h	g	g	g	g
gh	g	ph	f	g	b	g	g

In three of the branches above, these sounds are characterized by some kind of aspiration (breathiness or hissing quality). Sanskrit *bh* is a *b* followed by a puff of breath; Greek *ph* was a *p* followed by a puff of breath; Latin *f* belongs to a class of consonants, called fricatives, with a hissing quality due to release of air during their production (see further §3.12). On the other hand, English, Armenian, and some other branches do not show any aspiration here. It is generally agreed that the aspiration must have been originally present, but lost in the branches that no longer show it; the opposite direction of change is unlikely. We reconstruct five so-called *voiced aspirated stops*, symbolized **bh *dh *ĝh *gh *g^{w}h*. The voiced aspirates can also be written with superscript *h*'s (*b^{h} g^{h}* etc.); they were voiced stops followed by a puff of breath or a brief period of breathy voice (the latter technically called murmur). Indic (with its main ancient representative Sanskrit) is the only subbranch of the family that preserved them intact into the historical period; they are still found in many modern languages descended from Sanskrit, such as Hindi and Bengali.

(We may add parenthetically that in earlier Indo-European studies a fourth series of stops was reconstructed, the *voiceless aspirates *ph *th *kh* etc. The best evidence for them comes from Indo-Iranian and Greek, where however they can be explained as later, secondary developments. A few Indo-Europeanists still posit them for the proto-language. We will discuss these a bit more in §10.31.)

To sum up so far, PIE had the following fifteen-stop inventory:

	labial	dental	palatal	velar	labiovelar
voiceless	p	t	k̂	k	k^{w}
voiced	b	d	ĝ	g	g^{w}
voiced aspirated	bh	dh	ĝh	gh	g^{w}h

3.7. Following are representative cognate words to illustrate each of the correspondence sets so far discussed. If no English gloss (translation) is given for a particular form, it has the same meaning as its PIE ancestor. Not all the attested cognates are given in each set.

The forms cited as examples in this and the next few chapters may seem a bit bewildering at this stage, as we have not yet covered the various spelling systems of these languages, nor the sound changes that account for any deviations from a particular reconstructed PIE form. For the time being, such details are not significant and should be ignored; these lists are designed mainly to give a sense of the large body of evidence that the reconstructions are based on. In later chapters, we will have occasion to explicate the sound changes that caused any such deviations observed below. There are also a few forms in the lists below where an outcome is different from that predicted by the charts in §§3.4–6; these are typically due to a sound change conditioned by a particular neighboring sound and should not cause concern at this point.

As most of the IE language names are not assumed to be familiar at this stage, only the following abbreviations are used: Eng. = English; Gk. = Greek; Lat. = Latin; Vedic Skt. = Vedic Sanskrit (the oldest form of Sanskrit and the one generally cited in IE studies). Hyphens are used to separate prefixes and suffixes from root morphemes wherever this clarifies an example; a form ending in a hyphen means that normally the form had to have a grammatical ending attached to it, or that it was a prefix.

Voiceless stops

These typically remain unchanged, except in Germanic and Armenian, where they became fricatives or aspirates. The labial *p* is sometimes weakened or lost (Celtic, Armenian).

**p* **ped-*, **pod-* 'foot': Luvian *pāta-*, Vedic Skt. *pad-*, Gk. *pod-*, Lat. *ped-*, Armenian *otn*, Eng. *foot*, Tocharian A *pe*, Albanian *për-posh* 'under' (< **pēdsu* 'at the feet')

**t* **ters-* 'to dry': Vedic Skt. *tarṣ-áyati* 'makes thirsty', Gk. *térs-etai* 'becomes dry', Lat. *terra* '(dry) land', Eng. *thirst*, Armenian *t'aṙ-amim* 'I wilt', Albanian *ter* 'I dry'

**k̂* **k̂erd-* 'heart': Hieroglyphic Luvian *zārza*, Hittite *kard-*, Skt. *śrád-dhā-* 'putting one's heart (in), trust', Gk. *kard-íā*, Lat. *cord-*, Old Irish *cride*, Eng. *heart*, Armenian *sirt*, Tocharian B *kär-yāñ* 'hearts', Old Church Slavonic *srĭd-ĭce*, Lithuanian *širdìs*

**k* **kes-* 'comb': Hittite *kišš-*, Gk. *késkeon* (< **kes-kes-o-*) 'coarse flax prepared for spinning, tow', Middle Irish *cír* (< **kēs-rā*) 'comb', Old Eng. *heord* 'hair' (> Modern Eng. *hards* 'coarse refuse of flax'), Old Church Slavonic *kosa* 'hair', Lithuanian *kasà* 'braid'

**kʷ* **kʷi-*, **kʷo-* (interrogative pronoun stems): Hittite *kuit* 'what', Vedic Skt. *kás* 'who', Avestan *kō* 'who', Gk. *tí* 'what', Lat. *quid* 'what', Welsh *pwy* 'who', Armenian *k'ani* 'how much', Old Eng. *hwæt* 'what', Tocharian B *k̮ᵤse-* 'which', Old Church Slavonic *kŭ-to* 'who', Lithuanian *kàs* 'who', Albanian *kë* 'whom'

Voiced stops

These also typically remain unchanged, the main exceptions being Germanic, Armenian, and Tocharian, where they became voiceless:

**b* **bel-* 'strong, strength': Vedic Skt. *bálam* 'strength', Gk. *bel-tíōn* 'better', Lat. *dē-bilis* 'lacking strength', Old Church Slavonic *bolĭjĭ* 'bigger'

**d* **doru*, **deru* 'wood, tree': Hittite *tāru*, Vedic Skt. *dā́ru*, Avestan *dāuru*, Gk. *dóru*, Armenian *tram* 'firm', Old Irish *daur* 'oak', Eng. *tree*, Old Church Slavonic *drěvo*, Lithuanian *dervà*, Albanian *dru* 'wood'

**ĝ* **ĝonu*, **ĝenu* 'knee': Hittite *gēnu*, Vedic Skt. *jā́nu*, Avestan *žnūm* (accus.), Gk. *gónu*, Lat. *genū*, Armenian *cownr*, Eng. *knee*, Tocharian A *kanweṃ* 'the two knees'

**g* **gras-* 'eat': Vedic Skt. *grásate* 'eats, feeds', Gk. *grástis* 'green fodder, grass', Lat. *grāmen* (< **gras-men*) 'grass, fodder'

*g^w *g^w*en-* 'woman': Hittite ***kuinnaš***, Vedic Skt. ***jáni-***, Avestan ***jaini-***, Gk. ***gunḗ***, Old Irish ***ben***, Old Eng. ***cwēn*** (Mod. Eng. ***queen***), Armenian ***kin***, Tocharian B ***śana***, Old Church Slavonic ***žena***, Old Prussian ***genna***

Voiced aspirated stops

These are preserved intact only in Indic (as per §3.6 above). They fell together with the plain voiced stops in most of the other branches, but have reflexes distinct from those of the voiceless and plain voiced stops in Greek, Italic, Germanic, and Armenian (and Indic, of course).

bh* **bher-* 'carry': Vedic Skt. ***bhárāmi* 'I carry', Gk. ***phérō*** 'I carry', Lat. ***ferō*** 'I carry', Phrygian ***ab-beret*** 'he brought', Old Irish ***biru*** 'I carry', Armenian ***berem*** 'I carry', Eng. ***bear***, Tocharian A and B ***pär-***, Old Church Slavonic ***berǫ*** 'I take', Albanian ***bjer*** 'bring!'

dh* **medhu* 'honey; sweet drink': Luvian ***maddu* 'wine', Vedic Skt. ***mádhu*** 'honey', Gk. ***méthu*** 'wine', Old Irish ***mid*** 'mead', Eng. ***mead***, Tocharian B ***mit*** 'honey', Old Church Slavonic ***medŭ*** 'honey', Lithuanian ***medùs*** 'honey'

ĝh* **ĝheu-* 'pour': Vedic Skt. ***hūyáte* 'is poured', Avestan ***zaotar-*** 'priest (who pours libation)', Gk. ***khé(w)ō*** 'I pour', Lat. ***fūtis*** 'watering-can', Armenian ***joyl*** 'having been poured', Tocharian B ***kewu*** 'I will pour', Eng. ***ingot***

gh* **steigh-* 'go, climb': Vedic Skt. ***ati-ṣṭígham* 'to climb up', Gk. ***steíkhō*** 'I climb', Old Irish ***tíagu*** 'I go', Gothic ***steigan*** 'to climb', Old Church Slavonic ***stignǫti*** 'to come, arrive at', Lithuanian ***steigiúos*** 'I hurry', Albanian ***shteg*** 'path'

*g^wh *g^w*hen-* 'smite, slay': Hittite ***kuen-zi*** 'slays', Vedic Skt. ***hán-ti*** 'slays', Avestan ***jaiṇ-ti*** 'slays', Gk. ***-phonos*** '-slayer', Lat. ***dē-fen-dit*** 'beats off, defends', Old Irish ***gon-im*** 'I slay', Eng. ***bane***, Armenian ***ǰn-em*** 'I slay', Old Church Slavonic ***ženǫ*** 'I drive after, hunt', Lithuanian ***genù*** 'I drive'

"Centum" vs. "satem" development of the velars

3.8. The three series of velar consonants (palatals, velars, and labiovelars) collapsed to two in almost all the IE daughter languages, with either the palatals or the labiovelars merging with the plain velars. In the first case, the result was a plain velar series contrasting with a labiovelar series (*k g gh* and k^w g^w g^wh). In the second case, the result was a plain velar series contrasting with a palatal series (*k g gh* and *k̂ ĝ ĝh*); in branches exhibiting this development, as we saw above, the palatals typically went on to become affricates (*ch-* or *ts-*like sounds) and/or sibilants (*s-* and *sh-*like sounds). As a shorthand for referring to these two directions of development, Indo-Europeanists use the terms *centum* and *satem*, from the Latin and Avestan words for 'hundred' (*centum* and *satəm*, respectively), whose initial sounds come from PIE **k̂*. The Latin word begins with the sound *k* (spelled *c*) and therefore symbolizes the merger of palatal **k̂* with ordinary **k*, while in Avestan, **k̂* stayed distinct from **k* and became the sibilant *s*. The two developments are summarized below:

centum	**PIE**	**satem**
*k	*k̂	*k̂
	*k	*k
*k^{w}	*k^{w}	

3.9. For a long time it was thought that the distinction between centum and satem languages reflected an old dialectal division within IE, particularly since the two groups appeared not to overlap geographically: the centum branches (Greek, Italic, Celtic, Germanic) are more westerly than most satem branches (Indo-Iranian, Armenian, Balto-Slavic; exceptional is Albanian if satem, but see §19.9). However, a closer look at the material and some recent discoveries complicate things. Tocharian, located farther to the east than any other branch, is centum (if it can be called anything – ultimately all three series fell together as *k*, but the labiovelars were kept distinct until late in its prehistory; see §17.9). The Anatolian language Luvian has now been shown to preserve distinct reflexes of all three velar series in some phonetic environments (see §9.48). In three satem branches or subbranches, there is evidence that the plain velars and labiovelars were still distinct in some environments well into their later prehistories, meaning the eventual merger was a separate development in each: Indic (§10.37), Armenian (§16.12), and especially Albanian (§19.10). In a fourth, Balto-Slavic, many words actually show centum developments (see §18.5). It is therefore much more likely that each branch became centum or satem independently, although this view adds complications of its own. In any case, the terms centum and satem remain a useful descriptive shorthand.

3.10. Before leaving the realm of the PIE stop consonants, mention should be made of the **glottalic theory**, the most prominent alternative theory to the traditional view of the PIE stop system. Its starting point was a famous statement by the linguist Roman Jakobson in 1957 that the reconstructed consonant inventory of PIE was typologically improbable or impossible. This eventually spurred Tamaz V. Gamkrelidze and Vyacheslav V. Ivanov, and independently the American linguist Paul Hopper, to set up a different system in 1973. According to these scholars, PIE possessed a series of glottalized voiceless stops (stops followed by a brief closure of the glottis, symbolized *p' t' k'* etc.; technically called *ejectives*) in place of the traditional voiced stops *b d g* etc. They and their followers have averred that the resultant system is typologically more natural than the traditional one. Figuring into their arguments is the rarity of **b*, which appears in only a handful of reconstructed words; in their view, if we reconstruct glottalized **p'* instead of **b*, then PIE would have been just like some other languages with glottalized voiceless stops but lacking *p'*. They further claim that the glottalic system accounts for the curious fact (which we will get to in §4.9) that two plain voiced stops cannot co-occur in the same root (thus **deb-*, **ged-*, etc. are impossible PIE roots): if in fact the constraint was one against the co-occurrence of two *glottalized* consonants in the same root (**t'ep'-*, **k'et'-*, etc.), then that would be a familiar constraint known from other languages possessing such consonants.

3.11. The glottalic theory enjoyed a not insignificant following for a time, and still has adherents; but it has been rejected by most Indo-Europeanists. A full discussion cannot be embarked upon here, but the following points may be mentioned. Jakobson's original claim has since been falsified by the discovery of some languages having stop inventories structurally comparable to PIE. A second problem is the complete lack of direct comparative evidence for glottalized stops in PIE. None of the daughter languages has them except the Iranian language Ossetic, which acquired them in recent times from neighboring non-IE languages. (Some eastern dialects of Armenian are often claimed to have ejectives too, but in fact the relevant consonants are merely tense, that is, produced with simultaneous tightening of the glottis, a phonetically different phenomenon.) This makes accounting for the phonological histories of nearly all the branches much more complicated than under the traditional framework. Finally, the arguments based on the status of **b* are weak, for **b* is merely rare in PIE, not absent, and the statistical frequency of a sound does not necessarily indicate anything about that sound's history.

Fricatives

3.12. Fricatives are consonants produced with only partial closure of the vocal tract and typically having a hissing or buzzing quality. PIE possessed the sibilant fricative **s*, as in the root for 'sit', ***sed-***: the *s* is preserved intact in e.g. Vedic Skt. ***sáda*** 'sit!', Lat. ***sedēre*** 'to sit', Eng. ***sit***, and Old Church Slavonic ***sěděti*** 'to sit'. In some other languages, notably Greek, it became *h*: Gk. ***hézomai*** 'I sit down', Armenian ***hecanim*** 'I sit, ride'.

PIE **s* changed phonetically to **z* before voiced stops (by the same rule discussed below in §3.34): a form of the root for 'sit' is found in the compound ***ni-sd-o-*** 'where (the bird) sits down = nest', which was pronounced ***nizdo-***, with the *z* preserved intact in Old Church Slavonic ***gnězdo*** 'nest' (with later added *g-*) and Lithuanian ***lìzdas*** 'nest' (with later replacement of the initial *n-* by *l-*). In Vedic Skt. ***nīḍás*** and Lat. ***nīdus***, this **z* has disappeared but lengthened the preceding vowel.

Resonants: Liquids, nasals, and glides

3.13. PIE had six resonants, consonants produced with little obstruction of the flow of air and having a sonorous quality: the liquids **l* and **r*, the nasals **m* and **n*, and the glides (or semivowels) **i̯* and **u̯* (also written as in English, **y *w*). Technically the nasals are stops, but since air flows freely during their pronunciation (namely, through the nose), they behave like the liquids and glides and are always considered together with them in IE studies.

The liquids and nasals are preserved intact in most of the branches, though in Indo-Iranian **l* usually became *r*:

l* ****leuk-* 'light': Hittite ***lukke-*** 'kindle', Vedic Skt. ***rócate*** 'shines', Avestan ***raocaiieiti*** 'lights up', Gk. ***leukós*** 'bright', Lat. ***lūc-*** 'light', Old Irish ***luchair*** 'a shining', Armenian ***loys*** 'light', Eng. ***light***, Tocharian A and B ***luk-*** 'to shine', Old Church Slavonic ***luča*** 'beam of light' *r *pro, *prō* 'forward': Hittite *parā* 'forth', Vedic Skt. *prá*, Avestan *fra-*, Gk. *pró*, Lat. *prō* 'in front of', Old Irish *ro-* (perfective and intensive prefix on verbs), Eng. *fro*, Old Church Slavonic *pro-* 'through', Lithuanian *prã* 'past'

*m *men-* 'think': Vedic Skt. *mánas-* 'mind', Avestan *manah-* 'mind', Gk. *ménos* 'mental energy, spirit, wrath', Lat. *mēns* 'mind', Old Irish *do-moiniur* 'I think', Armenian *i-manam* 'I understand', Eng. *mind*, Old Church Slavonic *mĭnjǫ* 'I believe', Lithuanian *menù* 'I think'

*n *ne* 'not': Hittite *na-tta* 'not', Vedic Skt. *ná*, Avestan *na*, Lat. *ne-* (as in *ne-scīre* 'not to know'), Old Irish *ní* (< *nē), Old Eng. *ne*, Old Church Slavonic *ne*, Lithuanian *nè*

The glides underwent change more frequently than the other resonants. The palatal glide *i̯ sometimes weakened and disappeared, and the labiovelar glide *u̯ typically became a fricative *v* or *f*. Interestingly, only in West Germanic (which includes English) has PIE *u̯ survived unchanged to the present day, as *w*.

*i̯ *i̯ugom* 'a yoke': Hittite *iukan* (phonetically *yugan*), Vedic Skt. *yugám*, Gk. *zugón*, Lat. *iugum*, Welsh *iau*, Eng. *yoke*, Lithuanian *jùngas* (with added *n*)

*u̯ *u̯eĝh-* 'to lead, convey (in a vehicle)': Hieroglyphic Luvian *waza-* 'drive', Vedic Skt. *váhati* 'leads, brings', Avestan *vazaiti* 'leads, brings', Gk. (Pamphylian) *wekhetō* 'let him convey', Lat. *uehere* 'to convey', Old Irish *fén* (< *u̯eĝh-no-) 'wagon', Middle Dutch *wagen* 'wagon' (borrowed into Eng.), Old Church Slavonic *vezǫ* 'I convey', Lithuanian *vežù* 'I drive', Albanian *vjedh* 'I steal' (< *'lead away')

Syllabic resonants

3.14. When a resonant stood between two non-syllabic consonants (*CRC*) or between a consonant and a word-boundary (*-CR* or *RC-*), it became syllabic and functioned as a vowel. In IE studies, the syllabic liquids and nasals are conventionally represented with a little circle underneath (*l̥ *r̥ *m̥ *n̥). They were pronounced much like the liquids and nasals in the second syllable of the English words ***bottled***, ***buttered***, ***bottoms***, ***buttons*** as pronounced in colloquial speech.

In most of the daughter languages, the syllabic resonants *l̥ *r̥ *m̥ *n̥ developed prop vowels before them (such as Germanic *ul *ur *um *un). Sometimes the syllabic nasals lost their nasality and became plain vowels (as in Greek and Indo-Iranian, where *m̥ and *n̥ became *a*). Below are some representative correspondence sets:

*l̥ *u̯l̥kʷos* 'wolf': Hittite *walkuwa-* 'monster' (?), Vedic Skt. *vŕ̥kas*, Avestan *vəhrka-*, Old Church Slavonic *vlĭkŭ*, Lithuanian *vil̃kas*

*r̥ *mr̥-to-* 'dead': Vedic Skt. *mr̥tá-*, Avestan *mərəta-*, Gk. *brotós* (< *mrotós) 'mortal', Lat. *Morta* 'goddess of death', Armenian *mard* 'man', Eng. *murd-er*, Old Russian *mĭrtvŭ* 'dead', Lithuanian *mirtìs* 'death' *m̥ **dek̑m̥* 'ten': Vedic Skt. *dáśa*, Avestan *dasa*, Gk. *déka*, Lat. *decem*, Old Church Slavonic *desę-tĭ* (*ę* is a nasalized vowel), Lithuanian *dẽšimt*

*n̥ **n̥-* 'not, un-': Vedic Skt. *a(n)-*, Gk. *a(n)-*, Lat. *in-* (older *en-*), Old Irish *an-*, Eng. *un-*

The glides **i̯* and **u̯* also had syllabic variants – the vowels **i* and **u*. For comparative examples of their reflexes, see §3.26 below on vowels.

3.15. Earlier handbooks also reconstructed a series of long syllabic resonants, **l̥̄ *r̥̄ *m̥̄ *n̥̄*. These are nowadays understood to have been sequences of syllabic resonant plus laryngeal (see directly below): **l̥H *r̥H *m̥H *n̥H*. But the older notation can still be useful in some contexts.

Laryngeals

3.16. The so-called "laryngeals" are a class of sounds whose precise phonetic values are still not known. They are generally agreed to have been fricatives produced in the back of the mouth and throat, and are partly preserved as such in the oldest attested branch, Anatolian (e.g. as the velar fricative transliterated as *ḫ* in Hittite and Luvian). Outside Anatolian they have no certain consonantal reflexes, becoming vowels under certain conditions and leaving other, indirect traces. Their discovery by Ferdinand de Saussure represents one of the triumphs of historical linguistics; we will sketch his arguments in §§4.18–19.

In the standard theory, PIE had three of these sounds, represented abstractly as $*h_1$ $*h_2$ $*h_3$ (also written $*H_1$ $*H_2$ $*H_3$ or $*ə_1$ $*ə_2$ $*ə_3$, among other notations). The cover symbol *H* (less commonly *ə*) is used for a laryngeal that cannot or need not be specified.

3.17. When a laryngeal occurred between two non-syllabic sounds, it developed a prop vowel next to it (sometimes before, sometimes after), yielding what is often called a **vocalized** or **syllabic laryngeal**. Like syllabic resonants, vocalized laryngeals may be represented with circles under them: *h̥*$_1$ *h̥*$_2$ *h̥*$_3$ (cover symbol *H̥*), though we will not be doing that in this book except when necessary. Vocalized laryngeals became vowels in many of the branches, usually *a*, but *i* in Sanskrit. In Greek, each vocalized laryngeal had a different outcome, the valuable "triple reflex" *e a o* from $*h_1$ $*h_2$ $*h_3$ respectively. Some examples showing reflexes of vocalized laryngeals are as follows:

$*h_1$ **dhh$_1$s-* 'sacred, religious': Vedic Skt. *dhíṣ-ṇya-* 'devout', Gk. *thés-phatos* 'decreed by god', Lat. *fānum* (< **fas-no-* < **dhh$_1$s-no-*) 'temple'

$*h_2$ **sth$_2$-to-* 'standing, made to stand': Vedic Skt. *sthitá-*, Gk. *statós*, Lat. *status*, Welsh *(gwa)stad* 'standing firm, constant, level', Old Norse *staðr* 'obstinate, restive' (said of horses)

$*h_3$ **dh$_3$-ti-* 'gift': Vedic Skt. *díti-*, Gk. *dósis*, Lat. *datiō*

In Greek, Armenian, and Phrygian, laryngeals occurring at the beginning of a word before a consonant were also vocalized. Thus $^*h_2$*nēr* 'man' became Gk. *anḗr*, Phrygian *anar*, and Armenian *ayr* (from earlier **anir*). In the other branches, the laryngeals did not vocalize in this position and eventually disappeared, though they sometimes left indirect traces that will be discussed in the next chapter.

Behavior and effects of the non-syllabic laryngeals

3.18. There are three important sound changes undergone or induced by the laryngeals when they were not vocalized. The first of these happened already in PIE itself and is known as laryngeal **coloring.** This refers to the effects that two of the laryngeals, $^*h_2$ and $^*h_3$, induced on an adjacent short **e*: when next to $^*h_2$, **e* became "colored" to **a*, and when next to $^*h_3$, **e* became **o*. Thus $^*h_2$*ent-* 'front, forehead' became colored to $^*h_2$*ant-*, and $^*h_3$*erbh-* 'move from one social sphere into another' became colored to $^*h_3$*orbh-*. The first laryngeal, $^*h_1$, did not color; thus the *e* in $^*h_1$*esti* 'is' remained *e*.

The coloring effects of laryngeals are what gave them their name; they were dubbed "laryngeals" by Hermann Möller in 1911, inspired by an identically named class of sounds in Semitic languages with similar effects on neighboring vowels. When writing reconstructed forms where coloring could take place, some Indo-Europeanists write them with coloring, some without. In this book, we shall ordinarily write them without coloring (thus $^*h_2$*ent-* and $^*h_3$*erbh-*), as that usually makes word structures clearer (as we will see in the next chapter).

3.19. The second important development of the non-syllabic laryngeals was their **loss** when adjacent to a vowel. This process may have begun in PIE, but it did not run its full course until much later. Anatolian, importantly, still preserves consonantal reflexes of $^*h_2$ and (most likely) $^*h_3$ in many positions as a sound transliterated *ḫ*. Thus the Hittite outcomes of the forms $^*h_2$*ant-* and $^*h_3$*orbh-* mentioned above are *ḫant-* 'forehead' and *ḫarapp-* 'become separated' (the *o*-coloring effect of the third laryngeal is not directly visible in the second example because Hittite changed **o* to *a*). The oldest Indo-Iranian languages, Vedic Sanskrit and Old Avestan, also reflect consonantal laryngeals as hiatuses or glottal stops between vowels (see further below), and there is some evidence from Vedic that laryngeals after consonants still counted in poetry. But ultimately, all the consonantal laryngeals were lost in all the non-Anatolian branches. Thus $^*h_2$*ant-* and $^*h_3$*orbh-* became *ant-* and *orb-* in Latin *ante* 'before, in front' and *orbus* 'orphan'. As for the first laryngeal, it was lost even in Anatolian: thus $^*h_1$*esti* 'is' became Hittite *ēšzi*, Gk. *estí*, Lat. *est*.

3.20. If a laryngeal came after a vowel and either stood at the end of a word (*-VH*) or before another consonant (*VHC*), the loss of the laryngeal was accompanied by **compensatory lengthening** of the preceding vowel, yielding **V̄C* or **-V̄*. (Another term for this process is *contraction.*) Thus **dheh*$_1$*-mn̥* 'something placed' was contracted to **dhē-mn̥* (> Gk. (*aná-*)*thēma* 'offering'); **peh*$_2$*-s-* 'protect' was first colored to **pah*$_2$*-s-* and then was contracted to **pā-s-* (> Lat. *pās-tor* 'shepherd'); **deh*$_3$*-rom* 'gift' was first colored to **doh*$_3$*-rom* and then was contracted to **dō-rom* (> Gk. *dō̃ron*); and **pih*$_1$*-u̯erih*$_2$ 'fat' (feminine) underwent no coloring (since laryngeals did not color **i*) but did undergo contraction to **pī-u̯erī* (> Vedic Skt. *pī́varī*).

As a parallel to this development, compare the change from Old Eng. *niht* to Modern Eng. *night*, where the *-h-* has been lost in pronunciation and the preceding vowel lengthened (and later diphthongized). In Anatolian, as one might expect, compensatory lengthening did not happen where laryngeals were not lost; for example, PIE *$*peh_2$-s-* 'protect' above became Hittite *paḫš-*.

A laryngeal between two vowels (**VHV*) likewise disappeared, after coloring. Thus *$*dheh_1es$* 'you will put' and *$*steh_2onti$* 'they will stand' became first *$*dheh_1es$* (without coloring) and *$*stah_2onti$* (with coloring) and then **dhees* and **staonti*. The disappearance of the laryngeal and ultimate coalescence of the two vowels into a single long vowel happened at different times and with different effects in the daughter branches. In early Indo-Iranian poetry, these sequences must still be read as disyllables much of the time (so-called "laryngeal hiatus"; see further §§10.36 and 11.23). In Germanic and Balto-Slavic, long vowels going back to **VHV* have an extra mora (timing unit) of length compared with original long vowels. This may appear to be a specialized detail, but it turns out to have massive repercussions on the phonological and morphological history of Balto-Slavic (see further on this in chapter 18).

3.21. No other subject in IE phonology has been as contentious as the laryngeal theory. Resistance to accepting laryngeals altogether (partly because of their somewhat forbidding and algebraic look) has dwindled over time; the combined phonological and morphological evidence for their existence is irrefutable. A lot of Indo-European comparative linguistics is simply not possible without them, for they help to explain too many disparate phenomena too neatly to be dismissed. There are differences of opinion as to how many laryngeals to reconstruct for PIE, however; alternative minority views operate with anywhere from one to a dozen of them, or more. Some claim that the late Indo-European that developed after Anatolian split off had only one laryngeal. But the triple reflex in Greek makes this position very difficult to maintain.

As regards their phonetic character, one fairly widespread view has it that $*h_1$ was a simple *h* or a glottal stop [ʔ], $*h_2$ a voiceless pharyngeal fricative [ħ] (same sound as the Arabic letter *ḥā'*), and $*h_3$ a voiced pharyngeal fricative [ʕ] (same sound as Arabic *'ayn*); but there are other possibilities as well.

Consonant clusters

3.22. PIE was rich not only in consonants but also in consonant clusters, especially at the beginnings of words. Most languages that have clusters arrange the consonants in order of increasing sonority, and this was true of PIE also. Stops and fricatives are the least sonorous consonants, and generally come first, followed by resonants, which are more sonorous. The maximum number of consonants in a word-initial cluster appears to have been three; longer clusters are sometimes found word-internally.

3.23. The most common word-initial clusters are those where the second consonant is a resonant. Almost all the theoretically possible combinations are found: ***pro*** 'forward', ***dlegh-*** 'engage oneself', ***k^wrei-*** 'buy', ***dhu̯er-*** 'door', ***$ti̯eg^w$-*** 'revere', ***$g^wi̯eh_3$-*** 'live', ***$\hat{g}neh_3$-*** 'know', ***pneu-*** 'breathe', ***si̯uH-*** 'sew', ***sreu-*** 'flow', ***mreĝhu-*** 'short', ***$mleuh_2$-*** 'speak', ***$u̯leik^w$-*** 'flowing, liquid', ***$u̯reh_2d$-*** 'branch, root', *mneh$_2$- 'be mindful', *h$_2$ner- 'man', *h$_3$meiĝh- 'urinate', *h$_3$reĝ- 'stretch out the hands', *h$_1$leudh- 'go', *h$_1$i̯eh$_1$- 'throw', *h$_2$u̯es- 'spend the night'. Clusters in which the second consonant is a stop or laryngeal are rare unless the first sound is s: *sk̑eh$_2$i- 'shadow', *spend- 'pour a libation', *sh$_2$eh$_1$-i- 'bind', *tk̑ei- 'settle' (see §3.25 below), *pter- 'wing', *h$_3$bhel- 'be of use', *h$_1$sih$_1$- 'be' (optative pl. stem). The two liquids *l and *r, the glide *i̯, and the nasal *n did not begin consonant clusters word-initially.

Word-initial clusters with three consonants are also found; examples include *streng- 'squeeze, tie', *splei- 'split', *h$_1$si̯eh$_1$- 'be' (optative sing. stem), *h$_2$ster- 'star', and the imitative root *pster- 'sneeze'.

3.24. Word-final consonant clusters typically arose through suffixation, as in *eu̯ēĝhst (= *e-u̯ēĝh-s-t) 'conveyed' (3rd sing. aorist) and *bheronts (= *bher-ont-s) 'carrying' (nominative sing. masc. present participle). A number of these were subject to various rules of assimilation (compare §§3.34–35), but we do not really know how a form like *eu̯ēĝhst was pronounced.

"Thorn" clusters

3.25. The Indo-European languages exhibit a curious set of sound correspondences where Sanskrit has a cluster kṣ (pronounced ksh, [kʃ]) corresponding to various clusters in Greek and often single sounds in the other languages. A representative sample of these correspondences is given below; the words mean 'bear', 'earth, ground', and 'waste away, disappear'.

Hittite	Sanskrit	Avestan	Greek	Latin	Tocharian A
ḫartaggaš[1]	*ŕ̥kṣas*		*árktos*	*ursus*	
īn-zagan-[2]	*kṣam-*	*zam-*	*khthon-*	*hum-us*	*tkaṃ*
	kṣi-		*phthi-*	*si-tis*[3]	

[1] Phonetically *ḫartkaš*. [2] Cuneiform Luvian, '(putting) in the earth = inhumation'; see further below. [3] 'Thirst'.

Under the usual modern view, these correspondences descend from PIE clusters consisting of a dental followed by a velar. The order dental–velar is preserved only in Anatolian and Tocharian. The reconstructions of the forms above are *h$_2$r̥tk̑os, *dhĝhom-, and *dhg^{w}hi- (the choice of the specific dental and velar in each case is based on other comparative evidence). In the other branches, the two sounds metathesized (switched places), and the dental came to be pronounced as [θ], or its voiced equivalent [ð] if the cluster was a voiced cluster. (In some phonetic alphabets, the sound [θ] is represented by the symbol þ, called "thorn", hence the term "thorn cluster.") In many branches, the cluster was simplified to a single consonant. Under another view, though, the dentals in these clusters were pronounced [ts] or [dz], and were pronounced this way already in PIE before any metathesis had taken place. Recently, the American Indo-Europeanist and Anatolianist Craig Melchert has interpreted Cuneiform Luvian *īnzagan-* 'inhumation' as preserving precisely this stage: the word was probably pronounced [indzgan] and comes from the phrase **en dhĝhŏm* 'in the earth'.

The behavior of other consonant clusters is treated in §§3.34ff. below.

Vowels

3.26. PIE possessed five short vowels **i* **e* **a* **o* **u* (approximately equivalent to the first vowels of *bitter*, *better*, *groggy*, *older*, *super*). The vowel correspondences among the daughter languages present a very confusing picture, and it took over half a century for the relationships to be fully worked out. Several branches merged at least two of the vowels (typically *a* and *o*, as in Indo-Iranian, Germanic, and Balto-Slavic), and all the vowels were subjected to many sound changes in different phonetic environments. The following are examples of reconstructed words with each vowel:

**i* **mizdho*- 'reward': Avestan *miẓda-*, Gk. *misthós* 'wage, pay', Gothic *mizdo*, Old Church Slavonic *mĭzda*

**e* **$h_1$esti* 'is': Hittite *ēšzi*, Vedic Skt. *ásti*, Gk. *estí*, Lat. *est*, Old Irish *is*, Eng. *is*, Old Church Slavonic *jestŭ*, Lithuanian *ẽsti*

**a* **sal-* 'salt': Vedic Skt. *sal-ilá-* 'salty' (probable meaning), Gk. *hál-*, Lat. *sal-*, Armenian *ał*, Old Irish *sal-ann*, Eng. *salt*, Tocharian A *sāle*, Old Church Slavonic *solĭ*, Lithuanian (dialectal) *salià* 'sweetness'

**o* **g^wou-* 'cow': Lycian *wawa-*, Skt. *gáv-*, Gk. *bó(w)es* 'cows', Lat. *bouēs* 'cows', Old Irish *boin* 'for a cow', Armenian *kov*, Old Church Slavonic *gov-ęždĭ* 'bovine'

**u* **snusos* 'daughter-in-law': Vedic Skt. *snuṣā́*, Gk. *nuós*, Lat. *nurus*, Armenian *nu*, Old High German *snur*, Old Church Slavonic *snŭxa*, Albanian *nuse* 'bride'

3.27. PIE also had the long non-high vowels **ē* **ā* **ō*, pronounced similar to the short vowels but held for twice the length. The long vowels **ē* and **ō* are found especially in lengthened-grade forms (see §4.13):

**ē* **h_3rēĝs* 'king': Vedic Skt. *rā́ṭ*, Lat. *rēx*, Gaulish *-rīx* (in personal names)

ā* **nās-* 'nose': Vedic Skt. *nā́sā* (dual) 'two noses', Lat. *nāris* 'nostril' (nāsis*), Old Eng. *nōse* 'headland' (Old Eng. *nasu* 'nose' is from a different form **nas-*), Lithuanian *nósis* 'nose'

**ō* **su̯esōr* 'sister': Vedic Skt. *svásā*, Lat. *sorōr-*, Old Irish *siur*

Whether PIE had **ī* and **ū* is not fully certain because so many, if not all, of the putative examples may have come originally from **iH* or **uH*, which had not contracted to **ī* and **ū* until after the breakup of the family. (This is true of many of the traditional examples of **ē*, **ā*, and **ō* as well.) However, the long *ū* in the adverbs **nū* and **nūn* 'now' (as in Gk. *nũ(n)*, Vedic Skt. *nūn-ám* 'now', Lat. *nū-per* 'recently') is almost certainly not from **uH*, and thus represents a genuine old PIE **ū*. Other words, such as **mūs* 'mouse' (in e.g. Gk. *mũs*, Lat. *mūs*, Old Eng. *mūs*) and **dhĝhū-* 'fish' (in e.g. Gk. *ikhthũs*, Armenian *jow-kn*), may have contained a laryngeal. Also uncertain is the word **u̯īs* 'poison' (as in Avestan *vīš*, Lat. *uīr-us*, Middle Irish *fí*), which had a short-vowel variant **u̯is* (e.g. Vedic Skt. *viṣ-* 'excrement'); but similar words having long- and short-vowel variants are usually thought to have contained a laryngeal that disappeared under unknown conditions in PIE without compensatory lengthening. However, for the purposes of the phonological history of most of the daughter languages, we need not worry about these issues and can reconstruct **ī* and *ū*.

Some long vowels arose by contraction of two short vowels, especially in certain inflectional categories such as the thematic subjunctive (§5.55). Dispute surrounds most or all of the remaining long vowels: since the laryngeal theory demonstrated that long vowels could arise from an earlier sequence of short vowel plus laryngeal, some researchers have claimed that all PIE long vowels were once short vowels followed by laryngeal. But this is suspect without clear evidence underpinning it. Rewriting a long vowel in a traditional reconstruction as a sequence of short vowel plus laryngeal is useful if it provides fresh insight into either the morphological or the semantic makeup of the word; otherwise it is of no advantage.

Diphthongs

3.28. The non-high vowels **e *a *o* could combine with a following high vowel **i* or **u* to form six diphthongs: **ei *ai *oi *eu *au *ou*. Examples include ****ḱei-*** 'to lie' (in e.g. Gk. *keĩmai* 'I lie'), ****kaiko-*** 'one-eyed' (in e.g. Lat. *caecus* 'blind', Gothic *haihs* 'one-eyed'), **moino-* 'exchange, reciprocation' (in e.g. Archaic Lat. *moenus* 'duty, tribute, payment'), ****sreu-mn̥*** 'a flow' (in e.g. Gk. *rheũma*), ****sauso-*** 'dry' (in e.g. Gk. *haũos* and Lithuanian *saũsas* 'dry'), and ****$h_2$kous-*** 'hear' (in e.g. Gk. *akoúō* 'I hear'). Because the high vowel in such diphthongs is rather glide-like in pronunciation, it is common to see these diphthongs written **ei̯*, **eu̯*, etc. This is not done in the present work.

Long diphthongs, composed of a long vowel plus **i* or **u*, are rare. In PIE they typically arose by contraction or due to morphologically induced lengthening of a root vowel (the so-called lengthened-grade, discussed in the next chapter). In later dialectal PIE, various long diphthongs were created by contraction processes involving laryngeals. By the time of the attested histories of the daughter languages, however, the long diphthongs had usually been shortened or monophthongized, especially outside of Indo-Iranian. Examples include ****dēiḱ-s-*** 'showed' (aorist tense, in Avestan *dāiš* 'he showed'), the dative singular ending ****-ōi*** (in e.g. Gk. *hípp-ōi* 'for a horse'), and ****stēumi*** 'I praise' (in Vedic Skt. *stáumi*, Old Avestan *stāumī*). Some other cases are disputed, most prominently the words for 'sky, sky-god' and 'cow', which some reconstruct as **di̯ēus* and **g^wōus* and others as **di̯eus* and **g^wous*; see further discussion in §6.6.

"Schwa secundum"

3.29. In word-initial consonant clusters consisting of two stops plus a resonant, a prop vowel was introduced between the two stops to break up the cluster; this vowel is called "schwa secundum" (as opposed to the "schwa primum," the schwa that represents a laryngeal, §3.16). It is written with a little subscript $_e$ or schwa. For example, one of the forms of the numeral 'four' was _*k^wtu̯or-_, which developed a schwa secundum to become _*k^w_etu̯or-_ or _*$k^w_{\text{ə}}$tu̯or-_, yielding Lat. *quattuor* and Homeric Gk. *písures* (as opposed to Gk. *téssares* from a different form, _*k^wetu̯or-_).

Stress and accent

3.30. Most polysyllabic words have at least one syllable that is acoustically more prominent than the others; this is the stressed or accented syllable. Linguists distinguish broadly between stress-accent languages, where the primary feature of this syllable is greater volume (as in English or German), and pitch-accent languages, where the primary feature of this syllable is a different pitch or pitch contour from that of its neighbors (as in Ancient Greek or Japanese).

From the available comparative evidence, it is standardly agreed that PIE was a pitch-accent language. There are numerous indications that the accented syllable was higher in pitch than the surrounding syllables. Among the IE daughters, a pitch-accent system is found in Vedic Sanskrit, Ancient Greek, the Baltic languages, and some South Slavic languages, although none of these preserves the original system intact.

3.31. All full lexical content words in PIE (nouns, verbs, adjectives, and most adverbs) had an accented syllable. Finite verbs and the vocatives of nouns had idiosyncratic accentual properties; see §§5.63 and 6.7. A certain number of function words (some particles, pronouns, and conjunctions) had no stress and were clitics, that is, they could not stand alone and were phonologically attached to a neighboring stressed word with which they formed a single accentual unit. (Compare the *'em* in English *I see 'em,* which cannot stand on its own and is pronounced together with the preceding word *see.*) These are discussed in §§8.22–25.

3.32. An additional feature of the accent in PIE was that it was mobile, that is, its position was not predictable on the basis of any phonetic features of the word it appeared in. A mobile accentual system is continued in Hittite, Vedic Sanskrit, Greek, Tocharian, and parts of Balto-Slavic, but the other branches have developed fixed accent systems or systems in which accent position is predictable for other reasons. In mobile accent systems, words can be distinguished by the position of the accent alone: Vedic Skt. *úṣas* 'o dawn' (vocative sing.) vs. *uṣás* 'of the dawn'; Gk. *oíkoi* 'at home' vs. *oĩkoi* (with *oĩ* indicating accentuation of the first rather than second half of the diphthong) 'houses'; Russian *pisál* 'he was writing' vs. *písal* 'he was peeing'.

In this book, the accent will normally not be shown on reconstructed PIE forms unless it is important in context. Much of the time, in fact, we do not know on which syllable the accent fell.

Phonological Rules

3.33. As with all living languages, the pronunciation of the sounds of PIE varied depending on what other sounds they were combined with in any given word or phrase. This behavior can be captured in statements called phonological rules. Evidence for some of these rules is preserved in several of the daughter languages.

Except for certain basic and near-universal principles of syllabification, all phonological rules are the result of sound change. Some of the rules below represent features that were part of the living grammar of PIE, while others are fossilized remnants of older sound changes. It is not always possible to tell, for any given rule, which one we are dealing with. Thus the rules listed below may well belong to more than one chronological layer of the proto-language.

Rules of consonant clusters

Voicing assimilation

3.34. In a cluster of two consonants differing in voicing, the voicing of the first assimilated to (that is, became like) that of the second. Most frequently, the second consonant in such clusters is voiceless, causing the preceding consonant to become voiceless as well: ****leĝ-tó***- 'chosen' became ****lek-tó***- (Gk. *lektós*), and **h_1**ḗ**d-si*** 'you (sing.) eat' became ****h_1ḗt-si*** (Hittite *ēzzi* [pronounced *étsi*], Vedic Skt. *átsi*). The reverse development is seen in **ni-**sd**-o-* > **ni-**zd**-o-* 'nest' (cp. §3.12 above), as well as in Avestan *fra-**bd**a-* 'front of the foot' from **pro-**pd**-o-* (from the root **ped-* 'foot'). Assimilation of this sort, from right to left (the voicing feature can be thought of as spreading leftward), is called *regressive* or *anticipatory assimilation.*

3.35. Assimilation in the reverse direction, called *progressive* or *perseverative assimilation*, is found in one famous example known as **Bartholomae's Law**. This is reflected most clearly in Indo-Iranian; whether it was of PIE date is controversial. We will discuss it in §10.6.

Dental-plus-dental clusters

3.36. A sequence of two dental consonants was pronounced with an added sibilant inserted between them. Thus **-tt-* (from either **-tt-* or **-dt-*, by voicing assimilation) and **-dd-* were pronounced **-tst-* and **-dzd-*. The first was very common, as it happened anytime a root-final *t* or *d* was followed by a suffix beginning with *t* (of which there were many). This cluster survives as *tst* in Anatolian, but in the other branches it was simplified to *-tt-* (Indic), *-st-* (Iranian, Greek, Balto-Slavic), or *-ss-* (Italic, Celtic, Germanic). Thus **$h_1$ed-te(-)* 'eat! (pl.)' first became **$h_1$ette(-)* by voicing assimilation, and then **$h_1$etste(-)*, preserved in Old Hittite *ēzten* (pronounced *étsten*) but simplified in Vedic Skt. *attá*. Similarly, **h_1ḗd-ti* 'eats' > Lithuanian *ẽsti* and Old Church Slavonic *jastŭ*; **u̯id-to-* 'known' > **u̯itto-* > **u̯itsto-* > Gk. *(w)istós*, Old Irish *-fess*, and Germ. *ge-wiss* 'certain'.

Simplification of *_ss_

3.37. The cluster *_ss_, arising at morpheme boundaries where a suffix beginning with an _s_ was added to a root or stem ending in the same sound, was simplified to single *_s_. Thus the 2nd singular verb *_$h_1$es-si_ 'you are' was simplified to *_$h_1$esi_ already in PIE, as shown by Vedic Skt. _ási_ and Greek _eĩ_ (< *_ehi_ < *_esi_).

Stang's and Szemerényi's Laws

3.38. The Indo-Europeanist and Balticist Christian Stang noticed that certain word-final consonant clusters containing resonants appear to have simplified, with compensatory lengthening of a preceding short vowel. The best examples include the accusative singulars *_di̯ēm_ 'sky' and *_g^wōm_ 'cow' from earlier *_di̯eum_ and *_g^woum_ (yielding Vedic Skt. _dyā́m_ and _gā́m_, and Homeric Gk. _Zē̃n_ 'Zeus' and _bō̃n_). It also operated when the consonant preceding the _-m_ was a laryngeal, as witnessed by the feminine accusative singular in *_-eh_2m_ (see §6.70), which became *_-ām_ instead of disyllabic *_-ah_2m̥_ as expected by the ordinary rules of syllabification in PIE (see §3.42 below).

Similar to Stang's Law is **Szemerényi's Law**, named after the Hungarian linguist Oswald Szemerényi. It states that *_-VRs_ (where _R_ is a resonant) became *_-V̄R_. Thus an earlier *_p$h_2$ters_ 'father' and *_k̑u̯ons_ 'dog' became *_ph_2tēr_ and *_k̑u̯ōn_. The law was devised to explain morphological peculiarities of these words; see further §6.6.

The _boukólos_ rule

3.39. A labiovelar lost its labial element when adjacent to the vowel *_u_. This is an example of _dissimilation_, whereby two sounds that are alike in some way become less alike (both labiovelars and the vowel _u_ are pronounced with rounding of the lips). The classic example is Greek _bou-kólos_ 'cowherd' from *_g^wou-kolos_, dissimilated by the rule from *_g^wou-**k^w**olos_. If the labiovelar had been preserved and not undergone dissimilation, the word should have turned out as *_bou-pólos_ in Greek; compare the related term _ai-pólos_ 'goatherd' < *_ai(ĝ)-k^wolos_.

Other rules

3.40. Consonants at the ends of words were subject to special rules. Voicing distinctions in word-final stops were neutralized, so for example word-final _-t_ and _-d_ were pronounced the same. (Whether they were pronounced voiced or voiceless is a bit unclear.) Additionally, we know that word-final *_-n_ was lost after _ō_. Contrast Old Irish **_cú_** 'dog' (< *_k̑u̯ō_ < *_k̑u̯ō**n**_) and Lat. _homō_ 'man' (< *_(dh)ĝhemō_ < *_(dh)ĝhemō**n**_) with Gk. _humē̂n_ 'membrane' (< *_sumē**n**_) and Old Church Slavonic _imę_ 'name' (< *_n̥m-ē**n**_; the _-ę_ is a nasalized vowel). PIE forms where the *_-n_ disappeared, like the word for 'dog' above, are written by Indo-Europeanists variously with or without the _n_, or with _n_ in parentheses: *_k̑u̯ōn_ or *_k̑u̯ō_ or *_k̑u̯ō(n)_.

3.41. Osthoff's Law. The Indo-Europeanist Hermann Osthoff observed that in many IE languages, long vowels often became short before a resonant plus another consonant. Thus Gothic *winds* 'wind' (earlier **wend-*) and Lat. *uentus* 'wind' both have short vowels, although etymologically they come from **u̯ēnto-* (from even earlier **h₂u̯eh₁nto-*). Similarly, one of the tenses of the Greek verb (the aorist passive) has a stem vowel *-ē-* (as in *emígēn* 'I was mixed', *emígē* 'it was mixed'), which was shortened to *-e-* before the original 3rd plural ending **-nt* (**emigēnt* > **emigent* > *émigen* 'they were mixed'). Many of the examples of Osthoff's Law can be explained analogically, and it was not a general rule of PIE date (there is no evidence of it in Indo-Iranian or Tocharian). Such shortening is common cross-linguistically, so the attested examples of the "law" are probably independent developments; but the matter needs further investigation.

Syllabification

3.42. PIE grouped sounds into syllables in much the same way as Greek, Latin, Sanskrit, and many other languages. In any given sequence of consonants and vowels, the vowels constituted the syllabic peaks, and were linked to a preceding consonant (if one was available) which formed the onset (beginning) of a syllable. If two or more consonants occurred together in the middle of a word, they were usually split between two syllables. In the abstract, a word of the structure *VCCVCVCCVC* would have been syllabified *VC.CV.CVC.CVC.* It is possible that certain consonant clusters could group together in the middle of a word as the onset of a syllable; if so, by a universal phonological principle they would have also been able to form word-initial onsets.

Syllabification proceeded from right to left. Let us take a concrete example this time, the word **bherontsu* 'in the ones carrying'. First the vowels – the syllabic peaks – are located, and linked to a preceding consonant: *bhe ro su.* The remaining consonants are then attached to the preceding vowel: *bhe.ront.su.*

One problem currently under discussion concerns the precise rules for syllabifying an unbroken sequence of resonants (with or without laryngeals). It is usually assumed that as one proceeds from right to left, the first resonant or laryngeal in the sequence, as long as it is not followed by a vowel, is made syllabic, the second non-syllabic, and so on. (If the first resonant or laryngeal is followed by a vowel, it is made non-syllabic, while the next one to its left becomes syllabic, and so on.) This rule works for a word like **k̑u̯n̥bhi* 'with dogs', but not for a word like **i̯ungenti* 'they yoke' (which should come out as **iu̯n̥genti* by the usual rule). In the latter case, morphological analogy surely played a role, since the root that this form comes from is **i̯eug-* or **i̯ug-*, and **i̯ung-* is closer to the root in shape and sound than **iu̯n̥g-*.

Another problem is posed by words ending in **-iH*. This became *-ī* in some branches, but in others, especially Greek and Tocharian, the *-i-* was realized as non-syllabic (*i̯*) and the laryngeal was vocalized. For an example, see §6.71.

Sievers' and Lindeman's Laws

3.43. The Germanic philologist Eduard Sievers noticed that the weight of a syllable in PIE affected the pronunciation of following consonant clusters consisting of a consonant plus a glide before a vowel (e.g. *-ti̯o-, *-tu̯o-): if the syllable before the cluster was heavy (i.e. if it ended in -VCC or -V̄C), the vocalic equivalent of the glide was inserted into the cluster (yielding *-tii̯o-, *-tuu̯o-). Thus a pre-Germanic *har-jas 'army' became Gothic *harjis*, but *herdjas 'shepherd' became *herdijas, whence Gothic *hairdeis*. The twentieth-century Indologist Franklin Edgerton expanded Sievers' Law to include the liquids and nasals (leading to the term "Sievers–Edgerton" for the law), but closer examination has revealed Edgerton's extension to be incorrect.

3.44. Sievers' Law effects were largely undone in the daughter languages; the older Indo-Iranian languages still show frequent instances of it, but already they are replete with examples of analogical extensions of the law to phonetic environments where it did not originally apply, as well as with instances where its effects were erased. Teasing apart the original conditioning factors has been difficult, and some believe it was not a PIE rule at all, but developed independently in some of the daughter languages. According to the now generally accepted thesis of the late Austrian Indo-Europeanist Jochem Schindler, one of the conditions was that in PIE Sievers' Law only applied when the glide began the final syllable of the word; thus a word like Vedic Skt. *vaiśvānará-* 'belonging to all men' did not become *vaiśuvānará-. (A *v* in Sanskrit continues a *u̯* in PIE.) In fact, Schindler recognized that the process is essentially identical to a phenomenon known as **Lindeman's Law,** named after the contemporary Indo-Europeanist Fredrik Otto Lindeman, which states that monosyllables beginning with consonant plus glide (like *k̑u̯ō(n) 'dog') had the cluster broken up in the same way as Sievers' Law (*k̑uu̯ō(n)) if the word followed a word ending in a heavy syllable.

Lindeman's Law gave rise to so-called "Lindeman's Law variants," two forms of the same word whose distribution originally depended on the nature of the end of the preceding word. Descendants of both *k̑u̯ō(n) and *k̑uu̯ō(n) are preserved in Vedic Sanskrit as *śvá̄* and *śuvá̄* respectively. Sometimes one or the other variant became generalized as the only form in the language: Sanskrit eventually opted for monosyllabic *śvá̄*, while Greek opted for disyllabic *kúōn*. Similarly, *di̯ēus or *di̯eus 'sky, skygod' shows up in Vedic both as *dyáuṣ* and as *diyáuṣ*, but in Greek the monosyllabic form was the only one to survive, in the divine name *Zeús* (where the i̯ has affected the preceding consonant, forming z).

For Further Reading

There is no comprehensive, up-to-date account of PIE phonology written in English. The standard reference work is in German (Mayrhofer 1986), with an introduction by Warren Cowgill. A useful collection of technical articles in English, German, and French on various aspects of the laryngeal theory is Bammesberger 1988; a similar older collection, still very important, is Winter 1965. Lindeman 1987 (better than the revised 1997 edition) is also useful, although he believes in only one laryngeal for the non-Anatolian languages. The glottalic theory is most extensively presented in the first volume of Gamkrelidze and Ivanov 1984 (see Bibliography, ch. 2). A useful critical response to the glottalic theory can be found in the first part of Szemerényi 1985.

For Review

velar	resonant	"thorn cluster"	Osthoff's Law
voiced aspirate	syllabic resonant	long diphthong	Sievers' Law
centum	laryngeal	"schwa secundum"	Lindeman's Law variants
satem	vocalized laryngeal	voicing assimilation	
Roman Jakobson	coloring	Stang's Law	
Tamaz Gamkrelidze	compensatory lengthening	Szemerényi's Law	
Vyacheslav Ivanov		*boukólos* rule	

Exercises

1 Given the charts and accompanying discussion in §§3.4–6, reconstruct the initial stop that PIE had in the form ancestral to the forms in each of the following correspondence sets. If no gloss (translation) is given, the words mean the same as the English cognate. For English, be sure to think in terms of the pronunciation of the initial sound rather than its spelling. Ignore any material in parentheses.

- **a** Eng. *thin*, Lat. *tenuis*, Gk. *tanaós* 'tall'
- **b** Vedic Skt. *hávate* 'invokes', Avestan *zavaiti* 'invokes'
- **c** Eng. *tear* (from the eye), Gk. *dákru*, Welsh *deigryn*
- **d** Vedic Skt. *dhárṣati* 'is bold', Gk. *tharséō* 'am bold', Eng. *durst*, Lithuanian *drį̃sti* 'to dare'
- **e** Lat. *pūrus* 'pure', Welsh *ir* 'fresh, green'
- **f** Vedic Skt. *jámbhas* 'tooth', Gk. *gómphos* 'tooth', Eng. *comb*, Lithuanian *žam̃bas* 'sharp edge'
- **g** Gk. *khleúē* 'joke', Lithuanian *gláudoti* 'to joke', Eng. *glee*
- **h** Vedic Skt. *dhāyú-* 'thirsty', Armenian *(stn-)di* 'nursling', Lithuanian *dėlẽ* 'leech'
- **i** Eng. *quern* 'hand mill', Lithuanian *gìrnos*
- **j** Avestan *sraoni-* 'buttock', Welsh *clun* 'hip', Lithuanian *šlaunìs* 'hip'
- **k** Vedic Skt. *kā́mas* 'desire', Lat. *cārus* 'dear', Eng. *whore* (note: treat *wh-* as *h-*)
- **l** Gk. *gōleós* 'cave', Armenian *kaɫaɫ* 'lair', Lithuanian *guõlis* 'lair'
- **m** Lat. *fodiō* 'I dig', Welsh *bedd* 'grave', Lithuanian *bedù* 'I stick, dig'
- **n** Eng. *burn*, Lat. *for(ceps)* 'fire tongs', Vedic Skt. *ghr̥tám* 'clarified butter'
- **o** Vedic Skt. *karóti* 'does', Welsh *paraf* 'I accomplish', Lithuanian *kùrti* 'to make'
- **p** Vedic Skt. *pánthās* 'path', Armenian *hown* 'path', Eng. *find*

2 For each of the correspondence sets above in **1**, pick a language (from the languages used in the charts in §§3.4–6) in which a cognate is not given and predict what the initial sound of that cognate would be. For example, in **1a**, if there were a Lithuanian cognate, it would begin with *t*.

3 The following forms contain laryngeals. Indicate (1) what the forms became after coloring (if applicable), and (2) what the forms further became after laryngeal loss (and compensatory lengthening, if applicable). The first is done as an example.

a **u̯reh₂ĝhos* 'briar'
(1) colored to **u̯rah₂ĝhos*, which became (2) **u̯rāĝhos*

b **h₃ekʷih₁* 'both eyes'
c **dhoh₁ts* 'one that places'
d **h₂oĝmos* 'track, path'
e **protisth₂os* 'standing fast'
f **bhuh₂tos* 'having come into being'
g **h₃erō* 'large bird'
h **bheh₂mi* 'I say'
i **sneh₁si* 'you sew'
j **neh₂us* 'boat'
k **dhedheh₁eti* 'he will place'

4 The following forms were affected by the rule of voicing assimilation. State the outcome.

a **h₂eĝ-tó-* 'driven'
b **i̯unég-si* 'you yoke'
c **kʷid-kʷe* 'something'
d **o-sd-os* 'branch'
e **bhid-tó-* 'split'
f **ti̯egʷ-ter-* 'worshiper'

5 The following forms contain resonants, laryngeals, and high vowels. Apply the PIE rules of syllabification to figure out which of the resonants and laryngeals should be syllabic or vocalized, and which of the high vowels should be non-syllabic (i.e., glides). Use appropriate diacritic marks to indicate which resonants are syllabic and which high vowels are glides.

a **h₂nrbhi* 'with men'
b **h₂erh₃trom* 'plow'
c **k̂mtom* 'hundred'
d **h₂iuHon-* 'young'
e **h₂sntieh₂* 'being'
f **ĝhēimno-* 'wintry'

6 Observe the following forms:

a **h₂ekʷ-eh₂* > Lat. *aqua* 'water' (cp. **sal-* > Lat. *sal-* 'salt')
**h₂ēkʷ-i̯o-* > Old Norse *ægir* 'sea' (cp. **meh₁-ri-* > Old Norse *mærr* 'famous'; **ghan-* > Old Norse *gana* 'to gape')

b **e-ĝneh₃-s* > Gk. *é-gnō-s* 'you knew' (cp. **udōr* > Gk. *hudṓr* 'water')
**ĝnēh₃-s-* > Hittite *gane-š-* 'recognize' (cp. **u̯ēĝ-ti* > Hittite *wek-zi* 'demands'; **u̯edōr* 'waters' > Hittite *widār*)

c **u̯eh₂-n̥ti* > Hittite *waḫḫanzi* 'they turn' (cp. **albh-* > Hittite *alpi-* 'cloud')
**u̯ēh₂-ti* > Hittite *weḫzi* 'turns'

d **h₃est-e-* > Gk. *osté-on* 'bone' (cp. **o-sd-os* > Gk. *ózos* 'branch')
**h₃ēstoi̯o-* > Hittite *ḫeštāš* 'bone-house' (cp. **h₃erbh-* > Hittite *ḫarapp-* 'separate')

How do these forms show that coloring only affected short *e*?

4 Proto-Indo-European Morphology: Introduction

The Root and Indo-European Morphophonemics

4.1. Morphology is the study of the rules governing word-formation and inflection; the term also refers to the set of rules themselves in a given language. Words consist of one or more *morphemes*, the smallest meaningful units in a language. Morphemes can be whole words (e.g. Eng. *bed*, *succotash*, *sarsaparilla*) or parts of words such as affixes (e.g. the Eng. prefix *un-* and suffix *-ed*). In many languages, some morphemes can appear in different forms called *allomorphs* depending on their phonetic or morphological context (e.g. the Eng. prefix *in-* 'not' can appear as *in-*, *im-*, *il-*, *ir-*, as in *in-credible*, *im-perfect*, *il-logical*, *ir-replaceable*). The *morphophonemics* of a language is the set of rules determining the distribution of allomorphs.

A *root* is a morpheme from which semantically related words can be derived. The root itself does not usually exist as an independent form, but carries the semantic core of any word derived from it. In English, for example, the words *commit*, *emit*, *transmit*, *remission*, and *missive* are all derived from a root *mit* (borrowed from Latin) that conveys the basic meaning 'send'. When reconstructing the vocabulary of PIE, typically it is roots that are reconstructed in the first instance (see below, §4.11, for more on this). Since they did not stand alone, they are conventionally cited with an added hyphen (e.g. **sed-* 'sit'), indicating that suffixes had to be added to form free-standing words. Besides the attachment of suffixes (and sometimes, but more rarely, prefixes and infixes – affixes added into the middle of a root), word-formation in PIE often required modification of the shape of the root itself, in ways to be discussed further below.

Unlike sounds, morphemes do not necessarily change in an exceptionless and regular way over time. Changes may sometimes affect whole morphological systems, but very commonly they affect only individual words, as when the old irregular plural *kine* was replaced by the regular plural *cows* in English. Changes that affect individual words are by their nature sporadic, the results of such processes as analogy, paradigm leveling, and folk-etymology.

As with the discovery of the sounds of PIE, the determination of its morphemes and morphology was a long process, and is still going on today. The theory of ablaut (see below), in particular, took many decades to establish because of difficulties in reconstructing the PIE vowels. A guiding principle in historical morphology is that one should reconstruct morphology based on the *irregular* and *exceptional* forms, for these are most likely to be archaic and to preserve older patterns. Regular or predictable forms (like the Eng. 3rd singular present *takes* or the past tense *thawed*) are generated using the productive morphological rules of the language, and have no claim to being old; but irregular forms (like Eng. *is, sang*) must be memorized, generation after generation, and have a much greater chance of harking back to an earlier stage of a language's history. (The forms *is* and *sang*, in fact, directly continue forms in PIE itself.)

The Root

Canonical shape of the root

4.2. Every language has a particular "feel," a characteristic cut to its jib, that stems from phonological properties shared by the words in the language. These properties are a product of the language's phonological inventory, of its rules regarding combinations of sounds (called *phonotactic* rules), and of the basic structure of its morphemes.

The structure of most PIE roots can be boiled down to a single template, **CeC-*, where *C* stands for any consonant and *e* is the fundamental vowel (on which more below). This template could be modified in certain ways, especially by adding consonants either at the beginning or the end to form consonant clusters. Most commonly, a resonant could occur on either side of the vowel, resulting in roots of the shape **CReC-*, **CeRC-*, and **CReRC-*. (Both *i* and *u* can function as resonants following the *e*; recall §3.14.)

The following are some examples of PIE roots, arranged by structure (remember that voiced aspirates such as *bh* count as single consonants):

**CeC-* — **pet-* 'fly', **ped-* 'foot', **dheg^{w}h-* 'burn' (remember that *dh* and *g^{w}h* are single consonants), **seu-* 'press out juice', **bel-* 'strength', **$h_1$es-* 'be', **deh_3-* 'give', **u̯es-* 'buy, sell', **legh-* 'lie down', **sem-* 'one'

**CReC-* — **dhu̯er-* 'door', **sneh_2-* 'sew', **ti̯eg^w-* 'revere', **su̯ep-* 'sleep', **smei-* 'smile', **ĝneh_3-* 'know', **k̂leu-* 'hear', **sreu-* 'flow'

**CeRC-* — **dheiĝh-* 'shape with the hands', **derk̂-* 'see', **melĝ-* 'wipe', **meldh-* 'speak solemnly', **ĝembh-* 'bite', **$h_3$erbh-* 'change social status', **neh_3t-* 'buttocks'

**CReRC-* — **ghrendh-* 'grind', **kreuh_2-* 'gore', **su̯eh_2d-* 'sweet', **mleuh_2-* 'speak'

4.3. Roots could also have any of the basic structures above preceded by *s*. Some examples include **spek̂-* 'see', **steg-* 'cover', **sneig^{w}h-* 'snow', and **strenk-* 'tight'. A curious fact about such roots is that they sometimes appear without the initial *s-*, for reasons still not understood; these are called **s-mobile** roots. An example is the root **spek̂-* just mentioned: the *s-* is present in such forms as Av. *spasiieiti* 'looks at' and Lat. *speciō* 'I look at', but absent in Ved. *páśyati* 'sees'. Similarly, from **steg-* we have on the one hand Gk. *stégō* 'I cover', but on the other Lat. *toga* 'toga' (< *'covering'). The phenomenon was sporadic even within one and the same language: alongside the *s*-less Vedic form *páśyati* above, there is a causative form that has the *s-*, *spāśáyate* 'makes seen, shows', as well as a derived noun *spáś-* 'spy'. Such roots are often written with the *s* in parentheses: **(s)pek̂-*, **(s)teg-*.

As will be recalled from forms like **tk̂ei-* 'settle' and **pter-* 'wing' in §3.23, and by the existence of word-initial "thorn" clusters (§3.25), a few roots began with a cluster consisting of two stops.

Roots with laryngeals

4.4. Many roots, when first reconstructed in the nineteenth century, were seen to have a shape that did not adhere to the canonical structure. These mostly fell into two categories: vowel-initial roots, such as **ant-* 'front' and **od-* 'smell', and the so-called "long-vowel" roots ending in a long vowel, like **dhē-* 'put', **pā-* 'protect', and **dō-* 'give'. Thanks to the laryngeal theory, however, all these can be shown to be of the normal type. The vowel-initial roots originally began with a laryngeal that colored the adjacent vowel and later disappeared; thus **ant-* and **od-* were once **$h_2$ent-* (type **CeRC-*) and **$h_3$ed-* (**CeC-*). The long-vowel roots once ended with a laryngeal that also disappeared, but with coloring and compensatory lengthening; thus **dhē-*, **pā-*, and **dō-* were originally **dheh$_1$-*, **peh$_2$-*, and **deh$_3$-*, all of them thus also of the **CeC-* type.

4.5. While this sort of laryngeal "rewriting" can be done purely for theoretical purposes (out of the wish to reconstruct an internally consistent system), in many of these cases there is direct evidence to back it up. We saw in §§3.19–20 how the laryngeals in **$h_2$ent-* and **peh$_2$-* (traditionally **ant-* and **pā-*) are preserved in Hittite as *ḫ* in the words *ḫant-* 'front, forehead' and *paḫ-š-* (with a suffix) 'protect'. More difficulty is posed by roots traditionally reconstructed as beginning with *e-*, such as **es-* 'be'; this can be recast as **$h_1$es-*, but since **h_1* disappeared before a vowel everywhere (including Anatolian), evidence for the laryngeal here must come from indirect evidence. Such indirect evidence does in fact exist for many of these roots (an example is left for the exercises). Specialists differ on whether to rewrite all traditionally vowel-initial roots in this way when direct evidence of a laryngeal is lacking; the tendency is to add the laryngeal regardless, for the sake of structural uniformity.

4.6. A further class of roots, mostly beginning with a resonant in traditional reconstructions, have descendant forms with an initial vowel before the resonant in Greek and often Armenian and Phrygian (when there is evidence; not many remains of this language are preserved). Thus corresponding to Vedic Skt. *rudhirá-* 'red', *nár-* 'man', and *méh-* 'urinate' are Greek *eruthrós*, *aner-* (Armenian *ayr*, Phrygian *anar*), and *omeíkh-*. In earlier scholarship, the initial vowel was simply called "prothetic" – added on – and left unexplained. It has since been shown that these vowels in fact descended from laryngeals that had vocalized in Greek, Armenian, and Phrygian. For the three roots represented by these words, we now reconstruct **$h_1$reudh-*, **$h_2$ner-*, and **$h_3$meiĝh-*.

Independent evidence for the laryngeal in such roots (when the roots are not preserved in Anatolian) comes from certain compounds. Sanskrit has an adjective *sūnára-* 'mighty, fortunate', literally 'having good heroes' or 'good in manliness'; it is a compound of the prefix *su-* 'good' and the stem *nár-* that we just saw. The *u* of the prefix is normally short, and its length in *sūnára-* can only be explained by the laryngeal beginning the word for 'man': the sequence **su-h₂ner-* became **sūner-* after laryngeal loss with compensatory lengthening.

Structure of roots with laryngeals

4.7. The bulk of roots with laryngeals fall into the three types just introduced – **CeH-*, **HeC-*, and **HReC*. The mirror image of the last type, **CeRH*, is also common, as in **u̯emh₁-* 'vomit', **terh₂-* 'cross over, overcome', and **kelh₂-* 'cry out'. Less commonly, the laryngeal neighbored a stop, as in **h₃bhel-* 'be of use' and **pleth₂-* 'broad'. In all these cases, the laryngeal was either the first or last consonant of the root. Some roots contained a laryngeal before the final consonant, like **dheh₁s-* 'sacred' and **neh₃t-* 'buttocks'.

Roots ending in a laryngeal are often called **seṭ** roots (pronounced like Eng. *sate*), a term from traditional Sanskrit grammar, and those without such a laryngeal are called **aniṭ**. The terms *seṭ* and *aniṭ* mean 'with *i*' and 'without *i*', referring to the *i* that is the Sanskrit reflex of a vocalized laryngeal (cp. §4.18; see also §10.36).

Roots with a *as fundamental vowel*

4.8. A small but significant number of roots had *a* rather than *e* as the fundamental vowel. Examples include **mad-* 'be drunk', **nas-* 'nose', **sal-* 'salt', and **k̂as-* 'gray'. For reasons that are debated, initial *k-* is particularly common in this class of roots, as in **kadh-* 'protect', **kamp-* 'bend', and **kan-* 'sing'. As just discussed, many roots traditionally reconstructed with initial *a-*, such as **aĝ-* 'drive', are now usually thought to have begun originally with **h₂e-* (§4.4 above). For more on the behavior of these roots, see §4.17 below.

Root-structure constraints

4.9. Certain classes of consonants rarely or never co-occur within a given PIE root. There are not many securely reconstructible roots containing two plain (unaspirated) voiced stops (type **bed-*) or a voiceless stop and a voiced aspirate (type **bhet-* or **tebh-*, although the second of these is commonly found if preceded by an *s*, so **stebh-*). The source of these constraints is unknown, although similar constraints are known from other language families. See also §3.10.

Root "extensions" and "enlargements"

4.10. It is not uncommon for roots to appear with extra phonetic material (one or two sounds) added on to them, generally without any discernible change to the meaning of the root. These additional sounds are called "extensions" or "enlargements" (or "determinatives" in older literature). The root **(s)teu-* 'push, hit, thrust', for example, appears extended or enlarged as **(s)teu-k-*, **(s)teu-g-*, and **(s)teu-d-* (reflected respectively e.g. in Gk. *túkos* 'hammer', Eng. *stoke*, and Ved. *tudáti* 'beats'). The source and function of these extensions are not known.

4.11. Although most of the reconstructed PIE lexicon is in the form of roots, we can also reconstruct many whole words. Most are derived from known roots, but some words, apparently belonging to a very ancient layer of IE vocabulary, cannot be (at least not uncontroversially), e.g., **seh$_2$u̯l̥* 'sun', **dhugh$_2$tēr* 'daughter', **gheluneh$_2$* 'chin', **ag^{w}nos* 'lamb', and **u̯ortok̑os* 'quail'. A few, like the word for 'apple', **abel-*, and the word for 'ax', **pelek̑us*, have a shape that seems un-Indo-European and are thought by some to be prehistoric borrowings from non-IE languages. Such proposals are not unreasonable but can rarely be evaluated. (The case of **pelek̑us* is instructive: it was long thought to be a borrowing from a Semitic source akin to Akkadian *pilakku(m)* or *pilaqqu(m)*, but the Akkadian word was later shown to mean 'spindle', not 'ax'!)

Ablaut

4.12. Since *e* was the fundamental vowel of most PIE roots (§4.2), this is the vowel conventionally used when citing a root; so an IE dictionary entry for the root meaning 'sit' would have the headword **sed-*. Under certain conditions, however, this *e* could be replaced by other vowels. Specifically, a root could appear instead with short *o* (**sod-*), long *e* (**sēd-*), long *o* (**sōd-*), or no vowel at all (**sd-*). Broadly, the choice of vowel was determined by the type of word derived from the root. Different verb tenses, for example, called for different vowels in the root, as did different nominal (noun) inflections.

These changes in the root vowel constitute the system of vocalic alternations called **ablaut** (also called apophony or vowel gradation). Ablaut was central to PIE morphology, and its effects are still with us today. Consider the English forms *sing sang sung song*: between the consonants *s-* and *-ng* a different vowel appears depending on whether the form is a present-tense verb, a past-tense verb, a past participle, or a derived verbal noun. The particular vowels of these words, in fact, are descended directly from ablauting vowels of PIE.

4.13. The different ablaut variants of a root are called **grades**, and are named according to the vowel that appears. The citation form of a root (with *e*) is said to be in the ***e*-grade** or **full grade**, the basic ablaut grade. The other ablaut grades are the ***o*-grade, lengthened *e*-grade, lengthened *o*-grade**, and – when no ablauting vowel appears at all – **zero-grade.**

To illustrate, consider all the ablaut grades of the root **sed-* 'sit' again, together with some of their descendant forms:

e-grade (full grade) ****sed-***:	Lat. ***sed**-ēre* 'to sit', Gk. ***héd**-ra* 'seat', Eng. ***sit*** (*i* from earlier **e*)
o-grade ****sod-***:	Eng. ***sat*** (*a* from earlier **o*)
zero-grade ****sd-***:	**ni-**sd**-o-* 'where [the bird] sits down = nest' > Eng. *nest*

lengthened *e*-grade ***sēd-**: Lat. ***sēdēs*** 'seat', Eng. ***seat***
lengthened *o*-grade ***sōd-**: OE ***sōt*** > Eng. *soot* (*'accumulated stuff that sits on surfaces')

Roots were not the only morphemes that ablauted in PIE; many suffixes and inflectional endings also ablauted. As an example, we may list the guises taken by the stem of the Greek word for 'father', whose second syllable is an ablauting derivational suffix. The lengthened *e*-grade is seen in the nominative singular (subject case) ***patḗr*** 'father', the *e*-grade in the accusative singular (direct object case) ***patér-a***, the zero-grade in the genitive (possessive) singular ***patr-ós*** 'of a father', and the ordinary and lengthened *o*-grades in a compound adjective with nominative singular ***eu-pátōr*** 'having a good father, noble' and accusative singular ***eu-pátor-a***.

4.14. While theoretically any root of the normal type could appear in any ablaut grade, in practice this was not the case. Certain roots seem to have favored certain grades, sometimes appearing in one to the exclusion of all others. The root **$h_2$kous-* 'hear' (Gk. *akoúō* 'I hear', Goth. *hausjan* 'to hear', Eng. *hear*), for example, appeared only in the *o*-grade, as did the adjective **bhos-o-* 'naked' (Eng. *bare*) and the noun **u̯obhs-eh$_2$* 'wasp' (Avestan *vaβža-ka-*, Eng. *wasp*). Similarly, **bhuH-* 'grow, be' (Lat. *fu-tūrus* 'about to be', Eng. *be*) probably existed only in the zero-grade in PIE. Some roots may never have made lengthened-grade forms, while others seem to have had a certain propensity for them. Thus ablaut grades were not solely determined by the type of derivative formed from the root, but were also determined lexically.

No ablaut grade is limited to any part of speech or other morphological category, and the same morphological category may require different grades for different inflectional forms within that category (as with the nominative, accusative, and genitive of the noun for 'father' in the Greek example cited in §4.13 above). We therefore cannot confidently ascribe any particular meaning or semantic content to any of the ablaut grades.

Formation of the zero-grade

4.15. The zero-grade deserves some special comments because the deletion of the ablauting vowel often had effects on the syllabification of neighboring resonants in a root. In roots with a resonant directly before or after the ablauting vowel, the resonant would typically become syllabic or vocalized in the zero-grade. Thus the roots **ĝhel-* 'yellow', **k̂ens-* 'proclaim solemnly', and **k̂emh$_2$-* 'become tired' had zero-grades **ĝhl̥-*, **k̂n̥s-*, and **k̂m̥h$_2$-*; and **meĝh$_2$-* 'big' and **nes-* 'we' had zero-grades **m̥ĝh$_2$-* and **n̥s-*. (Most examples of syllabic resonants in PIE, in fact, occur in zero-grades.) In roots with a glide before the ablauting vowel, the glide became the corresponding high vowel (as per §3.14) in the zero-grade: thus **i̯es-* 'boil' and **su̯ep-* 'sleep' had zero-grades **is-* and **sup-*. (Note that a resonant preceding a diphthong stays non-syllabic in the root's zero-grade: thus the zero-grade of **trei-* 'three' and **k̂u̯eit-* 'white' were **tri-* and **k̂u̯it-*.) Laryngeals would become vocalized: the zero-grade of **dheh$_1$s-* 'sacred' was **dhh$_1$s-* with a vocalized (syllabic) **h̥$_1$* (recall §3.17).

Origin of ablaut

4.16. At the time of the breakup of PIE, ablaut was a morphologically conditioned process; but some of the grades may have originally come about through sound change. (In the histories of numerous languages, speakers have reinterpreted a phonological rule or result of a sound change as a morphological rule.) Most zero-grades are in unaccented syllables, which makes it likely that the zero-grade arose by vowel loss (syncope) in unaccented syllables. However, it should be noted that if this is true, it happened well before the stage of PIE accessible by reconstruction, since we can reconstruct some forms with accented zero-grade (such as **uĺ̥kʷos* 'wolf' and **h₂ŕ̥tk̂os* 'bear') or consisting only of zero-grades (e.g. **suHnus* 'son'). Accounts of the origin of the other grades are more speculative and will not be discussed here.

Ablaut of roots with root-vowel a

4.17. Although the evidence is sparse, it appears that roots with *a* as fundamental vowel also ablauted. The root **sal-* 'salt' had a zero-grade **sl̥-*, which underlies English *silt* and German *Sülze* 'pickled meat in aspic'; the root **nas-* 'nose' has lengthened-grade derivatives such as Latin *nār-ēs* 'the nostrils' and English *nose*, both from **nās-*; and the root **laku-* 'body of water' (Lat. *lacus* 'lake', Gk. *lákkos* 'pond') had an *o*-grade form **loku-* that became Scottish Gaelic *loch* 'lake'. The view that roots in *a* ablauted is not universally accepted, but these forms are difficult to explain otherwise.

Ablaut and the laryngeal theory

4.18. Ablaut was the key to deducing the existence of the laryngeals, an insight that we owe to the nineteenth-century Swiss linguist Ferdinand de Saussure. His reasoning bears relating; it is a brilliant example of straightforward but also very bold scientific thinking.

Sanskrit has a class of verbs (the seventh class) that contain a morpheme *-na-* infixed (i.e., inserted) into the root in the present tense, such as *yunakti* '(s)he joins' (the *-ti* is the ending for the 3rd person singular). It has another class (the ninth class) of verbs whose presents are formed with a suffix *-nā-*, such as *punāti* 'cleanses'. These classes differ systematically in the way they inflect in different morphological categories, as exemplified below:

present tense	future	infinitive
yunakti 'joins'	yokṣyati 'will join'	yoktum 'to join'
punāti 'cleanses'	paviṣyati 'will cleanse'	pavitum 'to cleanse'

If we remove what we know are infixes and suffixes from the first set, we get

yuk	yok	yok

– that is, zero-grade of the root in the first column and full grade in the other two (the *o* in Sanskrit goes back to PIE **eu*). This pattern was known also from other types of verbs.

Now the forms for the verb 'cleanse' behave oddly by comparison. The present seems to have a suffix *-nā-* before the endings rather than an infix *-na-* plus root-final consonant plus endings. In the other forms, *pav-* can go back to a full grade (it would continue PIE **peu̯-*), but the *-i-* added after it did not make *pavi-* look like a root form. But Saussure noticed that, at a more abstract level, the forms for 'cleanse' behaved identically to the forms for 'join'. In *yu-na-k-ti yo-k-ṣyati yo-k-tum* there was an element *-k-* before the endings; in *pav-i-ṣyati pav-i-tum* there was also an element, *-i-*, before the endings, and in *pu-nā-ti* one could think of the length of the vowel as an extra element too. Saussure reasoned that at some level, both verbs were formed in the same way, and that what seemed to be a *nā*-suffix in *punāti* was really the same *na*-infix seen in *yunakti*, plus something. He imagined there had been some segment – call it X – that had been the final consonant of the root for 'cleanse' and that had lengthened the infix *-na-* to *-nā-*, and had also become *-i-* between the consonants *v* and *ṣ*, and *v* and *t*, in the other two forms. Thus he reconstructed

*pu-na-X-ti	*peu̯X-syati	*peu̯X-tum

exactly parallel to

*yu-na-k-ti	*yeuk-syati	*yeuk-tum

In this way, it was revealed that the Sanskrit *nā*-class was exactly the same as the class formed with the infix *-na-*.

4.19. On the basis of this and many other pieces of evidence, Saussure deduced the existence of the laryngeals. He claimed there were two of them, and proposed that they patterned like resonants in having syllabic reflexes when between consonants (or sounds that could be consonantal, like the *u* in **peuX-syati*). Hermann Möller, one of the few people to pick up his theory at the time and develop it further, expanded the number to three in 1879; he was joined by a third scholar, Albert Cuny, at the close of the nineteenth century. Möller's and Cuny's ideas are quite close to those standardly accepted today.

But it was not until 1927, a good half-century after Saussure's proposals, that real vindication of the whole theory came. In that year, the young Polish linguist Jerzy Kuryłowicz published his discovery that the sound *ḫ* in the newly deciphered language Hittite appeared in many of the places that Saussure had predicted these mystery segments should have existed in PIE.

Saussure was at the ripe old age of 19 or 20 when he developed these ideas; he published his findings at age 21. What was new in his method was the application of the technique of internal reconstruction *to reconstructed PIE itself*, at the time a very radical thing to do – especially if it resulted in the positing of a set of consonants that had not survived as consonants into recorded history (as far as was then known). His starting point was the supposition that superficially different formations belonging to the same morphological categories had once been formed identically. Unfortunately, he did not live to see Kuryłowicz's work.

Morphological Categories of PIE

Word structure

4.20. The process of forming a word from a root or another word is called **derivation,** while the process of creating different grammatical forms of a given word is **inflection.** In English, prefixes like *anti-*, *con-*, *fore-*, and *hyper-*, and suffixes like *-ance*, *-ity*, *-ly*, and *-ness* are derivational morphemes; they are used to create new words. By contrast, suffixes like the plural *-(e)s* or the comparative suffix *-er* for adjectives are inflectional morphemes; adding them does not produce a new word, but just a different grammatical form of an already existing word.

Typically, a word in PIE consisted of three morphemes, root plus suffix plus ending, symbolized as $R + S + E$. (Prefixes and compounds will be treated below.) The suffix was a derivational morpheme, such as one used to form a present-tense stem or an abstract noun from a verbal root. (We know of one derivational *infix* that was inserted into the root, which we saw a preview of above in §4.18.) The ending (also called the *desinence*) was the inflection, which marked the grammatical function of the word (such as the nominative singular of a noun, or the 3rd person plural of a verb). All three of these elements could and did ablaut. To take an example, the word *_mn̥-téi-s_ 'of thought' consisted of the root *_men-_ 'think' in the zero-grade, followed by an ablauting suffix *_-t(e)i-_ (here in the full grade) that was used to form abstract nouns (§6.42), in turn followed by the inflectional ending *_-s_ of the genitive case (meaning 'of') in the zero-grade.

The suffix did not always appear overtly, in which case one sometimes speaks of *zero-suffixes*. For example, the form *_dem-s_ meant 'of the house' and consisted of the root *_dem-_ 'to build' in the *e*-grade plus the inflectional ending of the genitive singular, without an overt derivational suffix. Words could in fact be derived from one another simply by changing the ablaut or the position of the stress (or both) – a process known as *internal derivation*, much like *song* is derived from the verb *sing*. Internal derivation will be discussed in more detail in chapter 6.

Words could also be formed by **composition**, which includes prefixation and compounding. Not many PIE prefixes have been reconstructed, but one prefixal process known as **reduplication** was very common. In reduplication, a prefix was constructed consisting of a copy of the first consonant or consonant cluster of a root plus a vowel. Thus *_de-deh_$_3$*-* and *_ĝi-ĝn̥h_$_1$*-* are reduplicated forms of the roots *_deh_$_3$*-* 'give' and *_ĝenh_$_1$*-* 'beget', respectively. Compounding was most frequently seen in nouns and adjectives, but also occasionally in verbs; it will be discussed in the noun and verb chapters.

4.21. PIE was a richly inflected language. It possessed full sets of singular, dual, and plural endings in all three persons of the verb in several tenses, and at least eight (and possibly nine) cases in the noun, with somewhat less differentiation of cases in the dual and plural than in the singular. Adjectives and pronouns were fully inflected like nouns, as were the first four cardinal numerals. The functions of the case-endings of the noun, the personal endings of the verb, and the other verbal grammatical categories such as tense, voice, and mood, will be explained in detail in the two chapters to follow.

Thematic and athematic inflection

4.22. PIE nouns, adjectives, and verbs can be divided into two basic groups based on their inflectional patterns: those that had an ablauting short vowel, *e* or *o* (in shorthand, *-e/o-*), directly before the inflectional endings (the case-endings in nouns or adjectives, the personal endings in verbs), and those with no such vowel. This ablauting vowel is called the **thematic vowel**; words that inflect with it are termed **thematic**, and those inflecting without it are **athematic**.

For example, the Greek word *klṓps* 'thief' consists of the Greek (and IE) root *klep-* (in the lengthened *o*-grade) followed directly by the inflectional ending *-s*, which marks the nominative singular (or subject case). *Klṓps* is therefore an athematic nominative singular. By contrast, the Greek noun *nómos* 'law, custom' has the vowel *-o-* between the root (*nom-*, *o*-grade of *nem-*) and the ending. *Nómos* is therefore a thematic nominative singular.

4.23. Athematic declensions and conjugations are on the whole more complex than their thematic counterparts. Within athematic paradigms, there are alternations in ablaut and changes in the position of the accent; these will be fully discussed in the next two chapters. Athematic inflection appears to belong to a more ancient layer of IE nominal and verbal derivation than thematic inflection, and many athematic formations are moribund by the time they are attested, even in languages as archaic as Vedic Sanskrit. In the observable course of the histories of the older IE languages, thematic paradigms as a rule are outstripping and replacing athematic ones, giving thematic formations the appearance of young upstarts taking over the field. For example, the athematic Greek verb *seũ-tai* 'is hunted, chased', found only in Homer and some other early Greek poetry, was remade as – and replaced by – a thematic verb *seú-e-tai*. Similarly, prehistoric Greek had an athematic noun with stem **thes-* meaning 'god'; as a free-standing noun it was replaced by the thematic stem **thes-o-*, eventually becoming (after sound changes) Classical Greek *theós*. The older athematic stem survived only as a frozen member of compounds like *thés-phatos* 'decreed by god'. Thematic paradigms, unlike athematic ones, did not exhibit internal shifts in accent or alternations in ablaut grade and were thus arguably simpler for speakers to handle, which may partly explain their spread. The full reasons, however, are surely more complicated, as "simplicity" is a subjective and notoriously misleading yardstick in historical linguistics.

4.24. We are lucky to have a wealth of good comparative material on which to base our reconstructions of PIE morphology. The precise agreements among the ancient languages in nominal and verbal derivation and inflection are at times astounding, and leave little room for doubt about a great many aspects of the PIE morphological system. Many other aspects, however, are still the subject of controversy, and claims about them are more tentative. The next three chapters will provide an overview of the standard reconstruction of the PIE verbal, nominal, and pronominal systems, and the comparative evidence upon which it is based. Usually, only a selection of comparative data will be adduced in support of a given reconstruction so as not to swell the sizes of these chapters unmanageably; but where that would have sacrificed clarity or blunted the understanding of an important issue, it was thought better to give more information rather than less.

The material in the next few chapters is at any rate rather extensive, and is not meant to be learned all at once. Some of it is included primarily for reference. If it appears bewildering, the exercises can be used for orientation, since they focus on the most important points to be digested. As chapters 9 and following are worked through, with their sections on historical morphology, additional material from chapters 5–7 can be drawn in.

For Further Reading

Most studies in the realm of PIE morphology are devoted to specific aspects of it, such as noun or verb formation; references to such studies are given in the following chapters. No good general works on root structure or ablaut are found in English. For those who read French, influential is Chapter IX of Benveniste 1935 on root structure and root "enlargements." Kuryłowicz 1956, a highly complex work, will be impenetrable to introductory students, but is an important and famous treatment of ablaut. Ferdinand de Saussure's pioneering work on laryngeals was published as Saussure 1879, and Kuryłowicz's vindication can be read in Kuryłowicz 1927. Note also Anttila 1969, which concerns roots that show both *CReC* and *CeRC* forms and various related ablaut issues.

For Review

Know the meaning or significance of the following:

root	ablaut	Albert Cuny	composition
s-mobile	grade	Jerzy Kuryłowicz	thematic vowel
seṭ	Ferdinand de Saussure	derivation	thematic inflection
aniṭ	Hermann Möller	inflection	athematic inflection

Exercises

1 Recalling §3.23, indicate which of the following would be well-formed PIE roots:

a **streibh-* **b** **rdeu-* **c** **bhal-* **d** **$h_2$seup-* **e** **nregh-*

2 Which of the following would violate the root-structure constraints in §4.9?

a **kebh-* **b** **skebh-* **c** **kep-* **d** **gep-* **e** **beg-*

3 The following are some reconstructed roots in the full grade. Provide the zero-grade and the lengthened *o*-grade.

a *ĝheu- 'pour'
b *h_3ek^w- 'see'
c *k̂u̯en- 'holy'
d *skel- 'dry out'
e *bherĝh- 'bright'
f *keh_2d- 'care'
g *i̯es- 'boil'
h *dheb- 'thick'
i *$pleh_1$- 'fill'
j *ĝembh- 'bite'
k *$seng^wh$- 'sing'
l *h_1reudh- 'red'

4 For each of the roots in **3**, indicate what basic type they belong to (*CeC, *CReC, *CeRC, etc.). Ignore initial *s-* in consonant clusters.

5 Identify the ablaut grade that the following root forms appear in:

a *sōd- 'sit'
b *mr̥- 'waste away'
c *u̯oid- 'see'
d *stēu- 'praise'
e *ĝhel- 'yellow'
f *dik̂- 'point'

6 The Latin cognate of English *foam* is *spūma*. Explain the *f-/sp-* correspondence using material from this chapter as well as §3.4.

7 The following are older, "pre-laryngealistic" reconstructions of roots that are nowadays considered to have contained a laryngeal and the root vowel *e*. Rewrite the reconstructions using laryngeals.

a *kā- 'love'
b *ank- 'bend'
c *snē- 'spin, sew'
d *u̯ēr- 'water'
e *ok^w- 'see'
f *bhlāg- 'strike'

8 It was noted in §4.5 that the root for 'be' in PIE was *h_1es-.

a Give its zero-grade.
b Vedic Sanskrit has a prefix *a-* 'not, un-' and the present participle of the verb 'to be' is *sat-* 'being'. Given that the *a* in both these forms comes from PIE *n̥, and the present participle was formed from the zero-grade of the root, what would the PIE ancestors of *a-* and *sat-* have been?
c Vedic Skt. has a word *ā́sat-* 'monster', a compound of *a-* and *sat-* above. Provide a historical explanation for why the first *a* is long rather than short.

9 For each of the following English words, identify the morphemes, and specify which are derivational and which are inflectional.

a *capitalizes*
b *happier*
c *carrier*
d *angriest*
e *superpowers*
f *unbending*
g *disproportionate*
h *recklessness*
i *insurmountably*

10 The following are reconstructed words in PIE. Each consists of several morphemes, separated from each other by hyphens. One of the morphemes is a form of a root. Using your knowledge of ablaut and root structure, identify the root that the word is derived from, in the *e*-grade. Assume that long vowels are not induced by laryngeals.

Example: In *bhe-bhoid-e '(s)he has split', the underlying root must be *bheid- (*bhe-* and *-e* cannot be forms of roots because of their structure).

- **a** **n̥-dhgʷhi-to-m* 'imperishable'
- **b** **i̯eu̯-o-s* 'grain'
- **c** **dor-u* 'wood'
- **d** **u̯id-me* 'we know'
- **e** **gʷhn̥-t-osi̯o* 'of the slain one'
- **f** **u̯ōt-eno-s* 'enraged'
- **g** **de-dork̂-e* '(s)he has seen'

11 Identify the following forms as thematic or athematic. Each morpheme is separated by a hyphen.

- **a** **bher-e-si* 'you carry'
- **b** **k̂un-és* 'of the dog'
- **c** **mn̥-téi-s* 'of thought'
- **d** **u̯iHr-o-s* 'man, hero'
- **e** **e-steh₂-t* '(s)he stood'
- **f** **kʷel-o-nti* 'they turn'

5 The Verb

The Structure of the PIE Verb

5.1. Verbs in PIE and in most of the ancient IE daughter languages were inflected in dozens of forms. In this they were vastly different from Modern English verbs, barely any of which has more than five forms (e.g. *sing sings singing sang sung*). As stated in the preceding chapter, the grammatical categories that were distinguished in PIE verb inflection are **person** (first, second, and third), **number** (singular, dual, and plural), **tense**, **voice**, and **mood**. (On verbal aspect, see §5.10 below.)

Tense

5.2. Verbs in PIE could inflect in the **present** tense ('I go, am going'), the **imperfect** tense ('I was going', expressing ongoing or background action in past time), and the **aorist** tense ('I went', expressing one-time or completed action in past time). Traditional scholarship also recognizes a fourth tense, the **perfect**, but this is now viewed as a stative (see §5.53 below) that secondarily acquired use as a resultative past tense: 'I am in a state of having gone, I have gone'. There was probably also a **pluperfect**, a past of the perfect, though this is debated. Some further believe that PIE had a **future** (see §§5.39ff. below). Each of these tenses could distinguish various voices and moods (more limitedly, it appears, in the perfect), which are discussed in §§5.54ff.

5.3. The actual forms of the tenses and moods were made from **tense-stems**, of which there were three: the **present stem**, **aorist stem**, and **perfect stem**. There do not appear to have been conjugational classes in PIE as there were in, say, Latin. Rather, in one group of verbs, called **primary verbs**, the tense-stems were formed directly from the root. In another group, called **derived verbs**, the tense-stems were created secondarily by means of productive suffixes to express particular types of action or shades of meaning. These verbs included causatives, iteratives, desideratives, and denominatives, all of which will be discussed in due course.

Not every verb could form all three tense-stems. Quite a few did not form perfects, for example, and derived verbs only had present stems in PIE. (The daughter languages have often independently innovated additional tense-stems for these verbs.)

A few verbs exhibited *suppletion*, meaning they had different tense-stems formed from different roots. Examples of suppletive paradigms in English are *go/went* and *be/is/were*.

Voice

5.4. The voice (also called *diathesis*) of a verb indicates the role that the subject plays in the action. Two voices were distinguished in verbal inflection, **active** and **middle.** (On the passive, see below.) The difference in meaning between these two voices in PIE is not fully clear. In traditional grammatical usage, active means that the subject is doing the action rather than being acted upon, while middle means the subject is either acting upon itself or is in some other way "internal" to the action.

This rough guideline works reasonably well for verbs that could inflect in either voice. We can illustrate this with some active/middle verb pairs in Hittite. Sometimes the middle meant the same as the active but differed in not taking a direct object; in other words, the middle could express the intransitive of a transitive active, e.g. transitive active *irḫāizzi* 'sets an end to', intransitive middle *irḫāitta* 'comes to an end'. Second, the middle could express the reflexive sense of the active, where the subject acts on itself, e.g. active *nāi* 'leads', middle *neyari* 'leads oneself, turns (oneself) to'. Finally, the middle could have a reciprocal sense, e.g. active *zaḫḫiyaweni* 'we fight (someone)', middle *zaḫḫiyawaštati* 'we fight each other'. These uses of the middle are comparable to the reflexive in modern Romance, Slavic, and German, e.g. German *sich wenden* 'turn (oneself) to', *sich streiten* 'argue (with one another)'.

5.5. But in many other cases, the distinction between active and middle inflection was purely a formal one: there were some verbs that inflected only in the active and others only in the middle, without clear difference in meaning. Verbs having only middle inflection are often called **middle verbs.** (Students familiar with Latin can think of these as equivalent to the Latin deponent verbs – active in meaning but having only passive endings, which come historically from the PIE middle.) It is not fully clear whether their middle inflection stemmed from some aspect of their meaning, or whether it was purely arbitrary. On the one hand, as a group these verbs do tend to express various "internal" or intransitive notions like spatial movement, position of rest, emotions, sensory perception, speaking, giving off sound or light, and changes of state. (In technical terms, these are mostly "unaccusative" verbs.) However, active verbs could also express such notions. Compare the representative list of middle verbs in the left-hand column below with the active verbs on the right; the meanings are unaccusative in both cases, sometimes identical:

Middle	*Active*
Hittite *iyattari* 'goes'	Greek *eĩsi* 'goes'
Vedic Sanskrit *śáye* 'lies'	Vedic Sanskrit *sī́dati* 'sits'
Latin *uerētur* 'fears'	Greek *khaírei* 'rejoices'
Greek *dérketai* 'sees'	Latin *audit* 'hears'
Greek *eúkhetai* 'proclaims'	Hittite *memai* 'says'
Latin *moritur* 'dies'	Hittite *ḫarakzi* 'dies'

5.6. Further complicating our understanding of the middle is that some verbal roots had active inflection in one tense or mood, but middle in another. For instance, the Greek verb 'learn' has an active present *manthánō* 'I learn' but a middle future *mathḗsomai* 'I will learn'; this is a common pattern. The Old Irish verb *ad-cíu* 'I see' was active in the present indicative but middle in the present subjunctive (*ad-cear*); and the Tocharian A active present indicative *yäṣ* 'goes' has a middle present participle *ymāṃ* 'going'. (Again for students who know Latin, the Latin "semi-deponent" verbs, such as present [active] *audeō* 'I dare', perfect [passive] *ausus sum* 'I have dared', are comparable.)

5.7. The middle could also express the **passive** voice, which indicates that the subject is acted upon by someone else: 'is being fought', 'was washed'. A tradition of scholarship rejects positing a passive voice for PIE because there was no separate set of passive endings. But all the daughter languages that have a separate passive conjugation have developed it in whole or in part from the PIE middle endings, and it seems best to regard the middle as having been, in fact, a *mediopassive* or *middle-passive* – capable of expressing either voice depending on the context.

Mood

5.8. The mood in which a verb appears expresses the speaker's attitude or stance taken towards the action – whether (s)he is asserting that it is factual, or indicating a wish that it were or were not true, or reporting the action second-hand, or indicating a contrafactual condition. PIE possessed four moods: indicative, imperative, subjunctive, and optative.

5.9. All the daughter languages agree that the **indicative** was used to express matters of fact, and the **imperative** was used for issuing commands. The function of the **subjunctive** in PIE is less clear, but it was probably at least in part a future tense; see §5.56 for a full discussion. Finally, the **optative** was used to express wishes and various other non-factual modalities.

Aspect

5.10. Aspect is a grammatical category that refers to the type of action indicated by a verb. Actions can be done once or repeatedly, to completion or not, or be ongoing with neither a true beginning nor end. It is on the whole unclear what the aspectual system of PIE was; in part the difficulty lies in figuring out the niceties of aspectual differences in the earliest texts in the daughter languages. For example, part of the opening of the famous Rig Vedic hymn 1.32 that was quoted in §2.41 reads: "I (will) tell now the manly deeds of Indra, the foremost of which he <u>did</u> bearing a cudgel. He <u>slew</u> the serpent, <u>drilled</u> through to the waters, (and) <u>split</u> the belly of the mountains." The underlined verbs in the Sanskrit original are in the perfect, imperfect, perfect, and imperfect, respectively; yet any difference in aspectual sense eludes us.

According to the generally accepted view, the imperfect and aorist were distinct aspectually, the imperfect expressing incomplete or ongoing action in past time (imperfective aspect), the aorist indicating completed or punctual (one-time) action in past time (perfective aspect).

Since the lexical meanings of verbs can refer to momentary or to continuous actions or states, verbs also have a type of inherent aspect, a relationship to time that is independent of any particular usage in a sentence (i.e., independent of grammatical aspect). This lexically inherent aspect goes by its German technical name of **Aktionsart** ('type of action'), and has figured prominently in various theories about the structure of the PIE verbal system, especially by the late Karl Hoffmann and his followers in Germany and internationally. To explain why different roots formed different kinds of presents and aorists, Hoffmann proposed that the choice was based on the verb's Aktionsart. His basic idea was that if one adds personal endings to the plain root (i.e., without any additional derivational suffixes), the Aktionsart would determine whether the resultant formation was a present or an aorist: if the root had inherently durative Aktionsart, it would be a present (since durativity is imperfective, and the present is by nature imperfective); but if it had punctual Aktionsart, it would be an aorist (since inherent in the meaning was the completion of the act, i.e. perfectivity). The theory works well in some cases: for example, adding personal endings to **$h_1$ei-* 'go' and **$h_1$es-* 'be' makes a present, while doing so with **dheh$_1$-* 'put' and **deh$_3$-* 'give' makes an aorist. But there are also many exceptions requiring special explanations, and the matter continues to be researched.

Personal Endings

5.11. The persons of the verb were expressed with suffixes called **personal endings**. A complete set consisted of nine forms, the three persons in each of three numbers (singular, dual, and plural). PIE had several sets of personal endings. The most fundamental distinction was among those of the active voice, middle voice, and the perfect. Additionally, for each of the two voices active and middle, non-past or **primary** endings and past or **secondary** endings were distinguished. The primary endings were used for the present tense and the subjunctive mood, while the secondary endings were used for the two past tenses (imperfect and aorist) and for the optative mood. In sum there were five sets of personal endings with the following distribution:

Personal endings	*Where used*
primary active	present indicative active, active subjunctives
secondary active	imperfect and aorist indicative active, active optatives
primary middle	present indicative middle, middle subjunctives
secondary middle	imperfect and aorist indicative middle, middle optatives
perfect	perfect

(In Indo-Iranian, the subjunctive can also take secondary endings; see §5.55.) As an illustration, consider the following 3rd singular forms of the PIE verb 'turn': present indicative active **k^{w}ele-**ti*** (primary active ending), imperfect indicative active **k^{w}ele-**t*** (secondary active ending), present indicative middle **k^{w}ele-**tor*** (primary middle ending), imperfect indicative middle **k^{w}ele-**to*** (secondary middle ending), perfect **k^{w}ek^{w}ol-**e*** (perfect ending).

Not all of the endings can be reconstructed with equal certainty; the most secure are those of the singular and the 3rd person plural. We shall treat the active and middle personal endings first; the perfect endings will be discussed in §5.51.

Active endings

5.12. Below is a selection of the comparative evidence used to reconstruct the PIE primary and secondary active endings, whose reconstructions are given in the right-hand column. In these and the following tables, only forms relevant for the reconstructions are given, and the information is by no means exhaustive.

Primary (non-past) active endings

	Vedic Sanskrit		Greek		Gothic		PIE
sg. 1	*é-mi*	'I go'	*ei-mí*	'I am' etc.	*baira-m*	'I bear' etc.	**-mi*, **-h_2*[1]
2	*é-ṣi*	'you go'	*es-sí*		*bairi-s*		**-si*
3	*é-ti*	'(s)he/it goes'	*es-tí*		*bairi-þ*		**-ti*
du. 1	*i-vás*	'we both go'			*bair-os*		**-u̯e-*
2	*i-thás*	'you both go'	*es-tón*		*baira-ts*		**-to-*
3	*i-tás*	'they both go'	*es-tón*				**-to-*
pl. 1	*i-más(i)*	'we go'	*ei-més* (Doric)[2]		*baira-m*		**-me-*
2	*i-thá*	'you (pl.) go'	*es-té*		*bairi-þ*		**-te(-)*
3	*y-ánti*	'they go'	*entí* (Doric)		*baira-nd*		**-(é)nti*

[1] Not illustrated here; see below, §5.13. [2] Attic *es-mén*, with restored *s*.

Secondary (past) active endings

Note: the Vedic and Greek forms are imperfects meaning 'was/were carrying'; the Gothic forms are present optatives meaning 'would carry'. The vowels *a-* and *e-* at the beginning of the Sanskrit and Greek forms are explained in §5.44.

	Vedic Sanskrit	Greek	Gothic	PIE
sg. 1	*ábhara-m*	*éphero-n*		**-m*
2	*ábhara-s*	*éphere-s*	*bairai-s*	**-s*
3	*ábhara-t*	*éphere*	*bairai*	**-t*
du. 1	*ábharā-va*		*bairai-wa*	**-u̯e(-)*
2	*ábhara-tam*	*ephére-ton*	*bairai-ts*	**-to-*
3	*ábhara-tām*	*epheré-tēn*		**-teh_2-*
pl. 1	*ábharā-ma*	*ephéro-men*	*bairai-ma*	**-me(-)*
2	*ábhara-ta*	*ephére-te*	*bairai-þ*	**-te(-)*
3	*ábhara-n*	*éphero-n*	*bairai-na*	**-(é)nt*

Notes on the active endings

5.13. As can be seen, the primary and secondary active endings differ partly with respect to whether an *-*i* was added in PIE. This *-*i*, which marks primary active endings, has been termed the **"hic et nunc" particle** (Latin for "here and now"); it may be the same as the *-i* found attached to a number of pronominal and adverbial forms in various daughter languages, as in Greek *nū̆n-í* 'now'.

The reconstructions of the singular and the 3rd plural endings are uncontroversial. As for the other endings, the languages do not agree so precisely. For example, the daughter languages disagree whether the 1st dual, 2nd dual, and 1st plural primary endings ended in *-*s* or *-*n*. This disagreement even occurs between dialects of the same language, as seen in the first table above with Doric Gk. *ei-**més*** vs. Attic Gk. *es-**mén*** 'we are'. There was also *e/o* ablaut in the 1st dual and plural, as reflected e.g. in the 1st plural by Gk. *-mes*, *-men* vs. Lat. *-mus* < *-*mos*. To add yet one more complication, 2nd plurals and duals having a long vowel are found in Balto-Slavic and Germanic, e.g. Old High German *bintamēs* 'we bind' and Lith. reflexive *sùkotė-s* 'you (pl.) turn (yourselves)' (*ė* = long *e*). Some have concluded that PIE had long-vowel variants of these endings and have even sought to identify reflexes of them in other branches, but this is not certain.

The 1st singular primary ending *-*mi* was originally proper only to athematic presents (§§5.20ff.), while *-*h*$_2$ is the ending found in thematic presents (see §§5.28ff.) and in subjunctives (§5.55). Similarly, the 3rd plural endings *-*(é)nti* and *-*(é)nt* have the accented *é* only in athematic verbs.

Middle endings

5.14. The middle endings are more difficult to reconstruct than the active. The first chart below contains present middles: Vedic Skt. *bharé* and Gk. *phéromai* 'I carry (for myself), I gain', Tocharian A *träṅkmār* 'I say' (with a 3rd dual from another verb in Tocharian B, *nes-teṃ* 'both are'). The second chart contains the imperfect middles Vedic Skt. *ábhare* and Gk. *epherómēn* 'I was carrying (for myself)', and the Tocharian B preterite middle *kautāmai* 'I was split':

Primary (non-past) middle endings

		Ved.	Gk.	Toch. A	PIE
sg.	1	*bhár-e*	*phéro-mai*	*träṅk-mār*	*-*h*$_2$*er*
	2	*bhára-se*	*phére-ai*[1]	*träṅk-tār*	*-*th*$_2$*er*
	3	*bhára-te*	*phére-tai*	*träṅk-tär*	*-*or*, *-*tor*
du.	1	*bhárā-vahe*	*pheró-methon*		
	2	*bháre-the*	*phére-sthon*		
	3	*bháre-te*	*phére-sthon*	[*nes-teṃ*]	
pl.	1	*bhárā-mahe*	*pheró-metha*	*träṅk-ämtär*	*-*medhh*$_2$?
	2	*bhára-dhve*	*phére-sthe*	*träṅk-cär*	*-*dh(u)u̯e-* ?
	3	*bhára-nte*	*phéro-ntai*	*träṅk-äntär*	*-*ro(r?)*, *-*ntor*

Secondary (past) middle endings

	Ved.	Gk.	Toch. B	PIE
sg. 1	*ábhar-e*	*epheró-mēn*[2]	*kautā-mai*	*-h_2e
2	*ábhara-thās*	*ephér-ou*	*kautā-tai*	*-th_2e
3	*ábhara-ta*	*ephére-to*	*kautā-te*	*-*o*, *-*to*
du. 1	*ábharā-vahi*			
2	*ábhare-thām*	*ephére-sthon*		
3	*ábhare-tām*	*epheré-sthēn*[2]		
pl. 1	*ábharā-mahi*	*epheró-metha*	*kautā-mt(t)e*	*-$medhh_2$?
2	*ábhara-dhvam*	*ephére-sthe*	*kautā-t*	*-*dh(u)u̯e-* ?
3	*ábhara-nta*	*ephéro-nto*	*kautā-nte*	*-*ro*, *-*nto*

[1] Homeric (not actually attested for this verb). [2] Doric *-mān*, *-sthān*, which preserve the original vowel quality *ā*.

Reconstruction of the middle

5.15. Views diverge strongly on at least two essential points regarding the middle personal endings. The first concerns the primary tense-marker. Primary middles in Anatolian, Italic, Celtic, and Tocharian are characterized by endings with *-*r*, while Indo-Iranian, Greek, Germanic, and Albanian have or point to endings with *-*i*. The school of thought followed in the reconstructions above takes the *-*r* as the original primary middle marker, corresponding to the active primary marker *-*i*; under this view, the latter replaced *-*r* in branches like Indo-Iranian and Greek. Thus in the 3rd person singular, what was originally *-*to* + *-*r* (yielding ultimately Hitt. *-tari*, Lat. *-tur*, Old Irish *-tha(i)r*, Tocharian *-tär*, Phrygian *-tor*) was elsewhere remade as *-*to* + *-*i* (yielding Skt. and Avestan *-te*, Gk. *-tai* [or *-toi* in some dialects], Gothic *-da*). But other researchers, especially outside the United States, prefer to reconstruct the middle as having had the same primary marker *-*i* as the active, and to explain the *r*-endings as due to later developments.

A second issue is the descriptive fact that two unrelated sets of endings can be identified for the 2nd and 3rd singular and the 3rd plural. One, exemplified by Vedic and Greek, contains the same *-*s*-, *-*t*-, and *-*nt*- of the corresponding active endings, while the other, exemplified partly by the Tocharian paradigm above and by forms treated in the following discussion, resembles the endings of the IE perfect instead, which will occupy us later in §§5.51ff. The approach adopted here regards this latter set of endings as older, and the other set as replacements under the influence of the active. For a different view, see §5.18 below.

5.16. The **1st person singular** ended in *-h_2e (with or without primary marker). The laryngeal is the same as that seen in active *-h_2 in the thematic endings and the perfect (§§5.28, 5.51). In Toch. A *-mär* and Gk. *-mai*, the original ending was contaminated with the *-m-* of the active 1st sing. Likewise, the **2nd person singular** ending *-th_2e was variously remodeled or replaced, chiefly by a new ending *-*so*, yielding e.g. Ved. primary *-se* < *-*soi* and Gk. primary *-ai* < *-*sai* (replacing *-*soi*). In the **3rd person singular**, some forms in the daughter languages point to *-*o* (with or without primary marker), whereas others point to **-to*. Examples of the former include Cuneiform Luvian *ziy-ari* (with added *-ri*) 'lies' and Vedic Skt. *śáy-e* 'lies', both from **k̂ei̯-o(-)*, while **-to* is reflected in the 3rd singulars in the paradigms above.

The **1st person dual and plural** were probably the rhyming forms **-u̯edhh$_2$* and **-medhh$_2$*, respectively. No detailed reconstructions for the rest of the dual are possible. The **2nd person plural** was **-dhu̯e*, seen in the 2nd plurals above and in Cuneiform Luvian *-tuwa-ri* (with added *-ri*). The **3rd person plural** originally ended in **-ro* or **-ēro*, which only survives vestigially in forms like Vedic Skt. *duh-ré* 'they milk' (*-re* < **-roi*), Young Avestan *-mrauu-āire* 'they are spoken' (*-āire* < **-ēro-i*), and perhaps Tocharian B *stare* 'are' if this continues **sth$_2$-ro*, although other interpretations are possible. The newer ending was **-nto*, as in Ved. *-nte*, *-nta* and Gk. *-ntai*, *-nto* above.

5.17. The double set of 3rd-person endings is of particular interest because their descendants are distributionally and to some extent functionally distinct. In verbs that could take both endings, a contrast in voice can be seen such as that between Ved. *bruv-é* 'is called' (passive, no *t*) and *brū-té* 'calls' (not passive, with *t*); this is paralleled in Old Irish, where the passive also has no *t* (e.g. *ber-air* 'is carried') and where forms with *t* are simply middles (e.g. *seichi-thir* 'follows'). There is also evidence from Anatolian, Indo-Iranian, and Celtic that the distribution of these endings was determined by the formal class to which the verb belonged.

5.18. Since some of the athematic verbs that have *t*-less 3rd persons refer to states, such as most famously **k̂ei̯-o(-)* 'lies' above, several researchers in Germany have claimed that the *t*-less endings were part of a separate **stative** conjugation in PIE with endings **-h$_2$e* **-th$_2$e* **-o* in the singular and 3rd pl. **-(ē)ro*. Under this view, the stative conjugation represented a third voice alongside active and middle-passive, and the middle proper inflected with the endings **-h$_2$e* **-so* **-to* in the singular (with or without added primary marker) and **-nto* in the 3rd pl. This approach has gained numerous adherents, but the evidence for it is fairly slender. There is at any rate much contemporary research going into this and several allied issues involving the relationship of the middle to the active and the perfect. See also further §§5.28, 5.53, and 9.33.

The Present Stem

5.19. The present stem was used in PIE to form one primary tense, the present, and one secondary tense, the imperfect. Both of these could inflect in the active and middle voices. Along with the present tense in the indicative mood (used to express ordinary statements of fact), a present subjunctive, optative, imperative, and participle could also be formed from this stem.

Athematic presents

5.20. Like other verbal and nominal stems, present stems were either athematic or thematic (see §4.22), and there were a number of different types of each. We shall turn our attention first to the athematic presents, which were probably the older type.

5.21. Besides lacking a thematic vowel before the personal endings, the paradigms of athematic presents were characterized by changes in ablaut and typically by shifts in the position of the accent. The basic pattern is the same for all athematic presents: in the singular active, the root (or infix in the case of the nasal-infixed presents discussed below) receives the stress and is in the full grade; in the dual, plural, and in all middle forms the stress migrates rightward to the personal endings, and the root or infix is reduced to the zero-grade. Slightly different are the "Narten" presents discussed below in §5.23, but the basic distinction of a "strong" ablaut grade in the singular versus a "weaker" one in the dual, plural, and middle still obtains.

Root athematic presents

5.22. The simplest and most common athematic present was the root athematic present (or **root present** for short), formed by adding the personal endings directly to the root. There are two types of root presents. The more common type had accented root in the *e*-grade in the singular active, and unaccented root in the zero-grade in its dual, plural, and middle. A classic example is the verb 'be', **$h_1$es-*; paradigms from some of the daughter languages in the singular and plural are given below, together with the PIE reconstruction on the right. (Note that Eng. *am*, *is* is a direct continuation of PIE **$h_1$és-mi*, **$h_1$és-ti*.)

	Hitt.	Ved.	Gk.	Lat.	Goth.	OCS	PIE
sg. 1	*ēšmi*	*ásmi*	*eimí*	*sum*[3]	*im*	*jesmĭ*	**$h_1$és-mi*
2	*ēši*	*ási*	*eĩ, essí*[1]	*es*	*is*	*jesi*	**$h_1$és-si*[4]
3	*ēšzi*	*ásti*	*estí*	*est*	*ist*	*jestŭ*	**$h_1$és-ti*
pl. 1		*smás*	*esmén*	*sumus*	*sijum*	*jesmŭ*	**h_1s-mé(-)*
2		*sthá*	*esté*	*estis*	*sijuþ*	*jeste*	**h_1s-té(-)*
3	*ašanzi*	*sánti*	*eisí, entí*[2]	*sunt*	*sind*	*sǫtŭ*	**h_1s-énti*

[1] *eĩ* is Attic, *essí* is Homeric. [2] *eisí* is Attic, *entí* is Doric. [3] Archaic Lat. *esom*. [4] Became **$h_1$esi* by the rule in §3.37.

5.23. The second type of root present, only identified in the late 1960s by the Indo-Iranianist Johanna Narten and informally termed a **Narten present** in her honor, has the accent on the root throughout, but an alternation between lengthened *ē*-grade in the singular and ordinary *e*-grade elsewhere. Thus from **steu-* 'praise' was formed 3rd sing. **stḗu-ti*, 3rd pl. **stéu̯-n̥ti*. Note that the 3rd plural ending is **-n̥ti* instead of accented **-énti* in the ordinary type. The Narten presents are also called *acrostatic presents* (the term *acrostatic*, which will be properly introduced in the next chapter, means the accent remains on the root throughout the paradigm).

Ablaut of the Narten type may not have been limited to presents; see §5.47.

Other athematic presents

5.24. Two other main kinds of athematic presents are known, the nasal-infix presents and reduplicated athematic presents. As these are more complex formally than root athematics, they are often called *characterized presents*. The difference was significant and had consequences elsewhere in the verbal system; see §5.46.

5.25. Nasal-infix presents. An infix is a morpheme placed inside another morpheme. One PIE infix is known, used by certain roots to form present stems. It had the shape **-ne-* in the full grade and **-n-* in the zero-grade, whence the name *nasal present* for stems containing this infix. The distribution of the ablaut grades was the same as in root presents: full grade in the singular active, zero-grade elsewhere.

The infix was inserted into the zero-grade of the root, between its last two sounds (typically a resonant or high vowel followed by a consonant): thus from **i̯eug-* 'yoke', zero-grade **i̯ug-*, the 3rd sing. nasal present **i̯u-né-g-ti* 'yokes' was formed (> Vedic Skt. *yunákti*), with 3rd pl. **i̯u-n-g-énti* (> Vedic Skt. *yuñjánti*). Nasal-infix presents are typically active transitives, but beyond that we do not know what the meaning of the infix may once have been. Outside of Anatolian and Indo-Iranian, the infix no longer ablauts, as in Lat. *iungit* 'joins', pl. *iungunt*.

5.26. The daughter languages also have various other types of nasal presents that are ultimately related to the nasal-infix type. Two in particular may be mentioned: the suffixed **-neu-/-nu-* presents (e.g. Vedic Skt. *tanóti* 'stretches' ~ *tanvánti* 'they stretch'; Hittite *ar-nu-mi* 'I cause to go'; Gk. *ór-nū-mi* 'I rouse, incite'); and the so-called ninth class of Indo-Iranian verbs, with an ablauting suffix *-nā-/-nī-* that goes back to **-ne-H-/-n-H-* (that is, the nasal infix inserted before a root-final laryngeal), as in Vedic Skt. *punā́ti* 'cleanses' (**pu-né-*h_2*-ti*) ~ *punīmás* 'we cleanse' (**pu-n-*h_2*-mé-*). On this last type, recall the discussion in §4.18; the Sanskrit *tanóti* type will be dealt with in more detail in §10.42.

5.27. Reduplicated athematic presents. These are like ordinary root presents except that an additional syllable is added to the beginning that consists of the first consonant of the root plus an *e* or *i*. For example, the root **de*h_3*-* 'give' formed a reduplicated athematic present stem **de-de*h_3*-* in the singular and **de-d*h_3*-* in the dual and plural; this is reflected in Vedic *dá-dā-ti* 'gives' and *dá-d-ati* 'they give' (the latter from PIE **de-d*h_3*-n̥ti*).

In many examples of the type from the daughter languages, the reduplicating syllable has *-i-* rather than *-e-*, as in Vedic Skt. *jí-gā-ti* 'he goes' and Gk. *dí-dō-mi* 'I give'. This pattern probably spread from thematic reduplicated presents like Gk. *gígnomai* 'I become' (§5.36 below).

No reduplicated presents are known to have been made from vowel-initial roots in PIE (which were rare in any case). An apparent example like Vedic Skt. *íyarti* 'sets in motion' is historically *h_3*i-*h_3*er-ti*, from the laryngeal-initial root *h_3*er-* 'set in motion'.

Thematic presents

5.28. Thematic presents, like other thematic formations, have a theme or stem vowel, ablauting **-e/o-*, before the personal endings. The stress was fixed and the grade of the root did not change. The personal endings of thematic presents are the same as those of athematic presents except for the 1st person singular, which was *-h_2 (or *-oh_2 when we include the thematic vowel) rather than *-_mi_. This ending is ultimately the same as the 1st singular ending of the middle (*-h_2e), and in fact it is widely believed that the thematic conjugation had its origins in the middle.

The following are sample paradigms of the thematic conjugation, showing the verb meaning 'bear, carry' in Vedic, Greek, Gothic, and Old Church Slavonic, as well as the verb meaning 'drive, do' in Latin. In the right-hand column is the reconstructed thematic present of *_bher-_ 'bear, carry':

	Vedic Skt.	Gk.	Lat.	Goth.	OCS	PIE
sg. 1	_bhárāmi_	_phérō_	_agō_	_baira_	_berǫ_	*bhér-o-h_2
2	_bhárasi_	_phéreis_	_agis_	_bairis_	_bereši_	*bhér-e-si
3	_bhárati_	_phérei_	_agit_	_bairiþ_	_beretŭ_	*bhér-e-ti
du. 1	_bhárāvas_			_bairos_	_berevě_	*bhér-o-u̯e-
2	_bhárathas_	_phéreton_		_bairats_	_bereta_	*bhér-e-to-
3	_bháratas_	_phéreton_			_berete_	*bhér-e-to-
pl. 1	_bhárāmas(i)_	_phéromen_	_agimus_	_bairam_	_beremŭ_	*bhér-o-me-
2	_bháratha_	_phérete_	_agitis_	_bairiþ_	_berete_	*bhér-e-te(-)
3	_bháranti_	_phérousi_	_agunt_	_bairand_	_berǫtŭ_	*bhér-o-nti

5.29. The theme vowel was in the _o_-grade before the 1st person endings and the 3rd plural, i.e. before endings beginning with a resonant or laryngeal; the reason for this is not known. It was not an infrequent occurrence in the daughter languages that the athematic 1st singular ending _-mi_ was tacked on secondarily, as in Vedic _bhárāmi_ and Old Church Slavonic _berǫ_ (< *_bher-ōm(i)_) above.

We next survey the major types of thematic presents.

5.30. Simple thematic presents had full grade of the root, with the accent on it, followed by the theme vowel and the ending, as *_bhér-e-ti_ 'bears' above. It is noteworthy that simple thematic verbs are almost or completely absent from Anatolian.

5.31. The type known as **_tudáti_-presents** had zero-grade of the root and accent on the theme vowel. The name comes from a representative example in Sanskrit, Vedic _tudáti_ 'beats' < *_tud-é-ti_.

5.32. *_i̯e/o_-presents. A thematic suffix *-_i̯e/o_- is widely represented, appearing in several different functions. A number of verbs formed their ordinary presents with this suffix, e.g. *_leh_2-_ 'bark' had a present stem *_léh_2-i̯e-_ (as in Vedic Skt. _rā́yasi_ 'you bark', Lith. _lóju_ 'I bark'), and to *_men-_ 'think' the present was *_mn̥-i̯é-_ (as in Vedic Skt. _mányate_ 'thinks' and Gk. _maínetai_ 'is mad' < earlier *_man-i̯e-_ < *_mn̥-i̯e-_). These are usually termed **primary *_i̯e/o_-presents** (not to be confused with "primary" in the meaning "non-past"). The type with zero-grade of the root and accented suffix, characteristically used with intransitives, may have been restricted to middle inflection originally, which would explain why it came to be used to form the passive in Indo-Iranian.

5.33. A different but homophonous suffix, also accented, was used to form **denominative** verbs (verbs derived from nouns or other parts of speech, like English *to head*, *to chair*). These verbs were formed by adding the suffix **-i̯e/o-* directly to the stem of a noun. Thus from the noun **h₁neh₃mn-* 'name' (exact preform uncertain, see §6.36) was formed a denominative verb **h₁neh₃mn-i̯e/o-* 'to name', reflected in Hittite *lamn-iya-zzi* 'names' (from *lamn-* 'name', with *l* replacing *n*), Greek *onomaínō* 'I name' (< pre-Greek **enomn̥-i̯ō*), and Germanic **namnjan* 'to name' (in e.g. Gothic *namnjan*, Old High German *nemnen*, and Modern German *nennen*).

Denominative **i̯e/o*-verbs went on to become extremely productive in most of the daughter languages, and over time new denominative suffixes were created from them by resegmentation. For example, Greek made many denominatives from nouns whose stem ended in *-id-*; the resultant pre-Greek combination **-id-i̯e/o-* became (by regular sound changes) Gk. *-ize/o-*, and this was then reanalyzed as a separate denominative suffix in its own right. It eventually made its way into English as the all-purpose verbal suffix *-ize*, as in the Three Stooges' *moidalize*.

5.34. ***sk̑é/ó-presents.** PIE possessed an accented thematic suffix **-sk̑é/ó-*, added to the zero-grade of the root. The productive descendants of this formation differ in meaning from branch to branch. In Anatolian, the suffix indicates repeated, habitual, or background action, or action applied to more than one object, as in Hittite *walḫ-iški-zzi* 'beats (repeatedly), beats (several objects)'. The habitual or durative sense is also found in Homeric Greek (e.g. *pheúgeskon* 'they would (habitually) flee'). Note also its use in the existential verbs Palaic *iška* and Archaic Latin *escit* 'there is'. Other Latin verbs with the suffix, however, are inchoatives (indicating the beginning or inception of an action or state), e.g. *rubē-sc-ere* 'to grow red'. Several verbs having the suffix that are reconstructible for PIE refer to asking or wishing, indicating perhaps that the suffix also once had desiderative function. An example is **pr̥k̑-sk̑é-* 'ask' in Vedic Skt. *pr̥ccháti* 'asks', Lat. *poscit* 'asks', and German *forschen* 'to look into, research'.

5.35. Causative-iteratives. To form a verb meaning 'cause to do X', PIE took the *o*-grade of the root and added the accented thematic suffix **-éi̯e/o-*. Thus the causative of **sed-* 'sit' was **sod-éi̯e/o-* 'cause to sit' (> Old Irish [*ad-*]*suidi* 'makes sit', Gothic *satjan* 'to set, plant'); similarly, **u̯es-* 'clothe' has the causative **u̯os-éi̯e/o-* 'clothe, put on clothes' (> Hittite *waššezzi* 'he clothes', Vedic Skt. *vāsáyati* 'he clothes'). But almost all such formations in Greek, and many in Slavic, have iterative and not causative meaning, such as Gk. *phor-éō* 'I carry around, habitually carry' (from *phérein* 'to carry') and Old Church Slavonic *nositŭ* 'habitually carries' (from *nesti* 'to carry'). This feature is probably also of PIE date, hence the term "causative-iterative" for this class of verbs.

5.36. Reduplicated thematic presents. Unlike their athematic counterparts, reduplicated thematic presents were formed with **-i-* in the reduplicating syllable and had zero-grade of the root. Some examples include Gk. *gí-gn-o-mai* 'I am born' (root **ĝenh₁-* 'be born') and Lat. *si-st-ō* 'I stand' (root **steh₂-* 'stand').

5.37. Other presents. A suffix **-h₂-*, added to thematic adjectival stems (resulting in a sequence **-eh₂-*), was used to form a verb meaning 'to make something have the quality of the adjective'. Such a verb is called a **factitive.** This factitive suffix may have been further combined with the suffix **-i̯e/o-*. Thus from **neu̯-o-* 'new' was formed the factitive *neu̯-eh$_2$-(i̯e-) 'make new' in Hitt. *new-aḫḫ-* 'make new', Lat. *(re-)nou-ā-re* 'to make new' (*-ā-* < *-eh$_2$-).

There was also a **stative** suffix *-eh$_1$- (probably also followed by *-i̯e/o-) added to an adjectival root to form a verb meaning 'have the quality of the adjective', as in the cognate forms Lat. *rub-ē-re*, OHG *rot-ē-n*, and OCS *rŭděti*, all meaning 'to be red' from *h$_1$rudh-eh$_1$- (from the adjectival root *h$_1$reudh- 'red'). Note also Hittite *marš-e-* 'be false' (< *marša-* 'false'). The suffix appears in numerous other formations in the daughter languages, such as the Greek aorist passive suffix *-ē-* (§12.43) and probably the Armenian verbs in *-i-* (§16.37).

5.38. A number of other present-stem types are more marginally preserved, whose particular characteristics are unknown or disputed. These presents include the "*s*-presents," such as Gk. *a(w)éksō* 'I grow', Old English *weaxan* 'to grow' from PIE *h$_2$u̯og-s-, *h$_2$u̯eg-s-; the "*u*-presents," such as Hitt. *tarḫuzi* or *taruḫzi* (phonetically *tarḫ^{w}tsi*) 'overcomes, is able', Ved. *tū́r-v-ati* 'overcomes' from PIE *terh$_2$-u-, *tr̥h$_2$-u̯-; and presents with the addition of other sounds, such as *-d- and *-dh-.

Of greater import is a theory by the American Indo-Europeanist Jay Jasanoff that posits a class of presents having *o*-grade in the singular, *e*-grade in the dual and plural, and personal endings like those of the perfect. Discussion of this is deferred until the Anatolian chapter (§9.33) since the conjugation (assuming it existed) is best preserved in that branch.

5.39. Desideratives and futures. Several suffixes containing an *-s- have been reconstructed that were used to form desideratives, that is, verbs expressing desire or intent. Some of their descendants function as futures (see below), but it is not certain whether any of these were true futures in PIE. How, and whether, these future/desiderative formations are related to each other is still an open question.

5.40. Indo-Iranian, Balto-Slavic, and maybe Celtic point to a suffix *-si̯e/o- with future and desiderative meaning: Vedic Skt. *dā-syá-ti* 'he intends/wants to give' (later 'he will give'), Lithuanian *dúosiant-* 'about to give', Old Russian *byšęštĭ* 'future' (< *'about to be', from a participle *bhuH-si̯ont-), and Gaulish *pissíiumí* 'I will see'.

5.41. A reduplicated desiderative with *i*-reduplication and a suffix *-(h$_1$)se- is found in Indo-Iranian and Celtic. For example, from *g^{w}hen- 'slay' was formed *g^{w}hi-g^{w}hn̥-h$_1$se-ti, reflected in Vedic Skt. *jíghāṁsati* 'wants to slay' and the Old Irish future *(-)géna* 'he will slay' (from Celtic *g^{w}i-g^{w}nā-se-ti). The same suffix, without reduplication, is the source of Greek futures of the type Homeric *kaléō* 'I will call' < pre-Greek *kalesō < *kal-h$_1$se-.

5.42. An athematic future suffix in *-s- (without preceding laryngeal) is found in Italic (Umbr. *fu-s-t* 'he will be') and Baltic (Lith. *bùs* 'he will be'), while Greek has a thematic version that seems to have been middle in the first instance (e.g. *dḗk-s-o-mai* 'I will bite' to active present *dáknō* 'I bite'); cp. §5.6.

The imperfect and injunctive

5.43. The present stem was used to form not just the present tense but also the imperfect. As mentioned above, the imperfect is usually thought to have signified durative or repeated action in past time (*was going, used to go*). Formally it was usually identical to the present except that secondary endings were used instead of primary (so **-m*, **-s*, **-t* instead of **-mi*, **-si*, **-ti* in the active). The 1st singular **-m* is the same in both thematic and athematic imperfects. The original type is best preserved in Anatolian, Indo-Iranian, and Greek: for example, Hitt. (preterite) *daškinun* 'I (repeatedly) took', Vedic Skt. *ábharam* 'I was carrying', Av. *barəm* 'I was carrying', and Gk. *épheron* 'I was carrying'. (The Vedic and Greek forms begin with the augment **e-* explained in the next section.) Full paradigms were given above in §§5.12 and 5.14.

Outside of these branches, the IE imperfect has either been completely lost, or merged with the aorist. In those branches where the imperfect was lost, a new imperfect conjugation was often innovated (as in Italic and Slavic), sometimes of obscure origin (as in Celtic).

5.44. Indo-Iranian, Greek, Armenian, and Phrygian attest a prefix called the **augment** that was added to past-tense forms. It is reconstructible as **e-*, as in the imperfect **é-bher-e-t* 'he was carrying' (Vedic Skt. *ábharat*, Gk. *éphere*, Arm. *eber*) or the aorist **e-dheh*$_1$- 'placed' (Phrygian *edaes* 'he placed'). These branches have other features in common too, and may well have emerged out of a single dialect area of late PIE; thus it is often thought that the augment was an innovation peculiar to that dialect.

In Indo-Iranian and (especially Mycenaean and Homeric) Greek, past-tense forms can appear with or without the augment. The augmentless forms are called **injunctives**, and have been much discussed in the literature; figuring out their meaning and function has been very difficult. In Greek, injunctives appear especially in the older language of Homer (they are not recognized as a separate category in traditional grammar), where they are normally interchangeable with augmented forms but sometimes have "gnomic" force – that is, are used to express timeless truths. Vedic Sanskrit offers much more evidence for a "timeless" meaning of the injunctive as opposed to the augmented forms; see further §10.41. But its close relative Avestan has mostly dispensed with the augment and uses injunctives as past tenses, like Homer. The Mycenaean Greek evidence is somewhat ambiguous, while Phrygian and Armenian contribute little additional information. On the evidence of Vedic and the Homeric gnomic uses of the injunctive, the PIE category is widely regarded as having been used to refer to acts or events without reference to the time in which they occurred, as well as to facts and conditions having general validity. Under this view, the augment derives from a temporal particle that specified past tense (just like the "hic et nunc" particle specified non-past).

The Aorist Stem

5.45. PIE possessed several different aorist stem formations, some formally parallel to the present-stem types. Comparable to root athematic presents, for example, were root aorists. In addition, PIE possessed a special aorist suffix **-s-* used to form the so-called sigmatic or *s*-aorist. Some of the aorist formations persist even in languages where there is no longer an aorist proper, such as Latin, Old Irish, and Tocharian; in these languages, such forms are called preterites or perfects. In languages with the augment (see above), the aorist is augmented. The aorist indicative was inflected using the secondary personal endings.

The factors determining which aorist formation was chosen by which root are not fully clear. Normally, the same formation is not used for both present and aorist; one common pattern, for example, is an uncharacterized (root) aorist alongside a characterized present, e.g. Ved. root aorist *ádhāt* 'put' alongside reduplicated present *dádhāti* 'puts' (cf. §5.10 above on verbal Aktionsart).

5.46. Root aorist. The root aorist was formed by adding the secondary endings directly to the full grade of the root in the active singular, and to the zero-grade of the root elsewhere. Thus from **steh*$_2$- 'stand' was formed the root aorist **(e-)steh*$_2$*-t* 'he stood' (Vedic Skt. *ásthāt*, Doric Gk. *éstā*). Root aorists typically are made from roots that form characterized presents (see §5.24 on this term); Doric *éstā*, for example, is the aorist of the reduplicated present *hístāmi* 'I stand'.

5.47. Sigmatic or *s*-aorist. The PIE sigmatic or *s*-aorist was characterized by the addition of an *-*s*- to the verbal root. The root is in the lengthened *e*-grade in Indo-Iranian, Italic, and Slavic, as in Vedic Skt. *(á-)vākṣ-ur* (< **(é-)u̯ēĝh-s-*) 'they conveyed', Lat. *uēxī* 'I conveyed' (a perfect in Latin but originally an *s*-aorist), and Old Church Slavonic *věsomŭ* (< **u̯ēdh-s-me*) 'we led'. In Greek and in the *s*-aorist middle in Indo-Iranian, however, the root was in the full grade, as in Gk. *élekse* 'he said' (< **e-leg-s-*). The ablaut thus may have originally been of the "Narten" type (§5.23), with lengthened grade in the singular and full grade elsewhere.

The *s*-aorist eventually outstripped other kinds of aorists in Indo-Iranian, Greek, and Slavic. It is absent from Anatolian and Tocharian, where however there are preterites having an -*s* in the 3rd singular active (e.g. Hitt. *naiš* 'he brought', Toch. B *preksa* 'he asked' < **prēḱ-s-*). Possibly, these two branches reflect an earlier, rudimentary stage in the development of the *s*-aorist, and split off from the family before the *s*-aorist evolved further into its more familiar form.

5.48. Thematic aorist. The thematic aorist has a stem consisting of the zero-grade of the root plus thematic vowel. Although the formation is fairly common in several of the daughters, very few instances are found in more than one branch, leading most researchers to take a conservative approach and posit only one or two examples for the proto-language. Some would entirely deny it any status as a PIE formation, but at least one example seems quite secure, namely **(é-)h*$_1$*ludh-e-* 'went' (root **h*$_1$*leudh-* 'go') in Hom. *ḗluthe* 'came', Old Irish *luid* 'went', and Toch. A *läc* 'went out', the latter two forms occurring in branches in which thematic aorists are otherwise unproductive. Also frequently cited is **(é-)u̯id-e-* 'saw' (root **u̯eid-*) in Vedic Skt. *á-vidat* 'he found', Gk. *é-(w)ide* 'he saw', and Arm. *e-git* 'he found', but since the thematic aorist was productive in these branches, this example is less certain. (For a similar example, cf. §19.25.) The thematic aorist is regarded by some as originating in a thematization of the root aorist, and by others as having ultimately the same origin as the imperfect of *tudáti*-presents, with which it is formally identical.

5.49. Reduplicated aorist. On the basis of Indo-Iranian, Greek, and Tocharian A we can reconstruct a reduplicated thematic aorist for PIE. An example reconstructible for PIE, having *e* in the reduplicating syllable and zero-grade of the root, is **u̯e-uk*^{w}*-e-* 'spoke' (from the root **u̯ek*^{w}- 'speak'), seen in Vedic Skt. *(á)vocam* 'I spoke' and Gk. *(w)eĩpon* 'I spoke' (dissimilated from **(w)eũpon*). Aside from this example (and a very few others), reduplicated aorists typically have causative meaning, such as Vedic Skt. *á-pī-par-as* 'you made cross over', Gk. *dé-da-e* 'he taught' (< *'caused to know'), and Toch. A *śa-śärs* 'he made known'.

5.50. Long-vowel preterites. A variety of past-tense verb forms with long root vowel are found scattered among the branches. Particularly widely represented are forms reflecting **ē* in the root. A long-vowel preterite **lēĝ-* 'gathered, looked at' is reflected by Latin *lēg-ī* 'I gathered, read' (present *leg-ere* 'to gather'), Albanian *(mb)lodha* 'I gathered' (*o* < **ē* in Albanian), and Tocharian A *lyāk* 'saw'. According to one recent (and controversial) theory, these were originally imperfects of Narten presents, hence the lengthened grade. Other vowels are seen too, as in Greek *ánōge* 'he ordered', Gothic *mol* 'I/he ground' (present *mal-an* 'to grind'; the *o* is long), and Old Irish *fích* 'he fought' (present *fich-id* 'fights'). These all have diverse origins. Some, such as the Irish forms, are demonstrably more recent creations; others, such as the long-*ē* preterites, appear to be ancient. How they fit into the PIE verbal system is not known.

The Perfect Stem

5.51. The perfect stem was formed by reduplication, specifically, by doubling the first consonant of the root and inserting *e*. Characteristic of the perfect was the appearance of the root in the *o*-grade in the singular and accented; in the dual and plural, it was in the zero-grade and the endings were accented. Thus the perfect singular stem of **men-* 'think' was **me-món-*, and the dual and plural stem, **me-mn-´*.

The perfect had a special set of personal endings that closely resemble those of the middle:

	Perfect	*Primary middle*	*Secondary middle*
sg. 1	**-h₂e*	**-h₂er*	**-h₂e*
2	**-th₂e*	**-th₂er*	**-th₂e*
3	**-e*	**-or*	**-o*
pl. 1	**-me-*	**-medhh₂ ?*	**-medhh₂ ?*
2	**-e*	**-dh(u)u̯e- ?*	**-dh(u)u̯e- ?*
3	**-ēr, *-r̥s*	**-ro(r?)*	**-ro*

The close similarity of the perfect endings to the middle endings has generated much research and controversy; precisely what the connection between them is remains unclear. Not unconnected with the formal overlap of perfect and middle endings is the fact that some perfects have middle meaning (like Gk. *ólōla* 'I am lost', vs. the active present *óllumi* 'I lose, destroy'), or exist alongside middle presents (like Vedic Skt. *ruróca* 'shines', perfect of the middle present *rócate* 'shines') or middle root aorists (Vedic Skt. perfect *jujóṣa* 'enjoys' next to middle root aorist *ájuṣran* 'they took a liking to'). It has been speculated that the perfect and the middle endings were once a single set.

The following are some of the forms upon which this reconstruction has been based. They do not all have the same function (the Hittite forms are presents and the Gothic forms are preterites), more on which below in §5.53. The forms are Hitt. *wewakḫi* 'I demand', Vedic Skt. *jagáma* 'I went', Gk. *léloipa* 'I left', Lat. *meminī* 'I remember', and Goth. *haihait* 'I called, I named'. At the right is a reconstructed PIE paradigm.

	Hitt.	Ved.	Gk.	Lat.	Goth.	PIE
sg. 1	*(wewakḫi)*	*jagáma*	*léloipa*	*meminī*	*haihait*	**me-món-h₂e*
2	*(wewakti)*	*jagántha*	*léloipas*	*meministī*	*haihaist*	**me-món-th₂e*
3	*wewakki*	*jagā́ma*	*léloipe*	*meminit*	*haihait*	**me-món-e*
pl. 1		*jaganmá*	*leloípamen*	*meminimus*	*haihaitum*	**me-mn̥-mé(-)*
2		*jagmá*	*leloípate*	*meministis*	*haihaituþ*	**me-mn-é ?*
3		*jagmúr*	*leloípāsi*	*meminēre*[1]	*haihaitun*	**me-mn-ḗr*

[1] Older or poetic; ordinary Classical *meminērunt*.

Most of the languages have undone the original ablaut and have partially replaced the perfect endings with secondary endings, especially in the plural. It is not assured that Hitt. *wewakḫi* is in fact an old perfect, but formally it looks like one and has been included above for illustrative purposes.

5.52. One famous perfect does not exhibit reduplication, **u̯oid-h₂e* 'know' (from the root **u̯eid-* 'see'), becoming Vedic Skt. *véda*, Gk. *(w)oĩda*, Goth. *wait*, and Old Eng. *wāt* (continued in the modern British English phrase *God wot* 'God knows'). Compare the following paradigms:

	Ved.	Gk.	Goth.	PIE
sg. 1	*véda*	*(w)oĩda*	*wait*	**u̯óid-h₂e*
2	*véttha*	*(w)oĩstha*	*waist*	**u̯óid-th₂e*
3	*véda*	*(w)oĩde*	*wait*	**u̯óid-e*
pl. 1	*vidmá*	*(w)ídmen*	*witum*	**u̯id-mé(-)*
2	*vidá*	*(w)íste*	*wituþ*	**u̯id-é ?*
3	*vidúr*	*(w)ísāsi*	*witun*	**u̯id-ḗr*

This perfect is exceptional not only because of its lack of reduplication but also because of its meaning (not 'sees' or 'has seen' but 'knows'). These are widely thought to be archaic features, harking back, perhaps, to a time when the perfect had no reduplication; but this view is not universally held.

Meaning of the perfect

5.53. The perfect is formally best preserved in Indo-Iranian and Greek, and less well in Anatolian, Italic, Celtic, and Germanic. A number of archaic examples of the perfect, especially in Indo-Iranian and Greek, refer to states in present time. We saw this above (§5.51) in four perfects: Gk. *ólōla* 'I am lost', Vedic Skt. *ruróca* 'shines', Ved. *jujóṣa* 'enjoys', and Lat. *meminit* 'remembers'. (The Greek and Gothic cognates of *meminit* are also statives, meaning 'is mindful of': Gk. *mémone*, Goth. *man* 'thinks' [without reduplication].) Furthermore, the singular perfect endings are used to inflect a class of presents in Anatolian, the so-called *ḫi*-conjugation (to which Hittite *wewakki* in §5.51 belongs). While the relationship of the *ḫi*-conjugation to the perfect is unclear, all these facts together have led researchers to believe that the PIE perfect was a *stative*. In the daughter languages, however, except for relic forms like the ones just cited, perfects express past tense, and have often fallen together formally with the aorist into a single "preterite" tense. To explain this development, it is usually said that the PIE stative perfect had (or optionally had) resultative overtones ('is in a state resulting from having done X', therefore 'has done X').

Moods

Imperative

5.54. The imperative was used to express direct commands. The **athematic 2nd singular** imperative ending is reconstructible as **-dhi* and was added to the zero-grade of the root, as in Vedic Skt. *śru-dhí* 'listen!' and Gk. *í-thi* 'go!'. The **thematic 2nd singular** imperative was the bare thematic stem, as in Vedic Skt. *bhára* and Gk. *phére* 'carry!' from PIE **bhér-e*. The **2nd plural** imperative ended in **-te*: Vedic Skt. *bhárata* and Gk. *phérete*, both from **bhérete* '(you pl.) carry!'

PIE also had **3rd person** imperatives ending in **-u*, forming 3rd sing. **-tu* and 3rd pl. **-ntu*, as in Hittite *paiddu* 'let him go' and Vedic Skt. *ástu* 'it will be'. Another ending **-tōd* formed the so-called **future imperative**. This ending was indifferent to person and number and was used in commands that pertained to the more distant future or that were to remain always in force (as in laws). It is most clearly seen in Sanskrit and Italic, e.g. Vedic Skt. *dhattāt* 'you shall bestow (afterwards)', Archaic Latin *datōd* 'let him give, he shall give', Oscan *deiuatud* 'he shall swear'. In Greek the formation is also found, but only in the 3rd person (e.g. *pheré-tō* 'let him carry'), where – as also in Italic – it replaced **-tu*; and a few examples have recently come to light from Celtiberian (e.g. *tatuz*, phonetically probably [datuz], 'he will give').

Subjunctive

5.55. The subjunctive in PIE was formed by the addition of the thematic vowel to the verb stem (be it athematic or already thematic), followed apparently by primary endings (although in Indo-Iranian both primary and secondary endings were used; see below). In athematic verbs, the "strong" stem (the one having full grade of the root or ablauting portion of the stem) was used in all persons and numbers. Some reconstructed examples of 3rd sing. and 3rd pl. present subjunctives follow for the athematic presents of _*$h_1$es-_ 'be' and _*i̯eug-_ 'yoke' and the thematic present _*bher-_ 'carry':

	Indicative	*Subjunctive*
root present	_*$h_1$és-ti_	_*$h_1$és-e-ti_
	_*h_1s-énti_	_*$h_1$és-o-nti_
nasal-infix present	_*i̯u-né-g-ti_	_*i̯u-né-g-e-ti_
	*i̯u-n-g-énti	_*i̯u-né-g-o-nti_
thematic present	_*bhér-e-ti_	_*bhér-e-e-ti_ (= _*bhérēti_)
	*bhér-o-nti	_*bhér-o-o-nti_ (= _*bhérōnti_)

Adjusting for the fact that Vedic Sanskrit uses the secondary ending *-n* from _*-nt_ in the third plural, the right-hand column above yields the Vedic subjunctives *ásat(i)*, *ásan* (versus indicative *ásti*, *sánti*); *yunájati*, *yunájan* (versus indicative *yunákti*, *yuñjánti*); and *bhárāti*, *bhárān* (versus indicative *bhárati*, *bháranti*). Compare also Latin ***erit*** 'he will be', ***erunt*** 'they will be' (synchronically future, but historically subjunctive), and Greek *phérēi*, *phérōsi* (*-ōsi* < _*-ōnti_) for the thematic subjunctive.

As indicated by such first-person subjunctives as Vedic Skt. *kr̥ṇavā* 'I will do', Old Avestan *yaojā* 'I will yoke', Gk. *phérō* 'let me carry', and Lat. *erō* 'I will be', the 1st singular ended in _*-h_2_ (or _*-oh_2_ including the subjunctive vowel) rather than _*-mi_.

Subjunctives could also be formed in the same way from root and *s*-aorists, where likewise the full grade of the aorist stem was used.

5.56. Meaning of the subjunctive. The subjunctive was probably a future tense. Here one must be careful to avoid terminological confusion, as most of the forms called "subjunctives" in the daughter languages, which express a variety of modal meanings, have nothing to do with the PIE subjunctive, but come from the optative (see below) or elsewhere. The subjunctive in Indo-Iranian, Greek, and partly in Celtic is a continuation of the PIE subjunctive; in Indo-Iranian it usually has future meaning, as true also of many examples in Homer. In Latin, the descendants of the PIE subjunctive are futures. The PIE subjunctive is not preserved outside of these branches.

Optative

5.57. The optative was formed by adding an ablauting suffix _*-i̯eh_1-/-ih_1-_ to the relevant stem (present, aorist, or perfect), plus secondary personal endings. In most athematic verbs, this suffix was attached to the weak stem of the verb, and had the full-grade form _*-i̯eh_1-_ in the singular and zero-grade _*-ih_1-_ elsewhere. However, in Narten presents, being accented on the root, the suffix was in the zero-grade throughout. This was also true of thematic verbs, where the zero-grade of the suffix was used throughout, and added to the *o*-grade of the thematic vowel. Compare the following paradigms, showing the optatives of the athematic verb 'be' and the thematic verb 'bear' in PIE and selected daughter languages:

	Athematic optative				*Thematic optative*			
	Ved.	Gk.	Lat.	PIE	Ved.	Av.	Gk.	PIE
sg. 1	*syā́m*	*eíēn*	*siem*[1]	*h_1s-i̯éh_1-m	*bháreyam*		*phéroimi*[2]	*bhér-o-ih_1-m̥
2	*syā́s*	*eíēs*	*siēs*[1]	*h_1s-i̯éh_1-s	*bháres*	*barōiš*	*phérois*	*bhér-o-ih_1-s
3	*syā́t*	*eíē*	*siēt*[1]	*h_1s-i̯éh_1-t	*bháret*	*barōit̰*	*phéroi*	*bhér-o-ih_1-t
pl. 1	*syā́ma*	*eĩmen*	*sīmus*	*h_1s-ih_1-mé-	*bhárema*	*baraēma*[3]	*phéroimen*	*bhér-o-ih_1-me-
2	*syā́ta*	*eĩte*	*sītis*	*h_1s-ih_1-té-	*bháreta*		*phéroite*	*bhér-o-ih_1-te-
3	*syúr*	*eĩen*	*sient*[1]	*h_1s-ih_1-ént	*bháreyur*	*baraiiən*	*phéroien*	*bhér-o-ih_1-ent

[1] Archaic Latin; Classical *sim*, *sīs*, *sit*, 3rd pl. *sint*. [2] The *-mi* is an innovation; cp. Arcadian *ekselaunoia* 'I would drive out', with *-oia* from *-oih_1-m̥. [3] This form not actually attested for this verb.

Note that the 3rd plural was always *-ent (replaced in Sanskrit by a different ending) and never *-n̥t, even when unaccented. As mentioned above, the continuations of the PIE optative in the daughter languages are not always termed "optatives," but sometimes "subjunctives," as in Italic and Germanic. In Balto-Slavic the optative became the imperative and a new category in Lithuanian called the permissive, but also survived limitedly as a real optative in Old Prussian; see further §18.66. There is no trace of the optative in Anatolian. Interestingly, in the thematic optative the vowels *-o-ī-, resulting from *-o-ih_1-, were a disyllabic sequence and remained so for some time after the days of PIE, as shown by their treatment in Indo-Iranian, Greek, Balto-Slavic, and perhaps Germanic.

Non-finite Verbal Formations and Other Topics

We have now concluded our survey of the finite forms of the IE verb, that is, those that differentiate person and number. Two other sets of forms remain: infinitives and participles.

Infinitives

5.58. The infinitive is essentially a verbal noun, rendered either as 'to X' or 'X-ing' in English. The daughter languages exhibit a rather bewildering variety of infinitives. Typically they are frozen case-forms (usually accusatives, datives, or locatives) of nouns derived from verbal roots. The nominal formations in question are usually old, but which infinitive formations are of PIE date is uncertain. Represented in more than one daughter branch as true infinitives are the following:

1 The suffix *-dhi̯e- or *-dhi̯o-, appearing in both active and passive infinitives: Vedic Skt. *píba-dhyai* 'to drink', Umbr. *piha-fi* 'to propitiate', Toch. A and B *lkā-tsi* 'to look'.
2 Various case-forms of the noun suffix *-tu- (§6.42), e.g. Vedic Skt. *dā́-tum* 'to give', *pā́-tave* 'to drink, for drinking'.
3 Various case-forms of the noun suffix *-ti- (§6.42), e.g. Vedic Skt. *pī-táye* 'to drink, for drinking', Av. *kərə-tōe* 'to do', OCS *da-ti* 'to give', Lith, *bū́-ti* 'to be'.

4 Various case-forms of the complex *n*-stems (§6.34) *-*men*-, *-*sen*-, *-*ten*-, and *-*u̯en*-, e.g. Vedic Skt. *vid-máne* 'to find', Homeric Gk. *íd-menai* 'to know', the Gk. thematic infinitive ending -*ein* (< *-*e-sen*), OPers. *car-tanaiy* 'to do', Hitt. *laḫḫiya-uwanzi* 'to wage war', and Cypriot Gk. *do-wenai* 'to give'.

5.59. Several daughter branches have a specific infinitive formation often called the **supine** that is solely used with verbs of motion to indicate purpose, as Vedic (*áganma*) *právoḷhum* '(we went) to bring', Latin (*uēnērunt*) *questum* '(they came) to complain', Old Church Slavonic (*pridŭ*) *sŭpatŭ* 'I went (in order) to sleep'. Usually it is formed with the suffix *-*tum*, the accusative of the abstract noun suffix *-*tu*- mentioned above.

Participles

5.60. Participles are verbal adjectives. Like other adjectives, they inflect in the different nominal cases and numbers discussed in chapter 6.

The most widely represented participle is the ***nt*-participle**, found in virtually all the branches to form participles of active voice to present or aorist stems. The suffix was ablauting, appearing as *-*ent*- (perhaps also as *-*ont*-) and *-*nt*-. In athematic verbs, it was added to the weak present stem, as in **h_1s-(e)nt*- 'being' (> Vedic Skt. *sat*- 'being', Lat. *ab-sent*- 'being away, absent'), **dhe-dhh_1-(e)nt*- 'placing' (> Gk. *ti-thent*- 'placing'), and **i̯ung-(e)nt*- 'joining' (> Lat. *iungent*-). In thematic verbs, zero-grade *-*nt*- was added to the *o*-grade thematic vowel, as in **bher-o-nt*- 'carrying' (> Gk. *phéront*-, Goth. *bairand*-, and OCS *berǫšt*- from pre-Slavic **ber-ont-j*-). In Anatolian, however, this participle is semantically equivalent to the *-*tó*-verbal adjective (see §5.61 below), indicating completion and being passive when formed from transitive verbs, and active when formed from intransitive verbs: *kunānt*- '(having been) killed', *iyant*- '(having) gone'. Aorist active participles were formed similarly to present participles, as the root aorist participle meaning 'having stood' in Vedic Skt. *sthānt*- and Gk. *stant*-.

Several branches continue a **mediopassive participle** in *-*m(e)no*- or *-*m$h_1$no*- (its exact reconstruction is a matter of dispute), seen for example in Vedic Skt. *bhára-māṇa*- and Av. *barə-mna*- 'carrying (for oneself)', Gk. *pheró-menos* 'carrying (oneself), being carried', and OPruss. *poklausīmanas* 'heard'. In other branches only a few fossilized examples of it exist, such as Lat. *alu-mnus* 'fosterling' (lit. 'nurtured') and Arm. *anasown* 'animal' (lit. 'not talking', from *asem* 'I talk', as though from late PIE **n̥-aĝ-omno*-). Related is the **present passive participle** in *-*mo*- of Balto-Slavic and perhaps Anatolian: OCS *nĕsomŭ* 'being carried', Lith. *nẽšamas* 'being carried', and Cuneiform Luv. *kīšammi*- 'combed'.

A **perfect participle** with the ablauting suffix *-*u̯os-/-us*- is reflected in numerous branches. In PIE, it was added to the zero-grade of the perfect stem; the suffix was *-*u̯ōs* in the nominative singular masculine (neuter *-*us*, feminine *-*us-ih_2*); the accusative singular ended in *-*u̯os-m̥* (see §6.6 for the case-ending) and the other cases were added to the stem *-*us*-. This is directly reflected for example in Av. nomin. sing. *vīδuuå*, accus. *vīδuuåŋhəm*, stem *vīduš*- 'knowing' (from **u̯idu̯ōs* **u̯idu̯osm̥* **u̯idus*-). Compare also the Vedic stem *vidúṣ*- 'knowing'; Gk. masc. nomin. sing. *(w)eidṓs* and fem. *(w)iduĩa* (< **u̯idusih_2*) 'knowing'; and, further afield, Toch.

B masc. nomin. *lt-u* 'having come out', accus. *lt-uwes*, fem. *lt-usa*, and Lith. fem. *áug-us-i* 'having grown'.

Some branches also have evidence for a **preterite participle** in _*-lo-_: Arm. aorist participle *gereal* 'taken, having taken', OCS preterite participle *nes-lŭ* 'having carried', and Toch. A gerundive (verbal adjective) *ritwāl* 'united'.

5.61. In addition to the participles, PIE had **verbal adjectives** in _*-tó-_ and _*-nó-_, added to the zero-grade of a verbal root. These indicated completed action and were semantically like past participles in English: if the verb they were formed from was transitive (like *eat*), the verbal adjective was passive and past in tense (*eaten*), but if the verb was intransitive (like *go*), the verbal adjective was simply past in tense (*gone*). Thus the root _*g^{w}hen-_ 'kill' formed the verbal adjective _*g^{w}hn̥-tó-_ 'slain' in Vedic Skt. *hatá-* and Gk. *(-)phatós*, and the intransitive root _*g^{w}em-_ 'come' has _*g^{w}m̥-tó-_ '(having) come' in Vedic Skt. *gatá-*, Gk. *(-)batós*, and Lat. *uentus*. Less widespread than _*-tó-_ was _*-nó-_, whose participial function is clearest in Indo-Iranian, as in Vedic Skt. *bhin-ná-* '(having been) split' (< _*bhid-nó-_), but also in Germanic and Slavic in a longer form _*-enó-_ or _*-onó-_, as in Goth. *bit-ans*, Eng. *bitt-en* (< _*bhid-onó-_) and OCS *nes-enŭ* 'carried'. Similar forms, like _*pl̥h$_1$-nó-_ 'full', were once participles ('filled up') but have descendants that are only adjectives and no longer part of any verbal paradigm: Vedic Skt. *pūrṇá-*, Lat. *plēnus* (versus past participle *-plētus* 'filled'), Goth. *fulls* (double *-ll-* < _*-ln-_), Old Irish *lán*, and Lith. *pìlnas*.

Neither of these formations is found in Anatolian. For other uses of _*-tó-_, see §6.77.

Verbal composition

5.62. Verbs were often combined with adverbs to modify their meaning. Such adverbs were called *preverbs* and in the first instance remained separate words. Over time they tended to join with verbs as prefixes. As there are some interesting syntactic phenomena associated with this subject, we will defer discussion of preverbs until §§8.9ff.

Occasionally, verbs were compounded with a non-adverbial element, such as a noun. The most familiar example of this is the verb for 'believe, trust', _*k̑red dheh$_1$-_, literally 'place one's heart in', which became Vedic Skt. *śrád dadhāti* 'trusts, believes', Lat. *crēdō* 'I believe', and Old Irish *cretim* 'I believe'.

Prosodic status of verbs

5.63. There is good comparative evidence that finite verbs were prosodically weaker (that is, were pronounced with weaker stress or lower pitch) than other parts of speech, especially in main clauses. In Vedic Sanskrit, main-clause finite verbs that do not stand at the beginning of their clause (or a verse-line of poetry) are written in the manuscripts without accent marks. In Greek, the rules for accenting verbs are different from those for nouns, and resemble the accentuation of strings of clitics; this suggests an affinity between the prosody of verbs and the prosody of chains of weakly stressed or unstressed particles. In Germanic heroic poetry, fully stressed words alliterate with one another, but certain verbs, together with unstressed pronouns and particles, do not participate in alliteration; this suggests weaker prosodic status for those verbs. In certain Germanic languages, such as modern German, verbs are required to be the second syntactic unit in main clauses, which is the same position taken by many unstressed sentence particles elsewhere in Indo-European (Wackernagel's Law, see §§8.22ff.).

All these facts taken together suggest that finite verbs were in some way prosodically deficient in PIE. Whether verbs in PIE were true clitics, that is, had no stress and formed an accentual unit with a neighboring stressed word, is uncertain, but is a position defended by many Indo-Europeanists. However, it is clear that even if they could behave as clitics some of the time, they were fully stressed when moved to the front of a clause for emphasis or contrast, or when occurring in subordinate clauses. This is not too surprising, since weaker prosodic status of verbs (vis-à-vis nouns) is a common cross-linguistic phenomenon.

For Further Reading

Comprehensive recent works on the verb are wanting; the volumes on the verb in Brugmann 1897–1916 and Hirt 1927–37 (see Bibliography, ch. 1) are rather out of date. Books on the IE verb are generally specialized. Watkins 1969 is a very influential examination of the prehistory of PIE verbal inflection. Jasanoff 1978 is an in-depth study of the relationship between the stative and middle; see also his most recent work, Jasanoff 2003, a very thought-provoking and detailed theory on the prehistory of IE verbal morphology. Very useful and up-to-date – though in various places controversial – is Rix 2001, a dictionary of Indo-European verbal roots and reconstructed stem-forms.

For Review

Know the meaning or significance of the following:

tense-stem	mediopassive	primary endings	*tudáti*-present
primary verb	mood	secondary endings	**i̯e/o*-present
derived verb	indicative	"hic et nunc" particle	augment
voice	imperative	root present	injunctive
active	subjunctive	Narten present	sigmatic aorist
middle	optative	nasal infix	

Exercises

1 Name the function(s) of the following PIE suffixes:

a	**-nt-*	**d**	**-eh$_2$-(i̯e-)*	**g**	**-eh$_1$-(i̯e-)*	**j**	**-i̯e/o-*	**m**	**-i̯eh$_1$-/-ih$_1$-*
b	**-nó-*	**e**	**-ne-* (infix)	**h**	**e-* (prefix)	**k**	**-éi̯e-*	**n**	**-sk̑é/ó-*
c	**-u̯os-/-us-*	**f**	**-tó-*	**i**	**-si̯e/o-*	**l**	**-m(e)no-* or **-mh$_1$no-*		

2 Identify the following reconstructed PIE verb inflectional endings as specifically as possible:

a *-th$_2$er
b *-oh$_2$
c *-ti
d *-(t)o
e *-u̯e-
f *-(t)or
g *-m
h *-si
i *-s
j *-(é)nti
k *-tu
l *-te
m *-mi
n *-ntu
o *-ro
p *-(é)nt
q *-dhi
r *-t
s *-h$_2$er
t *-ēr, *-r̥s

In exercises **3–8**, indicate the position of the accent in each PIE form that you give.

3 The following verbal roots formed root presents of the ordinary (non-Narten) type in PIE. Provide all three singular forms and the 3rd plural in the present indicative active.

a *k̂tei- 'settle'
b *h$_2$u̯eh$_1$- 'blow'
c *su̯enh$_2$- 'make a sound'
d *h$_1$ei- 'go'
e *g^{w}hen- 'slay'
f *bhleh$_1$- 'weep'

4 The following verbal roots formed simple thematic presents. For each one, provide (1) the 1st and 2nd singular and 3rd plural present indicative active, and (2) the 3rd singular and 3rd plural imperfect indicative active. Include the augment where possible.

a *pek^w- 'cook'
b *pleu- 'swim'
c *bheidh- 'trust'
d *der- 'tear, flay'
e *leĝ- 'gather'
f *dheg^{w}h- 'burn'

5 The following verbal roots formed nasal-infix presents. For each one, provide (1) all three singular forms and the 3rd plural in the present subjunctive active, and (2) the present optative stems.

a *bheid- 'split'
b *peuh$_2$- 'cleanse'
c *k̂leu- 'hear'
d *k^{w}reih$_2$- 'exchange'
e *terd- 'bore'
f *h$_3$meiĝh- 'urinate'

6 The following roots formed perfects. Provide all three singular forms and the 3rd plural for each perfect.

a *h$_2$nek̂- 'reach, attain'
b *du̯ei- 'fear'
c *dhers- 'dare'
d *ĝenh$_1$- 'beget'
e *neig^w- 'wash'
f *g^{w}em- 'come, go'

7 Form the causative-iterative stem for each of the following verbal roots and give a translation.

a *bheudh- 'wake'
b *leuk- 'light'
c *i̯eudh- 'fight'
d *legh- 'lie'
e *demh$_2$- 'tame'
f *nek̂- 'disappear, come to harm'

8 The following are a mixture of thematic and strong athematic singular present stems. For each stem, (1) identify as specifically as possible the type of present it exemplifies, and (2) provide the singular and plural optative stems.

a *$\hat{g}\mathring{n}h_3$-$s\hat{k}\acute{e}$-* 'know'
b *$d\acute{\bar{e}}\hat{k}$-* 'receive'
c **pérd-e-* 'fart'
d **li-né-k^w-* 'leave'
e **$g^w\mathring{r}h_3$-é-* 'devour'
f **$m\mathring{r}$-i̯é-* 'disappear, die'
g **sél-* 'jump'
h **si-sd-e-* 'seat'
i **dhe-dheh$_1$-* 'put'

9 The following roots formed root aorists in PIE. Provide the 2nd singular indicative active for each. Include the augment.

a **peh$_3$-* 'drink'
b **der$\hat{k}$-* 'see'
c **dreh$_2$-* 'run'
d **k^wel-* 'turn'
e **k^wer-* 'cut'
f **$\hat{g}$enh$_1$-* 'beget'

10 The following roots formed *s*-aorists in PIE. Provide the 3rd singular indicative active for each. Include the augment.

a **h$_3$neid-* 'blame, scorn'
b **deu$\hat{k}$-* 'lead'
c **neiH-* 'lead'
d **h$_3$re$\hat{g}$-* 'direct, rule'
e **bher-* 'carry'
f **pre$\hat{k}$-* 'ask'

11 Based on the endings given in §5.14 and the ablaut information in §5.22, provide the singular and the 3rd plural present and imperfect indicative middle of the verb **mleuH-* 'speak'.

12 For **3a–c** and **4a–c**, give the stem of the present active participle.

13 For **6a–c**, give the nominative singular of the perfect participle.

14 Using the suffix **-tó-*, form the verbal adjectives of the roots in **9** above and translate them.

15 Given that **-ss-* was simplified to **-s-* in PIE (§3.37), how would you explain the Homeric form *essí* 'you (sing.) are', which looks as if it should come from **h$_1$es-si*? Do not assume any additional sound changes.

16 Vedic Sanskrit has an athematic verbal stem *duh-* 'to milk' (< PIE **dhugh-*, zero-grade of **dheugh-*) for which several variant forms are attested for the 3rd pl. present indicative middle, including *duháte*, *duhré*, and *duhráte*. In *duháte* and *duhráte*, the *a* is the Sanskrit outcome of **$\mathring{n}$*, and *e* comes from **oi*. Using §5.15 as a starting point, provide historical explanations for all three forms. Which do you think is the oldest?

17 No IE language preserves the Narten type of root present completely intact. It has been posited on the basis of such athematic present forms as the following: Lat. 2nd sing. *ēs* 'you eat' and 3rd sing. *ēs-t* 'he/she eats'; Vedic Skt. 3rd pl. *ad-ánti* 'they eat' (*ad-* < **h$_1$ed-*); Vedic Skt. 3rd sing. *mā́rṣ-ṭi* 'wipes' (*-ā-* < **-ē-*); Gk. 3rd sing. middle *hés-tai* 'puts on clothes' (*hes-* < **u̯es-*) and *keĩ-tai* 'lies (down)'. Discuss how these forms support the reconstruction of the Narten type of root present.

6 The Noun

Introduction

Case

6.1. Like verbs, PIE nouns were highly inflected. Nouns had case-endings that indicated their grammatical function, such as subject, direct object, indirect object, and possessive. Sure evidence exists for eight cases in PIE: **nominative** (subject of the sentence and predicate nominative), **vocative** (the case of direct address), **accusative** (direct object), **genitive** (possessive), **ablative** (source or place from which), **dative** (indirect object, possession, and beneficiary of an action), **instrumental** (means, accompaniment, and agent), and **locative** (place where). There may have also been a ninth case, the **directive** or allative (place to which). A few languages, such as Old Lithuanian, Tocharian, and Ossetic, developed additional cases that arose under the influence of neighboring, unrelated language groups (Finnic in the case of the first, Turkic in the case of the second, and Kartvelian in the case of the third).

Nominal declensions, like verbal conjugations, could be athematic or thematic. The latter gradually replaced the former in most branches, though not as quickly or thoroughly as thematic verbs replaced athematic verbs.

Number

6.2. Nouns were inflected in three numbers, singular, dual, and plural. The dual has tended to disappear, and several branches had lost it entirely or almost entirely by the time of their earliest attestations. Existing perhaps outside the singular–plural parameter was a category called the **collective**, which indicated a collection of entities treated as a unit (e.g., Latin *loca* '(group of) places', as opposed to the ordinary plural *locī*, singular *locus*). The collectives are only preserved as such in the archaic stages of a few branches, and were reanalyzed as singulars or plurals elsewhere. Interestingly, both Tocharian and Anatolian could form plurals to collectives, called **pluratives**; whether this is an inherited feature is not known, for it could have developed independently (as it later did in Celtic; cp. §14.66).

Gender

6.3. Most of the older IE languages show a three-way contrast in grammatical gender between masculine, feminine, and neuter. But the oldest preserved branch, Anatolian, has only a two-way distinction between animate or common gender and inanimate or neuter; the historical status of the feminine in Anatolian is disputed.

The neuter had the same endings as the animate (or masculine) except in the nominative, vocative, and accusative. These three cases are not formally distinguished from one another in neuters.

Athematic Nouns

6.4. Like athematic verbs, athematic nouns have inflectional endings added directly to a root or suffix without an intervening thematic vowel. Traditionally, those athematic nouns with stems ending in a consonant (called *consonant stems*) have been distinguished from those ending in *i* or *u* (the *i*-stems and *u*-stems) as well as from those ending in *ā* (< **e*h_2, the typically feminine *ā*-stems); but this distinction is both unnecessary and misleading, as it masks the fundamentally identical behavior of all these groups over against that of the thematic nouns. We will, however, leave the *ā*-stems to a separate later section (§6.70) for better treatment of certain complicating issues surrounding this class.

To understand athematic nominal inflection, one must distinguish between the so-called **strong** and **weak** cases. The strong cases differ from the weak cases typically in where the accent is located and which morpheme is in the full grade; most commonly, the full grade and the accent shift rightward in the weak cases, comparable to the shift seen in most athematic verbs. In the schematic diagram below, the strong cases are shaded:

	singular	dual	plural
nominative			
vocative			
accusative			
genitive			
ablative			
dative			
instrumental			
locative			

According to some theories, the accusative plural was strong as well. Standing somewhat apart was the ablaut of the locative singular; see §6.11.

Case-endings of athematic nouns

6.5. The reconstructions of the PIE case-endings are most secure for the singular and for the strong cases in the dual and plural. For the nominative and accusative, a distinction must be maintained between **animate** nouns (masculine or feminine) and **neuters** (or inanimates), as will become clear below.

First, we sketch the case-endings of representative daughter languages. The vocative has been omitted since the daughter languages usually used the nominative for the vocative (but see further below). Only those forms relevant to the reconstructions given later are shown.

The singular

Representative animate athematic paradigms are given in the chart below: Hitt. *ḫūmant-* 'every', Ved. *pad-* and Gk. *pod-* 'foot', Ved. *gopā-* 'cowherd, protector', Gk. *klōp-* 'thief', Av. *kəhrp-* 'body' and *nar-* 'man', and Lat. *uōc-* 'voice'. Baltic has clear cognate case-endings but not in any one paradigm, so a variety of forms are given that are glossed in the notes below. Case-forms in the individual languages that are either unattested or not useful for reconstruction are left blank in this and the following charts. No separate ablative is shown; see §6.8.

	Hitt.	Ved.	Av.	Gk.	Lat.	Baltic	PIE
nom.	*ḫūman-za*	*pā́d,* *gopā́-s*	*kərəf-š*	*poús,* *klṓp-s*	*uōx* (= *uōc-s*)	*viešpat-s*[3]	*-*s*
acc.	*ḫūmant-an*	*pā́d-am,* *gopā́-m*	*kəhrp-əm*	*pód-a*	*uōc-em*	*šùn-į,*[4] *smument-in*[5]	*-*m*
gen.	*ḫūmant-aš*	*pad-ás*	*kəhrp-ō*	*pod-ós*	*uōc-is*	*šuñ-s,*[4] *szird-es*[6]	*-*(é)s*
dat.		*pad-é*	*nair-e*		*uōc-ī*	*giwānt-ei*[7]	*-*ei*
instr.		*pad-ā́*	*kəhrp-a*				*-*(e)*h_1
loc.	*ḫūmant-i*	*pad-í*	*nair-i*	*pod-í*[1]	*uōc-e*[2]	*wieszpati-p*[8]	*-*i*

[1] Synchronically labeled dative: see §6.11. [2] Synchronically labeled ablative: see §6.11. [3] OLith., 'lord'. [4] Lith., 'dog'. [5] OPruss., 'man'. [6] OLith., 'of the heart'. [7] OPruss., 'for (one) living'. [8] OLith. adessive case, 'at the lord'.

6.6. In athematic nouns, the **animate nominative singular** ended in *-*s* and the **animate accusative singular** ended in *-*m* (or *-*m̥* after consonants). The **neuter nominative-accusative singular** had zero ending. Thus contrast Hittite neuter nomin. sing. *uttar* 'word', with zero ending, with animate nomin. sing. *ḫūmanza* 'every, all' above (phonetically *ḫūmant-š*; the odd-looking spelling *ḫūmanza* is due to limitations in the Hittite writing system on representing consonant clusters, cf. §9.30).

Athematic animate nouns ending in resonants show lengthened grade of the stem and lack **-s*, as for example Greek *patḗr* 'father'. It is widely held that these nominative singulars originally had ordinary full grade plus **-s* also, and that a sound change (Szemerényi's Law, §3.38) happened in PIE whereby the *-s* was lost with compensatory lengthening of the vowel: **ph$_2$t-ers* > **ph$_2$t-ēr*. Two important nouns are often reconstructed with both *-s* and lengthened grade in the nominative singular, **di̯ḗus* 'sky, sky-god' and **g^{w}ṓus* 'cow'. The lengthened grade, however, is found only in Indo-Iranian (Ved. *dyáuṣ*, *gáuṣ*, with *au* < **ēu*, **ōu*; Av. *gāuš*); Gk. *Zeús* 'Zeus' and *boús* 'cow' have short diphthongs, and the forms in the other languages point to short diphthongs also. Since full grade rather than lengthened grade is expected in the nominative singular, many researchers prefer to reconstruct **di̯éus*, **g^{w}óus* and take the lengthened forms in Indo-Iranian as innovatory.

6.7. In athematic animate nouns, the **vocative** ending was zero and there was retraction of the accent. What this meant for all practical intents and purposes is that the vocative was the same as the nominative without the **-s* or without lengthened grade: Gk. nomin. *pólis* 'city' but voc. *póli* '(o) city'; Ved. nomin. *hastī́* 'having a hand' (< **hastī́n*), voc. *hástin*. Vedic Sanskrit best preserves the accent retraction.

6.8. The **genitive** and **ablative** of athematic nouns were not distinguished from one another in PIE in the singular; they are often referred to together as the **genitive-ablative.** The ending was **-és* when accented, otherwise zero-grade **-s*. The first survives in genitives like Archaic Lat. *Vener-es* 'of Venus' (Classical Lat. *Veneris*), ON *feðr* 'of a father' (< pre-Germanic **patr-es*), and Lith. dialectal *dukter-ès* 'of a daughter'. Zero-grade **-s* is found for example in Hitt. *nekuz* (pronounced *nek^{w}ts*) 'of the evening' (< **nek^{w}t-s*) and OE *brōþor* 'of the brother' (< **bhrātr̥-s*). Some languages have a genitive going back to **-os*, spread perhaps from the thematic declension (§6.48): Homeric Gk. *géne-os* 'of a kind' and Ogam Irish *Lugudecc-as* 'of Lugaid' (personal name).

6.9. The **dative** ended in **-ei*, directly preserved for example in Archaic Lat. *Mārt-ei* 'for Mars', Oscan *Mamert-ei* 'for Mars', and OPruss. *giwānt-ei* 'for one living'.

6.10. The **instrumental** ending was **-h$_1$* or **-eh$_1$*. The bare laryngeal is found in archaic Vedic *i-* and *u*-stem instrumentals in *-ī* and *-ū* from **-i-h$_1$* and **-u-h$_1$*, e.g. *matī́* 'with thought'. The fuller form **-eh$_1$* is found in Indo-Iranian, e.g. in *vācā́* 'with speech' and perhaps in the first member of such Latin verbs as *rubē-facere* 'to redden', if this originally meant 'to make with redness' or the like.

6.11. Two types of **locative** are found. The first was formed with a suffix **-i*, as in Ved. *pad-í* 'on the foot', Lat. *ped-e* (synchronically called an ablative, but functionally instrumental, ablative, and locative) 'with/on the foot', and Gk. *pod-í* 'for the foot' (synchronically called a dative, but functionally dative, instrumental, and locative).

The second type is the **endingless locative**, which is interesting not only in being endingless, but in typically having full or lengthened grade of the stem, in contrast to the other weak cases. For example, the Vedic endingless locative of the word for 'name' is *nā́m-an*, whereas the weak stem is *nā́m-n-* with zero-grade of the *n*-stem suffix (see below on *n*-stems). Compare also Old Avestan *dąm* 'in the house' (< **dōm* or **dēm*) and Old Irish *talam* '(on the) earth' (< Common Celtic **talamon*, also an *n*-stem as in Vedic).

6.12. A ninth case, the **directive** (or allative), is posited by some on the basis primarily of Anatolian, the only branch in which it is still productive, at least in Old Hittite (e.g. *arun-a* 'to the sea', *parn-ā* 'to the house, homeward', with long *-ā* probably indicating stress; see §9.24). Elsewhere in IE there may be a few fossilized traces extended by the locative ending **-i*, such as Gk. *khamaí* 'to the ground' < **dhĝhm̥m-a*. Its PIE shape is uncertain; candidates include **-h₂(e)*, **-(e)h₂*, or simply **-a*.

The dual

6.13. Fewer cases were distinguished in the dual than in the singular. The **nominative, vocative,** and **accusative dual** ended in **-h₁* or **-h₁e* in animate nouns, and in **-ih₁* in neuters. The full animate form is reflected for example in OLith. *žmun-e* 'two men', while the neuter is found in Gk. *ósse* and OCS *oči* 'both eyes' (**h₃(e)kʷi̯-h̥₁* and **h₃ekʷi-h₁*, respectively, with different syllabification of the ending in the two languages), as well as Vedic Skt. *urv-ī́ rájas-ī* 'the two broad spaces'. Note also the number 'two' itself, **d(u)u̯oh₁* (becoming **d(u)u̯ō*).

The other cases of the dual cannot be reconstructed because the paradigms of the daughter languages differ too sharply from one another.

The plural

The cases of the plural also differ from one another across the daughter languages, especially outside the nominative, vocative, and accusative, making exact reconstruction uncertain in several instances. Below are some representative animate athematic plural paradigms for comparison: Hitt. *ḫūmant-* 'all', Ved. *pad-* and Gk. *pod-* 'foot', Av. *kəhrp-* 'body' (and other nouns glossed in the notes), Lat. *uōc-* 'voice', and Lith. *šun-* 'dog'.

	Hitt.	Ved.	Av.	Gk.	Lat.	Lith.	PIE
nom.	*ḫūmant-eš*	*pā́d-as*	*kəhrp-as-*[1]	*pód-es*		*šùn-es*	**-es*
acc.	*ḫūmant-uš*	*pad-ás*	*zəm-as-*[2]	*pód-as*		*šun-ìs*	**-n̥s*
gen.	*ḫūmant-an*	*pad-ā́m*	*kəhrp-ąm*	*pod-ō̃n*	*uōc-um*	*šun-ų̃*	**-ōm?*
dat.-abl.		*pad-bhyás*	*nərə-biiō*[3]		*bū-bus*[8]		**-bh(i̯)os*
instr.		*paḍ-bhís*	*haδ-bīš*[4]	*po-pi*[6]			**-bhi(-)*
loc.		*pat-sú*	*tanu-šu*[5]	*po-sí*[7]		*aki-sù*[9]	**-su*

[1] In the phrase *kəhrpas-ca* 'and bodies'. [2] In the phrase *zəmas-ca* 'and lands'. [3] 'For/From men'. [4] 'By (ones who are) being'. [5] 'In/On bodies'. [6] Mycenaean; phonetically *popphi*. [7] Synchronically labeled dative; cf. §6.11. [8] 'For/With cows'. [9] 'In the eyes'.

6.14. The **animate nominative** plural was **-es* and the **animate accusative** plural was **-ns* (probably from **-ms*, a combination of the accusative sing. **-m* and an old plural ending **-s*); after consonants this became **-n̥s*. The **vocative** plural was the same as the nominative, but probably with accent retraction.

6.15. The **neuter nominative-accusative** plural was **-h_2*, originally a collective and not a true plural (see §§6.68ff.): Hitt. *āššū* 'goods' (< **$h_1$es-u-h_2*), Ved. *paśumā́nt-i* 'having cattle' (*-i* from vocalized **-$\mathring{h}_2$*), and Homeric Gk. *géne-a* 'kinds'. (The similar-looking neuter plurals in forms like Lat. *gener-a* 'kinds' and OCS *sloves-a* 'words' actually go back to **-ā* < **-eh_2* and have been taken over from the thematic declension; see §6.54 below.)

Several archaic languages also have a neuter collective plural with a lengthened grade before a resonant, such as Hitt. *widār* 'waters' and Old Av. *aiiārə̄* 'days'. Probably these originally ended in the collective **-h_2* too, which at an early date assimilated to the preceding resonant: **ud-or-h_2* > **ud-ōr* 'waters' (> Gk. *húdōr* 'water', reinterpreted as a singular, and Hitt. *widār* with different ablaut).

6.16. The **genitive plural** is traditionally reconstructed as either **-om* or **-ōm*. On system-internal grounds, usually **-om* is preferred, but most of the daughter languages actually have **-ōm*; this is explained as an intrusion from the thematic declension (see below, §6.56), where the long vowel resulted from contraction of the thematic vowel **-o-* and the "real" athematic ending **-om*, as happened with a number of other thematic endings. It is possible that this replacement of **-om* by **-ōm* happened already in the proto-language, for no unambiguous examples of athematic genitives from **-om* are known from the daughter languages. Celtic and Slavic are potential exceptions, but the short vowel there has often been explained as due to secondary shortening of **-ōm*. As we will see in §6.56, **-ōm* is actually contracted from **-o-Hom*.

6.17. The **locative plural** is straightforwardly reconstructible as **-su*. An innovated variant **-si* is found in Greek, where it has become a dative, and in Albanian, where it has become the ablative in *-sh*. More problematic are the **instrumental, dative**, and **ablative plurals**. Most of the branches point to endings beginning with **-bh-*, e.g. Ved. instr. pl. *paḍ-bhís* 'with the feet', dat. and abl. pl. *pad-bhyás* 'for the feet', Mycenaean Gk. instr. pl. *po-pi* (which spells *popphi* < **pod-bhi*) 'with the feet', and Lat. dat. and abl. pl. *bū-bus* 'for/with cows'. But the two northern European branches Germanic and Balto-Slavic have endings beginning with *-m-*, e.g. inscriptional West Germanic dat. pl. *Afli-ms* 'for the Afli (goddesses)', OCS instr. pl. *synŭ-mi* (Lith. *sūnu-mìs*) 'with sons', and OCS dat. pl. *synŭ-mŭ* (Old Lith. *sūnú-mus*) 'for sons'. The *m*-endings may be an innovation of a late north-European IE dialect area.

Further confusing this picture is the fact that both **bh-* and **m*-elements also appear in a few cases that are *singular* and not plural in number, as the Armenian and OCS instrumental singular endings *-w* and *-mŭ* (e.g. Arm. *srti-w* 'with (the) heart', OCS *synŭ-mŭ* 'with (the) son') and residual forms in Greek like *ī-phi* 'with might'. Additionally, they appear in duals in Indo-Iranian and Balto-Slavic: Ved. instr. du. *pad-bhyā́m* 'with the two feet', OCS dat. du. *synŭ-ma* 'for the two sons', Lith. instr. du. *nakti-m̃* 'with two nights'. Finally, neither the **bh-* nor the **m*-endings are found in the oldest branch, Anatolian, which has no special endings for these cases.

All this taken together suggests that the **bh-* and **m*-endings developed late, probably after Anatolian split off from the family, and may have originally been postpositions or adverbs ultimately related to Eng. *by* and Germ. *mit* 'with'. (It is cross-linguistically common for postpositions to develop into case-endings.)

Other case-like elements

6.18. A number of suffixes are found scattered throughout the daughter languages that may or may not be descended from true case-endings in PIE. One example is *-*tos*, found in ablatival function in both singular and plural: Ved. *pat-tás* 'from the foot', pl. *patsu-tás* 'from the feet' (interestingly, added to the locative plural), and Lat. *caeli-tus* 'from heaven'. Another is a locative ending *-*dhi*, reflected by Gk. -*thi* and Arm. -*ǰ* (e.g. Gk. *ouranó-thi* 'in heaven', Arm. *tełwo-ǰ* 'in a place'). Certain others are marginally attested and typically show up in adverbs, such as *-*dhe* in Ved. *kú-ha* 'where' (with -*h*- from *-*dh*-), Av. *ku-dā* 'where', Lat. *un-de* 'whence', and OCS *kŭ-de* 'where'.

Athematic nominal stem formation

The accent-ablaut classes

6.19. Athematic nouns consist of a root and grammatical ending, often with a derivational suffix in between. The term **root noun** is used for an athematic noun consisting only of root and ending, without an overt derivational suffix; these nouns will be treated in a separate section (§§6.25ff.). We will first outline the properties of athematic nouns having all three morphemes.

As already alluded to, these three morphemes could each show up in different ablaut grades depending principally on the position of the accent, which could fall on any of the three. According to the standard theory, in any given case-form of an athematic noun the unstressed morphemes appeared in the zero-grade, while the stressed morphemes were in a grade "stronger" than zero-grade – that is, one with a vowel, generally *e*, but also *o*.

6.20. Four distinct classes of athematic nouns are recognized by most scholars, each characterized by a particular patterned distribution of accent and ablaut grades. They are termed *acrostatic*, *proterokinetic*, *amphikinetic* (or *holokinetic*), and *hysterokinetic* (equivalent terms for the last three are *proterodynamic*, *amphidynamic*, and *hysterodynamic*). In all of these but acrostatic (which has fixed accent on the root), the accent shifts rightward in the weak cases from its position in the strong cases. Some scholars recognize two more types, *mesostatic* and *teleutostatic*, for nouns that have fixed accent on the suffix and ending, respectively; but it is not certain that these existed in the proto-language, and they will be left out of our discussion.

The somewhat simplified pictorial overview below will make the basic schemes of the four classes clear. The shaded areas indicate the location of the accent in *R*oot or *S*uffix or *E*nding; the unshaded areas indicate no accent and usually zero-grade (with a couple of exceptions to be treated later). An example is given beneath each class, with the nominative exemplifying the strong cases and the genitive, the weak.

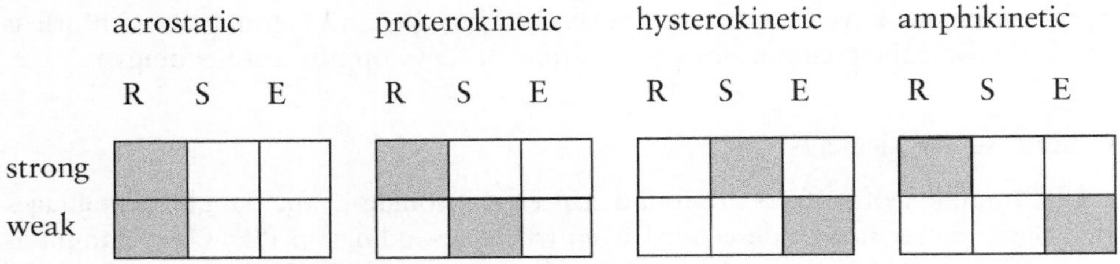
acrostatic
proterokinetic
hysterokinetic
amphikinetic
R S E
R S E
R S E
R S E
strong
weak

nom.	*nók^w-t-s 'night'	*mén-ti-s 'thought'	*ph_2-tér-s 'father'	*$h_2$éus-ōs 'dawn'
gen.	*nék^w-t-s	*m̥n̥-téi-s	*ph_2-tr-és	*$h_2$us-s-és

6.21. In **acrostatic** nouns, the root is accented throughout the paradigm, but with ablaut distinction between the strong and weak cases. The most common type had *o*-grade of the root in the strong cases and *e*-grade in the weak cases. The word for 'night' above is an example; the *o*-grade nominative is preserved e.g. in Lat. *nox*, and the genitive in Hitt. *nekuz* (phonetically *nek^{w}ts*) 'of eventide'. One well-known group of acrostatic nouns is a set of widely attested *u*-stem (§6.42) neuters such as *dóru 'wood', *$h_2$ói̯u 'life-force', and *ĝónu 'knee', reflected e.g. in Gk. *dóru* 'wood, spear', Ved. *ā́yu* 'life, life-force', and Gk. *gónu* 'knee'. In some branches, the *e*-grade of the oblique cases has been generalized or used as the basis for further derivation, e.g. Lith. *dervà* 'wood', Lat. *aeuum* 'age' (with *ae-* < *$h_1$ei-), and Lat. *genū* 'knee'; but sometimes it has been replaced by the zero-grade, on which see §6.27 below. Somewhat different was the word for 'liver', a neuter having lengthened grade in the nominative, *i̯ḗk^w-r̥ (> Av. *yākarə*, Gk. *hē̃par*, whence English words like *hepatitis*).

6.22. In **proterokinetic** nouns, the root is in the full grade and accented in the strong cases, and both accent and full grade shift to the suffix in the weak cases. Most *i*- and *u*-stems (§6.42) in Sanskrit appear to have been proterokinetic, such as Ved. nomin. *matís* 'thought', accus. *matím*, genit. *matés*, from PIE *mén-ti-s, *mén-ti-m, *m̥n̥-téi-s (Vedic has generalized the zero-grade of the root throughout the paradigm; see §6.42). Neuter proterokinetic nouns behaved the same way, as in the word for 'fire', nomin.-accus. *péh$_2$-u̯r̥, genit. *ph$_2$-u̯én-s (see §6.32 below).

6.23. In **hysterokinetic** nouns, the suffix is accented in the strong cases, the ending in the weak. The noun for 'father' is an example: nomin. sing. *ph$_2$-tér-s (the probable original form, later *ph$_2$-tḗr; recall §6.6), accus. sing. *ph$_2$-tér-m̥, genit. sing. *ph$_2$-tr-és, reflected almost exactly in Gk. *patḗr patéra patrós*. Another example is the noun for 'young bull', nomin. sing. *h_2uk^ws-ḗn, accus. *h_2uk^ws-én-m̥, genit. *h_2uk^ws-n-és, reflected almost exactly in Vedic Skt. *ukṣā́, ukṣáṇam, ukṣṇás*. The English descendant is *ox*, whose plural *ox-en* still preserves the old *n*-stem suffix (eventually reanalyzed as the pural ending).

6.24. In **amphikinetic** (or **holokinetic**) nouns, the root is accented in the strong cases, the ending in the weak, and the suffix is typically in the lengthened *o*-grade (rather than the expected zero-grade) in the nominative singular and ordinary *o*-grade in the accusative singular. The word for 'dawn' belongs here, nomin. sing. *$h_2$éus-ōs (Aeolic Gk. *aúōs*, Lat. *aurōr-a*), accus. sing. *$h_2$éus-os-m̥ (Ved. *uṣā́sam*, remade with zero-grade of the root), genit. sing. *$h_2$us-s-és (Ved. *uṣás*). Another famous example is the word for 'earth', nomin. **dhéĝhōm* (Hitt. *tēkan*), accus. **dhéĝhom-m* (> **dhéĝhōm* by Stang's Law, §3.38, to become ultimately Ved. *kṣā́m*), genit. **dhĝhm-és* (Hitt. *taknāš*, Ved. *jmás*). Yet another famous amphikinetic noun is the word for 'path', which will be discussed in §11.25.

6.25. We now turn to root nouns. They include many core vocabulary items that are surely ancient, such as **$h_3$ekʷ-* 'eye', **ped-* 'foot', and **dem-* 'house'. Two types can be recognized: those with fixed accent on the root (acrostatic) and those with mobile accent. Because of the lack of an overt derivational suffix, many researchers decline to assign the mobile type to any of the mobile accent-ablaut classes that we have just been discussing.

An example of an acrostatic root noun is **dem-* 'house' above, with nomin. sing. **dóm-s* (> **dōm* by Szemerényi's Law, §3.38), genit. sing. **dém-s*. The nominative singular became Arm. *town* 'house' and probably Gk. *dō̃* 'house', while the genitive is found in the famous phrase **dems potis* 'master of the house, lord, master' (Ved. *dám-patis*, Old Av. *dəṇg paiti-*, and Gk. *des-pótēs*, the source of Eng. *despot*). The mobile type can be represented by the word for 'sky, sky-god', nomin. sing. **di̯éu-s* (or **di̯ḗu-s*; recall §6.6), accus. **di̯éu̯-m̥* (which became **di̯ḗm* already in PIE by Stang's Law, §3.38), genit. **diu̯-és*. This is continued directly in Gk. *Zeús Zē̃n Di(w)-ós* and in Ved. *dyáuṣ dyā́m div-ás*.

6.26. Mobile root nouns often appear as the second members of compounds. Such root nouns were productively formed from verbal roots to indicate either the agent or the recipient (undergoer) of an action. Examples of such compounds include Ved. ***r̥tv-íj-*** 'sacrificing correctly' (**Hiĝ-*, zero-grade of **Hi̯aĝ-* 'worship, sacrifice'), Gk. ***sú-zug-*** 'yoked together' (root **i̯eug-* 'yoke, join'), Lat. *con-**iug**-* 'spouse' (< *'the one joined with', also from **i̯eug-*), and OIr. *druí*, genitive *druad* 'druid' (< **dru-**u̯id**-* 'seer/knower of the oak'; root **u̯eid-* 'see'). As some of these examples show, these forms often had adjectival function, and the zero-grade of the root was often generalized throughout the paradigm in the daughter languages. The ablaut alternations are better preserved in Vedic, as in nomin. *vr̥tra-hā́* 'slayer of Vr̥tra' (a demon), genit. *vr̥tra-ghn-ás* (< PIE **-gʷhēn *-gʷhn-es*).

6.27. Already in the proto-language, proterokinetic (or, in root nouns, mobile) inflection spread at the expense of acrostatic inflection in roots ending in a resonant or a resonant followed by another consonant. Thus alongside original acrostatic weak forms like genit. sing. **déru-s* and **dém-s*, new proterokinetic (mobile) forms **dr-éu-s* and **d(m̥)m-és* were created (the first seen e.g. in Ved. *drós* 'of the wood' and ultimately Eng. *tree*; the second seen in Arm. *tan* 'of the house'). Such remodelings led to a new class of proterokinetics that descriptively had *o*-grade of the root in the strong cases (as in the original acrostatic inflection) but zero-grade in the weak (as in the original proterokinetic inflection). Among animate nouns of this type, the best attested is the word for 'dog', nomin. **ḱu̯ṓ(n)* accus. **ḱu̯ón-m̥* genit. **ḱun-és*: Ved. *śvā́ śvā́n-am śún-as*, Gk. *kúōn kún-a kun-ós* (with the accusative stem remade using the weak stem).

6.28. Individual schools of thought differ on the specifics of these classes, as well as on their naturalness (cross-linguistic parallels are unfortunately lacking). The account here is based on the theory developed by German and Austrian researchers in the 1960s and 1970s (principally Jochem Schindler, Heiner Eichner, and Helmut

Rix) that has become in large measure accepted in the major European and American universities. Since no branch of the family preserves the original system intact (at least in the form predicted by the theory), most of it has had to be pieced together from a variety of sometimes contradictory evidence culled from different daughter languages. It is assumed that where daughter forms are at variance with this system (such as Ved. *matís* and *uṣā́sam* above), the discrepancy came about through the effects of analogy and paradigm leveling that changed the position of the accent and/or the distribution of full and zero-grades within a paradigm. Further research may well lead to modifications of the theory.

Internal derivation

6.29. One of the most interesting facts about the above system is that the accent-ablaut classes in PIE are thought to have stood in a derivational relationship with one another. The language could derive new nouns or adjectives simply by shifting the accent rightward and thereby changing the form's class membership. For example, one could shift the accent of an acrostatic noun rightward and create a proterokinetic or amphikinetic noun or adjective, and from proterokinetics one could derive amphikinetics or hysterokinetics in the same way. The resulting derivatives in general meant 'possessing, associated with' what was denoted by the original noun or adjective. This process is known as *internal derivation*, and was elucidated by the late Austrian Indo-Europeanist Jochem Schindler.

To illustrate, from an acrostatic noun could be derived a proterokinetic possessive adjective:

acrostatic **krót-u-s* genit. **krét-u-s* 'insight, intelligence' (Ved. *krátus*)

→ proterokinetic **krétus* genit. **kr̥t-éu-s* 'having mental force, strong' (Gk. *kratús* 'strong')

Similarly, from a proterokinetic noun could be derived an amphikinetic noun of appurtenance:

proterokinetic **bhléĝh-mn̥* 'sacred formulation' (Ved. *bráhmaṇ-*)

→ amphikinetic **bhléĝh-mō(n)* 'the one of the sacred formulation, priest' (Ved. *brahmáṇ-*)

This second type of internal derivation was quite common. Another such pair is Lat. *sēmen* 'seed' and its derivative *Sēmōn-ēs* 'deities of the seed'. From proterokinetic nouns could also be generated hysterokinetic derivatives, as in Gk. *pseũdos* 'false' and its derivative *pseudḗs* 'liar'.

6.30. Nouns could also be derived from a case-form of another noun, especially a locative. A prominent example is the derivation of the word for 'man, human' from the locative of the word for 'earth'. The amphikinetic noun **dhéĝhōm* 'earth' had an extended locative **dhĝhm-en* 'on the earth'; from this locative an amphikinetic noun meaning 'the one on/of the earth, earthling = man, human' was formed, **dhĝhémō(n)* genit. **dhĝhm̥nés*, becoming Lat. *homō* genit. *hominis*, and OE *guma* pl. *guman* (surviving in altered form as the *-groom* in the word *bridegroom*).

Athematic derivational suffixes

6.31. The most prominent athematic derivational suffixes ended in *n*, *r*, *s*, and *t*, forming nouns that were called *n*-stems, *r*-stems, etc. An archaic group of nouns, called **heteroclitic stems** (or heteroclites), had suffixes with different final consonants in the strong and weak cases. By far the best-known variety of heteroclites is the class of ***r/n*-stems**, neuter nouns ending in **-r* in the nominative-accusative singular and collective (§6.68) that is replaced by a stem in **-n-* in the other cases. A famous example is **u̯ód-r̥* 'water', stem **u̯éd-n-*, preserved almost exactly in Hitt. *wātar* genit. *witenaš*; note also that within Germanic we have both Eng. *water* (with *-r*) and ON *vatn* (with *-n*). Two other examples are Hitt. *ēšḫar* 'blood' genit. *išḫanaš*, and Lat. *femur* genit. *femin-is* 'thigh'. The class is widely productive in Anatolian and to a lesser degree in Avestan, but moribund in the other branches. In Greek, the *-n-* was remade into *-at-* (< **-n̥-t-*), yielding words like *húdōr* 'water' with stem *húdat-*.

6.32. A number of complex (compound) suffixes belong to this category. The richest representation of these is again provided by Anatolian, which reflects stems in **-mer/n-*, **-ser/n-*, **-ter/n-*, and **-u̯er/n-*. The last of these is found for instance in the word **peh$_2$-u̯r̥* 'fire', continued most faithfully in Hitt. *paḫḫur* genit. *paḫḫuenaš*; the alternation is preserved indirectly in Arm. *howr* 'fire' alongside its derivative *hn-ocʿ* 'oven' (< **hown-ocʿ*) with *-n-*, and in Eng. *fire* alongside Goth. *fon* 'fire'.

6.33. There may also have been an ***l/n*-stem**, the word for 'sun'. The forms in the daughter languages are quite diverse. Lat. *sōl*, Goth. *sauil*, Vedic Skt. *svàr* (phonetically *súvar*), and Av. *huuarə* (the last two with the Indo-Iranian change of **l* to *r*) reflect an old nominative ending in **-l*, probably **séh$_2$-u̯l̥* (or **sh$_2$-u̯ōl* in the case of Lat. *sōl*, which also differs from the rest in being masculine rather than neuter). This was refashioned by further suffixation and/or change in ablaut in such forms as Vedic Skt. *sū́ryas* (< **suh$_2$-l-*), Gk. *hḗlios* (Doric *ā(w)élios*), and Lith. *sáulė* (both < **sāu̯el-*). The original genitive **sh$_2$-u̯én-s* is directly reflected by the odd-looking Old Avestan form *x^{v}ə̄ṇg* (with *x^v-* < **su̯-*, simplified from **sh$_2$u̯-*, and *-ṇg* < **-n-s*). The oblique stem in **-n-* was also used to derive the Germanic words that include Goth. *sunno* and Eng. *sun*.

6.34. *n*-stems. Various types of animate and neuter suffixes ending in **-n* have been reconstructed, especially the compound suffixes **-men-*, **-sen-*, **-ten-*, and **-u̯en-*, all of which frequently show up as the basis for infinitival endings (see §5.58). The most familiar is the **neuter abstract noun suffix **-mn̥***, genit. sing. **-men-s*, referring to the act or result of the action of the verb. This yields for example the Vedic and Greek abstract nouns in *-ma* (e.g. Ved. *kár-ma* 'deed', lit. 'thing done', Gk. *thé-ma* 'theme', lit. 'thing placed') and the Latin abstracts in *-men* (e.g. Lat. *car-men* 'song' < **kan-mn̥* 'thing sung'). Some more archaic nouns consisted simply of an *n* preceded or followed by an ablauting vowel, such as **g^{w}reh$_2$u̯-ō(n)* 'pressing stone, millstone' (from **g^{w}r̥h$_2$u-* 'heavy', as in Ved. *gurú-*), becoming Ved. *grā́vāṇ-*, OIr. *bráu* (genit. *broon*), and Eng. *quern* 'hand mill'.

6.35. The so-called **Hoffmann suffix** (named after the late Indologist and Indo-Europeanist Karl Hoffmann) formed adjectives that indicated possession. It had the shape **-Hon-* alternating with zero-grade **-Hn-*. The PIE adjective for 'young' is a well-known example, made from the zero-grade of **h$_2$oi̯u* 'life-force': nomin. **h$_2$i̯u-Hō(n)* (Ved. *yúvā*), accus. **h$_2$i̯u-Hon-m̥* (Ved. *yúvānam*), genit. **h$_2$i̯u-Hn-es* (Ved. *yū́n-as*). This adjective thus originally meant 'having life-force, having vitality'.

6.36. A very widespread neuter *n*-stem noun is the word for 'name', but its precise reconstruction is disputed; two commonly adduced contenders are **h$_1$neh$_3$mn̥* and **h$_1$nomn̥*. The cognates include Hitt. *lāman* (dissimilated from earlier **nāman*), Ved. *nā́ma*, Greek *ónoma* (Laconian Gk. *énuma*, only in personal names and preserving an original *e-* that changed to *o-* elsewhere in Greek), Lat. *nōmen*, Goth. *namo*, Arm. *anown*, OIr. *ainm(m)*, Toch. A *ñom*, and OCS *imę*.

6.37. *r*-stems. Many stems ended in an **-r* that were not heteroclitic. The most common were the **agent-noun suffixes **-ter-* and **-tor-***. The first type, which was accented on the suffix and originally had zero-grade of the root (**dh$_3$-tḗr*), is represented for example by Ved. *dātā́* (with analogically introduced full-grade of the root as though from **deh$_3$-tér*) and Gk. *dotḗr*, while the second, which had root accent and full-grade of the root (**déh$_3$-tōr*), is represented by Ved. *dā́tā*, Gk. *dṓtōr*, and (with analogically introduced zero-grade) Lat. *dator*. All these forms mean 'giver, dispenser', but some researchers have claimed that there was a semantic distinction, with the first kind forming so-called non-event agent nouns ('one whose role is to give' even if he never has done so, cp. Eng. *toaster*, a machine whose function is to toast even if it has never been plugged in) and the second kind forming event agent nouns ('one who is a giver by virtue of having actually given something', cp. Eng. *grave-robber*). This claim is disputed. In Indo-Iranian, the two formations evince different syntactic behaviors: the first type took a genitive complement (*dātā́ vásūnām* [genit. pl.] 'giver of goods'), whereas the second took an accusative (*dā́tā vásūni*, but translated identically). How old this difference is is likewise unclear, as well as how the two formations are ultimately related to each other.

At least five **kinship terms** are also *r*-stems. Three of them, **ph$_2$tér-* 'father', **dhugh$_2$tér-* 'daughter', and **i̯énh$_2$ter-* or **i̯n̥h$_2$tér-* 'husband's brother's wife', contain an element **-h$_2$ter-*, of disputed interpretation. Under one view, **ph$_2$tér-* was originally an agent noun **ph$_2$-tér-* meaning 'the protector' or the like (from **peh$_2$-* 'protect'), from which **-h$_2$ter-* was later abstracted and spread to the other terms (for which no convincing root etymologies are known). Two other forms, for 'mother' and 'brother', are traditionally reconstructed as **mātér-* and **bhrā́ter-*, but given the existence of **-h$_2$ter-* above these are nowadays often thought to have been **meh$_2$tér-* and **bhréh$_2$ter-* instead. For 'mother', however, given the ubiquitous baby-talk syllable *ma*, some prefer to reconstruct **mah$_2$tér-* or even **mātér-* with no laryngeal.

An *r*-stem with simpler stem is the word for 'hand', **ĝhés-ōr* stem **ĝhes-r-*, seen in Hittite *kiššaraš* (phonetically *kisars*; the **-s* was added later) stem *kiš(š)r-*, Gk. *kheir-*, and Arm. *jeṙn* (< **ĝhesr-n-*).

6.38. *s*-stems. Neuters ending in *-os in the strong cases and having a stem *-es- in the weak cases, but with full grade of the root throughout (and therefore not falling readily into any of the accent-ablaut classes), are a common type of verbal abstract noun and were formed from the full grade of verbal roots. Thus from *ĝenh$_1$- 'be born' was formed *ĝénh$_1$-os 'birth, thing born, race, kind', stem *ĝenh$_1$-es-: Ved. *jánas-* 'race, clan', Gk. *génos* 'race, kind' (genitive *géne-os* < pre-Greek *gen-es-os), Lat. *genus* 'type', and Arm. *cin* 'birth'.

A simple suffix *-s- is found in some archaic nouns, such as *kreu̯h$_2$-s 'gore, bloody flesh' (Ved. *kráviṣ-*, Gk. *kréas*; the same root that yields English *raw*).

6.39. Animate *s*-stems having possessive semantics were formed from neuter *s*-stems by internal derivation (§6.29). Thus the neuter noun for 'grain', *k̂erh$_1$-os *k̂erh$_1$-es-, preserved in German *Hirse* 'millet', could form a noun or adjective *k̂erh$_1$-ḗs '(the one) associated with or possessing grain', whence the name of the Latin agricultural goddess *Cerēs*. Similarly, the neuter Greek noun *klé(w)os* 'fame' had a derivative *-klé(w)ēs* (contracted to *-klē̃s*) '-famed', common in names like *Sopho-klē̃s* 'famed for wisdom'.

A special *s*-stem was the suffix *-u̯os- used to form the perfect participle (§5.60).

6.40. *t*-stems. Athematic suffixes in *-t- are best known for forming feminine abstract nouns. The simple suffix is found for example in PIE *dek̂m̥-t- 'group of ten, decad' (from *dek̂m̥ 'ten'): Ved. *daśát-* and OCS (pl.) *desęte*. It is also found in the compound suffixes *-tāt- (probably from earlier *-teh$_2$-t-) and *-tūt- (*-tuh$_2$-t-), likewise used to form feminine abstracts; these are most familiar from Latin: *lībertāt-* 'freedom', *senec-tūt-* 'old age'. An unrelated suffix of some interest is *-it-, seen in PIE *melit- 'honey' and Hitt. *šeppit-* 'kind of grain'; perhaps it was a "foodstuff" suffix.

An important subset of the *t*-stems is comprised by the ***nt*-stems**, whose most conspicuous members are the participles formed to present and aorist tense-stems (see §5.60). Also worth mentioning is the **possessive suffix *-u̯ent-**, as in Hitt. *ēšḫar-want-* 'bloody' (*ēšḫar* 'blood'), Ved. *bhága-vant-* 'wealthy' (*bhágas* 'wealth'), and Gk. *niphó-(w)ent-* 'snowy' (*niph-* 'snow').

6.41. Reduplicated athematic nouns. A variety of reduplicated nouns are known from all stem-classes. One reconstructible for PIE is the word for 'beaver', *bhe-bhru- (a derivative of *bhreu- 'brown'): OHG *bibar*, Lith. *bẽbrus*, Ved. *babhrú-* 'brown'.

6.42. *i*- and *u*-stems. Two classes of athematic nouns that behaved in parallel were those whose suffix was *-i- or *-u- in the zero-grade and *-ei- *-eu- in the full grade. The most common type continues an earlier proterokinetic paradigm, with zero-grade *-i-s *-i-m and *-u-s *-u-m in the strong cases, and full grade in the weak cases (genit. *-ei-s *-eu-s). By the time of the daughter languages, however, these nouns do not ablaut in their root syllable. Thus Ved. *matí-* 'thought' is believed to continue a proterokinetic nomin. *mén-ti-s genit. *mn̥-téi-s, but the zero-grade *mn̥- (> Ved. *ma-*) has been generalized. (The same happened in Greek and other branches.) This is an example of the **verbal abstract nouns in *-ti-**, one of the most common groups of *i*-stems; also common were abstract nouns in *-tu-. Both of these types often appear in infinitives in the daughter languages (see §5.58).

Many adjectives made from roots having inherently adjectival meaning are simple *u*-stems, such as Lith. *dubùs* 'deep' and Ved. *gurú-* 'heavy'. On the *u*-stem proterokinetic nouns of the type **dóru* 'spear', see §6.21.

Thematic Nouns

6.43. Thematic nouns, like thematic verbs, are characterized by the presence of an ablauting stem **-e/o-* to which the case-endings are added. In practice, the stem is almost always **-o-*, and so these nouns are commonly referred to as **o-stems.** The case-endings are mostly the same as the athematic ones, but there are several notable differences, as we will see shortly. In many of the daughter languages, certain thematic case-endings were influenced or replaced by the corresponding pronominal case-endings (see §7.9); some common instances of this will be pointed out.

6.44. There are no certain accent–ablaut distinctions within thematic paradigms except in the vocative, where the accent was retracted. (But see also §6.66.) Most animate *o*-stems had masculine gender, but a number of them, including some kinship terms (e.g. **snusos* 'daughter-in-law') and a variety of tree names (e.g. **bhāĝos* 'oak, beech' and **kr̥nos* 'cornel cherry'), were feminine.

Case-endings of thematic nouns

6.45. Below is a comparative table of the athematic and most archaic thematic endings to illustrate the similarities and differences between the two classes:

	Singular		*Dual*		*Plural*	
	athem.	them.	athem.	them.	athem.	them.
nom. anim.	**-s*	**-os*	**-h_1(e)*	**-ō < *-o-h_1*	**-es*	**-ōs < *-o-es*
voc.	**-ø*	**-e*	**-h_1(e)*	**-ō < *-o-h_1*	**-es*	**-ōs < *-o-es*
acc. anim.	**-m*	**-om*	**-h_1(e)*	**-ō < *-o-h_1*	**-ns*	**-ons*
n.-a. neut.	**-ø*	**-om*	**-ih_1*	**-o-ih_1*	**-h_2*	**-ā < *-e-h_2*
gen.	**-s*	**-os ?*			**-ōm*	**-ōm < *-o-Hom*
abl.	**-s*	**-ōt < *-o-(h_2)at*			**-bh-*	**-o(i)bh-*
dat.	**-ei*	**-ōi < *-o-ei*			**-bh-*	**-o(i)bh-*
instr.	**-h_1*	**-ō < *-o-h_1*			**-bh-*	**-ōis*
loc.	**-i*	**-oi*			**-su*	**-oisu*

Singular

6.46. The following chart shows some of the comparative evidence for the singular declension of *o*-stems: the animates Hitt. *arunaš* 'sea', Ved. *vīrás* 'man', Av. *yasna-* 'sacrifice', Gk. *theós* 'god', Lat. *seruus* 'slave', Goth. *dags* 'day', OCS *gradŭ* 'city', and Lith. *výras* 'man'. The neuters and other special forms are glossed in the notes.

	Hitt.	Ved.	Av.	Gk.	Lat.	Goth.	OCS	Lith.
nom. anim.	*arun-aš*	*vīr-ás*	*yasn-ō*	*the-ós*	*seru-os*[12]	*dag-az*,[18] *dag-s*	*grad-ŭ*	*výr-as*
voc. anim.	*negn-a*[1]	*vī́r-a*		*ádelph-e*[9]	*seru-e*	*skalk*[19]	*grad-e*	*výr-e*
acc. anim.	*arun-an*	*vīr-ám*	*yasn-əm*	*the-ón*	*seru-om*[12]	*dag*	*grad-ŭ*	*výr-ą*, *deiw-an*[24]
n.-a. neut.	*pēd-an*[2]	*pad-ám*[3]	*xšaϑr-əm*[5]	*péd-on*[10]	*pers-om*[13]	*stain-a*[20]		*gijw-an*[25]
gen.	*arun-aš*	*vīr-ásya*	*ahur-ahiiā*[6]	*the-oĩo*[11]	*seru-ī*, *Popli-osio*[14]	*dag-s*[21]		
abl.		*vīr-ā́t*	*yasn-āt̰*		*Gnaiu-ōd*[15]		*grad-a*[23]	*výr-o*[23]
dat.		*vīr-ā́ya*	*yasn-āi*	*the-ō̃i*	*duen-ōi*[16]	*dag-a*	*grad-u*	*výr-ui*
instr.		*yajñ-ā́*[4]	*yasn-ā*[7]			*tag-u*[22]		*výr-u*
loc.	*arun-i*	*vīr-é*	*xšaϑr-ōi*[8]		*dom-ī*[17]		*grad-ě*	*nam-iẽ*[17]

[1] 'Brother'. [2] 'Place'. [3] 'Track'. [4] 'With a sacrifice'. [5] 'Rule'. [6] Old Avestan, 'of the lord'. [7] Old Avestan. [8] Old Avestan, 'in the rule'. [9] 'Brother'. [10] 'Ground'. [11] Homeric; Classical *theoũ*. [12] Archaic Lat.; Classical *seruus*, *seruum*. [13] Umbr., 'ground'. [14] Archaic Lat., 'of Publius'. [15] Archaic Lat., 'Gnaeus'. [16] Archaic Lat., 'for a good (man)'; Classical *bonō*. [17] 'At home'. [18] Runic. [19] 'Servant'. [20] 'Stone'. [21] Runic. [22] OHG, 'day'. [23] Synchronically genitive. [24] OPruss., 'god'. [25] OPruss., 'alive'.

6.47. There is complete agreement on the reconstruction of the **animate nominative, vocative, accusative**, and **neuter nominative-accusative singular**. Retraction of the accent in the vocative is evidenced by such forms as Ved. *vī́r-a* (vs. nomin. *vīrás*) and Gk. *ádelph-e* (vs. nomin. *adelphós*) above. Also uncontroversial are the reconstructions of the **dative, instrumental**, and **locative singular**, traditionally reconstructed as *-*ōi*, *-*ō*, and *-*oi*. The first two are likely contracted from *-*o-ei* and *-*o-*h_1. An ablaut variant *-*ei* in the locative is found especially in Italic, e.g. Oscan *comenei* 'in the assembly' and Lat. *domī* above. An *e*-grade variant instrumental in *-*e-*h_1 is also thought to underlie the Italic adverbs in *-*ē(d)* (which merged with the ablative and received the same dental as in the ablative), such as Lat. *rēctē* 'properly' (Archaic Lat. *rēctēd*). An important feature of the locative *-*o-i* is that it was disyllabic in PIE and remained so for some time after the proto-language, as reflected by intonational facts in Greek and Balto-Slavic.

6.48. The picture for the **genitive singular** is not quite as clear. The oldest ending was perhaps *-*os*, identical to the nominative, if Anatolian is any indication (e.g. Hitt. nomin. *arun-aš* 'sea', genit. *arun-aš*); and this ending may have infiltrated the athematic declension in several daughter languages, including Greek (see §6.8). But much more widely represented is *-*osi̯o*, represented by Ved. *vīr-ásya*, Av. *yasn-ahe*, Homeric Gk. *the-oĩo*, and Archaic Lat. *Popli-osio* above, as well as by Arm. *get-oy* 'of the river'. A similar suffix *-*oso* is reflected by OE (Northumbrian) *moncynn-æs* 'of mankind' (> Mod. Eng. *-'s*) and probably OPruss. *deiw-as* 'of god'; it is related to the pronominal genitive *-*eso* (see §7.8). A completely different genitive ending *-*ī* is found in Italic (Latin *uir-ī*), the closely allied Venetic (*Vineti* 'of Vinetos'), and Celtic (Ogam Ir. *maq(q)i* 'of the son').

6.49. Unlike the athematic ablative, the thematic **ablative singular** is distinct from the genitive. It was formed by suffixing an element variously reconstructed as *-*ad*, *-*at*, or *-h_2*et* (> *-h_2*at*) to the thematic vowel (the final consonant is uncertain due to the word-final voicing neutralization discussed in §3.40). This yielded a sequence *_-o-(h_2)ad/t_ that became _-āt_ in Vedic and _-āt̰_ in Old Avestan, and elsewhere contracted to *_-ōt_ (e.g. Archaic Lat. _Gnaiu-ōd_ 'by Gnaeus') or *_-āt_ in Balto-Slavic, where it became a genitive (OCS _grad-a_ 'of/from the city', Lith. _výr-o_ 'of/from the man'). This suffix may be related to the Slavic preposition *_otŭ_ 'from' (> Russ. _ot_). A laryngeal is likely because of the ending's intonational behavior in Baltic; additionally _-āt_ can have disyllabic scansion in Vedic poetry (though not, strangely, in Old Avestan).

Dual

6.50. The **nominative, vocative,** and **accusative animate dual** is traditionally reconstructed as *_-ō_, which is now thought to be from *_-o-h_1_ on the assumption that the ending contains the same dual suffix *_-h_1_ seen in the athematic declension. Examples of the thematic dual include Gk. _anthrṓp-ō_ 'two men', Ved. _dev-ā́_ 'two gods', OCS _grad-a_ 'two cities', and Lith. _výr-u_ 'two men'. The thematic **neuter** nom.-voc.-acc. dual ended in *_-o-ih_1_, as in Ved. _yug-é_ and OCS _iz-ě_ 'two yokes'. The other cases in the dual cannot be reconstructed with any certainty.

Plural

6.51. The following chart shows some of the comparative evidence for the plural of _o_-stems, using the same nouns as above except for Ved. _devás_ 'god' and Av. _daēuua-_ 'demon'. Other forms are glossed in the notes.

	Hitt.	Ved.	Av.	Gk.	Lat.	Goth.	OCS	Lith.
nom. anim.		_dev-ā́s_	_daēuu-ā̊ŋhō_	_the-oí_	_seru-ī, popl-oe_[9]	_dag-os_	_grad-i_	_výr-ai_
acc. anim.	_arun-uš_	_dev-ā́n_	_maṣ̌ii-ə̄ṇg_[3]	_the-oús, odel-ons_[6]	_seru-ōs_	_dag-ans_	_grad-y_	_výr-us, deiw-ans_[15]
neut. n.-a.	_pēd-a_[1]	_yug-ā́_[2]		_zug-á_[2]	_loc-a_[1]	_waurd-a_[13]	_měst-a_[1]	_slay-o_[16]
gen.	_arun-an_	_dev-ā́nām_	_daēuu-anąm_	_the-ō̃n_	_seru-om_[10]	_dag-a_[14]	_grad-ŭ_	_výr-ų_
dat.		_dev-ébhyas_	_daēuu-aēbiiō_		_Andetic-obos_[11]	_dag-am_	_grad-omŭ_	_výr-ams_
instr.		_dev-áis, dev-ébhis_	_yasn-āiš_[4]	_the-oĩs_[7]	_seru-īs, soki-ois_[12]			_výr-ais_
loc.		_dev-éṣu_	_asp-aēšu_[5]	_the-oĩsi_[8]			_grad-ěxŭ_	

[1] 'Places'. [2] 'Yokes'. [3] OAv., 'mortals'. [4] 'With sacrifices.' [5] 'Horses'. [6] Cretan, 'obols'. [7] Synchronically dative. [8] Dialectal; synchronically dative. [9] Archaic, preserved in Festus; 'people'. [10] Archaic Lat.; replaced by _-ōrum_. [11] Venetic, 'for the sons of Andetios' (?). [12] Archaic Lat. (inscriptional), 'for the friends'. [13] 'Words'. [14] ON, 'of days'. [15] OPruss., 'gods'. [16] OPruss., 'sled' (pl. in form but sing. in meaning).

6.52. The **animate nominative** and **vocative plural** was *_-ōs_ (contracted from *_-o-es_), as in Ved. _dev-ā́s_ 'gods', OIr. _(á) ḟir-u_ 'men!' (surviving as a vocative only), Goth. _dag-os_ 'days', and Osc. **Núvlan-ús** 'men from Nola' (the boldfacing is customary for transliterating words written in the native Oscan alphabet). To judge by the Ved. vocative _dévās_ 'gods!', the vocative plural had accent retraction like the singular. A doubled ending *_-ōsos_ is found in Indo-Iranian and Germanic: Ved. _dev-ā́sas_ 'gods', Av. _daēuu-ā̊ŋhō_ 'demons', and probably East Frisian _fisk-ar_ 'fishes'.

6.53. In at least five branches the pronominal nominative plural **-oi* (§7.9) replaced the original nominal ending. This probably came about in phrases consisting of a pronoun and noun, where the noun simply copied the pronominal ending: so a phrase **toi eḱu̯ōs* 'those horses, the horses' became **toi eḱu̯oi*. The ending is seen in Gk. *the-oí*, Lat. *seru-ī*, OCS *rab-i*, and Lith. *výr-ai* above, as well as Toch. B *yakwi* 'horses' (< **eḱu̯oi*) and OIr. *fir* 'men' (< **u̯ir-oi*); traces are also found in Albanian.

6.54. The **neuter nominative-accusative plural** was **-eh₂*, originally a collective (§§6.68ff.), as in Ved. *yug-ā́* 'yokes' and Osc. *comono* 'assemblies' (with *-o* < **-ā*).

6.55. The other thematic plural endings resemble the athematic endings, and generally consist of them added to the thematic vowel. The **animate accusative plural** was **-ons* (= **-o-ns*), as seen in OAv. *maṣ̌ii-ə̄ṇg*, Gk. (Cretan) *odel-ons*, Goth. *dag-ans*, and OPruss. *deiw-ans* above. A long version **-ōns*, which may or may not be of PIE date, is reflected for example in Ved. *dev-ā́n* (appearing as *dev-ā́ṃs* before certain consonants).

6.56. The thematic **genitive plural** was probably **-o-Hom* rather than the traditionally reconstructed **-o-om*, **-ōm*, because of the circumflex accent in Greek *-ō̃n* (representing *-óòn* < **-ó-Hom*) and Baltic (Lith. *-ũ*), the outcome in Germanic, and the disyllabic scansions in Indo-Iranian poetry (reflecting Indo-Iranian **-a'am*). Short **-(H)om* that appears to be reflected in Celtic and Slavic seems to be the result of secondary shortening in these branches.

6.57. As in the athematic declension, the thematic **dative and ablative plural** were generally formed with endings in **-bh-* or **-m-*, the latter only in Germanic and Balto-Slavic. Sometimes, as in Ved. dat pl. *dev-ébhyas* and Av. dat. pl. *daēuu-aēbiiō*, the ending was added to a stem in **-oi-* rather than the bare thematic stem. This recurs in the **locative plural** **-oi-su* (Ved. *dev-éṣu*, Av. *asp-aēšu*, dialectal Gk. *the-oĩsi* [dative, with *-si* replacing **-su*], and OCS *rab-ěxŭ*, with *-x-* from earlier **-s-*). A longer version **-ōi-* (presumably contracted from **-o-oi-*) of this stem-formant occurs in the only ending with no parallel in the athematic declension, the **instrumental plural** **-ōis* (Ved. *dev-áis*, Lith. *výr-ais*, Gk. *the-oĩs* [also dative]). This was subject to replacement by forms in **-oi-bhi-* or **-oi-mi-*, as in Ved. *dev-ébhis*.

Thematic nominal formations and suffixes

6.58. Some thematic nouns reconstructible for PIE are not derived from any known root, such as **u̯l̥kʷos* 'wolf', **h₂ŕ̥tḱos* 'bear', **snusós* 'daughter-in-law', and **agʷnos* 'lamb'. But most of the thematic nouns found in the daughter languages are derived from roots, either by adding the thematic vowel alone or by adding a suffix that itself ends in the thematic vowel. PIE had a large number of such suffixes, a few of which are given below. Some of the example forms are actually feminines ending with the suffix **-ā* (**-e-h₂*; see §§6.69–70).

Tomós and *tómos* nouns

6.59. These nouns, named after a Greek example of each type, were formed by adding the thematic vowel to the *o*-grade of the root. *Tomós* nouns had accented suffix and agential or active meaning (Gk. *tomós* means 'sharp', i.e. 'cutting', from *tem- 'cut'), while *tómos* nouns had root accent and resultative meaning (*tómos* means 'a slice', that is, a thing that results from cutting). The agential *tomós* nouns are particularly frequent as final compound members; an example is *-g^w*or(h_3)os* 'eating, devouring' (root *g^w*erh*$_3$- 'devour') in Gk. *dēmo-bóros* 'devouring the people' and Lat. *carni-uorus* 'eating meat, carnivorous'.

Possessive derivatives in *-*ó*-

6.60. Thematic nouns and adjectives indicating possession could be formed by adding the accented thematic vowel suffix *-*ó*- to an athematic noun stem, or by shifting the accent rightward to the thematic vowel of an already existing thematic noun (usually with additional modifications, see directly below). For example, the noun *g^w*i̯eh*$_2$- 'bowstring' (> Ved. *jyā́*) had zero-grade *g^w*ih*$_2$-, from which a thematic noun *g^w*ih*$_2$-*ó*- '(thing) having a bowstring' could be formed (> Gk. *biós* 'bow').

6.61. At other times, the ablaut grade of the base was "increased" a step (from zero to full or from full to lengthened), a very common type of formation called a **vrddhi-derivative**, after the Sanskrit word for 'growth'. Vrddhi-derivatives have a genitival or ablatival relationship to the noun from which they are formed: 'belonging to, of, (descended) from'. Thus from the thematic noun *su̯éḱuro- 'father-in-law' (Ved. *śváśura-*) could be formed a lengthened-grade vrddhi-derivative *su̯ēḱuró- 'pertaining to one's father-in-law' (> Skt. *śvāśura-* 'relating to one's father-in-law', OHG *swāgur* 'father-in-law's son = brother-in-law').

6.62. Sometimes a vrddhi-derivative was formed from a zero-grade and involved the insertion of the full-grade vowel in the "wrong" place. A famous example is the PIE word for 'god', *dei̯u̯-ó-s (Ved. *devás*, Av. *daēuua-* 'demon', Archaic Lat. accus. pl. *deiuōs* 'gods'). It was formed from the zero-grade *diu̯- of the noun *di̯ḗus 'sky', with the "wrong" full-grade *dei̯u̯- instead of *di̯eu-. Its literal meaning was 'one of, belonging to, or inhabiting the sky'.

Reduplicated thematic nouns

6.63. Just as some athematic nouns exhibit reduplication, so too do some thematic nouns. The most famous example, found throughout the family, is *k^w*e*-k^w*l-o*- 'wheel' (root *k^w*el(H)*- 'to turn'): Ved. *cakrám*, Gk. *kúklos*, Toch. A *kukäl* 'chariot', OE *hweohl* 'wheel', and perhaps Hitt. *kugullaš* 'ring-shaped bread, donut'. Additional examples include Ved. *ré-rih-a-* 'licking repeatedly', Av. *rą-rem-a-* 'resting', and OCS *gla-gol-ŭ* 'word' (< *gal-gal-o-, from *gal- 'to cry out'). It has been suggested that such forms had intensive or emotive force; *k^w*e*-k^w*l-o*- may have been an expressive neologism for a new gadget, the wheel, referring to the iterativity of its turning. (Recall on this point also §2.58.)

Nouns in *-*lo*-

6.64. This is widely found in diminutives in Italic, Germanic, and Balto-Slavic, such as the word for 'piglet': Lat. *porc-ulus*, OHG *farh-ali*, and Lith. *parš-ẽlis* (only the Latin form has actually remained thematic). It is also found added to verbal roots to make nouns of various kinds, such as **sed-lo-* (or feminine **sed-leh₂*) 'a seat' (from **sed-* 'sit') in e.g. Gk. *hellā́*, Lat. *sella*, and Goth. *sitls*.

Nouns in **-mo-*

6.65. This suffix was added to verbal roots to form a variety of action and event nouns. For example, the root *$*g^wher$-* 'to heat up' formed *$*g^wher$-mo-* or *$*g^whor$-mo-*, appearing as a noun meaning 'heat' (Ved. *gharmá-*, OPruss. *gorme*, Alb. *zjarm* 'fire') or an adjective meaning 'warm' (Gk. *thermós*, Lat. *formus*, Eng. *warm*, Arm. *ǰerm*). Some further examples from the individual languages include Gk. *gnṓ-mē* 'opinion' (Greek root *gnō-* 'know' < PIE *$*\hat{g}neh_3$-*), Lat. *fā-ma* 'fame, report, reputation' (Latin root *fā-* 'speak' < PIE root *$*bheh_2$-*), and Eng. *stream* (< **sreu-mo-*, from **sreu-* 'flow').

On the participial suffix **-mo-*, see §5.60.

Nouns in **-no-*

6.66. This suffix was added to verbal roots to form nouns of various sorts, such as Vedic *yajñá-* and Av. *yasna-* 'sacrifice, offering' (< **Hi̯aĝ-no-*, from **Hi̯aĝ-* 'to sacrifice'), and Lat. *dōnum* 'gift' (< *$*deh_3$-no-*, from *$*deh_3$-* 'to give'). One well-known trio of these nouns – the words for 'sleep' (**su̯ep-no-*), 'wagon' (**u̯eĝh-no-*), and 'price' (**u̯es-no-*) – is unusual in showing ablaut of the root. To use the first of these for illustration, the *e*-grade **su̯ep-no-* is found in OE *swefn* 'sleep, dream', the *o*-grade **su̯op-no-* in Arm. *kʿown* 'sleep', and the zero-grade **sup-no-* in Gk. *húpnos* 'sleep'.

On the passive verbal adjective suffix **-nó-*, see §5.61.

"Tool" nouns in **-tlo-*, **-dhlo-*, **-tro-*, **-dhro-*

6.67. These suffixes formed nouns indicating an instrument for accomplishing an action; normally they are neuters. Originally there were only the suffixes **-tlo-* and **-tro-*; **-dhlo-* and **-dhro-* arose secondarily by Bartholomae's Law (§§3.35, 10.6) and were later reanalyzed as independent suffixes. Examples of each suffix include *$*(s)neh_1$-tlo-* 'thing to sew with' (from *$*sneh_1$-* 'sew') in Eng. *needle*; *$*sth_2$-dhlom* 'place to stand things' (from *$*steh_2$-* 'stand') in Lat. *stabulum* 'place for animals to stand, stable, stall'; *$*h_2erh_3$-trom* 'a plow' (from *$*h_2erh_3$-* 'to plow') in Gk. *árotron*, Lat. *arātrum*, and OIr. *arathar*; and **k̂r(e)i-dhro-* 'sieve' (from **k̂rei-* 'to sift, strain') in Lat. *crībrum* and OE *hridder*.

The Collective and the Feminine

6.68. As noted above, the neuter plural was formed by adding *$*-h_2$*. A curious fact in Anatolian, Greek, and Old Avestan is that neuter plurals took singular verb agreement, as in the Greek phrase *tà zō̃ia trékhei* 'the animals (pl.) run (sing.)'. Additionally, in several branches (most notably Anatolian), animate nouns could form collective plurals in *-a* (< *$-(e)h_2$) alongside ordinary (distributive) plurals: Hitt. *alpaš* 'cloud', ordinary (distributive) plural *alpeš* 'clouds', collective *alpa* 'group of clouds'; Gk. *mērós* 'thigh', ordinary plural *mēroí* '(individual) thigh-pieces' (of a sacrificial animal), collective plural *mē͂ra* '(group of) thigh-pieces'; Lat. *locus* 'place', ordinary plural *locī*, collective *loca*. These facts have led many to hypothesize that *$-h_2$ was originally a collective suffix, and that PIE possessed a singular, dual, distributive plural, and collective.

6.69. The suffix *$-h_2$ is at least outwardly identical to an animate suffix *$-h_2$ that forms feminine nouns and abstract nouns. Its function as an abstract-noun suffix is found in all the branches including Anatolian, as in Luvian *zid-āḫ(-iša)* 'virility' (from *ziti-* 'man'), Lycian *pijata-* 'gift' (< **pii̯o-teh₂*), and Gk. (Doric) *tom-ā́* 'a cutting' (< **tom-eh₂*). The feminizing *$-h_2$, however, is found only outside Anatolian. If these two *h_2-suffixes are one and the same, as most researchers believe, then the collective *$-h_2$ early on acquired the additional function of marking the animate singulars of abstract nouns, and then later (after Anatolian broke off from the family) became specialized as a feminizing suffix.

It is not clear how this development is to be explained semantically. The use of abstract nouns to refer to an individual person belonging to or associated with that abstract entity has good parallels, as in Eng. *youth* 'state of being young' > 'a young individual', or Lat. *testimōnium* 'testimony' > French *témoin* 'witness'. But how such individualizing use might have been manifested in feminizing function is unclear.

The collective *$-h_2$ was restricted to the nominative and accusative of collectives, but in abstract and feminine forms it is found in all cases and numbers.

The ā*-stems*

6.70. The most widespread group of feminine nouns had a stem *$-eh_2$-, which contracted to *-*ā*-, the source of the *ā*-declensions that are characteristic of feminine nouns in so many of the daughter languages (Greek and Latin among them). This stem is either the feminizing suffix *$-h_2$ added to the thematic vowel, or simply the full grade of the feminizing suffix. Compare the paradigms below of Ved. *priyā́* 'dear', Av. *daēna* 'religion', Gk. *theā́* and Lat. *dea* 'goddess', Goth. *giba* 'gift', OCS *glava* 'head', and Lith. *dúona* 'bread'.

Singular

	Ved.	Av.	Gk.	Lat.	Goth.	OCS	Lith.
nom.	*priy-ā́*	*daēn-a*	*the-ā́*	*de-a*	*gib-a*	*glav-a*	*dúon-a*
voc.	*príy-ā*		*númph-a*[1]	*Turs-a*[3]		*žen-o*[5]	
acc.	*priy-ā́m*	*daēn-ąm*	*the-ā́n*	*de-am*	*gib-a*	*glav-ǫ*	*dúon-ą*
gen.	*priy-ā́yās*	*daēn-aiiå̄*	*the-ā͂s*	*de-ae*, *de-āī*[4]	*gib-os*		*dúon-os*
dat.	*priy-ā́yai*	*daēn-aiiāi*	*the-ā͂i*	*de-ae*	*gib-ai*	*glav-ě*	*dúon-ai*
instr.	*priy-ā́*, *priy-áyā*	*daēn-a*, *daēn-aiia*				*glav-ojǫ*	*dúon-a*
loc.	*priy-ā́yām*	*daēn-aiia*				*glav-ě*	*dúon-oje*

Plural

	Ved.	Av.	Gk.	Lat.	Goth.	OCS	Lith.
nom.	*priy-ā́s*	*daēn-å̄*	*the-aí*	*de-ae*	*gib-os*	*glav-y*	*dúon-os*
acc.	*priy-ā́s*	*daēn-å̄*	*the-ā́s*	*de-ās*	*gib-os*	*glav-y*	*dúon-as*
gen.	*priy-ā́nām*	*daēn-anąm*	*the-ō̃n*, *the-ā́ōn*[2]	*de-ārum*	*gib-o*	*glav-ŭ*	*dúon-ų*
dat.	*priy-ā́bhyas*	*daēn-ābiiō*	*the-aĩs(i)*	*de-īs*	*gib-om*	*glav-amŭ*	*dúon-oms*
instr.	*priy-ā́bhis*	*daēn-ābiš*	*the-ā́phi*[2]			*glav-ami*	*dúon-omis*
loc.	*priy-ā́su*	*daēn-āhu*				*glav-axŭ*	*dúon-ose*

[1] 'Bride', Homeric voc. [2] Homeric. [3] Umbrian, name of a goddess. [4] Archaic Lat.; note also the fixed phrase *pater famili-ās* 'head of the household'. [5] 'Woman'.

As can be seen, the *-eh_2-declension is athematic, with the case-endings added directly to the laryngeal. There is interestingly no *-*s* in the nominative singular. The vocative had retracted accentuation (preserved in Sanskrit and in a few words in Greek) and ended in *-*a* (whence the -*a* of Greek and Umbrian and the -*o* of OCS; elsewhere it was remade using the nominative ending). This *-*a* probably resulted from *-ah_2 with loss of the laryngeal before a pause. Some of the other forms in the charts above have been remade as well, such as the Latin genitive sing. *de-ae* (§13.38). Note that forms like the accusative singular *-eh_2-*m* do not appear as *-eh_2-*m̥*, as might be expected from the usual syllabification rules (§3.42), but rather remain *-eh_2-*m*, eventually to become *-*ām*. This is an example of Stang's Law (see §3.38). The accusative plural is also noteworthy: the daughter languages agree that the reconstructible ending is *-*ās* rather than *-*āns*, with the nasal lost early (*-eh_2*n̥s* > *-ah_2*n̥s* > *-ah_2*ns* by Stang's Law > *-*āns* > *-*ās*). Aside from the forms cited above, note also Celtic accusative plurals like Gaulish *mnas*, Old Irish *mná* 'women', and Old Irish *túatha* 'peoples', where by Celtic and Irish sound laws the final vowel must come from *-*ās* rather than *-*āns*. Sometimes the -*n*- was restored, notably in Greek (contrary to the appearance of *theā̃s* above; for the reason, see §12.50).

At an earlier stage there were potentially feminines formed simply by adding *-h_2 to a root, as in *g^w*en*-h_2 'woman', reflected directly by Ved. *jáni*- (with -*i*- < *h_2). (Gk. *gunḗ* and OCS *žena* come from later forms ending in *-eh_2.)

The *ā*-declension in the daughter languages is familiarly associated with thematic declensions, especially in adjectives where *o*-stem masculine and neuters form their feminines with *-*ā*- (e.g. Lat. *nouus* [masc.], *nouum* [neut.], *noua* [fem.]). It is also associated with feminine counterparts of *o*-stem animates (e.g. *ursa* 'she-bear' next to *ursus* '[he-]bear' in Latin). Both of these functions, however, may have arisen relatively late, as they are barely found in the earliest attested stages of these languages.

The devī́- *and* vr̥kī́-*feminines and other formations*

6.71. Beside bare *-eh_2- we can reconstruct a compound suffix *-*i̯*eh_2- that is also collective and feminizing. It existed in two types, represented on the one hand by Vedic *devī́* 'goddess', genit. *devyā́s*, and on the other by Vedic *vr̥kī́s* 'she-wolf', genit. *vr̥kyàs* (which spells *vr̥kías*). The *devī́*-type commonly forms feminines to athematic adjectives such as *nt*-participles; examples include Ved. *yuñjat-ī́* 'yoking (fem.)' (< *$\underset{\frown}{i}$ung-$\underset{\circ}{n}$t-ih_2) and Gk. *phérousa* 'carrying (fem.)' (< pre-Greek **bher-ont-i̯a*). (On the different syllabifications of *-ih_2, cp. §3.42.) There is no sure evidence of either of these types in Anatolian.

There are scattered vestiges of other feminine formations, of which we shall mention one. A feminine suffix **-s(o)r-*, derived from a word **soro-* 'woman', is indicated by the Indo-Iranian and Celtic feminine of the numerals 'three' and 'four', **t(r)i-sr-* and *k^wete-sr-* (Ved. *tisrás*, *cátasras*; Av. *tišrō*, *cataŋrō*, with *-ŋr-* from **-sr-*; Gaul. *tidres*; and OIr. *teoir*, *cetheoir*). It is also found as a feminizing suffix for certain Hittite nouns (see §9.44a), and may well be the second element in the kinship term **su̯e-sōr* 'sister', perhaps 'woman of one's own (kinship group)' (**su̯o-* 'one's own'; see §7.13).

Adjectives

6.72. Indo-European adjectives did not differ from nouns in declension, and could be thematic or athematic. To judge by the older IE languages, any adjective could also be used as a noun (like English *the good*, *the bad*, *and the ugly*). Sometimes the substantivization of an adjective (that is, the process of turning it into a noun) involved morphophonological changes, especially in an idiomatic meaning. Among the best-known of these is retraction of the accent when turning an adjective into a noun, as in Ved. *kr̥ṣṇá-* 'black' versus the noun *kŕ̥ṣṇa-* 'black antelope', and Gk. *dolikhós* 'long' versus *dólikhos* 'long race-course'.

Formation of adjectives

6.73. Adjectives could be formed by the addition of suffixes to roots or word-stems. While most of the adjectives so formed were *o*-stems (see the list starting in §6.74 below), many other adjectives were athematic. For example, a number of adjectives that were formed from roots of adjectival meaning were *u*-stems (as *su̯e$h_2$du-* 'sweet' > Vedic *svādú-*, Doric Gk. *hādús*), and we have seen various consonant-stem participles like those in **-nt-* and the feminine adjectives in *-ih_2-. A type of *i*-stem adjective of some interest is that exemplified by Latin *prō-clīu-is* 'steep' and *dē-pil-is* 'hairless': each of these is a compound formed from an *o*-stem noun (*clīu-us* 'a slope', *pilus* 'hair'), with the thematic declension replaced by *i*-stem endings when the noun formed a compound adjective. Aside from suffixation, athematic adjectives could be formed from athematic nouns by internal derivation, detailed in §6.29.

Adjectival suffixes

6.74. ***-i̯o-** and ***-ii̯o-**. Indo-Europeanists have traditionally reconstructed an all-purpose adjectival suffix **-i̯o-* underlying such forms as Hitt. *ištarniya-* 'central' (< *ištarna* 'between'), Ved. *dámiya-* 'domestic' (< *dám-* 'home'), *gávya-* 'pertaining to cows' (< *gáv-* 'cow'), and Lat. *ēgregius* 'outstanding' (< *ē grege* 'out of the herd'). But recent research suggests that PIE originally had two or more similar but functionally distinct suffixes. Probably the commonest was **-ii̯o-*, which formed adjectives of appurtenance or origin, and is partly or in whole derived from the locative ending **-i* plus the possessive suffix **-o-* or **-ó-* (§6.60). It was also in extensive use to form adjectives from compounds, such as Lat. *ēgregius* above. In several branches, the suffix was used to form patronymics ('son of . . .'), e.g. Homeric Gk. *Telamō̃n-ios Aías* 'Aias (Ajax) son of Telamon', Old Persian *Haxāmaniš-iya-* 'offspring of Achaemenes, Achaemenid', Lat. *Seru-ius* 'son of a slave (*seruus*), Servius'. A monosyllabic **-i̯o-* is found in some other formations, such as relational adjectives (most prominently **medh-i̯o-* 'middle' in e.g. Vedic Skt. *mádhya-*, Gk. *mésos*, and Gothic *midjis*, and **al-i̯o-* 'other', on which see §7.14) and various other items like Gk. *ápeiros* 'boundless' < **n̥-per-i̯o-*. But often it is hard to tell these apart, especially since **-i̯o-* was often pronounced **-ii̯o-* in the proto-language because of Sievers' Law (§§3.43ff.), and in many branches (such as Italic and Celtic) **-ii̯o-* replaced **-i̯o-*.

6.75. ****-ko-*.** This suffix is most commonly found added to nouns to indicate origin or material composition: Ved. *síndhu-ka-* 'from Sindh', Gk. *Libu-kós* 'Libyan', Gaulish (Latinized) *Are-mori-cī* 'those by the sea, Aremoricans', Goth. *staina-hs* 'stony'. It frequently appeared in a longer version ****-iko-*** as a suffix indicating appurtenance, as in Gk. *hipp-ikós* 'having to do with horses', Lat. *bell-icus* 'pertaining to war', and OE *gyd-ig* 'dizzy' (< Germanic **guđ-iga-* 'possessed by a god'; Mod. Eng. *giddy*).

Related is ****-isko-***, found in Germanic and Balto-Slavic to indicate affiliation or place of origin: OHG *diut-isc* 'pertaining to the (common) people' (> Mod. German *Deutsch* 'German'), OCS *rŭm-ĭskŭ* 'Roman', and Russ. *russkij* 'Russian'. This is the source of Mod. Eng. *-ish*.

6.76. ****-ro-*.** This suffix took part in the derivational system known as the Caland system (see §6.87). It was added to the zero-grade of an adjectival root to form that root's free-standing adjectival form, and was usually accented, as in ***h_1*rudh-ró-* 'red' (Ved. *rudhirá-* 'blood-red, bloody', Gk. *eruth-rós*, Lat. *ruber*) and ***h_2*r̥ĝ-ró-* 'swift; shining' (Ved. *r̥j-rá-*, Gk. *argós* < **argrós* 'swift').

6.77. ****-tó-*.** Aside from forming passive verbal adjectives (see §5.61), this suffix formed possessive adjectives, as in Lat. *barbā-tus* 'bearded', OCS *bogatŭ* 'wealthy' (from *bogŭ* 'wealth'), and Eng. *beard-ed*. For (unaccented?) **-to-* in superlatives and ordinals, see §6.81 and §§7.20, 7.22.

Comparison of adjectives

Comparative

6.78. Two suffixes are widely used as comparative markers in the IE languages. The first was an amphikinetically ablauting suffix **-i̯os-* (masculine nomin. **-i̯ōs*, weak cases **-is-*) added to the full grade of the root: Av. accus. sing. *nāid-iiå̄ŋhəm* 'weaker' (< Indo-Iranian **nādh-i̯ās-am*); Mycenaean Gk. *me-zo-e* '(two) bigger ones' (< pre-Greek **meg-i̯os-e*); Lat. *maior* (Archaic Lat. *maiōr*), neut. *maius* (**mag-i̯os-*), adverb *magis* 'more'; OIr. *sin-iu* 'older' (**sen-i̯ōs*, cp. Lat. *senior*); Goth. *manag-iz-* 'more'; and OCS *bol-ĭš-* 'bigger'.

6.79. The second comparative suffix was **-tero-*. This was not originally a comparative suffix: its basic function was to set off a member of a pair contrastively from the other member of the pair, as in Gk. *skaiós* 'left' vs. *deksiterós* 'right', i.e. 'the one on the right (as opposed to the one on the left)'. Thus a comparative like Gk. *sophṓ-teros* 'wiser' meant originally 'the wise one (of two people)', hence '(the one that is) more wise'. This suffix is continued by the comparative suffixes *-tara-* of Sanskrit and *-tero-* of Greek, and by such forms as Lat. *dē-ter-ior* 'farther down, lower, worse', OIr. *úachtar* 'higher part', and Eng. *far-ther*.

Superlative

6.80. To judge by the fact that some of the older IE languages could use the positive degree of an adjective plus a genitive plural noun to express the superlative of the adjective, PIE did not necessarily express the superlative degree by any change to the adjective. Thus Homeric Greek has *dī̃a theā́ōn* (genit. pl.) 'divine of/among goddesses = most divine goddess', and Hittite has *šallayaš* (genit. pl.) *šiunaš* (genit. pl.) *šalliš* 'great among the great gods = the greatest of the great gods'.

6.81. However, at least two suffixes are reconstructible that have a superlative function in the daughter languages. One is ***-m̥mo-**, seen in various forms and combinations: alone in Lat. *min-imus* 'least, smallest'; **-t-m̥mo-* in the Skt. superlative suffix *-tama-*; and **-is-m̥mo-* (a combination of the weak stem **-is-* of the comparative suffix and the superlative **-m̥mo-*) in Latin superlatives like *fort-issimus* 'strongest' and *maximus* 'biggest' (probably **magism̥mo-*). The other is the addition of **-to-* to the zero-grade **-is-* of the comparative suffix, yielding ***-isto-**, as found in the Skt. superlative suffix *-iṣṭha-*, Gk. *még-istos* 'greatest', and Goth. *bat-ista* 'best' (and continued by the Eng. superlative suffix *-est*). These superlative suffixes bear a striking resemblance to, and are perhaps ultimately identical with, certain ordinal numeral suffixes, e.g. **-isto-* in Eng. *first*; see §§7.19ff.

Nominal Composition and Other Topics

6.82. PIE possessed a rich set of compound noun formations. Compounds can be broadly classified into two types according to their meaning. In one type, which can be illustrated by *blackbird* '(a type of) black bird', the compound is essentially the sum of its parts, and its referent (a type of bird) is one of the compound members itself (usually the second one, as here). This type is called *endocentric* (or determinative). Examples of endocentric compounds from other IE languages include Skt. *Siṁha-puras* 'Lion City' (*Singapore*), Gaulish (Latinized) *Nouio-dūnum* 'New Fort', German *Blut-wurst* 'blood sausage', and OCS *dobro-děјanje* 'good works'.

The second type, which can be illustrated by another bird-name, *redthroat*, is more than the sum of its parts and refers to something outside itself: the referent is not a type of throat, but a type of bird possessing a red throat. Such compounds are called *exocentric* or possessive compounds, but in Indo-European circles they are typically called **bahuvrihis**, a term borrowed from Sanskrit (*bahuvrīhi-*, literally 'much-riced', i.e. 'having much rice' – itself an example of the type). Bahuvrihis are quite common in personal names: Gk. *Aristó-dēmos* 'best-people = having the best people', OIr. *Fer-gus* 'hero-strength = having a hero's strength', Cz. *Bohu-slav* 'having the fame of god', Lepontic *Uvamo-kozis* 'having supreme guests', and Eng. *Pea-body*. (Recall §2.48.)

6.83. It is frequently said that bahuvrihis typically have *o*-grade of the ablauting syllable of the second compound member. Such is indeed the case in such forms as Gk. *eu-pátōr* 'having a good father' (from *patḗr* 'father') and Umbrian *du-purs-* 'having two feet' (< **-pod-*). These *o*-grades are likely to be survivals of old amphikinetic inflection rather than engendered directly by the process of compounding; but the matter is in need of further investigation.

6.84. Some bahuvrihis had adverbs as the first compound member: Gk. *én-theos* 'having god within = inspired', Lat. *dē-plūmis* '(with) the feathers away = featherless', Gaul. *exs-ops* '(with) the eyes away = blind'.

6.85. PIE also had compounds in which one member was a verb or a verbal derivative that governed the other member. Having the verb as second compound member (type Eng. *bar-keep*, *cow-herd*) is quite common, e.g. Ved. *rathe-ṣṭhā́-* 'standing on a chariot, chariot-fighter', Lat. *armi-ger* 'one who bears arms', Arm. *ban-ber* 'word-carrier, messenger', and OCS *medv-ědĭ* 'honey-eater = bear'. More rarely, the verb is the first member (type Eng. *pick-pocket*), as in Gk. *pheré-oikos* 'carry-house = snail' and OCS *vě-glasŭ* 'know-voice = knowledgeable'.

6.86. Some adjectives and other parts of speech appear in a reduced form as prefixes. Some well-known examples include the zero-grade prefix **$h_1$su-* from the adjective **$h_1$esu-* 'good' (Skt. *su-*, Gk. *eu-*, OIr. *so-*, OCS *sŭ-*); the so-called "privative" or negating prefix **n̥-* 'not, un-' from **ne* 'not' (see §7.25); and the numeral prefix **tri-* 'three-' from **tréi̯es* 'three' (see §7.18).

The Caland system

6.87. The nineteenth-century Sanskritist Willem Caland noticed that adjectives in **-ro-* (§6.76) substituted an *-i-* for that suffix when they were the first member of a compound. For example, Av. *dərəzra-* 'strong' becomes *dərəzi-* in compounds like *dərəzi-raθa-* 'having a strong chariot', and Gk. *kūdrós* 'glorious' exists alongside *kūdi-áneira* 'bringing glory to men'. This rule of morphological replacement became known as "Caland's Law," and since Caland's time it has been discovered that several other suffixes participate in a so-called Caland system. Chief among these suffixes, besides **-ro-*, are the stative suffix **-eh_1-* and its relatives (§5.37), the adjectival suffix **-u-*, and several others. The roots involved are typically adjectival.

For Further Reading

As with the verb, no comprehensive treatment of the noun has been written in nearly a century. The accent-ablaut classes are the subject of many articles; the seminal ones are mostly in German by such authors as Jochem Schindler and Heiner Eichner, building on work by earlier scholars. Rieken 1999 is a massive study of Hittite athematic nouns and has an excellent detailed overview of the athematic accent-ablaut types. Nussbaum 1986 is a superb lexical and morphological study, treating many issues in the derivational relationships among IE nominal formations. Many of Nussbaum's articles concern nominal morphology and derivation and can be read with profit.

For Review

Know the meaning or significance of the following:

nominative	directive	endingless locative	heteroclitic
vocative	collective	root noun	*r/n*-stem
accusative	strong case	accent-ablaut class	Hoffmann suffix
genitive	weak case	acrostatic	*tomós/tómos* nouns
ablative	animate	proterokinetic	vrddhi-derivative
dative	masculine	amphikinetic	bahuvrihi
instrumental	feminine	hysterokinetic	Caland system
locative	neuter	internal derivation	

Exercises

1 The following are cases of the athematic noun **pod-* (**ped-*) 'foot'. Identify the case and number of each form:

a **pód-m̥* **b** **ped-bhi(-)* **c** **ped-ōm* **d** **ped-n̥s*

2 Below are given various case-forms of the animate *o*-stem noun **logos* 'word'. Identify the case and the number of each form. Some forms have more than one answer.

a **loĝosi̯o* **c** **loĝōs* **e** **loĝe* **g** **loĝoh$_1$*
b **loĝons* **d** **loĝos* **f** **loĝom* **h** **loĝōt*

3 For the neuter *o*-stem noun **deh$_3$nom* 'gift', give each form indicated below:

a nominative plural **b** accusative singular **c** dative singular

4 Using the information in §§6.45ff., give the full PIE singular and plural paradigms of the nouns in **2** and **3** above.

5 Below are given the nominative, accusative, and genitive singular of a variety of PIE athematic nouns. Identify the accent-ablaut class to which each noun belongs. Specify if the noun is a root noun.

a **péh$_3$-ti-s* **péh$_3$-ti-m* **ph$_3$-téi-s* 'a drink'
b **dhéh$_1$-mn̥* **dhéh$_1$-mn̥* **dhh$_1$-mén-s* 'something placed'

- **c** *-*stéh₂-s* *-*stéh₂-m̥* *-*sth₂-és* 'standing on . . .'
- **d** **h₂st-ḗr* **h₂st-ér-m̥* **h₂st-r-és* 'star'
- **e** **di̯ḗu-s* **di̯éu-m* **diu̯-és* 'sky, sky-god'
- **f** **dh₃-tḗr* **dh₃-tér-m̥* **dh₃-tr-és* 'giver'

6 Below are a set of nouns derived from verbs. Provide a translation of the nouns.

- **a** **ĝneh₃-* 'know': **ĝnéh₃-mn̥*
- **b** **ĝenh₁-* 'beget, create': **ĝénh₁-tōr*
- **c** **u̯ekʷ-* 'speak': **u̯ékʷ-os*, **u̯ékʷ-es-*
- **d** **gʷhen-* 'kill': **gʷhon-ós*
- **e** **peh₃-* 'drink': **peh₃-tlom*

7 Form the indicated derivative of the noun or adjective below.

- **a** **kʷtu̯r̥-ped-* 'having four feet': feminine
- **b** **h₂r̥tk̂os* 'bear': feminine
- **c** **smók̂r̥* 'beard': athematic adj. 'having a beard'

8 Mention was made above (§6.73) of *u*-stem adjectives formed from roots having adjectival meaning. The suffix *-*ro-* was also frequently used in this purpose. The distribution of these suffixes seems to have been phonologically conditioned by the sounds in the root. Based on the forms below, what restriction was placed on the kinds of roots to which *-*u-* could be attached?

**h₂reudh-* 'red': adjective **h₁rudh-ro-*
**su̯eh₂d-* 'sweet': adjective **su̯eh₂d-u-*
**ōk̂-* 'swift': adjective **ōk̂-u-*
**keud-* 'glorious': adjective **kud-ro-*
**mreĝh-* 'short': adjective **mr̥ĝh-u-*
**h₁lengʷh-* 'light, quick': adjective **h₁l̥n̥gʷh-u-*
**gheu-* 'be in awe of': adjective **gheu-ro-* 'causing awe'
**bherĝh-* 'high': adjective **bhr̥ĝh-u-*
**deuh₂-* 'long in duration': adjective **duh₂-ro-*
**anĝh-* 'tight, constricted': adjective **anĝh-u-*

9 Identify each of the following English compounds as either endocentric or exocentric.

- **a** *redhead*
- **b** *greenback*
- **c** *blueberry*
- **d** *whitecap*
- **e** *blackboard*
- **f** *yellowbelly*

7 Pronouns and Other Parts of Speech

Pronouns: Introduction

7.1. Pronouns present special difficulties to the comparatist. First of all, they easily come under analogical influence of each other. This is true especially of the personal pronouns: the accusative singulars of the first and second personal pronouns came to rhyme not only in English (*me thee*) but also in Hittite (*ammuk tuk*), Sanskrit (*mā́m tvā́m*), Greek (*emé sé*), and Russian (*menja tebja*), among many other languages; yet none of these formations is precisely cognate, and each is found only in its own branch of the family. Second, pronouns tend to attract ancillary emphatic particles or affixes of various kinds to give them greater saliency. This is true especially of deictic and demonstrative pronouns, as in dialectal English *this-(h)ere*, *that-(th)ere* replacing simple *this* and *that*. Third, pronouns tend to have a broad range of idiomatic uses that often make reconstruction of their original functions uncertain.

In spite of these difficulties, we are fairly well informed about the PIE pronominal system. We can reconstruct personal, reflexive, demonstrative, relative, and interrogative pronouns for the proto-language. We know that, like adjectives, pronouns were declined for case and number and (except for the personal and reflexive pronouns) for gender; and we know that the pronominal declensions differed from the nominal and adjectival declensions in several respects discussed below.

Personal Pronouns

7.2. The personal pronouns of the IE languages are of a somewhat paradoxical historical nature: probably no other set of words contains elements that are as ancient (they have been termed the "Devonian rocks" of the proto-language), yet at the same time they have undergone a great deal of analogical remodeling. Everywhere they are exceptional in the context of their language's grammar. In English, only the personal pronouns distinguish a subjective from an objective case (as in *I* vs. *me* and *she* vs. *her*), a retention of the fuller case-system that English once had. Going back a millennium, the Old English personal pronouns were the only words to have a set of dual forms alongside singular and plural – another archaism at the time. The use of more than one stem in any given paradigm (such as *I/me*, *we/us*), a phenomenon called *suppletion*, recurs throughout the family – and with exactly the same stems;

the suppletion is reconstructible for PIE and harks back to extremely old layers of the language's morphology.

But the amount of analogical refashioning that has occurred makes it impossible to reconstruct most pronominal forms with any certainty, aside from the bare stems. We know that PIE had complete singular, dual, and plural paradigms for the first and second personal pronouns, and had different paradigms for stressed and unstressed (enclitic) forms. We also know that PIE had no special forms for the third person, probably using demonstrative pronouns instead, such as *so *seh$_2$ *tod (see §7.10). There was also a reflexive pronoun that was indifferent to both person and number.

First person

7.3. A sampling of the comparative data for the first personal pronoun, in singular, dual, and plural, is as follows:

	Hitt.	Gk.	Ved.	Av.[3]	Lat.	Goth.	Arm.	Toch. B	OCS	Lith.
sg.										
nom.	*ūk*	*egṓ(n)*	*ahám*	*azəm*	*ego*	*ik*	*es*	*ñäś*	*azŭ*	*àš*
acc.	*ammuk*	*emé*	*mā́m*	*mąm*	*mē*	*mik*	*is*	*ñäś*	*mene*	*manè*
gen.	*ammēl*	*eméo*[1]	*máma*	*mana*	*meī*	*meina*	*im*	*ñi*	*mene*	*manę̃s*
dat.	*ammuk*	*emoí*	*máhyam*	*maibiiā*[4]	*mihī*	*mis*	*inj*		*mĭně*	*mán*
du.										
nom.		*nṓ*	*vā́m*	*vā*[4]		*wit*		*wene*	*vě*	*vēdu*[5]
acc.		*nṓ*	*āvā́m*	*əəāuuā*[4]		*ugkis*		*wene*	*na*	*nuodu*[5]
gen.		*nō̃in*	*āváyos*						*naju*	
dat.		*nō̃in*				*ugkis*			*nama*	
pl.										
nom.	*wēš*	*ámmes*[2]	*vayám*	*vaēm*	*nōs*	*weis*	*mekʿ*	*wes*	*my*	*mẽs*
acc.	*anzāš*	*ámme*[2]	*asmā́n*	*āhmā*[4]	*nōs*	*uns(is)*	*mez*	*wes*	*ny*	*mùs*
gen.	*anzēl*	*ámmōn*[2]	*asmā́kam*	*ahmākəm*	*nostrum*	*unsara*	*mer*	*wesi*	*nasŭ*	*mū́sų*
dat.	*anzāš*	*ámmi*[2]	*asmábhyam*	*ahmaibiiā*[4]	*nōbīs*	*uns(is)*	*mez*		*namŭ*	*mùms*

[1] Homeric. [2] Aeolic. [3] Young Avestan except where noted. [4] Old Avestan. [5] Dialectal.

Notes on the reconstruction of the first person

7.4. For the **nominative singular** of the first person singular, we reconstruct *eĝoh$_2$ (extended to *eĝh$_2$-om in e.g. Vedic *ahám*). The other cases are built from a different stem, *me- (sometimes extended to *eme-). The dual and plural contain at least two stems as well, one in *u̯e(i)- or similar for the nominative, and another in *n̥s- for the other cases. The **genitive singular** of the first person may have been *mene, to judge by the Indo-Iranian and Balto-Slavic forms above, as well as by Welsh *fy* 'my', which once ended in a nasal since it nasalizes the following sound (as *fy nghar* 'my car'; nasalization will be discussed in chapter 14). A **dative singular** *me-ĝh(i) is reflected in Indo-Iranian, Latin, and probably Armenian *inj* (< *eme-ĝh-). The **nominative dual** is fairly securely reconstructible as *u̯eh$_1$ (> *u̯ē), although the vowel is short in Germanic and Baltic. The **nominative plural** was probably **u̯ei*. The plural oblique cases are apparently ultimately based on a stem **n̥s-me-*; in some branches (Armenian, Baltic), only the second part of this seems to occur, perhaps under the influence of the 1st plural verbal endings in (*)*-me-*. The element **n̥s-* is the zero-grade of **nes*; this and other grades are found in the Latin pl. *nōs* and in a number of enclitic dual and plural forms.

Second person

7.5. A selection of the comparative data for the second person follows:

	Hitt.	Gk.	Ved.	Av.	Lat.	Goth.	Arm.	Toch. B	OCS	Lith.
sg.										
nom.	*zik*	*tú*[1]	*tvám*	*tū*	*tū*	*þu*	*dow*	*t(u)we*	*ty*	*tù*
acc.	*tuk*	*té*[1]	*tvā́m*	*θβąm*	*tē*	*þuk*	*kʿez*	*ci*	*tebe*	*tavè*
gen.	*tuēl*	*téos*[1]	*táva*	*tauua*	*tuī*	*þeina*	*kʿo*	*tañ*	*tebe*	*tavę̃s*
dat.	*tuk*	*toí*[1]	*túbhyam*	*taibiiā*[3]	*tibī*	*þus*	*kʿez*		*tebě*	*táu*
du.										
nom.		*sphṓ*	*yuvám*			*git*[4]		*yene*	*va*	*jùdu*
acc.		*sphṓ*	*yuvā́m*			*igqis*		*yene*	*va*	
gen.		*sphṓin*	*yuvós*	*yauuākəm*		*igqara*			*vaju*	
dat.		*sphṓin*				*igqis*			*vama*	
pl.										
nom.	*šumēš*	*úmmes*[2]	*yūyám*	*yūš*[3]	*uōs*	*jūs*	*dowkʿ*	*yes*	*vy*	*jū̃s*
acc.	*šumāš*	*úmme*[2]	*yuṣmā́n*		*uōs*	*izwis*	*jez*	*yes*	*vasŭ*	*jùs*
gen.	*šumenzan*	*ummō̃n*[2]	*yuṣmā́kam*	*yūšmākəm*	*uestrum*	*izwara*	*jer*	*yesi*	*vasŭ*	*jū́sų*
dat.	*šumāš*	*úmmi*[2]	*yuṣmábhyam*	*yūšmaibiiā*[3]	*uōbīs*	*izwis*	*jez*		*vamŭ*	*jùms*

[1] Doric. [2] Aeolic. [3] Old Avestan. [4] Old English.

Reconstruction of the second person

7.6. The singular forms of the second person are based on a stem in **tu-*. The dual and plural forms show mostly stems in **us-* and **i̯u-*. The nominative singular was perhaps **tuH*, with the laryngeal the source of the long vowel in most of the descendant forms. The oblique plural stem is usually reconstructed as **us-me-*, but it has been recently suggested by the American Indo-Europeanist Joshua Katz that this was remade (under the influence of the first person **n̥s-me-*) from **us-u̯e-*, reflected in Goth. *izwis* and related forms.

Enclitic personal pronouns

7.7. A number of the branches, in particular Anatolian, Indo-Iranian, Greek, Balto-Slavic, and Tocharian, distinguish fully stressed (emphatic or contrastive) personal pronouns from unstressed clitic object pronouns. For the dative of the first singular pronoun, for example, Hittite has the stressed form *ammuk* and clitic *-mu*, Greek has *emoí* and clitic *moi*, Vedic has *máhyam* and clitic *me*, and Lithuanian has *mán* and (Old Lith.) clitic *-m(i)*. Observe the forms below:

	1st person					*2nd person*				
	Hitt.	Gk.	Ved.	Av.	OCS	Hitt.	Gk.	Ved.	Av.	OCS
sg.										
acc.	*-mu*	*me*	*mā*	*mā*	*mę*	*-ta, -du-*[3]	*te*	*tvā*	*θβā*	*tę*
dat.	*-mu*	*moi*	*me*	*mōi,*[2] *mē*	*mi*	*-ta, -du-*[3]	*toi*	*te*	*tōi,*[2] *tē*	*ti*
gen.	*-mu*	*meu*[1]	*me*	*mōi,*[2] *mē*		*-ta, -du-*[3]	*seu*[1]	*te*	*tōi,*[2] *tē*	
du.										
A.D.G.			*nau*					*vām*		*va*
pl.										
acc.	*-naš*		*nas*	*nå̄*[2], *nō*	*ny*	*-šmaš*		*vas*	*vå̄*[2], *vō*	*vy*
D.G.	*-naš*		*nas*	*nə̄*[2], *nō*	*ny*	*-šmaš*		*vas*	*və̄*[2], *vō*	*vy*

[1] Homeric. [2] Old Avestan. [3] Used when together with the reflexive particle *-za*.

Not surprisingly, the clitic pronouns are mostly just reduced versions of the fuller forms. One can reconstruct for the singular of both persons **me* and **te* in the accusative and **moi* and **toi* in the dative and genitive (Gk. *meu* and *seu* are innovations); and for the plural, **nos* and **u̯os*. Old Avestan preserves distinct accusative forms *nå̄ vå̄* from long-vowel **nōs *u̯ōs* that have been compared with Latin *nōs* 'we, us' and *uōs* 'you'. The other Avestan forms in *-ə̄* and *-ō* come from short-vowel **-os*.

Anatolian, alone among the branches, has innovated a set of third-person clitic subject pronouns (e.g. Hitt. *-aš* 'he', *-e* 'they' [animate]). They are used only with certain kinds of intransitive verbs, as will be discussed in §9.11.

Possessive pronominal adjectives

7.8. The possessive adjectives for the singular personal pronouns are often formed by adding the thematic vowel to the genitive. Thus several first singular possessive adjectives are built to the enclitic genitive **moi* or **mei* (Lat. *meus* < **mei̯-o-*, OCS *mojĭ* < **moi̯-o-* is 'my'; so also, with different suffix, the Germanic family of Eng. *mine* < **mei-no-*). For the second person we can reconstruct **teu̯-o-* 'your' or **tu̯-o-* (> Ved. *tvá-*, Gk. *sós* [regular from **tu̯o-*], Lat. *tuus*, OCS *tvojĭ*), and in parallel for the reflexive, **seu̯-o-* or **su̯-o-* '(one's) own' (> Ved. *svá-*, Gk. *hós*, Lat. *suus*, OCS *svojĭ*). The dual and plural possessive adjectives vary from branch to branch, but were probably originally built comparably.

Other Pronouns and the Pronominal Declension

7.9. Among other PIE pronouns, the most easily reconstructible are the demonstratives in **so-*, **to-*, and **ei-*, the relative **(H)i̯o-*, the indefinite/interrogative **k*ʷ*o-*, and the reflexive **su̯e-* (all discussed below).

Several of the case-endings differ from those of the nominal and adjectival declensions. The neuter nominative-accusative singular ended not in **-m* but in **-d* (**tod*,

k^wid, etc.; also reconstructed as **tot*, *k^wit*; cf. §3.40). The genitive singular ending was **-eso*, as in OCS *česo* 'of what' and Goth. *þis* 'of the'. (In Germanic, this ending spread to the thematic noun declension: Goth. *dagis* 'of a day'.) The masculine nominative plural ending was **-oi* (so **toi*, *k^woi*, etc.), an ending that spread to the thematic noun declensions in several branches (§6.43). Finally, a genitive plural ending **-sōm* has been reconstructed on the basis of Hitt. *appen-zan* 'of those', Ved. *e-ṣā́m* 'of these', and Celtiberian *soi-sum* 'of these'.

A formant **-sm-* is found in several oblique cases in some of the languages: Ved. *asmin* and South Picene **esmen**, both locative singulars meaning 'in this'; OPruss. dative sing. *schismu* '(for) this', and probably Goth. dative sing. *þamma* 'for the, for this'. Surely related are forms without the *-s-* such as Lith. locative *tamè* 'in that'.

An additional peculiarity of the pronominal declensions is that, though basically thematic, they often show *i*-stem forms. Thus the interrogative pronoun *k^wo-* had nominative/accusative forms in *k^wi-* such as Av. *ciš* 'who?', Gk. *tís* 'who?' (in this language the *i*-stem forms were generalized throughout the paradigm), and Lat. *quid* 'what?' A stem **k̑i-* 'this' (see next section) is an *i*-stem, although the related emphatic particle **k̑e* (§7.29) ends in an *-e* that presupposes thematic forms as well.

Demonstrative pronouns

7.10. Widely represented are the two stems **so-* and **to-* meaning 'this, that' or 'the'. The first of these seems to have been marginalized early, and was incorporated already in PIE into the paradigm of **to-*, for which it formed the nominative masculine and feminine. We can thus reconstruct a pronoun with the nominatives **so* (masc.), *seh_2* (fem.), **tod* (neut.), becoming Ved. *sá sā́ tád*, Av. *hō hā tat̰*, Gk. *ho hē tó*, Goth. *sa so þata*, and Toch. B *se sā te*. Another stem **ei-* 'this' is reflected for example in Skt. *ay-ám* (masc.) *id-ám* (neut.); Av. *īm* (accus.) 'him'; Lat. *is ea id* 'this; he, she, it'; and Goth. *is* 'he'. A stem **k̑i-* 'this' is reflected principally in Balto-Slavic and Germanic (as in OCS *sĭ* 'this', Lith. *šìs* 'this', and Eng. *he*, and OHG *hiu-tagu* 'on this day, today' [> modern German *heute*]), and vestigially in such forms as Lat. *cis* 'on this side of'. Another pronominal stem, **eno-* or **ono-*, probably extensions of a stem **e-*, is found in Hitt. *ēni-* 'that one' and OCS *onŭ* 'that'.

Relative pronoun

7.11. Securely reconstructible is a relative pronominal stem **i̯o-* (or **Hi̯o-*; the presence of the laryngeal is disputed, and depends on one's interpretation of the initial *h-* of Greek *hó-*, cp. §12.22): Ved. *yá-*, Av. *ya-*, Gk. *hó-*, and Celtic **yo-* (in Gaulish *dugiionti-io* 'who serve'). Other branches have marshalled the indefinite/interrogative stem *k^wo-* (next section) into service as the relative pronoun.

Interrogative/indefinite pronoun

7.12. A stem *k^wo-* is widely attested, functioning both as an interrogative ('who, what?') and as an indefinite ('someone, something'): Ved. *kás* and Av. *kō* 'who?', Gk. adverbial interrogatives and indefinites in *po-* (e.g. *poũ* 'where?', *pōs* 'somehow'),

Goth. *ƕas* 'who?', OCS *kŭ-to* 'who?', and Lith. *kàs* 'who?'. The *i*-stem variant *k^wi-* is reflected in Hitt. and Luv. *kuiš* 'who?', Gk. *tís* 'who?', Lat. *quis* 'who?', OIr. *cia* 'who?', OE *hwī* 'how, why?', and OCS *čĭ-to* 'what?'. In the meaning 'anyone' or as an indefinite relative 'whoever' it is often doubled, as in Hitt. *kuiš kuiš*, Lat. *quisquis*, and Oscan *pitpit* 'whatever'. In several branches (Anatolian, Italic, Germanic, and Balto-Slavic), this stem is used for the relative pronoun, as in Eng. *which*.

Reflexive pronoun

7.13. A reflexive pronoun **su̯e-* (also **se-*) meaning '(one)self' has descendants in numerous branches: Ved. *sva-yám*, Av. *x^vāi* (dat.), Gk. (Pamphylian) *whe* (Classical Gk. *hé*), Lat. (accus.) *sē*, OIr. *fa(-dessin)*, and OCS (accus.) *sę*. It did not have a nominative case, did not distinguish number, and could be used with any of the three persons. The stem also formed the basis for the reflexive adjective **su̯o-* meaning '(one's) own', reflected in Ved. *svá-*, Gk. *heós*, Lat. *suus*, and OCS *svojĭ*. The syntax of the reflexive pronoun and adjective will be discussed in §8.18.

Pronominal adjectives

7.14. The best-attested pronominal adjective is **al-i̯o-* 'other' in Gk. *állos*, Lat. *alius*, Goth. *aljis*, OIr. *ail*, and Toch. B *alyek*.

Numerals

7.15. Numerals are technically adjectives or quantifiers, but morphologically they stand somewhat apart from other adjectives. The cardinal numerals were indeclinable except for 1–4, which not only declined but also distinguished gender.

7.16. No single form for the number 'one' can be reconstructed; there were at least two roots for the concept. The most widely represented is **oi-*, variously suffixed, especially as **oi-no-* (Lat. *ūnus*, OIr. *óen*, Goth. *ains* [Eng. *one*], OCS *inŭ* 'a certain one', and cp. Gk. *oinós* 'roll of one in dice'); **oi-ko-* and **oi-u̯o-* are also found (e.g. Ved. *éka-*, Av. *aēuua-*). The other root was **sem-*, the base of Gk. *heĩs* (**sem-s*), feminine *mía* (**sm-ih_2*), Arm. *mi*, and Toch. A *sas*, B *ṣe*. This root fundamentally expressed identity; it is the root of Eng. *same* and Lat. *similis* 'similar, like'.

7.17. A representative sampling of the cardinal numbers 2–10, 20, and 100 is given below. Blank spaces indicate that the relevant forms are not useful for reconstruction.

	Gk.	Ved.	Av.	Lat.	Welsh	Goth.	Arm.	Toch. A	OCS	Lith.
2	*dúō*	*dvā́(u)*	*duua*	*duo*	*dau*	*twai*	*erkow*	*wu*	*dŭva*	*dù*
3	*treĩs*	*tráyas*	*θrāiiō*	*trēs*	*tri*	*þreis*	*erekʿ*	*tre*	*trije*	*trỹs*
4	*téttares*	*catvā́ras*	*caθuuārō*	*quattuor*	*pedwar*	*fidwor*	*čorkʿ*	*śtwar*	*četyre*	*keturì*
5	*pénte*	*páñca*	*panca*	*quīnque*	*pump*	*fimf*	*hing*	*päñ*	*pętĭ*	*penkì*
6	*héks*	*ṣáṭ*	*xšuuaš*	*sex*	*chwech*	*saihs*	*vecʿ*	*ṣäk*	*šestĭ*	*šešì*

	Gk.	Ved.	Av.	Lat.	Welsh	Goth.	Arm.	Toch. A	OCS	Lith.
7	*heptá*	*saptá*	*hapta*	*septem*	*saith*	*sibun*	*ewtʿn*	*ṣpät*	*sedmĭ*	*septynì*
8	*oktṓ*	*aṣṭā́(u)*	*ašta*	*octō*	*wyth*	*ahtau*	*owtʿ*	*okät*	*osmĭ*	*aštuonì*
9	*enné(w)a*	*náva*	*nauua*	*nouem*	*naw*	*niun*	*inn*	*ñu*	*devętĭ*	*devynì*
10	*déka*	*dáśa*	*dasa*	*decem*	*deg*	*taihun*	*tasn*	*śäk*	*desętĭ*	*dẽšimt*
20	*wíkati*[1]	*viṁśatí-*	*vīsaiti*	*uīgintī*	*ugein(t)*[2]		*kʿsan*	*wiki*		
100	*hekatón*	*śatám*	*satəm*	*centum*	*cant*	*hund*		*känt*	*sŭto*	*šim̃tas*

[1] Doric. [2] Middle Welsh.

Based on these and some other data, we can reconstruct for the numerals 2–10 **d(u)u̯óh*$_1$, **tréi̯es*, **k*^{w}*étu̯ores*, **pénk*^{w}*e*, **su̯ék̂s*, **septḿ̥*, **ok̂tō(u)*, **néu̯n̥*, and **dék̂m̥*; for 20 **u̯īk̂m̥tī* (see below), and for 100 **k̂m̥tóm*. It is widely thought that the words for 20 and 100 are derivatives of the word for 10. Under this view, **u̯īk̂m̥tī* is a simplification of a dual **du̯ih*$_1$*-dk̂m̥t-ih*$_1$ 'two tens', and **k̂m̥tóm* is simplified from an earlier **dk̂m̥tóm*. Strictly speaking, the comparative evidence only supports a reconstruction **u̯īk̂n̥tī*, but most handbooks give **u̯īk̂m̥tī* because of the above analysis.

The numeral systems of the Anatolian languages are unfortunately almost entirely unknown. As clear descendants of PIE numerals we only have Hieroglyphic Luvian *tuwi-* 'two' and Hitt. *teriyaš* 'three' (genit. pl.), and maybe **šiptam-* 'seven' in Hitt. *šiptamiya-*, the name of a drink (perhaps containing seven ingredients; cp. Eng. *punch*, from Hindi *pañj* 'five').

As discussed in §6.71, the numerals '3' and '4' had special forms for the feminine with a suffix **-sr-*, as in Ved. *tisrás* '3' and *cátasras* '4'.

Numerals in composition

7.18. When combined with other words as prefixes, typically to form bahuvrihis (like *three-toed* in English), special forms of the numerals are sometimes found. The most securely reconstructible are: **du̯i-* 'two-' (as in Ved. *dvi-pád-* 'two-footed', Gk. *dí-pod-* 'two-footed', Archaic Lat. *dui-dent-* [Classical *bi-dent-*] '[sacrificial animal] having two teeth'); **tri-* 'three-' (as in Ved. *tri-pád-* 'three-footed', Gk. *trí-pod-* 'three-footed [table]', Lat. *tri-ped-* 'three-footed', Gaulish *tri-garanus* 'having three cranes'); and **k*^{w}*(e)tru-* or **k*^{w}*etu̯r̥-* 'four-' (as in Ved. *cátuṣ-pad-* 'four-footed', Av. *caθru-gaoša-* 'four-eared', Gk. *tetrá-pod-* 'four-footed', and Lat. *quadru-ped-* 'four-footed'). The zero-grade of **sem-* 'one', **sm̥-*, is found as a prefix meaning 'one-, as one, together, same': Ved. *sa-kŕ̥t* 'once', Gk. *há-ploos* 'one-fold, simple', *a-delphós* 'brother' (probably < **sm̥-g*^{w}*elbh-o-* '[the brother] having one [= the same] womb, uterine brother'), and Lat. *sim-plex* 'one-fold'.

Ordinal numerals

7.19. The ordinal numerals cannot be reconstructed with precision because of the great variety of formations exhibited by the daughter languages.

The ordinal 'first' was formed from a base **pr̥h*$_3$*-*, the zero-grade of a root **perh*$_2$*-* that is found in various adverbs and prepositions meaning 'forth, forward, front'; it is related to *_prŏ_ 'forth' (see §7.26 below). Widely represented are extensions of a stem *_pr̥h_2-u̯o-_ (as in Ved. _pū́rva-_ 'the first [of two]' and OCS _prĭvŭ_) and a stem *_pr̥h_2-mo-_ (e.g. Goth. _fruma_, Lith. _pìrmas_; compare also Lat. _prīmus_ from *_prīs-mo-_). Eng. _first_ is from *_pr̥h_2-isto-_.

No form for 'second' can be reconstructed. PIE may not have used a derivative of 'two', given that the daughters typically use unrelated expressions, such as ones historically meaning 'the other' (e.g. OIr. _ail_) or 'the following' (e.g. Lat. _secundus_).

7.20. The ordinals from 'third' through 'sixth' were probably formed with the suffixes *_-t-_ or *_-to-_: *_tr̥-t-_ or *_tri-t-_ 'third' (as in Ved. _tr̥tī́ya-_, Gk. _trítos_, and Lat. _tertius_); *_kʷetu̯r̥-t-_ or similar for 'fourth' (as in Gk. _tétartos_, OE _feorþa_, and OCS _četvrĭtŭ_); *_penkʷ-to-_ 'fifth' (as in Gk. _pémptos_ and Av. _puxδa-_); and *_su̯ek̂(s)-to-_ 'sixth' (as in Gk. _héktos_ and Lat. _sextus_).

7.21. The ordinals 'seventh' through 'tenth' were, it seems, originally created simply by suffixing the thematic vowel *_-o-_ to the cardinal. This is most clearly seen in 'eighth', which was *_ok̂tōu̯-o-_ or similar (as in Gk. _ógdo(w)os_ and Lat. _octāuus_). In the case of 'seventh' and 'tenth', the cardinals ended in syllabic *_-m̥_, and the combination *_-m̥-o-_ was realized as *_-m̥mo-_ phonetically: *_septm̥mo-_ (as in Gk. _hébdomos_, Lat. _septimus_, and OCS _sedmŭ_) and *_dek̂m̥mo-_ (as in Ved. _daśamá-_, Av. _dasəma-_, and Lat. _decimus_). Similarly, 'ninth' was *_neu̯n̥-o-_ originally, realized phonetically as *_neu̯n̥no-_, a form only preserved in Latin (_nōnus_, from *_nou̯enos_).

The forms *_septm̥mo-_ and *_dek̂m̥mo-_ were early on reanalyzed as *_septm̥-mo-_ and *_dek̂m̥-mo-_, and the apparent suffix *_-mo-_ that they seemed to contain then spread to neighboring ordinals in some branches, as in Ved. _aṣṭamá-_ and OCS _osmŭ_ 'eighth'. But in some branches it was the suffix *_-to-_ that spread in this way, as in Toch. A _ṣäptänt_ 'seventh', Lith. _deviñtas_ 'ninth', and Eng. _tithe_ 'a tenth part' (_tenth_ is a more recent creation).

7.22. Some of the suffixes used for the ordinals, especially *_-mo-_ and *_-to-_ (and *_-isto-_ in the Germanic words for 'first'), are identical to superlative suffixes. This overlap is seen in some of the higher numerals too, as in Vedic _śata-tamá-_ '100th', using the same suffix _-tama-_ as is used for superlatives. See also §6.77.

Adverbs

7.23. To judge by the evidence of the oldest daughter languages, PIE did not possess suffixes whose sole purpose was to change an adjective into an adverb (like Eng. _-ly_); rather, it used case-forms of nouns and adjectives in adverbial function. This method of forming adverbs is widely productive in all the daughter languages; since most such adverbs are relatively recent creations, few if any are of PIE date. One likely candidate is the neuter nominative-accusative singular of the adjective for 'great' used to mean 'greatly', *_meĝh_2_ (Hitt. _mēk_, Ved. _máhi_, Gk. _méga_, ON _mjǫk_). Adverbs formed from other case-forms can be exemplified by Lat. _rursus_ 'back(wards)' (nominative), _meritō_ 'deservedly' (ablative), and _quī_ 'how' (old instrumental).

7.24. Multiplicative adverbs for 'twice' and 'thrice' are securely reconstructible as *_du̯is_ and *_tris_: Ved. _dvís, trís_, Av. _biš θriš_, Gr. _dís trís_, Lat. _bis ter_ (< earlier _terr_ < *_ters_ < *_tris_).

Negation

7.25. The two nasals *n-* and *m-* begin certain adverbs expressing negation in the daughter languages. We can reconstruct a sentence negator **ne* 'not', reflected most directly in Germanic (e.g. OE *ne*), Balto-Slavic (e.g. OCS *ne* and Lith. *nè*), Ved. *ná*, and Lat. *ne-* (as in *ne-fās* 'not right, wrong'). The zero-grade of this word was used as a prefix, **n̥-* 'un-' (Hitt. *am-miyant-* 'not grown, young', Skt. and Gk. *a(n)-*, Lat. *in-*, Eng. *un-*). This prefix is called the **privative prefix**. Another negator, probably **mē* (as in Ved. *mā́*, Gk. *mḗ*, and, with different initial consonant, Lat. *nē* and Hitt. *lē*), was used with unaugmented (injunctive) verb forms in negative commands.

But many of the negative morphemes in the daughter languages are of more recent vintage and come from words or expressions that were not originally negative in force. People have a tendency to add additional emphasis to negatives (as in Eng. *not at all*, *not a whit*), and often the emphatic addition becomes reinterpreted as the actual negative if the phrase becomes stereotyped. A classic example of this comes from French: in the modern language, verbs are negated with a preceding *ne* (historically the true negator, from Latin *nōn*) and a following *pas*. The latter comes from the Latin noun (accus.) *passum* 'step' and was originally used to strengthen the negative force of *ne* with verbs of motion: 'not a step' = 'not at all'. But at some point the phrase *ne . . . pas* lost its literal meaning and the word *pas* was felt to convey negativity all on its own, whence its use in phrases like *pas mal* 'not bad'.

The older IE languages have many examples of this development as well. Probably the most famous is Greek *ou* or *ouk(í)* 'not'. The late American Indo-Europeanist Warren Cowgill incisively etymologized this as coming from a pre-Greek phrase **ne oi̯u kʷid*, essentially 'not on your life, not ever': **ne*, the historically "real" negator + **oi̯u* (< PIE **h₂oi̯u*) 'life, age', used adverbially and added to strengthen the negative + **kʷid*, an indefinite or generalizing particle. Ultimately the negative **ne* lost its salience and was dropped, and **oi̯u kʷid* became **oi̯ukid* (by the *boukólos* rule, §3.39), whence (by regular sound changes) *oukí* and the shorter forms *ouk* and *ou*.

Prepositions and Postpositions

7.26. A good number of words in PIE can be reconstructed that had both adverbial and postpositional function. As postpositions they followed their object, rather than preceding it as prepositions do; but in most of the daughter branches these postpositions eventually became prepositions. Only in Anatolian, Indo-Iranian, Sabellic, and vestigially in Latin and Greek is the old postpositional placement still seen. See further §8.8.

The following are some roots ancestral to many familiar prepositions; as always, descendant forms are given selectively. Unglossed descendant forms mean the same thing as the PIE form. Since prepositions usually develop idiomatic usages, the original sense of some of these roots is not certain.

*apo 'from': Ved. *ápa* 'away, forth', Gk. *apó* 'from', Lat. *ab* 'from', Eng. *of, off*
*en 'in': Gk. *en*, Lat. *in*, Arm. *i*, Welsh *yn*, Eng. *in*, OPruss. *en*, OCS *vŭ(n-)*
*en-ter 'within, inside' (derivative of *en): Ved. *antár* 'between', Lat. *inter* 'between, among', OIr. *eter* 'between', OHG *untar* 'between, among', Alb. *ndër* 'between, in'
*epi or *opi 'upon, by': Ved. *ápi* 'by, on', Gk. *epí* 'on', Lat. *ob* 'on, over against', Arm. *ew* 'and'
*kata or *km̥ta 'down': Hitt. *katta* 'with', Gk. *katá* 'down'
*kom 'with': Lat. *cum* 'with', OIr. *co* 'with', probably Gmc. prefix *ga- 'with'
*n̥dher, *n̥dhos 'under': Ved. *adhás*, Av. *aδairi*, Lat. *īnfr-ā*, Arm. *ənd*, Eng. *under*
*ni 'down, under': Ved. *ní*, Arm. *ni*; suffixed in Eng. *ne-ther*, OCS *ni-zŭ* 'down'
*per(i) 'around, through': Ved. *pári* 'around, forth', Gk. *perí* 'around', Lat. *per* 'through', OPruss. *per*, Alb. *për*
*prŏ̄ 'forth': Hitt. *parā*, Ved. *prá*, Gk. *pró*, Lat. *prō*, OIr. *ro-* (prefix and intensive particle), Goth. *fra-*, OPruss. *pra*, *pro* 'through'
*uper 'above': Ved. *upári*, Gk. *hupér*, Lat. *s-uper*, OIr. *for*, Arm. *(i) ver* 'up', Eng. *over*
*upo 'below': Ved. *úpa* 'up to', Gk. *hupó* 'below', Lat. *s-ub*, OIr. *fo*

Conjunctions and Interjections

7.27. Conjunctions tend not to be stable vocabulary items; new ones get created afresh out of other words. So, for example, English *and* developed out of an adverb or preposition cognate with Gk. *antí* '(over) against', and *but* out of a preposition or adverb meaning 'outside, except'. Similarly, we saw in the list above that the Armenian conjunction *ew* 'and' is derived from an adverb meaning 'upon' (*epi). A few conjunctions have been reconstructed for PIE, however, that are widely represented in the daughter languages. At least two of them were postpositive particles, being placed directly after the word (or first word of the phrase or clause) that was being conjoined or disjoined: the conjunctive particle *k^we 'and' (OHitt. *-ku*, Skt. and Av. *ca*, Gk. *te*, Lat. *-que*, Goth. *-h*) and the disjunctive particle *u̯ē 'or' (Skt. *vā*, Gk. *(w)ḗ*, Lat. *-ue*). (A well-known example of the postpositive usage is the opening of Vergil's *Aeneid* in Latin, *arma uirumque canō*, 'Arms and the man I sing'.) An adversative conjunction *h_2(e)u*, probably 'but, however', is found in Ved. *u*, Gk. *aũ*, and Lat. *au(-tem)*. For conjunctions introducing embedded (subordinate) clauses, the languages (and surely PIE itself) seem to have resorted to case-forms of various pronouns. Thus from the relative/interrogative stem *k^wo- we have a neuter accusative in Hitt. *kuit* 'because' and Lat. *quod* 'because', and a masculine accusative in Archaic Lat. *quom* 'when, since' (Classical *cum*).

The particle *k^we was also used as a generalizing particle, as evidenced by e.g. Ved. *yát kác ca* 'whatsoever' (relative and interrogative pronoun combined with *ca*), Lat. *quisque* 'each, every' (vs. *quis* 'who?'), and Goth. *ƕazuh* (< *k^wos-u-k^we) 'every' (vs. *ƕas* 'who?').

7.28. The languages also possess a variety of sentence-connecting particles, often translatable as 'and', two of which can be confidently reconstructed for PIE: *nu (preserved in Hittite and Tocharian B *nu*, in Vedic and Greek *nú*, and as *no-* in Old Irish and *nŭ* in Old Church Slavonic) and postpositive **de* (Gk. *dé*).

Particles

7.29. A number of unstressed words in the daughter languages used as sentence particles seem to be related to each other, although their functions – both in the daughter languages and in PIE – are often difficult to ascertain. A form **kem* or **km̥* is found in Hitt. *-kan*, Gk. *ke(n)*, and Ved. *kám*; it was perhaps a modal particle. An emphasizing particle **tar* is found in Luv. *-tar* and Homeric Gk. *tar* (usually written incorrectly as *t' ár* in editions of Homer); it appears to have been especially used with interrogatives (Luv. *kuiš-tar* = Homeric Gk. *tís tar* 'who [indeed]?'). Another emphasizing particle **ge* appears frequently after personal pronouns in Greek, as in *egṓge* 'I (for one), as for myself, I . . .', accusative *emége*, and may be the source of the velars found in the accusative of the first and second singular pronouns in certain languages: Hitt. *ammuk*, *tuk* 'me, thee', Gmc. **mik*, **þik* (becoming e.g. German *mich*, *dich*). Another particle **ghe* or **gho* is found in Ved. *(g)ha*, *ghā*, and OCS *že*. Lithuanian *ar̃*, a particle used when asking questions, and the Greek particle *ára* or *rhá*, may be related to each other. Finally, mention may be made of an emphatic particle **k̂e* (related to the pronominal stem **k̂i-*, §7.10): Hitt. *ki-nun* 'now', with the same elements reversed in Latin *nun-c* 'now'; Lat. *hī-c* 'this'; and Gk. *ekeĩnos* 'that' (**e-k̂e-eno-*; compare **k̂e-eno-* in the ON pronominal stem *hán-* 'he').

Interjections

7.30. It is perhaps indicative of some of the less pleasant aspects of life in the older IE societies that the one PIE interjection we can confidently reconstruct is an expression of woe or agony, **u̯ai*, preserved in Old Hitt. *uwai*, Lat. *uae*, Welsh *gwae*, Goth. *wai*, Eng. *woe*, Latv. *vai*, and, with further suffix for additional pathos, Av. *vaii-ōi*.

Many IE languages have a form like Eng. *oh!*, for which an ancestor **ō!* has been proposed. The laryngealistic rewriting of this as **eh₃!* requires no comment.

For Further Reading

Few book-length treatments of the words covered in this chapter exist except for the personal pronouns and the numerals. The reconstruction of the personal pronouns has been the subject of a fine recent dissertation, Katz 1998, which advances a host of new ideas. An earlier book-length study is Schmidt 1978. For the numerals, one should consult Gvozdanović 1992, which is a sundry collection of articles by different scholars on the numeral systems of each branch; the articles are not all of the same quality, but some are very valuable. A single-authored book-length treatment of issues pertaining to IE numerals is Szemerényi 1960, which should be treated with caution but has much interesting material. Warren Cowgill's etymology of Greek *ou* is in Cowgill 1960.

Exercises

1 What are the differences between the nominal and pronominal declensions?

2 Identify the following pronominal forms or stems. Be as specific as possible.

a	**so *seh$_2$ *tod*	**f**	**nos*	**k**	**moi*
b	**me-*	**g**	**ḱi-*	**l**	**n̥s-*
c	**(H)i̯o-*	**h**	**i̯u-*	**m**	**k^{w}o-*
d	**u̯os*	**i**	**ei-*	**n**	**u̯ei*
e	**su̯e-*	**j**	**te*	**o**	**tu-*

3 Provide the PIE reconstructions for the following pronominal forms or stems:

a 'other'
b 'I'
c 2nd person sing. dat. enclitic pronoun
d 1st person sing. genit. (not enclitic)
e 1st person sing. accus. enclitic pronoun

4 Discuss the etymological difference(s) between Ved. *eká-*, Greek *heĩs,* and Eng. *one.*

5 Provide the PIE reconstructions for the following numerals:

a	six	**c**	three	**e**	nine	**g**	hundred
b	ten	**d**	twenty	**f**	four	**h**	five

6 What do the prefixal forms **tri-*, **sm̥-*, **n̥-*, and **h$_1$su-* 'good' (§6.86) have in common?

7 Provide the PIE reconstructions for the following forms:

a	in	**c**	not	**e**	and	**g**	below
b	or	**d**	thrice	**f**	forth	**h**	greatly

8 Describe the formation of adverbs in PIE.

9 Comment on the Latin forms *quisquis* and *quisque* and their congeners from elsewhere in the IE family.

10 Describe Warren Cowgill's etymology of Greek *ou* 'not'.

8 Proto-Indo-European Syntax

Introduction

8.1. *Syntax* is the set of rules and principles for the combination of words into larger units – phrases, clauses, and sentences. The term also refers to the branch of linguistics that is concerned with syntactic systems as objects of study. In the comparative historical linguistics of the IE languages, we enter the field of *diachronic syntax*, the study of how syntactic systems change over time. This field and the allied enterprise of syntactic reconstruction raise certain methodological and practical issues that do not arise in diachronic phonology and morphology. We will briefly outline these issues here and then discuss them further below in §§8.12ff.

Morphemes and words are memorized and entered into the mental lexicon during language acquisition, but phrases, clauses, and sentences are not (except for fixed idioms). In the course of ordinary conversation, sentences are produced that have never been uttered before; clearly, a memorized body of sentences, no matter how extensive, would be of little use on its own in producing novel ones. This is how we know that there is a separate syntactic component of the grammar that encodes the procedures for generating phrases, clauses, and so forth. The rules constituting the syntax are deduced from the sentences that are heard during language acquisition in childhood.

8.2. Most contemporary syntactic theories are either wholly or partly the product of several decades of research spearheaded since the 1950s by Noam Chomsky, and constitute the field known as *generative grammar* or *generative syntax*. Though diverging from each other in many respects, all generative syntactic theories assume that the production of sentences is not done simply by stringing words together. First of all, sentence structure is not flat; rather, sentences are hierarchically organized into discrete units called *constituents* that have a particular internal structure and combine with one another in particular ways. In the sentence *The ugly duckling swam with the swans*, the noun phrase *the swans* is a constituent that is part of a larger constituent, the prepositional phrase *with the swans*, which in turn is part of the verb phrase (predicate) *swam with the swans*, which, finally, is combined with the subject noun phrase, *the ugly duckling*, to form a complete sentence.

8.3. According to linguistic theory, generating a sentence proceeds in several stages; in simplified terms, they are as follows. First, the sentence's constituents and subconstituents are arranged in a basic, *underlying* order; this order constitutes the sentence's *deep structure*. The underlying order may then be modified by the application of *movement* rules acting upon particular elements of the sentence. After these modifications, the relevant phonological and morphological rules are applied, with the final result being the *surface structure*, i.e., what is actually uttered.

Syntacticians try to deduce deep structures and the syntactic rules that act upon them by analyzing surface structures and gathering judgments from native speakers on the grammaticality of particular sentences. Since no native speakers of dead languages are around anymore, the whole enterprise of syntactic analysis of the older IE languages might appear to be doomed from the start. To be sure, the absence of native speakers will always impose certain limits on our knowledge; but that is no reason not to try to figure out as much as we can about the underlying machinery of those languages, utilizing what we know from the syntax of languages alive today. It so happens that many of the preserved texts are long and plentiful enough to allow quite a bit of solid theoretical syntactic analysis, and our analytical methods for doing this are only improving.

8.4. Textual genre is often raised as a problematic issue in these analyses. Many of the oldest preserved Indo-European literatures, such as the Rig Veda, are works of art whose style and mode of expression can be phenomenally inventive, both lexically and grammatically. However, this problem is sometimes overstated; it is incorrect to suppose – as many have – that poetic texts leave grammar by the wayside, and that poets were able to take "licenses" willy-nilly. The language of poetry is just as strictly rule-governed as ordinary speech: though certain constructions only occur in poetry (leading some scholars to speak of a *poetic grammar*), they are still possibilities afforded by the grammar of the language.

Some texts, especially the Gothic Bible and many Classical Armenian works, are translations that adhere closely to the word order and grammatical constructions of the original language. It is important when analyzing these texts not to make generalizations based on passages that are simply slavish imitations of another language. But since the match in word orders or grammatical constructions is never absolutely exact, and the differences can reflect particular syntactic features in the language of the translation, such texts are still of value in IE syntactic studies.

8.5. Only a few refined and theoretically sophisticated analyses of the syntax of older IE languages are available at present. This fact, coupled with our still limited (but growing) understanding of how syntax changes, prevents us from reconstructing PIE syntax in the same way that we can reconstruct PIE phonology and morphology. However, various syntactic patterns have long been known to be common to most or all the older IE languages, and were likely characteristic of PIE too; some of these will be outlined and exemplified below. Although much of nineteenth- and early twertieth-century syntactic studies of the IE languages focused on analyzing and cataloguing the functions of grammatical categories, such as the cases and moods, some figures of that time, especially Jacob Wackernagel and Berthold Delbrück, also made important discoveries concerning the behavior of constituents and word order. Though not formulated in the same terms as nowadays, their discoveries, such as Wackernagel's Law (§§8.22ff. below), have been extremely influential.

We will now proceed to survey more specific features usually thought to be part of the PIE syntactic system. Some abbreviations of textual references are not explained here, but can be found in the relevant later chapters.

Syntax of the Phrase

Noun phrases

8.6. Adjectival modifiers of nouns had to agree with their nouns in gender, number, and case. The languages differ as to whether modifiers usually precede or follow their nouns, and the order was surely flexible in PIE also; discourse and pragmatic factors dictated the relative ordering of words. Adjectives typically precede their nouns in Hittite, Vedic, and Germanic, and follow their nouns in Italic and Celtic; but in all these languages there are exceptions. In Celtic and Italic, for example, certain adjectives precede their nouns, while in Hittite, Vedic, and Italic, any noun can precede a modifier when one or the other element was being emphasized.

8.7. Common to all the older languages (and still found in modern Slavic) was the ability of nouns and their modifiers to be separated by intervening elements, yielding what are called discontinuous or distracted noun phrases (a construction called *hyperbaton* in Greek and Latin grammar): Cuneiform Luv. *alati awienta Wilušati* 'they came from steep Wilusa' (KBo 4.11:46), Gk. *ándra moi énnepe Moũsa polútropon* 'tell me, Muse, of the resourceful man' (*Odyssey* 1.1), Lat. *magnā cum laude* 'with great praise', Arm. *zyoys hatanem kenacʿ* 'I cut off the hope of life', Old Irish *Márta for slúaig saithiu* 'on the swarm of the host of March' (*Félire Oengusso*, March 31). Distraction of other types of phrases was common as well. The technical details of distraction are not well understood; in some cases, it is the result of part of a phrase being moved to a position of emphasis or contrast. Other cases are of a different nature; we will discuss one below in §8.10.

Prepositional and postpositional phrases

8.8. The elements traditionally classified as prepositions were most likely simply independent adverbs in PIE, a status they still largely have in Anatolian, Indo-Iranian, and the oldest Greek. From the comparative evidence it is not entirely clear whether these forms were prepositions, or rather occurred after their objects as postpositions; probably both patterns were current, though many researchers assume postpositional usage to be older. Anatolian and Vedic have almost exclusively postpositions and not prepositions, as in Hitt. *šuḫḫi šēr* 'on the roof' and Ved. *jánām̐ ánu* 'among men'. Avestan and Sabellic have a mixture of prepositions and postpositions. In the other older IE languages, prepositions are the rule, although some (e.g. Old Persian, Greek, and Latin) evince limited postpositional use, like Gk. *toútōn péri* 'about these things' and Lat. *mēcum* 'with me'. Similar mixed prepositional and postpositional use, with prepositions predominating, is familiar from many modern languages, including English and German.

Preverbs

8.9. Such adverbs, when used to modify the content of verbs, are called *preverbs*. In PIE, preverbs were still independent words, as reflected in Anatolian and older Indo-Iranian. In the examples below, the preverbs and verbs are underlined. (In the Hittite examples in this chapter, an equals sign is a modern orthographic convention for separating enclitic particles from preceding material. The other spelling conventions for transliterating Hittite, such as the use of capitalization, will be introduced in the next chapter and may be ignored for our present purposes.)

Old Hittite	*š=aš šarā* URU-*ya pait*[1] "and he went up to the city"
Vedic	*abhí yó mahinā́ dívaṃ mitró babhū́va saprátháḥ*[2] "Mitra the renowned who is superior to heaven by his greatness"
Old Avestan	*frō mā sāstū vahištā*[3] "let him teach me the best things"

[1] KBo 22.2 rev. B 17′ (Zalpa tale). [2] Rig Veda 3.59.7. [3] Yasna 45.6.

In the other branches, the preverbs became genuine prefixes attached to the verb. But archaic texts in Greek, Latin, and Old Irish show remnants of the older situation: Gk. *edētúos eks éron hénto* 'they put aside desire for food" (*Iliad* 1.469 and elsewhere), Archaic Lat. *ob uōs sacrō* "I entreat you" (Festus 206 L.; would be *uōs obsecrō* in Classical Latin), and perhaps OIr. *ad- cruth caín cichither* "fair form will be seen" (*Serglige Con Culainn* 694; but see §14.50a). Old Irish and Gothic allow certain clitics to intervene between preverb and verb, although the whole complex forms a single phonological word (the clitics are boldfaced in the following examples): OIr. *at**dom**-indnastar* 'that **I** be brought' (Milan glosses 39[d] 13), Goth. *frah ina ga-**u**-**ƕa**-sehvi* 'He asked him **if** he saw **anything**' (Mark 8:23). The so-called separable prefixes in Modern German and Dutch are either a direct continuation of the PIE situation, or comparable to it: German *auf-tragen* 'to assign', *er trägt auf* 'he assigns' = Dutch *op-dragen*, *hij draagt op*.

In languages where the preverb and the verb usually form a single word, such as Classical Greek, the separation of the two is called **tmesis**, literally 'a cutting'. The term is misleading; it arose from a traditional bias toward Classical Greek, which has been viewed as a standard from which Homeric Greek is "deviant," when in fact the classical language's loss of tmesis is what departs from the inherited situation.

8.10. Tmesis is a subtype of the general phenomenon of distraction discussed in §8.7, and examples of it can provide clear documentation of how not all instances of distraction are syntactically equal, except superficially. In the Avestan clause *apa vā yasāiti* 'or takes (it) away' (Yasna 11.5), the preverb *apa* 'away' is separated from its verb *yasāiti* 'takes' only because the clitic conjunction *vā* 'or' phonologically requires a single word to its left and therefore must intervene between the preverb and verb. (We will return to such clitics and their behavior in §8.22.) Syntactically quite distinct is a case like *pairi* *uši* *vāraiiaθβəm* 'cover (their) ears' (Yasht 1.27), where the preverb (*pairi*, literally 'around') has been fronted to the beginning of the clause for prominence or emphasis (by a process discussed in §8.19).

The vā́yav índraś ca *construction*

8.11. It was apparently a rule of PIE grammar that when two vocatives were conjoined, the one preceding the conjunction was put in the nominative rather than the vocative case. Almost all the examples of this come from Vedic, as in the phrase *vā́yav índraś ca* "o Indra and Vayu" after which the construction is named. In this example, the god Vāyu's name is in the vocative but Indra's is in the nominative, as it precedes the conjunction *ca* 'and'. The sole example outside Indo-Iranian is from an archaic passage in the *Iliad* (3.277): *Zeũ páter . . . Ēéliós te* 'Father Zeus (voc.) . . . and Helios (nomin.)'.

Syntax of the Clause

8.12. The reconstruction of the clausal syntax of PIE, for much of its recent history, has been concerned with establishing the **"basic word order"** of PIE and its daughters. This research program was born of linguistic typology, a field launched in the 1960s that has sought to determine universal patterns of linguistic structure. Most commonly the term "basic word order" has referred to the statistically most frequently observed word order in a given language (another sense of the term will be discussed further below). In the opinion of many scholars today, this approach (often called the typological approach) has led to an intellectual dead end. As a methodological preliminary, we devote some space here to a critique of it so that its mistakes can be learned from (not uncommonly, those same mistakes continue to be made).

First, word order is not equivalent to syntax, but is rather a byproduct of it. Word orders result from the application of syntactic rules, which arrange sentential elements into different functional positions. Pure statistical tallying up of word orders thus not only ignores actual syntax, but also ignores all the factors that intersect with syntax and cause different syntactic rules to apply under different discourse, pragmatic, and semantic conditions. In comparative linguistics, the typological approach has the additional problem of ignoring a fundamental aspect of the comparative method – namely, the identification of comparable structures in related languages on which to base reconstructions. In the domain of morphemes and words, that means cognate forms; in the domain of phrases and sentences, that means phrases and sentences that (broadly speaking) are used when talking about the same sorts of things in the same ways.

For example, both possible relative orders of verb and object (verb–object, object–verb) in the Homeric epics occur quite frequently. However, if one looks at a semantically restricted and well-defined sample, such as traditional sayings or proverbs, there is much more rigidity: the object almost always precedes the verb. The syntax of proverbs in Homer can then be compared with the syntax of proverbs in Vedic Sanskrit and other related languages, and it turns out that these sorts of sentences agree remarkably closely in their syntax across the older IE languages. Proverbs are a repository of traditional language, and often contain constructions that are rare elsewhere; and it is just those kinds of exceptional cases that are most valuable for the comparative method and for syntactic reconstruction (as we discussed in §4.1 with respect to morphology). In English, one syntactic fossil like *till death do us part* tells us more about the history of English syntax than a thousand sentences of newspaper prose.

8.13. A more modern definition of the term "basic word order" is a single underlying order in the deep structure from which all surface word orders in a language can be derived. According to many mainstream syntactic theories, the statistically most frequent surface word order is not necessarily the same as the basic underlying order. Word orders that are marked (that is, those that encode additional semantic content such as expressive contrast or the like) are derived by manipulation of basic word orders through syntactic movement; but, depending on the language (and the syntactician), unmarked orders may also differ from underlying orders. A refined analysis of texts in the daughter languages should be able to distinguish pragmatically neutral orders from those that are marked, and allow us to come up with syntactic movement rules that can then be compared with rules in other daughter languages. The existence of syntactic rules for the same semantic or pragmatic purpose (as for example the fronting of a verb to the beginning of a sentence for emphasis or contrast, discussed below in §8.19) in most or all the daughter languages could then be evidence for such a rule in PIE itself.

8.14. It is almost universally asserted that most of the ancient IE languages were verb-final, and that PIE was as well; more specifically, that they were SOV (Subject–Object–Verb). This assertion is made on the basis of sentences such as the following (the verbs are underlined):

Hittite — *nu=za* ^{MUŠ}*illuyankaš* ^{D}IM-*an* *taraḫta*[1]
"And the serpent overcame the Stormgod."

Vedic — *maruto ha enam na ajahuḥ*[2]
"Indeed the Maruts did not abandon him."

Latin — *Eumolpus tanquam litterārum stūdiōsus utīque ātrāmentum habet*[3]
"Eumolpus, so interested in learning, surely has (some) ink."

Runic — *ek hlewagastiz holtijaz horna tawido*[4]
"I, Hlewagastiz of Holt, made (this) horn."

Tocharian A — *kāsu ñom-klyu tsraṣiśśi śäk kälymentwaṃ sätkatär*[5]
"Good fame of the strong spreads out in ten directions."

[1] KBo 3.7 i 11 (Illuyanka myth, §3). [2] Aitareya-Brāhmaṇa 3.20. [3] Petronius, *Satyricon* 102. [4] Gallehus horn, normalized transliteration (see §15.39). [5] Puṇyavantajātaka 1 (see §17.32).

As a matter of fact, the claim that many or most of the older IE languages were verb-final has never been fully verified. Part of the problem with it is arriving at a clear definition of a verb-final language. In the strict sense, a verb-final language is one where the verb always comes at the end of each clause unless other factors intervene. The only well-known older PIE language that meets this criterion is Hittite. No matter what the genre, no matter how stylistically marked the text, the verb in Hittite is always clause-final, with one exception – when it is fronted to the beginning of the clause for emphasis or contrast (by the fronting rule that we will get to shortly). None of the other old IE languages behaves so rigidly (except for Insular Celtic, but that subbranch contains verb-*initial* languages; see §8.19); there is essentially no position in the clause (on the surface at least) where the verb cannot appear.

It is usually stated that in these languages, the pragmatically neutral order is SOV. This may, in fact, be true, at least of some of them (such as Latin); but with so many word-order permutations possible (and frequent), clearly they cannot be called "verb-final" in the same way as Hittite. There are any number of reasons, according to current theory, why a verb may or may not appear as the last word in its clause. Syntactic rules place the constituents of a clause in certain functional slots; superficially different linear positionings of a constituent can turn out, on closer examination, to be identical underlyingly, and vice versa.

The foregoing paragraphs, it must be repeated, do not represent the majority view, but are also not intended to claim that that view is wrong – just that it needs tighter formulation and convincing demonstration.

8.15. One usually thinks of clauses or sentences as containing a verb by definition, but in the older IE languages, many of their modern descendants, and doubtless in PIE itself, clauses could lack an overt verb. Chief among these are **nominal sentences**, in which the copula (the linking verb 'be') is understood but not overtly expressed: OHitt. *annaš=šiš* MUŠ-*aš* (KUB 1.16 ii 20) 'his mother (is) a snake' (recall §8.9 for the use of the equals sign), OPers. *manā pitā Vištāspa* 'my father (is) Vištāspa' (DSf 12–13), Gk. *emoì d' ákhos* 'and to me (there is) pain' (*Iliad* 5.759), Lat. *tū coniūnx* 'you (are) his wife' (Vergil, *Aeneid* 4.113), Toch. A *tsraṣiñ waste wrasaśśi* 'the strong (are) the protection of creatures' (Puṇyavantajātaka 2).

Subject–verb agreement

8.16. In clauses containing a verb, the subject (when expressed) had to agree with the verb in person and number. An apparent exception to this is the behavior of neuter plural subjects in Anatolian, Old Avestan, and Greek, which in these languages take singular verbs. In the following examples, the subjects are bold and the verbs are underlined: Hitt. ***apē=ya uddār*** (pl.) *QATAMMA* *lagāru* (sing.) "let also those words fall over likewise" (KUB 2.3 iii 21–22), Old Avestan ***yā*** (pl.) *zī vāuuərəzōi* (sing.) "the things which have been perpetrated" (Yasna 29.4), Greek ***hóssa te phúlla*** (pl.) ***kaì ánthea*** (pl.) *gígnetai* (sing.) *hṓrēi* "as many as the leaves and the flowers that appear in their season" (*Iliad* 2.468). But this phenomenon is likely due ultimately to the ancient status of the neuter plural as a collective; recall its history, discussed in §6.68.

8.17. Because the personal endings of verbs in the older IE languages encode the subject in them, it was not grammatically necessary to use an overt personal pronominal subject in addition. However, subject pronouns nonetheless occur; in the traditional grammars of these languages, overt subject pronouns are usually characterized as emphatic. (Terms like "emphasis" are rather blunt and can get overused, but they are a useful starting point on the way to more refined analyses.) When the Roman historian Sallust wrote *sīcutī ego accēpī* 'as I understand it' (*Bellum Catilinae* 6.1), the overt subject pronoun *ego* 'I' serves to contrast his own understanding with the opinion of others. While such contrast is certainly evident in many instances where a subject pronoun is expressed, it is not clear that overt subject pronouns are limited to contrastive or emphatic use, and it is often difficult or impossible to ascertain just why a writer used one. In nominal sentences, an overt pronominal subject is generally required for clarity, as in Old Persian *adam navama* 'I (am) the ninth' (DB 1.10).

8.18. The syntax of the reflexive possessive adjective **su̯o-* 'own' (§7.13) deserves a special note. Reflexive adjectives (and pronouns) refer back to the grammatical subject of a sentence. But the possessive **su̯o-* had broader usage, to judge by the daughter languages: it could refer back not to the grammatical subject, but to newly introduced discourse material or to an older topic that is returned to. As an example of the former, consider Rig Veda 8.2.7: *tráya índrasya sómāḥ sutā́saḥ santu devásya své kṣáye sutapā́vnaḥ* 'Let the three somas be pressed for the god Indra in the soma-drinker's **own** house' (translation following Brent Vine; soma was an intoxicating sacred drink). Here the grammatical subject is *tráya . . . sómāḥ* 'the three somas' and the possessive *své* refers to the soma-drinker, who is newly introduced. Similar behavior can be found in other older IE languages.

Basic movement processes

8.19. When a constituent or subconstituent appears in a position other than the usual one, syntacticians usually treat it as having been placed there by a movement rule. (Actually, many "usual" positionings of elements are also thought to arise by movement processes.) Typically, elements are moved leftward rather than rightward, by a process called **fronting**. The technical details do not concern us, but based on evidence from a variety of languages it is believed that the grammar provides a number of slots or "landing-sites" in the abstract syntactic representation of a sentence, which serve various functions and into which elements can be moved or to which elements can be adjoined. One such landing-site has been posited for the left edge of a sentence into which a constituent or subconstituent can be moved for emphasis or contrast; the process of fronting into this position is called **topicalization**. Some examples of clauses in which the verb has been topicalized follow (the emphasis or contrast does not always come across in translation):

Hittite *ḫalziššai=wa=tta* DINGIR^{MEŠ}*-aš attaš* ^{D}*Kumarbiš*[1]
"Kumarbi, the father of the gods, is calling you."

Old Av. *sraōtū sāsnā̊ fšə̄ŋ́hiiō suiiē taštō*[2]
"Let the bondsman (?), fashioned for benefit, hear the teachings."

Greek *ménei tò theĩon doulíāi per en phrení*[3]
"The divine (power), even when in bondage, stays in the mind."

Latin *fuimus Trōes, fuit Īlium*[4]
"We were (but no longer are) Trojans, Troy was (but no longer is)."

Armenian *erknēr erkin erknēr erkir*[5]
"In labor was heaven, in labor was earth."

[1] KUB 33.122 ii 11. [2] Yasna 49.9. [3] Aeschylus, *Agamemnon* 1084. [4] Vergil, *Aeneid* 2.325. [5] Movsēs Xorenacʿi 1.31 (see §16.46).

If verb-initial order generated in this way becomes stereotyped, it can be reanalyzed by learners as the neutral order; and in fact in Insular Celtic, VSO order became the norm for precisely this reason (the perhaps older verb-final order is still the rule in the Continental Celtic language Celtiberian). A similar reanalysis happened in Lycian; see §9.69. Certain verbs, especially existential verbs (e.g., 'there is') but also verbs of speaking and imperatives, preferentially occur clause-initially across all the IE languages: Skt. *āsīd rājā nalo nāma* 'there was a king named Nala' (*Mahābhārata* 3.53.1), Lat. *est in cōnspectū Tenedos nōtissima fāmā īnsula* 'within sight there is a most famous island, Tenedos' (Vergil, *Aeneid* 2.21–22), dialectal Old Russian *estĭ gradŭ mežu nobomŭ i zemleju* 'there is a city between heaven and earth' (Novgorod birch bark fragment 10.1).

Clause-initial position, as already noted, is a place of prominence not only for verbs, but for any constituent, as the following Hittite examples show: *irma=šmaš=kan dāḫḫun* "sickness I have taken away from you" (KBo 17.1 i 12′), *ammel=ma tarnumar ŪL pāi* "but my release he won't give" (KBo 32.15 iii 16), *šarā=kan namma eḫu* "come up again!" (KUB 33.84+ iv 11′). Topicalization was probably a syntactic process in PIE.

8.20. Another type of fronting that occurred in all known ancient IE daughter languages and is widely known from living languages too is **WH-movement**. This process has also been posited for the proto-language. WH-movement gets its name from the initial letters of English interrogatives such as *who*, *which*, *what*, which were shown in early generative syntactic work often to originate in deep structure in a later syntactic position than the one they occupy on the surface. Subsequent research has indicated that the syntactic slot to which interrogatives move (now called the *complementizer* position) can be occupied by other kinds of elements too, including relative pronouns and subordinating conjunctions. The complementizer position precedes the rest of the clausal positions proper, which is why in English and many other languages conjunctions such as *before*, *because*, *if*, *when*, and so forth appear first in their clause.

8.21. However, at least according to one analysis, in the older IE languages the complementizer position was preceded by the topicalization position; if the latter was filled by a topicalized element, the complementizer was no longer clause-initial. The following examples contain both a complementizer and a topicalized element; the topicalized element is underlined, the complementizer boldfaced:

Hittite *ammuqq=a* ***kuit*** *ḫarkun*[1]
"And also (that) **which** I had"

Vedic *jātám* ***yád*** *enam apáso ádhārayan*[2]
"**when** the craftsmen held him, just born"

Old Avestan *naēnaēstārō* ***yaθənā*** *vohunąm mahī*[3]
"**since** we are non-scorners of good things"

Latin *fēstō diē* ***sī*** *quid prodēgeris*[4]
"**if** you splurge a bit on a holiday"

[1] Apology of Hattusilis III, iv 69. [2] Rig Veda 3.2.7. [3] Yasna 35.2. [4] Plautus, *Aulularia* 380.

This marks a fundamental difference in syntactic behavior between the older IE languages and a language like English. In some languages, particularly Latin, syntactic movement can distribute numerous elements before the complementizer position, resulting sometimes in surface orders where all the words in a clause except one precede the complementizer (and, in some unusual poetic styles, where the complementizer even comes at the end of the clause). Whether this is due to the presence of multiple landing-sites in front of the complementizer position in this language, or to some other process, is not yet known. In the following conditional clauses from the Archaic Latin of Plautus, the subordinating conjunction *sī* 'if' can be preceded by some or all the other clausal constituents save the verb:

saluos domum ***sī*** *redierō* "**if** I shall have returned home safe"[1]
mē quoque ūnā ***sī*** *cum illō relinquerēs* "**if** you were to leave me together with him too"[2]
perfidia et peculātus ex urbe et auāritia ***sī*** *exulant* "**if** betrayal and embezzlement and greed are exiled from the city"[3]

[1] *Amphitruo* 584b. [2] *Captivi* 446. [3] *Persa* 555.

Wackernagel's Law and the placement of clitics

8.22. Perhaps the most famous feature of the clausal syntax of older IE languages is the positional behavior of *clitics*. As already mentioned a few times, these are unstressed words that cannot occur alone and must stand next to a stressed word (called the host; on chains of clitics see §8.25 below). Clitics include various conjunctions, unstressed pronouns, and a wide variety of particles having affective and logical functions that indicate, sometimes quite subtly, how thoughts relate to one another, the speaker's feelings about the content of what he or she is saying, and so forth. Some particles, such as Greek *gár* 'for' and Vedic *hí* 'for', have a lexical stress but behave syntactically like true clitics, and will be considered together with them in the following discussion.

It was observed by Jacob Wackernagel in the late nineteenth century that clitics have a tendency to appear second in their clause after the first stressed element. The phenomenon is called **Wackernagel's Law** in his honor. Observe the clitics (underlined) in the following sentences:

Hittite *kiēll=a parnaš ēšḫar papratar QATAMMA pattenuddu*[1]
"Of this house too may it likewise drive out the bloodshed (and) uncleanliness."

Vedic *ā́ tvā mántrāḥ kaviśastā́ vahantu*[2]
"Let the spells recited by the poets lead you hither."

Greek *ē̃mos d' ērigéneia phánē rhododáktulos Ēṓs*[3]
"but when early-born, rosy-fingered Dawn appeared"

Latin *tū autem in neruō iam iacēbis*[4]
"But you will soon be lying in custody."

Gothic *fram-uh þamma sokida Peilatus fraletan ina*[5]
"And at this Pilate sought to release him."

[1] KUB 7.41 ii 54–55. [2] Rig Veda 10.14.4. [3] *Iliad* 1.477 and passim. [4] Plautus, *Curculio* 718. [5] John 19:12.

Sometimes, however, one of these clitics appears as the third or fourth word in its clause. Recent research, especially by the American linguist Mark Hale, has shown that Wackernagel's Law actually involves several processes that usually, but not always, conspire to place unstressed particles in second position in the clause. His discoveries have explained the exceptions to a strict formulation of the law. A simplified account is presented here.

8.23. Three types of postpositive clitics (and clitic-positioning rules) can be distinguished. *Word-level clitics* modify or limit (or have scope over, in technical parlance) a single word or constituent, and are placed directly after the word or the first element of the constituent. Such clitics tend to have the function of emphasizing the word to which they are attached, or setting it in some kind of contrastive relief or focus (the clitic is boldfaced): Hitt. *nu=wa=za apun=**pat** eši* 'occupy **only** that (land)' (KUB 14.1 obv. 19), Ved. *pracyāváyanto ácyutā **cid*** 'the ones who move **even** unmovable things' (Rig Veda 1.85.4). If the word that such a particle modifies is first in its clause, then the particle appears (coincidentally) second in its clause: Ved. *sthirā́ **cid** ánnā dayate ví jámbhaiḥ* '**even** tough food he cuts apart with his teeth' (Rig Veda 4.7.10), Lat. *hoc **quoque** maleficium* 'this crime **too**' (Cicero, *Pro Roscio Amerino* 117). Such particles, when modifying a phrase, can often come second in the phrase, as in Gk. *én **ge** taĩs Thḗbais* 'in all of Thebes **indeed**' (Sophocles, *Oedipus Tyrannus* 1380). Some clitics, such as the descendants of PIE *$k^{w}e$ 'and', can act as word-level clitics as well as sentence connectors (see the next paragraph).

8.24. *Sentence-connective clitics* conjoin or disjoin clauses or sub-clausal constituents. Examples of these clitics are the various descendants of PIE *$k^{w}e$ 'and' and *u̯ē 'or' (see §7.27). They are attached to the first word of the constituent or clause being conjoined or disjoined, whether that is a single word (Ved. *ágna índraś **ca*** 'o Agni **and** Indra', Rig Veda 3.25.4), a phrase (Lat. *silua alta Iouis lūcus**ue** Diānae* 'the high forest of Jupiter **or** the grove of Diana', Vergil, *Aeneid* 3.681), or a clause

(Old Avestan *yā̊ zī āŋharə̄ yā̊scā həṇtī yā̊scā mazdā buuaiṇtī* 'indeed (those) who were **and** who are **and** who will be, o Mazda', Yasna 33.10).

8.25. Finally, *sentential clitics* are clitics whose scope is a whole clause or sentence. These include the unstressed personal pronouns as well as a variety of sentential adverbs that serve expressive functions and are often untranslatable into English. They are positioned in various ways. Some are placed after the first stressed word in a sentence and any emphatic or sentence-connective clitics associated with that word, while others (called "special clitics" in the technical literature) are positioned after a particular syntactic structural position in the clause. If the first word in a sentence is a proclitic, that is, an unstressed word that attaches phonologically to a following stressed word, the sentential clitic will of course not come directly after it, as in Gk. *eks hēméōn* ***gár*** *phāsi kák' émmenai* '**for** they say that bad things are from us' (*Odyssey* 1.33), where the proclitic *eks* 'from' is not a proper phonological host for the clitic *gár*. Sentential clitics occur not infrequently in strings or chains: Ved. *ná* ***vā́ u*** *etán mriyase* '**indeed** you do not die thereby' (Rig Veda 1.162.21), Gk. ***ẽ rhá nú moí ti*** *píthoio* 'may you **indeed now** trust **me somewhat**' (*Iliad* 4.93), Hitt. DUMU-*ŠU=ma=****wa=ššī=za=kan*** 'but his son **himself to him** . . .' (all the clitics after *-ma* 'but' are sentential; only *-ššī* 'to him' and *-za* 'himself' are translatable).

Subordinate clauses

Relative clauses

8.26. Relative clauses in numerous daughter languages share certain characteristics that are worth remarking on and are probably inherited. In the older IE languages, the relative clause often precedes the main clause (and the antecedent). The relative pronoun or adverb is often paired with a pronominal or adverbial antecedent, yielding what are called correlative structures of the type '(the one) who . . . , he . . .' or 'in the way which . . . , in that way . . .'. In the examples below, the relative clauses are underlined, and the relative pronoun and antecedent are boldfaced:

Vedic ***yéna*** *imā́ víśvā cyávanā kr̥tā́ni* . . . ***sá*** *janāsa índraḥ*[1]
"(The one) **by whom** all these things have been made to shake . . . **that**, people, (is) Indra."

Old Av. *at̰* ***yə̄ṇg*** *aṣ̌āat̰cā vōistā vaŋhə̄uščā dāθə̄ṇg manaŋhō ərəθβə̄ṇg mazdā ahurā* ***aēibiiō*** *pərənā āpanāiš kāməm xᵛā̊*[2]
"(Those) **whom** you know (to be) just in accordance with truth and with good thought (and) worthy, Ahura Mazda, fulfill **for them** (their) desire with profits." (tr. adapted from Humbach; see ch. 11)

Greek ***hós*** *ke theoĩs epipeíthētai, mála t' ékluon* ***autoĩ***[3]
"**Whoever** obeys the gods, they listen **to him** as well."

[1] Rig Veda 2.2.4. [2] Yasna 28.10. [3] *Iliad* 1.218.

Very characteristically, if the antecedent is a noun rather than a pronoun, it is placed within the relative clause and in the same case as the relative, sometimes repeated in the main clause. Thus instead of saying *The gods who gave us riches can take them away*, speakers of these languages would have said literally, *Which gods gave us riches, they/those gods can take them away*:

Hittite *nu=kan kāš* IM-*aš* ***kuēz** wappuwaz danza nu zik wappuaš* ᴰMAḪ *tuēl* ŠU-*TIKA dā*[1]
(lit.) "from **which** riverbank this clay (has been) taken, o genius of (that) riverbank, take (it) in your hand", i.e. "O genius of the riverbank from which this clay has been taken . . ."

Archaic Latin ***quem** agrum eōs uēndere herēdemque sequī licet, is ager uectīgal nei siet*[2]
"the field **which** (lit., which field) they are allowed to sell and pass to an heir, that field may not be taxable."

[1] Ritual of Tunnawi 1.30–32. [2] *Sententia Minuciorum*, CIL I² 584.5.

8.27. As can be seen from some of the examples so far quoted, the relative pronoun did not need to be the first member of its clause. In several of the ancient IE languages, the relative could be preceded at least by a topicalized element, just like the subordinating conjunctions discussed above. In Insular Celtic, the relative pronoun became fixed in second position of the clause, able to intervene between a preverb and following verb: Old Irish *ní latt aní ara-rethi* (Würzburg glosses 6ᵇ 22) "it is not yours that which you assail" (*ara-rethi* < Celtic **are-yo retesi*, where **-yo* is the relative pronoun). This happened prehistorically in Baltic as well: the inherited PIE relative pronominal stem **i̯o-* became attached to adjectives to make them definite (see next paragraph), and there are a few Old Lithuanian examples of participles beginning with preverbs where the relative pronoun occurs not at the end of the participle, but after the preverb, such as *nu-jam-lūdusam* 'saddened' (masc. dative sing. of the past active participle).

8.28. Independently in some daughter languages, the relative pronoun became reanalyzed as a marker of definiteness of an attributive adjective. Already in Old Avestan one comes across constructions that would have been an early stage in this development, such as *tāiš š́iiaoθanāiš yāiš vahištāiš* (Yasna 35.4) 'with the best works', lit. 'with the works which (are) best'. The relative pronoun *yāiš* has been attracted into the instrumental plural, the case of its antecedent *š́iiaoθanāiš* 'works'; earlier the construction would have been **tāiš š́iiaoθanāiš yā vahištā*, with the relative pronoun in the nominative plural (as subject of its clause) and the predicate adjective *vahištā* also in the nominative plural. Old Persian has examples like *karā haya manā* 'my army', lit. 'army which (is) mine', with an indeclinable relative *hya*; this developed ultimately into the Modern Persian *ezāfe* construction, as in *ketāb-e naw* 'the new book', where the particle *-e* marks definiteness of an attributive adjective and possession (*ketāb-e man* 'my book'). In Balto-Slavic, definite adjectives have an extra syllable beginning with *-j-*, from the PIE relative pronoun **i̯o-*: OCS *novyjĭ zavětŭ* 'the New Testament', Lith. (accus. sing.) *naũją̃jį var̃dą* 'the new name'. The Anatolian language Carian has recently been analyzed as having a similar construction, in phrases like *świnś upe arieś-χi ted* (M30) 'stele of Świn, father of Arie', where *arieś-χi ted* literally means 'of Arie who (is) the father' (with *-χi* continuing the other PIE relative pronominal stem, **kʷi-*).

Negation

8.29. As detailed in the previous chapter, for ordinary negation PIE had an adverb **ne* and a privative prefix **n̥-* 'un-'. In some cases, the privative prefix was used where one might expect the adverb. Comparative evidence suggests that certain classes of words were preferentially negated not with the adverb but with the privative prefix; among these words were participles and verbal adjectives. Greek and Latin, for example, ordinarily use their negative adverbs when negating participles, but some fixed archaic constructions point to an earlier time when the privative prefix was used instead, as Homeric Gk. *a-ékontos emeĩo* 'with me being unwilling, against my will', Lat. *mē īn-sciente* 'with me not knowing', ***in-uītus*** 'unwilling' (later replaced by *nōn uolēns* 'not willing'), ***im-prūdēns*** 'not knowing beforehand' (later *nōn prouidēns*). Compare also Av. ***an-usant-*** 'not wanting', Goth. ***un-agands*** 'not fearing'.

In clauses, the positioning of negation is complex. If the negation has scope over a single word or constituent, it usually directly precedes that constituent. Sentential negation typically directly precedes the verb, as in English. But it could also be moved toward the front of the sentence for emphasis.

Absolute constructions

8.30. An action, state, or event could be syntactically backgrounded using a construction called an absolute. Typically the absolute consisted of a noun modified by a participle – semantically equivalent to a subject plus verb – in an oblique case. Thus Latin has ablative absolutes (*hīs rēbus gestīs* lit. 'these things having been done', i.e. 'after these things were done' or 'because these things were done'), Greek has genitive absolutes (Homeric *aékontos emeĩo* 'with me being unwilling'), Vedic Sanskrit has locative absolutes (*ucchántyām uṣási* 'with dawn shining forth'), and Gothic and Old Church Slavonic have dative absolutes (Goth. *imma rodjandin* and OCS *jemu glagoljǫščemu* 'with him speaking, while he is/was speaking'). PIE surely had such constructions too, although which case or cases were used is debated. Opinions also differ as to how many of these are native in the languages in which they are attested.

Phrase and Sentence Prosody and the Interaction of Syntax and Phonology

8.31. An area that has received considerable attention in theoretical linguistics since the 1980s is the interaction of syntax and phonology, the so-called "phonology–syntax interface." Speech sounds in ordinary speech are grouped into hierarchically arranged levels of organization; this organization is termed the *prosody* (not to be confused with the rules of poetic meter, also called prosody). Each level of the prosody is called a *prosodic domain.* Syllables constitute the smallest prosodic domain; they combine to form words, which combine with clitics to form clitic groups; clitic groups and words, or words and words, form phonological phrases, which themselves combine to form intonational phrases. Each of these units is a level to which particular phonological rules are applied. For example, in clitic groups and certain other phrases in Vedic Sanskrit, a *t* will become *n* before a nasal, as in *prá tán me voco* 'proclaim that to me' (underlyingly *tát me*; Rig Veda 7.86.4). This same rule does not apply within the smaller prosodic domain of the word, as in *ātmā́* 'breath'. Within any prosodic domain larger than the word, a phonological rule will affect the *junctures* between words; such rules are usually called *sandhi rules.* Common types of phonological processes that can happen at word junctures include assimilation (as in Ved. *tán me* above, and as in the pronunciation of Eng. *I hit you* as [aj hɪtʃuw]) and resyllabification (as when *an ice man* sounds identical to *a nice man* in fluent speech).

8.32. The construction of prosodic domains above the level of the word is influenced by syntactic configuration. Under the usual assumptions about the mapping of syntactic structure onto the prosody, words belonging to the same constituent that start out as contiguous in the deep structure and stay contiguous throughout the derivation will tend to be grouped together as a single phonological unit, whereas words that only become contiguous through certain kinds of movement sometimes do not. In other words, syntactic movement can block the application of a particular sandhi rule, or can prevent a word from turning into a clitic. For example, in Greek, clitics normally receive no accent, but if two or more occur in a string, all but the last one get accented, as in *ei mḗ tís me theō̃n* 'if no one of the gods me . . .' (*Odyssey* 4.364). However, in a sequence like *douliāi per en phrení* 'even in bondage in the mind' (Aeschylus, *Agamemnon* 1084, quoted above in §8.19), there are two clitics in a row but the first is not accented. The reason is that *per* 'even' emphasizes *doulíāi* 'in bondage' and is phonologically attached to it, while *en* 'in' is a preposition that governs *phrení* 'the mind' and is proclitic to that word. The two resultant clitic groups [*doulíāi per*] and [*en phrení*] form two separate prosodic groups with what is called a prosodic boundary between them. (A prosodic boundary, incidentally, is not generally audible as a pause or other break.) We conclude that the rule placing an accent on the first of two successive clitics applies only if the two clitics belong to the same clitic group.

8.33. The writing systems of most languages do not consistently reflect the output of sandhi rules or related prosodic processes, but they do not entirely ignore them, either. In Hittite, chains of clitics (see §9.13) are written without word-breaks between the clitics, indicating that they all formed a clitic group that acted as a single phonological word. In medieval Irish manuscripts, prepositions are written together with following nouns as one word, indicating a similar prosodic fact for prepositional phrases. Greek and Latin inscriptions frequently show evidence of sandhi rules and prosodic groupings that are not reflected in the more rigid orthography of the standard literary tradition. For example, interpuncts (punctuation marks separating words) in Greek inscriptions are ordinarily not placed between a definite article and a following noun, or between a preposition and a following object. Latin inscriptions preserve spellings such as *quot per* 'because through (. . .)' where standard orthography demanded *quod per*; the less literary inscriber simply wrote as he spoke – with devoicing of the final *-d* before the following voiceless *p*, a sandhi rule about which the standard orthography provides no information. Sometimes authors who are linguistically more sensitive than most devise a phonetic spelling system that reflects external sandhi and related phenomena, such as the Old High German author Notker Labeo (see directly below) and the early Middle English author Orm (see §15.67). Most exceptional of all is the Sanskrit writing system (called Devanāgarī; see §10.57), which encodes sandhi phenomena in great detail; the received text of the Rig Veda has been of immense value in shedding light on the interaction of syntax and prosody in older IE languages.

8.34. One widely observed effect of the syntax on phonology involves the "heaviness" or "weight" of constituents. Noun phrases consisting of a bare noun, for example, are much more likely to enter into certain kinds of clitic groups than are noun phrases where the noun is modified by another element (called branching noun phrases). In punctuated Greek inscriptions, as we saw above, interpuncts do not ordinarily separate a definite article from a following noun; but an interpunct is present if the article is followed by a branching noun phrase, indicating a stronger prosodic break between the two. In Homer, we see a difference in the behavior of different types of prepositional phrases vis-à-vis the positioning of the sentence-connecting conjunction *dé*, an enclitic that normally occurs second in its clause. If the clause begins with a prepositional phrase consisting simply of a preposition plus bare noun, the clitic will follow the whole phrase (e.g. *eks pántōn* *dé* 'and of all', *Iliad* 4.96), whereas if the clause begins with a more complex phrase consisting of a preposition followed by an adjective-noun phrase, the clitic will come in between the preposition and the rest of the phrase (e.g. *dià* *dè* *khróa kalón* 'and into the fair flesh', *Iliad* 5.858). This has been interpreted to show that *eks pántōn* is prosodically cohesive enough to function as a single word for the purposes of clitic placement, while *dià khróa kalón* is not. A similar phenomenon is found in the Old High German of Notker Labeo: a definite article is written without an accent when preceding a simple noun phrase (e.g. *taz* *héiza fíur* 'the hot fire', J28), indicating clisis and destressing of the article, but is written with an accent when preceding more complex noun phrases (e.g. *díe* *uuîlsalda állero búrgô* 'the fortune of all cities', J19).

8.35. Metrics – the study of the rules and behavior of poetic meters – can be a valuable source of information about prosodic phonology. In certain Greek and Roman meters, for example, there is a rule that a sequence of two light syllables in particular verse-positions must belong to the same word. The rule, though, has an interesting exception: a word-break between the two syllables is allowed when one of them belongs to a proclitic (as in the sequence *ut opīniōne* 'that in [his] opinion', Plautus, *Miles Gloriosus* 1238). This means that the prosodic group consisting of proclitic plus word was tighter than that consisting of two full-content words – tight enough to behave, for the purposes of the poetic meter, as though there were no word-division. In the Old English epic poem *Beowulf*, whose poetry – like all older Germanic heroic poetry – is structured around stressed words alliterating with one another, weakly stressed and unstressed words like prepositions, pronouns, and certain adverbs do not participate in alliteration. Additionally, some verbs do not participate in it either, thus patterning with weakly stressed elements – a fact that is in agreement with the general propensity of verbs in IE to be more weakly stressed than nouns (as we saw in §5.63). Much of the poetry in the older IE languages remains to be exploited for similar information; the classical languages and Vedic have been most intensively studied in this regard but have themselves by no means yielded all their secrets.

8.36. It is reasonable to suppose that phonological and morphophonological processes such as prosodic domain formation and cliticization were conditioned in PIE by structural factors like those described in this section. There is as yet no theory of diachronic prosody – how prosodic systems change historically in the course of a language's development – and accounting for the phonology–syntax interface is the subject of ongoing debate in contemporary generative linguistics. As our understanding of some of these questions improves, and as the ancient IE texts are more closely scrutinized for the prosodic information they can provide, we will hopefully be able to determine which rules can be projected back onto PIE itself.

For Further Reading

Most grammars of Indo-European languages and introductory books on Indo-European give short shrift to syntax or neglect it altogether. The fundamental nineteenth- and early twentieth-century works, which are in German, mostly treat the usage of morphosyntactic categories. These include Wackernagel 1920 and Delbrück 1893–1900, a monumental work in three volumes. Wackernagel's Law was proposed in Wackernagel 1892. The modern age of IE syntax was ushered in by Calvert Watkins with his article on the Old Irish verbal complex (Watkins 1963); see also Watkins 1976, which lays out the problems with purely typological approaches to IE syntax and word order. Generative linguistic approaches have informed more recent studies such as Hale 1987 and Garrett 1990, both important and influential works. On the "phonology–syntax interface" in general, see the articles in Inkelas and Zec 1990.

For Review

Know the meaning or significance of the following:

constituent	*vā́yav índraś ca* construction	fronting	sentence-connective clitic
underlying movement	preverb	topicalization	sentential clitic
deep structure	tmesis	WH-movement	prosodic domain
surface structure	nominal sentence	Wackernagel's Law	sandhi rule
		word-level clitic	

Exercises

1 Briefly describe the syntactic behavior or significance of the following forms or constructions mentioned in the chapter:

a Lat. *magnā cum laude*
b Lat. *mēcum*
c Gk. *Zeũ páter . . . Ēéliós te*
d Hitt. *annaš=šiš* MUŠ-*aš*
e Skt. *āsīd rājā nalo nāma*
f Hitt. *-pat*
g PIE *$^*k^we$*
h Hitt. DUMU-*ŠU=ma=wa=šši=za=kan*
i Lat. *quem agrum . . . is ager . . .*
j Gk. *a-ékontos emeĩo*
k Ved. *prá tán me voco* (vs. *ātmā́*)
l OHG *díe uuîlsalda állero búrgô*

2 Determine the syntactic rule that is responsible for the position of the underlined forms in each of the following sentences from the Rig Veda:

a *divó no vr̥ṣṭím maruto rarīdhvaṃ* (5.83.6) "Give us the rain of heaven, o Maruts"
b *kvà idā́nīṃ sū́riaḥ* (1.35.7) "Where is the sun now?"
c *ví suparṇó antárikṣāṇi akhyad* (1.35.7) "The bird has looked out over the sky's regions" (*akhyad* = 'saw')
d *ráthaṃ kó nír avartayat* (10.135.5) "Who set the chariot rolling down?" (*kó* = 'who')

3 The sentence in **2b** above literally translates "Where now (the) sun". What kind of sentence is this?

4 In §8.8, the Greek postpositional phrase *toútōn péri* was mentioned. Where do you suppose the accent was in PIE, based on this evidence and on the discussion in §8.8?

9 Anatolian

Introduction

9.1. The Asian part of Turkey, called Anatolia in classical times, and parts of northern Syria are the home of the earliest attested Indo-European languages, together called Anatolian. Anatolian was not established as a branch of Indo-European until the twentieth century. Two letters found at Tell el-Amarna, Egypt, and written in Mesopotamian cuneiform script were the first documents to come to light that contained **Hittite**, now the most famous Anatolian language. Known as the Arzawa letters, they were published in 1902; the editor, Jorgen Knudtzon, identified the language as Indo-European, but this view was generally greeted with disbelief. In 1906, the first large-scale Hittite finds were made, in the central Turkish village of Boğazköy (now Boğazkale), roughly 90 miles east of Ankara. Excavations in that year uncovered about 10,000 cuneiform tablets and tablet fragments dating from the mid- to late second millennium BC; these finds still represent the bulk of our material in the language. It turned out that Boğazköy is on the site of Hattusas, the capital of the Hittite Kingdom (see below); the tablets were found in the remains of a royal archive. During the First World War, the Czech philologist Bedřich Hrozný deciphered the language and proved that it was Indo-European.

9.2. Since then other Anatolian languages, none as well preserved as Hittite, have been identified and have gradually been giving up their secrets: **Palaic** and **Cuneiform Luvian**, both also from the second millennium BC and written in the same cuneiform script as Hittite; **Hieroglyphic Luvian**, with remains from both the second and the first millennia BC and written in a native hieroglyphic script; and the first-millennium languages **Lycian** and **Lydian**, written in a Greek-derived alphabet. (Lycian was already known by the late nineteenth century, but its recognition as Anatolian did not come until later.) Three other languages of southern Anatolia – **Carian, Pisidian**, and **Sidetic** – belong to the family as well, but due to their fragmentary nature they are very poorly known. As we have come to understand the non-Hittite languages better, their importance for Anatolian and IE studies has increased tremendously. In the past, the focus of attention was the relationship between Hittite and IE, without concern for the intermediate stage of Common Anatolian; but we are now in a better position to reconstruct that stage.

9.3. Anatolian is one of the growth industries of IE studies. Almost since the time of its discovery, it has engendered vigorous debate about the structure of PIE and

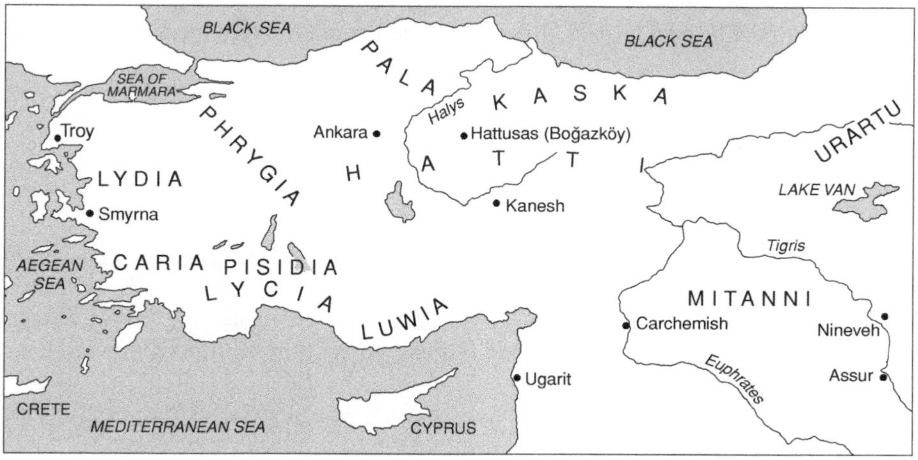

Map 9.1 Anatolia: combined view of the major principalities and historical regions of both the Bronze Age and the Hellenistic period

the subgrouping of the family. Our understanding of these matters is being continually revised because new inscriptions are discovered on a regular basis, and our interpretations of already-known texts and linguistic forms are constantly improving. Any historical account of the Anatolian languages is therefore somewhat provisional.

Anatolian, Indo-European, and "Indo-Hittite"

9.4. The main difficulty posed by Anatolian for Indo-Europeanists is the fact that its structure is quite different from that of PIE as traditionally reconstructed. One would ordinarily expect that the oldest known languages of the family should resemble the proto-language the most closely; and it is true that Anatolian does preserve a number of important archaisms, notably consonantal reflexes of at least one (and probably two) of the three laryngeals and productive classes of neuter *r/n*-stems. But most striking are the forms and categories that it does *not* have. Absent are such apparently bedrock IE formations as simple thematic verbs, the aorist, the perfect, the subjunctive, the optative, the dual, the **-tó*-verbal adjective, and the comparative in **-i̯os-*. Additionally, some inherited grammatical forms function differently from their congeners in the rest of IE: endings identifiable with those of the IE perfect are used to form a class of presents (the so-called *ḫi*-conjugation; §9.12); and the **-nt*-participle, which has active voice in the other IE languages, is passive in Anatolian.

One interpretation of these facts is that the forms missing from Anatolian were simply lost, and that the traditional reconstruction of PIE is perfectly valid. But evidence has been growing that Anatolian split off at a time when the development of some of these categories (such as the *s*-aorist) was only nascent. Under this view, PIE went through some subsequent development before achieving its "classic" look; the "missing data" of Anatolian are then partly attributable to loss, and partly to their not having existed yet. An early version of this theory was propounded by the

American Indo-Europeanist Edgar Sturtevant, who thought Anatolian was a sister of reconstructed PIE and that both were derived from a language he called **"Indo-Hittite"** (a term that later fell out of favor).

From PIE to Common Anatolian

Phonology

9.5. Anatolian is justly famous for being the only branch to preserve consonantal reflexes of the laryngeals. All scholars agree that $*h_2$ has a reflex in Hittite, Luvian, and Palaic as the sound transcribed *ḫ*, and in Lycian variously as *χ* (*x*), *k*, and *q*. It is also very probable that $*h_3$ was preserved as *ḫ* in Hittite, but not all have accepted this claim.

9.6. According to recent assessments of Luvian, Anatolian is also the only branch of IE that preserved the original three-way distinction among the velars; see further §9.48.

9.7. As for the other consonants, the voiced aspirated stops lost their aspiration and merged with the plain voiced stops. The liquids, nasals, and glide **u̯* generally stayed intact. Interestingly, no native Anatolian words began with *r* (except in clearly secondary cases), which has led some scholars to believe that PIE had no *r*-initial words either. Under this view, PIE words reconstructed with **r-* should be reconstructed as $*h_1r$-. But it has been observed that other languages in the same general region also lack words beginning with *r-*, including Hurrian, Armenian, and Greek (words beginning *rh-* in the latter come from initial clusters such as **sr-*; see §§12.19 and 22). Thus the lack of *r*-initial words in Anatolian, rather than reflecting something inherited from PIE, could be an areal feature.

9.8. Anatolian inherited all the PIE vowels, but in every language except Lycian **o* and **a* fell together as *a*. Long *ō* and *ā* also fell together, as *ā*.

Morphology

9.9. Anatolian nouns were richly inflected in the singular. All the PIE cases were represented, as well as a directive (or allative) case in **-a*, which indicated place to which; the directive was probably a case in PIE also, although most of the evidence for it comes from Anatolian (recall §6.12). The hallmark innovation of the Anatolian case system was the **ergative**, the case taken by neuter nouns when they were subjects of transitive verbs. The ergative was built with the Common Anatolian suffix **-ant-*, of disputed origin, plus animate nominative endings; examples include Hitt. erg. sg. *tuppi-anza* 'tablet' (phonetically *tuppiants*), erg. pl. *uttan-āntes̆* 'words', and Cuneiform Luvian erg. sg. *ḫaratn-antis̆* 'offense'. An ending **-ti* is reconstructed for the Common Anatolian ablative and instrumental, both singular and plural (e.g. Luv. *Wilus̆ati* 'from Wilusa'). In the plural, separate endings are reconstructible only for the nominative, accusative, genitive, and dative in Common Anatolian, and there is no trace of the other oblique plurals with suffixes beginning with **-m-* or **-bh-* (§6.17). Impressionistically, the plural has a more primitive look than elsewhere in IE.

The archaic *r/n*-stems (§6.31) are a large and productive class of nouns in Anatolian, reduced to a mere handful of forms in the rest of IE; for example, Luv. *kuršawar*, stem *kuršaw(a)n-* 'island' (from **kuršai-* 'cut', i.e. 'land cut off by water').

9.10. Anatolian preserves the distinction between distributive and collective plural in animate nouns (§6.68); thus Old Hittite *alpeš* 'clouds' vs. collective *alpa* 'group of clouds'. No direct reflex of the dual has been found. Whether the feminine exists in Anatolian in any way is debated (recall §6.69).

9.11. Among the striking features of the pronominal system is the development of clitic subject pronouns in the third person; elsewhere in IE, clitic pronouns are only found in oblique cases. The Anatolian subject pronouns are limited to use with a few classes of intransitive verbs. Among other features worthy of note in the pronominal system are a demonstrative stem **obo-* (< PIE **obho-*) meaning 'that' (> Hitt. *apā-*, Pal. *apa-*, Lyc. *ebe-*) and the odd *u*-vocalism of the 1st person pronoun **ug* 'I' and **emu* 'me' as opposed to PIE **eĝ-* and **eme* (Hitt. nomin. *ūk*, accus. *ammuk*; cp. Hieroglyphic Luv., Lyc., and Lyd. accus. *amu*). This *u* ultimately comes from the influence of **tu-* 'thee'; cp. §7.1.

Verbs

9.12. Anatolian verbs only inflected in two tenses, present and preterite, and in two voices, active and mediopassive. Thus there are far fewer verbal inflections in Anatolian than in the rest of IE. Among the types of present stems, simple thematic verbs are exceedingly rare or non-existent, but root athematic presents are very common. While the aorist as a category is not found, a few present stems appear to correspond to aorist stems in other languages, such as Lyc. *tadi* 'puts' (cp. Ved. aorist *(á)dhāt*). There was also an imperative, with 3rd person forms ending in *-*(t)u* (e.g. Hitt. *pau* 'let him give', *paiddu* 'let him go'; compare Ved. Skt. *étu* 'let him go').

But the morphological peculiarity for which the Anatolian verb is best known is the existence of two separate verbal conjugations, the ***mi*-conjugation** and the ***ḫi*-conjugation** (named after their respective Hittite 1st sing. present active endings). The *-mi* conjugation is unproblematic, continuing the familiar endings *-*mi* *-*si* *-*ti* etc. in the present and *-*m* *-*s* *-*t* etc. in the preterite. The *ḫi*-conjugation endings, however, are directly equatable with those of the IE perfect. How the *ḫi*-conjugation relates to the perfect is a major unsolved problem and bears on the very foundations of the IE verbal system. Under an older view, Anatolian turned the perfect into a present tense for one (diverse) group of verbs. Under a newer, still controversial view, the *ḫi*-conjugation continues a class of PIE presents and aorists that was allied with the perfect in complex ways; see §9.33 below. There are also many other theories.

Syntax

9.13. The Anatolian languages are syntactically quite similar to one another. Characteristic of Anatolian sentence structure is the clause-initial **clitic chain**: all clitic sentential conjunctions, clitic sentential adverbs, and clitic pronouns were attached to the first word of the clause in a particular fixed order, with the whole chain written as a single word. Thus in Hittite one can begin a sentence *kinun=ma=wa=tu=za* (the equals signs are used to indicate the clitic boundaries in Anatolian scholarship), where *kinun* means 'now', *-ma* is a clitic adversative conjunction meaning 'but', *-wa* is a quotative particle indicating that the sentence is quoted speech, *-tu* is the 2nd sing. accus. pronoun, and *-za* is a reflexive particle. Clauses are generally verb-final, although the verb or any other element in a clause could be fronted to the beginning of a clause for emphasis or topicalization. Also characteristic of Anatolian clauses was the almost universal use of a so-called sentence connective to begin any clause that was not discourse-initial; this conjunction served as an anchor for the clitic chain (in the absence of a fronted element filling that slot) and also connected each sentence to the previous one in continuous narrative. It roughly corresponded to 'and' or 'and then' in English, but is frequently untranslatable. The most familiar example is Hitt. *nu*, cognate with Eng. *now* (but not so translated).

9.14. We noted earlier the creation of the ergative case in Anatolian. Although the formal origin of this case is uncertain, it is evident that its creation was part of a larger change in Anatolian whose fulcrum was verb transitivity – specifically, the development of overt morphosyntactic marking of certain contrasts within this category. Thus the ergative distinguishes neuter subjects of transitive verbs from neuter subjects of intransitive verbs, which were not morphologically distinct from objects (the neuter nominative is identical with the accusative). Another new set of forms, the enclitic third-person subject pronouns (§9.11 above), made overt the distinction between the two basic types of intransitive verbs: unaccusatives and unergatives. (We met unaccusatives when discussing the PIE middle; see §5.5.) The subject of an unaccusative verb is not semantically an agent; underlyingly in fact it is an object, the undergoer of the action. Thus in the sentence *The tablet broke*, the subject *tablet* undergoes the breaking. With unergative verbs, however, the subject is the agent and is underlyingly the subject, as in *The king spoke.* Many languages make formal distinctions of some kind between these two types of intransitives. From a PIE view, the change can also be viewed a different way: the language went from not using clitic subject pronouns for *overt* subjects, to not using clitic subject pronouns for *underlying* subjects – and that only in the third person.

Hittite

9.15. Because of the extensive linguistic remains, far more is known about the Hittites than about the other Anatolian peoples; but little can be said about their origins. That they or their ancestors did not originally inhabit Anatolia is certain (in spite of the controversy mentioned in §2.71). Their designation for their country, *Ḫatti*, is taken over from the indigenous non-Indo-European Hattic people whom they encountered early and assimilated. The influence of Hattic culture was quite strong; preserved among the hundreds of ritual texts at Boğazköy are many of Hattic provenance. The Hittites, along with other Anatolian speakers, presumably came from the north, and were already settled in central Anatolia by about 1900 BC. Around this time Assyrian merchants were setting up colonies in the area, and in Assyrian documents from Kanesh (modern Kültepe, about 100 miles south-southeast of Boğazköy) the first

Hittite words appear, as loanwords – proper names and a few lexical borrowings, two of which are of some cultural significance: *išpa(t)ta(l)lu* 'nightwatch' (Hitt. **išpantalla-*, from *išpant-* 'night') and *išḫiu(l)lu* 'contract' (Hitt. *išḫiul*). The former is interesting in light of the fact that Anittas, the first Hittite king of whom we have records (see below), took enemy cities by night; the latter is revealing in light of the importance of the contract and other mutually binding arrangements in ancient IE societies (see §§2.11ff.).

Cultural and political history

9.16. At the dawn of Hittite history, the central part of Anatolia (the area known as Cappadocia in classical times) was divided into numerous small principalities. Hittite history is ushered in with the "Anittas text," the oldest surviving Hittite document, dating from the sixteenth century BC or earlier. It contains an account of how one Anittas and his father, Pithanas, king of a place called Kussara, vied against the other principalities for power. They were eventually victorious and set up their capital at Nesa (also called Kanesh). From the name Nesa comes the adverb *nešumnili* 'in Hittite'.

9.17. The connection between Anittas and the kings of the subsequent **Old Kingdom** is not known; he is not claimed by any of them as a forebear. The history of the Old Kingdom apparently starts with Hattusilis I, who moved the capital to Hattusas and also began a southward territorial expansion into what is now northern Syria. His son Mursilis I pressed into Mesopotamia and even sacked Babylon. The Old Kingdom culminated with the reign of the powerful king Telipinus in the fifteenth century BC.

During the early years of the **Middle Kingdom**, the state prospered at first but then was beset by invaders from every direction; records even speak of Hattusas getting sacked and burned. A strong king came to the rescue, Suppiluliumas I, who ascended the throne around 1380 BC. With his reign the **New Kingdom** or Hittite Empire began – the most powerful period in the history of the Hittites. For nearly two centuries the Hittite Empire was one of the most influential states in the ancient Near East. Eventually, though, it fell victim to invasions from the north, ending with the destruction of Hattusas around 1200 BC. While this did not spell the end of Hittite civilization, it did terminate the production of Hittite texts, since Hattusas had been the center of the Hittite scribal chancelleries.

9.18. Various principalities of the former empire remained intact until near the end of the eighth century BC and called themselves Hittites, most prominently a state in northern Syria with its capital at Karkamish (Carchemish) on the Euphrates. Their chancellery language was not Hittite, however, but Hieroglyphic Luvian. After the Assyrians conquered Syria in the late eighth century, we never again hear of anyone called Hittite.

The linguistic stages of Hittite

9.19. Hittite is divided into three periods that correspond to the three political periods outlined above: **Old Hittite**, the language of the Old Kingdom (c. 1570–1450 BC);

Middle Hittite (c. 1450–1380 BC); and **Neo-Hittite** (c. 1350–1200 BC), beginning with the death of Suppiluliumas I (documents from his reign are linguistically still Middle Hittite). About four centuries separate the oldest Old Hittite from the latest Neo-Hittite – about as much time as separates present-day English from the language of Shakespeare.

Except for one bronze tablet, all surviving Hittite texts are inscribed on clay. The dating of Hittite texts and the description of Old, Middle, and Neo-Hittite have been hampered by the fact that texts were often recopied and modernized. Many tablets inscribed during the New Kingdom contain Neo-Hittite versions of Old and Middle Hittite originals and present a mixture of archaic and modernized forms. Greater accuracy in dating has been achieved largely through advances in *paleography*, the study of sign-shapes and their evolution. We now know in considerable detail the relative chronology of different cuneiform sign-shapes and of various external features of the tablets. The earliest style (or *ductus*) of Hittite cuneiform is called **Old Script**, followed by **Middle Script** and **New Script**.

9.20. The Hittite corpus spans a wide range of genres. Most plentiful are ritual texts, containing instructions (some quite lengthy) on how to conduct the rituals and festivals of the Hittite state religion. Of great importance to historians of the Ancient Near East are the numerous treaties, decrees, annals of kings, official letters, and a sizeable law code. We also have many myths, omens, and medical texts.

Copies of the cuneiform tablets have been published in several collections since the early 1900s; published tablets are identified by an abbreviation of the collection, the volume number, and the tablet number. Thus the catalogue number of the text sample in §9.44 below, KBo 17.1 (or KBo XVII 1), means the first tablet in the 17th volume of the collection *Keilschrifttexte aus Boghazköy* (*Cuneiform Texts from Boghazköy*). Reference may then be made to column and line numbers: KBo 17.1 iii 12 refers to line 12 in column 3. All the Hittite texts were organized into a thematic (genre-based) catalogue by Emmanuel Laroche called CTH (*Catalogue des textes hittites*: Laroche 1971); it is now standard practice to give the CTH number for any text being discussed.

Cuneiform writing and its transcription

9.21. Before proceeding with our historical grammatical sketch, we will introduce the nature of, and problems with, the writing system and the transcription of it. Hittite was written in the Mesopotamian cuneiform script. This script was probably invented by the Sumerians; Sumerian is at any rate the first language recorded in it that we can read, beginning at the end of the fourth millennium BC. Over the ensuing millennium and a half it was adopted by many other cultures of the Ancient Near East. The designation *cuneiform* comes from Latin *cuneus* 'wedge', after the wedge-shaped marks made by a reed stylus pressing into soft clay. The clay tablet was the writing medium *par excellence* in a region where both clay and the sunshine needed to harden it were abundant.

Cuneiform writing was originally designed for keeping mercantile records and consisted of symbols for numbers and pictorial depictions of trade items. But it eventually spread into other spheres of life, necessitating the representation of abstract concepts for which pictures could not be drawn. As a result, by about 2800 BC the script had developed into a partly phonetic system in which individual signs could be read as *ideograms* (also called *logograms*, representations of whole words or concepts) or as *syllabograms* (representing individual syllables). For example, the sign for the Sumerian word for 'mouth', pronounced *ka*, could be used logographically to represent the concept 'mouth' or syllabographically to represent the syllable *ka* in some other (longer) word. In essence, what the Sumerians developed was a rebus system, similar to English word-games where a picture of an eye can be used to represent the concept 'eye', the pronoun 'I', or the syllable [aj] in some longer word. Over time the system increased greatly in complexity, with some syllables represented by any of numerous signs, and with many signs having multiple values.

9.22. From the Sumerians the script spread by c. 2400 BC to the Akkadians, whose language was Semitic (Sumerian is not certainly related to any known language family). The Akkadians took over the whole system, and continued to use many of the signs in their ideographic Sumerian values as a kind of shorthand; these are called *Sumerograms*. However, since Akkadians read Sumerograms out loud in Akkadian, it was often convenient to the reader to indicate what the inflections of the underlying Akkadian words were. This was done by adding a sign or two indicating the Akkadian inflectional ending. This extra information is known as a *phonetic complement*. (The use of phonetic complements, incidentally, is also characteristic of Japanese writing; and for a parallel from English, compare the addition of letters in the ordinal numerals *2nd*, *3rd*, *4th*, etc.)

One version of Akkadian cuneiform, known as Old Babylonian, was adopted by the Hittites sometime before 1600 BC. They took the above practices one step further: they used both Sumerian and Akkadian words (the latter called *Akkadograms*) as a shorthand, and sometimes attached Hittite phonetic complements to them. Thus in a Hittite text, theoretically any given sign could stand for a Sumerian word, a syllable of a Sumerian word, a syllable of an Akkadian word or phonetic complement, or a syllable of a Hittite word or phonetic complement.

9.23. In transliterating Anatolian cuneiform texts, the three languages Sumerian, Akkadian, and Hittite (or Luvian or Palaic) are conventionally differentiated by contrastive use of capitalization and italics. These and other conventions are best explained using an illustrative example (KBo 3.4 ii 41f.):

na-aš-ma-at-ta ^{URU}KÙ.BABBAR-ša-aš ZAG-aš ku-iš *BE-LU* ma-ni-in-ku-wa-an nu ERÍN^{MEŠ} ANŠE.KUR.RA^{MEŠ} a-pé-e-da-ni ú-e-ek-ti

"or whichever border-guard of Hattusas is near you, (if) you ask for infantry and chariot-fighters from him"

Hyphens are used to separate the transcriptions of individual cuneiform signs: thus the first word, *na-aš-ma-at-ta*, is written with five signs. (As we will discuss below in §§9.30 and 31, individual cuneiform signs often represented sequences of two speech sounds.) Signs used to write Hittite are transcribed in lower case (such as the first word); Sumerograms are in roman upper case (as ZAG); and Akkadograms are in italic upper case (as *BE-LU*). When a Sumerian word consists of more than one sign, periods are used instead of hyphens to mark the sign boundaries (as ANŠE.KUR.RA). Hittite phonetic complements are joined to a preceding Sumerogram or Akkadogram with a hyphen: ZAG-*aš* consists of the Sumerogram ZAG 'border' plus the Hittite phonetic complement -*aš* indicating genitive singular (the underlying Hittite word is *irḫaš*), and ^{URU}KÙ.BABBAR-*ša-aš* represents *Ḫattušaš* 'of Hattusas', where the last syllable of the Hittite word (-*ša-aš*) is added to the Sumerogram as a phonetic complement.

A superscript sign preceding a word, as in this last example (^{URU}), is called a *determiner* (or *determinative*) and indicates the general semantic class to which the word belongs. In this example, ^{URU} (literally 'city') indicates the name of a city. The superscript signs that follow a word are usually Sumerian grammatical endings (or Akkadian, if they are italicized); the one occurring in our example (^{MEŠ}) is a Sumerian plural marker.

9.24. The system of transcribing sign by sign shown above, called *narrow transcription*, is often clumsy (although it is used for all editions of Hittite texts); it can be normalized by "erasing" the hyphens and redundant vowels (*broad transcription*). Thus the word *ma-ni-in-ku-wa-an* above can be normalized as *maninkuwan*. In a word like *ḫa-a-ra-aš* 'eagle' or *ma-a-an* 'when, if', the extra vowel sign for *a* must be taken seriously, for this was how the Hittites wrote long (and possibly also stressed) vowels; these words are normalized as *ḫāraš* and *mān*. (The technical term for the use of an extra vowel sign is *scriptio plena*, 'full writing'.) Double consonants are written double in both kinds of transcription, as the difference between single and double consonants is significant (see §9.31 below): *šu-up-pi-iš* = *šuppiš* 'pure'. In all the forms cited below, broad transcription will be used, as is standard.

The letters used in transcription have their Latin values except *z*, which represents *ts* (as in German). The letters *š* and *ḫ* probably represent *s* and the velar fricative [x] (as in German *Bach*). Diacritics and subscript numerals are used to differentiate homophonous cuneiform signs (e.g. *gú* [or gu_2], *gù* [or gu_3], gu_4, etc.)

Phonology

9.25. Only some of the numerous sound changes undergone by Hittite will be outlined here. In the stop system, the palatal and plain velar stops merged into plain velars as in centum languages; compare ***kāš*** 'this' (< **k̂os*) with ***lukke-*** 'to kindle' (**loukei̯e-*), both spelled with *k*. The labiovelars preserved their labial element and are usually written with the sign *ku*: ***kuiš*** 'who' < **$k^w$is*, ***kuenzi*** 'kills' < **g^whenti*.

9.26. A characteristic consonant change is the development of **t* to *ts* (written *z*) before an *i*. The 3rd sing. and pl. primary personal endings **-ti* and **-nti* thus become *-zi* and *-nzi* in Hittite, as in *ēšzi* 'is' and *ašanzi* 'are' (cp. Ved. *ásti*, *sánti*). Also characteristic of Hittite is the dissimilatory change of **u̯* to *m* when next to *u*. Thus the 1st pl. primary verb ending *-weni* appears as *-m(m)eni* in verbs like *arnummeni* 'we stir, move'.

9.27. Hittite preserves the second and probably also the third laryngeal as *ḫ*, as in *paḫḫur* 'fire' < **peh₂u̯r̥* and *ḫāraš* 'eagle' < **h₃er-*.

9.28. The syllabic resonants developed an *a* in front of them, as in ***palḫi-*** 'broad' < **pl̥h₂-i-*, ***kard-*** 'heart' < **k̂r̥d-*, and ***anzāš*** 'us' < **n̥sos*.

9.29. The Common Anatolian vowels underwent complex changes in Hittite, of which we may mention the following. Short **e* became *a* in several environments, especially before sonorants, although the conditioning factors have not been fully worked out. Examples include *anda* 'in, into' < PIE **endo*; *tarku-* 'to dance' < **terk^w-* ('twist' in PIE; cp. the name of the English dance!); and *daššu-* 'massive' < **dens-*. Short **e* also generally became *a* when unaccented: the 1st and 2nd pl. endings *-weni* and *-teni* appear in Old Hittite as *-wani* and *-tani* when the verbal root is stressed. Short accented **ó* became *ā*: *wātar* 'water' < **u̯ódr̥*, *kunānt-* 'killed' < **g^{w}hnónt-* (with *o*-grade of the participial ending as in Greek *-ont-*).

Hittite phonology and the cuneiform syllabary

9.30. In their phonetic values, cuneiform signs constituted a syllabary, not an alphabet: signs stood for syllables and not individual sounds (except vowels). Signs represented single vowels (V), sequences of consonant + vowel (CV), vowel + consonant (VC), or consonant + vowel + consonant (CVC). Not all theoretically possible combinations are found.

Such a spelling system has limitations. Since no cuneiform signs stand for consonantal sounds alone, a syllabary cannot unambiguously represent word-initial or word-final consonant clusters, or word-internal clusters of more than two consonants. From comparative evidence and from spelling fluctuations in Hittite texts, it is certain that Hittite inherited such clusters, but it is not always known whether they were preserved as such in speech. A clear example where a word-final cluster was still pronounced intact is the 3rd singular preterite of the verb 'come', which was written either *a-ar-aš* or *a-ar-ša*, suggesting that the real pronunciation was [ars]; the extra *a* was a "dummy" or "empty" vowel, forced upon the scribes by the limitations of the writing system. Usually the vowel appearing in clusters was *a*, but in those containing *s* and a stop it was generally *i* instead, and the interpretation of these spellings has been more controversial. Thus the preterite of the verb 'die' is always written *ak-ki-iš*, not **ak-ka-aš* or **ak-ša*, and the noun *išpantuzzi-* 'libation vessel', cognate with the Greek verb *spéndō* 'I pour a libation', is never written with *ašp-* or *šap-* or the like. In such cases the *i* probably was not simply graphic, but really pronounced. The "sprouting" of a front vowel before or within an *s*-cluster is easy to parallel from other languages, as in the Hungarian and Spanish versions of the name *Stephen* – *István* and *Estebán*, respectively.

9.31. The Akkadian syllabary distinguished voiced from voiceless consonants in its CV signs (e.g., *pa* and *ba*), but the Hittites did not avail themselves of this distinction in any systematic way. Crucially, there is no correlation between the sign used and whether the relevant sound comes from a voiced or voiceless consonant in PIE. For example, *a-ta-an-zi* and *a-da-an-zi* 'they eat' are both attested spellings of a word that etymologically contains *d* (from **h$_1$ed-* 'eat').

What the Hittites did instead was make a systematic distinction between consonants written single between vowels (*V-CV*) and consonants written double (*VC-CV*). Consonants written single correspond to PIE voiced stops, while those written double correspond to voiceless stops. Thus the single *t* or *d* in *a-ta-an-zi* and *a-da-an-zi*, which comes from **d*, contrasts with the double *-tt-* or *-dd-* in a word like *ar-nu-ut-tu* or *ar-nu-ud-du* 'let him bring', which comes from **t.* This fact is known as **Sturtevant's Law**, after the American Indo-Europeanist Edgar Sturtevant. What these spellings represent phonetically is still being debated.

Morphology

Verbs

9.32. As in Common Anatolian, Hittite verbs were conjugated only in the indicative mood, in the present and preterite tenses, and in the active and middle (mediopassive) voices. There was also an active and middle imperative for all persons. Mention has already been made of the *mi*- and *ḫi*-conjugations; the endings of both are alike in the plural and middle, and often a verb belonging to one conjugation acquired endings of the other conjugation by analogy, especially in later texts. Sample active paradigms are given below for the *mi*-verb *ēpmi* 'I take, seize' and the *ḫi*-verb *ārḫi* 'I reach, arrive at'. To exemplify the middle, the paradigm of *arḫaḫari* 'I stand' is given; variant forms of the 3rd singular, without *-t-*, are illustrated with relevant forms of *kišḫaḫari* 'I become'. Bracketed forms are not actually attested for these verbs:

		Active		*Middle*
		mi-conjugation	*ḫi*-conjugation	
Present	sg. 1	*ēpmi*	*ārḫi*	*arḫari*,[1] *arḫaḫari*
	2	*ēpši*	*ārti*	*artati*
	3	*ēpzi*	*ari, āri*	*arta(ri), kīša(ri)*
	pl. 1	*appueni*	*arweni*	*arwašta*
	2	*apteni*	*arteni*	[*arduma*]
	3	*appanzi*	*aranzi*	*aranta, arantari*
Preterite	sg. 1	*ēppun*	*ārḫun*	*arḫati*,[1] *arḫaḫat*
	2	*ēpta*	[*ārta*]	*artat(i)*
	3	*ēpta*	*āraš*	*artat, kišat(i)*
	pl. 1	*ēppuen*	*erwen*	*arwaštat*
	2	*ēpten*	[*erten*]	[*ardumat*]
	3	*ēppir*	*erir*	*arantat, arantati*

[1] Old Hittite.

To the active forms above may be added the imperatives, which in the 2nd singular are the base stem (*ēp*) and in the 2nd plural end in *-ten* (*ēpten*, *arten*); in the 3rd person, a *-u* appears in place of the *-i* of the indicative (sing. *ēpdu*, *aru*; pl. *appandu*).

9.33. There is considerable variation in ablaut in root athematic verbs of both conjugations. For example, alongside the forms *appueni apteni* above are also found ***ē**ppueni* and ***ē**pteni*. The 3rd singular present tense of ablauting *mi*-verbs often has *e*-vocalism that contrasts with either *a*-vocalism or no vowel in the plural: compare the singular/plural pairs ***ē**šzi* 'is' ~ ***a**šanzi* 'they are', ***ē**kuzi* 'drinks' ~ ***a**kuwanzi* 'they drink',

kuenzi 'kills' ~ ***kunanzi*** 'they kill'. Some ablauting *ḫi*-verbs have the opposite pattern: *šakki* 'knows' ~ *šekkanzi* 'they know'. Others have *a*-vocalism throughout, sometimes with a contrast of single versus double consonant: *āki* 'dies' ~ *akkanzi* 'they die'.

An *a* ~ *e* alternation in Anatolian likely continues an **o* ~ **e* alternation in PIE. This is reminiscent of the fact that several dozen verbal roots show an interchange of *o*- and *e*-grade in cognate present-tense forms in other daughter languages: Goth. *graban* 'to dig' (< **ghrobh-*) vs. OCS *po-grebǫ* 'I dig' (< **ghrebh-*); OIr. *melid* 'grinds' (< **melh₂-*) vs. Goth. *malan* 'to grind' (< **molh₂-*); Gk. *a(w)éksomai* 'I grow' (< **h₂u̯eks-*) vs. Goth. *wahsan* 'to grow' (= Eng. *wax*; < **h₂u̯oks-*). To explain these verbs and the ablaut of the *ḫi*-conjugation, it has been suggested by the American Indo-Europeanist Jay Jasanoff that PIE had a class of presents, the **h₂e-conjugation**, with *o*-grade in the singular and *e*-grade in the dual and plural that originally inflected with endings like the perfect. This idea has not found universal acceptance but has been gaining adherents, and the research it has spawned has been shedding light on the relationships among the *ḫi*-conjugation, the perfect, and the middle.

9.34. Besides root athematic verbs, there are several types of derived stems. Two kinds of nasal presents are found, both conjugating as *mi*-verbs, those with infix *-nin-* and those with suffix *-nu-*; both form causatives, such as *ḫarnink-* 'destroy' (< *ḫark-* 'perish') and *arnu-* 'bring' (< *ar-* 'reach' above). The PIE factitive suffix **-eh₂-* (§5.37) is faithfully continued in Hittite as *-aḫḫ-*, as in *idālawaḫḫ-* 'do bad, do evil' (< *idālu-* 'evil'); the factitives conjugate first as *ḫi*-verbs and later also as *mi*-verbs. Among thematic verbal suffixes, one that is particularly widespread is *-(i)ške-* (< PIE **-sk̂e-*), which could be freely attached to any verb stem to form what is standardly called an iterative. The term is misleading, for – as alluded to in §5.34 – the suffix was used to indicate not only repeated action, but also background action, action lasting over a long time (durative), and action undertaken by several subjects or applied to several objects (distributive). Thus *uw-anzi* 'they look' ~ *ušk-andu* 'let them (all) look', *memai* 'says' ~ *memišk-ezzi* 'says (many things)'.

9.35. Hittite verbs also had an infinitive in *-anna* (e.g. *adanna* 'to eat') or *-wanzi* (e.g. *iyawanzi* 'to bring'), used much like the English infinitive; a supine in *-wan*, used only with the verb *dāi-* 'place' in a construction meaning 'begin to . . .' (e.g. *memiškiwan dāi* 'he begins to speak'); and the *nt*-participle, which (unlike elsewhere in IE) is a past passive participle when added to transitive verbs (e.g. *kunānt-* '[having been] killed' from *kuen-* 'kill') but active when added to intransitives (e.g. *pānt-* '[having] gone' from *pāi-* 'go'). It is functionally equivalent to the PIE **tó*-verbal adjective, which is not found in Anatolian.

9.36. That Hittite inherited mobile accentual paradigms is clear from the shift of long vowels in such pairs as Old Hitt. *dāḫḫe* 'I take' ~ *tumēni* 'we take' (**dóh₃-h₂e* vs. **dh₃-u̯éni*) and *ēšzi* 'is' ~ *ašānt-* 'having been' (**h₁és-ti* **h₁s-ónt-*).

Nouns

9.37. A representative selection of Hittite noun and adjective declensions is given below. Paradigms are given for *antuḫšaš* 'man', *ḫalkiš* 'grain', *ḫaššuš* 'king' (attested only in the singular), *idālu-* 'evil', *ḫūmant-* 'every, all', and *uttar* 'word, speech'. All are common-gender except *uttar*.

	a-stem	*i*-stem	*u*-stem noun	*u*-stem adj.	*nt*-stem	*r/n*-stem
singular						
N	*antuḫšaš*	*ḫalkiš*	*ḫaššuš*	*idāluš*	*ḫūmanza*	*uttar*
V			*ḫaššue*			
A	*antuḫšan*	*ḫalkin*	*ḫaššun*	*idālun*	*ḫūmandan*	*uttar*
G	*antuḫšaš*	*ḫalkiaš*	*ḫaššuwaš*	*idālawaš*	*ḫūmandaš*	*uddanaš*
D-L	*antuḫši*		*ḫaššui*	*idālawi*	*ḫūmanti*	*uddani*
Ab	*antuḫšaz*	*ḫalkiyaz*	*ḫaššuwaz*	*idālawaz*	*ḫūmandaz*	*uddanaz*
I		*ḫalkit*		*idālawit*		*uddanit*

	a-stem	*i*-stem	*u*-stem adj.	*nt*-stem	*r/n*-stem
plural					
N	*antuḫšeš*	*ḫalkiš*	*idālawēš*	*ḫūmanteš*	*uddār*
A	*antuḫšuš*	*ḫalkiuš*	*idālamuš*	*ḫūmanduš*	*uddār*
G	*antuḫšaš*		*idālawaš*	*ḫūmandaš*	*uddanaš*
D-L	*antuḫšaš*		*idālawaš*	*ḫūmandaš*	*uddanaš*
Ab			*idālawaz*		

9.38. As in Common Anatolian, Hittite nouns distinguished more cases in the singular than in the plural. Over the course of the language's attested history, certain case distinctions in the singular disappeared as well. The ablative took over the functions of the instrumental, and the directive disappeared, its function taken over by the dative-locative.

The genitive plural in Old Hittite ended in *-an* (< **-ōm*), as in *šiunan* 'of the gods', but this got replaced by the *-aš* of the dative-locative, as in the paradigms above. The accusative plural ending *-uš* appears to be the regular outcome of PIE **-n̥s*; the *u*-stem accus. pl. *-amuš* is dissimilated from **-awuš* (from PIE **-eu̯-n̥s*) by the sound change noted above in §9.26. Not represented in the particular paradigms above is the Old Hittite directive which ended in *-a* (as in *aruna* 'to the sea'). Also not represented is the ergative, which ended in *-anza*, as in *paḫḫuenanza* 'fire'.

9.39. Hittite, as well as the other Anatolian languages, has a much more robust class of *r/n*-stems than the other IE languages. Aside from such basic inherited nouns as *paḫḫur* genit. *paḫḫuenaš* 'fire', *ēšḫar išḫanaš* 'blood', and *wātar wetenaš* 'water', derivatives using the suffixes *-ātar* and *-ēššar* were freely formed, e.g. *paprātar paprannaš* 'defilement' and *uppeššar/uppešnaš* 'sending, message'.

9.40. Remains of mobile accentual paradigms are preserved in such pairs as *wātar* (sing.) 'water' ~ *widār* (collective pl.) 'waters' (< **u̯ódr̥ *u̯edṓr*) and *tēkan* (nominative sing.) 'earth' ~ *taknī* (dative sing.) (< **dhéĝhōm *dhĝhméi*).

Syntax

9.41. Like the other Anatolian languages, Hittite clauses (except those at the start of a discourse or a major section in a text) typically begin with a sentence connective to which one or more clitics could be attached in a clitic chain. The most common sentence connective was *nu*; Old Hittite also had *ta* and *šu*. The initial position in the sentence, i.e. the place held by the sentence connective, could also be filled with another element in the sentence that was topicalized or fronted for emphasis or contrast; and such an element could also host the clitic chain. Various examples can be seen in the text sample below.

9.42. The order of clitics in the clitic chain was fixed: first the conjunctions *-(y)a* 'and', *-a* 'but', or *-ma* 'but'; then the quotative particle *-wa(r)*, used to indicate that the clause in which it appears is directly quoted speech; the enclitic pronouns (with forms of the 3rd person preceding the other two persons); the reflexive particle *-za*; and finally the still imperfectly understood local particles *-kan* or *-šan* (also *-(a)šta* and *-(a)pa* in the older language).

9.43. The syntax of relative clauses is of some interest. If the relative pronoun is the first word in its clause (or is preceded only by a sentence connective with or without attached clitics), then it is indefinite: ***kue*** GAL$^{\text{ḪI.A}}$ *akkuškizzi ta apie=pat ekuzi* '**whichever** cups he usually drinks from, he shall drink from those' (KBo 19.74 iv 33′–34′); *nu=mu=kan* ***kuiš*** *idaluš memiaš* ZI-*ni anda n=an=mu* DINGIR^{MEŠ} EGIR-*pa* SIG$_5$-*aḫḫanzi šarlanzi* '**whichever** bad word (is) in my soul, the gods will alleviate it (and) remove it" (KUB 6.45+ iii 46–47). However, if it is preceded by any stressed elements in its clause, it is definite: GU$_4$*=ya=wa=mu* ***kuin*** *tet nu=war=an=mu uppi* 'And the cow **that** you promised me, send it to me' (Maşat 75/14 obv. 14–16). As is typically the case in older IE languages, the relative clause precedes the main clause.

Old Hittite text sample

9.44. Below is an excerpt from the Old Hittite Ritual for the Royal Couple, KBo 17.1 (CTH 324), column III, lines 1–13, following the edition of Otten and Souček 1969. This passage is taken from the middle of the ritual; previously prepared items – an eagle and clay figurines representing an army – are here manipulated in the performance of sympathetic magic (somewhat similar to voodoo).

The passage is given below in narrow transcription; broad transcription is used in the notes (where equals signs mark off the clitics). Brackets enclose missing parts of the tablet that have been restored by conjecture; material inside the bracketed sections that is further enclosed in parentheses has been supplied from identical passages in duplicate copies (in this case, the fragments KBo 19.3 and 19.6). The horizontal lines are paragraph dividers in the original.

[ma-a-a]ḫ-ḫa-an-da ^{d}UTU-uš ^{d}IŠKUR-aš ne-e-pí-iš te-e[(-kán-na)]
2 uk-tu-u-ri LUGAL-uš SAL.LUGAL-aš-ša DUMU^{MEŠ}-ša uk-tu-u-ri-eš a-š[(a-a)]n-d[u]

---

ta nam-ma ^{MUŠEN}ḫa-a-ra-na-an ne-e-pí-ša tar-na-aḫ-ḫi
4 a-ap-pa-an-an-da-ma-aš-še ke-e me-e-ma-aḫ-ḫi na-at-ta-an ú-uk
t[(ar-na-a)]ḫ-ḫu-un LUGAL-ša-an SAL.LUGAL-ša tar-na-aš nu i-it ^{d}UTU-i
6 ^{d}IŠKUR-ya me-e-m[(i-i)]š-ki ^{d}UTU-uš ^{d}IŠKUR-aš ma-a-an uk-tu-u-ri-eš
LUGAL-uš SAL.LUGAL-aš-ša *QA-TAM-MA* uk-tu-u-ri-eš a-ša-an-tu

---

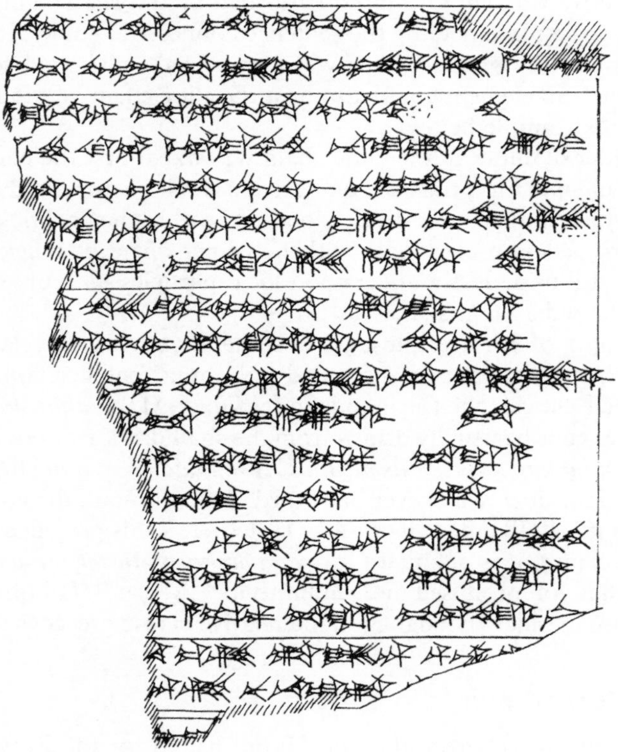

Figure 9.1 One of the fragments composing KBo 17.1. The top line begins in the middle of line 1: the broken sign is UTU, followed closely by *uš* and then a short word-break. Underneath UTU is the right part of LUGAL in line 2 followed again by *uš*. Note the "right justification" of several of the lines, where the last sign or signs of a line were delayed until near the edge of the tablet. Drawing from Heinrich Otten, *Keilschrifttexte aus Boghazköi*, vol. 17 (Berlin: Mann, 1969), p. 3. Reproduced by permission.

8 ú-i-il-na-aš ERÍN^{MEŠ}-an te-eš-šu-um-mi-uš-ša ta-ak-na-a
ḫa-ri-e-mi tu-uš tar-ma-e-mi ta ki-iš-ša-an te-e-mi
10 ^{d}UTU-uš ^{d}IŠKUR-aš ka-a-š[(a LU)]GAL-i SAL.LUGAL-ri DUMU^{MEŠ}-ma-aš-ša
^{URU}Ḫa-at-tu-ši
e-er-ma-aš-me-et e-eš-ḫ[(ar-š)]a-me-et i-da-a-lu-uš-me-et
12 ḫa-tu-ka-aš-me-et ḫa-ri-[(e-nu-u)]n ta-at a-ap-pa ša-ra-a
le-e ú-e-ez-zi

(The priest speaks:) "Just as the Sungod (and) the Stormgod, heaven and earth (2) (are) eternal, so may the king and queen and (their) children be eternal!"

(3) Then I release the eagle to the sky, (4) and after it I speak these (words): "I did not release it – the king and queen released it. Go! Say to the Sungod and the

Stormgod, 'Just as the Sungod and the Stormgod (are) eternal, (7) let the king and queen likewise be eternal!'"

(8) I bury the clay soldiers and the pots into the earth, and I nail them fast. Then I speak as follows: (10) "Sungod, Stormgod, I have just buried the disease, bloodshed, evil, (and) fright of the king, queen, and their sons in the city of Ḫattuša. Let it not come up again!"

9.44a. Notes (through beginning of line 9 only). **1–2. nēpiš:** 'sky, heaven', a neuter *s*-stem from PIE **nebh-es-* 'cloud'; cp. Ved. *nábhas-* and Gk. *néphos*. **tēkann=a:** 'and earth'; *tēkan* is from PIE **dheĝhōm*, and the clitic conjunction *-a* means 'and' and doubles the preceding consonant (as also in the phrase 'king and queen' in the next line). After a vowel and sometimes Sumerograms (e.g. line 6) it is written *-ya*. **uktūri:** 'eternal', Old Hitt. neuter collective pl. **LUGAL-uš SAL.LUGAL-ašš=a:** 'king and queen'; the underlying Hittite is *ḫaššuš *ḫaššuššarašš=a*. SAL (or MUNUS) is the Sumerogram for 'woman'. The ending *-ššaraš* comes from PIE **soro-* 'woman', which had marginal use as a feminizing suffix (§6.71). **ašandu:** 3rd pl. imperative, 'let them be', spelled *ašantu* in line 7.

3–4. ta: Old Hitt. sentence connective. ^{MUŠEN}**ḫāranan:** 'eagle', accus. sing. *n*-stem; cognate with Gk. *órn-īth-* 'bird' and the second syllable of German *Adl-er* 'eagle' (< Middle High German *adel-ar* 'noble *Aar* [eagle]'). ^{MUŠEN} is the Sumerian determiner for bird-names. **nēpiša:** 'to the sky', directive case. **tarnaḫḫi:** 'I release', 1st sing. present of the *ḫi*-conjugation, like *mēmaḫḫi* 'I say' in the next line. **āppananda=ma=šše:** 'And/but (*-ma*) after (*āppananda*) it (*-šše*)'. **kē:** neut. pl., 'these things'; PIE pronominal stem **k̂i-* (§7.10). **natta=an:** 'not' plus the clitic animate object pronoun referring to the eagle, 'it'. **ūk:** emphatic 1st sing. pronoun, 'I' (§9.11).

5–6. LUGAL-š=an SAL.LUGAL-š=a: underlying Hittite is *ḫaššuš=an *ḫassuššarašš=a* 'the king and (*-a*) the queen it (*-an*, i.e. the eagle) . . .' **tarnaš:** 'released', 3rd sing. preterite; singular because the subject 'king and queen' are treated grammatically as a unit. **īt:** 'go', suppletive imperative to the verb *pāi-* 'go' from PIE **h_1i-dhi* (Ved. *ihí*, Gk. *íthi*). **mān:** 'just as', originally a reduced form of *maḫḫanda* (line 1). ^{d}**UTU-i** ^{d}**IŠKUR=ya:** 'to the Stormgod and the Sungod'. The determiner ^{d}, short for Sumerian DINGIR 'god', precedes divine names. The phonetic complement *-i* is the Hittite dative singular ending; *-ya* means 'and'. ^{d}UTU-*uš* in line 6 is the nominative sing. **mēmiški:** 'say, speak', sing. imperative of the iterative of *memai-* 'speak', here perhaps with an inceptive meaning: 'begin to speak'.

7–9. *QATAMMA*: 'likewise', Akkadian adverb. **uīlnaš:** 'of clay', genit. sing. The sentence does not begin with a connective because it starts a new section (§9.41). **ERÍN**^{MEŠ}**-an:** 'troops'; plural in Sumerian (^{MEŠ}), but singular in Hittite, hence the accus. sing. ending *-an*. **teššummiušš=a:** 'and the pots', accus. pl. **taknā:** 'into the earth', directive of *tēkan* (stem *takn-*); the spelling *ták-na-a* instead of *ták-na* probably indicates stress on the ending, consistent with the presumed amphikinetic paradigm of the noun; see §6.24. **ḫariemi:** 'I bury'.

Luvian

9.45. Luvian (or Luwian) is attested in two closely related dialects, Cuneiform and Hieroglyphic. The language was spoken over a wide territory, especially to the south of the Hittites but also to the west. Evidence has been mounting that the fabled city of Troy, on the northwest coast of Turkey, was Luvian-speaking (see further below). As the Hittites spread south and west over Anatolia, they became strongly influenced by Luvian culture and borrowed many words, especially in the domain of religion and cult. Luvian was employed in rituals adopted by the Hittites, and most preserved Cuneiform Luvian is embedded in Hittite ritual texts from the Middle and Neo-Hittite periods.

Hieroglyphic Luvian is the only Anatolian dialect attested in both the second and first millennia BC. It is written in a native hieroglyphic script that was developed by the fourteenth century BC, although during the Hittite Empire was mostly limited to writing proper names on seals. Hieroglyphic Luvian inscriptions begin to appear on stone faces and rocks starting around the thirteenth century BC, but are infrequent before the destruction of Hattusas shortly after 1200 BC, after which Hittite ceased to be the official language of culture. The Luvian of the hieroglyphs then filled this role – a shift that in some respects was not sudden: already in the later Neo-Hittite texts there is a steady increase of Luvianisms. The majority of Hieroglyphic Luvian inscriptions date from the ninth to the seventh centuries BC, although some of the dates are being revised and may be earlier. The inscriptions include historical accounts and economic records.

9.46. Both forms of Luvian present certain difficulties. Cuneiform Luvian script is the same as Hittite script, but the meanings of many words are still opaque. The hieroglyphic script, like cuneiform, consists of characters used both logographically and syllabically; unfortunately, it is phonetically much less highly developed than cuneiform. The syllabic signs only stand for single vowels or CV sequences, and no effort is made to distinguish long vowels or many other basic phonetic facts. Since the hieroglyphic script gives so little information about the pronunciation of the language, almost all our phonetic knowledge has been gleaned from Cuneiform Luvian (the two varieties of Luvian are phonologically nearly identical). Major breakthroughs in the past few decades have improved the readings of a number of hieroglyphic signs, but some remain undeciphered.

The Trojan connection

9.47. Evidence has gradually been growing that the Trojans spoke an Anatolian language, perhaps Luvian. Troy is now generally identified with an Anatolian city called Wilusa (*Wiluša*), whose name is strongly reminiscent of *Wílion*, the early form of *Ílion*, a Greek word for Troy. One of the kings of the Hittite Empire, Muwatallis, is remembered for the treaty he sealed with one Alaksandus of Wilusa; the name is probably to be identified with Aleksandros, the Greek name for the Trojan prince Paris. In one passage of Luvian poetry (cited in §8.7), Wilusa is called 'steep', an epithet also used of the city by Homer. In 1995 a seal inscribed in Luvian was unearthed on the site of Homer's Troy, the first written object to be found there; though tantalizing, this does not yet prove that the Trojans spoke Luvian.

Developments from Common Anatolian to Luvian

Grammatically, Luvian is very similar to Hittite, but there are some differences in the phonology and morphology.

Phonology

9.48. Luvian (and perhaps Lycian) is valuable in preserving three separate outcomes of the three PIE velar series, if limitedly (only the voiceless set and only in certain contexts). As in Hittite, the plain velar **k* and the labiovelar *k^w remain intact: *kīšammi-* 'combed' < **kes-* (cp. OCS *češǫ* 'I comb'); and *kuiš* 'who' < *k^w*is* (cp. Lat. *quis* 'who'). Unlike Hittite, **k̑* remained distinct from **k* and became *z* (pronounced *ts*) before an original *e*, *i*, or *y*: *ziyari* 'lies' < **k̑ei̯-o-*, *zi-* 'this' < **k̑i-*, Hieroglyphic *wazi-* 'request' (?) < **u̯ek̑-i̯e-*. The voiced velars show no distinction, however. Both **ĝ(h)* and **g(h)* disappear before a front vowel or a *y*, as in *iššara-* 'hand' < **ĝhes-ro-* (cp. Hitt. *kiššar-*, Gk. *kheír* < **ĝhes-r-*), Hieroglyphic *waza-* 'drive' < **u̯eĝh-i̯e-*, and *ipala-* 'left(-hand)' < **geibh-* (cp. Norwegian dialectal *keiva* 'left hand'). Otherwise both remain *k* (spelling *k* or *g*), e.g. *kuttaššara-* 'orthostat' (a large megalithic slab) < **ĝhou-t-* (root **ĝheu-* 'pour') and Hieroglyphic *gurta-* 'citadel' < **ghr̥dho-* (cp. Russ. *gorod* 'city'). The voiced labiovelar *g^w*(h)* usually became *w*, as in *wāna-* 'woman' < *g^w*en-*.

9.49. A characteristic feature of Luvian phonology is a change known as **Čop's Law**, after the Slovenian Indo-Europeanist Bojan Čop. Under this rule, an original stressed **é* before a voiced stop, resonant, or *s* became *a*, and the following consonant is written double. (The consonant may have undergone fortition or "strengthening" of some sort, such as devoicing or doubling.) Thus PIE **médhu* 'sweet drink' became *maddu* 'wine'; **mélit-* 'honey' became *mallit-*; and **u̯és-* 'good' shows up in *waššar-* 'favor'. A limited version of this change may have already happened in word-initial position in Common Anatolian, but this is uncertain.

9.50. Lenition. Luvian and Lycian provide almost all the evidence for a set of lenition ("weakening") rules in Common Anatolian, which voiced an intervocalic stop after a long stressed vowel or when between two unstressed vowels. Orthographically, such stops were written single, rather than double as was usually the case with the reflexes of voiceless stops. The lenition also affected laryngeals, which are written as single in such positions rather than double; this could also indicate voicing. It has been proposed that this lenition is of Common Anatolian date, but this is controversial; the best evidence for the lenition rules comes from Luvian and its close relative Lycian. Thus Luvian *mallitati* 'with honey' (instr. sing.) has single *t's* following original unstressed vowels (earlier **mélitoti*); compare also Lycian *tadi* 'puts' (< Common Anatolian **dḗti* < PIE **dhéh*$_1$*ti*).

9.51. Differences between Cuneiform and Hieroglyphic Luvian. As briefly noted earlier, Hieroglyphic and Cuneiform Luvian are closely related dialects, but they do differ in several telling details. In Hieroglyphic Luvian, intervocalic *d* was weakened to a sound that was often indicated in writing by *r*, as in *pa+ra/i-* (phonetically *para-*) 'foot' < **podo-*. The genitive was not lost in Hieroglyphic Luvian as it was in Cuneiform, though Hieroglyphic also frequently used relational adjectives as its sister dialect did. There were also minor differences in the declension of pronouns. One noteworthy lexical difference is that the words for 'heaven' reflect different ablaut grades: Cuneiform *tappaš-* from **nebes-* (with Čop's Law) and Hieroglyphic *tipas-* from **nēbhes-*; the original paradigm was an acrostatic *s*-stem, nomin. sg. **nḗbh-os*, weak stem **nébh-es-*. But both languages share the innovation of changing the initial *n- in this word (cp. Hitt. *nēpiš-*, OCS *nebes-*) to a dental stop (interestingly paralleled by Lith. *debesìs* 'cloud').

Morphology

9.52. The noun has some peculiarities from the Hittite point of view. There was no genitive case in Cuneiform Luvian; to show possession, the language instead turned the noun into a relational adjective having the suffix *-ašša-* or *-iya-* (< PIE **-i̯o-*). Thus the noun *tiyamm(i)-* 'earth' formed the relational adjective *tiyammašša-* 'pertaining to the earth, of the earth'. Such relational adjectives are not exact equivalents of genitives, since they cannot distinguish between the singular 'of the X' and the plural 'of the X-es'; Luvian solved this problem by adding the relational adjective suffix to an old animate accusative plural ending **-anza* (< **-ns*) if the base noun was plural. Thus the word for 'ritual' was *malḫašša*, which always declined in the plural; its relational adjective was *malḫašš-anz-ašša-* 'pertaining to the ritual'. The animate accusative plural **-ns* wound up having important other uses too, as the Luvians decided to use it as a base for remaking the animate plural paradigm, whence for instance a new animate pl. nominative in *-inzi* (on the first *-i-*, see §9.54 below; the second *-i* might continue the pronominal plural **-oi*, but this is uncertain).

9.53. Neuter nouns in the nomin.-accus. singular regularly appear with a particle *-ša* attached, quite probably from an old neuter demonstrative **sod*. An example is *wār-ša* 'water' (< **u̯oh*$_1$*r̥*, cp. Ved. *vā́r*). As elsewhere in Anatolian, neuters are declined in an ergative case when functioning as the subject of a transitive verb.

9.54. Another peculiarity of Luvian nominal declension not found in Hittite is that most animate nouns and adjectives formed their nominatives and accusatives with a stem *-ī-*, even if they were not normally *i*-stems. Thus the relational adjective *tiyammašša-* 'of the earth' above has a nominative sing. *tiyammaššiš*. This is also the norm in Lycian and Lydian. The origins of this phenomenon (termed "*i*-mutation") are debated.

9.55. In verbal morphology, Luvian differs from Hittite especially in the 1st person present active endings. The singular normally ends in *-wi*, as in *ḫapiui* 'I bind' and *arkamanallaui* 'I bear tribute'; and the plural is *-unni*, related to Hitt. *-wani* (e.g. *mammalḫunni* 'we crush'). Luvian has an unexplained 3rd plural preterite ending *-aunta* (e.g. *nakkušāūnta* 'they furnished a scapegoat', Hieroglyphic Luvian *wa/i-la-u-ta* 'they died', phonetically *walaunta*). Luvian kept **t* intact before *i*, unlike Hittite, so the 3rd sing. and pl. of the *mi*-conjugation are still *-ti* and *-nti*: *īti* 'goes' (cp. Lat. *it*), *ḫišḫiyanti* 'they bind' (vs. Hitt. *išḫiyanzi*). Because of the limited remains of the language, not all forms of the verbal paradigm are known.

9.56. Not much is known about the non-finite formations in Luvian. It has a participle in *-mma-* (or *-mmi-*) that functions like *-ant-* in Hittite or **-tó-* elsewhere in IE: *kīšammi-* 'combed', *dūpaimmi-* 'beaten'. The source may be PIE **-mo-* that yields passive participles in Balto-Slavic (§5.60), but this is disputed. (This feature is shared by Lycian.) An infinitive in *-una* is also found (e.g. *aduna* 'to eat'), probably an old directive case of a verbal noun in **-war*, stem **-un-*.

Cuneiform Luvian text sample

9.57. From the Dūpaduparša Ritual, KUB 9.6 + 35.39 i 23f. The ritual is written mostly in Hittite, with spells and incantations in Luvian spoken by the "old woman" (^{SAL}ŠU.GI) who officiated over the ritual. Restorations have been made on the basis of parallel passages elsewhere on the tablet. The interpretation of several forms is tentative. An 'x' stands for an unreadable sign.

ku-iš ḫi-i-ru-ta-ni[-ya-at-t]a ti-wa-ta-ni-ya-at-ta
24 na-a-nu-um-pa-ta ma-a[d-du-ú-]in-zi ma-al-li-ti-in-zi
da-a-i-ni-in-zi x[ ]x-al-la-an-zi a-ar-ši-ya-an-du
26 [t]a-a-i-in-ti-ya[-ta ma-al-li a-i-]ya-ru ta-pa-a-ru-wa
[ḫi-ru-]ú-ta [ta-ta-ar-ri-ya-am-na u-w]a-la-an-te-ya
28 ḫu-u-i-it-wa[-li-e-ya -ḫ]i-e-ya na-a-ni-e-ya
na-a-na-aš-ri[-e-ya]
30 lu-u-la-ḫi-e-ya ḫ[a-pí-ri-e-ya ku-wa-ar-š]a-aš-sa-an
tu-ú-li-ya-aš-ša-a[n

Whoever has cursed (or) sworn, (24) then now let the . . . of wine, of honey, (25) of oil flow! (26) Let them become oil (and) honey – the . . . s, (27) the oaths (and) curses of the dead (28) (and) of the living, of the . . . , of a brother, (29) of a sister, . . . (30) of the mountain-dwellers, of the people of the plain, of the army, (31) of the assembly . . .

9.57a. Notes. 23. kuiš: 'who, whoever', PIE **$k^{w}$is* (Hitt. *kuiš*). **ḫīrutaniyatta:** 'has cursed', preterite 3rd sing., to be analyzed as *ḫīrut-aniya-tta*, a denominative verb from the noun *ḫīrut-* 'curse'. The ending *-tta* is the 3rd sing. preterite ending, from PIE **-to*, and *-aniy(a)-* is a denominative suffix that ultimately comes from PIE **-i̯e/o-* (§5.33). The noun *ḫīrut-* 'curse' (nomin. pl. *ḫirūta* below in line 27) comes from **h_2ēru-t-* (with long *ē* not colored by the laryngeal) and is probably cognate with Gk. (Arcadian) *(kat-)arw(-os)* 'accursed'. **tiwataniyatta:** 'has sworn, cursed', a 3rd sing. preterite denominative like the preceding, from *tiwat-* 'Sungod' (**diu̯-ot-*, like Lat. *dīu-it-* 'wealthy'). It has been suggested that it originally meant something like 'call upon god' in a bad sense, like the Oscan verb *deiua-* 'curse' from the word for 'god'.

24–25. nānum=pa=ta: a chain consisting of *nānun* 'now' plus a conjunction *-pa* plus a particle *-ta* that seems to mean 'then' or the like. **maddūinzi:** 'of wine', nomin. pl. of *madduwi(ya)-*, adjective formed from *maddu* 'wine', PIE **medhu-*, with geminate *-dd-* and *-a-* by Čop's Law (§9.49 above). **mallitinzi:** 'of honey', nomin. pl. of *malliti(ya)-*, from *mallit-* 'honey', PIE **melit-*, with geminate *-ll-* and *-a-* by Čop's Law. **dāininzi:** 'of oil', nomin. pl. of *dāini(ya)-*, from *dāin-* 'oil'. **āršiyandu:** 'let (them) flow' or 'let (them) make them flow', 3rd pl. imperative; cp. Hittite *aršiya-* 'cause to flow'.

26–27. tāīn=tiy=ata: 'oil' (nomin. sing.) plus the reflexive particle *-ti* plus the clitic pronoun *-ata* 'they, them', with a *y*-glide written between them. The clitic pronoun "doubles" the subject and is required when the subject (*tapāruwa hirūta* and so forth) is shifted to the end of the sentence (technically, when it is right-dislocated). **aiyaru:** 'let become', 3rd sing. imperative; singular verb agreeing with a neuter plural subject, an archaic IE syntactic feature (§§6.68, 8.16). **tapāruwa:** of unknown meaning, but apparently designating something bad; the first in a string of neuter plurals. **tatarriyamna:** 'curses' (the restoration is tentative); lit. '(bad) things that get said', from *tatarriya-* 'say' (cp. Hitt. *tar-anzi* 'they say'). **uwalanteya:** 'of the dead', neut. pl. of a relational adjective in **-i̯o-*, as are all the following words. The base *uwalant-* 'dead' is perhaps the clearest Luvian example of an old participle in *-nt-*, §9.4.

28–31. ḫūītwalieya: 'of the living', from *ḫuitwal-* 'alive', related to Hitt. *ḫuišu-*, *ḫuišwant-* 'living, alive', with unclear morphological details. **nānieya:** 'of a brother', adjective from an unattested **nani-* that would be the Luvian cognate of Hitt. *negnaš* 'brother' (interestingly not the PIE word). **nānašrieya:** 'of a sister', from the 'brother' word plus the feminizing suffix *-šri-*; see note to line 2 of the Hittite text above. **lūlaḫieya:** 'of those living in the mountains'. **ḫapirieya:** 'of those living on the plain'. **kuwaršaššan:** 'of the army'; apparently the *-an* in this and the following word is a mistake for *-a*, since they should both still be neuter plural. **tūliyaššan:** 'of the assembly'. The rest of the line is unclear.

Hieroglyphic Luvian text sample

9.58. The block inscription HAMA 2 (conventionally, Hieroglyphic Luvian inscriptions are named using capital letters), from Hama (ancient Hamath) in western Syria, c. 830 BC. To reduce somewhat the inscrutability of the transcriptional conventions, the following points may be noted. Ideograms are rendered as Latin words in capitals; those used as determiners are put in parentheses and without a break separating them from the word they are determining. Quote marks indicate the addition of a pair of curly marks to a sign, indicating explicitly that it is a determiner. Slashes indicate multiple possible phonetic readings of a single sign (e.g. *wa/i* can be read *wa* or *wi*); a plus sign indicates that two signs are joined.

The transliteration follows the edition of Hawkins 2000.

1 EGO-*mi* MAGNUS+*ra/i-tà-mi-sa u+ra/i-hi-li-ni-sa* (INFANS)*ni-za-sa i-ma-tú-wa/i-ni*(REGIO) REX
2 *a-wa/i á-mu* AEDIFICARE+*MI-ha za-'* ("CASTRUM")*ha+ra/i-ni-sà-za la-ka-wa/i-ni-sà-ha-wa/i*(REGIO) FLUMEN.REGIO-*tà-i-sà*
3 REL-*za i-zi-i-tà a-tá-ha-wa/i ni-ki-ma-sa*(REGIO)

I (am) Uratamis, son of Urhilina, Hathamite king. I myself built this fortress, which he of the Laka river-land made, and in addition the land Nikima.

9.58a. 1. EGO-mi: phonetically *amu=mi*; *-mi* is the 1st sg. dative reflexive pronoun. Hieroglyphic Luvian syntax had the curious requirement that the dative reflexive pronoun be used in sentences with the verb 'be' (whether expressed or not) if the subject was 1st or 2nd person. **ni-za-sa:** abbreviation of *ni-mu-wa/i-za-sa* (phonetically *nimuwizas*) 'son'. The word may mean 'not (sexually) mature'; *muwa-* is an Anatolian morpheme in words having to do with virile might (PIE root **muH-*) and *ni-* appears to be a negative morpheme, but the formal details are unclear. The *-sa* of this and Uratamis's name represents the *-s* of the animate nomin. sg. (the *-a* is an empty vowel), while in Urhilina's name it is the genit. sg. **i-ma-tú-wa/i-ni:** 'Hathamite', containing the adjectival suffix *-(u)wanni-* (geminates are always written single in HLuv.) for forming ethnonyms, from earlier **-u̯én-(i)-* that underwent Čop's Law (§9.49). The nominative ending *-sa* was not written.

Figure 9.2 The Hieroglyphic Luvian inscription HAMA 2. Each line of text is divided into vertical groupings that are read top to bottom, and successively from right to left in the first line. The direction is reversed in each successive line; faces always point away from the direction of writing (facing the approaching eyes of the reader, as it were). The first group of signs is in the upper right with the figure pointing at himself (EGO) followed by the rectangular signs below that (*mi*). Drawing by David Hawkins from Hawkins 2000 (vol. 1, part 3, plate 222). Reproduced by permission of the publisher.

2. a-wa/i: chain consisting of the sentence-initial conjunction *a-* (left untranslated; cp. Hitt. *nu*) plus the quotative particle *-wa* (Hitt. *-wa(r)*), since the king's words are being quoted. **á-mu:** 'I', Hitt. *ammuk* (with added *-k* from the nominative *ūk*); used emphatically. **AEDIFICARE+*MI*-ha:** 'I built', with pret. 1st sing. ending *-ha*, cp. Hitt. *-ḫḫa*, from PIE $*\text{-}h_2e$. Phonetically probably *tamaha* (cp. Gk. *démō* 'I build'), with *MI* a kind of phonetic indicator of the *-m-*. **za-':** 'this', CLuv. *zā-*, Hitt. *kā-* < **k̂o-*; the acute accent represents an extra sign without phonetic value that was probably used as a space-filler for aesthetic purposes (the Luvians liked the vertical space to be filled evenly). **ha+ra/i-ni-sà-za:** 'fortress'. **la-ka-wa/i-ni-sà-ha-wa/i** = *lakawanis* 'of Laka' plus the connecting particle *-ha* 'and, also' (cognate with the Hitt. conjunction *-a* that geminates a preceding consonant) and the quotative particle *-wa*. **FLUMEN.REGIO-tà-i-sà:** phonetically *hapatais* 'of the river-land', animate nomin. sg., contracted from **hapata-iy-i-s*, an *-i̯i̯o-*adjective with *i*-mutation (*-i̯i̯-i- replacing *-i̯i̯-o-) built to *hapata-* 'river-land', cp. Hitt. *ḫap-* 'river' < $*h_2eb\text{-}$ (the source also of Welsh *afon* 'river' and the name of the river *Avon*).

3. REL-za: REL is the transliteration of the ideogram standing for the relative pronoun, and *-za* (also *-sa*) is a suffix added to neuter nominative-accusative singulars in Luvian.

i-zi-i-tà: 'made', 3rd sing. pret. of *izzi(ya)-* 'make', of uncertain etymology. Though the second syllable was long (*izzīta*, syncopated from *izziyata*), the repeated *i* is probably not a marker of length (which was otherwise not done) but added for the aesthetic purpose of filling up the available space. **a-tá-ha-wa/i:** a chain beginning with *a-tá* (phonetically *anta*) 'within; in addition' (cp. Hitt. *anda*; PIE *endo) plus the particles *-ha* and *-wa* again.

Palaic

9.59. Palaic is known from only eleven ritual and mythological texts written down during Old Hittite times. The language seems to have become extinct rather early, and has in fact been called the first Indo-European language to die out. The name comes from Palā, the Hittite name of a region probably in north-central Anatolia across the Halys River in the area known in classical times as Paphlagonia (a name plausibly interpreted as deriving from a reduplicated version of Palā, *pa-pla- or the like).

9.60. Palaic is on the whole quite similar to Hittite. A striking phonological feature is the continuation of the sequence *-eh$_2$-i̯e- in derived verbs as *-āga-*. As in Hittite and Luvian, short accented vowels in open syllables are written long, as in the genitive singular of the word for 'eagle', *ḫāranaš* < *h$_3$óron-; contrast the nomin. sing. *ḫarāš=kuwar=zi* in the text below, where the accent seems to have shifted to before the following enclitic *-kuwar*.

Palaic text sample

9.61. KUB 32.18 i 5′ff. (The symbol ′ means the top part of the tablet is broken off and lines have been numbered from the beginning of the surviving part of the tablet.) The text is too poorly understood to provide a complete translation. Line 7′ is essentially identical to a passage from the Hittite Telipinu myth (KUB 19.10) which states, *eter n=e UL išpier ekuier=ma n=e=za UL ḫaššikir* "They ate, (but) they were not satisfied; they drank, (but) they were not satisfied." This seems to be a mythological theme of Common Anatolian date. An 'x' stands for an unreadable sign.

]x-na-ku-pa-an-ta šu-wa-a-ru! ša-a-ú-i[
6′]an-za ma-a-ar-za ma-a-aḫ-la-an-za a-an-ti-en-ta ma-a[-ar-ḫa-aš
[a-]ta-a-an-ti ni-ip-pa-ši mu-ša-a-an-ti a-ḫu-wa-an-ti ni-ip-pa-aš ḫa-ša-an-ti

---

8′ [ti-]ya-az-ku-wa-ar ú-e-er-ti ka-a-at-ku-wa-a-at ku-it a-ta-a-an-ti
[ni-]ip-pa-ši mu-ša-a-an-ti a-ḫu-wa-a-an-ti ni-ip-pa-aš ḫa-ša-a-an-ti
10′ x ḫa-ra-a-aš-ku-wa-ar-zi pa-na-a-ga-an-zi ši-i-it-tu-wa-ra-an
[ši-]it-ta-an ḫa-pí-it-ta-la-an-ku-wa-ra-an ši-it-ta-an

9.61a. Notes. 5′–7′. šuwāru: 'full', neuter nomin.-accus. sing., cp. German *schwer* 'heavy', Lith. *svarùs* 'heavy'. The raised exclamation point is a convention indicating that the scribe wrote a different sign by mistake. **šāui[:** probably the word for 'horn', whose collective plural is *šāwidār*; cp. Hitt. *šāwatar* 'horn'. Note that if this interpretation is correct, we have a reference here to a 'full horn' or cornucopia. **mārza:** something edible. **āntienta:** 'they go in', if it is to be segmented *ānt-yenta* (cp. Hitt. *anda* 'in, into' and Hitt. *ianzi*, *ienzi* 'they go' < root *$h_1$ei-* 'go', cp. Lat. *eunt* 'they go'). **mārhaš:** 'the gods'. **atānti:** 'they eat', Hitt. *atanzi*, PIE *$h_1$edn̥ti*. Note the scriptio plena in the ending *-ānti* in this and the next verb (and more consistently in lines 8′ ff.), which probably indicates stress. **nippaši:** to be segmented *ni=ppa=ši*, of which *ni-* is the negative 'not', *-ppa* is a conjunction meaning 'but', and *-ši* is probably a reflexive particle (note that the Hittite word for 'eat one's fill', *ḫaššikke-*, is also used with a reflexive particle). **mušānti:** 'they eat their fill, become satisfied'; cp. Greek *amustí* 'at one draught'. **aḫuwanti:** 'they drink', Hitt. *akuwanzi*; Palaic lenited (weakened) the intervocalic labiovelar to *-ḫu-* (PIE *h_1eg^wh- 'drink', also in Lat. *ēb-rius* 'drunk'). **nippaš:** *ni=pp(a)=aš* 'but they not'; *-aš* is probably a 3rd pl. subject pronoun. **ḫašanti:** 'they drink their fill, become satisfied', cp. Hitt. *ḫaššikke-* 'eat one's fill'.

8′–11′. **tiyaz:** 'the Sungod', PIE **diu̯ots*, cp. Luv. *Tiwaz*. The particle *-kuwar* may be emphatic: 'the Sungod himself'. **uērti:** 'announces, says'; cp. Hitt. *weriya-* 'say'. **kātkuwāt:** *kāt* means 'this', nomin.-accus. sing. neuter (or maybe plural); the rest is unclear. **panāganzi:** 'appearing' or the like; animate nomin. sing. present participle, with the *-i* probably an empty vowel, from **-ant-s* (in Hittite, this would have been written *-anza* with an empty *-a*). The stem goes back to something like *panáh$_2$i̯e-, with the Palaic outcome of *-ah$_2$i̯e- discussed above. **šīttuwaran šittan:** unclear in meaning, but probably a middle verb form *šīttuwar* (plus clitic pronoun *-an*) followed by a 2nd pl. imperative (active) *šittan* from the same verb. The alternation in voice is strongly reminiscent of Cuneiform Luvian *azzaštan* . . . *nīš aztūwari* 'Eat! (2nd pl. imperative active) . . . You do not eat' (2nd pl. middle) in KUB 9.31 ii 26–28. **ḫapittalan:** 'member, limb, joint'; cp. Hitt. *ḫapp-eššar* 'limb, joint' with different suffix.

Lycian

9.62. Lycian was spoken in Lycia, a country on the southwest Anatolian coast in a rugged area between the Gulf of Fethiye and the Gulf of Antalya. It is attested almost solely on coin legends and short tomb inscriptions from the fifth and fourth centuries BC in a Greek-derived alphabet. Only two extensive texts have been found, the Xanthos Stele, containing a historical account, and the Letoon Trilingual, concerning the establishment of a cult of Leto and written in Lycian, Greek, and Aramaic. The Trilingual, not surprisingly, has been crucial for understanding the language. The Lycian on two sides of the Xanthos Stele is different from the usual sort and is called **Milyan** or Lycian B (with Lycian A being the ordinary form of Lycian). Lycian is closely related to Luvian, but contrary to some claims cannot be derived directly from the Luvian known to us, as shown by certain differences especially in phonology and morphology.

9.63. The letters used in the traditional transcription of the Lycian alphabet do not all match their probable pronunciations very well. The letter transcribed as χ was not a fricative but a stop; what are written as voiced stops were pronounced as fricatives (so, e.g., *d* stands for ð); and *z* represents a voiceless affricate *ts* as in Hittite. Additionally, after nasals or nasalized vowels, it appears that stops were voiced even if they were written voiceless. For example, the possessive suffix *-wãt(i)-* (PIE **-u̯ent-*, §6.40) was pronounced *-wãd-* (with nasalized *a*). Etymological *d*'s show up spelled as *t*'s in this position too, as in *ñte* 'in' < **endo* (cp. Hitt. *anda*, Gk. *endo-*).

9.64. As might be expected of a language closely allied with Luvian, the three original voiceless velar series have distinct reflexes. The old palatal velar **k̂* became *s*, as in the verb *si-* 'lie' from **k̂ei-* (cp. Luvian *zi-* seen above, §9.48). The ordinary velar **k* remains *k* in all positions, but ***k^w becomes *t* in Lycian A before front vowels, as in *ti-* 'who, which' < ***k^w*i-* 'who, which' (compare §12.15 for the same development in Greek). Our information on the voiced velars is meager, but from what we have it appears that they pattern with Luvian. For example, ***g^w also became *w*, as in *wawa-* 'cow' < ***g^w*ou-*.

9.65. Consonantal reflexes of the second laryngeal are well attested; ***h_2 became a stop variously spelled *k*, *q*, and *χ*, with the precise conditioning factors still not worked out. Examples include *χñt-* 'front' (cp. Hitt. *ḫant-*) and *Trqqas* (stem *Trqqñt-*), the name of the Stormgod (cp. Luv. *Tarḫunt-*) < **tr̥*h_2*u̯ent-*. The latter example suggests that *q* is a labialized outcome of the laryngeal before the glide **u̯*.

9.66. The fate of vocalized laryngeals in Anatolian is the subject of controversy. Figuring in the debate is a well-known word in Lycian A, *kbatra-* 'daughter' (PIE **dhugh*$_2$*ter-*), which most likely preserves the ***h_2 as the first *-a-*. An early **dugatr(a)-* lost its internal *g*, becoming **du̯atra-*; in Lycian A, the cluster **du̯-* became *kb-* (compare the word for 'two', *kbi-* < **du̯i-*), so **du̯atra-* then became *kbatra-*.

9.67. Unaccented vowels in various positions underwent syncope (loss), although the exact conditions still have to be worked out: *ahñtãi* 'property' < **ahãntãi* < **asant-* 'existing'; *pddẽ* 'place' < **pedom*; *θθẽ* 'votive object' < **dVhẽ* or **tVhẽ*. As these last two examples show, this syncope produced various unusual word-initial consonant clusters, giving Lycian part of its characteristic look. The final consonant in consonant clusters is often written double, as in both *Trqqas* and *pddẽ*; the reasons for this are not fully clear.

9.68. Lycian provides crucial evidence for the existence of the vowel **o* in Common Anatolian, for it is the only language in which this vowel did not merge with *a* either in pronunciation or in spelling. (As the cuneiform syllabary had no signs for *o*, we cannot be absolutely sure that *a* was not sometimes used to write the vowel *o*.) Its outcome in Lycian was *e*, as in the preterite 3rd sing. verbal ending *-te* from **-to*, the neuter nomin.-accus. ending *-ẽ* from **-om*, and words like *ñte* 'in, into' < **endo*; contrast for all of these Hittite and Luvian *-ta*, *-an*, and *anda*.

9.69. Lycian syntax differs from the syntax of its Anatolian sisters in not having verb-final clause structure. Verbs appear near the front of the clause, preceded by topicalized or focused elements and certain conjunctions. Apparently, the option of fronting verbs for emphasis (§8.19) was generalized in this language.

Lycian text sample

9.70. The beginning of the Letoon Trilingual. The translation below loosely follows an unpublished one by Craig Melchert (used here by permission). Each clause is put on a separate line below for clarity.

ẽke Trm̃misñ χssaθrapazate Pigesere Katamlah tideimi
sẽ=ñne ñte-pddẽ-hadẽ Trm̃mile pddẽnehm̃mis Ijeru se-Natrbbijẽmi
sej-Arñna asaχlazu Erttimeli
me-hñti-tubedẽ arus sej-epewẽtlm̃mẽi Arñnãi

m̃maitẽ kumezijẽ θθẽ χñtawati χbidẽñni sej-Arᴋᴋazuma χñtawati
sẽ=ñn=aitẽ kumazu mahãna ebette Eseimiju Qñturahahñ tideimi
se=de Eseimijaje χuwati-ti

When Pigesere (Pixodaros) son of Katamle (Hekatomnos) ruled as satrap of Lycia (2) and he installed for the Lycians Hieron and Natrbbijẽmi (Apollodotos) as commissioners (3) and for Xanthos Artemelis as governor, (4) the free citizenry (?) and the dependents of Xanthos came to an agreement (5) and they made a sacred cult installation for the (gods) King of Kaunos and King Arkazuma. (6) And they made Simias son of Kondorasis priest for these gods, (7) and the ones who succeed Simias.

9.70a. Notes (through line 5 only). **1. ẽke:** 'when'. **Trm̃misñ:** 'Lycia', accus. sing. **χssaθrapazate:** 'ruled as satrap', 3rd sing. preterite. A satrap was a local governor in ancient Persia; it is ultimately an Iranian word (**xšaθra-pā-* 'protector of a province'; cp. Old Pers. *xšaçapāvā*). **tideimi:** 'son', perhaps from a mediopassive participle of a verb **tid(e)i-* 'suckle'.

2. sẽ=ñne: lit. 'and (*se*) him (*-ẽ*) them (*-ñne*)', clause-initial clitic chain. The clitic object pronoun *-ẽ* 'him' (< **-om*, cognate with Hitt. *-an*) doubles the direct object *Ijeru*, and the clitic pronoun *-ñne* 'them' doubles the indirect object *Trm̃mile*. Such clitic doubling is obligatory in Lycian syntax. **ñte-pddẽ-hadẽ:** 'installed, commissioned'; *ñte-* is a preverb cognate with Hitt. *anda* 'in, into'; *pddẽ* is accus. sing. of the noun meaning 'place' and seems to form part of a compound verb, the other part being *hadẽ* 'let go of, left'; literally then 'left in place'. **Trm̃mile:** 'for the Lycians', dat. pl.; cp. *Trm̃misñ* in the preceding line. **pddẽnehm̃mis:** 'commissioners', accus. pl. The second half of it, *-hm̃mi-*, is the mediopassive participle of *ha-* 'let, leave' seen above. **Ijeru se-Natrbbijẽmi:** 'Hieron and Natrbbijẽmi'; the first is a Greek name, the second is translated in the Greek version of the inscriptions as Apollodotos ('given by Apollo'), meaning that *Natr-* is an Anatolian god corresponding to Apollo, and *-bbijẽmi* is *pijẽmi-* 'given' (with *p-* voiced to *b-* following the *-r* of *Natr-*), the participle of *pije-* 'give' (cp. Hitt. *pāi* 'gives').

3–5. sej-Arñna: 'and for Xanthos', dat. pl. (with singular meaning); the *-j* of *sej* is just a hiatus-filling glide between vowels. **asaχlazu:** 'governor'. **Erttimeli:** 'Artemelis', Greek name. **me-hñti-tubedẽ:** 'they made an agreement'; *me-* is a conjunction that introduces a main clause following a dependent clause; *hñti-* may consist of *hñ-* 'together' plus the reflexive particle *-ti* (Hitt. *-za*, Luv. *-ti*). **arus:** uncertain, here rendered as 'citizenry'. **sej-epewẽtlm̃mẽi:** 'and the *períoikoi*', the neighboring dependent population; ultimately a participle of an unknown verb. **Arñnãi:** 'of Xanthos', genit. pl. **m̃maitẽ:** a verb form of uncertain meaning. **kumezijẽ:** 'sacred', derived from *kumaza-* 'priest' with the same "occupational" suffix *-aza-* as in the word for 'governor' in line 3. **θθẽ:** 'cult offering, installation'; cp. Lydian *taśev* 'stele'. **χñtawati:** 'king', dat. sing.; probably literally 'the one who is in front/foremost', cp. Hitt. and Luv. *ḫant-* 'front'. **χbidẽñni:** 'of Kaunos', a deity. **sej-Arᴋᴋazuma:** 'and Arkazuma', dat. sing.; a name or title of a deity, with ᴋᴋ representing some kind of rare velar rendered in Greek by a *g*.

Lydian

9.71. Lydia, located on the west-central Anatolian coast, was inhabited in the first millennium BC by an Anatolian people who left behind a little over 100 texts in an alphabet similar to eastern varieties of the Greek alphabet, as well as in the Old Phrygian alphabet. The texts are mostly from the fifth and fourth centuries BC in Sardis, the capital of Lydia. A few others are dated to as early as the eighth century BC. The inscriptions, carved on stone, include dedicatory formulas, decrees, and epitaphs. The language is difficult to figure out due to the small size of the corpus – the smallest in Anatolian after Palaic. A number of the inscriptions are in verse, which has allowed an analysis of the language's stress placement.

9.72. Lydian had the voiceless stops *p* (written *b*) *t k* and a stop transliterated as *q* that was probably a labiovelar. Under certain conditions, such as after nasals (as in Lycian), stops were voiced. The letter transliterated as *d* was actually a fricative, probably ð (as in Eng. *this*). There were two sibilants, transcribed *ś* and *s*: confusingly, it now appears that the first one stands for the ordinary dental or alveolar sibilant *s*, while the second stands for a palatal sibilant of some kind. The symbol λ is used to represent what was probably a palatalized *l*. The pronunciation of the symbol transcribed as a lower-case Greek letter nu, *ν*, is uncertain; its only clear source is a word-final nasal.

9.73. Lydian underwent loss of unstressed vowels, as in *alarmś* 'self' < **-mos*, *bidν* 'I gave' < **piyom*, and *ẽtamν* 'designation' < **ẽtamẽν*. The nasalized vowels *ã* and *ẽ* occur as in Lycian. As shown by *bidν* < **piyom* above and by other examples like *dẽt* 'movable property' < **yont-* 'going', Lydian underwent the unusual change **y* > *d* (ð). An interesting feature of Lydian verbs, coincidentally found also in Baltic (§18.66), is that the present 3rd-person forms are the same in the singular and plural. The preterite 3rd person shows an ending *-l*.

9.74. Not much of the morphology of Lydian has been preserved, but that which has survived is consistent with the other Anatolian languages. In nouns, the animate nomin. sing. ended in *-ś* or *-s*, essentially unchanged from PIE, while neuter nouns and adjectives end in *-d*, which has spread from the pronominal neuter nomin.-accus. ending **-d*. As in Luvian, there was no genitive. Possession was expressed by a relational adjective in *-l*, as in *bakillλ* 'of Bacchus', or (less commonly) *-si-* (etymologically the same as Luvian *-ašša-*).

Lydian text sample

9.75. The Lydian-Aramaic bilingual epitaph from Sardis, on a marble stele dated to about 400 BC. Parts of the Aramaic version are not well understood, hence some of the uncertainty in the translation. The Lydian version is probably missing a line at the beginning. The equals signs have been added to show clitic boundaries.

[o]raλ islλ bakillλ est mrud eśś=k [wãnaś] laqrisa=k qela=k kud=k=it ist esλ wãn[aλ] bλtarwod ak=ad manelid kumlilid silukalid ak=id n[ãqis] esλ mruλ buk esλ wãnaλ buk esvav laqirisav buk=it kud ist esλ wãnaλ bλtarwod ak=t=in nãqis qelλk fẽnsλifid fak=mλ artimuś ibśimsis artimu=k kulumsis aaraλ biraλ=k kλidaλ kofuλ=k qiraλ qelλ=k bilλ wcbaqẽnt

. . . during the month of Bacchus. This stele and this [tomb] and *laqrisa* and land (?), (and?) as it . . . from (?) this tomb, it (is) of Manes (son) of Kumlis (son) of Silukas. But (?) should anyone (be?) at this stele or at this tomb or at these *laqirisa* or indeed as it belongs in this tomb (??), should anyone violate against the land,

Figure 9.3 The Lydian bilingual. The Lydian text is the upper part, beginning in the upper right and reading from right to left (the first easily visible letters are the A and Λ of *oraλ*). Photograph from W. H. Buckler, *Sardis,* Vol. VI: *Lydian Inscriptions*, Part II (Leiden: Brill, 1924).

Artemis of Ephesus and Artemis the Koloan will trample (?) on his yard and house, earth and water, property and land.

9.75a. Notes. oraλ: 'month'. **islλ:** some sort of participle. **bakillλ:** 'of Bacchus'; see §9.74. **est:** 'this', neuter; the *-t* is a suffixed neuter nomin.-accus. ending ultimately from PIE **-d*. The pronoun *es-* has been plausibly etymologized as cognate with Hitt. *aši* 'the aforementioned'. **mrud:** 'stele', shortened form of *mruwaad*. **eśś=k:** 'and this'; *-k* is the conjunction 'and' < PIE **kʷe*. **wãnaś:** 'tomb'. **laqrisa:** part of the tomb or tomb complex. The spelling *laqirisa* further in the inscription is an error or reflects epenthesis. **qela:** usually interpreted to mean 'land', but uncertain. **kud=k=it:** *kud* is apparently a conjunction, perhaps 'as'; *-it* is 'it'. **ist:** perhaps 'from', from **eks* (cp. Lat. *ex* 'out of, from'). **eśλ wãnaλ:** 'this tomb', object of *ist*. **bλtarwod:** a verb of unknown meaning. **ak=ad:** *ak* is apparently a sentence connective like Hittite *nu*; *-ad* is an enclitic neuter pronoun. **manelid:** 'of Manes', relational adjective in the neuter, modifying *-ad*; the following two words are relational adjectives also, functioning as patronymics. **nãqis:** 'whoever, anyone', from earlier **nãvqis*, with the same morphemes (in reverse order) as Latin *quisnam* 'whoever'. **buk:** 'or'. **esvav:** 'these', genit. pl.; since the nasal transliterated as nu (ν) seems to come from original word-final nasals (§9.72), the original form was **esom*, which, after syncope to **esν*, was recharacterized with the productive ending *-aν*. **fẽnsλifid:** perhaps 'violates'. **fak:** a variant of *ak* (for the *f-*, cp. Luv. and Palaic *-pa* 'but, and'). **artimuś ibśimsis:** 'Artemis of Ephesus', local goddess. **aaraλ:** 'yard'. **biraλ:** 'house', cp. Hitt. *pēr* 'house'. **kλidaλ:** 'earth'; a suggested cognate is Eng. *clay*. **kofuλ:** 'water', perhaps cognate with Armenian *cov* 'sea'. Note the rhyming pair *aaraλ biraλ* and the alliterative pair *kλidaλ kofuλ*, poetic features. **qiraλ:** 'property', perhaps specifically immovable property. **qelλ=k bilλ:** the Aramaic here has 'and whatever is his', which would mean that *qel* is not a form of *qela* 'ground' but rather a form of *qeśi* 'whatever'. **wcbaqẽnt:** perhaps 'trample', but uncertain. Lycian does not distinguish between 3rd sing. and 3rd pl. verbs.

Carian, Pisidian, and Sidetic

9.76. As mentioned at the outset of this chapter, three very fragmentarily attested languages of southwest Anatolia also belong to the Anatolian branch: Carian, Pisidian, and Sidetic. All three appear to be allied with Luvian, though the limited attestation does not yet allow any firm conclusions about subgrouping.

Caria was a region in the extreme southwest of Anatolia, to the north and west of Lycia. A few inscriptions from about the fourth and third centuries BC have been found there, but most of the Carian corpus comes from Egypt, where a number of Carian immigrants settled and left epitaphs and graffiti dating from the seventh to the fourth centuries BC. Recent advances in the decipherment of the Carian alphabet have allowed some preliminary grammatical analysis. The claim that Carian is Anatolian was originally based on the presence of relational adjectives of the Luvian type, and with a related suffix *-ś*. To this can be added some cognates with other Anatolian languages, like *χi* 'who' (cp. Hitt. *kuiš*, and recall also §8.28) and *ted* 'father' (cp. Lyc. *tede-*, Cuneiform Luv. *tātiš*).

Pisidia, located east of Caria and north of Lycia, is the site of a little over thirty tomb inscriptions from perhaps the third or second centuries BC in a Greek-derived alphabet. Finally, Sidetic, the least well attested Anatolian language (if it is Anatolian), is known from a half-dozen inscriptions from the third century BC found in Side, on the Pamphylian coast. The identification of both Pisidian and Sidetic as Anatolian rests mostly on the presence of relational adjectives in *-s*. Note also Sidetic *maśara*, apparently meaning 'gods', which is related to Lycian *mahãna* (which appeared above in §9.70, line 6).

For Further Reading

Most of the important general reference works on the Anatolian languages are in German. An exception is the excellent historical phonology by H. Craig Melchert (1994) and the historical phonology of Hittite by Sara Kimball (1995). Fundamental for Anatolian studies are good textual editions; these are scattered among innumerable journals and other publications, but a number of important ones can be found in the 40-plus volumes of the ongoing series *Studien zu den Boğazköy-Texten* (*StBoT* for short; published by Harrassowitz in Wiesbaden). This series also contains the complete Cuneiform Luvian corpus (Starke 1984) and the complete Palaic corpus with glossary (Carruba 1970). Note also the monograph series *Texte der Hethiter* (Heidelberg: Carl Winter), as well as the recently begun *Dresdner Beiträge zur Hethitologie* (now published by Harrassowitz in Wiesbaden), many volumes of which contain transliterations of published collections of the tablets. The only complete dictionary of Hittite is Friedrich 1952–66, which is rather out of date; two larger works are in progress, Friedrich and Kammenhuber 1975– and Güterbock and Hoffner 1980– (beginning with the letter L), both with significantly fuller entries but far from being finished. No complete etymological dictionary of Hittite has yet been written. Puhvel 1984– , which has copious textual citations, is moving close to completion, as is Tischler 1977– (in German); Kloekhorst 2008 covers only those words considered by the author to be (directly or indirectly) of IE origin and opens with a lengthy historical grammar. A number of his views about historical phonology and morphology must be treated with caution, but it is otherwise a very useful and up-to-date work. Hittite is now very well served by an exhaustive synchronic grammar in English (Hoffner and Melchert 2008), which has superseded the previous concise but useful standard reference grammar, Friedrich 1974. Melchert 1993 is a complete dictionary of Cuneiform Luvian, with etymological notes; for general linguistic, historical, and cultural information on the Luvians see also Melchert 2003. Almost all the first-millennium-BC Hieroglyphic Luvian corpus has appeared in an exquisite new edition (Çambel 1999 and Hawkins 2000). The only grammar of Lycian, with texts, is Neumann 1969; the Lydian corpus and grammar are contained in Gusmani 1964 (plus supplements). A complete Lycian dictionary, with etymologies, is now Melchert 2004. Carian is now served by an excellent new edition of the inscriptions with detailed philological and linguistic commentary, Adiego 2007.

A comprehensive and up-to-date book on Anatolian historical morphology is still lacking. For athematic nouns in Hittite, see now Rieken 1999 (see Bibliography, ch. 6), and for Luvian, see Starke 1990, though not all his views have been followed. Anatolian syntax took a large leap forward with Garrett 1990 (see Bibliography, ch. 8), a pathbreaking doctoral thesis; he has since written additional articles on the subject.

Emmanuel Laroche's *Catalogue des textes hittites* (see §9.20) is being periodically updated electronically at http://www.asor.org/HITTITE/CTHHP.html. Another important online resource for Hittite textual studies is the portal at www.hethiter.net.

For Review

Know the meaning or significance of the following:

Boğazköy	sentence connective	phonetic complement	Sturtevant's Law
Bedřich Hrozný	cuneiform	Akkadogram	*mi*-conjugation
Indo-Hittite	ductus	determiner	*ḫi*-conjugation
ḫ	ideogram	scriptio plena	Wilusa
ergative	syllabogram	syllabary	Čop's Law
clitic chain	Sumerogram		lenition

Exercises

1 Explain briefly the significance of the following forms mentioned in the chapter:

- **a** OHitt. *alpa*
- **b** Hitt. *ūk*
- **c** Assyrian *išpa(t)ta(l)lu*
- **d** Hitt. *ēšzi*
- **e** Hitt. *wātar*
- **f** Hitt. *memiškezzi*
- **g** HLuv. *ziyari*
- **h** HLuv. *maddu*
- **i** Pal. *-āga-*
- **j** Lyc. *ñte*
- **k** Lyc. *Trqqas*
- **l** Lyc. *kbatra-*

2 For each of the boldfaced segments or sequences in the following Hittite words, determine whether they would be expected to continue a voiced or voiceless stop in PIE. Where necessary, indicate if no such determination is possible purely from the spelling.

a *e**k**an* 'ice'
b *ā**pp**a* 'back'
c ***t**ūwa-* 'far'
d ***p**ēr* 'house'
e *a**tt**a-* 'father'
f ***g**arāp-* 'devour'
g *ḫa**p**a-* 'river'
h ***d**aššu-* 'mighty'
i *i**d**ālu-* 'evil'
j *dalu**g**a-* 'long'
k *pē**t**an* 'place'
l *za**kk**ar* 'feces'

3 The following are singular active verb forms in Hittite. For each, indicate whether it belongs to the *mi-* or the *ḫi*-conjugation. Hyphens have been added before the inflectional endings.

a *zāi-tti* 'you cross'
b *dankueš-zi* 'it grows dark'
c *punuš-ta* '(s)he asked'
d *paḫšanu-ddu* 'let him/her protect'
e *ḫāš-i* 'opens'
f *lā-ši* 'you unbind'
g *pā-u* 'let him/her give'
h *peda-ḫḫun* 'I took away'

4 Convert lines 10–13 in the Hittite text sample (§9.44) into broad transcription. Do not worry about clitic boundaries.

5 A Hittite passage (KBo 3.60 ii 2–5) reads: *ku-iš iš-tar-ni-iš-mi an-tu-wa-aḫ-ḫi-iš a-ri ša-na-ap az-zi-kán-zi ma-a-an ú-wa-ar-kán-ta-an an-tu-uḫ-ša-an ú-wa-an-zi na-an-kán ku-na-an-zi ša-na-ap a-ta-a-an-zi* "Whatever man comes among them, they eat him. If they see a fat man, they kill him and they eat him." Based on your knowledge of Hittite morphology and syntax, determine the Hittite for 'they see', 'they kill', and 'they eat' (two forms for the last one).

6 The Anatolian descendants of PIE *$*deh_3$- 'give', such as Hitt. *dā-*, mean 'take', unlike in the rest of the IE languages. In light of §2.11, provide an explanation for this fact.

7 Identify the merisms (§2.43) in the second half of the Luvian text sample (§9.57).

8 Name one or more ways that Luvian and Lycian provide important phonological information about PIE.

PIE Vocabulary I: Man, Woman, Kinship

From this chapter forward, a list of roughly a dozen basic roots and lexemes in the proto-language will be given for memorization. Each list will pertain to a particular semantic category. English descendants of the roots are given in SMALL CAPITALS; these are native English or (occasionally) borrowings from Old Norse. When the gloss of a root is at the same time its English descendant, the gloss is given in small capitals. No attempt is made to be exhaustive in listing cognates.

**dhĝhemon-* 'human being': Lat. *homō*, OLith. *žmuõ*, OE *guma* (> *bride*GROOM)
**$h_2$ner-* 'man, hero': Ved. *nár-*, Gk. *anḗr* (*andr-*), Lat. *Ner-ō* (personal name)
**u̯iH-ro-* 'man': Ved. *vīrás*, Lat. *uir*, OIr. *fer*, Eng. WERE*wolf*
**g^wenh_2* 'woman': Ved. *gnā́*, Gk. *gunḗ*, OCS *žena*, Eng. QUEEN
**p$h_2$tér-* 'FATHER': Ved. *pitár-*, Gk. *patḗr*, Lat. *pater*
**meh$_2$tér-* 'MOTHER': Ved. *mātár-*, Lat. *māter*
**suHnú-* 'SON': Ved. *sūnú-*, Lith. *sūnùs*
**dhugh$_2$ter-* 'DAUGHTER': Ved. *duhitár-*, Gk. *thugátēr*
**bhréh$_2$ter-* 'BROTHER': Ved. *bhrā́tar-*, Lat. *frāter*
**su̯esor-* 'SISTER': Ved. *svásār-*, Lat. *soror*
**nepot-* 'NEPHEW, grandson': Ved. *nápāt-*, Lat. *nepōs*

10 Indo-Iranian I: Indic

Introduction to Indo-Iranian

10.1. The Indo-Iranian branch consists of two subbranches, Indic and Iranian, and perhaps also a third, Nuristani (see below). Indo-Iranian languages are and have been spoken not only in the present-day countries of India and Iran, but over a wide expanse of Asia from the Black Sea to western China. The branch is bested only by Anatolian as the oldest in the family, with the earliest datable remains dating to the fourteenth century BC. This chapter begins with an overview of Indo-Iranian historical grammar and then covers the development of Indic; Iranian is left for the next chapter.

10.2. The best-known early Indo-Iranian language is **Sanskrit.** Its oldest known variety is **Vedic** Sanskrit, preserved in the early collection of hymns known as the Rig Veda and in subsequent literature discussed in more detail below. In this chapter as elsewhere in the book, most cited Sanskrit forms will be taken from Vedic and labeled as such; a form labeled "Sanskrit" is not attested until the later Classical Sanskrit language.

Although Sanskrit has held uncommon esteem throughout the history of IE studies, its linguistic testimony must be balanced against that of its sister **Avestan,** the oldest preserved Iranian language. Understanding of the Avestan corpus has advanced remarkably in recent decades, and **Old** or **Gathic Avestan,** the oldest preserved stage of the language, is structurally very close to Vedic but more archaic in several important respects. The French Indo-Europeanist Émile Benveniste once wrote that "the testimony of Vedic is valuable for its richness, the testimony of Avestan for its fidelity." The only other older Iranian language preserved in any significant amount is the later **Old Persian,** the language of royal inscriptions from the Achaemenid dynasty starting in the late sixth century BC. Old Persian is the only Indo-Iranian language whose remains are securely datable.

10.3. Several languages spoken in a remote region of Afghanistan belong to a group called **Nuristani** (formerly Kafiri; also sometimes Dardic, a term now properly used of a subbranch of Indic that includes Kashmiri). Many specialists have thought that these languages constitute a separate branch of Indo-Iranian. The fact that they have been poorly studied (they are spoken in inaccessible and war-torn areas) and have no older literature has made their classification difficult. On the one hand, they share several basic sound changes with Iranian, but on the other they preserve some features of reconstructed Proto-Indo-Iranian that are not found elsewhere in the branch.

10.4. It is widely thought that Indo-Iranian forms a subgroup with Greek, Armenian, and Phrygian. The morphological structure of Greek and older Indo-Iranian languages agree in many striking details, and Greek shares numerous similarities with the fragmentary Phrygian as well as the more distant Armenian. However, the issue has not been settled, and for our purposes it is best to regard all four of these as separate branches, even if closely allied at some level.

From PIE to Indo-Iranian

The following is an overview of the major developments from PIE to Proto-Indo-Iranian, that is, the developments that are shared by both Indic and Iranian.

Phonology

Consonants

10.5. Velars. The defining change to the consonant inventory in Indo-Iranian is its development of the PIE velars. Indo-Iranian is a satem branch (§3.8); it affricated the palatal velars *k̂ *ĝ *ĝh to *ć *ȷ́ *ȷ́h, and merged the PIE plain velars *k *g *gh and labiovelars *k^w *g^w *g^wh into just a series of plain velars (*k *g *gh). It appears, though, that this merger was completed independently in early Indic and Iranian; see §10.37 below. These plain velars, when before a front vowel (*i or *e) or the glide *i̯, were then palatalized to the affricates *c *j and *jh (the traditional Indo-Iranian writing of phonetic [č ǰ $ǰ^h$], pronounced like English *ch* and *j*). This palatalization is often called the **Law of Palatals**.

To illustrate: PIE *dek̂m̥ 'ten' became Indo-Ir. *daća (Ved. *dáśa*, Av. *dasa*); ***ghous-** 'hear' became Indo-Ir. ***ghauš-** (Ved. *ghóṣas* 'noise', Av. *gaoša* 'ear'); and ***g^wōus** (or ***g^wous**, §6.6) 'cow' became Indo-Ir. ***gāuš** (Ved. *gáuṣ*, Av. *gāuš*). The Law of Palatals can be illustrated by the development of the first sound in the weak perfect stem ***k^we-k^wr-** 'did' > pre-Indo-Ir. ***ke-kr-** > ***ce-kr-** > Indo-Ir. ***ca-kr-** (Ved. *cakr-*, Av. and OPers. *caxr-*), and in ***ki̯eu-** > Ved. *cyav-ante* 'they move', Av. *śiiauu-āi* 'I want to drive'.

10.6. Voiced aspirates. The voiced aspirates were preserved intact in Indo-Iranian and remain to the present day in Indic, the only IE subbranch still to have them. (In Iranian, the aspiration was lost; see §11.2.) However, if a voiced aspirate was immediately followed by a voiceless unaspirated consonant, a change known as **Bartholomae's Law** (after the nineteenth- and twentieth-century German linguist Christian Bartholornae) took place, whereby the aspiration moved to the end of the cluster and the voiceless consonant became voiced. Thus a cluster *ght became *gdh, as in Ved. *mugdhá-* 'dazed' < *mugh-tó- and Old Avestan *aogədā* 'he spoke' (phonetically *aogdā*) < Indo-Ir. *augdha < pre-Indo-Ir. *augh-to.

Bartholomae's Law is particularly interesting in how it affected **dental-plus-dental clusters.** Recall that dental-plus-dental clusters sprouted a sibilant between the dentals in PIE (§3.36), so **tt* > **tst* and **dd* > **dzd*. In the case of **dht*, by a combination of this rule and Bartholomae's Law, this cluster became **dzdh* in Indo-Iranian. In Indic, all these clusters lost the sibilant (so **tst* > *tt*, **dzd* > *dd*, and **dzdh* > *ddh*), whereas in Iranian, they lost the first dental (so **tst* > *st*, **dzd* > *zd*, and **dzdh* > **zdh* and then ultimately *zd*). Thus for example Ved. *vittá-* 'known' and Av. *vista-* come from **u̯id-tó-*; OPers. *azdā* 'known' and Ved. *addhā́* 'surely' come from pre-Indo-Ir. **adh-tā*. Note that the name of the Buddha contains an example of Bartholomae's Law (Classical Skt. *buddha-* 'awakened, enlightened').

10.7. Resonants. The two nasals **m* and **n* are preserved intact in all positions: ***mr̥tii̯o**- 'mortal' > OPers. ***martiya-***, ****ne*** 'not' > Ved. ***ná***, accusative sing. *-***om*** > Av. -***əm***.

10.8. The fate of the two liquids **r* and **l* is more difficult to ascertain. Iranian and the core of Vedic Sanskrit point to them having merged as **r*: PIE **k^{w}el-eti* 'turns, moves' > Ved. *cárati*, Av. *caraiti*; **bhreh$_2$ter-* 'brother' > Av. and OPers. *brātar-*. But many varieties of Indic, especially those spoken farther to the east, show *l* as an outcome of both liquids, and some words in Iranian have been claimed to preserve *l* from IE **l* (though this is rather doubtful). It may be that the liquids merged as **r* in the western dialect area that would become Iranian and the western dialects of Indic, but merged as **l* in the east, with the original distinction perhaps maintained in the middle. For fuller discussion of the Indic situation, see §10.34.

10.9. As for the **syllabic resonants**, syllabic **r̥* and **l̥* merged as **r̥*: **bhr̥ĝhent-* 'high, mighty' > Ved. *br̥hánt-*, Av. *bərəzant̰-*; **u̯l̥k^{w}os* 'wolf' > Ved. *vŕ̥kas*, Av. *vəhrka-*. The syllabic nasals both became **a*: PIE **septm̥* 'seven' > Ved. *saptá*, Av. *hapta*; PIE **n̥-* 'not, un-' > Ved. and Av. *a-*. When followed by a laryngeal, the result was a long syllabic resonant: **dl̥h$_1$gho-* 'long' > Indo-Ir. **dr̥̄gha-* (> Ved. *dīrghá-*, Old Av. *darəga-*).

10.10. "Ruki" and creation of *š. Indo-Iranian created a new sibilant phoneme **š* (**ž* before voiced consonants) from several sources. One source was **s* when preceded by **r* **u* **k* or **i*, a change sometimes known as the "ruki-rule" (compare Balto-Slavic for a similar change, §18.6). This Indo-Iranian **š* became Skt. *ṣ* and Av. *š*, as in Ved. *tŕ̥ṣṇā*, Young Av. *taršna-* 'thirst' < **tr̥s-n-* (root **ters-* 'dry' as in Eng. *thirst*) and Ved. *vakṣayam* 'I cause to grow', Old Av. *vaxšat̰* 'he will grow' (**h$_2$u̯eks-*, compare Eng. *wax*). In Iranian, **š* also arose after labial consonants, as in the Avestan nomin. sing. *āfš* 'water' (stem *āp-*).

As expected by the IE voicing assimilation rule (§3.34), the voiced variant **ž* is the outcome before a voiced stop; this is preserved in Avestan but only indirectly attested in Sanskrit, e.g. **mizdho-* 'reward' > Av. *mižda-* but Ved. *mīḍhám* 'prize' (< pre-Vedic **mižḍhá-*; cp. Gk. *misthós* 'pay'; and see further §10.33).

10.11. The second source of **š* or **ž* is the old palatal velars when they stood before a dental. The voiceless version is illustrated for example by Ved. *naṣṭá-*, Av. *našta-* 'died, disappeared' < PIE **neḱtó-*.

10.12. The third source of **š* was as part of the development of the PIE "thorn" clusters (§3.25), which became in all cases *kṣ* in Sanskrit but *š*, *xš*, or *γž* in Iranian: compare Ved. ***kṣétram*** 'settlement', ***kṣáyati*** 'has power', and ***kṣárati*** 'flows' with

Av. *šōiθra-*, Old Pers. *xšāyaθiya-* 'king', and Young Av. *γžar-* 'flow' (PIE **tk̂ei-*, **tkei-*, **dhgʷher-*).

10.13. Laryngeals. To judge by the metrical evidence from the Rig Veda and the Gathas in Old Avestan, both consonantal and vocalic reflexes of the laryngeals were still present in Indo-Iranian, though whether the three-fold distinction was still preserved is not known. The vocalic laryngeals became **i*, preserved in Indic but mostly lost in Iranian. See further §§10.36 and 11.7.

Vowels

10.14. Vowel merger. The defining change in the Indo-Iranian vowel system was the merger of all non-high vowels of PIE, **e* **o* **a*, into a mid to low central vowel that is written **a*. Thus PIE **bher-onti* 'they bear' became OPers. *bar-antiy*, **mad-* 'wet' became Ved. *mad-ati* 'is drunk', and **potnih₂* 'lady, mistress' became Av. *paθnī*. Analogously, long **ē* **ō* **ā* all fell together as **ā*: PIE aorist **eu̯ēĝhst* 'he conveyed' > Ved. *ávāṭ*, **māter-* (**meh₂-ter-*) 'mother' > Av. *mātar-*, and **ok̂tō* 'eight' > Ved. *aṣṭā́*. The vowel merger only happened after the Law of Palatals and Brugmann's Law (see §10.16 immediately below) had run their course.

10.15. As a result of this merger, the PIE diphthongs **ei* **ai* **oi* all became **ai*, and **eu* **au* **ou* all became **au*. In Sanskrit, **ai* and **au* were monophthongized to *e* and *o*, as discussed further below (§10.38); but they were still diphthongs in the earliest preserved Indic, the fourteenth-century-BC cuneiform documents described in §§10.21ff., and also remained diphthongs in Iranian (see §11.8).

10.16. Brugmann's Law. Before the vowel merger noted above, an original **o* in open syllables became lengthened to **ō*, later becoming *ā* by the merger of long vowels. This is known as Brugmann's Law, after its discoverer, the German Indo-Europeanist Karl Brugmann. Thus the 3rd sing. perfect **kʷekʷóre* '(s)he did' (syllabified as **kʷe.kʷó.re*) became Ved. *cakā́ra*, while the 1st singular **kʷekʷórh₂e* 'I did' (syllabified as **kʷe.kʷór.h₂e*) became *cakára*. Other examples include Ved. *dā́ru*, Av. *dāuru*, OPers. *dāru* 'wood' < **doru* and the passive aorists Ved. *ávāci* 'was said', OAv. *vācī* 'was named' < **(e)u̯okʷi*.

Morphology

10.17. Indo-Iranian has changed the PIE morphological system (as presented in chapters 4–7) only in detail. Thematic and athematic inflection are alive and well in both nouns and verbs, as are all three numbers of singular, dual, and plural. All the tense, mood, and voice categories in the verb, as well as the cases in the noun, are still in use. See the separate discussions in this and the next chapter, where paradigms and other details will also be given.

10.18. In the noun, an important innovation in inflection is the creation of a genitive plural ending **-nām* used with vocalic stems, as Ved. *nadī́nām* 'of rivers'. In verbs, the chief innovation was the creation of a passive conjugation with the suffix **-yá-* (a specialization of the PIE accented intransitive suffix **-i̯é/ó-*; see §5.32) with middle inflection, as in Ved. *kri-yá-nte* 'they are made', Av. *kiriieṇte* 'they are made' < Indo-Ir. **kr̥-i̯á-*.

Syntax

10.19. Of great interest for comparative IE syntax is the study of clitic placement in Indo-Iranian, which has shed a great deal of light on Wackernagel's Law, as was discussed in detail in §§8.22–25. Vedic Sanskrit in particular is extremely valuable in this regard because the spelling system quite exactingly reflects the operation of sandhi rules (see §10.40 below), whose application is influenced by syntactic movement and constituency, as we have seen in chapter 8 (§§8.31ff.).

Indic (Indo-Aryan)

10.20. Indic (also called Indo-Aryan; see further below) tribes entered India probably during the early to mid-second millennium BC, migrating from the Iranian plateau northwest of present-day Pakistan into the Punjab in eastern Pakistan, northwest of modern India. One of the hymns of the Rig Veda (1.131) alludes to a legendary journey that may be a distant memory of this migration. The Indus River valley, to the south of the Punjab, had already been the site of an extensive early urban civilization which flourished from c. 2400 to 2000 BC, gradually declining over the next half-millennium. This people left behind short inscriptions in a language that has yet to be deciphered; judging by the material and cultural remains, the Indus Valley Civilization was not Indo-European, but may have been Dravidian. Whether the demise of this civilization was due to the encroaching Indo-Aryans, as used to be thought, or rather to internal or climatic factors, as is generally argued nowadays, is uncertain. The Indus Valley script died with the civilization that had invented it; writing would not return to India until well over a millennium later.

The Mitanni texts

10.21. The earliest Indo-Iranian has been found, of all places, in the Near East. Hittite and Hurrian texts from Anatolia and Syria contain words cited from an early Indo-Iranian language that was spoken by overlords of the Hurrians when they were united into an empire called Mitanni (or Mittani). The Hurrians were a non-Indo-European people probably originating east of the Tigris River who spread westward to become one of the dominant powers in the ancient Near East in the second millennium BC. Starting around 1600 BC their homeland of Hurri was settled by an Indo-Iranian people that was skilled in horse-breeding and chariot-warfare; by perhaps 1500 BC this people had apparently become an elite ruling class among the Hurrians. Under the feudal state that they founded, called Mitanni, the Hurrian lands were united into an empire that lasted until its conquest by the Hittites about 1360 BC.

10.22. From this otherwise unknown language are preserved personal names, divine names, and technical terms pertaining to horse-racing. Names of some numerals are found in compounds referring to laps around a race course, such as *a-i-ka-wa-ar-ta-an-na* '(of) one lap', *pa-an-za-wa-ar-ta-an-na* '(of) five laps', and *na-a-wa-ar-ta-an-na* '(of) nine laps' (compare Ved. *éka-* 'one', *páñca* 'five', *náva* 'nine', and later [post-Vedic] Sanskrit *vartanam* 'a turning'). In a treaty between Mitanni and the Hittites, the gods who are called to witness include *mi-it-ra-*, *u-ru-wa-na-*, *in-dar*, and *na-ša-at-ti-ya-*; their names correspond closely to the Vedic gods Mitra, Varuna, Indra, and the divine twins the Nāsatyas. And in slightly later Babylonian texts are found the color terms *baprunnu*, *binkarannu*, and *barittanu* describing horses, which can be equated with Ved. *babhrú-* 'brown', *piṅgalá-* 'reddish', and *palitá-* 'gray'.

Most of the words could be either Indic or Iranian, but *a-i-ka-* 'one' points to Indic origin, since 'one' in Iranian is **aiwa-* rather than **aika-*. Note also that the Iranian word for 'lap' or 'turn' (Av. *uruuaēsa-*) is formed quite differently from the one in the Mitanni speech or Vedic. Various characteristics of the onomastics and divine names also indicate Indic rather than Iranian provenance.

Sanskrit

10.23. The earliest Indic language in which we have significant remains is **Sanskrit**. This term has both a broad and a narrow sense. Broadly, it refers to any language or dialect belonging to **Old Indic**, the linguistically oldest preserved stage of Indic; as it happens, we have only two major dialects belonging to this stage (Vedic and Classical Sanskrit), and they are nearly identical formally. More narrowly, it refers to the somewhat artificial literary language (Classical Sanskrit) discussed below in §10.27, as opposed to the earlier Vedic that we will treat in the next section. We will use the term in its broad sense. ("Old Indic" is especially commonly used in German-speaking lands, where it is rendered in German as *Altindisch*.)

Sanskrit has held a strong grip on the development of IE studies. Even before comparative linguistics came into existence, one can get a feel for the pedestal that Sanskrit would later occupy from Sir William Jones's famous pronouncement in 1786 (quoted in full in §1.14): "The *Sanscrit* language, whatever be its antiquity, is of a wonderful structure: more perfect than the *Greek*, more copious than the *Latin* . . ." As the nascent field of IE studies got its start some decades later, philologists accorded it the greatest importance for the reconstruction of PIE, and early models of PIE differed only in minor detail from Sanskrit itself. The realization, by the 1870s, that Sanskrit too had undergone considerable change (especially in its phonological system), and was not a pristine and unblemished continuation of the parent language, transformed IE studies and solved a number of problems. But far from being "dethroned" thereby, Sanskrit has retained a certain pre-eminence because of, among other things, the age of its oldest texts and the richness and transparency of its morphology.

The Rig Veda

10.24. The earliest preserved Sanskrit is called **Vedic**, after the Vedas or collection of sacred lore (*véda-* means 'knowledge'). The oldest Veda is the Rig Veda (also spelled

Rigveda or R̥gveda), a collection of 1,028 hymns collected in ten books called maṇḍalas. Books II–VII are linguistically the most archaic and are known as the **Family Books**, as each was composed by a particular family of poets. We cannot assign precise dates to the hymns of the Rig Veda; like the Homeric epics, parts of it were composed at different periods and it was transmitted orally over many generations before eventually being committed to writing. But it is reasonable to suppose that the whole collection was completed by the end of the second millennium BC.

The Rig Veda is of paramount importance to IE studies, and it continues to contribute insights into all matters of comparative IE linguistics, poetics, and culture. A difficult text, not all its verses are fully understood. The Vedic poets strove for a deliberately obscure style often densely packed with allusions that are hard for modern readers to recover without careful study of the interconnections among verbal concepts and formulae. (Recall the discussion of one such case in §2.40.)

Other Vedic literature

10.25. The other three Vedas were assembled after the Rig Veda was, and are linguistically younger: the Sāma Veda, Yajur Veda, and Atharva Veda. The verses of the Sāma Veda are drawn almost entirely from the Rig Veda but arranged differently, while the Yajur Veda, divided into the so-called White and Black Yajur Veda, contains not only metrical texts but also explanatory prose commentaries that had accreted onto the transmission of the hymns; this is the earliest preserved Vedic prose. The Atharva Veda contains hymns as well as charms and magical incantations of a more popular and folkloristic type. Exegetical texts like those in the Black Yajur Veda, as well as ritual directions by the brahmans (priests), developed into separate prose works called Brāhmaṇas. Parallel exegetical traditions developed into other genres of early prose writings – the Āraṇyakas, Upaniṣads, and Sūtras. All these texts are important for understanding the often obscure ritual references in the Vedic hymns themselves, and they contain a wealth of information on early myth and legend that has not yet been fully mined. One sub-genre of the Sūtras, the Gr̥hya-Sūtras or 'household Sūtras', spawned a set of law texts, the Dharmaśāstras, most importantly the Mānavadharmaśāstra or Code of Manu, which contains much ancient legal material of great value for the comparative study of IE law. All these works seem to have been completed by the mid-first millennium BC.

Pāṇinian Grammar

10.26. In the fifth century BC or thereabouts, a grammarian named Pāṇini codified a set of rules for Sanskrit in a work called the Aṣṭādhyāyī. This was the culmination of a long grammatical tradition that is one of the intellectual wonders of the ancient world: it is a highly precise and thorough description of the structure of Sanskrit somewhat resembling modern generative grammar. Roots were set up together with rules for deriving words from them, and the pronunciation of sounds was described in detail. While the analyses are often different from those of modern western linguistics, the work of Pāṇini is very valuable and remained the most advanced linguistic analysis of any kind until the twentieth century.

Classical Sanskrit

10.27. In practical terms, Pāṇini's codification fossilized the written language; thus was born Classical Sanskrit, a language that became a vehicle for scholarly, religious, and literary discourse, and which is still used today to a certain extent. It achieved a role analogous to that of Latin in Europe during the Middle Ages. Classical Sanskrit is the language of the two surviving Indian epics, the *Mahābhārata* and *Rāmāyaṇa*; the latter was authored by one Vālmīki, while the former, which is roughly eight times the length of the *Iliad* and *Odyssey* combined, was composed and embellished over many centuries. Some of its material is quite ancient and valuable for Indo-European studies. One episode in the *Mahābhārata* has become particularly famous, the philosophical discourse known as the Bhagavad-Gītā, 'the song of the lord'.

Classical Sanskrit is also the language of the lyric poetry known as *kāvya*, written in a deliberately difficult and ornate style. The greatest master of *kāvya* was Kālidāsa, the author of such poems as the *Meghadūta*. He was also the pre-eminent Classical dramatist; his most famous play, *Śakuntalā*, would later inspire Goethe and other German Romantics. Finally, a gigantic mass of philosophical, scientific, religious, grammatical, mathematical, astronomical, and medical literature is written in Classical Sanskrit, as well as tales and fables such as those of the *Hitopadeśa* and *Pañcatantra*, stemming ultimately from the same source as the fables of Aesop.

Classical Sanskrit is not a linear descendant of Vedic, but more like a niece; there are a (very) few formal differences between the paradigms of the two languages. In spite of the great formal similarity, there are many differences in usage and idiom; for example, Classical Sanskrit tended to avoid using finite verbs, favoring instead nominal constructions of various types and non-finite verbal forms.

The terms "Aryan" and "Indo-Aryan"

10.28. As noted above, Indic is also called Indo-Aryan. The term "Aryan" has had a rather complicated history. The Sanskrit word *ā́rya-*, the source of the English word, was the self-designation of the Vedic Indic people and has a cognate in Iranian **arya-*, where it is also a self-designation. Both the Indic and Iranian terms descend from a form **ă̄rya-* that was used by the Indo-Iranian tribes to refer to themselves. (It is also the source of the country-name *Iran*, from a phrase meaning 'kingdom of the Aryans'.) In the west, various translations of Ved. *ā́rya-* have been used, most commonly 'nobleman', although we really do not know what its original meaning was. During the nineteenth century, it was proposed that this had been not only the Indo-Iranian tribal self-designation but also the self-designation of the Proto-Indo-Europeans themselves. (This theory has since been abandoned.) "Aryan" then came to be used in scholarship to refer to Indo-European. Some decades later it was further proposed that the PIE homeland had been located in northern Europe (also a theory no longer accepted), leading to speculations that the Proto-Indo-Europeans had been of a Nordic racial type. In this way "Aryan" developed yet another, purely racialist meaning, probably the most familiar one today. In Indo-European studies, "Aryan" (and *Arisch* in German) and "Indo-Aryan" have been frequently used in their older senses – "Aryan" to refer to Indo-Iranian (less commonly, Indo-European) and "Indo-Aryan" to refer to Indic.

Sanskrit phonology

Sanskrit historical phonology is very rich and complicated; only important highlights and a few of the more noteworthy details will be discussed here.

General remarks on the consonants

10.29. Sanskrit is the only known older IE language in which the PIE voiced aspirates remain unchanged, though it also made some rather sweeping innovations elsewhere in the system. We find three new series of consonants: voiceless aspirated stops (*ph th* etc.); a set of alveo-palatal affricates (usually just called the "palatals," *c ch j jh ñ*); and a set of retroflex consonants, dentals pronounced with the tip of the tongue curled backwards and written in Roman transcription with a dot under the letter (*ṭ ṭh ḍ ḍh ṇ*). The number of nasals increased to five, one for each of the resultant places of articulation. There was also a symbol called *anusvāra* (indicated in transcription as *ṃ* or *ṁ*) and one called *anunāsika* (indicated by *m̐*) that stood for either a reduced nasal sound or nasalization of a preceding vowel. Partly counterbalancing these additions was the satem merger of the PIE labiovelars with the plain velars. The outcome of all these innovations was a neat 25-member system of stops and affricates:

	labial	palatal	retroflex	dental	velar
voiceless	p	c	ṭ	t	k
voiceless aspirated	ph	ch	ṭh	th	kh
voiced	b	j	ḍ	d	g
voiced aspirated	bh	jh	ḍh	dh	gh
nasal	m	ñ	ṇ	n	ṅ

Under certain conditions, the voiced aspirates were reduced to just *h* before vowels, as in the imperative *ihí* 'go!' < *$^*h_1$i-dhi* and the verbal adjective *hitá-* 'placed' from the Sanskrit root *dhā-* 'place'.

The Indo-Iranian velars **k *g *gh* (from PIE **k/k*^{w}, **g/g*^{w}, **gh/g*^{w}*h* when not before front vowels) remained unchanged, as did the palatals **c* and **j* from palatalized **k* and **g*. The affricate **ć* (from PIE **k̂*) became a palatal sibilant transliterated as *ś* (see §10.35 below), while its voiced counterpart **ȷ́* (from PIE **ĝ*) fell together with **j* and became *j*. Aspirated **jh* (< palatalized **gh/g*^{w}*h*) and **ȷ́h* (< **ĝh*) fell together as *h*: *sáhas* 'victory' < **seĝh-os*, *hánti* 'slays' < **g*^{w}*hen-ti*.

Grassmann's Law

10.30. The Indo-Europeanist Hermann Grassmann discovered that the first in a sequence of two aspirated stops that were separated by an intervening sound or sounds lost its aspiration in Sanskrit. Thus PIE **bheudh-eti* 'wakes up' became Ved.

bódhati, and the participle *bhudh-tó- became *buddha-* 'awakened' (undergoing Bartholomae's Law also). Grassmann also discovered the same kind of aspiration dissimilation in Greek, though independent of the Indic change (see §12.14).

Voiceless aspirates

10.31. A number of voiceless aspirates arose out of a combination of voiceless stop plus second laryngeal; for example, *pleth$_2$- 'broad' > Ved. *prathi-mán-* 'width', *sth$_2$-tó- 'stood' > Ved. *sthi-tá-*. In some seemingly identical phonetic environments, however, aspiration did not occur, as in *pitár-* 'father' < *ph$_2$tér-. The details are still insufficiently understood, but most Indo-Europeanists believe the voiceless aspirates to be the result of secondary developments rather than inherited from PIE, as used to be thought (recall §3.6).

Dental plus dental

10.32. PIE *TsT and *DzD from dental plus dental sequences (§3.36) lost the internal sibilant in Indic: Ved. *vr̥t-tá-* 'turned' < *u̯r̥t-tó-, *vit-tá-* 'found' < *u̯id-tó-.

Retroflex stops

10.33. The retroflex consonants arose under a variety of conditions, most notably from assimilation to a preceding Indo-Iranian *š or *ž (§§10.10ff.), as in PIE *ok̂tō 'eight' > Indo-Ir. *aćtā > *aštā- > Ved. *aṣṭā́*, and PIE *h$_1$us-no- 'burned' > Indo-Ir. *ušná- > Ved. *uṣṇá-* 'hot'. Since *r* was retroflex, *n* became retroflex *ṇ* after *r* or *r̥*, as in *dur-ṇā́man-* 'having a bad name', *pr̥ṇā́ti* 'fills'. Note also PIE *nizdos 'nest' > Indo-Ir. *niždás > pre-Sanskrit *nižḍás > Ved. *nīḍás*, where the sound that originally caused the *d* to become retroflex has disappeared (recall §10.10), with compensatory lengthening of the preceding vowel.

Many other words with retroflex stops were borrowed from Dravidian languages to the south. As the Indic tribes moved southward, the number of such loans increased, resulting in a general expansion of retroflexion that even affected originally non-retroflex dentals in native Sanskrit words.

Resonants

10.34. As stated earlier, the outcomes of PIE *l and *r appear to have varied dialectally. In Sanskrit, both largely merged as *r. However, forms with *l* are found abundantly, such as *ślókas* 'poem, type of verse-line' from *k̂leu- 'to hear'. But these are rarer in the oldest parts of the Rig Veda, suggesting that they belong to a later infusion of dialectal material from a different part of India, probably the east (Middle Indic inscriptions from the east show a preponderance of *l*). Doublets are not infrequent, as Ved. *riptá-* 'smeared' alongside *liptá-* (< PIE root *leip- 'to smear, stick').

The syllabic *r̥ inherited into Sanskrit is often seen rendered in English orthography as *ri*, hence spellings like *Sanskrit*, *Prakrit*, and *Krishna* (Skt. *saṃskr̥tam*, *prākr̥tam*, *Kr̥ṣṇas*). The source of this *ri* is a later development in pronunciation in India.

Sibilants

10.35. In addition to the ordinary sibilant _*s_ inherited from PIE, Sanskrit has two other sibilants of the _sh_ variety, a palatal _ś_ and a farther-back retroflex _ṣ_ (often written _sh_ in older handbooks). The first is the ordinary development of PIE _*k̂_, while the second continues Indo-Iranian _*š_ and represents either PIE _*s_ with "ruki" (§10.10) or PIE _*k̂_ in certain environments.

Laryngeals

10.36. The laryngeals were lost in their non-syllabic (consonantal) variants, although not until fairly late; the Rig Veda preserves many words that must scan as though a laryngeal or some remnant of a laryngeal (like a glottal stop) were still present between vowels, a phenomenon called **laryngeal hiatus**. For example, _vā́tas_ 'wind' must sometimes scan trisyllabically as _va'atas_, which comes from earlier _*waHatas_ (< PIE _*h_2u̯eh_1n̥tos_). The vocalic laryngeals are continued as the vowel _i_ (or sometimes _ī_, perhaps originally only in final syllables): _pitár-_ 'father' < _*p$h_2$tér-_; _ábravīt_ 'said' < _*e-breu̯H-t_. Traces of word-initial laryngeals are preserved indirectly in the lengthening of preceding vowels in compounds, e.g. _sūnára-_ 'mighty' < _*$h_1$su-$h_2$nero-_, literally 'having good manliness' (_*$h_1$su-_ 'good' + _*$h_2$ner-o-_ 'manliness', from _*$h_2$ner-_ 'man'). Word-final laryngeals after consonants are preserved as _-i_: _máhi_ 'great' = Greek _méga_, both from _*meĝh_2_.

10.37. The "long" syllabic resonants, from original syllabic resonants followed by laryngeals, became _īr_ or _ūr_ before consonants (e.g. _śīrtá-_ 'mixed' < _*k̂r̥$h_2$tó-_; _pūrṇá-_ 'full' < _*pl̥$h_1$nó-_) and _ir_ or _ur_ before vowels (_tiráte_ 'overcomes' < _*tr̥h_2-é-_; _purás_ 'fort' [genitive sing.] < _*pl̥H-és_). As these examples show, the _u_-quality outcomes were induced by a preceding labial, while the _i_-outcomes are seen elsewhere (with some exceptions that arose through analogical interference). Particularly interesting are words like _gurú-_ 'heavy' < _*g^{w}r̥h_2-u-_, where the labialization that induced the _u_-quality was that of the preceding labiovelar. In other words, at the time of the split of _*r̥H_ or its immediate descendant into _ir_ and _ur_, which happened only in Indic (Iranian has a different outcome), the labiovelars were still distinct from the plain velars in at least this environment.

Glides and vowels

10.38. The glide _*i̯_ stayed intact (written _y_), while _*u̯_ became a sound transcribed as _v_ but still pronounced _w_: _yugám_ 'yoke' < _*i̯ugom_, _vanóti_ 'wins' < _*u̯en-_ (cp. Eng. _win_). After the Indo-Iranian merger of PIE _*e *o_ and _*a_, not much else happened to the vowels except that the Indo-Iranian diphthongs _*ai_ and _*au_ monophthongized to _e_ and _o_, respectively. Both these vowels were pronounced long and are often transcribed _ē_ and _ō_ in older handbooks. The earliest preserved Indic from the Mitanni documents shows these diphthongs still intact: _a-i-ka-_ 'one', later Ved. _éka-_. An example of _*au_ becoming _o_ is the name of the sacred intoxicating drink _sómas_ 'soma' from _*saumas_ (cp. Av. _haoma-_).

The PIE long diphthongs **ēi *ōi* became Skt. *ai*, and **ēu *ōu* became Skt. *au* (transcribed as *āi* and *āu* in older handbooks): Ved. *s*-aorist *ánaikṣīt* '(s)he washed' < PIE **e-nēig^w-s-*; Ved. *o*-stem instr. pl. *-ais* < PIE **-ōis*; Ved. *gáuṣ* 'cow' < pre-Indo-Iranian **g^{w}ōus*.

Accent

10.39. As was noted in §3.32, Vedic preserves the PIE mobile pitch-accent system. The accent markings used in the native script and the Indian grammarians' terms for those markings suggest that syllables preceding the accented syllable had low tone, and that during the pronunciation of the accented syllable the pitch rose, reaching a peak at its end and at the beginning of the next syllable, after which it fell again. The pitch-accent system changed into a stress-accent system in later Sanskrit.

Sandhi

10.40. In colloquial English, the final consonant of a word like *hit* is pronounced differently depending on what sound follows: contrast *hit me* [hɪʔmij], where the *t* is reduced to a glottal stop, with *hit ya* [hɪtʃə], where the *t* merges with the following *y* to form *ch*. As already noted in §8.31 (and cf. also §8.33), the rules governing such changes in pronunciation at word or morpheme boundaries are called sandhi rules, from Sanskrit *saṃdhí-* 'putting together, transition'. In Sanskrit, these rules are very numerous, and differ depending on whether the boundary occurs inside a word (*internal sandhi*) or between words (*external sandhi*). To give an idea of the phenomenon, consider what happens in external sandhi to word-final *-as*, as in the nomin. sing. of the word *devás* 'god': this form becomes *devá* before most vowels or before *s* plus stop, *deváś* before a *c*, *deváḥ* before any other voiceless consonant or a pause (the *ḥ* is simply pronounced *h*), and *devó* before a voiced consonant. The Sanskrit sandhi rules are to some extent inherited from common Indo-Iranian, to judge by various traces in Avestan.

External sandhi, especially outside the more artificial language of Classical Sanskrit poetry, did not occur between just any pair of words; its occurrence was governed by syntactic and prosodic conditions that are just beginning to be understood.

Morphology

10.41. Sanskrit has the greatest number of grammatical forms of any ancient Indo-European language. Nouns and pronouns are inflected in eight cases in singular, dual, and plural (the dual and plural in the noun do not have as many case distinctions, however). Personal pronouns have separate fully stressed and enclitic (reduced, unstressed) paradigms. Verb tense-stems were still generally built by derivation from roots, as in reconstructed PIE. Verbs in Vedic could be conjugated in six tenses (present, imperfect, aorist, future, perfect, and pluperfect; a seventh, called the conditional, is met with once in the Rig Veda and only rarely thereafter) and in three voices (active, middle, and passive); as in PIE, though, not all verbs were conjugable in all the tenses or voices. There were five moods: indicative, subjunctive, optative, imperative, and precative, a specialized development of the optative. The augment (Ved. *a-*) could be attached to secondary tenses (imperfect, aorist, pluperfect); when it was lacking, the form is called an **injunctive** (recall §5.44). Though the account does not work equally well in all cases, the injunctive is usually regarded as referring to acts or states that have a certain "timeless" quality or where no specific time-reference is made, as in maxims, descriptions of general characteristics of gods or nature (or in mentioning the deeds of gods without reference to when the deeds actually happened), legal or customary sayings, and so forth. Thus at Rig Veda 8.42.6 the sage Vasiṣṭha is spoken of with the words *evā́gnim̐ sahasyàṃ vasiṣṭho . . .* ***staut*** "thus Vasiṣṭha praises/has (always) praised/will praise mighty Agni," where the aorist injunctive *staut* is different from the indicative *astaut*, which would mean 'praised (once or at a specific point in the past)'. The injunctive is also used in prohibitions with the negative *mā́*, as in *mā́ na indra párā* ***vr̥ṇak*** "Do not abandon us, o Indra!" (present injunctive 2nd sing.). The subjunctive in Vedic was less a separate mood and more a simple future tense, while the category that is called the future behaved more like a desiderative or volitional ('I intend to . . .', 'I want to . . .'). The aorist and subjunctive fall into obsolescence in Classical Sanskrit, which relies heavily upon nominal and participial forms to express many concepts that Vedic used finite verb forms to impart. See further §10.47.

Verbs

10.42. Present stem classes. Traditional Sanskrit grammar divides the present stems of verbs into ten classes, which may be exemplified as follows:

I	*bhárati* 'bears'	VI	*tudáti* 'beats'
II	*ásti* 'is'	VII	*yunákti* 'yokes'
III	*dádhāti* 'puts'	VIII	*tanóti* 'stretches'
IV	*náhyati* 'binds'	IX	*gr̥bhṇā́ti* 'seizes'
V	*śr̥ṇóti* 'hears'	X	*coráyati* 'steals'

From the IE point of view, several of these can be combined. Classes I, IV, VI, and X are all thematic verbs: simple thematics in Class I, verbs in **-i̯e/o-* in Class IV, verbs accented on the suffix in Class VI and usually having zero-grade of the root (called the *tudáti*-class for PIE after the example above; see §5.31), and various derived forms with the suffix *-aya-* in Class X. The other classes are athematic. Class II contains root presents, and Class III reduplicated athematics. Classes VII and IX are nasal-infix presents (§4.18): Class IX contains seṭ (laryngeal-final) roots (thus *gr̥bhṇā́ti* 'seizes' < **ghr̥bh-né-*h_2*-ti*, root **ghrebh*h_2*-*), while in Class VII the roots end in some other consonant (so *yunákti* 'yokes' < **i̯u-ne-g-ti*, root **i̯eug-*). The nasal present **k̑l̥-né-u-ti* 'hears' (Ved. *śr̥ṇóti*; root **k̑leu-*) was the likely model for a whole new class of presents formed by adding **-neu-* to a root; these became the verbs of Class V and most of Class VIII (the latter containing roots that already had an *n* in them from the point of view of the Sanskrit grammarians; thus *tanóti* above was formed from the Sanskrit root *tan*, while in IE terms it was really a **-neu-*present formed from the zero-grade **tn̥-*).

The following sample paradigms will illustrate the Vedic active and middle present tense forms of five of the verb classes: *bhárāmi* 'I bear', *dvéṣmi* 'I hate', *śr̥ṇómi* 'I hear', *yunájmi* 'I yoke', and *gr̥bhṇā́mi* 'I seize'.

	I	II	V	VII	IX
Active					
sg. 1	*bhárāmi*	*dvéṣmi*	*śr̥ṇómi*	*yunájmi*	*gr̥bhṇā́mi*
2	*bhárasi*	*dvékṣi*	*śr̥ṇóṣi*	*yunákṣi*	*gr̥bhṇā́si*
3	*bhárati*	*dvéṣṭi*	*śr̥ṇóti*	*yunákti*	*gr̥bhṇā́ti*
du. 1	*bhárāvas*	*dviṣvás*	*śr̥ṇvás*	*yuñjvás*	*gr̥bhṇīvás*
2	*bhárathas*	*dviṣṭhás*	*śr̥ṇuthás*	*yuṅkthás*	*gr̥bhṇīthás*
3	*bháratas*	*dviṣṭás*	*śr̥ṇutás*	*yuṅktás*	*gr̥bhṇītás*
pl. 1	*bhárāmas(i)*	*dviṣmás(i)*	*śr̥ṇmás(i)*	*yuñjmás*	*gr̥bhṇīmás(i)*
2	*bháratha*	*dviṣṭhá(na)*	*śr̥ṇuthá*	*yuṅkthá*	*gr̥bhṇīthá(na)*
3	*bháranti*	*dviṣánti*	*śr̥ṇvánti*	*yuñjánti*	*gr̥bhṇánti*
Middle					
sg.					
1	*bháre*	*dviṣé*	*śr̥ṇvé*	*yuñjé*	*gr̥bhṇé*
2	*bhárase*	*dvikṣé*	*śr̥ṇuṣé*	*yuṅkṣé*	*gr̥bhṇīṣé*
3	*bhárate*	*dviṣṭé*	*śr̥ṇvé, śr̥ṇuté*	*yuṅkté*	*gr̥bhṇīté*
du. 1	*bhárāvahe*	*dviṣváhe*	*śr̥ṇváhe*	*yuñjváhe*	*gr̥bhṇīváhe*
2	*bhárethe*	*dviṣā́the*	*śr̥ṇvā́the*	*yuñjā́the*	*gr̥bhṇā́the*
3	*bhárete*	*dviṣā́te*	*śr̥ṇvā́te*	*yuñjā́te*	*gr̥bhṇā́te*
pl. 1	*bhárāmahe*	*dviṣmáhe*	*śr̥ṇmáhe*	*yuñjmáhe*	*gr̥bhṇīmáhe*
2	*bháradhve*	*dviḍḍhvé*	*śr̥ṇudhvé*	*yuṅgdhvé*	*gr̥bhṇīdhvé*
3	*bhárante*	*dviṣáte*	*śr̥ṇváte, śr̥ṇviré*	*yuñjáte*	*gr̥bhṇáte*

The forms *śr̥ṇvé* and *śr̥ṇviré* are archaic *t*-less 3rd person middles (see §5.15). Vedic and Avestan are both important sources of information on these forms in IE. Note also such forms from Class II as 3rd sing. *śáy-e* 'lies', pl. *śé-re* (from **k̂éi̯-oi* and **k̂éi-roi*), and from Avestan, *mruii-e* 'it is announced', *sōi-re* 'they lie'.

10.43. Aorists. The PIE categories of root, thematic, reduplicated, and *s*- (sigmatic) aorist are all found in Sanskrit. A curious formation is the aorist passive in *-i* with old *o*-grade of the root, e.g. *śrā́v-i* 'he was heard' (**k̂lou̯-*); there are several competing theories about the formation's origin. Below are singular and plural paradigms of the root aorist *ásthām* 'I stood' and the sigmatic aorists *ávākṣam* 'I conveyed' and (middle) *ástoṣi* 'I praised'. The forms not attested for these particular roots are in brackets, and forms not attested for any root are left blank.

	Active		*Middle*	
	root	sigmatic	root	sigmatic
sg. 1	*ásthām*	[*ávākṣam*]		*ástoṣi*
2	*ásthās*	[*ávāṭ*]	*ásthithās*	[*ástoṣṭhās*]
3	*ásthāt*	*ávāṭ*	*ásthita*	*ástoṣṭa*

pl. 1	*ásthāma*	[*ávākṣma*]	[*ásthimahi*]	[*ástoṣmahi*]
2	*ásthāta*	[*ávāṣṭa*]		*ástoḍhvam*
3	*ásthur*	*ávākṣur*	*ásthiran*	*ástoṣata*

10.44. Other verbal morphology. A few of the other verbal formations in Sanskrit may be mentioned here; this is only a selection. The IE perfect is alive and well and frequently still has stative meaning (§5.53) in Vedic. Two passive verbal adjectives are found, one in *-ná-* and one in *-tá-*, both of good PIE provenance (§5.61). An indeclinable participle known as the gerund grew to be extremely important, especially in the Classical language; it usually indicated action prior to that of the main verb: *ha-tvā́* 'having slain', *saṃ-gŕ̥bh-ya* 'gathering, having gathered'. Vedic possessed a large number of infinitives, often with several attested for a single root; by contrast, only one infinitive is found in Classical Sanskrit, in *-tum* (e.g. *ótum* 'to weave'), interestingly just barely attested in the Rig Veda though likely inherited (§5.59).

10.45. An important characteristic of Vedic Sanskrit finite verbs is that they are not marked with accents when they occur in main clauses, unless they are the first word in the clause or verse-line (the *pāda*). This is not to say that such verbs were fully unstressed, as is often stated in the literature. But it does indicate that they were prosodically weaker and probably had lower pitch. The feature is shared with the vocative case of nouns.

Nouns and other parts of speech

10.46. The eight cases of the noun were nominative, vocative, accusative, instrumental, dative, ablative, genitive, and locative. All the PIE declensional types are found: consonant-stems, *i*-stems, *u*-stems, long *ī*-stems, *a*-stems (from PIE *o*-stems), and *ā*-stems, as well as a few residual heteroclitic *r/n*-stems. Vedic preserves some of the mobile accent paradigms that are reconstructed for PIE, although it has innovated in many details. It also preserves the two different types of feminine *ī*-stems, the so-called *devī́-* and *vr̥kī́*-types (after the words for 'goddess' and 'she-wolf', respectively); see §6.71.

Vocatives are accented uniformly on the first syllable, a feature inherited from PIE but only residually present in the other languages. Compare nomin. sing. Ved. *pitā́*, Gk. *patḗr* 'father' with voc. Ved. *pítar*, Gk. *páter*.

The following sample paradigms illustrate typical nouns of several classes: *devás* 'god', *śúcis* 'bright', *priyā́* 'dear', *adán* 'eating', and *pitā́* 'father':

		a-stem	*i*-stem	*ā*-stem	*nt*-stem	*r*-stem
Sg.	N	*devás*	*śúcis*	*priyā́*	*adán*	*pitā́*
	V	*déva*	*śúce*	*príye*	*ádan*	*pítar*
	A	*devám*	*śúcim*	*priyā́m*	*adántam*	*pitáram*
	I	*devéna, devā́*	*śúcinā, śúcyā*	*priyáyā*	*adatā́*	*pitrā́*
	D	*devā́ya*	*śúcaye*	*priyā́yai*	*adaté*	*pitré*
	Ab	*devā́t*	*śúces*	*priyā́yās*	*adatás*	*pitúr*
	G	*devásya*	*śúces*	*priyā́yās*	*adatás*	*pitúr*
	L	*devé*	*śúcau*	*priyā́yām*	*adatí*	*pitári*

Du.	N-A	*devā́(u)*	*śúcī*	*priyé*	*adántā*	*pitárā*
	V	*dévā(u)*	*śúcī*	*príye*	*ádantā*	*pítarā*
	I-D-Ab	*devā́bhyām*	*śúcibhyām*	*priyā́bhyām*	*adádbhyām*	*pitṛ́bhyām*
	G-L	*deváyos*	*śúcyos*	*priyáyos*	*adatós*	*pitrós*
Pl.	N	*devā́s, devā́sas*	*śúcayas*	*priyā́s*	*adántas*	*pitáras*
	V	*dévās(as)*	*śúcayas*	*príyās*	*ádantas*	*pítaras*
	A	*devā́n*	*śúcīn*	*priyā́s*	*adatás*	*pitṝ́n*
	I	*deváis, devébhis*	*śúcibhis*	*priyā́bhis*	*adádbhis*	*pitṛ́bhis*
	D-Ab	*devébhyas*	*śúcibhyas*	*priyā́bhyas*	*adádbhyas*	*pitṛ́bhyas*
	G	*devā́nām*	*śúcīnām*	*priyā́ṇām*	*adatā́m*	*pitṝ́ṇā́m*
	L	*devéṣu*	*śúciṣu*	*priyā́su*	*adátsu*	*pitṛ́ṣu*

That the accusative plurals in *-n* once ended in **-ns* reveals itself in certain sandhi contexts, such as *devā́ṃs tvám* 'gods you . . .', *nṝ́ṁḥ pāhi* 'protect men', *sárgāṁ̐r íva* 'like streams' (with *-ḥ* and *-r* from **-s*).

10.47. Compounding in Classical Sanskrit. The more artificial and ornate styles of Classical Sanskrit are famous for the proliferation of lengthy compound nominal forms. Particularly common is the stringing together of words into one great possessive compound (bahuvrihi) modifying some other word in the sentence. Such compounds, of theoretically limitless length, often correspond to whole clauses or sentences in English. A common type is a basically tripartite compound X-Y-Z with the middle member a passive participle, the whole functioning as an adjective meaning 'having (one's) Z Y-ed by X'. In the *Buddhacarita* (*Life of Buddha*) by Aśvaghoṣa, for example, a steed is described as *laghuśayyāstaraṇopagūḍhapṛṣṭa-* '(whose) back (*pṛṣṭa-*) was covered (*upagūḍha-*) by a short (*laghu-*) bed (*śayyā-*) blanket (*āstaraṇa-*)', and a beautiful woman is compared to a river that is *ṛjuṣaḍpadapaṅktijuṣṭapadmā* '(having) lotuses (*padma-*) that were enjoyed (*juṣṭa-*) by a collection (*paṅkti-*) of bees (*ṣaḍpada-*, lit. six-footers) in a row (*ṛju-*)'. In addition to bahuvrihis, the language was fond of compounds expressing essentially a list of things, such as *rogaśokaparītāpabandhanavyasanāni* 'disease (*roga-*), pain (*śoka-*), grief (*parītāpa-*), captivity (*bandhana-*), (and) misfortune (*vyasana-*)'.

Given the Classical authors' penchant for detailed word-painting, these compounds provided a flexible template for extraordinarily rich and dense descriptive passages in both prose and poetry. A consequence of the wide use of such nominalizing, which extended far beyond what we have described here, is a marked decrease in the use of finite verbs. This went hand-in-hand with a simplification of the verbal system that was occurring in the spoken language at the same time; see §10.56 below for more on this.

Pronouns

10.48. As noted above, personal pronouns come in two types in Vedic: fully stressed forms in all the cases but the vocative (for example, *tvám* 'thou', *yuvám* 'you two', and *yūyám* 'ye'), and unstressed enclitic forms occurring only in the accusative, dative, and genitive (such as the accusatives *tvā*, dual *vām*, and plural *vas*). The enclitic forms could not be placed at the beginning of a sentence or clause.

10.49. Most of the other pronouns are of IE ancestry as well. Etymologically most obvious are the demonstrative pronoun *sá* (masc.), *sā́* (fem.), *tád* (neut.) 'the, this' (exactly cognate with Gk. *ho hē tó*; §7.10); the interrogative pronoun masc. *kás*, fem. *kā́*, neut. *kád* (Classical *kim*) 'who, what' from the interrogative stem *k^wo- (§7.12); and the relative pronoun *yás yā́ yád* 'who, which, that' (IE **i̯o-*, §7.11).

Syntax

10.50. Vedic syntax is quite similar to that of the other IE languages of comparable date. The many inflections rendered word order fairly free, although recent research is increasingly showing that the freedom was not as great as used to be thought. As in related languages, the beginning of a sentence was a place of prominence; verbs normally come last, but could be fronted for emphasis. Of particular interest is the complex set of rules for the placement of clitics (including both the clitic pronouns and a variety of conjunctions and sentential particles), as discussed in §§8.22ff.

Vedic text sample

10.51. Verses 11–13 of Rig Veda 10.90, the so-called Puruṣa Hymn. This hymn is a creation myth, and describes the primeval man, Puruṣa, seen as the source of the universe (see §2.32). Verse 12 provides an etiological myth of the traditional caste system of Indian society.

11 yát púruṣaṃ ví ádadhuḥ katidhā́ ví akalpayan
múkhaṃ kím asya káu bāhū́ kā́ ūrū́ pā́dā ucyete

12 brāhmaṇò 'sya múkham āsīd bāhū́ rājanyàḥ kr̥táḥ
ūrū́ tád asya yád váiśyaḥ padbhyā́ṃ śūdró ajāyata

13 candrámā mánaso jātáś cákṣoḥ sū́ryo ajāyata
múkhād índraś ca agníś ca prāṇā́d vāyúr ajāyata

11 When they divided up Puruṣa, how many pieces did they make him into?
What was his mouth, what were his arms, what his thighs, his feet called?

12 His face was the priestly caste, his arms became the princely caste,
his thighs (became) the third caste, from his feet the fourth caste was born.

13 The moon was born from his mind, the sun was born from his eye;
from his face Indra and Agni, from his breath Vāyu was born.

10.51a. Notes. 11. yát: 'when'. Historically this is the neuter accus. sing. of the relative pronoun, which came to be used as a sort of all-purpose conjunction. **ví ádadhuḥ:** 'they put apart, divided'; *ví* 'apart' plus the 3rd pl. imperfect of *dádhāmi* 'I place' (cp. Gk. *títhēmi*).

katidhā́: 'into how many parts?' **ví akalpayan:** 3rd pl. imperfect, 'they made into', from *kalpáyati*, of disputed etymology; it may be a causative that contains the same *-p-* found in such causatives as *sthā-p-áyati* 'causes to stand' (from *sthā-* 'stand'). **kím:** 'what?' Notice that interrogative words do not need to be sentence-initial as they normally are in English. **asya:** 'his', enclitic pronoun, genit. sing. **bāhū́, ūrū́, pā́dā:** 'arms, thighs, feet', all nomin. duals; the lengthening of the final vowels was induced by the PIE dual ending *-h_1 (§6.13). **ucyete:** 'are called', 3rd dual present passive of the root *vac-* 'call, speak, say', PIE **u̯ekʷ-*, also the root of Gk. *(w)épos* 'word, speech, epic poem' and Lat. *uōx* 'voice' < **u̯ōkʷ-s*.

12. brāhmaṇò: 'pertaining to the brahmans, priestly, priestly caste'. The word is a vrddhi-derivative of *brahmáṇ-* 'brahman', itself an amphikinetic (possessive) derivative meaning 'the one of the formulation', from the neuter noun *bráhmaṇ-* 'sacred formulation' (recall §6.29). *Brāhmaṇò 'sya* is the sandhi outcome of underlying *brāhmaṇás asya*. **āsīd:** 3rd sing. imperfect of *ásti* 'is'. The expected athematic form *ā́s* (< **e-$h_1$es-t*) is only marginally preserved in the Rig Veda, replaced nearly everywhere by *ā́sīt*, an innovation formed with the ending *-īt*. This ending was originally proper only to laryngeal-final roots (< **-H-t*). **kr̥táḥ:** '(was) made', *tó*-verbal adjective of *kr̥-* 'do, make'. **tád . . . yád:** literally 'it (was his thighs) that (became) the third caste'. **váísyaḥ:** 'one who has settled (on the soil), farmer, peasant', a member of the third caste in Indian society; from PIE **u̯eiḱ-* 'live, dwell', cp. Gk. *(w)oĩkos* 'home'. **ajāyata:** 'was born', imperfect of *jan-* 'beget', PIE root **ĝenh₁-*.

13. mánaso: 'from his mind', abl. sing. of *mánas-* 'mind' (Gk. *ménos* 'mental spirit, fighting spirit'). **cákṣoḥ:** 'from his eye', ablative sg. **agníś:** Agni, god of fire (cp. Lat. *ignis*, Lith. *ugnìs*). **vāyúr:** Vāyu, god of the wind; PIE **h_2u̯eh_1-i̯u-*, from **h_2u̯eh_1-* 'blow', whose *nt*-derivative **h_2u̯eh_1-n̥t-o-* gives Ved. *vā́tas* (sometimes read as a trisyllable *va'atas*; §10.36), Lat. *uentus*, and Eng. *wind*. The second laryngeal at the beginning is directly reflected by Hitt. *ḫūwant-* 'wind' and the Gk. present *á(w)ē-si* 'blows' (=Ved. *vā́-ti*).

Middle Indic

10.52. Even as early a text as the Rig Veda is not filled exclusively with archaic Sanskrit forms, but contains (especially in the later books) many that belong to stages of Indic that had undergone additional sound changes. These stages are collectively referred to as **Middle Indic** or **Prakrit**. Throughout the history of Indian literature, Sanskrit and Middle Indic words and texts have coexisted; Middle Indic is thus less a chronological term than one referring to a particular cluster of linguistic developments. The Prakrits, or Middle Indic dialects, are often named after particular regions, but their use spread beyond the purely regional to become characteristic of specific literary genres. For example, in Classical Sanskrit drama different dialects represent the speech of different classes of people: the fairly conservative western dialect Śaurasenī is used for women and the northeastern dialect Māgadhī for lowborn buffoons. (Compare the use of Doric Greek as the language of the choruses in Greek drama.)

10.53. The term *Prakrit* comes from the Sanskrit word *prākr̥tam*, 'made before, original, low, vernacular'; this word was opposed to *saṃskr̥tam*, 'put together', hence 'adorned, perfected', already a term for the sacred literary language in Vedic times. The distinction between Classical and Vulgar Latin discussed in chapter 13 is comparable; and just as regional varieties of Vulgar Latin developed into the modern Romance languages, so too did the Prakrits eventually yield the modern Indo-Aryan languages. In literary works, Prakrits are used especially in Sanskrit drama, particularly the east-central variety called Mahārāṣṭrī that was also used in writing Prakrit poetry. A closely allied variety known as Ardhamāgadhī is the language of the Jain canon (Jainism is an ascetic philosophy and religion that developed around the sixth century BC).

The Prakrits were not spoken just within the confines of India, but spread also into Central Asia. Worthy of mention is the variety spoken around Niya, a site along the Silk Road on the edge of the Tarim Basin in what is now western China. Preserved in hundreds of documents from the third century AD, Niya Prakrit has been receiving attention recently because it developed somewhat apart from the Prakrits of India.

The Aśokan inscriptions

10.54. Our first datable written connected texts in an Indic language are a set of royal rock inscriptions set up in northwest, central, and northeast India by the emperor Aśoka probably around the mid-third century BC. Aśoka was the third emperor of the Maurya dynasty (c. 325–183 BC), under whose rule India was unified for the first time. The inscriptions are all identical in content but evince regional linguistic differences that are valuable for the comparative study of early Middle Indic dialects. Two inscriptions in the extreme northwest are written in a substantially different dialect, called Gāndhārī.

Pāli

10.55. The immense corpus of canonical and post-canonical works of Theravada Buddhism (an early form of Buddhism now most prominent in Southeast Asia) was written in the variety of Middle Indic known as Pāli. The literary form of this language was fixed relatively early, and by comparison with other Middle Indic dialects it is rather conservative. Tradition says it was the language of the Buddha himself, who came from eastern India, but the features of Pāli are in fact central and western. As Buddhism spread throughout Central and Southeast Asia during the first millennium AD, Pāli spread with it; the impact of its vocabulary on the languages of this area was significant, and the scripts in which Pāli was written were adopted for writing many languages of Central and Southeast Asia (see further below).

Pāli preserves some archaic features that are drawn from an early Indic dialect different from either Vedic or Classical Sanskrit, or both. For example, the PIE "thorn" clusters all became the voiceless cluster *kṣ* in Sanskrit, but the ones that were originally voiced clusters sometimes remain voiced in Pāli (as they did also in Iranian), as in Pāli *ug-gharati, pag-gharati* 'oozes' < Indo-Ir. **gžharati* (cp. Av. *γžar-* 'flow', and contrast Ved. *kṣárati* 'flows'; the PIE root is **dhg^{w}her-*). Another archaism is the short *i* in the first syllable of the verb *kiṇāti* 'buys' from PIE **k^{w}ri-neh$_2$-ti*; in Classical Sanskrit the *i* was secondarily lengthened under the influence of the verbal adjective *krītá-* 'bought' to *krīṇā́ti*. (This archaism is also preserved in Vedic; though Classical Sanskrit spelling is used in writing the Vedas, the metrical scansion reveals the true quantity of the *i* as short.)

Middle Indic linguistic developments

10.56. Characteristic of Middle Indic historical phonology were the simplification of Sanskrit consonant clusters; the loss of most final consonants; and the weakening or loss of single consonants between vowels. In morphology, both noun and verb inflection was simplified, partly due to the loss of final consonants. Noun cases and stem-classes fell together, and athematic nouns became thematic. In verbs, the several past tenses merged into a single preterite, and the present stem replaced the root as the basic form from which to derive other verbal forms. A new syntactic system known as split ergativity arose, whereby (broadly speaking) the grammatical case taken by a subject depends on the tense of the verb: in the present tense, the subject is in the nominative, whereas in the past tense, the subject is in the same case as objects. This came about through the reanalysis of a construction that was already common in Classical Sanskrit, whereby the past passive participle was used to express actions in past time rather than a past-tense finite verb. Thus to say 'Indra slew the serpent', one said literally 'By Indra the serpent (was) slain', with the logical subject (Indra) in the instrumental case. Over time, the logical subject in such constructions became reanalyzed as the grammatical subject. The resulting system is characteristic of the modern Indo-Aryan languages, and was already developing in the later Prakrits.

Development and spread of Indian scripts

10.57. In the earliest inscriptions, two scripts are found, Brāhmī and Kharoṣṭhī. The latter was limited to writing Gāndhārī in northwest India until the fifth century AD, and died out thereafter. Brāhmī was to enjoy much greater fortunes. Its origins have been the subject of controversy, though it is most likely derived, at least in part, from a Semitic alphabet. By around the third century AD, it had evolved into a northern and a southern form. The northern form eventually spawned Devanāgarī, the script of Sanskrit and Hindi. Buddhist missionaries carried related offshoots with them into Central Asia, where they became used for writing Tocharian, Khotanese (a Middle Iranian language), and Tibetan. Knowledge of the script spread as far as Japan, where it greatly influenced the development and organization of the *kana* syllabaries (whose symbols, though, are derived from Chinese).

The southern form, whose signs basically look more rounded, developed into the scripts used for the Dravidian languages in southern India, such as Telugu, Tamil, Kannaḍa, and Malayalam, as well as of the Indic language Sinhalese in Sri Lanka. A variety of the southern type from about the sixth century spread to Southeast Asia and is the source of the modern scripts of Thailand, Myanmar, Cambodia, and Laos.

Modern (New) Indo-Aryan

10.58. Between a fifth and a sixth of the world's population speaks a Modern Indic language. A listing of the languages would include well over 200 names, although many of them form large dialect continua without clear divisions. The classification

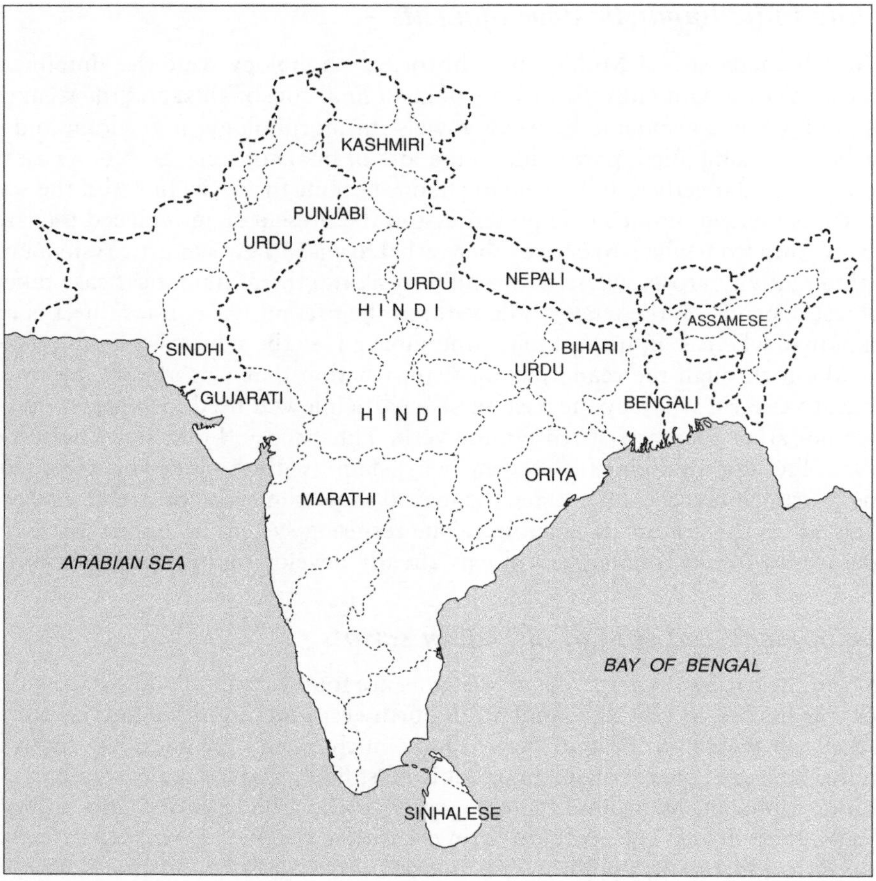

Map 10.1 Modern Indo-Aryan languages

of most of the modern languages is made on the basis of broad geographic areas (zones), including Eastern, Central, Northern, Northwest, and Southern.

The Modern Indo-Aryan languages have continued some of the developments described above for Middle Indic. Diphthongs were often monophthongized and short vowels deleted; final stops and even whole final syllables were often lost. Nominal inflections were reduced in many dialects to just two cases, a direct and an oblique; the number of grammatical genders was reduced to two or, in some areas, none at all. Inflected tenses and moods in the verb were widely replaced by analytical (periphrastic) constructions using a helping verb. These developments had all largely taken place by the time of **Apabraṁśa** (Sanskrit for 'corruption'), a language occurring in several regional varieties that formed the transitional stage between the Prakrits and the modern languages. It developed toward the end of the first millennium AD.

10.59. The **Eastern Zone** includes **Bengali** (Bāṅglā), spoken in Bangladesh and northeastern India. Bengali literature is among the oldest of the modern Indo-Aryan languages, starting in the tenth or eleventh century. Linguistically, Bengali is notable for being rather conservative in nominal inflection, with some nouns inflecting in up to six cases; but it has lost grammatical gender. Closely related to Bengali is **Assamese**, spoken in the state of Assam in eastern India; it also has a relatively rich inflectional system for nouns, and is noteworthy in having lost the retroflex stops. Also belonging to this branch are **Bihari** (Bihārī) and **Oriya** (Orīyā).

10.60. The **Central Zone** includes, most famously, **Hindi-Urdu** or Hindustani. This represents two literary languages (Hindi and Urdu) of what is essentially a single spoken language. Hindi is spoken across northern India, while Urdu is spoken in northern India and Pakistan (where it is the national language). Literary Hindi is heavily influenced by Sanskrit and written in the same script, while Urdu is rich in Persian and Arabic loanwords and is written in a modified Perso-Arabic script. **Gujarati** (Gujarātī), spoken in Gujarat and the neighboring states of Maharashtra and Rajasthan, preserves all three genders in the noun, unlike Hindi, which only has two (masculine and feminine). **Punjabi** (Panjābī), spoken in the Punjab in northwest India and Pakistan, has developed tones on vowels that originally neighbored voiced aspirated stops; for example, initial voiced aspirated stops have became voiced stops with a low tone on the following vowel. Also belonging to the Central Zone is **Romani** (or Romany), the language of the Roma or Gypsies, spoken now primarily in Europe. It apparently separated from the other Central languages around 1000; its modern varieties have borrowed heavily from the languages of the regions where the Roma settled.

10.61. Most prominent of the **Northern Zone** languages is **Nepali** (Nepālī), spoken primarily in Nepal and northeast India.

10.62. The **Northwestern Zone** includes the **Dardic** languages, especially **Kashmiri** (Kashmirī), spoken in northwest India and Pakistan. The Dardic languages share several features with neighboring Iranian languages; Kashmiri, for example, has merged the voiced aspirated stops with the plain voiced stops, probably under Iranian influence. **Sindhi** (Sindhī) is spoken mostly in the Sindh region of Pakistan; it is unusually conservative in retaining final short vowels, but has innovated strikingly in developing a series of implosive stops.

At the other end of the subcontinent is **Sinhalese** (Sinhālā), spoken on the island of Sri Lanka. The ancestors of the Sinhalese came from northern India and colonized the island probably in the fifth century BC. Some inscriptions in an early form of the language, in the Brāhmī alphabet, have been dated to the second century BC; substantial amounts of Buddhist literature were being produced from around AD 1000. Sinhalese merged the aspirated and unaspirated stops.

10.63. Finally, the **Southern Zone** contains **Marathi** (Marāṭhī), spoken in Maharashtra and adjacent states.

For Further Reading

The literature on Sanskrit and Indic is vast; there is, however, no complete comparative grammar, and few major reference works that are either in English or up-to-date. A notable exception is the standard Sanskrit grammar, Whitney 1896 (still exceptional in spite of its age) and, specifically for Vedic, Macdonell 1910 (which lists all the forms that occur, by category) and the smaller (but still very useful) Macdonell 1916. The standard introductory selection of Rig Vedic hymns, with translations, notes, and glossary, is Macdonell 1917. The one comprehensive Sanskrit comparative grammar is in German and incomplete (Wackernagel and Debrunner 1896–); the most recent volume appeared in 1964, and volumes on the verb and syntax are still lacking. The standard edition of the Rig Veda in transliteration is Aufrecht 1877, and the most commonly used scholarly translation is Geldner 1951–7, unhappily out of print. Readers of French may profitably avail themselves of the 17 volumes of translations of various Vedic hymns and commentary in Renou 1955–69. A new complete translation in English, currently in preparation by the American Indologists Joel Brereton and Stephanie Jamison, will supersede all previous ones when it is finished. Hermann Grassmann's dictionary of the Rig Veda (Grassmann 1873) lists every form and gives the surrounding context for many passages; it is still immensely useful in spite of its often out-of-date definitions. A newly finished and very up-to-date etymological dictionary of both the Vedic and the Classical languages is Mayrhofer 1986–2001. Sanskrit syntax is given fundamental treatment in Delbrück 1888; for more modern analyses of Wackernagel's Law in Vedic and related phenomena, see Hale 1987 (see Bibliography, ch. 8) and subsequent works. A useful new historical and grammatical account of Pāli is Oberlies 2001. The articles of the late Karl Hoffmann on both Indic and Iranian are masterful; they are collected in Hoffmann 1975–92.

For Review

Know the meaning or significance of the following:

Rig Veda	"ruki"	Aryan	sandhi
Nuristani	Brugmann's Law	Indo-Aryan	injunctive
Law of Palatals	Mitanni	retroflex	Middle Indic
Bartholomae's Law	Pāṇini	laryngeal hiatus	Aśoka

Exercises

1 Give the outcomes of the following PIE forms in Sanskrit after the operation of Brugmann's Law, changes to the velars, vowel mergers, monophthongization of diphthongs, and changes to the resonants. (Don't forget to apply any relevant pre-Indo-Iranian changes.) Show or describe the intermediate steps. For the purpose of this exercise, both **r* and **l* became *r*.

Example: **ĝenos* 'tribe, kind, family' became *janas* (**ĝ* became *j* and the two mid vowels became *a*)

- **a** *g^w*olbhom* 'womb'
- **b** **bhagos* 'portion, good fortune'
- **c** **dhermn̥* 'law'
- **d** **ĝhenu* 'jaw'
- **e** **meĝhorēĝō* 'great king'
- **f** *k^w*ormn̥* 'doing, action'
- **g** **semsk*^{w}*r̥tom* 'thing put together'
- **h** **niru̯e*h_2*nom* 'blowing out, extinction'
- **i** **u̯eidos* 'knowledge'
- **j** **i̯eugom* 'yoking, joining'

2 Vedic has a family of words that includes an adjective *drógha-* 'deceitful' and a root noun *drúh-* 'deceit'.

a Which PIE velar or velars are the possible sources for the root-final consonant in this family of words?
b Part of the paradigm of *drúh-* is accus. sing. *drúham*, nomin. pl. *drúhas*, accus. pl. *druhás*. Are any of these forms not predicted by the operation of regular sound changes?
c Provide an explanation for any unpredicted forms you identified in **b**.

3 **a** The neuter of the Classical Skt. interrogative pronoun, *kim* (§10.49), is odd from the point of view of historical Sanskrit phonology. What is odd about it? Can you suggest an explanation?
b The form *kim* is also odd from the point of view of PIE morphology. Why?

4 What would have been the outcome in Sanskrit of the boldfaced sequences in the following PIE forms?

a **h_1**eisi*** 'you go'
b ****isn**ont-* 'setting in motion'
c **di**k̂to**-* 'indicated, pointed'
d **u̯**isto**-* 'active'
e ****u̯r̥n**euti* 'covers'
f **h_2**usto**-* 'having shined'
g **h_2**uks**ont-* 'growing'
h **h_2**u̯r̥sto**-* 'having rained'

5 By Bartholomae's Law and any other relevant sound changes, what would be the outcome in Sanskrit of the following words?

a **rudhto-* 'obstructed'
b **labhto-* 'taken'
c **mr̥dhto-* 'neglected'
d **dughto-* 'milked'

6 A special case involving Bartholomae's Law is the outcome of the cluster **-ĝht-*. Based on the following forms, what was the outcome of this cluster? (Ignore the retroflection of the *ṣ* in *áṣāḍha-*.)

**n̥seĝhto-* > *áṣāḍha-* 'invincible'
**$h_3$miĝhto-* > *mīḍhá-* 'urinated'
**uĝhto-* > *ūḍhá-* 'conveyed'
**dr̥ĝhto-* > *dr̥ḍhá-* 'strong' (*r̥* scans long)

7 Apply Grassmann's Law and any other relevant sound changes to the following forms to produce their outcome in Sanskrit:

a **dhedheh$_1$mi* 'I place'
b **dhuĝhroi* 'milks'
c **bheudhetoi* 'wakes up'
d **edheg^{w}het* 'was burning'
e **gheghose* 'has eaten' (note: apply Grassmann's Law first)

8 As seen in the chart in §10.46, the accusative singular of consonant stems ends in *-am* (*adántam, pitáram*). Given Indo-Iranian sound changes, is this expected? If not, say what should have been the outcome, and give an explanation for the form actually occurring. Do not suggest additional sound changes to account for it.

9 Identify the class to which the following Sanskrit verbs belong and indicate the type of IE present stem that it continues.

a *ā́ste* 'sits' (middle)
b *bhinátti* 'splits' (cp. passive *bhidyáte* 'is split')
c *pádyate* 'goes' (middle)
d *nudáti* 'pushes'
e *pácati* 'cooks'
f *pr̥ṇā́ti* 'fills' (cp. passive *pūryáte* 'is filled')
g *bíbharti* 'carries' (cp. passive verbal adjective *bhr̥tá-* 'carried')
h *hinóti* 'impels' (cp. 1st pl. root aorist *áhema*)

10 One important group of Sanskrit verbs not mentioned in the chapter are the causatives, formed with the suffix *-áya-*. Observe the following pairs of causatives and past participles:

pav-áyati 'causes to cleanse'	*pū-tá-* 'cleansed'
jar-áyati 'makes old'	*jīr-ṇá-* 'aged'
mān-áyati 'makes thought (highly of)'	*ma-tá-* 'thought'
yāj-áyati 'causes to worship'	*iṣ-ṭá-* 'worshiped'

Given your knowledge of the PIE causative and of sound changes in Indo-Iranian, provide an explanation for the difference in root vocalism (*-a-* vs. *-ā-*) in these causatives.

11 **a** The Vedic text sample in §10.51 contains one verb form showing accent (*ádadhuḥ*) and four verb forms not showing accent (*akalpayan, ucyete, āsīd, ajāyata*). Explain why some of these are written with an accent and some without.
b In another Rig Vedic hymn (10.129.2) there is a sentence that reads, *ā́nīd avātám̐ svadháyā tád ékam̐* 'That one breathed by its own power, without wind'. Why is the verb *ā́nīd* 'breathed' accented?

PIE Vocabulary II: Animals

**ek̂u̯os* 'horse': Ved. *áśva-*, Gk. *híppos*, Lat. *equus*
**g^w^ou-* 'COW': Ved. *gav-*, Gk. *boũs*, Lat. *bōs* (*bou-*)
**$h_2$ou̯i-* 'sheep': Lycian *χawa-*, Ved. *ávi-*, Lat. *ouis*, Eng. EWE
**k̂u̯ōn* 'dog, HOUND': Hitt. *kuwan-*, Ved. *śvā́*, Gk. *kúōn*, Lat. *canis*
**suHs* 'pig': Gk. *hũs*, Lat. *sūs*, Eng. SOW
**ĝhans-* 'GOOSE': Ved. *haṁsás*, Lat. *ānser*, OCS *gǫsĭ*
**h_2ŕ̥tk̂os* 'bear': Hitt. *ḫartaqqaš*, Ved. *ŕ̥kṣas*, Gk. *árktos*, Lat. *ursus*
**u̯l̥k^w^os* 'WOLF': Hitt. *walkuwa-* 'monster' (?), Gk. *lúkos*, Lat. *lupus*
**mūs* 'MOUSE': Gk. *mũs*, Lat. *mūs*, OCS *myšĭ*

11 Indo-Iranian II: Iranian

Introduction

11.1. Languages bearing the designation "Iranian" are by no means limited geographically to Iran. Since ancient times Iranian languages have been spoken over a large section of southwestern and central Asia – from Armenia and Mesopotamia in the west, to the Persian Gulf in the south, all the way into Chinese Turkestan in the east, and well to the north of what is now Iran, Afghanistan, and Tajikistan (the only modern countries whose official languages are Iranian). Chronologically, the Iranian subbranch is divided into **Old Iranian** (until c. 400 BC), **Middle Iranian** (c. 400 BC–c. AD 900), and the modern Iranian languages. By dialect-area it is divided into East and West Iranian, or into Southwest, Central, and Northeast Iranian.

The study of the Iranian languages has made remarkable strides in the last century. The discovery of several Middle Iranian languages in the early 1900s coupled with a steady advance in philological methods in Avestan studies has put Iranian linguistics on an equal footing with Indic. As noted in the previous chapter, Iranian preserves some archaic features that were lost in Indic (see the fuller discussion in §11.25 below), but unfortunately the Old Avestan corpus, the most archaic textual material in Iranian, is very small.

Most of this chapter will concern the two Old Iranian languages Avestan and Old Persian, the only ones in which we have texts. We know of several other contemporaneous languages, including Median (§11.29) and Scythian (preserved in some glosses and proper names), spoken in the extreme northwest of Iranian territory. Scythian may have been the Iranian language that came into contact with the early Slavs and from which the latter obtained a few loanwords (see §18.20).

Basic Iranian phonological characteristics

Several features distinguish the Iranian subgroup from Indic; these are innovations that occurred after the Common Indo-Iranian period, or retention of Common Indo-Iranian features that were changed in Indic.

11.2. Deaspiration of voiced aspirates. The voiced aspirates lost their aspiration and became ordinary voiced stops, as in Av. *baraiṇti* and OPers. *bara(n)tiy* 'they carry' < Indo-Ir. **bharanti*.

11.3. Spirantization of voiceless stops. Characteristic of Iranian is the development of stops into fricatives in many environments. In the case of the voiceless stops **p *t *k*, they became the fricatives *f θ* (= [θ] Eng. *th*) and *x* (= [x] German *ch*) before non-syllabic consonants, as in Av. and OPers. *fra-* 'forth, forward' from Indo-Ir. **pra-*, Av. *caθuuārō* 'four' from Indo-Ir. **catu̯āras*; and Av. *xrūra-* 'bloody' from Indo-Ir. **krūra-*.

11.4. Development of the palatals. The Indo-Iranian palatals **ć* and **j́(h)* (from PIE **k̂* and **ĝ(h)*, recall §10.5) became Avestan and Median *s* and *z* and Old Persian *θ* and *d*; their intermediate Common Iranian stage may have been the affricates **ts* and **dz*.

11.5. Weakening of **s* to *h*. The old sibilant **s* became weakened to *h* before vowels or resonants in Iranian, as in Av. *hənti* 'they are' (< Indo-Ir. **santi*) and *ahmi* 'I am' (< **asmi*). This development is similar to that of Greek, as we will see in the next chapter.

11.6. Dental-plus-dental clusters and Bartholomae's Law. As discussed in §10.6, the Indo-Iranian outcomes of the PIE dental-plus-dental clusters, namely **-tst-* (< PIE **-t-t-* and **-d-t-*) and **-dzd(h)-*, lost the initial dental in Iranian and became *-st-* or *-zd-*: Av. *vista-* 'known' (cp. Ved. *vittá-*; Indo-Ir. **u̯itsta-* < PIE **u̯id-to-*), OPers. *azdā* 'known' (cp. Ved. *addhā́* 'surely'; Indo-Ir. **adzdhā* < earlier **adh-tā*). The progressive voicing assimilation induced by Bartholomae's Law is preserved in Iranian not only in the cluster *-zd-*, but in other clusters as well. In Old Avestan it is still regularly preserved in all contexts, as in *aogədā* (phonetically *aogdā*) 'he said' < **augh-ta* and *aoγžā* 'you said' < **augh-ša*. But in Young Avestan its effects were largely undone by analogy (for example, 'he said' is *aoxta*).

11.7. Laryngeals. Vocalized laryngeals were lost word-medially in Iranian, as in Av. *duxtar-* 'daughter' (vs. Ved. *duhitár-* < **dhugh₂ter-*), but apparently preserved elsewhere on occasion, as *i* (e.g. in the 1st pl. middle verb ending *-maiδi*, cp. Ved. *-mahi* < **-medhh₂*, and perhaps in Young Av. *pitā* 'father' < **ph₂tḗr*, although Old Avestan has *ptā*). The laryngeals in their non-vocalized form left traces in two important ways. First, **h₂* aspirated a preceding voiceless stop, e.g. genit. sing. *paθō* 'path' < PIE **pn̥t-h₂-es*; and second, Old Avestan preserves so-called laryngeal hiatus (see further §11.23) like Vedic but more faithfully.

11.8. Preservation of diphthongs. In contrast to Sanskrit, Iranian preserved the Indo-Iranian diphthongs **ai* and **au*. These are written as *aē* and *ao* in Avestan, *ai* and *au* in Old Persian: Av. *daēuua-* 'demon', OPers. *daiva-* 'evil god' (vs. Ved. *devás* 'god'); Av. *haoma-*, OPers. *hauma-* 'sacred intoxicating drink' (vs. Ved. *sómas*). Later in Middle Iranian times (§11.35 below), these diphthongs were monophthongized as they had been in Sanskrit.

Avestan

11.9. Avestan is the language of the **Avesta**, the collection of sacred texts of the Zoroastrian religion. The full Pahlavi (Middle Persian) name, *abestāg u zand*, meaning 'text and commentary', was mistakenly rendered as *Zend-Avesta* in Europe; *Zend* was further misunderstood as a language name, and for well over a century Avestan was known as "Zend." Avestan was introduced to Europe by the French scholar Abraham Hyacinthe Anquetil du Perron (or Duperron), who journeyed to India in 1754 to learn about Zoroastrianism from the Parsis (Zoroastrians who had migrated to India in the tenth century) and published the first Avestan texts and translations in 1771. Avestan is classified as East Iranian, and it is believed to have been spoken in an area from the Aral Sea to what is now easternmost Iran.

Zoroastrianism and the Avesta

11.10. Zoroaster or Zarathuštra (Av. *Zaraθuštra-*; Zoroaster is the Greek rendering of his name) was a prophet who founded the Mazdayasnian religion (more familiarly called Zoroastrianism). The dates of his life are unknown, although linguistic and comparative evidence points to the late second millennium BC. The Mazdayasnian religion eventually spread throughout pre-Islamic Iran and adjacent territories. Zoroastrians believe in a cosmic dualism in which good spirits (*ahura-*) and evil spirits or demons (*daēuua-*) are in constant conflict, a conflict that will ultimately end with the triumph of good. A supreme being who heads the good spirits is worshiped, Ahura Mazda or 'wise lord' (Av. *ahurō mazdā̊*, OPers. *Auramazdā*, ModPers. *Ohrmazd*), whence the term *Mazdayasnian* (*yasna-* means 'worship, sacrifice').

The roots of Zoroastrianism are the inherited Indo-Iranian religion that became Hinduism in India, but Zarathuštra's teachings resulted in many changes, including some that reversed or rejected traditional concepts. The most familiar example is the Avestan word for 'demon' mentioned above, *daēuua-*, which is the inherited word for 'god' (cp. Ved. *devás*). Nonetheless, many myths in the Rig Veda have analogues in the Avesta, and cognate phrases and formulas are found abundantly in both works (e.g. Ved. *r̥tám̥ sapāmi* 'I honor truth' ≈ Old Av. *aṣ̌əm haptī* 'he honors truth'). Thus the Avesta importantly continues a common inherited religious poetic tradition.

The Avesta consists of several separate texts: the Yasna (the liturgy, containing formulaic prayers and hymns); the Yašts (poems, some lengthy, celebrating particular deities and their deeds); the Vidēvdāt or Vendidad (a legal text concerning punishment and purification); the Khorde Avesta (miscellaneous short prayers); the Nīrangestān (ritual rules and legal matters); and various other texts.

11.11. The linguistically oldest Avestan, called **Old** or **Gathic Avestan**, is confined mostly to the core of the Yasna, namely Yasna 28–34, 43–51, and 53. These sections constitute the five Gathas (or Gāthās; *gāθā* 'song') traditionally ascribed to Zarathuštra himself. Also in Old Avestan is the prose ritual text called the Yasna Haptaŋhāiti or 'Yasna of the seven chapters' (Yasna 35.3–41), as well as four sacred formulas preserved in Yasna 27 and 54. Old Avestan, as mentioned in the preceding chapter, is grammatically comparable to the language of the Rig Veda. It is therefore usually assumed to be of about the same age, perhaps dating to the late second millennium BC.

11.12. The rest of the Avesta is written in **Young Avestan**. As Young Avestan is structurally more archaic than our earliest Old Persian, it is probably several centuries older; a reasonable estimate puts it at the ninth or eighth century BC. It is not a linear descendant of Old Avestan (just as Classical Sanskrit is not a linear descendant but rather a "niece" of Vedic Sanskrit), at least not in the form in which Old Avestan has come down to us. The two varieties differ from each other in several details, some of which will be noted below (and recall §11.6).

Textual transmission

11.13. Anyone working with Avestan materials needs to be aware of the quality of their transmission, which is sometimes poor. The existing manuscripts are thought to go back ultimately to an edition compiled in Persia during the Sassanian dynasty (AD 224–652). By this point, Avestan had been long dead as a spoken language, and was only used in reciting the sacred religious texts. No direct copy of the putative Sassanian archetype exists; the surviving manuscripts stem from a much later descendant dating to the eleventh century or thereabouts. The earliest preserved Avestan manuscript dates only to the year 1288, and some of the most important other manuscripts were not produced until the 1600s and 1700s. Clearly, there has been plenty of opportunity for errors to enter into the transmission, both modernizations under the influence of modern speakers and miscopyings.

11.14. To make matters more difficult, modernizations and other modifications were not confined to the period in which the texts were transmitted in written form, but extend throughout their entire history. Internal linguistic and orthographic evidence indicates that, well after the first several centuries of oral composition, recomposition, and transmission, the texts were redacted by scholars (called *diaskeuasts* in Avestan scholarship, from Greek *diaskeuázō* 'set in order, edit a literary work') in an effort to produce a kind of school-text that preserved the liturgical pronunciation (which is usually thought to have been slow and musical) and made it more linguistically transparent. These scholars probably still spoke Young but not Old Avestan. The changes they wrought were far-reaching and often based on false or (from our point of view) pseudo-scientific analysis of the language, as well as on influence from the Young Avestan that they spoke. For example, Avestan, in keeping with inherited practice, could separate preverbs from verbs with intervening material (tmesis, §8.9); in Young Avestan, but not Old Avestan, a separated preverb could be repeated before the verb. The diaskeuasts introduced repeated preverbs into the Old Avestan text in such cases, which we know are artificial additions because they ruin the meter. (The first verse of Yasna 48.7 has two such preverbs, *nī aēšəmō nī.diiātąm paitī rəməm paitī.siiōdūm* "Let wrath be laid down! Cut up fury," where the second *nī* and the second *paitī* are redactional additions, increasing the line from its required eleven syllables to fourteen!) A good deal of the modern philology of the Gathic texts is devoted to untangling these diaskeuastic modifications.

Because much of the editorial work happened during the Young Avestan period, Old Avestan has a strongly Young Avestan phonetic cast that represents secondary overlayering and adaptation. Some have argued, in fact, that the oldest Zoroastrian texts were composed already in late Common Iranian times. For example, words beginning in Iranian with the disyllabic sequence **ju'a-* (with hiatus from **juHa-*) still scan disyllabically in the Gathas; later this sequence became monosyllabic

**i̯ua-*, the ancestor of both Avestan *zba-* (the spelling in the transmitted text) *and* of Old Persian *za-*. All this indicates that the text preserves (underneath the modernizations) a stage from a time before the common ancestor of Avestan and Old Persian split. (If that is true, then Young Avestan actually *is* a lineal descendant of Old Avestan.) Thus the participle *zbaiieṇtē* 'for him invoking' at Yasna 49.12 must be read **zuu̯aiieṇtē* (probably really **zuu̯aiantai* if one undoes the vowel changes).

Script

11.15. An alphabetic script was invented, perhaps in the fourth century, for the express purpose of recording the recitation of the Avestan texts; some of the letters were taken from those of "Book Pahlavi" (see §11.42 below) while the rest were invented afresh. To preserve the recitation accurately, the script was devised to encode much of the phonetic detail of Avestan. (Contrast this with scripts devised by native speakers of a language, which rarely encode such detail because any native speaker can supply the missing information.) Unfortunately the script does not encode all the phonetic information we might like to have; in particular, there is no indication of the placement or nature of the word-stress, for example. (Such information can be gleaned indirectly from variations in vowel quantity: a form like *dātaras-ca* 'and the creators' has its second vowel shortened from expected **dātāras-ca* presumably because the clitic *-ca* threw the accent forward to **dātārás-ca*. See also §11.22.) The phonetic detail and certain orthographic conventions lend an unfamiliar look to the spelling of many words that are in fact little different from their Sanskrit cognates, like the instr. pl. *daēuuaēibiš* 'by the demons' (Ved. *devébhis* 'by the gods') and the noun *iθiiejah-* 'danger' (Ved. *tyájas-*): *uu* and *ii* represent the glides *w* and *y*; *aē* represents the diphthong *ai*; and an extra *i* before a consonant indicates palatalization of that consonant.

In the manuscripts, words are separated from each other by dots (.), which also regularly appear between the members of a compound (such as *aspō.gar-* 'devouring horses'), and occasionally at or near other morpheme boundaries, such as before an inflectional ending (e.g. OAv. *dīdraγžō.duiiē* 'you [pl.] wish to hold firmly'). In the standard transcription of Avestan, it is customary to include such dots only when they occur inside a word.

Phonology

Consonants

11.16. Velars. Below is a tabular comparison of the Sanskrit and Avestan outcomes of the velars:

PIE	Skt.	Av.
*k, $^*k^w$	k	k
*g, $^*g^w$	g	g
*gh, $^*g^wh$	gh	g

*k, *k^w before front V	c	c
*g, *g^w before front V	j	j
*gh, *g^{w}h before front V	h	j
*k̂	ś	s
*ĝ	j	z
*ĝh	h	z

The development of the velars in Avestan is thus fairly straightforward. The Iranian velar stops **k* and **g* (representing PIE **k* **k^w* **g* **g^w* **gh* **g^{w}h*) and affricates **c* and **j* (representing the same PIE sounds, but before front vowels) remained intact as *k g c j*. The PIE palatals, which had become **ć* and **ʄ* in Indo-Iranian, became the sibilants *s* and *z* in Avestan (their outcomes in Old Persian are different; see §11.32), as in *sōire* 'they lie' (Ved. *śére*, PIE **k̂ei-ro-*) and *zairi-* 'yellow, golden' (Ved. *hári-*, PIE **ĝhel-*). Thus Avestan kept three distinct reflexes of palatals, velars before front vowels, and velars elsewhere, in contrast to Sanskrit, which partially merged the first two.

11.17. Spirantization of voiced stops. The spirantization of the voiceless stops has already been dealt with (§11.3). The voiced Indo-Ir. stops *b d g* became fricatives in many environments in YAv., especially word-internally and before voiced consonants of various kinds. These are written *β δ γ*, representing phonetic [v ð ɣ], as in *gərəβnā-* 'seize' (Ved. *gr̥bhṇā́-*), *daδāiti* 'gives; puts' (Ved. *dádāti*, *dádhāti*), and *γ(ə)nā* 'woman' (Ved. *gnā́-*).

11.18. Iranian **h*. Important for the general look of the language is the further development of Iranian **h* from PIE **s*. Word-internally before *a* it became a sound transliterated as *ŋh*, as in *aŋhaṯ* 'he will be', the 3rd sing. pres. subjunctive of *ah-* 'be' (cp. Ved. *ásat* 'will be'). A PIE sequence **su̯* became a sound transliterated *x^v*, as in *x^{v}aŋhar-* 'sister' < **su̯esor-*.

Vowels

11.19. Development of **a*. The development of the vowels in Avestan is complex. We here list some of the changes to affect just one of them, Indo-Ir. **a*. This vowel generally remained intact, but became a sound written *ə* before a nasal, as in the accus. sing. ending *-əm* (Ved. *-am*) and the noun *nəmō* 'reverence' (Ved. *námas*). The sequence **-an-* before a coronal fricative (*s, z, θ*) became *ą*, representing a nasalized *a*, as in *mąθra-* 'formulation' (Ved. *mántra-*) and *fšuiiąs* 'cattle-herder' < **pk̂u-i̯ent-s* (from **pek̂u* 'cattle, livestock'; cp. Lat. *pecū* 'cattle'). Final *-as*, most common in the nomin. sing. of thematic masculine nouns and adjectives, became *-ō*, as in *daēuuō* 'demon'; this development also happened before a morpheme boundary in compounds, e.g. *aspō.gar-* 'devouring horses'. A particularly unusual-looking development is the Old Avestan outcome *-ə̄ṇg* from Indo-Iranian **-ans*, as in the accus. pl. *daēuu-ə̄ṇg* 'demons' < PIE **dei̯u-ons*, in the genit. sing. *x^{v}ə̄ṇg* 'of the sun' < Indo-Ir. **su̯ans* or **suHans*, and in the phrase *də̄ṇg paiti-* 'lord of the house' < Indo-Ir. **dans pati-*, PIE **dems potis* (cp. Ved. *dám-patis*, Gk. *des-pótēs* 'master, lord').

11.20. Long **ā* normally remained, but also became *ą* before nasals sometimes (e.g. the accus. sing. *daēnąm* 'religion' < **-ām*). Before **s* it became a sound transliterated as *å*, as in the feminine nomin. pl. *tå* 'these' (Ved. *tā́s*) and the feminine genit. pl. *yåŋhąm* 'of which' (Ved. *yā́sām*).

11.21. Final vowels. A characteristic difference between Old and Young Avestan is the treatment of original Indo-Iranian final vowels. In Old Avestan, the outcomes of all original final vowels are written long, regardless of the original quantity, while in Young Avestan they are written short (except for monosyllables). Hence the contrasts between Old Av. *astī* 'is', YAv. *asti* (**-i*); Old Av. *uxδā* 'words', YAv. *uxδa* (neut. pl. **-ā* < PIE **-eh*$_2$); Old Av. dat. pl. *-aēšū*, YAv. *-aēšu* (< **-aisu* < PIE **-oisu*); Old Av. voc. *ahurā* 'o lord', YAv. *ahura* (**-a* < PIE **-e*); and instr. sing. Old Av. *aṣ̌ī* 'with a reward', YAv. *paiti* 'with a master' (< **-ī* < PIE **-ih*$_1$). It is usually thought that the length of Old Avestan final vowels is artificial and was introduced into the redactional tradition well after the Old Avestan period, perhaps as an indication of recitational practice (recall §11.14 above). There is in fact evidence that final long vowels in polysyllables were shortened in the ancestor of both Old and Young Avestan.

11.22. Development of **r̥*. The reflex of syllabic **r̥* is written *ərə*, as in *kərəta-* 'done' (Ved. *kr̥tá-*). An interesting development is that an accented **ŕ̥* was devoiced before a following voiceless stop, becoming a sound or sound sequence written *əhr* (e.g. *vəhrka-* 'wolf', cp. Ved. *vŕ̥ka-*), and if the stop was a *t*, the combination produced a *sh*-like sound written with a letter transliterated as *ṣ̌*. This happened not only with stressed syllabic **ŕ̥* but also with **-ár-*: *maṣ̌iia-* 'mortal' (cp. Ved. *mártya-*); *aməṣ̌a-* 'immortal' (cp. Ved. *amŕ̥ta-*).

Note incidentally that these last changes provide important evidence for the existence of a mobile accentual system in early Iranian. A mobile accent is found today in Pashto and a few other modern Iranian languages.

11.23. Laryngeal hiatus. The poetic meter of the Gathas shows that, as in Vedic, certain long vowels count as two vowels (i.e., two syllables) with a hiatus (presumably a glottal stop) between them. The hiatus corresponds to a former laryngeal; we therefore call this phenomenon **laryngeal hiatus.** Thus the nomin.-accus. sing. *då* 'gift' must scan as two syllables, i.e. *da'ā* (from **da'ō* < **deh*$_2$*-os*), whereas the 2nd sing. aorist injunctive *då* 'you give/gave, you put' does not, as it comes from **deh*$_3$*s* or **dheh*$_1$*s*, both monosyllables. The poetry of the Gathas is very consistent in preserving laryngeal hiatus where it would be expected on etymological grounds – far more consistent in fact than the Rig Veda, making Old Avestan extremely valuable for the laryngeal theory.

11.24. Sandhi. The complicated external sandhi found in Sanskrit is not present in Avestan. Thus the nominative singular of the word for demon is always *daēuuō*, though its Vedic counterpart ('god') was *devó* only before voiced consonants, and otherwise could be *devá*, *devás*, *deváḥ*, or *deváś*. But etymological final *-s*'s reappear sometimes, especially when a clitic follows, as in *daēuuas.ca* 'and the demon' (cp. Ved. *deváś ca*), but sporadically also in other contexts, as in *hauuaiiåsə tanuuō* 'of one's own body' (otherwise *hauuaiiå*). All word-final *t*'s are written with a modified *t* that is transliterated as *t̰*; this may have been an unreleased *t*. Note, though, the treatment in clitic groups such as *ad-āiš* 'so through them', versus *at̰* 'so' when alone.

Morphology

11.25. Due to the relative paucity of material, not all inflectional endings are attested; but it is clear that the morphological system of Old and Young Avestan is essentially the same as that of Vedic Sanskrit, with only some minor differences in detail. Notably though, Avestan, in particular Old Avestan, preserves some archaic features that are not found in Vedic. (Interestingly, most of these features are not found in Young Avestan either, making the latter in some sense closer to Vedic than to Old Avestan.) Some of these may be briefly noted. The first singular present indicative of thematic verbs ended usually in *-ā* in Old Avestan (e.g. *pərəsā* 'I ask') but always *-āmi* in Young Avestan (e.g. *barāmi* 'I carry'); Old Av. *-ā* thus preserves the PIE thematic ending **-oh₂* unextended by the athematic ending **-mi* (recall §5.29). Avestan preserves traces of proterokinetic inflection in *r/n*-stems, a feature lost in Indic; Old Avestan also has proterokinetic inflection of *u*-stems. Thus YAv. *aiiarə* 'day', genit. *aiiąn* < **ai̯ans* has proterokinetic genitive in **-s*, as seen also in the Old Av. genit. *pasə̄uš* < Indo-Ir. **pas-aus* of *pasu-* 'cattle'; the latter has been remade to hysterokinetic *pasuuō* < **pas-u̯as* in Young Avestan. The word for 'path', nomin. *paṇtā̊*, accus. *paṇtąm*, genit. *paθō* famously preserves the amphikinetic ablaut of its PIE ancestor, **pént-oh₂-s *pént-oh₂-m̥ *pn̥t-h₂-és*, down to the location of the laryngeal in all the forms: the ending *-ąm* of the accusative scans with laryngeal hiatus, and the laryngeal aspirated the preceding *t* to produce *ϑ* in the oblique stem, but not in the strong stem where it was separated from the *t* by a vowel. Finally, Old Avestan preserves a distinction among three possessive pronouns (*ma-* 'my', *ϑβa-* 'your', *xᵛa-* '(one's) own') while Young Avestan has only *hauua-* for all three (remade from the same **hu̯a-* as OAv. *xᵛa-*).

But retained archaisms are always balanced by innovations; one which may be mentioned is the Young Avestan extension of the final *-t̰* of the thematic ablative singular ending *-āt̰* to athematic ablatives (where it replaced the final **-s* used for both the genitive and the ablative), as in *nərət̰* 'from a man' (vs. genit. *nərəš*). This development is also in Old Persian, and may be a common innovation of the two languages.

Old Avestan text sample

11.26. Stanza 4 from Yasna 44, called the Tat̰.θβā.pərəsā Hāiti after its opening words. The poet is asking his patron for a reward for singing his praises and alludes to the fact that a patron who did not remunerate his poet was subject to punishment. Such a reciprocity relation between poet and patron was important in ancient Indo-European cultures; see §2.38.

The translation here is modeled on that of Helmut Humbach.

tat̰ θβā pərəsā ərəš mōi vaocā ahurā
kasnā dərətā zą̄mcā adə̄ nabā̊scā
auuapastōiš kə̄ apō uruuarā̊scā
kə̄ vātāi duuąnmaibiiascā yaogət̰ āsū
kasnā vaŋhə̄uš mazdā dą̄miš manaŋhō

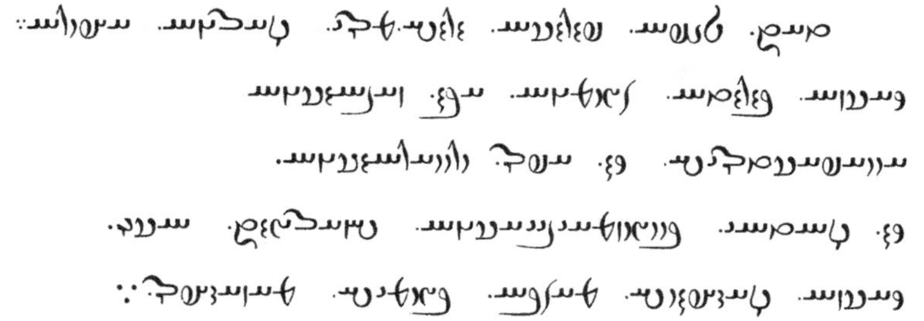

Figure 11.1 Yasna 44.4 in Avestan script, read from right to left. Reproduced with slight alterations from Geldner 1886–96, vol. 1, p. 148.

> This I ask you, tell me straight, Lord:
> Who holds firm both the earth and the heavens
> from falling? Who (holds firm) the waters and plants?
> Who yokes the two swift ones to the wind and the clouds?
> Who (is) the creator of good thought, o Wise One?

11.26a. Notes. taṯ: 'this, that', Ved. *tát*. All the stanzas but the last one in this hymn begin with this line. **θβā:** 'you', accus. sing. enclitic pronoun, Ved. *tvā*. **pərəsā:** 'I ask', 1st sing. present, with *-ā* from PIE *$-oh_2$ without the addition of *-mi* (vs. Ved. *pr̥cchā́mi*); §11.25. **ərəš:** 'straight, correctly', related to *ərəzu-* 'straight', Ved. *r̥jú-*. **mōi:** 'me', 1st sing. dat. enclitic pronoun, Ved. *me*; *ōi* and not *aē* was the Avestan outcome of Indo-Ir. **ai* in word-final position and in closed syllables. **vaocā:** 'tell', aorist imperative; Ved. *voca*. This is a reduplicated aorist, PIE *$\underaccent{\frown}{u}e\text{-}uk^w$-. Note that the etymologically short final vowel is long here (recall §11.12).

kasnā: 'who', literally 'which man, which person', combination of the masc. nomin. sing. of the interrogative pronoun plus the nomin. sing. of the word for 'man', *nā* (< *$h_2n\bar{e}r$) cliticized and having little meaning. The interrogative has the form *kas-* in close sandhi before the enclitic (see §11.24), and appears alone as *kə̄* below. **dərətā:** 'holds firm, keeps', 3rd sing. aorist middle injunctive, PIE **dhr̥-to*. **zə̨mcā:** accus. sing. of 'earth' (= Ved. *kṣā́m*) plus enclitic conjunction *-cā* 'and' (PIE *k^we). The sequence *-cā* . . . *-cā* means 'both . . . and', as elsewhere in IE. **adə̄:** 'below', a word occurring only here; cognate with Ved. *adhás* 'below'. **nabå̊scā:** 'and heavens', accus. pl.; the *-s* only shows up before enclitics.

auuapastōiš: 'from falling', genit. sing. of a *ti*-abstract noun consisting of the prefix *auua-* 'down' plus either **pad-ti-* (from *pad-* 'fall') or **pat-ti-* (from *pat-* 'fly, fall'). **apō:** 'waters', accus. pl., Ved. *apás*. **uruuarå̊scā:** 'and plants'. The same phrase is in Vedic: *apáśca urvárāśca* 'waters and (plantable) fields' (Atharva Veda 10.10.8). Indo-Iranian **urvarā-* is related to Gk. *ároura* 'plowland' and OIr. *arbor* 'grain', though the details are uncertain.

vātāi: 'wind', dat. sing.; the first syllable scans as two syllables because of laryngeal hiatus (PIE *$h_2\underaccent{\frown}{u}eh_1\mathring{n}to$-). **duuąnmaibiiascā:** 'and clouds', dat. pl. of the *n*-stem *duuąnman-*. Elsewhere the word has the stem *dunman-*. It is related to Ved. *dhvan-* 'make smoke, form clouds', from PIE *$dh\underaccent{\frown}{u}enh_2$-, and perhaps ultimately to PIE *$dhuh_2$-*mo-* 'smoke' (> Lat. *fūmus*). **yaogəṯ:** 'yokes', 3rd sing. aorist injunctive. **āsū:** 'the two swift ones', neuter accus. dual, referring to the two horses of a team, or perhaps to two teams. Compare Rig Veda 3.35.4 *yunajmi hárī āśū́* 'I yoke the two swift steeds'.

vaŋhə̄uš: 'good', genit. sing. of *vaŋhu-* or *vohu-* 'good' (= Ved. *vásu-*, from PIE *$\underaccent{\frown}{u}esu$-), modifying *manaŋhō* 'thought', genit. of *manō* (= Ved. *mánas*, from PIE **men-os-*, from

men-* 'to think'). 'Good thought' (nomin. *vohū manō*) was a central Zoroastrian concept and one of the manifestations of the Wise Lord, Ahura Mazda. **mazdā: 'wise', cp. Ved. *medhā́-* 'wisdom'; both from an Indo-Iranian phrase **mn̥s dhā-* 'put (one's) mind'. **dąmiš:** 'creator', from *dā-* (PIE **dheh₁-*) 'put, create' with the rare suffix **-mi-* that also appears in the Gk. cognate *thémis* 'right, law' (*'something set down', PIE **dhh₁-mi-*).

Young Avestan text sample

11.27. From Yašt 14 (the Bahirām Yašt), excerpt from verse 40. An Iranian descendant of the IE dragon-slaying myth (see chapter 2).

yim θraētaonō taxmō barat̰
yō janat̰ ažīm dahākəm
θrizafanəm θrikamərəδəm
xšuuaš.ašīm hazaŋrā.yaoxštīm
aš.aojaŋhəm daēuuīm drujəm
aγəm gaēθāuuiiō druuaṇtəm

(. . . the power and the force) which mighty Thraetaona had, who slew the serpent Dahaka, the three-jawed, three-headed, six-eyed, thousand-skilled, the extremely powerful demoniacal monster, evil (and) sacrilegious to living beings . . .

11.27a. Notes. θraētaonō: Thraētaona, a mythical Iranian dragon-slaying hero. **janat̰ ažīm:** 'slew the serpent', cognate with Ved. *áhann áhim* in the related Vedic dragon-slaying myth (though the verb form is slightly different, being a thematic rather than an athematic imperfect). The Iranian serpent's name is (Aži) Dahāka. **θrizafanəm:** 'having three jaws', composed of *θri-* 'three' and *zafan-*, from *zafarə* 'jaw', probably an *r/n*-stem, though only the form *zafarə* is attested. **θrikamərəδəm:** 'three-headed'; *kamərəδa-* is a special word for the head of a demon. The body-parts of demons had names different from those of corresponding human body-parts. **xšuuaš.ašīm:** 'having six eyes'; *xšuuaš* is 'six', cp. Vedic *ṣáṭ*, PIE **su̯ek̂s*, and *aši-* is 'eye', cp. Ved. *ákṣi*. **hazaŋrā.yaoxštīm:** 'having a thousand skills'; *hazaŋrā-* 'thousand' is cognate with Ved. *sahásra-*. **aš.aojaŋhəm:** 'very powerful', containing the prefix *aš-* 'very' and *aojah-* 'strength' (cp. Ved. *ójas-*). **daēuuīm:** 'demoniacal', from Iranian **dai̯u̯i̯am*, a *-i̯o-* adjective formed from **dai̯u̯a-* (cp. Ved. *devá-* 'god'). **drujəm:** 'monster, lie'; the Iranian term **druj-* or **drug-* refers to all manner of evil things, especially the Lie, the arch-enemy of Truth (Av. *aṣ̌a-*) in the polarized Zoroastrian world. **gaēθāuuiiō:** 'living beings', dat. pl., with *-āuuiiō* a variant of Young Av. **-ābiiō* (Ved. *-ābhyas*). **druuaṇtəm:** 'lying, deceptive', a **-u̯ent-* possessive adjective (§6.40) formed from **drug-* (see above).

Old Persian

11.28. Old Persian is the language of the royal inscriptions of the Achaemenid dynasty of the ancient Persian Empire. The Old Persian inscriptions have the distinction of being the only preserved Old Iranian texts that are authentic originals, written by the very people who spoke the language and free from copyists' errors. The inscriptions come from various sites in western Iran, especially Bisotun (Bīsotūn, also spelled Behistūn, Bīsitūn), Persepolis, Susa, and Hamadan. Most belong to

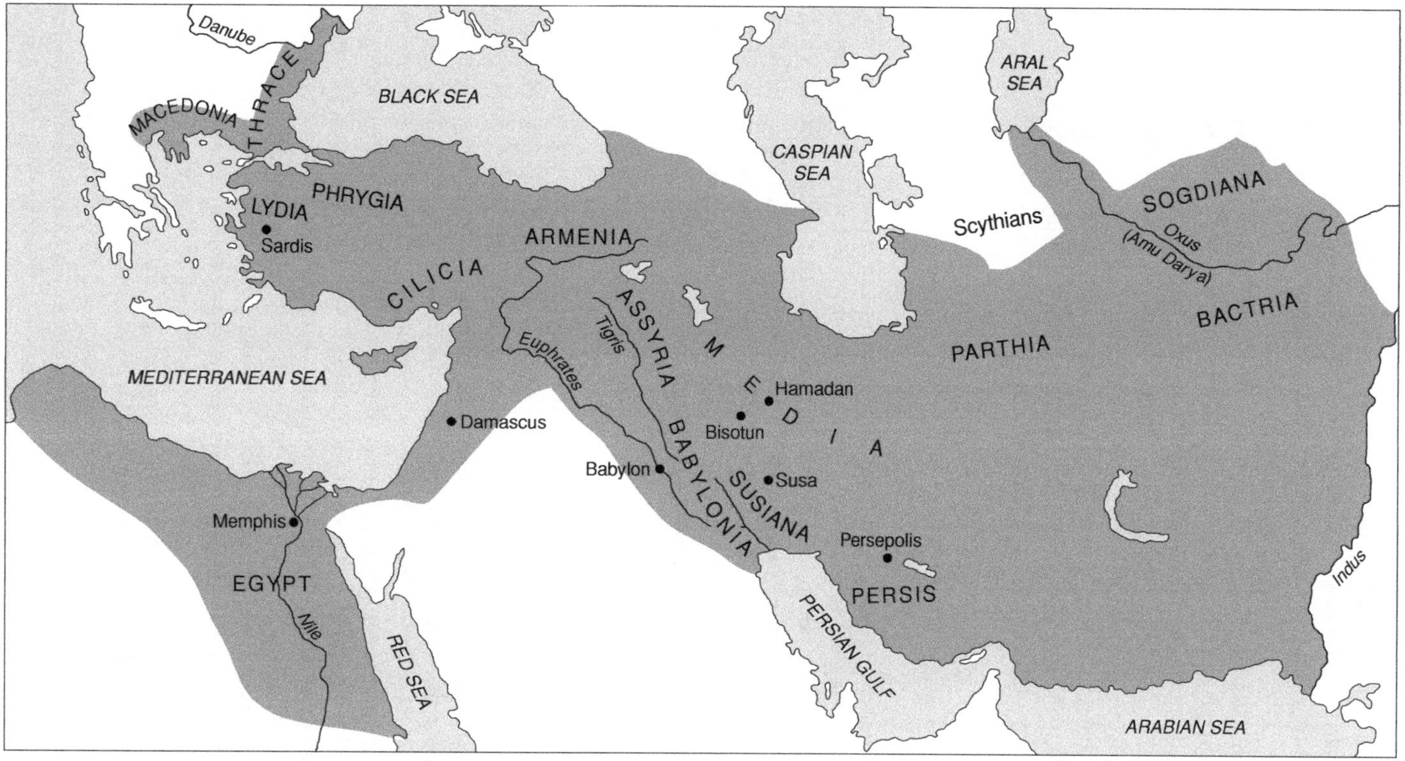

Map 11.1 The Persian Empire under Darius I

Darius I (reigned 521–486 BC) and his son Xerxes I (reigned 486–465), but inscriptions continue almost to the end of the Achaemenid dynasty, the last ones belonging to Artaxerxes III (reigned 359–338). Over this nearly 200-year period, the language changed quite a bit. The language of the inscriptions of Darius and Xerxes was a courtly one, a bit archaizing and containing many Median elements (see the next section), but already in Xerxes' time certain developments common to the Middle Iranian languages were starting to creep in. By the time of Artaxerxes III the language looks already more like Middle Persian than an Old Iranian language. It had undergone a number of sound changes, including the monophthongization of diphthongs and the erosion of final syllables (and with them, of the case system). Even the oldest Old Persian is not very archaic compared with Avestan, being typologically quite like late Young Avestan. This suggests that Young Avestan and early Old Persian were roughly contemporaneous. Old Persian belongs to the Southwest branch of Iranian.

Median

11.29. Old Persian contains a fair amount of admixture from Median, the language of the earlier Median Empire (c. 700–522 BC) in northwestern Iranian territory. Almost all our knowledge of Median comes from these loanwords, which afford us a partial view of the sound changes that Median underwent and therefore of its filiation within Iranian. Thus the Median loan *aspa* 'horse' (native OPers. *asa*) shows that the language patterned with Central Iranian, where IE **k̑u̯* became *sp* (not *s* as in the southwest, where Old Persian was spoken).

The Old Persian script

11.30. Old Persian is written in a cuneiform script that is imitative of Mesopotamian cuneiform, but the actual signs are wholly different. It is a relatively simple syllabary that was apparently designed just for this language. A poorly understood passage of the great Bisotun inscription of Darius I has the king claiming that he devised the script, which could be true. (An inscription purporting to be of the earlier king Cyrus the Great has been shown to postdate his reign.) Old Persian cuneiform was the first cuneiform script to be deciphered; the early breakthroughs were made in 1802 and subsequent years by a German school-teacher named Georg Friedrich Grotefend. The existence of bi- and trilingual inscriptions in Old Persian, Akkadian, and Elamite (the language of Persia before it was taken over by the Persians, and subsequently used by them as a court language; it has no known relatives) then paved the way for unlocking the secrets of Mesopotamian cuneiform.

11.31. The script is not well suited for writing Old Persian, and its limitations hamper the analysis of the language's phonology. Like Mesopotamian cuneiform, the symbols are syllabic, not alphabetic. Only signs for vowels and for sequences of consonant plus vowel (CV) were used. A complete set of CV signs was devised where the vowel was *a*, but where the vowel was *i* or *u* only a subset of the possibilities are represented. Since there were no VC signs, the use of "empty" or "dummy" vowels was frequent, as in the spelling *vi-ša-ta-a-sa-pa-ha-ya-a* for the dat. sing. *Vištāspahayā* 'for/of Hystaspes' (the father of Darius I). As this example also shows, long *ā* was represented by adding an extra *a*. Where comparative evidence from Avestan would lead one to expect the presence of *h*, no *h* is actually written before certain sounds; thus the Old Persian equivalent of Avestan *Ahurō Mazdā̊* 'Ahura Mazda' is always written *Auramazdā*. Either the *h* was pronounced but not written, or it was simply not there at all. For this reason, one often sees transcriptions like *A*^{h}*uramazdā* to indicate that etymologically an *h* is expected, but not present in the script. The same is true for *n* at the ends of syllables, as in *atar* (*a*^{n}*tar*) 'between'. Sometimes the Akkadian and Elamite renderings of Old Persian names provide clues, but the spellings here are often so varied that they are not as helpful as one would wish. No information on the placement or nature of the stress is available; however, some sandhi phenomena are preserved (see below).

Characteristics of Old Persian

Phonology

11.32. The outcomes of the IE palatals differ considerably from Avestan. In Old Persian, PIE **k̂* and **ĝ* became *θ* and *d*, respectively, in contrast with Avestan *s* and *z*: **u̯ik̂*- 'all' > OPers. *viθ*- (Av. *vīs*-), **eĝh*$_2$*om* 'I' > OPers. *adam* (Av. *azəm*).

11.33. Also characteristic of Old Persian is the development of the sequence **tr* to *ç* (via an intermediate stage **θr*; *ç* is the standard transcription of a sign in the Old Persian script whose phonetic value has yet to be determined). Compare Vedic *kṣatrám* 'kingdom' with Av. *xšaθra*- but OPers. *xšaça*-.

Morphology

11.34. Our picture of the morphology of Old Persian has many gaps because of the small corpus, but the forms we do have are in close agreement with Avestan, especially in the verb. The Old Persian noun, however, has undergone more case syncretism (merging of different cases) than Young Avestan. The dative has been replaced by the genitive, and the ablative has mostly merged with the instrumental and the locative. The relative pronoun had the stem *haya-/taya-* instead of the usual *ya*- in the rest of Indo-Iranian; it also functioned as a kind of definite article and as a particle that was inserted between a noun and a following modifier or appositive, as in *Gaumāta haya maguš* 'Gaumata the priest' (originally meaning *'Gaumata, who [is] a priest'). In Modern Persian, this is continued by the so-called *ezāfe* construction, which utilizes a particle *-(y)e* to connect attributive adjectives and possessives to nouns, as in *mard-e īrānī* 'the Iranian man'.

11.35. Other developments include the loss of a distinction between aorist and imperfect; the spread of *a*-stems replacing other stem-types in the noun; and the later contraction of **-iya*- to *-ī*-. A development of interest from the viewpoint of Modern Persian is the beginnings of a periphrastic perfect, where the past passive participle was used with a noun in the genitive functioning as the agent, as in *taya manā kartam* 'what (was) done by me' = 'what I have done'. The oblique form *manā* 'by me' eventually became reinterpreted as a subject case, yielding *man* 'I' in Modern

Persian. Nowadays one says *man kard-am* 'I have done', where *-am* is a 1st sing. ending added to what was originally a non-finite verb form (a participle; the *-am* in OPers. *kartam* was a neuter sing. ending that was later lost).

Old Persian text sample

11.36. Two excerpts from column I of the great inscription of Darius I inscribed on a steep polished cliff-face at Bisotun, along a caravan route between Baghdad and Tehran. The inscription is trilingual, in Old Persian, Elamite, and Akkadian. The bulk of the inscription details Darius's battles and conquests. The translation is Roland Kent's, with a few modifications. Note that most of the lines end in the middle of a word that then spills over onto the beginning of the next line.

1 adam Dārayavauš xšāyaθiya vazarka xšāyaθiya xšāyaθiy-
2 ānām xšāyaθiya Pārsaiy xšāyaθiya dahyūnām Višt-
3 āspahyā puça Aršāmahyā napā Haxāmanišiya . . .
20 . . . θātiy Dārayava-
21 uš xšāyaθiya atar imā dahyāva martiya haya āgriya āha avam u-
22 bartam abaram haya arika āha avam ufrastam aparsam vašnā Auramazdā-
23 ha imā dahyāva tayanā manā dātā apariyāya yaθāšām hacāma aθah-
24 ya avaθā akunavayatā . . .

1–3. I am Darius the great king, king of kings, king in Persia, king of countries, son of Hystaspes, grandson of Arsames, an Achaemenid.
20–24. Darius the king announces: Within these countries, the man who was loyal (?), him I rewarded well; who was evil, him I punished well; by the favor of Ahuramazda these countries that abided by my law, as was said to them by me, thus was it done.

11.36a. Notes. 1–3. adam: 'I', cp. Av. *azəm*. **Dārayavauš:** 'Darius', lit. 'upholding the good', composed of *dāraya-* 'uphold' (cp. Ved. *dhārā́yati* 'upholds') and *vau-* 'good' (cp. Ved. *vásu-* 'good'; one expects OPers. **vahuš*, but no *h* is ever written). **xšāyaθiya:** 'king', cp. Ved. *kṣáyati* 'rules'; the genit. pl. *xšāyaθiyānām* straddles the end of the line. The Modern Persian descendant is *šāh* 'shah'. **vazarka:** 'great'; the suffix *-ka-* achieved enormous productivity in Iranian for forming nouns, especially from Middle Iranian times on. **Pārsaiy:** 'Persia', loc. sing. **-oi*; strictly speaking, just one province of the Persian (Achaemenid) Empire. **dahyūnām:** 'of the countries', genit. pl.; cp. OAv. *dax́iiu-* 'country'. **Vištāspahyā:** 'of Vištaspa', Gk. Hystaspes; genit. sing. (**-osi̯o*). The name means 'having unharnessed/free horses' (*aspa* 'horse' is a Median loanword; see §11.29). **puça:** 'son', Av. *puθra-*, Ved. *putrás*, from **put-lo-*; also found in Oscan *puclom* (accus. sing.). **napā:** 'grandson', PIE **nepōt-*. **Haxāmanišiya:** 'of Haxāmaniš, Achaemenid', Gk. Achaemenes; relational adjective in *-iya-* (PIE **-i̯o-*).

20–24. θātiy: 'says'. **atar:** 'within, among', probably spelling *antar* (= Ved. *antár*, Lat. *inter*; PIE **enter*). **martiya:** 'mortal, man', Ved. *mártya-*, Av. *maṣ̌iia-*. **haya:** 'who', relative and indefinite pronoun. **āha:** 'was', imperfect 3rd sing. as though from Indo-Ir. **āsat* (thematic, in contrast to athematic Av. *ās* and the rare Vedic *ā́s* from **āst*, i.e. **a-as-t*). **avam:** 'that (man)', accus. sing. masc. of *ava-*, demonstrative pronoun, cp. Av. *auua-* 'that'. **ubartam:** lit. 'well-carried, well-held', from *u-* 'well' (Av. *hu-*, Ved. *su-*) plus *bartam*, *to*-verbal adjective of *bar-* 'carry'. Note the etymological figure with the verb *abaram* 'I carried, held', which is of

Indo-Iranian date: Av. *hubərətąm barāṯ* '(who) may hold us well-held' at Yasht 13.18, Ved. *súbhr̥tam bibhárti* 'carries (him) well-carried' at Rig Veda 4.50.7. **ufrastam:** 'well punished', also spelled *ufraštam*; *frasta-* literally 'interrogated', from *fraθ-* (PIE **preḱ-* 'ask'; Av. *fras-*, German *fragen*). **aparsam:** 'I punished', imperfect of *fraθ-*; the verb makes an etymological figure with the preceding adjective, *ufrastam aparsam*. **apariyāya:** 'they went around, abided by', 3rd pl. imperfect with final nasal lost or not written; a curious form, apparently containing a double augment: *a-pari-a-aya(n)*, before and after the preverb *pari* 'around' (Av. *pairi*, Gk. *perí* 'around'). **yaθāšām:** consists of *yaθā* 'as' (correlative with *avaθā* 'so, thus, in that way') plus *-šām* 'to them, of them', genit. pl. demonstrative pronoun. **hacāma:** consists of *hacā* 'with, by' (cp. Ved. *sácā*) plus the enclitic ablative *-ma* 'me' (cp. Av. *maṯ*). **akunavayatā:** 'were done, made', spells *akunavayantā*, a 3rd pl. optative middle added to an augmented (imperfect) stem. Such a formation is unusual in Indo-European, but other examples are known from Iranian. Here the optative functions as a past tense.

Middle and Modern Iranian

11.37. Middle Iranian refers collectively to the stages of the Iranian languages that share a set of phonological and morphological developments as compared with Old Iranian, including especially the monophthongization of the diphthongs *ai* and *au* to *ē* and *ō*, the loss of many or most of the tenses, and (particularly in the west) the reduction of the case-system in nouns. Broadly, two groups of Middle Iranian languages can be distinguished, **East** and **West**, though the terms are not fully accurate geographically (some East Middle Iranian languages were spoken farther to the west than the West Middle Iranian languages!). This period saw the greatest geographical distribution of Iranian languages, from the northwest coast of the Black Sea to China. The later migratory waves of Turkic peoples into this territory caused the Iranian populations to shrink considerably, but even today most of this area still has at least some pockets of Iranian speakers.

Middle Persian was the only Middle Iranian language about which anything was known until spectacular finds in the twentieth century added several more to the roster: Parthian, Sogdian, Choresmian, Bactrian, Khotanese, and Tumshuqese. Most of these were unearthed in Chinese Turkestan (southwest Xinjiang in western China) – some on the same expeditions that saw the unearthing of the Tocharian languages. Only Middle Persian and Sogdian are known to have close living relatives. Other Middle Iranian languages, such as Sarmatian and Alanic, are known only indirectly and have no preserved literature.

11.38. Most of the Middle Iranian languages were written in scripts derived from the Aramaic alphabet. Aramaic had been one of the official languages of the Persian Empire, and continued to be used in the empire's former territories. Like all Semitic alphabets, it possessed no signs for short vowels and no unambiguous signs for long vowels, rendering it ineffective for recording certain phonetic features of the relevant languages.

West Middle Iranian

11.39. In West Middle Iranian, a stress accent developed on the penultimate or antepenultimate syllable, and final (unaccented) syllables were generally dropped.

Nominal inflections were reduced to a system of two cases. The verbal system was more conservative, but the future, aorist, and perfect were lost.

11.40. Parthia was a historical region corresponding to present-day northeastern Iran and neighboring parts of Turkmenistan; in it was spoken **Parthian**, the official language of the Arsacid dynasty (247 BC–AD 224). The Arsacids themselves were not from Parthia, but when they conquered the Parthians they took over their language. Most of the Parthian we have is preserved in documents from Xinjiang, but there are also some important early royal inscriptions from about 140 BC on. Parthian vocabulary strongly influenced Middle Persian "Book Pahlavi" (see directly below).

11.41. Middle Persian was the official language of the Sassanian dynasty (AD 224–652), but is also known from literature in the ninth and tenth centuries. It was the cult language of Manicheism (or Manichaeism) in Persia, a syncretistic religious movement founded by the Babylonian-born prophet Mani (also Manes or Manichaeus, c. 215–276) and combining the dualism of Zoroastrianism with certain elements of Babylonian religion, Buddhism, and even Christianity. The religion found a wide following in Central Asia and India, as well as for a time in the West (St. Augustine was once a Manichean).

Neither of the two types of Middle Persian discussed below stems directly from the language of the Old Persian Achaemenid inscriptions. Because the literary dialects of Persian, throughout its history, were used for official and administrative purposes, each stage incorporated forms from whatever other Iranian languages were useful at the time for broadest comprehensibility.

11.42. The language of the Zoroastrian Middle Persian texts or "books" is also called **Pahlavi** (a Middle Iranian descendant of Old Persian *Parθava* 'Parthian'), a term often applied to Middle Persian as a whole. This "Book Pahlavi" is the standardized written form, using a historicizing orthography developed before Sassanian times. The existence of a Pahlavi translation of the Avesta, with commentary, makes the language valuable for Old Iranian studies. But the script of "Book Pahlavi" is notoriously difficult, since several originally distinct letters have merged, leading to multiple ambiguities in readings. Most of the texts may have been written down in the ninth century from oral traditions, but the surviving manuscripts only date from the fourteenth century, after many corruptions had entered the transmission.

11.43. A much better picture of the pronunciation and vocabulary of Middle Persian comes from the **Manichean Middle Persian** texts, written in a Syriac form of the Aramaic script. It is also a much purer form of the language, as it does not contain the numerous Parthian and Avestan loans that were absorbed into Pahlavi.

East Middle Iranian

11.44. East Middle Iranian was more conservative than West Middle Iranian, as it generally preserved final vocalic endings and, with them, most of the inherited case system in nouns (especially in Khotanese and Sogdian). The verbal system underwent reduction similar to West Middle Iranian.

11.45. The least conservative East Middle Iranian language is **Bactrian**, spoken in the historical region of Bactria between the Oxus River (now the Amu Darya) and the Hindu Kush. Once a remote province of the Persian Empire, it became part of the Hellenistic world after the conquest of Alexander the Great in 331 BC. About 200 years later invaders called the Kushans established an empire there, replacing Greek with Bactrian as the official language but using the Greek alphabet to write it. Bactrian was known for a long time only from coin legends until a 25-line royal inscription was discovered in northeastern Afghanistan and published in 1951. Recent discoveries have added hundreds of well-preserved legal documents to the roster, as well as additional inscriptions.

11.46. Two languages, **Khotanese** and **Tumshuqese**, are known from finds in Chinese Turkestan and are collectively referred to as **Saka**. Remains of Tumshuqese were discovered in several villages near Kucha, and while our knowledge of it is slim, it is clearly more archaic than Khotanese. The latter is known from much larger finds; it was spoken in the medieval kingdom of Khotan (centered around the present-day city of Hetian on the southern Silk Road). The Khotanese documents include Buddhist texts, letters, and legal documents and date from the seventh to the tenth centuries. Both Khotanese and Tumshuqese are written in varieties of the Brāhmī alphabet (see §10.57). Neither language has any living descendants, but Wakhi, spoken today a bit to the west in the Wakhan corridor of northeast Afghanistan, is closely allied (see §11.53 below). Khotanese preserves six cases in the noun and several noun classes; it has also preserved all the moods in the verb, but lost most of the tenses.

11.47. Sogdia or Sogdiana, where **Sogdian** was spoken, is an ancient land in Central Asia already mentioned in the Old Persian inscriptions. Its capital was Samarkand (now in Uzbekistan), which became an important node on the Silk Road. Sogdian merchant colonies were established to the east, and Sogdian practically became a trade language of Chinese Turkestan. It is preserved in Manichean, Christian, and above all Buddhist texts, especially from the Turfan Oasis and Dunhuang deep inside Xinjiang and Gansu provinces, respectively. It is also preserved in non-religious writings. Like Khotanese, it is rather conservative in retaining most nominal cases. It is particularly striking in having innovated a very rich verb system. A variety of Sogdian different from the preserved variety was ancestral to modern Yaghnobi (see §11.53 below).

11.48. The inhabitants of the medieval land of Choresm (Khwarezm), located along the Amu Darya south of the Aral Sea along the present-day Turkmenistan–Uzbekistan border, spoke **Choresmian** (also Chorasmian or Khwarezmian). The language is known mostly from an interlinear translation of a medieval Arabic encyclopedia written in 1135, although scattered writings from much earlier have been found on a variety of materials. Linguistically it is similar to Sogdian, but has undergone further development.

Modern Iranian

11.49. The modern Iranian languages share the syntactic phenomenon known as split ergativity, wherein the subject of a past-tense verb is in an oblique case, while the object appears in the nominative case (normally used for the subject). This is a development from an Old Iranian stylistic feature (shared also by Sanskrit

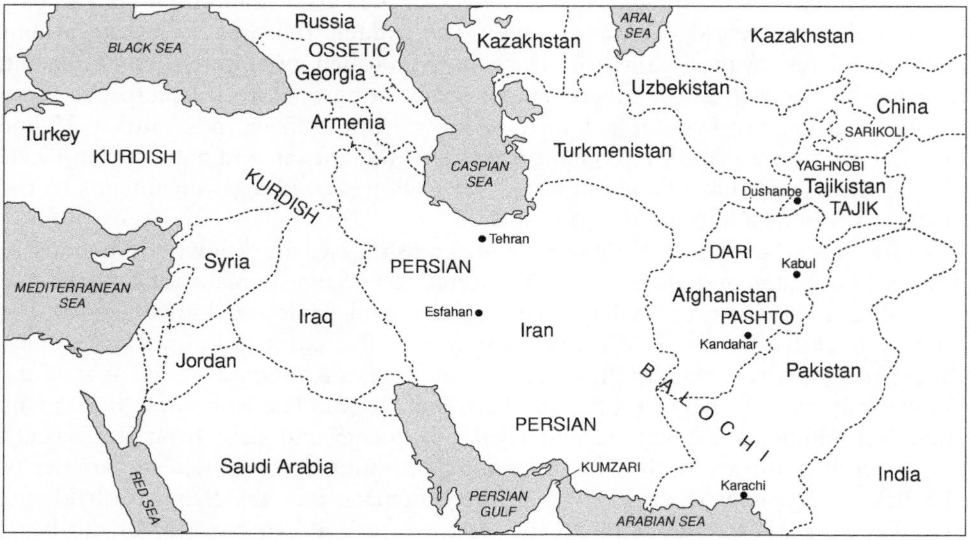

Map 11.2 Selected Modern Iranian languages

and likewise continuing as split ergativity in many modern Indo-Aryan languages) whereby past participles were used instead of finite past-tense verbs to express actions in past time (cp. §10.56).

Modern Iranian languages are spoken over a wide area, from the Caucasus in the northwest (where Ossetic is spoken) to northern Oman in the south (where Kumzārī is spoken) to Xinjiang in the east (where Sarikolī is spoken). We will only mention the more prominent Modern Iranian languages below.

11.50. Modern West Iranian. By far the most familiar language is **Modern Persian** or Farsi (Fārsī), the national language of Iran and one of the two national languages of Afghanistan. The variety spoken in Afghanistan is also called Dari. A dialect of Persian known as **Tajiki** (older Tadzhiki) is spoken in Tajikistan and neighboring countries. Two other modern West Iranian languages deserve mention, **Kurdish** (Kurdī) and **Balochi** or Baluchi (Balōčī). Kurdish is spoken in Iraq, Iran, Turkey, and Russia; Balochi is spoken primarily in Balochistan (Baluchistan) in southeast Iran and southwest Pakistan.

11.51. Modern East Iranian. The other national language of Afghanistan, **Pashto** (Paṣ̌tō, also spelled Pushtu in older literature), is the most populous East Iranian language and, aside from Persian, the modern Iranian language with the longest and finest literary tradition (from the sixteenth century). Pashto is the only modern Iranian language to have accent oppositions in morphological classes. This system very indirectly continues the mobile accent of older Iranian.

11.52. Ossetic, with half a million speakers in Turkey and Georgia, is of interest because of its isolation from other Iranian languages over the last two millennia; it is the last remnant of the essentially unknown Middle Iranian dialect area that included Sarmatian, and is said to descend from Alanic. It has taken on many features of the neighboring Caucasian languages, such as glottalized consonants and a system of nine cases in the noun. It has also preserved the inherited subjunctive and optative as distinct moods, making it one of the rare modern languages to do so (the others being Albanian and one or two other Iranian languages).

11.53. Two other Modern East Iranian languages, **Yaghnobi** (Yaghnōbī), spoken by a small population in Tajikistan, and **Wakhi** (Wakhī), spoken in the Pamir and far western China, deserve mention for linguistic reasons. Yaghnobi is surely descended from an unknown (non-literary) variety of Sogdian, and is the only modern Iranian language that still uses the augment to mark past-tense verb forms. Wakhi is important for preserving some archaic features not even found in Avestan, such as past participles in *-n-* that go back to the PIE suffix **-nó-* (§5.61), not otherwise found as a participial suffix in Iranian.

For Further Reading

All the Iranian languages, literatures, and cultures, past and present, are treated exhaustively in the ongoing *Encyclopaedia Iranica* (Yarshater 1982–), although many years will pass before it is completed. The languages are given very able and up-to-date historical treatment in the articles in Schmitt 1989. The only complete dictionary of Avestan is Bartholomae 1904, which also contains Old Persian; it is now to some extent out of date. A good etymological dictionary of the Iranian verb has just been published (Cheung 2007) but no complete etymological dictionary of any Iranian language. If one knows the Sanskrit cognate of an Iranian word, etymological information can be found under the Sanskrit word in Manfred Mayrhofer's etymological dictionary of Sanskrit (see the previous chapter). The one complete grammar of Avestan is also an older work, Reichelt 1909; for Old Avestan, see Beekes 1988, and for an exhaustive treatment of the history of the Avestan vowels see de Vaan 2003. The standard critical edition of the Avesta is Geldner 1886–96, whose introduction contains an important philological evaluation of the manuscripts and their relationships to one another. A superb historical grammar of Avestan is Hoffmann and Forssman 2004. Avestan morphology has been the subject of two recent excellent studies in French, Kellens 1974 (root nouns) and Kellens 1984 (the verb). The difficulty of the Gathas has led to many differing interpretations, and several translations with commentary are available, including Insler 1975 and Humbach 1991. The texts, grammar, and vocabulary of Old Persian are easily accessible in Kent 1953, though a few additional texts have been discovered since. The corpus of Iranian inscriptions has been appearing in the ongoing *Corpus Inscriptionum Iranicarum* (London, 1955–). Many excellent articles on Iranian by Karl Hoffmann can be found in Hoffmann 1975–92 (see Bibliography, ch. 10).

For Review

Know the meaning or significance of the following:

Old Iranian	Zoroastrianism	Achaemenid
Middle Iranian	Gathas	Georg Friedrich Grotefend
Avesta	laryngeal hiatus	Pahlavi

Exercises

1 Using the table in §11.16, for each of the following Sanskrit–Avestan cognate sets determine which PIE velar underlies the boldfaced segments. Some forms may have more than one answer.

a Av. ***k**ainiiā-*, Ved. ***k**anyā̀* 'unmarried girl'
b Av. *ra**z**išta-*, Ved. *rá**j**iṣṭha-* 'most upright'
c Av. ***z**araniia-*, Ved. ***h**íraṇya-* 'golden'
d Av. ***z**an**g**a-* 'ankle', Ved. ***j**áṅ**gh**ā-* 'lower leg' (two different velars)
e Av. ***k**arša-* 'furrow', Ved. ***k**r̥ṣáti* 'cuts a furrow'
f Av. *ha**c**aite*, Ved. *sa**c**ate* 'accompanies'
g Av. *dādarə**s**a*, Ved. *dadár**ś**a* 'I saw'
h Av. *ao**j**ō*, Ved. *ó**j**as* 'power'
i Av. ***j**aiṇti*, Ved. ***h**ánti* 'smites'
j Av. ***g**ənā*, Ved. ***g**nā́-* 'woman'
k Av. ***g**arəma-*, Ved. ***gh**armám* 'heat'
l Av. *-maē**z**aiti*, Ved. *mé**h**ati* 'urinates'
m Av. *adru**j**iiaṇt-* 'not deceitful', Ved. *drú**h**yati* 'deceives'
n Av. *-**z**ānaiti* 'recognizes', Ved. ***j**ānā́ti* 'knows'
o Av. ***s**āstī*, Ved. ***ś**āste* 'teaches'
p Av. ***c**isti-*, Ved. ***c**íttis* 'thought'

2 Below are given various Vedic words. Predict what the Avestan cognates would look like based on the sound changes enumerated in §§11.2–8 and 16–22.

a *spr̥dh-* 'eagerness'
b *trātā́* 'protector'
c *śróta* 'you (pl.) hear'
d *bháram* 'I carried'
e *mātáras* 'mothers' (nomin. pl.)
f *dhenú-* 'female'
g *tvā́m* 'you' (accus. sing.)
h *mā́sam* 'month' (accus. sing.)

3 The "Hoffmann" suffix (§6.35) was originally identified on the basis of the Old Avestan word *mąθrā* (nomin. sing.), stem *mąθrān-* 'possessing a *mąθra-* or religious formulation (mantra)'. The *ā* in the nominative and accusative scans in the Gathas as two syllables. Explain how this fact allows us to deduce the shape of the suffix.

4 Avestan has the form *kəhrpəm* 'body', accusative singular of a root noun whose cognate in Vedic only occurs in the instrumental singular, *kr̥pā́*. Given the rules in §11.22, what would you predict the Vedic accusative singular to have been?

5 Given §10.37 and the forms below, what was the Avestan outcome of syllabic resonant plus laryngeal before vowel?

a Av. *tarō*, Ved. *tirás* 'through'
b Av. *garō*, Ved. *gíras* 'praises' (noun)
c Av. *parō*, Ved. *purás* 'in front'
d Av. *-sparat̰*, Ved. *sphurat* 'hurried'

6 **a** Given that Ved. *khā́-* 'well' is cognate with Av. *xā-*, and that Ved. *pathás* 'from the path' is cognate with Av. *paθō*, and finally that Ved. *śaphá-* 'hoof' is cognate with Av. *safa-*, what were the Avestan outcomes of the Indo-Iranian voiceless aspirated stops?

b What would you reconstruct as the Indo-Iranian ancestor of Ved. *kumbhá-* 'pot' and Av. *xumba-*? Explain.

c The word for 'path' in Vedic has nomin. sing. *pánthās*, accus. sing. *pánthām*, and weak stem *path-*. Contrast this with its Avestan cognate, discussed in §11.25. How do you account for the *-th-* in the Vedic nominative and accusative forms?

7 Comment on each of the following morphological differences between Vedic and Avestan:

a athematic ablative singular: Ved. *mánasas*, Av. *manaŋhaṯ*

b perfect participle: Ved. *vidvā́n, vidvā́ṁsam, vidúṣ-*, Av. *viduuå, viduuåŋhəm, viduš-*

c *r/n*-stem nominative sing.: Ved. *yákr̥t* 'liver', *śákr̥t* 'excrement'; Av. *baēuuarə* 'myriad', *aiiarə* 'day' (ignore the schwa)

d *r/n*-stem instrumental pl.: Ved. *udá-bhis* 'with waters' (from **udn̥-*), Av. *baēuuarə-bīš* 'with myriads' (ignore differences in the endings)

8 **a** The Old Avestan 2nd sing. imperative of the verb 'be' is *zdī*. What is its history?

b A supposed sound law of PIE date was Siebs's Law, whereby a voiced aspirate became unvoiced following **s*. Comment on the validity of this law in light of forms like *zdī* and *mižda-* 'reward' (§10.10).

9 Given the remarks in §11.31 and the example there, render the first three lines of the Old Persian selection in §11.36 as you believe they would have been written in the Old Persian syllabary. Use hyphens to separate signs in the syllabary. Remember there are no signs representing consonants standing alone or vowel-consonant sequences. Assume that where a *Ci* or *Cu* sign is needed, it exists.

PIE Vocabulary III: Food and Agriculture

**aĝros* 'field': Gk. *agrós*, Lat. *ager* (*agr-*), Eng. ACRE
**$h_2$erh$_3$-* 'plow': Gk. *aróō* 'I plow', Lat. *arāre* 'to plow'
**i̯ugom* 'YOKE': Ved. *yugám*, Gk. *zugón*, Lat. *iugum*
**seh$_1$-* 'SOW (seed)': Lat. *sē-men* 'seed', Lith. *sė́ju* 'I sow'
**ĝr̥h$_2$-no-* 'grain': Lat. *grānum*, Eng. CORN
**$h_2$melĝ-* 'MILK': Gk. *amélgō* 'I milk', Lat. *mulgēre* 'to milk'
**melit-* 'honey': Hitt. *milit-*, Gk. *méli* (*mélit-*), Lat. *mel*, Eng. MIL*dew*
**medhu-* 'sweet drink': Luv. *mattu-* 'wine', Ved. *mádhu-* 'honey', Gk. *méthu* 'wine', Eng. MEAD
**sal-* 'SALT': Gk. *háls*, Lat. *sāl* (*sal-*), OCS *solĭ*
**melh$_2$-* 'grind': Hitt. *mallai* 'grinds', Gk. *múlē* 'mill', Lat. *molō* 'I grind', Eng. MEAL

12 Greek

Introduction

12.1. It is a remarkable fact that Greek has remained Greek over its 3300-year written history. Throughout this time, its dialects never developed into mutually incomprehensible languages, and are at all times recognizably woven out of the same linguistic fabric.

We do not know when Greek (or pre-Greek) speakers first came to Greece nor what languages were spoken there before. Much has been written about the pre-Greek linguistic situation, most of it speculative and inconclusive. For example, it is usually claimed that a number of words containing an element *-nth-* come from a pre-Greek substrate language, such as *Kórinthos* 'Corinth', *labúrinthos* 'labyrinth', and *asáminthos* 'bathtub'; but we can say nothing conclusive about such words or the language(s) they may have come from.

By the time we first meet Greek in written documents, in the second half of the second millennium BC, Greece and parts of the western coast of Asia Minor were already Greek-speaking. The earliest preserved Greek is written in **Mycenaean** (or Mycenean), the official dialect of the Mycenaean civilization. Mycenaean inscriptions are preserved on clay tablets and ceramic vessels found on the isle of Crete (primarily at Knossos) and the mainland (primarily at Pylos), always from Mycenaean royal cities. The dating of the Mycenaean tablets has been in flux for some decades, but it appears that the island inscriptions are older than the mainland ones, the oldest confirmed being the so-called Room of the Chariot Tablets from Knossos (c. 1400–1350 BC); the Pylos tablets date to c. 1200 BC. Mycenaean is most closely related to Arcado-Cypriot (see below on the classification of the Greek dialects).

12.2. Mycenaean is written in a syllabic script called Linear B, whose decipherment was announced by Michael Ventris in 1952. It was developed from the earlier Linear A script, which was used to write the language of the Minoan civilization but remains undeciphered. The Linear B syllabary is poorly suited to writing Greek. It contains only signs representing single vowels or open syllables (consonant–vowel), does not distinguish between short and long vowels, between *r* and *l*, or usually between voiced, voiceless, or aspirated stops. Consonants at the ends of syllables are rarely written. Because most of the texts are inventories (lists of offerings, to cite a common type), our knowledge about the structure of this dialect is limited. Nonetheless, what we do have is extremely valuable, as the dialect is a full 500 years older than the next-oldest inscriptions of any length. Mycenaean is famous for preserving the inherited labiovelars as a distinct series of stops (transliterated with the letter *q*), unlike the later dialects (see §12.16), and it has many inflections, words, and phrases found otherwise only in the Homeric epics.

12.3. The period from the demise of Mycenaean civilization to the earliest appearance of alphabetic Greek in the eighth century BC has traditionally been called the "Greek Dark Ages." During this time Greece plunged largely into illiteracy and stagnation; there was a drastic drop in population and much movement of refugees, and a unified Greek civilization no longer existed. Nonetheless, at least one inscription from the period is known, a skewer found in Cyprus with a name incised in the Cypriot syllabary (see below) and dated to about 1050 BC.

The cultural regionalism that began in the "Dark Ages" persisted for many centuries, and in no way is this better reflected than linguistically: the history of post-Mycenaean Greek is essentially the history of its local dialects, even well into the Classical period (480–323 BC). Not until the following age, the Hellenistic period, would Greece again become both culturally and linguistically unified.

12.4. The period from the appearance of the first alphabetic inscriptions, in the early eighth century BC, to 480 BC is termed the **Archaic period.** Near the beginning of this time is probably when the earliest known Greek literary works – the two surviving Greek epics, the *Iliad* and the *Odyssey* – reached their present form. The language of these poems, called **Epic** (or Homeric), is a literary mixture from a variety of different periods. Representing the culmination of a long oral-poetic tradition stretching back into the dim past, the epics were not composed by a single person; the bard "Homer" was as remote and shadowy to the ancients as he is to us, and may well be a fiction. Rather, they were elaborated regionally by generations of illiterate poets until they were finally committed to writing perhaps around 700 BC. Aside from their status as two of the greatest works of literature ever composed in the Indo-European-speaking world, the *Iliad* and the *Odyssey* are of supreme importance for Indo-Europeanists because of their seemingly inexhaustible supply of archaic forms, phrases, and cultural material. Some phrases and turns of language in the epics date to before Mycenaean times, and scattered throughout are some inherited poetic formulae from PIE. We will discuss the study of these works in more detail in §§12.58ff.

Epic is also the language of the thirty-three so-called Homeric hymns, each addressed to a specific deity, and of the works of the first Greek author whose name we know, Hesiod (late eighth century BC). Some of the Homeric hymns contain important ancient material, but all of them were composed much later than the two epics.

Epic has at its base the dialect called **Ionic**, the variety of Greek spoken in Ionia (the coast of western Asia Minor), the island of Euboea, and the Cyclades islands in the Aegean Sea. Epic also contained, mixed in with Ionic, a substrate of **Aeolic** forms. Aeolic was a group of dialects spoken on the island of Lesbos and over the mainland Greek areas of Thessaly and Boeotia. Particularly prominent in other literature from the Archaic period is the Aeolic dialect of Lesbos, called **Lesbian**, in which was written the lyric poetry of such figures as Sappho, Alcaeus, and Stesichorus from the seventh and sixth centuries BC.

The Classical period

12.5. Due to the cultural and political hegemony enjoyed by Athens in the fifth century BC, it was **Attic**, the dialect of Athens, that became the standard literary language during the **Classical period** (480–323 BC). Attic was closely related to Ionic, and the two form a group called **Attic-Ionic**. Early on Attic became the language of drama (essentially an Athenian creation), as represented by the tragedies of Aeschylus, Sophocles, and Euripides, and the comedies of Aristophanes. Soon it became used for prose as well, by historians like Thucydides and Xenophon; philosophers like Plato, Aristotle, Theophrastus, and Epicurus; orators like Isocrates and Demosthenes; and hundreds of other authors. But the earliest Greek prose, that of philosophers such as Heraclitus, was written in Ionic.

12.6. Attic-Ionic, the Aeolic dialects, and Mycenaean are all part of the **East Greek** dialect group, which includes also the non-literary dialects **Arcado-Cypriot**

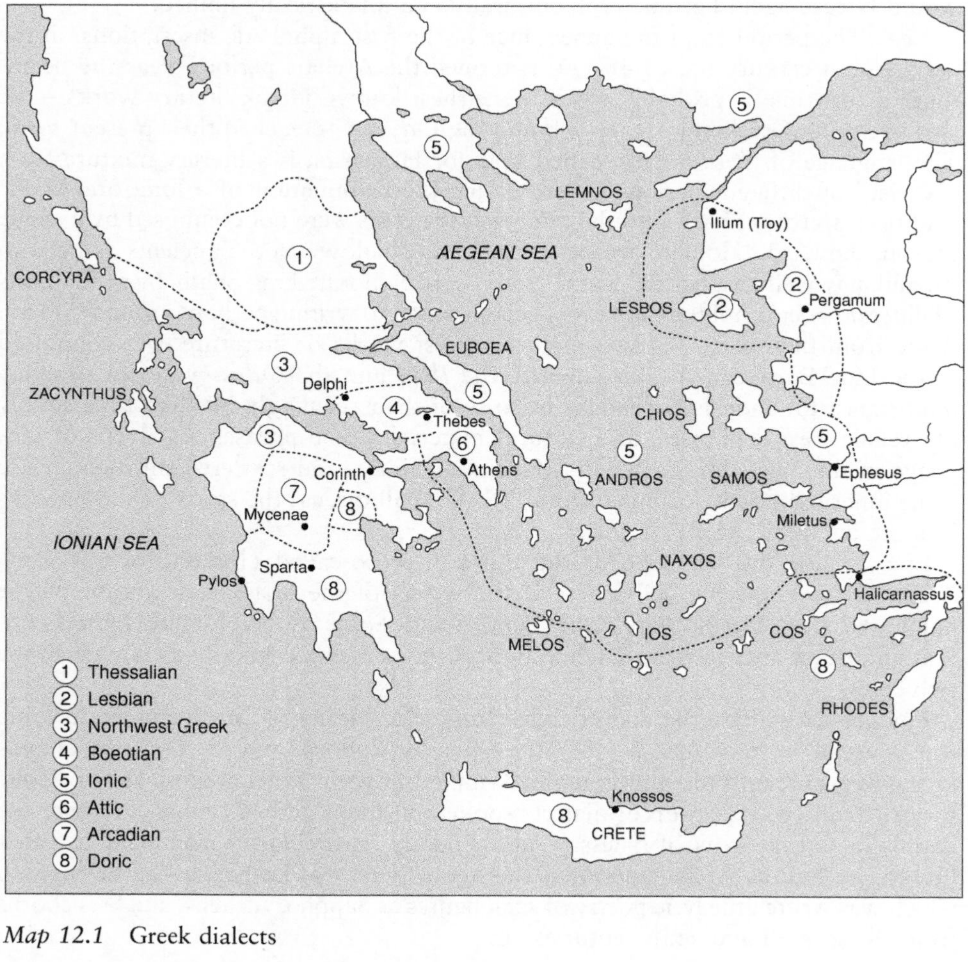

Map 12.1 Greek dialects

(or Arcado-Cyprian, consisting of Arcadian, spoken in the central Greek region of Arcadia, and the closely related Cypriot, spoken in the farther-flung island of Cyprus, and both closely akin to Mycenaean) and **Pamphylian** (from the southern Turkish coast; not a pure East Greek dialect, but a curious blend of Arcado-Cypriot, Aeolic, and Doric). The other group is **West Greek**, which contains dialects spoken generally to the south and west of East Greek: in the Peloponnese (Sparta), on many islands of the southern Aegean Sea, and in most of the Greek colonies in Sicily and Italy (where some of the oldest alphabetic Greek inscriptions hail from). Most of the West Greek dialects belong to the group called **Doric**. Doric was traditionally the language of lyric poetry (aside from Sappho and the others mentioned above) and of the choral lyric passages in drama. One of the most important lyric poets for IE studies is Pindar, who reworked and incorporated much ancient material in his compositions. All the non-literary dialects are attested in alphabetic inscriptions except Mycenaean and Cypriot; the latter is written in a syllabary derived from Linear A.

Although Attic became the literary norm and is the most familiar Greek dialect, the other dialects are often more important for Indo-Europeanists, for they preserve various features that were altered or lost in Attic. We will note examples of this where relevant in the pages to follow.

The Greek alphabet

12.7. The early first millennium BC saw the rise of the Phoenicians, a people who originated in Lebanon but spread westward as highly successful maritime merchants. Their language belongs to the Semitic family and was closely related to Hebrew and Canaanite. They established outposts throughout the Mediterranean basin, the most famous of which was Carthage, and everywhere they went they brought not only goods for sale, but a far more precious item too – their alphabet. The Greek alphabet is an adaptation of the Phoenician alphabet, a historical fact that made its way into Greek folklore in the form of the alphabet's legendary Phoenician inventor, Cadmus (< Phoenician **qadm* 'east'). There are several versions of the early Greek alphabet, and where and when the Greeks first learned it from the Phoenicians is controversial. The oldest known examples of alphabetic Greek have been found in Euboea and Italy, and date from the early eighth century BC.

The regional Greek alphabets are mostly classifiable into an eastern and a western group. While a western alphabet used by Greek colonists in Italy is what gave rise to the Latin alphabet (see further §§13.1–2), it was a form of the eastern alphabet that won out in Greece itself, slowly displacing the others beginning in the fifth century BC.

12.8. Like the related alphabets of modern Hebrew and Arabic, the Phoenician alphabet only had letters for consonants; the crucial innovation on the part of the Greeks was to use certain letters solely for vowel sounds. The Greek vowel letters Α Ε Ι Ο Υ (upsilon) and (in the eastern alphabet) Η (eta) are adaptations of Phoenician letters for consonant sounds that were not present in Greek. One inherited letter, digamma (F), represented *w* and is not part of the canonical Greek alphabet, since *w* was lost early from the eventually standard dialect of Attic-Ionic;

but digamma is common in inscriptions in other dialects. The last four letters of the Greek alphabet, Φ X Ψ Ω (*phi*, *khi*, *psi*, *omega*, standing for *ph*, *kh*, *ps*, *ō*), are additions.

From PIE to Greek

Greek and the other Indo-European languages

12.9. As mentioned in §10.4, many have thought that Greek, Armenian, Indo-Iranian, and the poorly known Phrygian form a subgroup within Indo-European because of a number of mostly morphological features shared among them. Most of these features are shared between Greek and Indo-Iranian, but that may simply reflect the fact that these two branches are attested many centuries before the oldest Phrygian, and over a millennium before the oldest Armenian.

12.10. We may list some of the language's most noteworthy features differentiating it from the other branches. Greek is characterized by a triple reflex of the vocalized laryngeals, the loss of most word-final consonants, the devoicing of the voiced aspirates, and special developments of **i̯*. In morphology, the middle and the passive voice were differentiated in the future and the aorist, an aorist passive morpheme *-(th)ē-* was created, and the locative plural ending **-su* was replaced with *-si*.

Phonology

Greek phonological inventory

12.11. Attic Greek of the fifth century BC had the following consonant inventory. There were four series of stops: the voiceless stops *p t k*, the voiced stops *b d g*, the voiceless aspirated stops p^h t^h k^h (usually transliterated *ph th kh*), and the voiced nasal stops *m n* and *ŋ* (the last only before a velar; pronounced like the *ng* of *sing* and written in Greek with a gamma, γ). There was also a voiceless sibilant *s*, and the voiceless glottal fricative *h*, which occurred word-initially and at the beginning of the second member of compounds. There were two liquids, *l* and *r*, the latter always aspirated or voiceless in word-initial position (see further §12.20); this was represented by the Romans as *rh-*, whence the spelling of such Greek-derived English words as *rhetoric* and *rhapsody*.

12.12. At the beginning of the Classical period, Attic Greek had five short vowels, phonetically [i e a o u], and seven long vowels, [iː eː aː oː uː ɛː ɔː], in addition to many diphthongs mentioned below. The two Greek long-vowel letters, H and Ω, stand for the long vowels [ɛː ɔː]. Long [eː oː] were written *ei* and *ou*, the so-called "spurious diphthongs"; these digraphs (combinations of two letters representing one sound) were also used to represent what had originally been true diphthongs [ei] and [ou] from PIE **ei* and **ou*. Greek still had plenty of other diphthongs to go around: *ai āi ēi oi ōi ui; au eu ēu ōu* (also *āu* outside Attic-Ionic); these also eventually developed into monophthongs.

During or before the early Classical period, perhaps as early as the sixth century, the high back vowel [u], short and long, became fronted to [y], as in French *une* or German *Brüder*. After this change, the long [oː] mentioned above developed further into [uː].

The complex early Classical vowel inventory was strongly reduced in the medieval period; see §§12.55ff. below.

Development of the PIE consonants into Greek

Stops

12.13. Greek is a centum language (§3.8), merging the PIE palatals with the plain velars. It continues the PIE voiceless and plain voiced series of stops unchanged, but devoiced the voiced aspirates. After the changes to the labiovelars (§12.15 below), the language had the stops *p t k b d g ph th kh*. Though we think of *ph th kh* nowadays as the fricatives [f θ x], they were not pronounced as such until the early Christian era. Greek is the only language outside of Indic to preserve this series as aspirated stops.

12.14. Like Indic but independently, Greek shows the effects of **Grassmann's Law**, or aspiration dissimilation (§10.30). In an original sequence of two aspirated stops separated by one or more segments (_*Th . . . Th_), the first lost its aspiration. Thus a reduplicated present like _*dhi-dheh$_1$-mi_ (< _*dhe-dheh$_1$-mi_; cf. §5.27) first became pre-Greek _*thi-thē-mi_ and then, by Grassmann's Law, *títhēmi* 'I place'.

12.15. Among the stops, only the labiovelars have a particularly complicated history, and their development was different from dialect to dialect. The Attic-Ionic outcomes, illustrated in the tabular overview below, are dentals before an *e* (as well as *i* in the case of _*k^w_), and labials before vowels and before most consonants.

	before *e*	before *i*	before back V or C
_*k^w_	*te* 'and' < _*k^{w}e_	*tís* 'who?' < _*k^{w}is_	*póteros* 'which (of two)' (< _*k^{w}o-tero-_) *pémptos* 'fifth' (< _*penk^{w}tos_)
_*g^w_	*adelphós* 'brother' < _*sm̥-g^{w}elbhos_ 'of the same womb'	*bíos* 'life' < _*g^{w}ih$_3$os_	*boũs* 'cow' < _*g^{w}ōus_ *bállō* 'I throw' (< _*g^{w}l̥-i̯ō_)
_*g^{w}h_	*theínō* 'I kill' < _*g^{w}hen-i̯ō_	*óphis* 'snake' < _*og^{w}his_	*nẽphō* 'I go without drink' < _*ne-eg^{w}h-ō_ *phrḗn* 'midriff' < _*g^{w}hrēn_

12.16. Before the decipherment of Mycenaean, it had been assumed that the labiovelars were still intact in Proto-Greek (the common ancestor of the attested Greek dialects) even though none of the dialects then known actually preserved them as labiovelars. This assumption had been made because it was the easiest way to explain certain consonant alternations within the dialects (such as Attic *téll-ō* 'I accomplish' ~ *humno-pólos* 'composing songs') and certain sound corres-pondences between dialects (such as Attic *tís* 'who?' = Thessalian *kís*; Attic *téssares* 'four' = Lesbian *péssures*). Mycenaean proved this hypothesis correct: it still preserved the labiovelars intact, or at least preserved them systematically as something different from labials, dentals, or plain velars. In transliterations of Mycenaean, they are represented with the letter *q*, as in *qe-to-ro-po-pi* (= *k^w^etropopphi*) 'with four-footed (chattels)'.

12.17. All non-nasal stops were lost word-finally except in unstressed words like the preposition *ek* 'out of': **tod* 'the, this' (neuter) > *tó*, **ébheret* 'he was carrying' (imperfect) > *éphere*, *hupódra* 'looking from underneath' < **upo-dr̥k̂* (root **derk̂-* 'see').

Sibilant *s

12.18. The sibilant **s* was generally preserved word-finally and next to stop consonants, as in *génos* 'kind' and *kákistos* 'worst'. Elsewhere it became *h*, as in *heptá* 'seven' < **septm̥*. This *h* had a tendency to disappear: it was lost between vowels except in Mycenaean (so pre-Greek **skelesa* 'legs' became *skeleha* in Mycenaean, written *ke-re-a*$_2$, with *a*$_2$ representing *ha*) and was lost word-initially before vowels in Ionic and some other dialects (a phenomenon called *psilosis*). The voiced variant **z* in PIE that occurred before a voiced stop (§3.12) stayed intact in the sequence *-zd-*, which is written in Greek with the single letter zeta (ζ, *z*), as in *hízō* (phonetically *hízdō*) 'I set' < **sizd-* < reduplicated **si-sd-*.

12.19. Initial clusters beginning with **s-* plus resonant or the glide **u̯-* lost the sibilant (again via an intermediate stage with *h-*), e.g. *niph-* 'snow' < **snig^w^h-* (cp. Eng. *snow*), *lḗgō* 'I abate' < **sleh*$_1$*g-* (cp. Eng. *slack*). In the case of **sr-*, the aspiration remained, hence the spelling *rh-* (§12.11), as in *rhéō* 'I flow' < **sreu̯ō*; this is also seen in some dialect inscriptions in the case of the other liquid *l*, as in Argolic *lhabṓn* 'having taken' < earlier **slab-*. The erstwhile presence of the *s* is also indicated by instances in Homer where a phrase must scan as though the *s* were still there (though not written). In internal position, these clusters sometimes become a geminate resonant, as in Homeric *éllabon* 'I took' from earlier **e-slab-om* and Homeric *érree* 'it was flowing' < **e-sreu̯-et*.

Liquids and nasals

12.20. The liquids and nasals are preserved intact in Greek, except that final **-m* became *-n*, as in the imperfect 1st sing. *épheron* 'I was carrying' < **ébherom*. The nasal **n* assimilated to the place of articulation of a following stop, as in *pémptos* 'fifth' < **penptos* < **penk^w^tos* and *ánkūra* 'anchor', pronounced [aŋk-] and written with gamma (ἄγκῡρα).

12.21. By the historical period the **syllabic nasals** had lost their nasality and show up in most dialects simply as *a*: **pod-m̥* 'foot' (accus. sing.) > *pód-a*; **n̥-dhg^w^hitom* 'imperishable' > *á-phthiton*. Likewise, the **syllabic liquids** developed an epenthetic vowel *a*, either before or after the liquid: **k̂r̥d-* 'heart' > *kardíā* (also *kradíē* in Homer); **pl̥th*$_2$*-u-* 'broad' > *platús*. Dialectally the epenthetic vowel was *o*, as in Cypriot *kórza* 'heart'. The syllabic liquids were thus still present in Common Greek, since the outcomes differ from dialect to dialect. There is also metrical evidence from the Homeric epics that **r̥* was still **r̥* at the time that certain formulaic phrases made their way into the epic repertory. For example, in the phrase *lipoũs' androtē̃ta* *kaì hḗbēn* 'leaving behind manhood and youth', which describes the departing soul of the Greek warrior Patroclus when he is killed by the Trojan Hector (*Iliad* 16.857) and later the soul of Hector when the latter is killed by the avenging Achilles (*Iliad* 22.363), the first syllable of the noun *androtē̃ta* 'manhood' must scan as short, which makes sense only if this phrase was incorporated into epic language when the combining form of the word for 'man' was still **anr̥-* (syllabified *a.nr̥-*). These two deaths are at the very heart of the plot of the *Iliad*, so it would make sense that these phrases would belong to a very old layer of epic language.

The later development to *andro-* (via **anro-*) illustrates another change: between a liquid and a nasal, a voiced stop arose, *d* if the nasal was *n* and *b* if *m*. Compare also ***ambrosíā*** 'ambrosia' < **amrotíā*, ultimately < **n̥-mr̥-t-* 'undying'.

Glides

12.22. In traditional reconstructions before the laryngeal theory became widely accepted, it appeared that the glide **i̯* at the beginning of a word had two outcomes, *h-* (e.g. *hág-ios* 'sacred' from PIE **i̯aĝ-*, cp. Vedic *yájate* 'worships') or *z-* (e.g. *zugón* 'yoke' < PIE **i̯ugom*, cp. Eng. *yoke*). Nowadays the difference is attributed to the presence or absence of a preceding laryngeal, the standard account being that **Hi̯-* > *h-* (**i̯aĝ-* is nowadays usually reconstructed as **Hi̯aĝ-*) but **i̯-* > *z-* (whence the more "modern" reconstruction of **i̯aĝ-* as **Hi̯aĝ-*); but not all are agreed that this is the case. Word-internally, **i̯* disappeared, but had various effects on preceding consonants, on which see §12.26.

The glide **u̯* was lost in standard Attic-Ionic, but in numerous other dialects it is preserved as *w* (digamma), as in Arcadian and Thessalian *woikos* 'house' (Attic-Ionic *oĩkos*; cp. Latin *uīcus* 'homestead'). It also became *h-* before *r*, yielding (like **sr*, §12.19) the sound spelled *rh-*, e.g. *rhḗtōr* 'public speaker' < pre-Greek **u̯rē-tōr* (root **u̯erh₁-* 'speak'). Although no digamma is used in the written transmission of the Homeric poems, the scansion of many lines demands that a *w* be read where it is etymologically expected. For historical purposes, Indo-Europeanists often cite Greek forms that once contained a digamma, or that are attested dialectally with one, with a parenthetical *w*, e.g. *(w)oĩda* 'I know', *é(w)idon* 'I saw'.

Laryngeals

12.23. Although there is controversy concerning the details, Greek is of paramount importance for reconstructing the PIE laryngeals – arguably more important than any other language in the family. In the standard account, Greek uniquely has three distinct descendants (the "triple reflex") of the three laryngeals when they were vocalized: vocalized $*h_1$ $*h_2$ $*h_3$ became *e a o*, as in the passive verbal adjectives *thetós* 'placed' ($*dhh_1$*-tó-*), *statós* 'stood, made to stand' ($*sth_2$*-tó-*), and *dotós* 'given' ($*dh_3$*-tó-*).

12.24. These three outcomes are also found in word-initial position before consonants (usually resonants), as in ***anḗr*** 'man' from $*h_2$*nḗr*, ***érebos*** 'darkness' < $*h_1reg^{w}$-, and *óphelos* 'advantage' < $*h_3$*bhel-*. Until the advent of the laryngeal theory, the source of these initial vowels was not understood; they were simply labeled "prothetic vowels" – vowels tacked on. Much more limited vocalic reflexes of such laryngeals are found in Armenian and Phrygian (see §§16.21, 20.5).

12.25. Additionally, sequences of syllabic resonant plus laryngeal (the "long syllabic resonants", §3.15) also have a triple reflex, depending on the laryngeal – another feature unique among the IE languages (though see §20.5): *_ĝn̥h_$_1$_-tós_ 'born' > _(-)gnētos_, *_tl̥h_$_2$_-tós_ 'endured' > Doric _(-)tlātos_, *_ĝn̥h_$_3$_-tós_ 'known' > _(-)gnōtos_. Sometimes, the outcome is a disyllabic sequence _eRe, aRa, oRo_, as in **_génesis_** 'birth' < *_ĝń̥h_$_1$_-ti-_ and **_kámatos_** 'toil' < *_ḱḿ̥h_$_2$_-to-_; this was probably the outcome when the original sequence was accented, but the matter is disputed.

Consonant clusters

12.26. A few of the major sound changes affecting consonant clusters and somewhat obscuring the IE state of affairs may be briefly mentioned. Most complicated, but also probably most widespread, are the changes that happened in consonant clusters ending in the glide *_i̯_, examples of which can be drawn abundantly from present stems of verbs formed with the suffix *_-i̯e/o-_ (see §§5.32–33) and feminine derivatives in *_-i̯a_ (< *_-ih_$_2$, see §6.71). Selected examples of the outcomes in the Attic dialect are given below:

pre-Greek	Greek	pre-Greek	Greek
*_klep-i̯ō_	_kléptō_ 'I steal'	*_ti̯eg_^{w}_-o-_	_sébomai_ 'I worship'
*_ḱi̯-āmer-_	_tḗmeron_ 'today'	*_medhi̯os_	_mésos_ 'middle'
*_phulak-i̯ō_	_phulátt-ō_ 'I guard'	*_melit-i̯a_	_mélitta_ 'honey-bee'
*_di̯ēus_	_Zeús_ 'Zeus'	*_onomn̥n-i̯ō_	_onomaín-ō_ 'I name'
*_nig_^{w}_-i̯ō_	_níz-ō_ 'I wash'	*_leu̯n̥n-i̯a_	_léaina_ 'lioness'

As a side-note concerning English etymology, the Ionic outcome corresponding to Attic _-tt-_ was _-ss-_, and sometimes English has borrowed the Ionic form of a word rather than an Attic one, such as the name _Melissa_ ('honey-bee', vs. Attic _mélitta_ above). Sometimes English borrowed both, as in _glossary_ (Ionic _glõssa_ 'tongue') but _polyglot_ (Attic _glõtta_).

12.27. In East Greek, including Attic, the change of *_t_ to _s_ happened not just before *_i̯_, but also before *_i_, as in the *_ti_-abstract nouns. These nouns all end in _-sis_ in Greek, whence many English borrowings like _basis_ and _prognosis_ (Gk. _básis, prógnōsis_ < PIE *_g_^{w}_m̥-ti-_, *_(-)ĝn̥h_$_3$_-ti-_). This change is also seen in the 3rd pl. primary ending *_-nti_, which became first *_-nsi_; then the _n_ disappeared, compensatorily lengthening the preceding vowel if there was one. Thus the thematic 3rd pl. active ending in Attic is _-ousi_, as in _phér-ousi_ 'they carry' < *_pher-onsi_ < *_pher-onti_ (in Doric, the form is still _phéronti_).

12.28. The PIE clusters of two dentals (§3.36) became _st_ in Greek, as in _(w)ístōr_ 'judge' < *_u̯idtōr_ 'knower' (of right and wrong).

Development of the PIE vowels into Greek

12.29. Greek preserves the PIE vowels and diphthongs (including the long diphthongs) more faithfully than any other IE language. Because of this, ablaut is reflected particularly clearly, since the ablauting vowels _e_ and _o_ are kept distinct from one another (in contrast to Indo-Iranian), and *o* is distinct from *a* (in contrast to Germanic, Balto-Slavic, and most of Indo-Iranian and Anatolian).

The short vowels are preserved intact in such words as *tís* 'who?' (**kʷis*), *pénte* 'five' (**penkʷe*), *hágios* 'sacred' (**Hi̯aĝ-*), *nóstos* 'homecoming' (**nos-tos*), and *gónu* 'knee' (**ĝonu*). The long vowels (whether from original long vowels or from sequences of short vowel plus laryngeal) are preserved in such words as *ī́os* 'poison' (**u̯īs-o-* or **u̯iHs-o-*), *patḗr* 'father' (**ph₂tḗr*), Doric *hādús* 'sweet' (**su̯ādú-* < **su̯eh₂du-*), *ōkús* 'swift' (**ōk̂ús*), and *ikhthū̃s* 'fish' (**ĝhdhūs* or **ĝhdhuHs*).

The one characteristic point on which Attic-Ionic innovated is in the treatment of **ā*, which frequently became *ē* in this dialect group (e.g. *mḗtēr* 'mother' vs. Doric *mā́tēr*). In Ionic this change happened across the board, while in Attic it did not affect **ā* after the sounds *e*, *i*, or *r* (hence Ionic *neēníēs* 'young man' and *hṓrē* 'season' but Attic *neāníās*, *hṓrā*).

Diphthongs

12.30. Both short and long diphthongs are faithfully preserved in Greek: **ei *ai *oi* in *leípō* 'I leave' (**leikʷ-*), *lai(w)ós* 'left' (**laiu̯os*), and *léloipa* 'I left' (**le-loikʷ-*); and **eu *au *ou* in *rheũma* 'stream' (**sreu-mn̥*), *haũos* 'dry' (**saus-o-*), and *akoúō* 'I hear' (**h₂kous-*). By the fifth century BC, the diphthongs *ei* and *ou* had been monophthongized to [eː] and [oː], long vowels that already existed in the language because they had arisen from certain vowel contractions and other changes. (The spellings *ei* and *ou* for [eː] and [oː] are therefore often called "spurious diphthongs," as we saw in §12.12.)

Long diphthongs are continued in such forms as the dative singular of *o*-stems like *anthrṓp-ōi* 'for the man'. Starting around the third century BC, however, the *i* in the long diphthongs *āi ēi ōi* ceased to be pronounced, whence the orthographic convention in Greek of placing the *i* underneath the long-vowel letter (ᾳ ῃ ῳ). This convention is not followed in all modern texts, and postdates Classical Greek.

The accent

12.31. Ancient Greek, like Vedic Sanskrit and some Balto-Slavic languages, had a mobile pitch-accent. (Modern Greek, though, has a stress-accent like English.) In most dialects the position of the accent was not usually predictable except in verbs. Judging by ancient descriptions, the accented syllable had higher pitch than unaccented syllables, and is ordinarily marked with an acute accent (´). Syllables containing long vowels and diphthongs could have the high pitch on either the first or the second half (technically called the mora) of the syllable; accent on the first mora is denoted by a circumflex accent (˜). Thus *aí* is different from *aĩ*, the latter representing *ái* (high pitch on the first mora). Since Byzantine times it has been customary to write an acute accent on a final syllable as a grave (`) when another word follows: *theā́* 'goddess' but *theā̀ Thétis* 'the goddess Thetis'. But there is no unambiguous evidence that the grave represents a different kind of accent from the acute.

12.32. A small handful of particles, pronouns, and short verb forms are clitic and do not receive an accent; however, if they occur in groups of two or more, then all but the last one receive an acute, as in the string *gar te me phēsi* becoming *gár té mé* *phēsi* in the Homeric text (§12.65) at the end of the chapter. Some of the rules for the accentuation of clitic chains are strongly reminiscent of the rules for verbal accentuation; it may be that verbs themselves were weakly stressed or unaccented in the prehistory of Greek. This would be paralleled by the weaker phonetic status of verbs in Vedic and elsewhere in IE (§5.63).

Morphology

The verb

12.33. The morphology of the Greek verb is very close to that of Sanskrit and of reconstructed PIE. Verbs in Greek do not belong to "conjugations" as in a language like Latin (see §§13.12ff.); rather, for the old core of verbs, tense-stems are derived directly from roots. Greek has innovated chiefly by expanding the number of forms of the verb: it has a true future tense, and it has created a new passive, distinct from the middle, in the future and aorist. The Greek verb had up to six so-called principal parts or stems: the present (e.g. *gráphō* 'I write'), a future (*grápsō* 'I will write'), an aorist active or middle (active *égrapsa* 'I wrote'), a perfect active (*gégrapha* 'I have written'), a perfect mediopassive (*gégrammai* 'I have written for myself, I have been written'), and an aorist passive (*egráphēn* or *egráphthēn* 'I was written'). All tenses having secondary endings (imperfect, aorist, pluperfect) were prefixed with the augment *e-* in the indicative mood, although in Homer (and occasionally in other poets) this is sometimes lacking. Most of the time augmentless forms have no discernible difference in meaning from augmented ones.

12.34. Most IE present classes are still found in Greek, although the number of athematic verbs has been much reduced, with some types such as nasal-infix presents barely found. Two notable innovations in the present stems are the combination of reduplication with the suffix *-skō* (< **-sk̑e/o-*; e.g. *mi-mnḗ-skō* 'I remind') and the double nasal presents with both nasal infix and nasal suffix *-anō* (e.g. *li-m-p-ánō* 'I leave', Greek root *leip-*).

12.35. The primary personal endings. Primary active and middle endings in thematic and athematic verbs are exemplified below by the present indicative of the verbs *phēmí* 'I say', *dídomai* 'I give (for myself), I am given', *phérō* 'I carry', *phéromai* 'I carry (for myself), I am carried'. Dual endings are not given.

		Athematic		**Thematic**	
		Active	*Mediopassive*	*Active*	*Mediopassive*
sing.	1	phēmí[1]	dídomai	phérō	phéromai
	2	phḗis[2]	dídosai	phéreis	phérēi[5]
	3	phēsí[1]	dídotai	phérei	phéretai
pl.	1	phamén	didómetha	phéromen	pherómetha
	2	phaté	dídosthe	phérete	phéresthe
	3	phāsí[3]	dídontai	phérousi[4]	phérontai

[1] Doric preserves the original vowel in *phāmí, phātí.* [2] Remade from **phēs.* [3] Doric *phantí.* [4] Doric has *phéronti.* [5] Homeric has *phéreai.*

12.36. The primary active athematic endings are easily derivable from PIE (see §§5.12ff.) except for the 2nd sing. *-s*. The expected ending *-si* occurs only in dialectal *essí* 'you are' (and even here has been restored by analogy; cf. §3.37); elsewhere, the secondary ending *-s* seems to have infiltrated the primary paradigm. In the thematic conjugation, both the 2nd and 3rd singular are of uncertain origin; we would expect 2nd sing. **-ei* (< **-ehi* < **-e-si*) and 3rd sing. **-eti* (Attic **-esi*).

12.37. The primary middle endings show much more innovation than the active endings. To cite one example, the 1st sing. *-mai* is a refashioning of earlier **-ai* under the influence of the active ending *-mi*; this *-ai* in turn is a combination of the PIE 1st sing. middle ending **-h_2e* (> **-a*) and primary active particle **-i* (§5.13), which in Greek and several other branches replaced the original primary middle marker **-r*. The 3rd person endings *-tai* and *-ntai* are a replacement of *-toi* and *-ntoi* (ultimately PIE **-(n)to* plus **-i*), which were still preserved in Mycenaean and Arcado-Cypriot (e.g. Arcado-Cypriot *keitoi* 'lies').

12.38. The secondary personal endings. Below is a chart illustrating the secondary endings, from the imperfect tenses of the verbs given previously: *éphēn* 'I was saying', *edidómēn* 'I was giving (for myself), I was being given', etc.

		Athematic		Thematic	
		Active	*Mediopassive*	*Active*	*Mediopassive*
sing.	1	éphēn	edidómēn[2]	épheron	epherómēn[2]
	2	éphēs	edídoso	épheres	ephérou[3]
	3	éphē[1]	edídoto	éphere	ephéreto
pl.	1	éphamen	edidómetha	ephéromen	epherómetha
	2	éphate	edídosthe	ephérete	ephéresthe
	3	éphasan	edídonto	épheron	ephéronto

[1] Doric *éphā*. [2] Doric *edidómān, epherómān*. [3] Earlier **ephereo* < **ephereso*.

12.39. The secondary active endings are mostly the predicted outcomes from the corresponding endings in PIE, except for the 3rd pl. athematic ending *-san*, which has been taken over from the *s*-aorist (see below). The secondary mediopassive endings have been refashioned since PIE times, just like their primary counterparts.

12.40. The perfect. The perfect is fairly well preserved, although the old alternation between *o*-grade and zero-grade has mostly been leveled out in favor of the *o*-grade, except in some archaic forms found especially in Homer. In the verb *(w)oĩda* 'I know', historically a perfect without reduplication but thought of as a present in Greek, the IE ablaut relationships are still clear: singular *(w)oĩda (w)oĩstha (w)oĩde*, plural *(w)ídmen (w)íste (w)ísāsi* (Doric *ísanti*).

Greek also has three different pluperfect formations, none of which has a clear claim to being very ancient. A future perfect, formed to the perfect mediopassive stem, is also an innovation within Greek.

12.41. The aorist. Greek preserves all the PIE aorist categories. The thematic aorist in Greek, as in PIE, has the same endings as the imperfect, e.g. sing. *élip-on -es -e*, pl. *elíp-omen -ete -on*, the aorist of *leípō* 'I leave'. The root and *s*-aorist deserve more attention; sample paradigms are reproduced below (*éstēn* 'I stood', *edómēn* 'I gave (for myself)', *épleksa* 'I wove', *epleksámēn* 'I wove for myself').

		Root aorist		s-Aorist	
		Active[1]	*Middle*	*Active*	*Middle*
sing.	1	éstēn	edómēn[2]	épleksa	epleksámēn[2]
	2	éstēs	édou	épleksas	epléksō[3]
	3	éstē	édoto	éplekse	epléksato
pl.	1	éstēmen	edómetha	epléksamen	epleksámetha
	2	éstēte	édosthe	epléksate	epléksasthe
	3	éstēsan[1]	édonto	épleksan	epléksanto

[1] Doric has *ā* instead of *ē* and 3rd pl. *éstan*. [2] Doric has *edómān, epleksámān*. [3] Earlier **epleksao* < **epleksaso*.

12.42. In the root aorist, the Doric 3rd plural is noteworthy in preserving the zero-grade of the root (Doric *éstan*, from **e-sth₂-nt*, with vocalized laryngeal). The *s*-aorist has undergone some remodeling since PIE times. The full grade has been generalized at the expense of the lengthened grade, and the *-a* that was the regular outcome of old 1st sing. **-m̥* and 3rd pl. **-n̥t* spread to most of the other persons and numbers to become the characteristic vowel of this tense. The middle endings in the aorist are the ordinary secondary middle endings already discussed.

12.43. The **aorist passive** was usually formed with a suffix *-thē-* (e.g. *egráphthēn* 'I was written'), but in several older verbs the suffix was just *-ē-*. Curiously it had active personal endings and the participle is formed with the historically active suffix *-nt-* (e.g. *graphthént-* 'having been written'), and some archaic aorist passives such as *edáēn* 'I learned' and *ephánēn* 'I appeared' are not even passive in meaning. It is a descendant of the PIE stative in **-eh₁-* (§5.37).

12.44. The future. Most Greek futures are sigmatic, formed with a thematic suffix *-se/o-*: *lū́ō* 'I release' (present), *lū́sō* 'I will release' (future). The source of the Greek sigmatic future is controversial, but most likely continues one of the PIE desiderative formations in **-s-*, probably **-h₁se-* (§5.41). Greek has invented a future passive by adding this *-se/o-* to the (unaugmented) aorist passive stem: aorist passive *e-tīmḗthē-n* 'I was honored', future passive *tīmēthḗ-somai* 'I will be honored'. This is a fairly recent innovation; it is barely attested in Homer.

12.45. The subjunctive and optative. Greek has inherited the PIE subjunctive in both athematic and thematic verb stems, where it typically has modal force and not future force. Athematic stems in Homer still fairly commonly form "short-vowel" subjunctives that reflect the PIE subjunctive vowel **-e/o-*, as in Homeric *stḗ-o-men* 'let us stand' (aorist athematic stem *stē-*). In thematic stems, the contraction of the thematic vowel with the subjunctive vowel led to a subjunctive in long *-ō-* and *-ē-*, as in *phér-ō-men* 'let us carry' < **pher-o-o-men*.

The optative has also been inherited intact. The ablaut **-i̯eh₁-/*-ih₁-* is preserved in athematic forms like the present optative 1st sing. *eíēn* 'may I be' (**h₁s-i̯eh₁-m*), 1st pl. *eĩmen* 'may we be' (**h₁s-ih₁-me-*), and the expected optative of thematic stems, **-o-ih₁-*, is continued by Greek *-oi-*, as in *phér-oi-men* 'may we carry'.

12.46. Imperative. Greek has 2nd and 3rd person imperatives in the present, aorist, and perfect, in all voices. While several of these are new creations, the endings are mostly familiar from PIE. The athematic 2nd sing. **-dhi* is continued as *-thi* in a few athematic forms (e.g. *í-thi* 'go!'), while the thematic is endingless (*phére* 'carry!'). The 2nd pl. active ends in *-te* everywhere, as expected (*phérete* 'carry!').

12.47. Infinitives and participles. Infinitives and participles are very numerous in Greek, being formed from all the verb-stems. Greek active infinitives contain a suffix **-en*, **-men*, or **-ai*, sometimes in combinations like *-(e)nai* or *-menai*. In Attic, **-en* (probably < **-hen* < **-sen*) is found in thematic verbs, as in *phérein* 'to carry' < **pher-e-en* (cp. Mycenaean *e-re-e* 'to row' = *erehen*), while **-nai* is found in athematic verbs (*didó-nai* 'to give'). These endings are mostly creations within Greek, as are the peculiarly abundant participles, of which ten are formally distinguished. Except for the perfect, the active participles have a stem in *-nt-* which is inherited from PIE (such as the present *gráphont-* 'writing' and aorist *grápsant-* 'having written'), and except for the aorist passive, the middle and passive participles have a stem in *-meno-*, likewise inherited (such as the present mediopassive *graphómenos* 'being written' and future middle *grapsómenos* 'about to write for oneself'). The inherited perfect active participial stem **-u̯os-* has been refashioned to **-u̯ot-* (with a *-t-* of disputed origin) except in Mycenaean, which continues the older form as *-woh-* (e.g. *te-tu-ko-wo-a₂* = *tetukhwoha*, neuter pl. of the Mycenaean perfect participle of *teúkhō* 'I fashion, craft').

The noun

12.48. In contrast to the verb, which has gained a number of forms since PIE times, the number of Greek noun forms has shrunk somewhat. The nominative, vocative, accusative, and genitive are preserved intact. The function of the ablative has been taken over by the genitive (the two were not always distinct in PIE), though Mycenaean might still have a separate ablative. The case called the dative in Greek grammar combines the functions of the old dative, instrumental, and locative, and formally continues the PIE dative or locative in the singular (depending on the declension) and the instrumental or locative in the plural (depending on the declension and dialect; in Mycenaean the two are still distinct). A separate locative is still used for place-names and in some locational adverbs. An ending *-phi* (< PIE *-bhi-) is still productive in Myceanaean for the instrumental plural and occurs in Homer as well, where however it is indifferent to number (so *ĩphi* 'with might' sing. and *naũphi* 'with ships' pl.; compare the analogues in Vedic Sanskrit in §6.17).

12.49. The following are the paradigms for the nouns *lúkos* 'wolf', *hṓrā* 'season' and *sōtḗr* 'savior'.

	o-stem		*ā-stem*		*Consonant stem*	
	sing.	pl.	sing.	pl.	sing.	pl.
nom.	lúkos	lúkoi	hṓrā	hō̃rai	sōtḗr	sōtē̃res
voc.	lúke	lúkoi	hṓrā	hō̃rai	sō̃ter	sōtē̃res
gen.	lúkou	lúkōn	hṓrās	hōrō̃n[1]	sōtē̃ros	sōtḗrōn
dat.	lúkōi	lúkois	hṓrāi	hṓrais	sōtē̃ri	sōtē̃rsi
acc.	lúkon	lúkous	hṓrān	hṓrās	sōtē̃ra	sōtē̃ras

[1] Homeric *hōrā́ōn*.

12.50. The *o*-stem singular endings directly continue the relevant PIE endings discussed in §§6.45ff. The nominative plural in *-oi* is taken over from the pronominal declension, as in several other branches (§6.53). The noun *hṓrā* was chosen above because it preserves PIE **ā*; in practice, though, most nouns of this declension have *-ē-* instead of *-ā-* in Attic-Ionic because of the change discussed in §12.29. The *o*-stem and *ā*-stem accusative plurals *-ous* and *-ās* arose by sound change from **-ons* and **-ans* (shortened from **-āns* by Osthoff's Law, §3.41), endings that are preserved intact in Cretan (the Doric dialect of Crete). Note that the nasal in the feminine accus. pl. **-ans* is a Greek innovation, copied over from the *o*-stem ending **-ons*, since the original nasal was lost already in Indo-European (§6.70). (We know that the insertion of the nasal was already of Common Greek date, and not just a Cretan one, because **-ās* would have become **-ēs* in Attic-Ionic, not *-ās*.) Consonant-stem inflection is more straightforward than in PIE, since the endings no longer ablaut (though the stems sometimes do, e.g. *kúōn* 'dog', stem *kun-*; *patḗr* 'father', stem *patr-*). The dative singular ending *-i* is from the PIE locative, which ousted the original dative in *-ei*, which is still in Mycenaean (see the Mycenaean text sample in §12.66 for an example and further discussion).

12.51. Greek still preserves the dual. The nominative-accusative ending **-h_1e* is preserved intact in athematic nouns as *-e* (e.g. *pód-e* 'both feet'); the thematic ending **-oh_1* is also faithfully preserved as *-ō* (e.g. *híppō* 'two horses').

Syntax

12.52. Because of its rich inflectional system, sentences in Greek, as in most other older IE languages, have many possible word orders. In poetry such as Pindar's, this freedom is stretched to its limits, but even here some theoretically possible word orders are not found, showing that certain orders were probably not grammatical. In particular, the order of clitic particles was constrained, as in other languages like Vedic and Hittite. The number of these particles was large; they conveyed various shades of meaning and are often difficult or impossible to translate. These particles, together with certain unstressed pronouns and conjunctions, tend to be grouped together near the beginning of the sentence after the first fully stressed word by Wackernagel's Law (§§8.22ff.). The rules of clitic placement, however, are not always that easy to divine, as they differ somewhat from author to author and dialect to dialect. In their essentials, though, their behavior is clearly comparable with clitic placement in Indo-Iranian, Celtic, and elsewhere.

12.53. A neuter plural subject takes a singular, and not a plural, verb, as in the phrase *tà zȭia* (pl.) *trékhei* (sing.) 'the animals run'. This is also the case in Old Avestan and Hittite (cp. §6.68) and is an inherited feature.

Greek after the Classical Period

The Hellenistic period and the Koine

12.54. Toward the middle of the first millennium BC the prestige of Greek language and culture was extending outside the confines of the local Greek city-states. Both had been carried to the shores of Italy by colonists starting in the eighth century BC, where they would soon exercise considerable influence over the Etruscans and other indigenous peoples. Of even greater importance for the fortunes of Greek was the adoption of Attic-Ionic by around the fifth century as the official language of the court in Macedon, a kingdom to the north of Greece. When Macedon's power expanded in the fourth century under Philip II and his son Alexander III (the Great), Greek language and culture spread over an enormous area of the ancient world and ushered in the **Hellenistic period**, whose beginning is traditionally dated to the year of Alexander's death in 323 BC. During this time, Greek was spoken as far south as Egypt and as far east as Bactria. A uniform and somewhat simplified variety of spoken Greek called **Koine** (short for *hē koinḕ diálektos*, 'the common language') established itself as the medium of communication. It was based mostly on Attic but had admixtures from Ionic and other non-Attic elements. As it became the standard administrative language, almost all the other Greek dialects died out, the one exception being the Doric dialect Laconian (living on nowadays as Tsakonian) and perhaps the Doric spoken by Greek settlers in Calabria (southern Italy), though this is controversial.

The Koine was used until around the reign of Justinian I in the sixth century AD; it is the language of the Septuagint and the New Testament, and was used by some authors such as the historian Polybius and the philosopher Epictetus. But most writers after the first century AD reacted against it and returned to pure Attic, including such familiar figures as Plutarch, Galen, Euclid, and Ptolemy. Mention should also be made of Hesychius, an Alexandrian glossator who compiled a lexicon of rare words probably in the fifth century AD. His lexicon, while sometimes faulty, contains a prodigious number of dialectal forms and words from other languages that are only poorly known, and is of great value for Greek dialectology and IE studies.

12.55. Characteristics of the Koine. Most important for the later history of Greek were the changes that the Koine underwent in its phonology. First, the numerous distinctions among the vowels were reduced: *ei*, *ē*, and *i* all became pronounced [i]; *ai* and *e* merged as [ɛ]; and *oi* and *u* merged as [y] (pronounced *ü* as in German). Over time, distinctions in quantity were lost; and the pitch-accent was replaced with a stress-accent. The aspirated stops *ph th kh* became fricatives [f θ x], and the voiced stops *b d g* became voiced fricatives [v ð ɣ]. In the morphology, the dual number and the optative mood were lost and the distinction between perfect and aorist was given up, with verbs retaining only one of the two past-tense stems (usually the aorist).

Byzantine Greek

12.56. The purist reaction alluded to above resulted in the adoption of an artificial archaizing literary language based on Classical Attic. This continued to be used as an administrative and literary language in the Byzantine period (roughly from the reign of the emperor Justinian I in the sixth century AD to the fall of Constantinople in 1453). The gap between the written and spoken languages widened with time, and as the Byzantine empire disintegrated and educational standards declined, spoken usages infiltrated the written language in ever larger numbers. Spelling errors (among other evidence) indicate that the two high vowels [i] and [y] merged as [i]. Additionally the dative case was lost in nouns, and the infinitive began to be replaced with other constructions found also in other languages of the region, such as Bulgarian; see further §19.5.

Modern Greek

12.57. Aside from Tsakonian in the eastern Peloponnese and perhaps the Greek dialects of southern Italy, the varieties of Modern Greek are all descended from the Koine. Following the establishment of the new Greek state after the yoke of Turkish rule was cast off in 1828, a new literary standard called the **Katharevusa** ('purified') was created that was purged of foreign elements and drew on Ancient Greek for both vocabulary and inflections. The variety of Greek spoken in the Peloponnese became the spoken standard, known as **Demotic**. In 1976, Demotic also replaced the Katharevusa as the written standard, although the two varieties had essentially merged by then anyway; the result of their convergence is often called Standard Modern Greek (*Koiní Neoelliniki*).

The Philology of Homer and Its Pitfalls

12.58. Because of the importance of the Homeric poems for the historical study of both Greek and PIE, it is essential to have some knowledge of the difficulties peculiar to these texts. In particular, the epics contain forms that are artificial and consequently of little or no historical value for comparative linguistics. We will present a sampling below.

12.59. The Homeric poems in their present form represent the accumulated labor of many generations of bards from different parts of eastern Greece. The result was a mixture of forms from different dialects and from different chronological stages. Each poet drew on a repertory of inherited and memorized formulaic poetic language, but in composing the epics in performance would inject newer material of his own devising. Bards constantly adapted the poetic language, and to make the verses scan they would sometimes create forms that from a historical point of view are wrong.

As noted earlier, the dialect of the epics is Ionic, with admixture from Aeolic and Mycenaean. Alongside Ionic forms like *téssares* 'four' and *hēmeĩs* 'we' are found the Aeolic equivalents *písures* and *ámmes*. Aeolic and Ionic forms sometimes coexist in the same line, and there are even words that are artificial hodge-podges of morphemes from both Aeolic and Ionic, such as the dative plural *stḗthessin* 'in (one's) chest', which has the Aeolic dative plural ending *-essi* plus an *-n* that many inflections have in Attic-Ionic.

12.60. Lines of Greek poetry were structured according to particular sequences of light (⏑) and heavy (–) syllables. A light syllable was one ending in a short vowel; all others counted as heavy. Syllable division ignored word-breaks; thus *ptolíethron épersen* 'he sacked the city' is syllabified *pto.li.eth.ro.ne.per.sen.* Heavy and light syllables are organized into basic units called feet, of which two occur in Homer: the dactyl (– ⏑ ⏑) and the spondee (– –). A line of Homeric poetry contains six feet, most of which can be either dactyls or spondees, whence the name of the meter, *dactylic hexameter*.

12.61. Discrepancies between how a particular Homeric line is written and how it scans are common. Often, this is due to modernized spelling, in which older forms that did scan were replaced with newer forms that do not. For example, the *o*-stem genitive singular ended in disyllabic *-oio* in its oldest Homeric form (< PIE *-*os̯io*) and monosyllabic *-ou* in later Attic-Ionic. But there was also an intermediate stage, namely disyllabic *-oo* (two short syllables), a form that is nowhere preserved in the written tradition but whose former presence in some passages is betrayed by a mismatch between the spelling and the meter. Thus *Odyssey* 10.60 contains the phrase *Aiólou klutà dṓmata* 'famed dwellings of Aeolus', where *Aiólou* cannot scan as written because it would form the sequence – ⏑ –, which is not allowed in the dactylic hexameter. But restoring the genitive ending *-oo* solves the problem: *Aióloo klutà* (syllabified again without regard to word-breaks: *ai.o.lo.ok.lu.ta*) yields two dactyls, – ⏑ ⏑ | – ⏑ ⏑.

12.62. The earlier presence of digamma (*w*) explains some other peculiarities. Normally in Greek poetry, a short vowel at the end of a word is elided (not pronounced) before a word beginning with a vowel; thus the sequence *me ō̃ka* in line 416 in §12.65 below is written (and read) *m' ō̃ka*. There are many exceptions to this in Homer, but usually they are due to the earlier presence of a digamma that blocked elision. An example is the phrase *Hēphaístoio ánaktos* 'of Hephaistos the king', where if we restore the digamma that originally began the word for 'king', the irregularity disappears: (*)*Hēphaístoio wánaktos*.

12.63. A number of artificialities of the Epic language are due to so-called poetic "licenses." Poetic licenses are conceived as the conscious bending of rules of phonology or grammar to make a word fit the meter. The bards presumably could not do this willy-nilly; they took advantage of pre-existing and naturally occurring variants and then extended the properties of those variants analogically. One famous such license in Homer is poetic lengthening, the lengthening typically of the initial syllable of a word that could not otherwise have fit the meter, e.g. *Āpóllōna* 'Apollo' (accus. sing., for *Apóllōna*).

12.64. Finally, the alphabet used in the earliest stages of the written transmission of the epics did not distinguish short from long *e* and *o*, and words were written together without a break. These facts led to numerous errors on the part of copyists, including the creation of ghost-forms. An example is the story of the two nearly identical Greek adjectives meaning 'horrible, chilling', *kruóeis* and *okruóeis*. Both are descendants of PIE **kreus-* 'freeze', but the *o-* of *okruóeis* has no obvious source. Philological examination of the Homeric passages containing the problematic form *okruóeis* reveals two interesting facts: first, the word preceding *okruóeis* is always an *o*-stem genitive singular ending in *-ou* (e.g. in the phrase *epidēmíou okruóentos* 'of chilling civil [war]'); and second, this syllable must scan light to fit the meter, whereas normally (since it is a diphthong) it should scan heavy. Now, as just discussed above, the ending *-ou* is of somewhat recent vintage in Homer; it was earlier *-oo*, which is the ending we would expect to have been current at the time of the composition of much of the epics. If we combine the expected ending with the unproblematic form of the adjective, we would get the phrase *epidēmíoo kruóentos*, which happens to scan perfectly. For this scenario to work, all we need is an explanation for how *epidēmíoo kruóentos* became corrupted to *epidēmíou okruóentos*. The explanation is straightforward: since the earliest Greek texts were written without word-divisions, this would have been transmitted as *epidēmiookruoentos*, and later copyists who only knew the newer genitive singular ending *-ou* misparsed the sequence *. . . ookru . . .*, thinking that the second *o* was part of the following word and that the first *o* was meant to be the ending *-ou*. We conclude that there was originally just one adjective for 'chilling', *kruóeis*; the *o-* of *okruóeis* has no etymological significance, and the word entered Greek through a copyist's error. (Some authorities believe that this sort of error could already have arisen during the preliterate, oral transmission of the text through singers' misunderstandings rather than copyists' errors.)

Homeric Greek text sample

12.65. *Iliad* 9.410ff. Achilles describes his double fate.

μήτηρ γάρ τέ μέ φησι θεὰ Θέτις ἀργυρόπεζα
διχθαδίας κῆρας φερέμεν θανάτοιο τέλοσδε·
εἰ μέν κ' αὖθι μένων Τρώων πόλιν ἀμφιμάχωμαι,
ὤλετο μέν μοι νόστος, ἀτὰρ κλέος ἄφθιτον ἔσται·
εἰ δέ κεν οἴκαδ' ἵκωμι φίλην ἐς πατρίδα γαῖαν,
ὤλετο μοι κλέος ἐσθλόν, ἐπὶ δηρὸν δέ μοι αἰὼν
ἔσσεται, οὐδὲ κέ μ' ὦκα τέλος θανάτοιο κιχείη.

mḗtēr gár té mé phēsi theà Thétis argurópeza
dikhthadías kē̃ras pherémen thanátoio télosde:
ei mén k' aũthi ménōn Trṓōn pólin amphimákhōmai,
ṓleto mén moi nóstos, atàr kléos áphthiton éstai;
ei dé ken oíkad' híkōmi phílēn es patrída gaîan,
ṓletó moi kléos esthlón, epì dēròn dé moi aiṑn
éssetai, oudé ké m' ō̃ka télos thanátoio kikheíē.

For my mother, the silver-footed goddess Thetis, says to me
that (I) have a double fate towards the end of death.
If, on the one hand, staying here I fight beside the city of the Trojans,
my homecoming is lost, but I will have imperishable fame;
on the other hand, if I go home to my beloved fatherland,
noble fame is lost for me, but my life will be long,
and the end of death would not come swiftly to me.

12.65a. Notes. 410. mḗtēr: 'mother'; Doric *mā́tēr*. **gár té mé:** string of clitics placed after the first stressed word in the sentence (cp. Anatolian, §9.13): *gar* = 'for' (explanatory particle); *te* = 'and' (PIE $*k^we$, also in Lat. *-que*, Skt. *ca*), connecting this sentence to the preceding and not translated here; and *me* is the accus. enclitic pronoun 'me', the subject of the following clause of indirect statement, where the main verb is an infinitive (cp. English *I consider him to be dishonest*). The pronoun has moved out of the clause of indirect statement and into the main clause (clitic raising). **phēsi:** 'says', clitic verb form; Doric *phātí*, PIE $*bheh_2\text{-}ti$, cognate with Lat. *fā-tur* 'speaks'. **theà:** 'goddess' ($*dhh_1s\text{-}\bar{a}$); not related to Latin *dea* 'goddess', but rather to Lat. *fēstus* 'holy, festal' < $*dheh_1s\text{-}$ 'sacred' and *fānum* 'temple' < $*dhh_1s\text{-}no\text{-}$.

411–12. dikhthadías kē̃ras: 'double fates', object of *pherémen* 'to carry, have', an Aeolic infinitive (Attic *phérein*). **thanátoio:** 'of death', with the archaic genit. *-oio* (§6.48). **télosde:** 'to the end, to completion'; *-de* indicates place to which (also line 414, *oíkad(e)* 'homewards'); it is probably related to Eng. *to*. **ei mén:** 'if, on the one hand . . .' **k':** elided form of *ke*, a particle (variant *ken* line 414) used in certain conditional clauses; maybe related to Hittite *-kan*, Ved. *kám* (§7.29). **ménōn:** 'remaining, staying', pres. partic. (stem *ménont-*), cognate with Lat. *maneō* 'I remain'. **amphimákhōmai:** 'I fight around, fight beside', pres. subjunc. mid.; *amphi-* comes from $*h_2\text{m̥}bhi\text{-}$, whence German *um* 'around', Old High German *umbi*, and the *om-* of Eng. *ombudsman* (a borrowing from Swedish).

413–14. ō̃leto: 'is lost', 3rd sing. aorist middle of *óllumai* 'am lost'. **moi:** 'to/for me', clitic dat. 1st sing. pronoun; dative of possession ('my homecoming') or dative of reference ('as for me . . .'). **nóstos:** 'homecoming', a rare IE formation, with the **-to-*suffix added to the *o*-grade of the root (root **nes-* 'arrive home safely', also in Gk. *néomai* 'I come home safely' < **nesomai*, and the name *Nés-tōr*). **kléos áphthiton:** 'imperishable fame', directly from PIE **k̑leu̯os n̥dhgʷhitom* (see §2.37). This is its only occurrence in Homer. **éstai:** 'will be', shorter form of *éssetai* (line 416), future of the verb *es-* 'be', middle alongside the active present (cp. §5.6). **dé:** 'but', a particle functioning both as adversative and as sentence connector. **híkōmi:** 'I come, arrive at', pres. subjunc. In Attic the form would be *hī́kō*; the addition of the athematic 1st sing. ending *-mi* is a Homeric feature. **phílēn es patrída gaĩan:** 'to (my) beloved fatherland'. The adjective (*phílēn*) has been moved out of the prepositional phrase, a common stylistic feature in the early IE languages (cp. Latin *magnā cum laude* 'with great (*magnā*) praise'; recall §8.7).

415–16. epì dēròn: 'for a long time'; *dērón* is from earlier **du̯āron*. The second syllable of *epí* scans long, which can only be explained if the cluster *du̯-* was still present at the time of the composition of this line or phrase (the syllabification being *e.pid.u̯ē.ron*). The adjective comes from $*du̯eh_2\text{-}ro\text{-}$, whose zero-grade $*duh_2\text{-}ro\text{-}$ is seen in Lat. *dūrus* 'enduring'. **aiȭn:** 'life, lifetime', borrowed into Eng. as *(a)eon*; ultimately < PIE $*h_2oi̯u$ 'life, life-force'; see also next. **oudé:** 'and . . . not, nor', combination of *dé* (line 414) and the negative *ou* 'not', also ultimately < $*h_2oi̯u$ 'life' (see §7.25). **ō̃ka:** 'swiftly', related to the adjective *ōkús*, PIE **ōk̑ú-* (Ved. *āśú-* 'swift', Lat. *ōc-ior* 'more swiftly').

Mycenaean text sample

12.66. One of the tablets found at Pylos, PY Ta 722, an inventory of vessels and furniture. "FOOTSTOOL" refers to a pictogram representing a footstool.

ta-ra-nu a-ja-me-no e-re-pa-te-jo a-to-ro-qo i-qo-qe po-ru-po-de-qe po-ni-ke-qe
FOOTSTOOL I
ta-ra-nu a-ja-me-no e-re-pa-te-jo ka-ra-a-pi re-wo-te-jo so-we-no-qe
FOOTSTOOL I
ta-ra-nu a-ja-me-no e-re-pa-te-ja-pi ka-ru-pi
FOOTSTOOL I

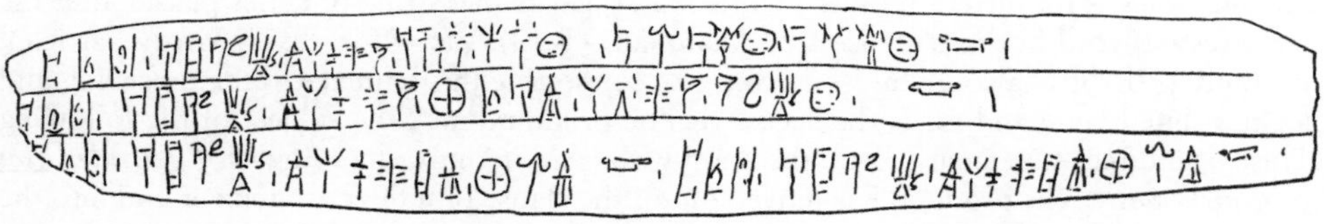

Figure 12.1 The Pylos tablet Ta 722. The "footstool" pictogram is the second-rightmost sign on each line. Drawing from Emmett L. Bennett, Jr., *The Pylos Tablets: Texts of the Inscriptions Found 1939–1954* (Princeton: Princeton University Press, 1954), p. 87. Reproduced by permission of the publisher.

One footstool inlaid with (a picture of) a man, horse, octopus, and palm tree (?) in ivory. One footstool inlaid with ivory lions' heads and grooves (?). One footstool inlaid with ivory nuts (?).

12.66a. Notes. 1. ta-ra-nu: *thrānus* 'footstool', otherwise only in Homer (*thrē̃nus*). **a-ja-me-no:** 'inlaid', mediopassive participle in *-menos* to an otherwise unknown verb. **e-re-pa-te-jo:** *elephanteiōi* '(made of) ivory' (adj.), dat. sing. In the next line, *e-re-pa-te-jo* spells the dat. pl. *elephanteiois.* **a-to-ro-qo:** *anthrōq^{w}ōi* 'man', dat. sing. The Myc. form shows that the *-p-* in the Classical form *ánthrōpos* comes from a labiovelar, but the source of this word is still disputed. **i-qo-qe:** *hiqq^{w}ōi-q^{w}e* 'and horse', dat. sing.; Classical *híppōi te.* The Myc. spelling system is like Latin in showing that this conjunction (= Lat. *-que*) was enclitic and pronounced together with the preceding form as a single word. The *h* and the *i* of Gk. *híppos* are irregular and still unexplained: we would expect **ep(p)os* (PIE **ek̑u̯os*). **po-ru-po-de-qe:** *polupodei-q^{w}e* 'and octopus', dat. sing.; this and the following form are important in showing the inherited dat. sing. ending *-ei* (spelled *-e*), replaced in the rest of Greek (and in some Myc. texts) by the locative *-i*, except for trace survivals like the Cypriot name *Diwei-philos* 'dear to Zeus'. The word for 'octopus' is Classical *polúpous* (*polúpod-*), lit. 'many-footed'. **po-ni-ke-qe:** *phoinikei-q^{w}e*, either 'and palm-tree' or 'and griffin', Classical *phoĩniks.* There follows a pictogram of a footstool.

2. ka-ra-a-pi: *karāhaphi* 'with heads', instr. pl., with Myc. instr. pl. ending *-phi*, surviving in Homer as an instr. ending in both sing. and pl. The first *a* may or may not be real; compare the two Homeric stem forms *karēat-* and *krāat-*. The forms are ultimately from PIE **k̑r̥h$_2$-es* 'head' (> Ved. *śíras*). **re-wo-te-jo:** *lewonteiois* '(in the shape of) lions' (adj.), dat. pl. modifying *elephanteiois.* **so-we-no-qe:** 'and grooves'; probably the same word as Attic *sōlḗn* 'pipe, groove' < **sōlwēn.*

3. e-re-pa-te-ja-pi: *elephanteiāphi*, fem. instr. pl. **ka-ru-pi:** disputed; it could be an instr. pl. of an otherwise unknown *u*-stem noun **karu-* 'nut' (cp. Classical *káruon* 'nut'), or of an otherwise unknown **kalu-* 'flower-bud' (cp. Classical *káluks*). The inscription closes with a fourth line identical to the third.

Cretan text sample

12.67. Excerpt (V 28–44) from the Gortynian law-code, fifth or sixth century BC. Cretan is a Doric dialect with several interesting archaic features.

Ai de k' oi epiballontes oi men leiōnti datēththai ta krēmata, oi de mē, dikaksai ton dikastān epi toil leionsi datēththai ēmen ta krēmata tauta, prin ka dattontai. Ai de

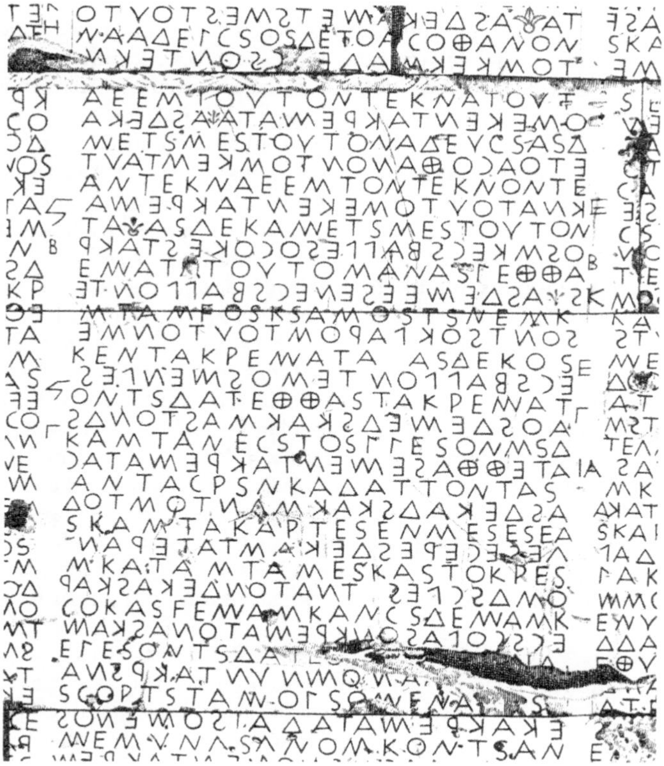

Figure 12.2 Column V of the Gortynian law-code. Line 28 is the second full line of text after the second horizontal seam between two blocks of stone; our excerpt begins after a small space two-thirds through the line. It reads at first left-to-right and then switches direction every line (boustrophedon). The alphabet is among the most archaic of the Greek alphabets, having several letters close in shape to their Phoenician sources. Iota looks like an S, pi like a C, sigma like an M, and theta like a circle enclosing a cross; E and O are used for both short and long *e* and *o*. Drawing reproduced from Margarita Guarducci, *Inscriptiones Creticae opera et consilio Friderici Halbherr collectae,* IV: *Tituli Gortynii* (Rome: Libreria dello Stato, 1950), pp. 142–3 (foldout).

ka dikaksantos tō dikastā kartei enseiēi ē agēi ē perēi, deka statērans katastāsei kai tō krēios diplei. Tnātōn de kai karpō kai wēmās kanpidēmās kēpipolaiōn krēmatōn, ai ka mē leiōnti datē[ththai - - ton dikast]ān omnunta krīnai porti ta mōliomena.

If some of the heirs at law want to divide the property but others do not, the judge shall decree that this property belongs to those wanting to divide it, until they divide it. And if, after the judge has made a judgment, anyone should rush in by force and either drive or carry off (anything), he shall pay ten staters and double the value. And concerning livestock and produce and clothing and ornaments and movable wealth, if they do not want to divide (it) . . . the judge swearing by oath shall decide with reference to the pleadings.

12.67a. Notes (selective). **First sentence. oi:** 'the', masc. nomin. pl., Attic *hoi*. Cretan has lost *h*-. **epiballontes:** 'heirs at law', literally 'the ones devolving', a telescoping of a longer expression like 'the ones to whom the inheritance devolves'. **leiō̃nti:** 'want', 3rd pl. pres. subjunctive of a Doric verb *leíō* or *lō̃* 'I want', of unclear origin. Note retention of *-ti* in the ending (vs. Attic *-si* with loss of nasal, §12.27). **toil:** 'the', dat. pl., assimilated from *tois* to the initial *l*- of the following word (a Cretan, as well as a Homeric, feature). **leionsi:** 'ones wanting', dat. pl. pres. participle; note the retained cluster *-ns-*, characteristic of Cretan and some other Doric dialects. The dative is used to indicate possession. **datēththai:** 'to divide', pres. infinitive middle, with *-thth-* corresponding to *-sth-* in Attic-Ionic. **dattontai:** 'they divide', aor. subjunctive middle, with *-tt-* corresponding to Attic-Ionic *-s(s)-*.

Second sentence. dikaksantos tō dikastā: 'with the judge having decided', genitive absolute construction, corresponding to the ablative absolute in Latin. **kartei:** 'with force', Attic *krátei*. **statērans:** 'staters', a unit of currency, accus. pl., showing Cretan retention of *-ns*.

Third sentence. tnātōn: 'livestock', literally 'things that can perish', genit. pl.; cp. Attic *thnētós* 'mortal', and the phrase *zō̃ia pánta thnētà kaì phutá* 'all living things that die and grow', i.e. 'all living things, animals and plants', in Plato. **wēmās:** 'clothing', genit. sing., a neuter *n*-stem in the nomin.-accus. (*wēma* = Attic *heĩma*, from **u̯es-mn̥*), but the genit. sing. is from an *ā*-stem **wēmā*. Compare Attic *gnō̃ma* 'mark, token' alongside *gnṓmē* 'opinion' (an *ā*-stem). The same is true of *anpidēmās* below. Note the preservation of initial *w*- in Cretan. **kanpidēmās kēpipolaiōn krēmatōn:** the first two *k*-'s are from elided *kai* 'and'; *anpidēmās* (genit. sing.) would be Attic **amphidēmēs*, literally 'a thing that binds around', and *epipolaiōn krēmatōn* is the Cretan equivalent (genit. pl.) of Attic *épipla* 'utensils, movable property'.

omnunta: 'swearing', from *ómnūmi*, cognate with Ved. *ámīti* 'swears' < **h_3emh_3-*. **krīnai:** 'to decide', aor. infinitive, Attic verb *krī́nein*; root **krei-* 'to sift' as in Lat. *crībrum* 'sieve'. **porti:** 'towards, against, in reference to', Homeric *protí*, Attic *prós* (< **proti̯*, the sandhi variant before a vowel); cp. Ved. *práti*. **mōliomena:** 'pleadings', pres. mediopassive participle of *mōliō* 'I plead', a verb known only from Cretan and one gloss in Hesychius.

For Further Reading

The literature on the history of Greek is immense, and familiarity with the Greek alphabet is necessary for using any of it. The most exhaustive comparative grammar is Schwyzer 1939–71; more up-to-date, and the best recent historical grammar, is Rix 1992. In English one may consult Sihler 1995, the most recent combined Greek and Latin historical grammar; an earlier antecedent is the classic Meillet and Vendryes 1968. Two complete etymological dictionaries are available, one in French (Chantraine 1968–80) and one in German (Frisk 1960–72). The best overall description of the historical phonology of Greek is Lejeune 1972. A famous study of the pronunciation of Ancient Greek is Allen 1987, to which can now be added Devine and Stephens 1994, a fascinating if difficult work that attempts to reconstruct all levels of the prosodic phonology of Ancient Greek. Peters 1980 is a famous technical study of the history of the laryngeals in Greek. Useful for Indo-Europeanists is Risch 1974, a catalogue of Homeric forms arranged by formation and with historical commentary. Chantraine 1953–8 is indispensable for serious students of Homeric language, as are two exhaustive commentaries on the *Iliad* and *Odyssey* in English (Kirk et al. 1985–93 and Heubeck et al. 1988–92); the introductory essay to vol. 4 of Kirk 1985–93, by Richard Janko, contains a very useful overview of the study of Homeric diction, poetics, and textual transmission. For the dialects, Buck 1955 is still eminently useful, though it lacks Mycenaean and some of the interpretations have been superseded. A more recently edited selection can be found in Duhoux 1984. Schmitt 1977 contains short but useful summaries of the dialectal developments, including Mycenaean. The standard compendium on Mycenaean, written by the decipherers themselves and including a history of the decipherment, grammar, edition of the entire corpus then known, and vocabulary, is Ventris and Chadwick 1973.

For Review

Know the meaning and significance of the following:

Mycenaean	Epic	psilosis
Linear B	Phoenicians	triple reflex of laryngeals
"Greek Dark Ages"	Grassmann's Law	Koine

Exercises

1 Discuss the fates of the following PIE sounds in Greek:

a **u̯* **b** **h_2* **c** **k^w* **d** **s* **e** **dh* **f** **m̥*

2 Using your knowledge of Greek sound laws, produce the Greek outcomes of the following PIE forms. Do not worry about accents or the Attic-Ionic change of **ā* to **ē*.

a	**$h_1$le-$h_1$ludh-* 'come' (perfect stem)	**g**	**h_2u̯e$h_1$ti* 'blows'
b	**deh_3-rom* 'gift'	**h**	**h_2i-$h_2$eus-oh_2* 'I stay the night'
c	**h_2u̯oideh_2* 'song'	**i**	**$h_2$en$h_1$mos* 'wind'
d	**g^welbhus* 'womb'	**j**	**bheidhoh_2* 'I trust'
e	**tn̥tos* 'stretched'	**k**	**neu̯os* 'new'
f	**bhn̥ĝhus* 'thick'	**l**	**n̥g^wēn* 'gland'

3 Demonstrate that Grassmann's Law in Greek was a separate change from Grassmann's Law in Sanskrit.

4 Using the following three forms, formulate rules for the outcome of the PIE labiovelars in front of nasals: *ómma* 'eye' < **h_3ok^w-mn̥*, *amnós* 'lamb' < *ag^wnos*, *ophnís* 'plowshare' < **u̯og^wh-ni-*.

5 **a** The account given of Grassmann's Law in §12.14 is not quite complete. Expand it to account for the fact that pre-Greek **si-sgh-ō* became Greek *ískhō* 'I hold' and pre-Greek **song^{w}hā* became Greek *omphḗ* 'voice'.

b Greek has a verb *ékhō* 'I have', future *héksō*. Given your answer to **5a**, and given the fact that the future of *gráphō* 'I write' is *grápsō*, reconstruct what the present and future of 'have' would have been before the advent of Greek sound changes.

c From the point of view of your expanded formulation of Grassmann's Law, what is curious about the word *theós* 'god' < **dhh₁s-os*?

6 a Given that PIE **su̯eh₂du-* 'sweet' became Gk. *hēdús*, PIE **su̯e* 'himself, herself' became Gk. *he*, and PIE **su̯eḱuros* 'father-in-law' became *hekurós*, what was the outcome of PIE **su̯-* in Greek?

b The second syllable of the phrase *phíle hekuré* 'dear father-in-law' (*Iliad* 3.172) scans long, which is unexpected for a short vowel in an open syllable. Provide a historical explanation for this scansion.

7 a Mention was made in §12.30 of the so-called "spurious diphthongs." Below are a number of examples of words containing the spurious diphthongs *ei* and *ou*. From this list, determine the sources of these diphthongs. The reconstructions are pre-Greek but not necessarily PIE. Ignore accents.

**esmi* 'I am' > *eimí*
**sems* 'one' (masc.) > *heĩs*
**tons* 'the' (masc. accus. pl.) > *toús*
**kteni̯ō* 'I kill' > *kteínō*
**phtheri̯ō* 'I destroy' > *phtheírō*
**orsā* 'tail' > *ourā́*
**koru̯ā* 'girl' > *koúrē* (Epic, Ionic)
**enemsm̥* 'I doled out' > *éneima*
**edersm̥* 'I flayed' > *édeira*
**kseni̯os* > *kseĩnos* 'guest' (Epic, Ionic)
**ghesr-n̥s* 'hands' (accus. pl.) > *kheĩras*
**oru̯os* 'boundary' > *oũros* (Epic, Ionic)

b The verbal root **du̯ei-* 'fear' formed a perfect. What would the singular and plural perfect stems have been in PIE?

c In Homer, two perfect forms from this verb are 1st sing. *deídoika* (the *-k-* is a late addition) and 1st pl. *deídimen* (*-men* is the inflectional ending). Account for the first syllable *dei-*.

d Account for the vocalism of the first member of the compound *theou-dḗs* 'fearing god' (contrast *theo-trephḗs* 'feeding the gods').

8 In Homer, the thematic verb *hépomai* 'I follow' conjugates in the singular and plural of the present as follows: (singular) *hépomai hépeai hépetai*; (plural) *hepómetha hépesthe hépontai*. The root in PIE and pre-Greek was **sekʷ-*.

a According to Greek sound changes, what ought the 2nd and 3rd singular and the 2nd plural have been?

b Provide an explanation for the actually occurring forms of the 2nd and 3rd singular and the 2nd plural.

9 Below are several words or phrases from the Homeric epics and their metrical scansions, which are unexpected in one or more ways. For each phrase, indicate what is unexpected about the scansion and provide a historical explanation for it.

a *órea niphóenta* 'snowy mountains' (*Odyssey* 19.338; *órea* = 'mountains', *niphóenta* = 'snowy') scans ⏑ ⏑ – ⏑ ⏑ – ⏑
b *éban oĩkónde* 'they went home' (*Odyssey* 1.424; *éban* = 'they went') scans ⏑ – – – ⏑
c *es díphron árnas* 'to the chariot lambs' (*Iliad* 3.310) scans – – – – – (cp. lack of elision in *te arnõn* 'and of the lambs' at 4.158)
d *parékhēi* 'provides' (*Odyssey* 19.113) scans – ⏑ ⏑ (don't worry about the last syllable; *par-* is a preverb meaning 'by'; use your answer to **5b** to help you)

10 Provide a historical explanation of the form *-peza* '-footed' in *argurópeza* 'silver-footed', at the end of line 410 of the excerpt from Homer in §12.65. (Hint: see §6.71.)

11 Account for the boldfaced consonant clusters in the following words by positing a sound change not mentioned in the chapter.

*a**ndr**ós* 'man' (genit. sing.; *h_2*nr-ós*)
*á**mbr**otos* 'immortal' (earliest form **n̥-mr̥tos*, with dialectal change of **r̥* > *ro*)

12 The Greek thematic optative in the first person singular active ended in *-oimi* (e.g. *phér-oimi* 'may I carry'). The Arcadian dialect has a different ending, as in *ekselaun-oia* 'I would drive out'. Which of these endings, *-oimi* or *-oia*, is older from the IE point of view? Provide a historical explanation for both forms.

PIE Vocabulary IV: The Body

*h_3*ek*^{w}- 'EYE; to see': Lat. *oc-ulus*, OCS *oči* (dual)
*h_3*bhrū-* 'BROW': Ved. *bhrū́-*, Gk. *ophrū̃s*
*h_2*ous-*, *h_2*eus-* 'EAR': Gk. *oũs*, Lat. *auris*
**nas-* 'NOSE': Ved. *nas-*, Lat. *nāris*, OCS *nosŭ*
**dn̥ĝhū-* 'TONGUE': Lat. *lingua* (Archaic *dingua*), OIr. *teng*
*h_1*dont-* 'TOOTH': Ved. *dant-*, Gk. *odṓn* (*odónt-*), Lat. *dēns* (*dent-*)
**ĝonu* 'KNEE': Ved. *jā́nu*, Gk. *gónu*, Lat. *genū*
**pod-*, **ped-* 'FOOT': Ved. *pad-*, Gk. *poús* (*pod-*), Lat. *pēs* (*ped-*)
**k̂erd-* 'HEART': Hitt. *kard-*, Gk. *kardíā*, Lat. *cor* (*cord-*)
**esh*$_2$*r̥* 'blood': Hitt. *ēšhar*, Gk. *éar*, Latv. *asins*
**dak̂ru-* 'TEAR': Gk. *dákru*, Lat. *lacruma*
*h_2*ost-* 'bone': Hitt. *ḫastāi-*, Gk. *ostéon*, Lat. *os*
*h_1*orĝhi-* 'testicle': Av. *ərəzi-*, Arm. *orji-*, Gk. *órkhis*, Alb. *herdhe*
**ors-* 'ARSE': Hitt. *ārraš*, Gk. *ourā́* 'tail'

13 Italic

Introduction

13.1. The Italic languages comprise most of the ancient Indo-European languages of Italy, as well as the modern-day descendants of one of those languages, namely Latin. Though Latin was destined to outshine its more obscure sister languages, its origins were humble. A casual observer of the linguistic and cultural milieu of early first-millennium-BC Italy would not have been led to predict greater fortunes for it than for its neighboring relatives; it was just one of a number of minor local languages in the center of the Italian peninsula spoken by predominantly pastoral tribes living in small agricultural settlements.

The Italic peoples were not indigenous to Italy, but arrived from the north probably by 1000 BC and slowly worked their way southward. North and central Italy had earlier been settled by successive waves of immigrants from across the Alps, while the southern regions, including Sicily, were partly under different cultural influence, being in contact with Aegean peoples to the east at least as early as the Sicilian Copper Age (c. 2500–2000 BC). Archaeological evidence points to widespread cultural exchange throughout the region, making it all the more difficult to link the known Italic peoples of historical times with specific prehistoric cultures.

By the early eighth century BC, Greek colonists from Chalcis in Euboea (northeastern Greece) had settled in Pithekoussai (modern Ischia, an island off the Italian coast by the Bay of Naples) and Cumae (on the coast near Naples), as well as other areas of the southern Italian coast and Sicily. These colonists brought a western Greek form of the alphabet with them (see §12.7), which soon spread rapidly into Italy. Alphabetic Greek inscriptions – among the oldest known – have been found on Italian soil dating to the eighth century BC, and the first inscriptions in the non-Greek languages of Italy appear around the same time or even slightly before. (One recently discovered inscription from Gabii, an ancient town near Rome, is already from c. 770 BC; it reads *euoi*, and although the language is uncertain, it is the oldest piece of alphabetic writing yet discovered that has vowels.)

13.2. Early on the Greeks came into contact with the southernmost settlements of the **Etruscans**, an ancient people whose homeland, Etruria (modern Tuscany), was located in northwestern Italy, bordering on Latium (to its south) and Umbria (to its east). Their culture was the dominant one in Italy from about the eighth century BC on; by the sixth century, Etruscan settlements flourished along most of the length of the western part of the peninsula. From the Greeks the Etruscans picked up the alphabet and many other aspects of Greek culture. The Etruscans never developed a centralized state, but their impact on the fledgling civilization of the Romans was tremendous. Among other things, the Romans and many other peoples of Italy may have the Etruscans to thank for their knowledge of the alphabet. As Rome's power grew, the culture of the Etruscans waned, disappearing by about 100 BC. Etruscan slowly died out as well over the course of the next one to two centuries; the first-century-AD emperor Claudius (died 54) is said to have written a dictionary of the language based on interviews with the last surviving speakers. But it may have continued to be used in religious rituals for some time after that.

The Etruscan language was not Italic, nor even Indo-European. Although there is no dearth of inscriptions (over 13,000 have been found), they are mostly short dedicatory or funeral inscriptions containing only proper names, and the few longer texts are not well understood. The origin of the Etruscans, in fact, has been controversial since ancient times, with one school claiming they came to Italy from Asia Minor and another claiming they were a pre-Indo-European people indigenous to Italy. On the one hand, the testimony of the Greek historian Herodotus (who claimed they came from Anatolia), certain cultural practices (such as divination by inspection of the liver of a sacrificial animal), the presence of some Anatolian loanwords in Etruscan, and some modern genetic studies support the theory of an origin from Asia Minor. On the other hand, there is no archaeological evidence of a migration, and Etruscan culture seems to grow organically from an earlier culture of north-central Italy called Villanovan. The existence of **Lemnian**, a language very similar to Etruscan and preserved on a stele and a few minor vase inscriptions on Lemnos (an island off the coast of Asia Minor) from the seventh or sixth century BC, does not settle the issue: it may have been simply the language of a group of colonists from Italy. Aside from Lemnian, the only relative of Etruscan is **Raetic**, a very similar language spoken in extreme northern Italy and neighboring areas.

13.3. Latin and the languages most closely related to it (of which only Faliscan is known) form the **Latino-Faliscan** branch of Italic and were spoken originally in a small region of west-central Italy south of Etruria. The languages comprising the other subbranch of Italic, **Sabellic** (also known as Osco-Umbrian), were spoken over a considerably larger area of central and later southern Italy. Given the significant differences between the two linguistic groups already in the sixth century BC, Italic linguistic unity probably ended at the close of the second millennium BC. Some scholars have given these differences even greater weight and reject the notion of a single Proto-Italic language; according to this opinion, Latino-Faliscan and Sabellic belong to two separate branches of IE that partially converged due to later mutual influence. But this is a controversial view, and we shall assume a Common Italic stage in all that follows.

13.4. The seventh century BC saw the first inscriptions in Latin, and by the end of the sixth century the alphabet had spread eastward through Italy to the other coast, where the Piceni lived (§13.75), and northeastward into the territory of the Veneti (see below). The Samnites (whose language we call Oscan) and the Umbrians probably had the alphabet at this point also, but our earliest records in these languages come a bit later. As is customary in the field of Italic philology, when citing

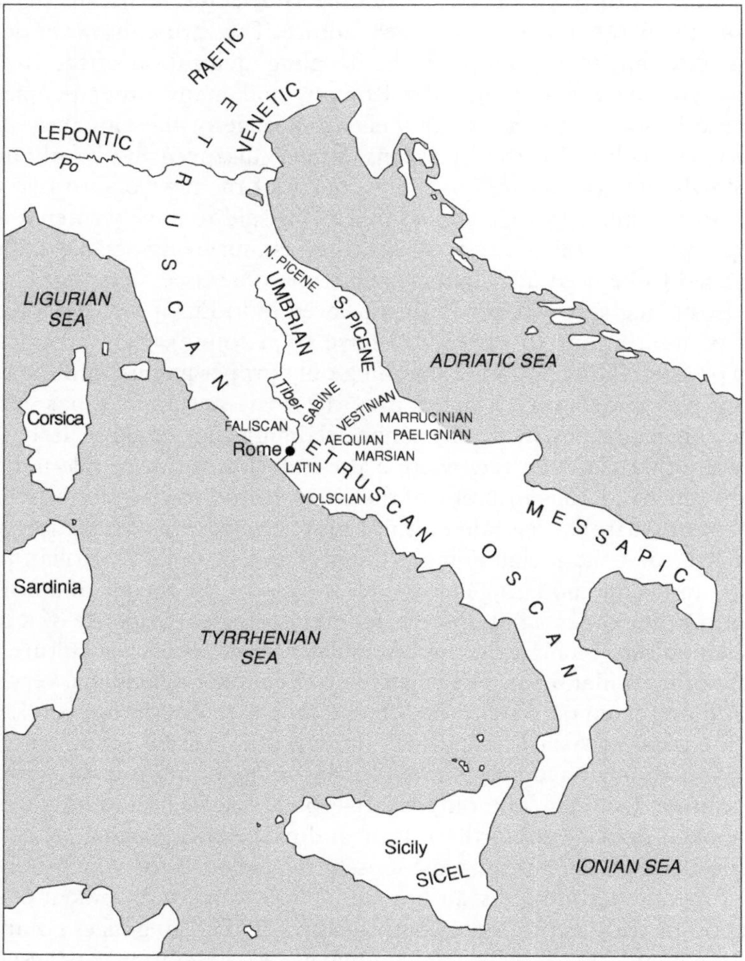

Map 13.1 Languages of ancient Italy before Roman expansion

forms from a non-Latin inscription in a local non-Latin alphabet, boldface will be used.

In the extreme northeast of Italy lived a people known in ancient times as the Veneti, along the northern and northwestern shores of the Adriatic Sea. Their language, **Venetic**, bears close affinities with Italic and may belong to it but is not known well enough for this to be certain. It is treated in chapter 20.

"Italo-Celtic"

13.5. Italic shares several innovative features with Celtic, such as the *o*-stem genitive singular in *-*ī* (e.g., Lat. *uir-ī* 'of a man', Ogam Irish *maq(q)i* 'of the son'), an innovated conglomerate superlative suffix _*-is-m̥mo-_ (as in Lat. _maximus_ 'greatest' < _*mag(i)samos_ < _*mag-is-m̥mo-_, Gaulish place-name _Ouxisamē_ 'highest' < _*ups-is-m̥mo-_, cp. Gk. _hups-ēlós_ 'high'), and a subjunctive morpheme _*-ā-_ (as in Archaic Latin _fer-ā-t_ 'he may carry', Old Irish _beraid_ 'he may carry'). These shared features have led many Indo-Europeanists to posit an "Italo-Celtic" subgroup or dialect area of Indo-European. However, the hypothesis of an Italo-Celtic unity has never gained universal approval.

From PIE to Italic

Phonology

13.6. Stops. Italic is a centum branch, and therefore the palatal stops and the plain velars fell together as plain velars, as in the word _centum_ itself, Latin for '100', from PIE _*k̂m̥tom_ (the _c_ in the spelling of the word was pronounced _k_ in pre-imperial Latin, still surviving today in Sardinian: see §13.49 below). The remaining PIE plain voiceless and voiced stops remained unchanged in Italic. The labiovelars have divergent developments in Latino-Faliscan and Sabellic (§§13.24 and 61).

The characteristic look of the Italic languages is due partly to the widespread presence of the voiceless fricative _f_, which is the most common reflex of the voiced aspirates across the family. This fricative also arose due to a variety of developments specific to individual Italic languages, especially involving _s_ in certain consonant clusters, such as the change of initial _*sr-_ to _fr-_ in Latin and the change of _*ns_ to _f_ in some contexts in Sabellic.

13.7. Dental-plus-dental sequences in the parent language became _*ss_ in Italic, as in Lat. _fissus_ 'split' < _*bhid-to-_. The consonant cluster _*-tl-_ became _*-kl-_, as in Osc. **puklum** (accus. sing.) 'son' < _*putlo-_ and Lat. _pōculum_ 'cup' (earlier _pōclum_, which is how the word scans in early Latin poetry) < _*pōtlom_. It is not infrequently claimed that the change _*tl_ > _*kl_ postdated the Common Italic period, the main piece of evidence being the Etruscan word _putlumza_, purportedly a borrowing of _*pōtlom_, the prehistoric ancestor of Lat. _pōculum_. However, this is highly uncertain for various reasons (not the least being that the Etruscan word appears in a single early inscription whose interpretation is uncertain).

13.8. Resonants. The consonantal liquids, nasals, and glides remain unchanged: Osc. **anamúm** 'breath' (_*$h_2$enh$_1$mo-_), Lat. _alter_ 'the other' (_*al-tero-_), _iugum_ 'yoke' (_*i̯ugom_), Umbr. _uiro_ 'men' (_*u̯ir-o-_). Syllabic liquids developed a prothetic _o_ before them (_or ol_), whereas syllabic nasals developed an _e_ (_em en_): Lat. _cord-_ 'heart' (_*k̂r̥d-_), _**mollis**_ 'soft' (_*ml̥d-u̯i-_), _**septem**_ 'seven' (_*septm̥_), _**nōmen**_ 'name' (_*$h_1$neh$_3$mn̥_). The outcome of syllabic nasals in word-initial syllables in Sabellic may have been different, however. According to a widely held view, the outcome there was _an_ and _am_, as in Osc. **fangvam** (accus.) 'tongue' (cp. Lat. _lingua_, Archaic Lat. _dingua_, PIE _*dn̥ĝhu-_) and Umbr. _ander_ 'between' (cp. Lat. _inter_, PIE _*n̥ter_). This view is not universally accepted, as the relevant forms have alternate explanations and it adds some unnecessary and unlikely complications to Italic historical phonology.

13.9. Sibilants. Proto-Italic appears to have preserved the sibilant *s in most positions, but in the later histories of the daughter languages it was often subject to changes. Most famous among these was *rhotacism*, whereby *s* became voiced to *z* and then became *r* (see §§13.30, 13.68), which affected (to varying degrees) Latin, Umbrian, and Oscan. In consonant clusters, especially involving resonants, *s* tended to be unstable, especially in Latin; see §13.31.

13.10. Laryngeals. The laryngeals were lost in their non-vocalized form, but the vocalized laryngeals are preserved as *a*, as in Lat. *status* 'stood' (*sth_2-to-), *datus* 'given' (*dh_3-to-), and Osc. **anamúm** 'breath' (*h_2enh_1mo-; in Lat. *anima* 'breath' the internal vowel weakened to *-i-* as per §13.32). The outcome of syllabic resonant plus laryngeal (the "long" syllabic resonants) was *Rā* or *aRa*, the latter probably when under the accent: Lat. *(g)nātus* 'born' (*$\hat{g}\d{n}h_1$-tó-), *strātus* 'strewn' (*$st\d{r}h_3$-tó-), and *palma* 'palm' from earlier *palama (*$p\d{l}h_2$-meh_2, cp. Gk. *palámē*).

13.11. Vowels. Except for *eu, which fell together with *ou, the vowels and diphthongs were all preserved intact and are kept most faithfully in Oscan. In Latin, they subsequently underwent significant modification; see §§13.32ff. The mobile pitch-accent of PIE (§§3.30ff.) was replaced by a stress-accent on the first syllable of the word in Italic. This situation still obtained in early Latin, but was later replaced by the classical stress pattern (see §13.36 below).

Verbal morphology

13.12. Of considerable interest are the substantial innovations in the verbal system, which will be described here at some length, with certain details left for later. Broadly, Italic reorganized (1) the PIE present formations into a neat system of four conjugations, each characterized by a particular stem-vowel to which the personal endings were added; and (2) the PIE tense-aspect system into one based on the aspectual opposition between imperfective and perfective, with each of these having a future and a past tense.

The four conjugations

13.13. With few exceptions, all Italic verbs belong to one of four classes or conjugations characterized by the stem-vowels *ā*, *ē*, *e*, and *ī*. Compare:

Conj.	Latin	Oscan	Umbrian
I	*port-ā-re* 'to carry'	**faam-a-t** 'commands'	*port-a-tu* 'let him carry'
II	*hab-ē-re* 'to have'	**fat-í-um** 'to speak'	*hab-e* 'has'
III	*sist-e-re* 'to place'	*did-e-st* 'he will give'	**sest-e** 'you place'
IV	*aud-ī-re* 'to hear'	**sakruv-i-t** 'consecrates'	*persnimu* 'pray!'

The rise of the conjugational system was due almost entirely to sound change. (All the examples in the following discussion are taken from Latin.) The first conjugation stem-vowel *-ā-* comes primarily from contraction of the sequence *-ā-i̯e-, which itself comes from various sources: denominative verbs from *ā*-stem nouns and adjectives (e.g. *cūrā-re* 'to take care' from *cūra* 'care'), factitive verbs from *o*-stems (e.g. *nouā-re* 'to make new' < **neu̯-eh₂-i̯e-*, cp. Hitt. *new-aḫḫ-*), and *-*i̯e/o*-presents from other types of verbs (e.g. *tonā-re* 'to thunder' < **(s)tonh₂-i̯e-*).

The second conjugation stem-vowel -*ē*- comes from the contraction of the causative suffix *-*éi̯e*- (§5.35, e.g. *mon-ē-re* 'warn' < **mon-éi̯e-*, literally 'cause to think') and from the stative suffix *-*eh₁-i̯e*- (§5.37, e.g. *alb-ē-re* 'to be white' and *sed-ē-re* 'to be sitting').

The third conjugation consists mostly of old thematic presents of various kinds (e.g. *ag-e-re* 'to drive, do' < **h₂eĝ-e-*; *bib-e-re* 'to drink' < **pi-ph₃-e-*; *albēsc-e-re* 'to grow white' < **albh-eh₁-sk̂e-*), as well as a number of originally athematic presents that later became thematized, such as *find-e-re* 'split' < **bhi-n-d-*.

Presents formed with the suffix *-*i̯e/o*- added directly to the root have a more complicated history than the other kinds of *-*i̯e/o*-presents treated above. Such presents wound up in the fourth conjugation if the root they were added to was heavy, that is, ended in a consonant cluster, had a long vowel or diphthong, or consisted of two syllables (e.g. *sanc-ī-re* 'to ratify' < **sank-i̯e-*, *sepel-ī-re* 'to bury' < **sepel-i̯e-*). Otherwise they fell into a special class of the third conjugation that will be treated in §13.39 below, such as *fug-e-re* 'flee' < **bhug-i̯e-*.

The rest of the fourth conjugation consists of denominatives from both *i*-stems and *o*-stems (the first e.g. in *moll-ī-re* 'to soften' < *mollis* 'soft'; the second e.g. in *seru-ī-re* 'be a servant (to), serve' < *seruus* 'slave').

13.14. Very few athematic verbs still inflect athematically in Italic; relics include the Latin verbs *es-se* 'to be', *ī-re* 'to go', and *uel-le* 'to want'.

The Italic tense-aspect system

13.15. The Italic tense-aspect system was based on an opposition between imperfective and perfective, each having a future and a past tense. The basic imperfective tense was the present (Lat. *portō* 'I carry, am carrying'), whose corresponding past tense was the imperfect (*portābam* 'I was carrying, used to carry') and whose future was the ordinary future (*portābō* 'I will carry'). The basic perfective tense was the perfect (*portāuī* 'I carried, have carried'), whose past tense was the pluperfect (*portāueram* 'I had carried') and whose future was the future perfect (*portāuerō* 'I shall have carried'). Each of these tenses except the two futures was also fitted out with a subjunctive.

The imperfect and future

13.16. The PIE imperfect was lost without a trace in Italic. A suffixal morpheme *-*f*-, an Italic invention derived from the PIE root **bhuH*- 'be, become', was used to form the imperfect and (in Latino-Faliscan only) the future. The imperfect used the stem *-*fā*-, while the future used the stem *-*fe*- (probably from an old subjunctive **bhu(H)-e-*; see directly below): Lat. imperfect *port-ā-bat* 'he was carrying', Umbr. **fu-fans** 'they were'; Lat. future *port-ā-bit* 'he will carry', Fal. *care-fo* 'I will do without'. The future is also formed (in Sabellic exclusively, and in Latin vestigially) with the suffix -*s*-, e.g. Archaic Lat. *fax-ō* 'I will do' (**fak-s-*), Osc. *dide-s-t* 'he will give', Umbr. **prupeha-s-t** 'he will purify before'. This is a continuation of one of the PIE future or desiderative formations in *-*s*- (§§5.39ff.). Finally, the old PIE subjunctive, where it survives, became a future in Italic: for example, the PIE thematic verb *h_2eĝ-e-* 'drive' formed a subjunctive with stem *h_2eĝ-e-e-*, which became the future stem *ag-ē-* 'will drive' of the Latin verb *agere* 'to drive'. Note also the future *erit* 'he will be' (Archaic Lat. *esed*) from the athematic subjunctive **$h_1$es-e-* (cp. Ved. *ásati*).

The Italic imperfect in *-*fā-*, as well as forms like the Latin imperfect stem *erā-* 'was', attest to the presence of a formation known as the *ā*-preterite. Its origins are unclear, though it has been compared to scattered past-tense forms elsewhere in the family that have a stem in *-ā-*, such as Doric Greek *erruā* 'it flowed' and Old Church Slavonic aorists like *sŭpa-* 'slept'.

The perfect system

13.17. The Italic perfect is a conglomeration of the IE perfect and aorist. All the Italic languages have a reduplicated perfect (Lat. *dedit* 'he gave', Fal. *peparai* 'I gave birth to', Osc. perfect subjunctive *fefacid* 'he might make', Umbr. *dede* 'he gave'), a non-reduplicated or de-reduplicated perfect (Osc. **(kúm-)bened** 'agreed', Umbr. *benust* 'will have come', Lat. *tulī* 'I brought'), and a long-vowel perfect (Lat. *ēgit* 'he drove, did', Osc. *hipid* 'had' [< **hēb-*], Umbr. **(pru-)sikurent** 'they will have announced'). The old stative meaning of the perfect is still visible in such forms as Lat. *meminī* 'I remember' (PIE **me-mon-*), but as a rule the Italic perfect is a past tense.

13.18. The pluperfect and future perfect were both formed with a morpheme *-*s-*. The pluperfect, attested only in Latin, can be exemplified by Lat. *fu-eram* 'I had been' from earlier **fu-isam*. The future perfect, which happens to be particularly well attested in Sabellic, can be exemplified by Lat. *fu-erit* (< earlier **fu-iset*) 'he will have been' and Osc. *fefacust* 'he will have done'.

The subjunctive

13.19. The Italic subjunctive is not a continuation of the PIE subjunctive, which became a future (see above). There are at least three subjunctive morphemes found in Italic, of which one continues the PIE athematic optative and the other two are of unknown origin. Their distribution is complex and need not be entered into here in detail; a few examples will suffice. The PIE optative morpheme is seen, with ablaut still intact, in Archaic Lat. *siēs* 'may you be' (**h_1s-i̯eh_1-s*), pl. *sītis* 'may you [pl.] be' (**h_1s-ih_1-te-*); but the zero-grade *-ī-* was generalized elsewhere. The so-called *ā*-subjunctive, also found in Celtic, is seen for example in the Lat. pres. subj. *habe-ā-s* '(that) you have' and the Osc. pres. subj. **pútí-a-d** '(that) he be able'. Finally, the *ē*-subjunctive, which has no sure analogues outside Italic, is seen for example in the Lat. imperfect subj. *es-sē-s* 'you would be' and the Umbr. perfect subj. *herii-ei* 'he should want'.

Personal endings

13.20. The old distinction between primary and secondary personal endings has traces in the third person, such as in Faliscan *fifiqod* 'they fashioned', with *-od* from secondary *-*ont* and not primary *-*onti*. The dual has disappeared. Like Anatolian, Tocharian, and Celtic, Italic generalized PIE *-*r* as the marker of the mediopassive (called simply the passive in Italic linguistics). Some verbs, such as *sequor* 'I follow', inflected only in the passive, and are called "deponent" in traditional Latin grammar; these are often the descendants of PIE middle verbs (see §5.5).

Participles and infinitives

13.21. The IE present active participle in *-*nt-* is well preserved, as in Lat. *port-ant-* 'carrying', but only traces are found of the mediopassive participle in *-*m(h₁)no-* (such as *alumnus* 'nursling, foster-son', literally 'one [being] nurtured'). The PIE infinitive in *-*dhi̯-* (§5.58) is found in Sabellic (see below §13.64). The other Italic active infinitives, *-se* in Latin (e.g. *es-se* 'to be') and *-*om* in Sabellic (e.g. Umbr. *er-om* 'to be'), descend from nominal formations and are not ancient. The Italic perfect passive participle in *-*to-*, such as Lat. *cap-tus* 'taken' and Umbr. *uirseto* 'seen' (< **u̯id-ē-to-*), directly continues the PIE verbal adjective in *-*tó-* (§5.61). Italic also created a future passive participle or gerundive in *-*nd-*, of unclear origin: Lat. *dēlendus* '(about) to be destroyed', Osc. **úpsannam** 'to be done'.

Nominal morphology

13.22. All the PIE nominal stem-classes are preserved in Italic, including even traces of the archaic *r/n*-stems (§6.31), as in Lat. *femur* 'thigh', stem *femin-*, and Umbrian **utur** 'water', stem *un-* (< **utn-*). The Latino-Faliscan and Sabellic branches differ in certain details of nominal inflection, but as an aggregate they show that Italic inherited the PIE case-endings with little change. The instrumental had been lost by the historical period (though examples still survive in adverbial use, such as Lat. *bene* 'well') and its functions taken over by the ablative. The functions of the locative, too, were mostly taken over by the ablative, though it still survives as a productive separate case in place-names and certain nouns, e.g. Lat. *Rōmae* 'in Rome', *rūrī* 'in the country', Osc. **mefiaí víaí** 'in the middle of the road'. The final dental of the *o*-stem ablative singular ending *-*ōt* (§6.49) spread to the ablative of all the declensions: Osc. *toutad* 'by the people', Archaic Lat. *magistrātūd* 'with the office of a magistrate'. There is no dual.

13.23. As noted above, a peculiarity that Latino-Faliscan *o*-stem nouns share with Venetic, Messapic, and Celtic is a genitive singular ending *-*ī* (e.g. Lat. *uir-ī* 'of a man', Fal. *Marci* 'of Marcus'), which is of uncertain origin. Alongside this, however, the more familiar genitive in *-*osi̯o* was inherited as well, but preserved only in proper names, as in Archaic Latin *Popliosio Valesiosio* 'of Publius Valerius' and Faliscan *Kaisiosio* 'of Kaisios'. Neither occurs in Sabellic.

Latino-Faliscan

13.24. The Latino-Faliscan subbranch of Italic comprised Latin and Faliscan. In the mid-first millennium BC they were neighboring languages in a small area of west-central Italy. Because of the few remains in Faliscan, Latin is usually our only witness for Latino-Faliscan innovations. One difference between Latino-Faliscan and Sabellic that is immediately diagnostic is the divergent treatment of the labiovelars: they became labial stops in Sabellic (*k^w > *p*, *g^w > *b*) but not in Latino-Faliscan (*k^w remained, and *g^w > *u̯*). Thus for instance *k^we 'and' became Latin *-que* and Faliscan *-cue*, but Osc. *-pe*. See also §13.61.

Latin

13.25. Latin derives its name from Latium, a region of west-central Italy cut through by the lower part of the river Tiber as it flows westward to the Tyrrhenian Sea. One of the tribes in this area, around the Alban Hills, were the Latini, who eventually became dominant in central Italy and beyond.

The period of Latin from the earliest inscriptions to about the mid-second century BC is called **Archaic Latin** (also Old Latin). Some scholars use the term **Very Old Latin** for the language's first remains, which are found in scattered inscriptions dating from the last quarter of the seventh century BC to the fifth century BC. Inscriptions become relatively copious only in the third century BC, a century that also marks the beginning of preserved Latin literature. The earliest surviving literary fragments come from Livius Andronicus (born c. 284 BC); he is traditionally credited with being the first to set the Latin language to Greek meters. About two generations later came the comic playwright Plautus (254?–184? BC), the first author whose works survive in considerable quantity; his plays are followed by those of Terence (c. 195–159 BC). Also important for this time are such poets as Ennius, Accius, and Lucilius; of their works we unfortunately possess only single lines or short passages quoted by later writers. Latin prose begins with Cato the Elder (234–149 BC), whose book on agriculture, *Dē Agrī Cultūrā*, is of immense value for historians of Latin language, culture, and religion.

13.26. The Archaic period was followed by the period of **Classical Latin**, traditionally divided into the Golden and Silver Ages. The Golden Age, lasting until the death of the poet Ovid in AD 17, saw for example the orations and other works of Cicero; the military commentaries of Caesar; the histories of Livy; and the poetry of Lucretius, Catullus, Horace, and Vergil. The Silver Age, dating until the death of the emperor Marcus Aurelius in 180, contains such literature as the tragedies and philosophical writings of Seneca; the novel *Satyricon* of Petronius; the *Natural History* of Pliny the Elder; the satires of Juvenal; and the histories of Tacitus and Suetonius. After this period came **Late Latin**, during which a large amount of early Christian literature was written, as by St. Augustine and St. Jerome.

Mention should be made here of the lexicographer Sextus Pompeius Festus, who lived and wrote sometime between AD 100 and 400. His *On the Meaning of Words* is an enormously important dictionary of archaic words and forms, containing a wealth of information also on older Roman legal and religious practice. It survives only in fragments, but we also have an abridged version of the whole work made by the eighth-century Lombard historian Paul the Deacon.

During this time the colloquial Latin spoken throughout the Empire, known as **Vulgar Latin,** was beginning to develop into the different dialects that would later become the Romance languages. See §§13.44ff. below.

Phonological developments of Latin

Consonants

13.27. The main hallmark of Latin consonantism that sets it apart from its sister Italic languages, including the closely related Faliscan, is the outcome of the PIE voiced aspirates in word-internal position. In the other Italic dialects, these simply show up written as *f*. In Latin, that is the usual outcome word-initially, but word-internally the outcome is typically a voiced stop, as in ***nebula*** 'cloud' < **nebh-oleh₂*, ***medius*** 'middle' < **medhii̯o-*, ***angustus*** 'narrow' < **anĝhos-*, and ***ninguit*** 'it snows' < **sni-n-gʷh-eti*. The details of these developments are left as an exercise at the end of this chapter.

13.28. Among the other changes to affect stops may be mentioned the loss of word-final *-d* after long vowels, as in the Classical Latin *o*-stem ablative sing. *-ō* from earlier *-ōd* (cp. Archaic *Gnaiuōd* 'from Gnaeus'). Also, as noted in §13.24, PIE **gʷ* became the glide *u̯*, as in *ueniō* 'I come' < **gʷem-i̯ō*.

13.29. Consonant clusters. Among the many changes to consonant clusters, a few of special interest will be briefly mentioned. Voiced stops were lost before **i̯* or assimilated to it, as in the name of the god Jupiter, *Iūpiter*, stem *Iou-*, from **di̯eu̯-* (Archaic genitive sing. *Diouos* 'of Jove') and in the comparative *maior* 'greater' (really *maiior*, with a geminate glide from the consonant cluster of earlier **magi̯os-*). The similar cluster **du̯* became *b* at the beginning of a word, as in ***bellum*** 'war' (Archaic and poetic ***duellum***), and *u̯* word-internally, as in *suāuis* 'sweet' < **su̯ādu̯is*.

13.30. Rhotacism and other changes to *s*. Latin famously changed the sibilant *s* to *r* between vowels, a change known as *rhotacism*. Thus *mūs* 'mouse' has the plural *mūrēs* (< **mūs-ēs*), *genus* 'kind, race' (**genos*) has the plural *genera* (**genesa*), and the infinitive *-se* of *es-se* 'to be' appears as *-re* in vowel-stem verbs such as *amā-re* 'to love' and *dūce-re* 'to lead'. This change happened during the historical period; early inscriptions still have intervocalic *s* (e.g. Archaic *iouesat* 'swears', Classical *iūrat*). Cicero noted in a letter that a certain Papirius Crassus officially changed the spelling of his name from Papisius in 339 BC, so the change probably happened not long before then.

13.31. In many other environments, especially next to a resonant, **s* assimilated, disappeared, or was changed to another sound. It disappeared in words beginning **sm-*, **sn-*, and **sl-*, as in *mīrus* 'wonderful' < **smei-ro-* (contrast Eng. *smile* < **smei-l-*), *nix* (stem *niu-*) 'snow' < **snigʷh-* (contrast Eng. *snow*, Russ. *sneg*), and *laxus* 'slack' < **slag-so-* < **slh₁g-* (contrast Eng. *slack*). The group **sr* became *fr* word-initially (as in *frīgus* 'chill' < **srīg-*) but *br* word-internally (as in *cōn-sobrīnus* 'cousin' < **-su̯esr-*, zero-grade of **su̯esōr* 'sister'). In clusters where the liquid was first and the *s* second, the *s* assimilated to the liquid, a well-known example being *terra* 'land, earth' from **tersā*, root **ters-* 'dry'. Originally the word was simply the adjective 'dry', metonymically transferred to the ground – an example of what is called a *transferred epithet*.

Mention may also be made of the voiced allophone **z* in consonant clusters: in Latin this disappeared with compensatory lengthening of the preceding vowel, as in *nīdus* 'nest' < **nizdos.*

Vowels

13.32. As stated above, Italic transformed the mobile accent system of PIE into a system characterized by stress on initial syllables. In Latin, this resulted in the weakening of vowels in non-initial syllables. The rules are rather complex, but in general terms a short vowel in an open syllable was weakened eventually to *i*. Thus compare ***amīcus*** 'friend' with ***inimīcus*** 'enemy', ***legō*** 'I choose' with ***colligō*** 'I collect', and ***locus*** 'place' with ***īlicō*** 'on the spot, right away'. In closed syllables, *a* was weakened to *e*, as in ***affectus*** 'affected' beside ***factus*** 'done', ***ineptus*** 'inept' beside ***aptus*** 'apt', while *o* was weakened to *u*, as in ***onustus*** 'burdensome' from **onos* 'burden' (Classical *onus*). In final syllables, the same rules usually apply, as in *artifex* 'craftsman' from **arti-fak-s* (from the bases *art-* 'skill' and *fac-* 'make, do') and ***seruus*** 'slave' from earlier (Archaic) ***seruos***; but before *-s* and *-t*, *e* weakened to *i*, as in ***legis*** 'you (sing.) lead' and ***legit*** 'he leads' from **leges* and **leget* (with the thematic vowel **-e-*). In inscriptions from the Archaic period, many of these vowel weakenings had not yet happened.

13.33. Among some of the many other changes to vowels, two more may also be mentioned. An original *o* became *u* before final consonants: contrast Archaic Latin ***malos*** 'bad' (nomin. sing.) with Classical ***malus***, and Archaic ***seruom*** 'slave' (accus. sing.) with ***seruum***. An old *e* before nasals usually became raised to *i*, as in the preposition ***in*** 'in' from older ***en*** (preserved in inscriptions). The opposite change *i > e* happened before **z* from rhotacized *s*: genit. sing. *cineris* 'of ash' < **kinizes* < **kinises* (compare nomin. sing. *cinis*).

13.34. Long vowels and diphthongs. Long vowels were shortened in the late Archaic period in final syllables before any consonant except *s*. Thus contrast the 2nd sing. subjunctive *dūcās* '[that] you carry' with the 1st and 3rd singulars *dūcam* and *dūcat*.

13.35. Several of the old diphthongs were monophthongized to long vowels in Latin; those that survived were *ai* (spelled *ae* after the Archaic period), *au*, and in some cases, *oi* (spelled *oe*). The diphthong *ei* became *ī* (as in the dative ending of *patr-ī* 'for the father', cp. Archaic *Castorei* 'for Castor'), while *oi* became either *ī* (e.g. in the ablative pl. of *o*-stems, e.g. Classical *meīs sociīs* 'with my companions' but Archaic *meois sokiois*) or *ū* (as in *ūnus* 'one', Archaic accus. sing. *oino*[*m*]); it also sometimes remained unchanged, as in *foedus* 'treaty' and *moenia* 'walls'. PIE **eu* fell together with **ou* in Italic (§13.11), and **ou* later became *ū*, as in *ūrere* 'to burn' (**$h_1$eus-e-*) and *iūmenta* 'teams (of oxen)' < Archaic *iouxmenta*.

13.36. Stress. The vowel weakenings in non-initial syllables discussed above indicate that the stress in early Latin was still on the first syllable, as in Italic (§13.11). In Classical Latin, however, the stress fell on the antepenult (third-to-last syllable) unless the following syllable was heavy. Thus *ánima* 'breath', *amā́bitur* 'he will be loved', and *adipīscíminī* 'you (pl.) are approaching' were all stressed on the antepenult, while *deā́rum* 'of goddesses', *amābúntur* 'they will be loved', and *adipī́scor*

'I approach' were stressed on the penult. Latin borrowings into English are often stressed according to these rules.

Morphological developments of Latin

Latin morphology differs little from the picture outlined above for Common Italic. We may mention a few details.

Nouns

13.37. Traditional Latin grammar divides nouns into five declensions. The first continues the PIE *ā*-stems and consists mostly of feminines. The second continues the *o*-stems, and consists mostly of masculines and neuters. The third continues the consonant stems as well as the *i*-stems, while the *u*-stems become the Latin fourth declension. The fifth declension is not an inherited type, but a medley of various formations that, due to sound change, all came to have a stem in *-ē-*. The five declensions may all be illustrated by the paradigms given below of the nouns *terra* 'land', ***lupus*** 'wolf', ***bellum*** 'war' (neuter; given where different from *lupus*), *rēx* 'king' (and for *i*-stem forms, ***turris*** 'tower', where different), ***currus*** 'chariot' (and neuter *cornū* 'horn'), and *diēs* 'day'. Endings that are Archaic or poetic are given in parentheses:

		I	II	III	IV	V
sg.	N	*terr-a*	*lup-us (-os), bell-um (-om)*	*rēx*	*curr-us, corn-ū*	*di-ēs*
	V	*terr-a*	*lup-e*	*rēx*	*curr-us, corn-ū*	*di-ēs*
	G	*terr-ae (-āī, -ās)*	*lup-ī (-osio)*	*rēg-is (-es, -os)*	*curr-ūs (-uos)*	*di-ēī*
	D	*terr-ae*	*lup-ō (-ōi)*	*rēg-ī (-ei)*	*curr-uī, corn-ū*	*di-ēī*
	Ac	*terr-am*	*lup-um (-om)*	*rēg-em, turr-im*	*curr-um, corn-ū*	*di-em*
	Ab	*terr-ā (-ād)*	*lup-ō (-ōd)*	*rēg-e (-ed), turr-ī (-īd)*	*curr-ū (-ūd)*	*di-ē*
pl.	NV	*terr-ae*	*lup-ī (-ei, -oe), bell-a*	*rēg-ēs*	*curr-ūs, corn-ua*	*di-ēs*
	G	*terr-ārum*	*lup-ōrum (-ōrom, -um, -om)*	*rēg-um (-om), turr-ium*	*curr-uum (-uom)*	*di-ērum*
	D	*terr-īs*	*lup-īs (-ois)*	*rēg-ibus*	*curr-ibus*	*di-ēbus*
	Ac	*terr-ās*	*lup-ōs, bell-a*	*rēg-ēs, turr-īs*	*curr-ūs, corn-ua*	*di-ēs*
	Ab	*terr-īs*	*lup-īs (-eis)*	*rēg-ibus*	*curr-ibus (-ibos)*	*di-ēbus*

13.38. A few remarks may be appended. In the first declension, the genitive singular ending *-ās* (as in the fixed phrase ***pater familiās*** 'head of a household') is the oldest; the Classical ending *-ae* (< earlier *-āī*) comes from the spread of the genitive *-ī* of the second declension (this ending also spread to the fifth, whence *-ēī*). In the second declension, the original *o*-stem nominative plural **-ōs* was replaced by the pronominal nomin. pl. in *-*oi*, as happened in a number of other IE languages too (§6.53). Two genitive plurals in the *o*-stems are found, an older (in Classical times, poetic) one in *-um* (earlier *-om*), and a longer one in *-ōrum*, formed by analogy to *-ārum* in the first declension (itself from *-*āsōm*). In the third declension, noteworthy is the presence of genitive singulars in *-*es* (which became the standard *-is*) as well as *-*os* (as in Greek; limited to a few inscriptional attestations). The older ablatives all ended in *-d* (as per §13.22).

A locative case is still found vestigially in the first three declensions: *Rōm-ae* 'in Rome', *dom-ī* 'at home', *rūr-ī* 'in the country'.

Verbs

13.39. The Latin verbal system is the same as that described above for Italic (§§13.13ff.). The paradigms below will illustrate the active and passive forms in the present tense; the verbs are *amāre* 'to love' (first conjugation), *habēre* 'to have' (second), *dūcere* 'to lead' (third), *capere* 'to take' (third *-iō*), *audīre* 'to hear' (fourth), and *esse* 'to be' (athematic). Archaic or poetic forms are indicated in parentheses and in the notes.

		I	II	III	III *-iō*	IV	Athem.
Active							
sg.	1	*am-ō* 'I love'	*hab-eō* 'I have'	*dūc-ō* 'I lead'	*cap-iō* 'I take'	*aud-iō* 'I hear'	*sum*[1] 'I am'
	2	*am-ās*	*hab-ēs*	*dūc-is*	*cap-is*	*aud-īs*	*es*
	3	*am-at*	*hab-et*	*dūc-it*	*cap-it*	*aud-it*	*est*
pl.	1	*am-āmus*	*hab-ēmus*	*dūc-imus*	*cap-imus*	*aud-īmus*	*sumus*
	2	*am-ātis*	*hab-ētis*	*dūc-itis*	*cap-itis*	*aud-ītis*	*estis*
	3	*am-ant*	*hab-ent*	*dūc-unt*[2]	*cap-iunt*	*aud-iunt*[3]	*sunt*
Passive							
sg.	1	*am-or* 'I am loved'	*habeor* 'I am had'	*dūcor* 'I am led'	*capior* 'I am taken'	*audior* 'I am heard'	
	2	*am-āris* (*-āre*)	*habēris* (*-ēre*)	*dūceris* (*-ere*)	*caperis* (*-ere*)	*audīris* (*-īre*)	
	3	*amātur*	*habētur*	*dūcitur*	*capitur*	*audītur*[4]	*ītur*[5]
pl.	1	*amāmur*	*habēmur*	*dūcimur*	*capimur*	*audīmur*	
	2	*amāminī*	*habēminī*	*dūciminī*	*capiminī*	*audīminī*	
	3	*amantur*	*habentur*	*dūcuntur*	*capiuntur*	*audiuntur*	

[1] Archaic *esom.* [2] Archaic *ueiuont* 'they live'. [3] Archaic *cōsentiont* 'they agree' . [4] Archaic *nancītor* 'he obtains'. [5] From *īre* 'to go', meaning 'one goes, people go'; archaic *eitur*.

The verbs like *capere* are descended from *-*i̯e/o*-presents where the suffix *-*i̯e/o*- followed a light root (see §13.13); they take regular 3rd-conjugation endings except in the 1st person sing. and the 3rd pl. The 2nd sing. passive ending in *-re* is the older form, continuing *-*se*; the regular Classical ending *-ris* is an example of double marking, since it ends with an added 2nd sing. active ending *-s*. The 3rd person endings in *-t* and *-nt* continue the PIE primary endings *-*ti* and *-*nti*.

The perfect

13.40. Several of the types of perfect stems still resist straightforward historical explanation. Probably the most important of these is the so-called *v*-perfect, exemplified by such forms as *portāu-ī* 'I carried', *nēu-ī* 'I sewed', and *audīu-ī* 'I heard'. It might be connected with the *-u* in Sanskrit perfects like Ved. *dadáu* 'I/he gave' (root *dā-*), *tastháu* 'I stood' (root *sthā-*), but this is controversial. It is also possible the *-u-* got its start on Italic soil, generalized from forms like *fuī* 'I was'. Not found in Sabellic (perhaps by accident) are perfects that continue *s*-aorists, such as *uēxī* 'I conveyed' (< **u̯eĝh-s-*; §5.47).

13.41. The endings of the perfect are still recognizably descended from the PIE perfect endings, being conspicuously different from the regular active and passive endings, as illustrated by the paradigm of *gnōu-ī* 'I have learned, I know' (Archaic or poetic forms given in parentheses):

	Singular	Plural
1	*gnōu-ī* (*-ei*)	*gnōu-imus*
2	*gnōu-istī* (*-istei*)	*gnōu-istis*
3	*gnōu-it* (*-et*, *-eit*)	*gnōu-ērunt* (*-ēre*, *-ērai*)

One can see lurking under these the PIE endings **-h_2e* (> **-a*), **-(s)th_2e* (> **-sta*), **-e* in the singular, all extended by the primary active particle **-i* (§5.13), and an altered version of the 3rd plural ending **-ēr* (extended by the non-perfect 3rd pl. ending *-unt* in the familiar Classical ending *-ērunt*).

The later history of Latin

Vulgar Latin

13.42. Most of the Latin that has come down to us consists of literature in an elevated style. A few works, such as the comedies of Plautus, the novel *Satyricon* of Petronius, and some letters of Cicero, contain colloquial language, and many inscriptions reflect the spoken idiom of the day. The spoken form of Latin, especially from about the third century AD on, is called **Vulgar Latin** (*uulgāris* 'pertaining to the common people') and forms the basis of the modern Romance languages (§§13.44ff.).

Among the more extensive remains of early Vulgar Latin are the citations of "incorrect" forms collected in a work called the *Appendix Probī*, long thought to have been written in the fourth century but probably dating from the sixth. It is preserved as an appendix attached to a manuscript of a grammatical treatise by the first-century grammarian Valerius Probus. The *Appendix* consists of lists of words in their correct Classical spellings followed by their incorrect counterparts, such as *speculum non speclum* (indicating that *speculum* and not *speclum* is the correct spelling of the word for 'mirror'). The *Appendix*'s efforts were all in vain, for the "incorrect" spellings reflect pronunciations and forms that would all win out in the Romance languages. Thus for example the form *speclum* (and not *speculum*) is the ancestor of Italian *specchio* 'mirror'.

Developments of Vulgar Latin

13.43. Unstressed vowels in internal syllables were often syncopated (lost), as in *speclum* just discussed. The distinction in length between long and short vowels was lost, but in an interestingly skewed fashion in most areas. Though long and short *a* fell together as one might expect, short *i* fell together with long *ē* as a tense [e], and their back counterparts (short *u* and long *ō*) fell together as tense [o]. Latin short *e* and *o* became lax [ɛ] and [ɔ], while the two long high vowels *ī* and *ū* became [i] and [u]. The general pattern of the mergers can be exemplified by the following words in Spanish: contrast ***el*** 'the' (Lat. ***ille***) and *vendo* 'I buy' (Lat. *uēndō*) with ***siete*** 'seven' (Lat. ***septem***), and contrast ***boca*** 'mouth' (Lat. ***bucca***) and ***olla*** 'pot' (Lat. ***ōlla***) with ***puerta*** 'door' (Lat. ***porta***). Since Oscan shows some of the same mergers of the mid and high vowels, it has been speculated that these changes in Vulgar Latin pronunciation started in southern Italy and spread from there. Most diphthongs became monophthongized: the diphthong *oe*, for example, became *e*, as in Italian *pena* 'sorrow' from Lat. *poena* 'punishment'. In most areas where Vulgar Latin was spoken, the velars became palatalized before front vowels, for example turning into [t^s] (spelled *c*) in Old Spanish *ciento* and Old French *cent* 'hundred' and [č] in Italian *cento* (all from Lat. *centum*).

There were also many changes in morphology. The number of cases in the noun was reduced, with prepositional phrases often taking over their functions: if one gave something 'to the king', one said *ad regem* rather than the dative *regī*. In most areas (except Romania; see §13.51 below) only two cases, the nominative and accusative, survived in nouns, and by the time the Romance languages are first attested this distinction too had been lost (except in Old French and Old Provençal, where it persisted until the later Middle Ages). In pronouns, though, some case distinctions have been maintained everywhere to the present day. (The general development mirrors that from Old to Middle English; see §15.65.) Verbs did not go through as much formal reduction as nouns did, but periphrastic constructions (that is, constructions using "helping" verbs, as in English *I have seen*) became quite common. Typical of these were the compound perfect tense consisting of *habēre* 'to have' plus the past participle (e.g. French *j'ai chanté* 'I have sung' < *ego habeō cantātum*) and the compound future tense consisting of an infinitive plus *habēre* (e.g. French *chanterai* and Spanish *cantaré* 'I will sing' < *cantāre habeō*).

The Romance languages

13.44. The fragmentation of the Roman Empire in the fifth century and the incursion of non-Latin-speaking peoples into former Roman territories created excellent conditions for the differentiation of Vulgar Latin (itself not uniform to begin with) into local dialects that became more and more distinct over time. Their modern descendants are the **Romance languages** (from Vulgar Latin **romanicus* 'Roman', i.e. vernacular). Though they form a basically unbroken continuum from the Iberian peninsula to the Balkans, it is convenient to organize them into the branches that are given below.

No texts in any of the vernacular descendants of Vulgar Latin survive from before the ninth century, and it is possible that none were written down before then. The language of administration and the Church was always Latin, and only when the vernaculars had diverged so much from Latin that ordinary people could no longer understand it did the need arise to use the vernaculars in writing and in the Church.

Gallo-Romance

13.45. The earliest Romance language to be attested is **French**, a northern variety of which first appears in writing in the Strasbourg Oaths in or around the year 842. It is surely no accident that this is the first Romance language to have been written down, as it had diverged more strongly from Latin than the other varieties closer to Italy. Literary remains of French remain meager, however, until the twelfth century. The language is known as **Old French** until the early 1400s.

The part of Europe that is now called France had several varieties of Romance, collectively termed Gallo-Romance. In central France, especially around Paris, was spoken a variety that would become the dominant dialect already in the twelfth and thirteenth centuries and which developed into modern standard French. In the far north was **Norman French**, which spread to England following its conquest in 1066 by William the Bastard (as he is called in contemporaneous official documents, but now more familiar as "the Conqueror"). The Norman French that developed in England is often called **Anglo-Norman**, which flourished for at least two centuries before its eventual eclipse by Middle English. Another northern Gallo-Romance variety is **Walloon**, spoken in Belgium. In the south were spoken varieties of French termed *langue d'oc* or **Occitan**, an important language of poetry in the Middle Ages until southern France was taken over by the north in the early 1200s. (The term *langue d'oc* refers to the way of saying 'yes' in this region, *oc* < Lat. *hoc* 'this'; the northern half of the country spoke *langue d'oïl*, their word for 'yes' being *oïl* [> modern *oui*] from Lat. *hoc ille* [*fecit*] 'he [did] this'.) Occitan varieties are still spoken in southern France, the most prominent one being **Provençal** in the Provence and neighboring regions, attested from as early as the tenth century.

Ibero-Romance

13.46. The Romance language spoken by the greatest number of people worldwide, **Spanish**, is first attested in the form of glosses on Latin texts dating probably to the mid-eleventh century. The earliest Spanish does not evince many dialect differences, but the famous twelfth- or early thirteenth-century epic poem *Cantar de mío Cid* (*Song of My Cid*, or *El Cid* for short) is in an early variety of **Castilian**, the dialect that would eventually become the standard.

As in France, the Romance varieties spoken in Spain are not homogeneous. In the northeast is **Catalan**, for centuries the official language of the kingdom of Aragon (until 1749). It is first attested in the twelfth century; before that, Catalan poets had written in Provençal. As this last fact attests, Catalan occupies an intermediate linguistic position between Spanish and the varieties of Occitan, although Spanish influence has grown over time. In the south, now-extinct Romance varieties collectively called **Mozarabic** were spoken; they were heavily influenced by the Arabic of Spain's Moorish invaders.

13.47. The northwestern dialects of Spain, especially Galician, are historically varieties of **Portuguese**, nowadays the second-most populous Romance language. Galician and Portuguese were a unitary language until the 1400s, called **Gallego-Portuguese**; scattered words in this language are recorded already in the late ninth century. The earliest true text dates to the late twelfth or early thirteenth century, and for two hundred years Gallego-Portuguese enjoyed a high literary prestige throughout most of the Iberian peninsula. Eventually Portuguese and Galician diverged; Portuguese formed its own literary standard beginning in the fifteenth and sixteenth centuries, soon eclipsing Galician on the European and the world stage. Brazilian Portuguese has itself diverged somewhat from European Portuguese in phonology and syntax.

Italian

13.48. Italy has held a patchwork of dialects for most of the past millennium. The earliest records that can securely be called **Italian** are in the form of court records from the tenth century. The dialect of Florence became the basis of the standard literary language beginning in the thirteenth century; it was phonologically more conservative in several respects than other dialects, but admixtures of forms from them have continued to shape the standard.

Sardinian

13.49. The island of Sardinia, a Carthaginian colony before it became Roman territory soon after Carthage's defeat in the First Punic War (264–241 BC), is where **Sardinian** is spoken today. Sardinian is attested quite early, near the end of the eleventh century, but little literature has ever been written in it. The north-central dialect Logudorese is remarkably conservative in one famous respect: the velars did not become palatalized before front vowels (§13.43), as in their word for 'hundred', *kentu* (Lat. *centum*).

Rhaeto-Romance

13.50. This branch of Romance comprises languages spoken in northeastern Italy and Switzerland. In the former may be mentioned **Ladin** (Dolomite Mountains) and **Friulian** (Friuli-Venezia Giulia region, attested since the thirteenth century), while in the eastern Swiss canton of Grisons (Graubünden) is spoken **Romansh**, one of the four national languages of Switzerland and attested since the sixteenth century.

Romanian

13.51. Romanian (or Rumanian), spoken in Romania, Moldova, and neighboring areas, descends from the Latin of the Roman provinces of Dacia and Illyricum. Beginning in the third century, the region fell out of Roman control and was taken over successively by Goths, Bulgaria, Hungary, the Ottoman Empire, and Russia. The linguistic influence especially of Slavic and Hungarian was far-reaching. The first Romanian text dates only from 1521; the Cyrillic alphabet was used until 1859. All of the numerous divergent dialects of Romanian are nearly extinct except for the standard, called Daco-Romanian. A noteworthy conservative feature of Romanian is the preservation of the neuter gender and three case-distinctions in nouns, including limited use of a separate vocative.

Archaic Latin text sample A

13.52. The so-called Duenos inscription, found in Rome, inscribed around a terracotta vessel consisting of three small bowls joined together and dating to *c.* 500 BC. Only the first and third lines are mostly uncontroversial in their interpretation;

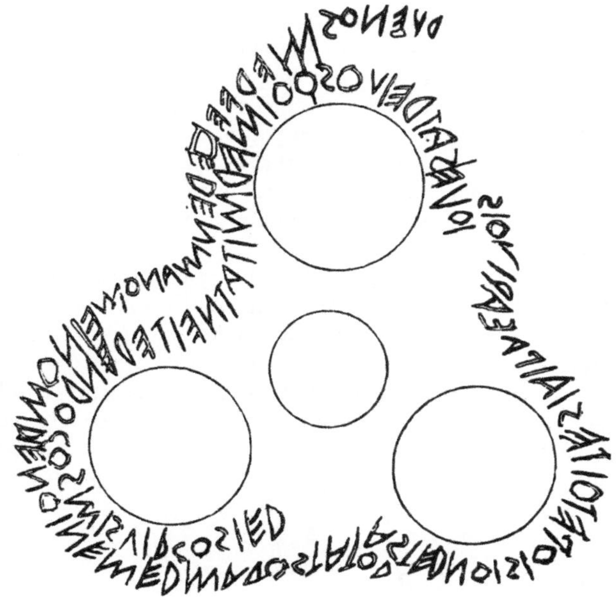

Figure 13.1 The Duenos inscription. The text starts at the top and goes around counterclockwise from there. The three larger circles represent the three connected pots around which the inscription is written. Drawing from Atilius Degrassi, *Inscriptiones latinae liberae rei publicae: Imagines* (Berlin: de Gruyter, 1965), p. 261. Reproduced by permission of the publisher.

the second will not be treated here. The original has no word-divisions. Latin inscriptions are collected in the multi-volume *Corpus Inscriptionum Latinarum* (CIL): this one is CIL I^2 4.

iouesatdeiuosqoimedmitatneitedendocosmisuircosied
astednoisiopetoitesiaipacariuois
duenosmedfecedenmanomeinomduenoinemedmalostatod

The first and third lines with word-divisions added read as follows:

iouesat deiuos qoi med mitat nei ted endo cosmis uirco sied
duenos med feced en manom einom duenoi ne med malos tatod

He who gives (?) me swears by the gods: if a girl is not nice to you, [. . .]
A good (man) made me for "good going" for a good (man). Let no bad (man) steal me.

13.52a. Notes. 1. iouesat: Classical *iūrat*, 'swears'; intervocalic *s* is still unrhotacized, and contraction of the sequence *-oue-* to *-ū-* has not happened yet either. **deiuos:** 'gods', accus. pl., Classical *deōs*. **qoi:** '(he) who', Classical *quī*, relative pronoun. **med:** *mēd*, 'me', Archaic accus. sing.; Classical *mē*. The *-d* is secondary and of uncertain origin, but may have spread from the ablative (also *mēd*, ultimately from PIE **med*). **mitat:** 3rd sing. of an Archaic Latin verb, probably meaning 'gives' or 'sends' or the like. It may be related to Classical Latin *mittere* 'to send'. **nei:** 'if not', Classical *nī*. **ted endo:** 'toward you', with postposed preposition *endo*, Archaic for *in*. The form *tēd* is parallel to *mēd* above. **cosmis:** 'nice', Classical *cōmis*, with the cluster *-sm-* still preserved. **uirco:** 'girl', Classical *uirgō*. Since Etruscan only had voiceless stops and the Romans borrowed that language's alphabet, they used C early on for both *c* and *g*; later they created G, probably by adding a stroke to C. Cp. the abbreviation C. for the name Gaius. **sied:** 3rd sing. present subjunctive of *esse* 'to be', with *-d* from PIE secondary **-t*.

2. duenos: 'good', Classical *bonus* (*du̯* regularly became *b-*); used as a noun. The dative *duenōi* a few words later preserves the long diphthong *-ōi* (Classical *bonō*). **feced:** 'made', 3rd sing. perfect; Classical *fēcit*. **en manom einom:** of disputed interpretation; perhaps 'for good going'. Under this interpretation, *en* is the preposition *in* 'in'; *manom* (*mānom*) is the accusative of *mānus* 'good', a rare adjective that had died out by the Classical period, though related words survived (e.g. *immānis* 'savage'); and *einom* is a verbal abstract noun from the root **$h_1$ei-* 'go'. **ne:** *nē*, negative with the imperative at the end of the line. **malos:** 'a bad (man)', Classical *malus*. **tatod:** 3rd sing. imperative of an otherwise unattested verb **tāre* 'to steal', cp. Hitt. *tāiēzzi* 'steals'.

Archaic Latin text sample B

13.53. Excerpt from the so-called suovitaurilia prayer, recorded by Marcus Porcius Cato (Cato the Elder), *Dē Agrī Cultūrā* (*On Agriculture*) 141.1ff. This was a prayer to Mars on the occasion of the purification of a field, during which a sow (*sūs*), sheep (*ouis*), and bull (*taurus*) were sacrificed. The prayer has phraseology that is in places identical to that seen in the selection from the Umbrian Iguvine Tables below, and which has further analogues in Indo-Iranian (see the Notes). The repetitive language is typical of sacral poetic style; note also the alliterating pairs as in the Umbrian and South Picene texts further below (*uiduertātem uastitūdinemque*, *pāstōrēs pecuaque*, etc.).

Mārs pater tē precor quaesōque utī siēs uolēns propitius mihi domō familiaeque nostrae, [. . .] utī tū morbōs uīsōs inuīsōsque uiduertātem uastitūdinemque calamitātem intemperiāsque dēfendās prohibessīs āuerruncāsque utīque tū frūgēs frūmenta uīnēta uirgultaque grandīre beneque ēuenīre sīrīs pāstōrēs pecuaque salua seruassīs duīsque bonam salūtem ualētūdinemque mihi domō familiaeque nostrae [. . .]

Father Mars, I beseech and entreat you, that you be willing (and) propitious to me, (my) house and our household, [. . .] that you ward off diseases seen and unseen, banish barrenness and devastation, and sweep away destruction and bad weather, and that you allow the fruits and grains, the vineyards and shrubbery to grow tall and come out well, that you protect shepherds and livestock, and that you give good safety and health to me, (my) home and our household [. . .]

13.53a. Notes. Mārs pater: also *Mārspiter*, cp. *Iū-piter* and Gk. *Zeũ páter*. **precor:** 'I beseech', a deponent (§13.20) 1st sing. present, from PIE *prek̂- 'ask' (which also formed a *sk̂e*-present *pr̥k̂-sk̂e- in Lat. *poscō* 'I demand'). **-que:** 'and', cognate with Gk. *te*, Skt. *ca*; §7.27. **utī:** 'that', conjunction. **siēs:** '(that) you be', Archaic subjunctive, Classical Latin *sīs*, a continuation of the IE optative *h_1s-i̯eh_1-s (§13.19); cp. Ved. *syā́s*. **uolēns:** 'willing', present participle of *uolō* 'I want', an athematic verb. **mihi:** 'to me', dat. sing., probably from earlier *mehei < *meĝh(e)i, cp. Ved. dat. *máhy-am*. **domō:** 'to (my) home', dat. sing. of *domus* 'house'; PIE root *dem-. **familiae:** 'household', dat. sing., derived from *famulus* 'household slave'. **morbōs:** 'diseases', *o*-stem accus. pl.; the ending was earlier *-ōns (§6.55). **uīsōs:** 'seen', not directly from expected *u̯id-to- (which should have given *u̯isso-) but apparently remade to the full-grade *u̯eid-to-. **uiduertātem:** 'barrenness'; the word only occurs here and was built to *uiduus* 'bereft' on the model of its semantic opposite *ūbertāt-* 'richness'. *Viduus* in turn comes from *uidua* 'widow' (PIE *u̯idheu̯eh_2, the source of Eng. *widow*). **dēfendās prohibessīs āuerruncās:** '(that) you ward off, banish, sweep away'; these verbs are not entirely synonymous, as each goes with a particular evil. The forms *dēfendās* and *āuerruncās* are ordinary *ā*-subjunctives (§13.19), while *prohibessīs* is an Archaic Latin subjunctive containing the PIE optative morpheme (*-ī-* < *-ih_1-) added to an *-s-* or *-ss-* of uncertain origin. **grandīre:** 'to grow tall', a denominative from the *i*-stem adjective *grandis* 'tall'. **bene:** 'well'; the earlier form was *duenē*, and if we restore that here we get *duenēque ēuenīre sīrīs*, with a lovely succession of long and short *e*'s and *i*'s. **ēuenīre:** 'to come out', a compound of *uenīre* 'come', PIE *g^wem- (> Goth. *qiman*, Eng. *come*, Ved. root *gam-*). **sīrīs:** '(that) you allow'. **pāstōrēs pecuaque:** 'shepherds and livestock'; the phrase signifies movable wealth in the form of slaves (which shepherds were considered in archaic Roman society) and livestock, or two-footed and four-footed wealth. Recall §2.10. Both *pāstōrēs* and *pecua* are good PIE inheritances: *peh_2- 'protect' (Ved. *pā-*, with *-s-* also in Hitt. *paḫš-* with the laryngeal preserved) and *pek̂u- (Ved. *páśu* 'cattle', German *Vieh* 'animal, cattle', Eng. *fee*). **salua seruassīs:** '(that) you protect, keep safe', an inherited Italic sacral formula, seen also below in Umbrian *saluo seritu*. **duīs:** '(that) you give', an Archaic subjunctive of *dare* 'give'; of disputed origin. **bonam:** 'good'; earlier *duenam (see the Duenos inscription above).

Faliscan

13.54. Faliscan was spoken by a people known in ancient times as the Falisci, in and around the city of Falerii (nowadays Cività Castellana), about 60 km north of Rome in southern Etruria. It is known from about 300 inscriptions from the seventh to the second centuries BC. With a few notable exceptions, the inscriptions are mostly quite short, and our knowledge of the language correspondingly scanty. The Falisci were closely related to the Latini, and their language was quite close to Latin as well, as for example in its treatment of the voiceless labiovelar stop *k^w, which was preserved as such and not changed into a labial stop (§13.24). It does not pattern with Latin in all matters of phonology, however: unlike Latin and like Sabellic, for example, the voiced aspirates became *f* word-internally, as in *pipafo* 'I will drink' (with *-f-* from *-*bh*-) and *efiles* 'officials, aediles' (with *-f-* from *-*dh*-). In word-initial position, the voiced aspirates often became *h*-, as in *huticilom* 'a little cash' in the text sample below (with *h*- from **ĝh*-).

Faliscan text sample

13.55. The so-called Ceres inscription, found at Falerii; c. 600 BC. The triple dots are interpuncts, punctuation marks used in ancient inscriptions to separate words or phrases. Letters within brackets have been conjecturally restored.

ceres ⁝ farme[la]tom ⁝ louf[i]rui[no]m ⁝ [ ]rad
euios ⁝ mamazextosmedf[if]iqod ⁝
prauiosurnam ⁝ soci[ai]pordedkarai ⁝
eqournela[ti]telafitaidupes ⁝
arcentelomhuticilom ⁝ pe ⁝ parai[ ]douiad

Let (?) Ceres [. . .] ground grain, Bacchus wine.
Mama (and?) Zextos Euios fashioned me.
Prauios gave the urn to his dear girlfriend.
I, a little *titela*-urn, . . .
have given birth to a little money. May it give (?).

13.55a. Notes. ceres: 'Ceres', the goddess of grain; from PIE **keres* (cp. Hitt. *karaš* 'grain'). **far:** 'grain', Lat. *far*, Eng. *bar-ley*. **me[la]tom:** 'ground', if correctly restored (= Lat. *molitum*, PIE **melh₂*- 'grind'); 'ground' is a frequent epithet of words for 'grain' in Italic, especially in religious contexts. **louf[i]r:** 'Bacchus', the Faliscan form of the native Italic word for the god of wine; cp. Lat. *Līber*, with Lat. *-b-* and Fal. *-f-* from **-dh-*. **[ ]rad:** 3rd sing. of some verb, probably subjunctive; 'let . . .' or 'may . . .'. **euios mamazextos:** probably Euios is the family name going with two first names, Mama and Zextos; but uncertain. **med:** 'me', cp. Archaic Lat. *mēd*; see §13.52a above. **f[if]iqod:** 'have fashioned', most likely a 3rd pl. like Lat. *-unt* (Archaic Lat. *-ont*), without the nasal written, and from secondary **-nt* rather than primary *-nti* (where the *-t-* would have remained). The *-q-* stands for *-g-* (compare *eqo* for *ego* two lines below), and the form seems to be a reduplicated perfect of the Faliscan equivalent of

Figure 13.2 The Ceres inscription. The text begins right below the center and curves counterclockwise around the bottom of the bowl. Drawing reproduced from O. A. Danielsson and G. Herbig, *Corpus Inscriptionum Etruscarum*, vol. 2, part 2, fascicle 1 (Leipzig: Barth, 1912), no. 8079 (p. 23).

Lat. *fingō* 'fashion, create' (PIE $*dhei\hat{g}h$-, Eng. *dough*). **soci[ai]:** 'girlfriend', dat. sing., Lat. *sociae*, ultimately from PIE $*sek^{w}$- 'follow, accompany'. The separation of the noun from its modifier *karai* 'dear' by an intervening verb is a common poetic stylistic device in the older IE languages. **porded:** 'gave', 3rd sing. **karai:** 'dear', dat. sing. fem., Lat. *cārae*; from PIE $*keh_2$- 'love, desire' (> Ved. *kā́mas* 'love', Eng. *whore* [prehistorically 'girlfriend' or 'beloved']). **urnela:** 'little urn', a diminutive like the following *[ti]tela*. The remainder of the line is not understood. **arcentelom:** 'little bit of money', cp. Lat. *argentum* 'silver'. **huticilom:** basically means the same thing as *arcentelom*; *hut-* may be the Faliscan cognate of the Latin root *fud-* 'pour' (nasal-infix present *fundō* 'I pour'); therefore *huticilom* is literally 'a little pourable stuff', i.e. liquid assets (same metaphor as in English!). The IE root is $*\hat{g}heu$- (Gk. *khé(w)ō* 'I pour', Eng. *in-got*). **peparai:** 'I have given birth to', reduplicated perfect 1st sing. with the archaic ending *-ai* < $*$-h_2e plus the *hic et nunc* particle *-i* (§5.13; cp. also §13.41); cp. Lat. *pariō* 'I give birth' and *parēns* 'parent'. Why an interpunct separates the reduplicating syllable from the rest of the word is uncertain. **]douiad:** maybe a 3rd sing. subjunctive of the Faliscan cognate of Lat. *dō* 'I give', reminiscent of the Archaic Lat. subjunctive *duit* (see §13.53a).

Sabellic (Osco-Umbrian)

13.56. The Sabellic languages derive their name from the Sabelli, another name for the Samnites; both names are in turn etymologically connected with the name of the Sabines. The Sabellic-speaking peoples originally inhabited an area to the east and northeast of Latium, but a subgroup of them that spoke Oscan migrated southward into Campania around the middle of the first millennium BC. After this migration, Sabellic languages were spread out over most of Italy except along the western coastal strip; centuries later they would be eclipsed by Latin and would die out.

Common Sabellic developments

13.57. Superficially, the Sabellic languages, especially Umbrian, look strikingly different from Latin because of the far-reaching effects of a few basic sound changes. Sabellic in general also presents considerable divergences from Latin in nominal and verbal morphology. However, peeling away these differences one finds that the Sabellic languages really behave much the same as Latin.

Sabellic phonology

13.58. Due first of all to the limited number of inscriptions we have in Sabellic, and second to their inconsistent spelling, any sketch of Sabellic phonology, both historical and synchronic, must be tentative. The following conclusions are among the most secure.

13.59. The voiced aspirates became *f* not only word-initially (as usually in Latin) but also word-internally: Osc. **prúfatted** 'he approved' (cp. Lat. *probāuit*, from **probh-*), **mefiaí** 'in the middle' (Lat. *media-* < **medhii̯ā-*), and Umbr. **vufru** 'votive' (< **u̯og^{w}h-ro-*, cp. Lat. *uou-ēre* 'to vow'). As usually in Latin, **gh* became *h* word-initially: Osc. **húrz** 'yard' (cp. Lat. *hortus* < **ĝhort-*).

13.60. This development of voiced aspirates to *f* word-internally gives the Sabellic languages a preponderance of *f*'s not seen in Latin. As if this were not enough, the cluster **ns* became *f* much of the time as well – an unusual development whose details in the different languages are complex. In Proto-Sabellic, it appears that only final **-ns* became *-f*, as in the consonant-stem accusative plural *-f* < **-ns*, syncopated (by the rule in the next section) from Italic **-ens* (< PIE **-n̥s*), as in Umbr. *nerf* and SPic. **nerf** 'magistrates' < **ner-en-s* (root **h$_2$ner-* 'man'). In Oscan, the outcome *-f* in accusative plurals has been obscured by the addition of an analogical *-s*, yielding *-ss*, e.g. **feíhúss** 'walls' < **feihōf-s* (root **dheiĝh-* 'form with the hands, build'). The old nominative singular ending **-nt-s* of present participles became *-f* also, via a simplification to **-ns*, as in Osc. **staef** 'standing, existing, established' < **sta-ē-ns*, Umbr. **zeřef** 'sitting' < **seden(t)s*, as did nominative singulars of animate *n*-stems that had the nomin. sing. ending *-s* secondarily added to them, e.g. Osc. **úíttiuf** 'use' < **oitiōns* (cf. Lat. *ūtiō*, which is more archaic in lacking *-n* in the nominative singular [recall §3.40] and in not adding an *-s*). In Umbrian and South Picene the change **ns > f* was extended to other contexts also, as for instance in South Picene **múfqlúm** 'monument' (probable meaning) from **mons-klo-* or **mons-tlo-*, cp. Lat. *mōnstrum* 'sign, portent'.

13.61. Also characteristic of Sabellic, as mentioned in §13.24, is the development of the labiovelars to labial stops: Osc. fem. accus. sing. **paam** 'whom' (Lat. *quam*), Osc. **biítam** 'life' (Lat. *uītam*) < **g^{w}ih$_3$-*. The syllabic nasals may have developed differently in Sabellic vis-à-vis Latino-Faliscan, as discussed in §13.8.

13.62. Two important developments of the vowel system may also be mentioned. First is the syncope (loss) of short vowels in final closed syllables, as illustrated by Osc. nomin. pl. **humuns** 'people' (< **homones*) and Osc. nomin. sing. **húrz** 'yard' (pronounced *horts*, from **hortos*). Second is the change of final **-ā* to a rounded **å̄* ([ɔ], as in Eng. *law*), written in the various alphabets usually as *o* or *u*: Osc. **víú** 'road' (**uiā*, cp. Lat. *uia*), Umbr. **mutu** 'punishment' (**moltā*), *toto* 'tribe' (**toutā*).

Morphology

13.63. The Sabellic languages preserve distinctions between primary and secondary verbal endings in the third person. The active plural primary ending is *-nt* (as in Osc. present indicative **stahínt** 'they stand'), while the secondary ending is *-ns* (as in Osc. imperfect subjunctive **patensíns** 'they would open'), whose relationship to the inherited secondary ending **-nt* is disputed (either *-ns* is the regular development of **-nt*, or **-nt* first became weakened to **-n(n)* – a change paralleled elsewhere – to which the nominative plural **-(e)s* was analogically added as a copy of the termination of plural *n*-stem subjects in *-n(e)s*). Umbrian has a further distinction, lost elsewhere in Sabellic, in the passive (see §13.73).

13.64. Not found in Latino-Faliscan is an infinitive in *-fi-* from PIE **-dhi̯-* (§5.58), which can have active or passive meaning: Osc. **sakrafír** 'to consecrate, be consecrated' and Umbr. *pihafi* 'to be offered'.

13.65. Perfects in Sabellic exhibit several formations not occurring in Latin, some found only in individual Sabellic languages to the exclusion of others. Oscan and Umbrian both have an *f*-perfect (e.g. Osc. *fu-fens* 'they were', Umbr. *andirsa-fust* 'he will have taken around'), while a *tt*-perfect is found only in Oscan (e.g. **prúfatted** 'it approved') and the so-called *nki̯*-perfect is found only in Umbrian (the *k* in that sequence became a sibilant, e.g. *combifia-nsiust* 'he will have announced'). The origins of these perfect formations are disputed.

13.66. The system of nominal inflection is quite similar to that of Latin with the exception of some endings. The *o*-stem genitive singular has been replaced by the *i*-stem ending *-eis*: Osc. **sakarakleís** 'of the temple', Umbr. *popler* 'of the people' (< **popleis*, contrast Lat. *populī*). Unlike Latin, Sabellic preserves the inherited *o*-stem nominative pl. ending **-ōs*: Osc. **Núvlanús** 'the inhabitants of Nola', South Picene **safinús** 'Sabines'. And judging from Umbrian, it also preserves the inherited distinction between the nominative and vocative singular of feminine *ā*-stems, which were *-ā* and **-a*, respectively: contrast Umbrian nominative **mutu** 'punishment' (**-u** < **-ā*, §13.62) with the vocative *Tursa* (a proper name).

Umbrian

13.67. Umbrian is almost entirely known from the seven Iguvine Tables, discovered in 1444 in the Italian town of Gubbio (in classical times Iguvium), about 160 km north of Rome near Perugia. It is said that the original number of tablets was nine and that two were later lost after their discovery, although there is evidence that this is erroneous. The Iguvine Tables constitute the longest text in any non-Latin language of Italy, containing a set of ritual instructions for a class of priests called the Atiedian Brethren and containing about 4000 words in all. The content is immensely valuable for our knowledge of native Italic religion and cultic practice, about which the Romans themselves did not tell us much (as a result of the Hellenization of Roman religion). Not all the tablets were inscribed at the same time: tables V and VIb are linguistically more recent and easier to understand. Tables VI and VII are in the Latin alphabet and were probably written down shortly after the Social War (90–87 BC) but copied from an older original. The rest are in the native Umbrian alphabet and are conventionally transliterated in boldface.

Umbrian is otherwise known from a few dozen scattered inscriptions from the sixth to the first centuries BC. Already by the time of its earliest attestation the language had undergone many of the phonological reductions that make it look more unlike Latin than any other Italic dialect. Some of these are listed below.

Consonants

13.68. As in Latin, *s* was rhotacized between vowels, e.g. *erom* 'to be' (**esom*), but in later Umbrian at the ends of words too, as in the phrase *pre uereir treblaneir* 'before the Trebulan gate' (written **preueres treplanes** in the older portions of the Iguvine Tables), with the ablative pl. ending *-eir* < **-eis*. The stop *d* became spirantized between vowels and sometimes before consonants to a voiced fricative sound written *rs* in the Latin alphabet and with a modified *r*, transcribed **ř**, in the native alphabet, as in *dirsa* (**teřa**) 'he should give' (**didāt*) and *arsfertur* (**ařfertur**) 'priest' (< **ad-fer-tōr*).

13.69. We saw above (§13.60) the change of final **-ns* to *-f* in Proto-Sabellic. In Umbrian, the same thing happened to the sequence **-nss-* word-internally, as in the past participle *spefa* 'sprinkled, scattered' < **spenssā-* < **spend-t-* (recall that double dentals became *ss* in Italic; §13.7). Curiously, **-ns-* did not undergo this change, but developed to *-nts-* (written **nz** or *ns*), as in **anzeriatu** or *anseriato* 'to observe' < **an-seriā-tum*, and **uze** (with the nasal not written) or *onse* 'on the shoulder' < **omse* < **omesei* (cp. Lat. *(h)umerus* 'shoulder').

13.70. Various consonant-cluster simplifications further altered the look of the language. They can be exemplified by such forms as *ape* 'when' < **atpe* < **atk*^{w}*e* (cp. Lat. *atque* 'and'); *une* 'water' (ablative) < **udni*; **testru** 'to the right' < **dekstero-* (cp. Lat. *dexter*); and **kumatir** 'crumbled' < **kommal(a)teis*.

13.71. Later Umbrian palatalized *k* before front vowels or **i̯* to a sound written with a letter transliterated as **ç** (native alphabet) or *ś* (Latin alphabet): **façia** 'let him make' < **fak-i̯ād*; *śihitu* 'girded' (**kink-to-*); **çerfe** 'of Ceres' (**kerezeis*).

Vowels

13.72. Short vowels in many interior syllables, especially before single consonants, were lost, as in *actud* 'let him do' (**agetōd*, cp. Lat. *agitō*) and **vitlaf** 'yearlings' above (**u̯itelāns*). Whereas Oscan retains the diphthongs intact, Umbrian monophthongized them: *ocrer* 'of the mount' < **ocreis*; *preplohotatu* 'let him trample' < **prai-plautātōd* (with *-oho-* rendering ō); **ueres** 'gates' (abl. pl.) < **u̯erois*; and **muneklu** 'little gift' < **moi-ni-tlom*.

Morphology

13.73. Noteworthy in Umbrian is a distinction in the 3rd person mediopassive endings between primary *-ter*, found in present indicatives like **herter** 'there is need', and secondary *-tur*, found in the subjunctive, as in **emantur** 'let them take'.

Umbrian text sample

13.74. From the Iguvine Tables, tablet VIa, lines 27–31. This section contains a prayer to Jupiter Grabovius, an Umbrian deity. The dots are interpuncts.

(27) . . . dei . crabouie . persei . tuer . perscler . uaseto . est . pesetomest . peretomest (28) frosetomest . daetomest . tuer . perscler . uirseto . auirseto . uas . est . di . grabouie . persei . mersei . esu . bue (29) peracrei . pihaclu . pihafei . di . grabouie . pihatu . ocre . fisei . pihatu . tota . iouina . di . grabouie . pihatu . ocrer (30) fisier . totar . iouinar . nome . nerf . arsmo . ueiro pequo . castruo . fri . pihatu . futu . fos . pacer . pase . tua . ocre fisi (31) tote . iiouine . erer . nomne . erar . nomne . di . grabouie . saluo . seritu . ocre . fisi . salua . seritu . tota . iiouina .

(27) . . . Jupiter Grabovius, if in your sacrifice (anything) has been done wrongly, mistaken, transgressed, (28) deceived, left out, (if) in your ritual there is a seen or unseen flaw, Jupiter Grabovius, if it be right for this (29) yearling ox as purificatory offering to be purified, Jupiter Grabovius, purify the Fisian Mount, purify the Iguvine state. Jupiter Grabovius, purify the name of the Fisian Mount (and) of the Iguvine state, purify the magistrates (and) formulations, men (and) cattle, heads (of grain) (and) fruits. Be favorable (and) propitious in your peace to the Fisian Mount, (31) to the Iguvine state, to the name of that, to the name of this. Jupiter Grabovius, keep safe the Fisian Mount, keep safe the Iguvine state.

13.74a. Notes. 27. dei crabouie: 'Jupiter Grabovius', voc. sing. It has been suggested, speculatively but intriguingly, that *Grabovius* is from Illyrian (presumably via Messapic, cp. §20.21) and means 'of the oak', cp. Illyrian *grabion* 'oak wood', Polish *grabowy* 'made of white beechwood', Modern Greek (Epirotic) *grabos* 'type of oak'. Oak in various ancient IE societies is mythologically associated with the god of thunder (§2.21). Alternatively, connection with an Etruscan god with the unfortunate name *Crap* has also been suggested, but we know nothing about this deity – which might be a good thing. **persei:** 'if', also *pirsi*; apparently from **k^wid-id*, cp. Lat. *quid* 'what'; see §13.68 on *rs* from intervocalic **d*. **tuer**

perscler: 'of your sacrifice', genit. sing., with rhotacism of the original final **-s*. **uaseto est:** 'there has been a fault'; should be *uasetomest* like the following with the neuter sing. *-m* intact. **pesetomest:** 'has been mistaken', cognate with Lat. *peccātum est* 'it has been sinned', but with stem vowel *-ē-* rather than *-ā-*. **peretomest:** 'has been transgressed', lit. 'gone through' (**per-ei-*).

28. frosetomest: 'has been deceived'; *fros-* seems equatable with Lat. *fraud-* 'fraud'. **daetomest:** 'has been left out'. **uirseto:** 'seen' < **uidētom*, a different formation from Lat. *uīsum* 'seen' (**ueid-tom*). For the phrase 'seen (or) unseen fault', compare Lat. *morbōs uīsōs inuīsōsque* 'seen and unseen diseases' in the suovitaurilia prayer above (§13.53). **mersei:** *mers sei*, '(if) it be right'. The first word is from **medos*, from the root **med-* 'to take appropriate measures', and *sei* is the 3rd sing. subjunctive of 'to be', equivalent to Lat. *sit*. **esu bue:** 'with this ox', abl. sing.

29. peracrei: 'yearling', abl. sing.; assimilated from *peraknei*, its form in older parts of the Tables. The root *-akn-* 'year' is dissimilated from the same **atn-* that became Lat. *annus* 'year'. **pihaclu:** 'offering', Lat. *piāculum*. **pihafei:** 'to be purified', passive infinitive in *-f(e)i* (§13.64). **pihatu:** 'purify', 3rd sing. imperative but used like a 2nd sing. **ocre fisei:** 'the Fisian mount', accus. sing., again without writing final *-m*. **tota:** 'people, state', accus. sing.; cp. Gaulish *Teutatis* 'god of the people'. **iouina:** 'Iguvine'. The adjective was originally **ikuvin-**, the usual spelling in the older parts of the Tables; the change to *iou-* may reflect folk-etymological association with *iou-* 'Jove'.

30–31. nome: 'name', accus. sing., cp. Lat. *nōmen*. **nerf:** 'magistrates', accus. pl., from IE **$h_2$ner-* 'man, hero'. The word is common to all Sabellic languages (including South Picene), but is not found in Latin except in the personal name *Nerō*, originally 'having manly strength' or the like. **arsmo:** 'formulations', accus. pl. **ueiro pequo:** 'men and livestock', a phrase inherited from PIE; it occurs in Indo-Iranian as a term for movable wealth, as in Av. *pasu vīra*. **castruo:** 'heads' (of grain), neut. accus. pl. of a *u*-stem < **kastruu̯ā*. **fri:** 'fruits', accus. pl. (final *-f* not written), cp. *frū-* in Latin *frūctus* 'fruit'. **futu:** 'let there be', 3rd sing. imperative of *fu-* 'be' (in Lat. *fu-tūrus* 'about to be'; PIE **bhuH-*, also in Eng. *be*). **pase:** 'in peace', abl. **saluo:** 'safe, whole', Lat. *saluus*. **seritu:** 'hold, keep, preserve', 3rd sing. imperative. The phrase *saluo seritu* is the same as Lat. *salua seruassīs* in the suovitaurilia prayer above.

South Picene

13.75. South Picene is known from nearly two dozen inscriptions from an area in east-central Italy called Picenum in ancient times; the inhabitants were called the Piceni. Although South Picene inscriptions have been known for some time, due to difficulties posed by the script they remained essentially a closed book until very recently. In the 1980s it was finally realized that two symbols (· and :) that had always been assumed to be interpuncts were instead the letters *o* and *f*; needless to say, this discovery dramatically improved our ability to read these texts, and further advances in interpretation have been continuing apace. Our South Picene documents date from the beginning of the sixth to the third century BC; the earliest ones are among our oldest preserved texts in any Sabellic language.

South Picene appears to be more closely related to Umbrian than to Oscan. It is unrelated to another language of the region called North Picene, a non-IE language preserved in a single unintelligible text.

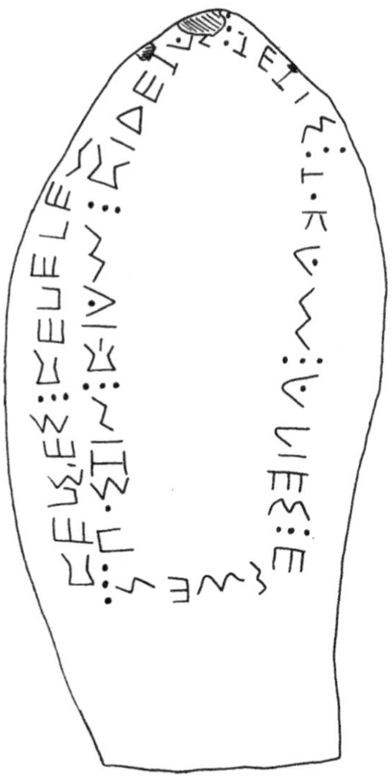

Figure 13.3 The South Picene inscription Sp TE 2. The inscription begins near the bottom of the inner of the two vertical lines of text on the left (right above the vertically stacked triple dots) and proceeds upwards and then clockwise around. Drawing reproduced from Marinetti 1985, p. 204. Reproduced by permission of the publisher.

South Picene text sample

13.76. The inscription Sp TE 2, a gravestone found in Bellante near Teramo, south of Piceno. The inscription is poetry in the archaic Italic strophic style (see §§2.42ff.); except for the first word it consists of alliterative word-pairs (***viam videtas***, ***tetis tokam***, etc.).

postin : viam : videtas : tetis : tokam : alies : esmen : vepses : vepeten

Along the road you see the "toga" of Titus Alius (?) buried (?) in this tomb.

13.76a. Notes. postin: 'along', Umbrian **pustin. videtas:** probably 'you see', 2nd pl., equivalent to Lat. *videtis* 'you (pl.) see'; passers-by are the addressees. **tetis alies:** apparently the name, in the genitive, of the man buried there. **tokam:** cognate with Lat. *togam* (accus. sing.), but the exact sense is uncertain ('covering'? The root is **(s)teg-* 'cover'). In many early Italic inscriptions *k* or *c* was used for voiced *g*. **esmen:** locative of the demonstrative stem *e-*, cp. Umbr. *esme*; superficially similar to Sanskrit *asmin* 'in this' (§7.9) but probably not of identical origin. It is thought to continue **esmeien*, the earlier locative **esmei* plus the postposition *-en* 'in'. **vepses:** perhaps 'buried'; unclear. It might be a past participle of the sort seen in Lat. *lāpsus* 'slipped'. **vepeten:** perhaps 'tomb', with locative in *-en*.

Oscan

13.77. Oscan is known from close to 400 mostly short inscriptions from central and southern Italy dating primarily from the fourth century BC into the first century AD. There are far more Oscan inscriptions than Umbrian ones, but they are mostly quite short and so our knowledge of the language is less secure.

13.78. Oscan is on the whole more conservative than Latin in its vowels, and more conservative than Umbrian in many other phonological respects. It has suffered very little phonetic reduction since Common Sabellic times. It even underwent at least one change going in the opposite direction – the epenthesis (insertion) of a vowel to break up consonant clusters consisting of a resonant and another consonant, as in **aragetud** 'with money' (cp. Lat. *argentō*) and **sakarater** 'it is consecrated' (cp. Lat. *sacrātur*).

13.79. The alphabets used to write Oscan do not distinguish the differences in the vowels equally well. In the north, where the "North Oscan" idioms of Paelignian, Marrucinian, and the other languages enumerated below in §13.81 were spoken, the Latin alphabet was used, which distinguished five vowels (*i e a o u*). In the central part of Oscan territory (Campania), where the Oscans were in contact with the Etruscans, they used a modified version of the Etruscan alphabet that is often referred to as the Oscan national alphabet; this is usually transliterated in boldface. In the south (as in Bruttium and Lucania), the Greek alphabet was used in the early inscriptions, and later the Latin alphabet.

Oscan text sample

13.80. The inscription Po 3, from Pompeii; first century BC. Some expressions are translations of Latin administrative phraseology. Note that some words are split up across the end of a line.

v . aadirans . v . eítiuvam . paam
vereiiaí . púmpaiianaí . trístaa
mentud . deded . eísak . eítiuvad
v . viínikiís . mr . kvaísstur . púmp
aiians . trííbúm . ekak . kúmben
nieís . tanginud . úpsannam
deded . ísídum . prúfatted

The money that V(ibius) Atranus, (son) of V(ibius), gave to the Pompeiian community in his will – with that money V(ibius) Vinicius, (son) of M(aras), the Pompeiian quaestor, gave, with agreement of the assembly, (for) this house to be built. The same one approved (it).

Figure 13.4 The Oscan inscription Po 3. The lines read from right to left. Note that what looks like an R in this alphabet is actually a D, and vice versa. The dot above a V and the very short horizontal stroke extending rightward from the stem of an I are the signs conventionally transliterated by an acute accent. Drawing from Iohannes Zvetaieff, *Sylloge Inscriptionum Oscarum ad Archetyporum et Librorum Fidem* (St. Petersburg: Brockhaus, 1878), plate XI.

13.80a. Notes (selective). **eítiuvam:** 'money', lit. 'movable (wealth)', from *ei-* 'go'. It is from earlier **eítuvam*; the *-t-* became *-ti̯-* before the *-u-*, as in varieties of English where *tune* is pronounced *tyune*. **paam:** 'which', PIE **kʷām*; relative adjective modifying *eítiuvam*, so literally "Which money V. A. gave . . ." Both *eítiuvam* and the subject of the relative clause appear before the relativizer; recall §8.26. **vereiiaí:** 'gatekeepers', dat. sing. of an abstract noun referring to a class of youths having some connection with gates. **púmpaiianaí:** 'Pompeiian'; the word is derived from the numeral 'five', which would have been ***púmpe. trístaamentud:** 'by testimony, in the will', abl. sing. of the Osc. cognate of Lat. *testāmentum*, both from **tri-st-* 'stand by as the third', i.e. to witness; the sequence **tris-* became **ters-* and then *tes-* in Latin by a sound change. **deded:** 'gave', 3rd sing. perfect (= Lat. *dedit*, Archaic Lat. *dedet*); the old perfect ending **-e(i)* has been replaced with the aorist **-et*. **eísak:** 'with that', fem. abl. sing., from **eisād-k*, the *-k* being cognate with the particle *-c* in such Latin demonstratives as *hic* 'this', *nunc* 'now', etc. The accus. *ekak* below is from **ekām-k* with loss of the nasal. **kvaísstur:** 'quaestor', an official charged with tax-collection and other financial duties. The Oscan word is borrowed from Lat. *quaestor*. **trííbúm:** 'house', from **trēbom*, from a root **treb-* found in Eng. *thorpe*. **kúmbennieís:** 'of the senate', genit. sing.; a noun formed from *kum-* 'together' (Lat. *con-*, *com-*) and *ben-* 'come' (PIE **gʷem-*). **tanginud:** 'by decision', abl. sing. *-ud* < **-ōd*. Phonetically this begins *tang-*, from the same root as Eng. *think*. The Oscan phrase *kúmbennieís tancinud* is a loan-translation of the Latin bureaucratic phrase *senātūs sententiā*. **úpsannam:** 'to be built'; *-annam* is equivalent to the Latin gerundive (future passive participle) in *-andam*. The Oscan root *úps-* is cognate with Lat. *opus* 'work'. The Oscan phrase *úpsannam deded* is a loan-translation of Lat. *faciendam cūrāuit* 'saw to it that . . . be done'. **ísídum:** 'the same one', equivalent to Lat. *is* 'he, that one' plus the Oscan equivalent of *īdem* 'the same (one)'. **prúfatted:** 'approved', an Oscan *tt*-perfect (§13.65), from *prúfa-* = Lat. *probā-*.

Other Sabellic Languages

13.81. Besides Oscan, Umbrian, and South Picene, scattered inscriptions in over half a dozen other Sabellic languages from central Italy east of Rome are known, collectively called "North Oscan." Best attested is **Paelignian**, known from about two dozen inscriptions in the Abruzzi region of eastern Italy; it is thought to be a form of Oscan by some, though its exact affiliation is not clear. Not far away were a cluster of other quite similar languages: **Marsian**, in which we have close to a dozen inscriptions; **Marrucinian** (a half-dozen); **Vestinian** (two inscriptions); and one inscription each in **Aequian**, **Sabine**, and **Volscian**, the latter spoken to the south of Latin.

Furthermore, we have about a half-dozen inscriptions from Campania from the sixth and fifth centuries BC in a language called "**Pre-Samnite**," which may have been a form of South Picene.

For Further Reading

Several books treat the history of Greek and Latin together; two were mentioned in the previous chapter (Meillet and Vendryes 1968 and Sihler 1995). The most accessible book in English on the history of Latin has been Palmer 1954, which has an appendix of archaic texts; to this may now be added Baldi 1999. The standard comparative grammar of Latin is Leumann 1977, exhaustive but largely eschewing laryngeals; more up-to-date, though smaller, is Meiser 1998. Both books will be at least partly superseded by a new comprehensive comparative grammar, in outline form, by Michael Weiss (Weiss to appear). A detailed investigation of the outcomes of the laryngeals in Latin is Schrijver 1991. The two standard etymological dictionaries of Latin are Ernout and Meillet 1979 and Walde and Hofmann 1938–56; the former contains a wealth of cultural information alongside the purely linguistic. Most of the important Archaic Latin texts are collected, with linguistic commentary, in Ernout 1947; see also, more recently, Wachter 1987 and Vine 1993, as well as now Hartmann 2005.

A vast resource on the antiquities of ancient Italy is the multi-volume *Popoli e civiltà dell'Italia antica* (Rome: Biblioteca di Storia Patria, 1974–92), of which vol. 6 contains descriptions of all the languages. An excellent and readable overview of the Sabellic languages is now Wallace 2007, which includes analyses of many inscriptions and inscriptional excerpts. The most up-to-date collection of all the Sabellic inscriptions is Rix 2002, which contains the raw texts with references to secondary literature but no commentary. The standard collection of all the Italic dialect inscriptions known by the early 1950s is Vetter 1953, which has interlinear Latin translations and some commentary; it was supplemented by Poccetti 1979. The Faliscan corpus is in Giacomelli 1963. For Oscan and Umbrian, still very useful because of its thorough grammatical descriptions is Buck 1928, which contains most of the important inscriptions plus translations and a glossary. Of the many editions of the Umbrian Iguvine Tables, Poultney 1959 is the most accessible, and has an English translation. Meiser 1986 is a useful recent phonological history of Umbrian. A dictionary of Sabellic, with grammatical and etymological discussion, is Untermann 2000. The South Picene corpus is handsomely edited in Marinetti 1985.

For Review

Know the meaning or significance of the following:

Etruscan	rhotacism	Vulgar Latin	Sabellic
"Italo-Celtic"	Festus	*Appendix Probi*	Iguvine Tables

Exercises

1 Using the sound and morphological changes introduced in this chapter, determine the Latin outcomes of the following PIE forms. In **a** and **e**, the final *-i* disappeared prehistorically.

a *_h_2eĝonti_ 'they drive'
b *_p$h_2$tres_ 'of the father'
c *_$h_1$si$h_1$mos_ 'may we be'
d *_tr̥$h_2$ns-pr̥te$h_2$tiō_ 'act of carrying across'
e *_deuk̂eti_ 'he leads'
f *_loukei̯oh_2_ 'I make shine'
g *_duk̂tos_ 'led'
h *_str̥$h_3$tos_ 'laid, strewn'
i *_g^wih_3u̯os_ 'alive'
j *_ek̂u̯om_ 'horse' (accus.)
k *_n̥ter_ 'between'

2 The outcomes of the PIE voiced aspirated stops in Latin are fairly complex. Using the data below, answer the questions that follow.

*_bhāĝos_ > _fāgus_ 'beech'
*_bhrātēr_ > _frāter_ 'brother'
*_bheremos_ > _ferimus_ 'we bear'
*_$h_3$erbhos_ > _orbus_ 'orphan'
*_albhos_ > _albus_ 'white'
*_dhu$h_2$mos_ > _fūmus_ 'smoke'
*_dhightos_ > _fictus_ 'fashioned by hand'
*_medhii̯os_ > _medius_ 'middle'
*_u̯idheu̯eh_2_ > _uidua_ 'widow'
*_oudhes-_ > _ūber-_ 'udder'
*_i̯oudhei̯oh_2_ > Archaic _ioubeo_ 'I command'
*_$h_1$leudheros_ > _līber_ 'free'
*_$h_1$rudhē-_ > _rubē-(facere)_ 'to redden'
*_ĝhiems_ > _hiems_ 'winter'
*_ghostis_ > _hostis_ 'stranger, enemy'
*_ghabhē-_ > _habē-_ 'have'
*_ghu-n-d-_ > _fund-_ 'pour'
*_ghu̯er-_ > _fera_ 'wild animal'
*_u̯eĝheti_ > _uehit_ 'conveys'
*_dhinĝh-_ > _fing-_ 'make with the hands'
*_g^whormos_ > _formus_ 'warm'
*_sning^{w}heti_ > _ninguit_ 'it snows'
*_snig^{w}hm̥_ > _niuem_ 'snow'

a Treating *_gh_ and *_ĝh_ as the same thing, determine the word-initial outcomes of each aspirated stop.
b Again treating *_gh_ and *_ĝh_ as the same thing, determine the word-internal outcomes of each aspirated stop.
c It was mentioned in §2.15 that Eng. *law* comes from the root 'to lay down', a root that has also been forwarded as the source of the Latin word for 'law', *lex* (stem *leg-*). The root in question is *_legh-_. Why is this etymology of the Latin word problematic?

3 In the Introduction (§1.1) and elsewhere in this book it has been mentioned that Lat. *deus* 'god' is not related to its Greek synonym *theós.* Explain why this is so.

4 Explain the historical relationships between the words in each of the following pairs or triplets. For example, if the pair were *dīcit* '(s)he says' : *dictus* 'said' (past participle), the answer would be that the *ī/i* alternation probably continues PIE ablaut, namely full grade (present tense, thematic) and zero-grade (*_-to-_ verbal adjective), which means *ī* is from *_ei_ (§13.35). Not all the answers involve matters of PIE date.

- **a** *ūrit* '(s)he burns', *ustus* '(having been) burned'
- **b** *precēs* 'prayers' (nomin. pl.), *procus* 'suitor'
- **c** *tegit* '(s)he covers', *toga* 'toga' (< *'covering'), *tēgula* 'roofing tile'
- **d** *fīdit* '(s)he trusts', *foedus* 'treaty', *fidēs* 'faith, trust'
- **e** *iungit* '(s)he joins, yokes', *coniugem* 'spouse' (accus. sg.; *con-* 'with')
- **f** *fūner-is* 'of a funeral (gen. sg.)', *fūnes-tus* 'funerary'

5 In the Latin suovitaurilia prayer (§13.53), you met the forms *-**que*** and *ē-**uen**-īre*, where the *-qu-* and *-u-* (which stands for the glide *w*) go back to IE *k^w and *g^w, respectively. Now consider three other Latin words:

bōs 'cow'
coquīna 'kitchen' (earlier **quoquīna*)
popīna 'hash-house'

The latter two forms go back to an Italic root *$k^w ek^w$- or *$k^w ok^w$- meaning 'cook'. Which of these three forms (*bōs*, **quoquīna*, *popīna*) show(s) the genuine Latin outcome(s) of the labiovelars in question? What explanation can you offer for the forms that do not?

6 **a** Analyze the excerpt from the suovitaurilia prayer (§13.53) in light of the strophic poetic style discussed in §§2.42–44. Note especially pairs or triplets of words that echo each other phonetically or syntactically.
b Cato's text has *bonam* in the last line of the excerpt; as the Notes indicate, this is from earlier **duenam*. If we restore **duenam* here, how would that fit in with the phonetic figures that you just discussed?

7 Latin has pairs such as the following, in which the first word is a derivative with a **no*-suffix and the second word is a diminutive of the first: *tignum* 'plank' : *tigillum* 'small plank'; *pugnus* 'fist' : *pugillus* 'handful' (< *'little fist'). Latin also has pairs where the first member has undergone sound change, such as *scamnum* 'stool' : *scabillum* 'low stool'.

- **a** What would *scamnum* have originally been, and what sound change occurred to give the attested form?
- **b** Another pair where the non-diminutive has undergone sound change is *pānis* 'bread' : *pastillus* 'medicinal tablet' (< *'small loaf'). What would *pānis* have been originally, and what sound change(s) occurred to give the attested form?
- **c** Latin also has the pair *pīlum* '(large) pestle' (with an *l*-suffix instead of an *n*-suffix) : *pistillum* '(small) pestle'. What would *pīlum* have been originally, and what sound change(s) occurred to give the attested form? (Ignore §13.7 for the purposes of this problem.)
- **d** Comparable to the above is the pair *āla* 'wing' : *axilla* 'little wing'. What would *āla* have been originally, and what sound change(s) happened to give the attested form?

e How does the sound change you came up with for **d** explain the difference between the prefix in the verbs *ex-portāre* 'to carry out' and *ē-lūcēre* 'to shine out'?

f What additional sound change is needed to explain the compound verb *ē-numerāre* 'to count out'?

g An inscription from the third century BC has the form *losna* (from slightly earlier **lousna*) 'moon', which became Classical Latin *lūna*. This is from the same root seen in *lūc-ēre* 'to make shine' < **louk-ēre*. What does this inscriptional form tell us about the order of events making up the sound change in **f**?

8 Observe the following pairs of Latin forms:

ag-ere 'to do' : *āc-tus* '(having been) done'
fra-n-g-ere 'to break' : *frāc-tus* '(having been) broken'
leg-ere 'to choose' : *lēc-tus* '(having been) chosen'

The lengthened vowels in the past participles are unexpected. Contrast *fac-tus* '(having been) made' from *fac-ere* 'to make' and *iac-tus* 'thrown' from *iac-ere* 'to throw'. It has been claimed that in Latin, a vowel before a voiced stop became lengthened when that stop was devoiced before a voiceless consonant ("Lachmann's Law"). What rule in PIE phonology might pose difficulties for this claim?

9 How do we know that *duenoi* in the third line of the Duenos inscription (§13.52) had a long diphthong *-ōi* rather than *-oi*, as per the notes?

10 Using the information in §13.13, indicate into which of the four Latin conjugations the following PIE verb forms would have fallen:

a **h₁rudh-eh₁-i̯e-* 'be red' **c** **pekʷ-e-ti* 'cooks'
b **dok̂-éi̯e-* 'show' **d** *. . . *-eh₂-i̯e-*

11 Based on §13.13 and your knowledge of PIE and Latin sound changes, into which of the four conjugations would the following PIE athematic verbs have fallen?

a **bhleh₁-ti* 'weeps' **b** **bheh₂-ti* 'speaks' **c** **neh₁-ti* 'sew'

PIE Vocabulary V: Body Functions and States

**gʷih₃u̯o-* 'alive': Ved. *jīvá-*, Gk. *bíos* 'life', Lat. *uīuus*, Eng. QUICK
**h₂enh₁-* 'breathe': Ved. *ániti* 'breathes', Gk. *ánemos* 'wind', Lat. *anima* 'breath'
**su̯ep-* 'sleep': Ved. *svápnas*, Gk. *húpnos*, Lat. *somnus*
**su̯eid-* 'SWEAT': Ved. *svédate* 'sweats', Lat. *sūdor*
**h₁ed-* 'EAT': Hitt. *ēdmi* 'I eat', Ved. *ádmi* 'I eat', Gk. *édomai* 'I will eat', Lat. *edō* 'I eat'
**peh₃-* 'drink': Hitt. *pāši* 'swallows', Ved. *pā́ti* 'drinks', Lat. *pōtus* 'a drink'
**ĝenh₁-* 'give birth': Ved. *jánati* 'gives birth', Gk. *génesis* 'birth, beginning', Lat. *genus* 'race, kind'

**u̯eid-* 'see': Ved. *ávidat* 'found', Gk. *é(w)idon* 'I saw', Lat. *uideō* 'I see', OCS *viděti* 'to see'
**k̑leu-* 'hear': Ved. *śr̥ṇóti* 'hears', Gk. *klũthi* 'hear!', OIr. *ro-cluinethar* 'hears', Lith. *klausýti* 'to hear'
**men-* 'think': Ved. *manyáte* 'thinks', Gk. *maínomai* 'I go mad', Lat. *mēns* (*ment-*) 'mind', Eng. MIND
**u̯emh₁-* 'vomit': Gk. *(w)émein* 'to vomit', Lat. *uomere* 'to vomit'
**perd-* 'FART': Ved. *párdate* 'farts', Gk. *pérdetai*
**mer-* 'die': Gk. *ámbrotos* 'immortal', Lat. *mors* (*mort-*) 'death', Eng. MURDER

14 Celtic

Introduction

14.1. The Celtic languages hold a special place in the early history of Indo-European linguistics because they presented the first real challenge to the nascent science. The demonstration that Irish and its relatives are related to the likes of Greek, Latin, and Sanskrit was a genuine triumph; for while it is obvious that Greek, Latin, and Sanskrit are related to each other, it is not at all obvious that they have anything to do with Irish or Welsh – languages that, on the surface at least, are bafflingly different. We will discuss how the puzzle was solved below when we talk about Insular Celtic (§§14.21ff.).

14.2. The Celtic languages that have survived in unbroken tradition until the present day are confined to a small corner of northwestern Europe – Irish Gaelic in Ireland, Scottish Gaelic in Scotland, Welsh in Wales, and Breton in Brittany (northwest France); the total number of their speakers does not exceed one million. Such meager numbers give little indication of the erstwhile glory of this branch of Indo-European. For hundreds of years before the expansion of late republican Rome in the first century BC, Celtic tribes dominated much of Europe. Archaeologically, it appears that the prehistoric Celts are to be identified with the later stages of the Hallstatt culture (c. 1200–500 BC), located in what is now southern Germany, Austria, and Bohemia (western Czech Republic). By the end of this period, Celtic tribes had spread outward in almost all directions, first westward into France, Belgium, Spain, and the British Isles, and then, by about 400 BC, southward into northern Italy and southeast into the Balkans and beyond, with one group (the Galatians) eventually winding up in Asia Minor (see further below).

After Julius Caesar's conquest of Gaul (ancient France) by 50 BC and the emperor Claudius's subjugation of Britain roughly a century later, most of this Celtic-speaking territory was assimilated to the Roman world. Latin became the dominant language; Gaulish and the other **Continental Celtic** languages eventually died out. The other branch of Celtic, **Insular Celtic**, to which all the modern Celtic languages belong, continued to flourish in the British Isles, especially in Ireland, whose separation from Britain by the Irish Channel insulated it somewhat from the Romans and, later, from the Anglo-Saxons. Ireland in fact is the home of the first vernacular literature written in medieval Europe, that is, literature that was not written in an official language of the Church (Latin in the West).

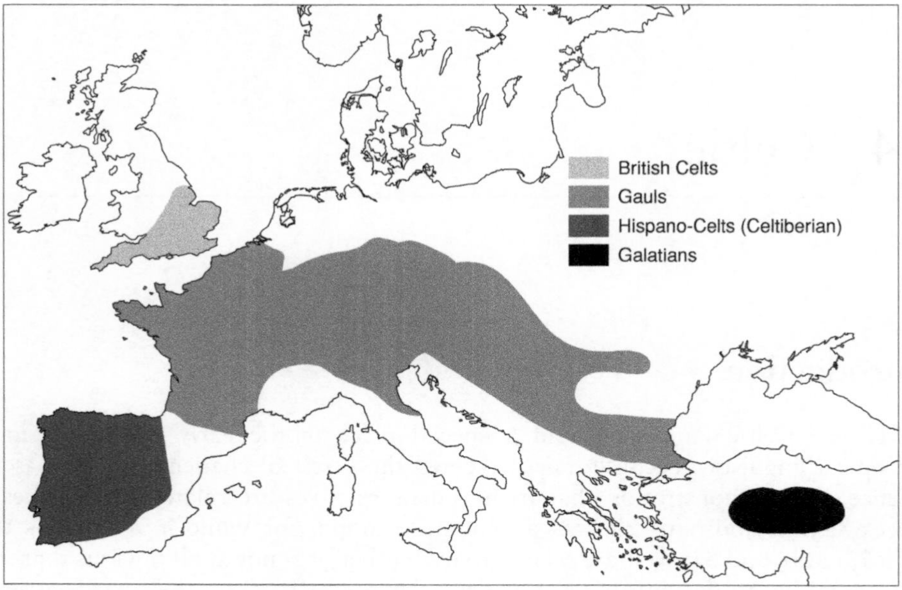

Map 14.1 The Celts

But eventually the expansion of English cultural hegemony reduced the number of Celtic speakers in Ireland and elsewhere in the British Isles. The situation is no better in France, where Breton, spoken by descendants of British Celts, suffers under the comparable cultural dominance of French.

Celtic and other branches of Indo-European

14.3. Celtic shares several features with Italic, leading some scholars to claim that the two branches formed an "Italo-Celtic" subgroup of Indo-European. But the validity of this claim is in doubt, even after decades of controversy. See §13.5 for a more detailed discussion.

From PIE to Celtic

Phonology

Stops

14.4. Celtic is a centum branch, having merged the palatal velars with the ordinary velars. A defining change was the loss of **p* in most positions, as in OIr. *athair* 'father' < ***ph₂tēr***. At an early date, the voiced labiovelar $*g^w$ became *b* (e.g. $*\boldsymbol{g^w}$***en-*** 'woman' > OIr. and W. ***ben***); interestingly, the other labiovelars remained intact as labiovelars until much later. Following the change of *g^w to *b*, the voiced aspirates lost their aspiration, as in OIr. ***biru*** 'I carry' < **bher-oh*$_2$, Middle Ir. ***daig*** 'fire' < **dheg*^{w}*h-i-*, and Middle W. ***gell*** 'yellow' < **ĝhel-*.

A double-dental sequence (§3.36) became *-ss-* in Celtic (pronounced as a single *s* by the historical period): OIr. ***-fess*** 'known' < **u̯id-to-*, W. ***gwŷs*** 'summons, writ' < **u̯id-tu-*.

Laryngeals

14.5. Laryngeals were lost except when vocalized, in which case they became **a*, as in most of the other branches (e.g. **ph*$_2$*tēr* > OIr. ***athair***, cp. Lat. *pater*, Eng. *father*).

Resonants

14.6. The nonsyllabic resonants stayed unchanged except for final **-m*, which became *-n* in Insular Celtic and some varieties of Gaulish. The syllabic liquids are a difficult domain of Celtic phonology because of their multiple outcomes. Sometimes **r̥* **l̥* became **ri* **li*: OIr. ***cride*** 'heart' < **k̑r̥d-i̯o-* (cp. Gk. *kardíā*); Gaul. ***litano-*** and W. ***llydan*** 'wide' < **pl̥tano-* (cp. Gk. *platús* 'broad'). But the outcomes **ar* **al* are also found: Gaul. ***Arto-***, W. ***arth***, OIr. ***art*** 'bear' (whence the name *Art*) < **h*$_2$*r̥tk̑o-*; OIr. ***tart*** 'thirst' < **tr̥sto-* (cp. Ved. *tr̥ṣṭá-* 'dry', Eng. *thirst*).

The syllabic nasals are more straightforward: **m̥* and **n̥* became **am* and **an*: Gaul. ***ambi-*** 'around', W. ***am*** < **h*$_2$*m̥bhi*; OIr. and W. ***an-*** 'not, un-' < **n̥-*. In Irish, as recent research has shown, these were sometimes raised to *em/en* or *im/in*, especially before voiced stops, as in *imb* 'around'.

14.7. The "long" syllabic resonants **r̥̄* **l̥̄* **m̥̄* **n̥̄* (from sequences of syllabic resonant plus laryngeal; see §3.15) typically turn into the relevant resonant followed by *ā*, as in Italic: Gaulish city name (Latinized) *(Medio-)****lānum*** 'middle of the plain, Milan' < **pl̥h*$_2$*no-* (cp. Lat. *plānum* 'plain'); OIr. ***grán*** 'grain' (the acute accent indicates length), W. ***grawn*** 'grain' < **ĝr̥h*$_2$*no-* (cp. Lat. *grānum* 'grain', Eng. *corn*); OIr. ***gnáth*** 'known, customary' < **ĝn̥h*$_3$*to-* (cp. Gk. *gnōtós* 'known').

Vowels

14.8. The IE vowel system remained largely unchanged. The main early shift was made by **ō*, which became **ū* in final syllables, as in the 1st sing. ending in Gaul. ***delgu*** 'I hold' and OIr. ***biru*** 'I carry'. It became **ā* elsewhere: **mōros* 'great' > Celtic **māros*, as in the Gaulish personal name *Sego-****māros*** 'great in strength', Archaic OIr. ***már*** 'great', and W. ***mawr*** 'great'; cp. Gk. *enkhesí-mōros* 'great with the ash spear'.

Morphology and syntax

Verbs

14.9. Most of the verbal formations of PIE survive into Celtic in one form or another, including athematic verbs, aorists, perfects, thematic subjunctives, and middles. The optative, though, has disappeared, as have participles (though a few old participles are preserved vestigially as nouns, such as OIr. *carae* 'friend' from the present participle **karant-* 'loving'). Dual verb endings were also lost (but not dual noun endings), although there is disputed evidence of a dual in Gaulish. The Celtic imperfects are of unknown origin and must be innovations. Like Italic, Celtic has a derivational suffix in *-ā-* from PIE *$*$-eh_2$-* (§5.37) for forming denominative verbs, as well as a subjunctive morpheme in *-ā-* of uncertain origin (cp. §13.19).

Nouns

14.10. The new finds from Celtiberian have shown that Celtic inherited the PIE case-system intact in the singular. Like Italic, Celtic has an *o*-stem genitive singular in **-ī* (e.g. Primitive [inscriptional] Ir. *maq(q)i* 'of the son').

Syntax

14.11. Insular Celtic is unusual among the older IE branches in that verbs are generally clause-initial. (The possible source of this order was discussed in §8.19.) An interesting and archaic feature of Gaulish and Insular Celtic word order was the position of the relative pronoun. In these languages, an indeclinable relative **yo* (from the relative pronominal stem **i̯o-*, §7.11) was placed after the first element in a relative clause. This is attested directly in such forms as Gaul. *dugiionti-io* 'who serve', and (somewhat obscured after sound changes) Old W. *issid* (Mod. W. *sydd*) 'who is' < **esti-yo*. In Celtiberian, however, declined forms of the relative pronoun are still found, such as the dative *iomui* 'for whom', and its placement seems to have been freer.

Continental Celtic

14.12. The Celtic languages spoken in continental Europe until the first few centuries AD, all of them extinct, are referred to as Continental Celtic and were spoken by people called *Keltoí* by the Greeks and *Gallī* or *Galatae* by the Romans. Chief among the Continental Celtic languages is **Gaulish**. The Gauls were a powerful Celtic people consisting of hundreds of tribes spread throughout much of Europe; as noted above, their territory stretched from Gaul (ancient France) through Switzerland and northern Italy into Hungary, with one major group settling in the third century BC in Galatia in central Anatolia. (The *Gal-* of Galatia is related to *Gallī*; its inhabitants are the Galatians addressed in an epistle of Paul in the New Testament.) Many of the Gaulish tribes were aggressive marauders, as exemplified by the Galatians, who wreaked havoc on many principalities in Asia Minor, and famously by the band of Gauls that penetrated deep into Italy in the early fourth century BC and sacked Rome in 390 or thereabouts. But the tides of history eventually turned against them; they were subdued by Julius Caesar by 50 BC and gradually assimilated into Roman culture. Gaulish was still spoken in isolated pockets probably until around AD 500, or even later in Asia Minor.

Gaulish inscriptions are written in both the Greek and Italic scripts. The number of known inscriptions has grown dramatically since the mid-twentieth century. In addition to the inscriptional remains, many Gaulish proper names are preserved in Greek and Roman historical and geographical writings.

14.13. Inscriptions in a Celtic language called **Lepontic** (also called Cisalpine Gaulish) have been found in northern Italy; it may or may not be a dialect of Gaulish. The earliest Lepontic inscriptions date to the sixth century BC and represent our oldest preserved Celtic. Most of the Lepontic inscriptions are funerary and contain little more than personal names.

14.14. Last of the Continental Celtic languages is **Celtiberian** (or Hispano-Celtic), spoken by Celtic peoples who migrated into northeast Spain in the mid-first millennium BC. Most of the nearly 120 extant Celtiberian inscriptions are very brief; the language has been seriously studied only since 1970, when an extensive bronze inscription was found in the village of Botorrita (ancient Contrebia Belaisca), 20 km south of Zaragoza in northeast Spain. An even longer second inscription was found at the same site in 1992, but disappointingly consists almost entirely of personal names. About three other inscriptions of some length are known, two from south of Zaragoza and one that recently came to light in New York City and was published in 1993. The Celtiberian inscriptions date to the second and first centuries BC.

14.15. The script of most of the Celtiberian inscriptions was borrowed from a neighboring non-Indo-European people, the Iberians, who lived along the eastern Spanish coast and acquired an alphabet from either the Greeks or the Phoenicians or both. They modified it in certain ways so that it became partly a syllabary: vowels and resonants were indicated by single letter signs, while stop consonants were only indicated by signs that represented the combination of a stop plus a following vowel. No distinction was made between voiced and voiceless stops, so a sign like *ta* stood for both *ta* and *da*.

14.16. A very poorly attested IE language called **Lusitanian** is documented in Portugal. Although some say it is a relative of Celtiberian, this is very uncertain. Lusitanian will be discussed in chapter 20. On the southernmost tip of the Iberian peninsula was spoken another poorly known language called **Tartessian**, which has some Celtic linguistic material in its personal names.

Continental Celtic grammar

14.17. We cannot compile anything resembling a complete grammar of either Gaulish or Celtiberian. It does not appear that the two languages were particularly close. Of the two, Celtiberian was the more conservative; as noted above (§14.10), it preserved PIE nominal inflection practically intact. Even the ablative and instrumental, which had merged in Hittite and Greek a millennium earlier, are still preserved in Celtiberian separately as *-uz* and *-u* in *o*-stem nouns (< late PIE *-*ōd* and *-*ō*). The dual is still a living category in nouns. Celtiberian also preserved the labiovelars as such (as in the conjunction ***-cue*** 'and' < ****k***^{w}*e*), while Gaulish changed them to labials (as in ***pissíiumí*** 'I see' < ****k***^{w}*i*-). Since Brittonic also changed the labiovelars to labials (§14.54), some specialists view Gaulish as a Brittonic language, but this claim has not won general acceptance.

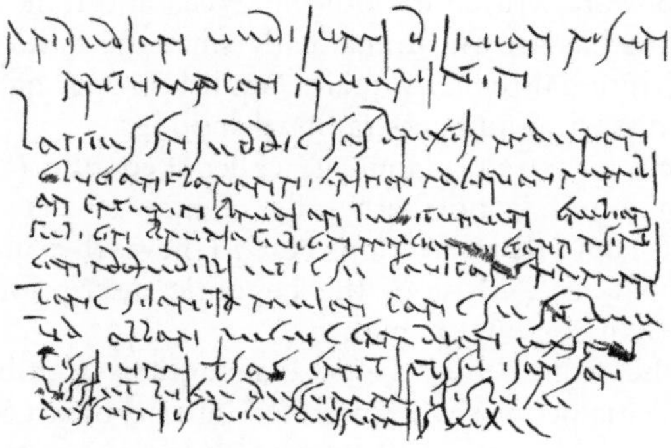

Figure 14.1 The Chamalières inscription, written in an ancient cursive form of the Latin alphabet that has no relationship to our modern cursive script. The excerpt begins at the end of the sixth line from the bottom (the smudge comes between the *n* and *c* of *toncnaman*). An I twice the height of a normal I is rendered as *í* in the transliteration. Drawing by R. Marichal, from Pierre-Yves Lambert, *Recueil des inscriptions gauloises,* vol. II, fasc. 2: *Textes gallo-latins sur* instrumentum (Paris: CNRS, 2002), p. 271. Reproduced by permission of the publisher.

Gaulish text sample

14.18. An excerpt from the inscription found in Chamalières in Clermont-Ferrand (southeast France), written on a lead tablet in the early first century AD and deposited in a spring. In ancient Mediterranean cultures, this was standard practice for prayers, curses, and other texts addressed to underworld deities. This tablet was written apparently on behalf of some men seeking beneficial action from the gods. There are no word-divisions in the original, and not all the forms are understood, so no translation is given.

[. . .] toncnaman
toncsiíontío meíon ponc sesit buetid ollon reguc cambion exsops
pissíiumí [. . .]

14.18a. Notes. toncnaman: a noun in the accus. sing. forming an etymological figure with the following verb; perhaps 'oath'. **toncsiíontío:** a 3rd pl. verb *toncsiíont(i)* 'they will swear' (?), containing the future morpheme **-si̯e-* (§5.40), with the relative pronominal clitic *-ío* 'who' or 'which' attached (PIE **i̯o-*). Perhaps '. . . the oath which they will swear . . .'. **ponc:** 'when' or the like, from **kwom-k̂(e)* (accus. sing. of the relative pronoun plus the deictic particle **k̂e*, §7.29); cp. Lat. *tunc* 'then' < **tom-k̂(e)*. **buetid:** 3rd sing. *buet* 'will be' plus clitic subject pronoun *-id* 'it'. **ollon:** 'all, whole'. **reguc cambion:** probably 'I straighten the crooked'; *regu* is 1st sing. from the root **$h_3$reĝ-*, seen also in Lat. *regō* 'I direct', and *cambion* is from the Celtic root **kamb-* 'crooked', also referring to back-and-forth motion and exchange. It is ultimately the source of Eng. *change* via Late Latin *cambiāre* 'to exchange', a borrowing from Celtic. The reason for the *-c* at the end of *reguc* is disputed. **exsops:** 'blind', literally '(having) the eyes (*-ops*) out (*exs-*)'. The French word for 'blind', *aveugle*, from Vulgar Latin

Figure 14.2 The front side of the first Botorrita inscription. The inscription reads from left to right; most word-divisions are indicated by double dots (though these are missing after the first word). Drawing from Untermann 1997, vol. 4, p. 567. Copyright Dr. Ludwig Reichert Verlag Wiesbaden. Reproduced by permission of the publisher.

ab-oculus*, may ultimately be a loan-translation of this Gaulish word, though other explanations are also possible. **pissíiumí: 'I will see', 3rd sing. future, from pre-Celtic **k^wid-si̯ō(-mi)*. The root is the source of OIr. *(ad-)cí* 'sees'. The last four words are thus '(And) I (shall) straighten the crooked; blind, I shall see'.

Celtiberian text sample

14.19. The first three lines of the first Botorrita inscription. The transliteration makes use of the most recent discoveries, using *b* for the signs formerly transliterated with *p*, and using *s* and *z* instead of *ś* and *s* (*z* represents either [z] or [ð]). A very tentative translation is given, mostly following Wolfgang Meid, *Celtiberian Inscriptions* (1994).

tiricantam bercunetacam tocoitoscue sarniciocue sua combalcez nelitom
necue to uertaunei litom necue taunei litom necue masnai tizaunei litom soz aucu
arestalo tamai uta oscuez stena uerzoniti silabur sleitom conscilitom cabizeti

Concerning the region (?) pertaining to the **berguneta* of Tocoit- and Sarnicios, it has been thus decreed as non-permitted:
It is neither permitted to put (things) upon, nor is it permitted to do (work?), nor is it permitted to cause damage by destruction.
And whoever contravenes these things, he shall take cut-up . . . silver . . .

14.19a. Notes. tiricantam: uncertain; translated by Meid 'region', but it has been recently suggested to be the number 'thirty' in the sense of a group of thirty people (a council?) or other societal division (cp. the tradition that Romulus divided the Roman populace into thirty groups). Cp. OIr. *tríchat-* < Celt. **trī-kant-* 'thirty' < PIE **trī-dk̑m̥t-*. **bercunetacam:** phonetically probably *bergunetacam* and apparently containing the root for 'hill', *berg-* (PIE **bherĝh-*, cp. German *Berg* 'mountain'); maybe 'hilly'. **tocoitoscue sarniciocue:** 'both of T. and of S.'; *-cue . . . -cue* are like Lat. *-que . . . -que* 'both . . . and', from PIE **k^we*. **sua combalcez:** contains the notion 'it has been thus decreed' or the like, but grammatically unclear; could also be read *compalcez*, *complacez*. *Sua* may be comparable to Goth. *swa*, Eng. *so*; *combalcez* may be a 3rd sing. past-tense verb with ending from **-t*. The exact phrase *tiricantam . . . sua combal*[*ce*]*z* recurs on another Celtiberian inscription. **nelitom:** 'not allowed', from the same root as Eng. *let.* **necue . . . necue:** 'neither . . . nor', cp. Lat. *neque . . . neque.* **to uertaunei:** perhaps literally 'the putting-upon', if phonetically *to uerdaunei*, with *uer-* 'over, above' (cp. the Gaulish name *Ver-cingeto-rīx* 'far-stepping king') and *daunei* an infinitive meaning 'to do, place, put' from **dheh₁-* 'place, put'. The infinitive suffix *-unei* may be dissimilated from **-mn-ei.* **litom:** 'allowed'. **masnai:** dative, perhaps from a noun **mad-snā-* related to OIr. *maidid* 'breaks'. **tizaunei:** another infinitive. The rest of the line and the beginning of the next are unclear. The reading *arestalo* is uncertain (*arestaso* is also possible). **uta:** 'and', cp. Ved. *utá* 'and'. **oscuez:** 'whoever', formally like Gk. *hós-tis* < **i̯os-kʷis.* **uerzoniti:** 'over-seeks, contravenes', another verb with the prefix *uer-*. **silabur:** 'silver', a cultural loanword also found in Germanic and Balto-Slavic (cp. Goth. *silubr*, Russ. *serebro*). **cabizeti:** 'he shall take'.

Insular Celtic

14.20. Insular Celtic consists of two subbranches, **Goidelic** and **Brittonic**. Goidelic contains Old Irish and its descendants: Irish Gaelic, Scottish Gaelic, and Manx. Brittonic (or Brythonic) contains Welsh, Breton, Cornish, and perhaps the language of the Picts (see §14.53). (Manx and Cornish both died out in recent times, though there have been attempts to revive them.) Goidelic and Brittonic are often called "Q-Celtic" and "P-Celtic" because of their respective treatment of the PIE labiovelars: Goidelic turned the labiovelars into velars, while Brittonic turned them into labials.

While Continental Celtic languages look basically like other old Indo-European languages, with Insular Celtic the story is quite different. Irish and Welsh, to put it bluntly, look bizarre when compared to languages like Greek and Latin. This is mostly due to a massive set of sound changes that occurred in rather quick succession over the course of a few centuries, and to which we now turn.

Phonology

Insular Celtic consonant mutations

14.21. The single most striking feature of the Insular Celtic languages from the early medieval period onward is the system of initial consonant mutations: word-initial consonants change depending on what word precedes, or depending simply on grammatical roles. To take Modern Welsh as an example, the word *car* 'car' can appear as *car*, *gar*, *nghar*, or *char*: *eu **car** nhw* 'their car', *y **gar*** 'the car', *fy **nghar** i* 'my car', *ei **char** hi* 'her car'. Similarly, in Old Irish, the number *sé* 'six' causes no change in a following consonant (*sé guth* 'six voices'), whereas *cóic* 'five' causes a following stop consonant to become a fricative (written *cóic gotha* 'five voices' but pronounced [ɣoθə] with a voiced velar fricative), while *secht* 'seven' causes the consonant to become nasalized (*secht ngotha* 'seven voices'). The system seems at first glance utterly capricious, the contexts in which mutation occurs completely arbitrary.

14.22. But behind many capricious linguistic systems lie less capricious origins. We owe the unraveling of this particular mystery to Franz Bopp, one of the founders of IE linguistics in Germany in the early nineteenth century. Until his work, there was no consensus that the Celtic languages were even Indo-European. Bopp's fundamental breakthrough was to notice systematic correspondences between the Celtic mutations and certain facts in Greek, Latin, and Sanskrit. Specifically, an Irish word caused a following consonant to become a fricative when the Sanskrit cognate form ended in a vowel, and an Irish word caused nasalization when its cognate ended in a nasal; in all other cases, no mutation happened. For instance, consider the mutations induced (or not induced) by the Old Irish forms below in light of the final sounds of their Sanskrit and Latin cognates:

Skt.	***asya*** 'his'	OIr.	*a **guth*** [ɣʊθ] 'his voice'
	eṣām 'their'		*a **nguth*** 'their voice'
	asyāḥ 'her'		*a **guth*** 'her voice' (no mutation)
Lat.	***quīnque*** 'five'	OIr.	*cóic **gotha*** [ɣoθə] 'five voices'
	septem 'seven'		*secht **ngotha*** 'seven voices'
	sex 'six'		*sé **gotha*** 'six voices' (no mutation)

The mutations were thus revealed to preserve vestiges of final syllables in prehistoric Celtic: the nasalization in a phrase like *a nguth* is a relic of the nasal that once ended the possessive *a* 'their'. (In effect, the mutations are remnants of old sandhi rules.) The overall system is the same in the other Insular Celtic languages, though differing in detail. The mutation that causes a following consonant to become a fricative is called **lenition**, and the mutation that adds a nasal before a following sound is called **nasalization**. The mutations also happened word-internally.

Insular Celtic vowel changes

14.23. The "old Indo-European" look of Insular Celtic was also dramatically altered by a series of changes to the vowels, in particular the loss of most final syllables (apocope), the loss of internal vowels (syncope), and umlaut (called in Celtic studies vowel "affection" and "infection," and sometimes "vowel harmony"). Some of these changes happened in the common Insular Celtic period, but others were later parallel and independent developments (arising no doubt from some favorable initial conditions already present in common Insular Celtic).

14.24. The various umlauts were the first to take place. Their details, as well as those of the initial consonant mutations, are discussed individually for Irish and Welsh below. Following the umlauts, both Goidelic and Brittonic underwent apocope and syncope. Syncope in Irish hit every other syllable after the initial (stressed) syllable, e.g. pre-OIr. **cossamil* 'similar' > OIr. *cosmil*; **ancossamili* 'dissimilar' (pl.) > OIr. *écsamli*. In Brittonic, syncope hit unstressed syllables directly before stressed syllables, but was a bit more sensitive to word-structure, as in the British king's name *Cunobelī́nos* becoming **Cun-belī́nos* (whence Welsh *Cynfelyn* and English *Cymbeline*), rather than expected **Cuno-blī́nos* (which would have become **Cyneflyn*).

Morphology

Verbs

14.25. Much inherited IE verbal morphology is preserved intact in Insular Celtic, generally more faithfully in Goidelic than in Brittonic. Both Irish and Welsh continue the *s*-aorist as two types of preterite, an *s*-preterite (e.g. OIr. *mórais* 'he magnified', Middle W. *kereis* 'he loved') and a *t*-preterite (e.g. OIr. *birt* 'he carried', Middle W. *cant* 'he sang'), the latter being a special development of the *s*-preterite in resonant-final roots. The PIE perfect is continued by another preterite, the reduplicated preterite (although Brittonic barely has any examples): Middle W. *ciglef*, OIr. *(ro-)chúala* 'I heard', both ultimately from PIE **k̂e-k̂lou̯-*. (In the Irish form, the diphthong *úa* is ultimately from the sequence **-ek-* in **keklou-*.) Both Irish and Welsh have a so-called *s*-subjunctive, from the PIE *s*-aorist subjunctive (e.g. OIr. indicative *guidiu* 'I pray', *s*-subjunctive *gess*; Middle W. indicative *car* 'loves', subj. *carho* [with *-h-* < **-s-*]). Insular Celtic has a 3rd person passive used as an impersonal, while the **to*-verbal adjective is continued as a passive preterite (e.g. OIr. *-críth* 'was bought' < $*k^{w}rih_2$*-to-*; Middle W. *caffat* 'was had'). The IE future (or desiderative) formations were mostly lost in Brittonic, but survive as futures in Irish (§14.41). A morphological innovation in the Insular Celtic verb is the use of the preverb **ro-* to mark perfective aspect (OIr. *ro-*, W. *ry-*; from IE **pro-*).

The hallmark of the verb in the older stages of Insular Celtic is the distinction between the so-called absolute and conjunct verb-forms: most verb-forms existed in two variants, one used clause-initially and the other when certain elements preceded. This feature is far more characteristic of Irish than Brittonic, and will be discussed in the Irish section.

Infixed pronouns

14.26. Object pronouns in the Insular Celtic languages are often inserted between the preverb and verb, and are called infixed pronouns. Thus in Old Irish, to say 'does not strike' one said *ní-ben*, while 'does not strike me' was *ní-m ben* (with the initial *b-* pronounced as the fricative [β]) and 'does not strike him' was *ní-mben* (where *mb* was pronounced [mb]). Similarly, from *ad-cí* 'sees' one could form *atot-chí* 'sees you' and *at-chí* 'sees it'. As forms like *ní-mben* show, the presence of an infixed pronoun is sometimes betrayed only by the mutation of the initial consonant of the verbal root (after the preverb).

Conjugated prepositions

14.27. Characteristic of Insular Celtic is the fusion of prepositions with personal pronominal objects, resulting in prepositions that are "conjugated" in the three persons, singular and plural, like verbs. An example from Middle Welsh, the conjugation of the preposition *ar* 'on', is given below; the forms *arnam* and *arnunt* have taken over endings from the verbal conjugations:

	sing.	*pl.*
1	*arnaf* 'on me'	*arnam*, *arnan* 'on us'
2	*arnat* 'on you'	*arnawch* 'on you'
3	*arnaw* 'on him'	*arnadut*, *arnunt* 'on them'
	arnei, *erni* 'on her'	

Goidelic: Old Irish and Its Descendants

History of Irish

14.28. Proto-Goidelic, the prehistoric ancestor of Irish, was spoken in Ireland at least by the beginning of the Christian era, if not earlier. The earliest preserved Irish is the language of the 300 or so stone inscriptions written in the Ogam (or Ogham) alphabet, which consists of strokes and notches chiseled along and across a central line, usually the edge of a stone (unfortunately the part that gets weathered and damaged most easily). The origin of the Ogam script is not known for certain; the inscriptions hail mostly from southern Ireland and date from about the fourth to the seventh centuries AD, with the bulk of them coming from the fifth and sixth. The stage of Irish at this time is called **Primitive Irish** (or Ogam Irish). Its earliest specimens do not yet show the effects of apocope, syncope, or vowel affection (e.g. *maq(q)i* 'of the son', OIr. *maicc*; *Lugudeccas* 'of Lugudecca', OIr. *Luigdech*; *velitas* 'of a bard', OIr. *filed*). While this allows us to date certain sound changes that happened during or later than the Primitive Irish period, the value of the inscriptions is offset by their extremely inconsistent spelling and their brevity, as they are all short burial inscriptions consisting almost solely of proper names.

The conversion of Ireland to Christianity in the fifth century resulted in the introduction of the Roman alphabet. Irish clerics learned the alphabet from monks in western Britain, who spoke early Welsh or its immediate ancestor. The fifth and sixth centuries saw not only significant alterations to the cultural landscape of the Emerald Isle, but also radical changes in the Irish language. Broadly, it was during this time that Irish changed from looking roughly like Gaulish or Latin to looking like Irish. The **Old Irish** period begins with the earliest datable literature, written at the end of the sixth century or the start of the seventh but preserved only in much later manuscripts. The early part of this period, into the first quarter of the seventh century, is called **Archaic Old Irish**, followed by **Classical Old Irish**, which lasted until the mid-900s.

14.29. Several manuscripts preserved on the Continent containing glosses on the Scriptures and other Latin texts represent the most important source of information on Old Irish. The major ones are the Würzburg, Milan, St. Gall, and Turin glosses. These manuscripts were brought to the Continent by Irish missionaries and other religious figures in the eighth and ninth centuries and are our only contemporary documentation of the Classical language. The Würzburg glosses are written very accurately, and their spelling is considered to be the Classical norm. Because the glosses were not understood on the Continent, these manuscripts were not used in later centuries and survived in good shape. By contrast, manuscripts of the same age do not survive from Ireland itself since they became worn out from continuous use. Copying and recopying often introduced corruptions and modernized spellings. These medieval (and even early modern) manuscripts are the ones that contain all preserved Old Irish literature, such as the saga of the *Táin Bó Cuailgne* (*The Cattle-Raid of Cooley*) and other tales, heroic poetry, and legal, historical, and grammatical texts.

14.30. Lasting from the tenth to the thirteenth centuries was **Middle Irish**, which saw changes to the morphological system that were as far-reaching as the phonological changes of the Primitive Irish period. By the end of the thirteenth century the language was effectively as it is today. The **Modern Irish** period begins with the codification of a normative form of the language by bards and other literary elite in the thirteenth century. The bards' literary guild collapsed in the early 1600s, after which texts in different regional varieties appear – the dialects of Munster, Connacht, and Ulster that are still with us.

14.31. It was also during the seventeenth century that Ireland received an English-speaking ruling class; by the next century the status of Irish had deteriorated and it became primarily a language of the rural poor. A tragic blow was the devastation wreaked by the Potato Famine in 1845–49, which ravaged especially this population; over a million died outright, and another million and a half emigrated to America or elsewhere. Today, no more than 70,000 people comprise the Irish-speaking communities called the *Gaeltacht.* While a larger number have learned Irish as a second language, its future is cloudy.

Irish is often called "Gaelic," though this is not strictly speaking correct. "Gaelic" is properly used in combination, as in "Irish Gaelic" or "Scottish Gaelic"; it is a general term that is more or less synonymous with Goidelic. (It derives, in fact, from the Scottish Gaelic descendant of Old Irish *Goídel.*)

Phonological developments of Old Irish

Consonants

14.32. The labiovelars of Goidelic were changed to ordinary velars during the early history of Irish. Ogam Irish has a separate letter for k^w that is transliterated Q, as in the frequent word *maq(q)i* 'of the son' < *$*mak^{(w)}k^w\bar{\imath}$* (Classical OIr. *maicc*), and a special name is preserved for another letter that must have represented g^w before it shifted to *g*.

Lenition and nasalization are the main changes to have affected consonants during the historical period. Both changes were conditioned by the preceding sound; the conditioning sound could be in the same word as the affected consonant, or separated from it by a word-boundary. But not just any word-boundary was "invisible" for the purposes of lenition and nasalization – only those in particular syntactic or prosodic groups. Thus lenition or nasalization could apply across the boundary between noun and a following adjective, and after proclitics of various kinds – the definite article, possessive pronouns, certain conjunctions, and infixed pronouns; but they could not apply across two different phrases.

14.33. Lenition. Lenition turned originally intervocalic stops into fricatives, as in ***cath*** 'battle' < ****katus*** and ***in chinn*** 'of the head' < **sindī* ***k**^w**ennī**.* In the case of voiced stops, the difference between the lenited and unlenited versions is not indicated in the orthography, hence *bó* 'cow' begins with *b*, but in *a bó* 'his cow' it begins with a bilabial fricative [β] (similar to Eng. *v*). The fricatives *s* and *f* when lenited became *h* (written *ṡ*) and zero (written *ḟ*), and the nasals and liquids when lenited were lenis (less strongly articulated) versions of the corresponding unlenited nasals and liquids. These facts are all still true of modern Irish dialects.

14.34. Nasalization. The other consonant mutation, nasalization, affected only stops and vowels. It occurred when the final sound of the preceding word was a nasal consonant in prehistoric Irish. Nasalization had three effects. It changed voiced stops to nasal stops, for example *dán* 'gift' but *in ndán* 'the gift' (accus. sing.; *nd* = [n]) < pre-Irish **sindan dānan*. It changed voiceless stops to voiced stops (not represented in the spelling), for example *túath* 'people' but *in túaith* 'the people' (accus. sing.), pronounced *in dúaith*, ultimately from earlier **sindān toutān*. Finally, it prefixed an *n* to a vowel, for example *ech* 'horse' but *in n-ech* 'the horse' (accus. sing.) < earlier **sindan ek^{w}an*. The only other mutation to be noted is that a word-initial vowel is prefixed with *h* following a word that does not lenite or nasalize, as in *úa hAirt* 'grandson of Art, O'Hart'.

14.35. Palatalization. A front vowel (*i* or *e*) following a consonant palatalized that consonant, that is, moved its point of articulation closer to the palate. In the early stages of this change, only *i*'s in certain syllables had this effect; as time went by, palatalization spread to other contexts. The end result was that consonants, aside from being lenited, unlenited, and nasalized, now came in two other guises, palatalized and non-palatalized (or "slender" and "broad," as Celticists refer to them). Palatalization is indicated in the orthography by writing an *i* before the relevant consonant (but this is not done consistently): for example, *-beir* 'carries', with palatalized (and lenited, since postvocalic) *r* that used to be followed by a front vowel (**bhereti*; cp. the absolute form *berid*). The *b* is also palatalized because it occurs before the vowel *e*, but this is not specially shown in the script.

Vowels

14.36. The main Irish changes to the Common Celtic vowel system are as follows. An **o* in an unstressed syllable became *a*, as in the Ogam consonant-stem genitive singular *Lugudeccas* 'of Luigdech', with *-as* < **-os*. These *a*'s mostly disappeared but not before causing *a*-affection (see below). The *u*-diphthongs **eu* and **ou* were monophthongized to *ó* (as in Archaic OIr. *tóth* 'tribe' from **toutā*), later diphthongized to *úa* (hence classical *túath*). The diphthong **ei* became *é* or (after the archaic period) *ía* depending on whether the vowel that originally stood in the following syllable was front or back, respectively: thus *tégi* or *-téig* 'you (sing.) go' < **(s)teigh-es(i)* but *tíagu* 'I go' < **(s)teigh-ō*.

14.37. Vowel affection. The vowels were also subject to various umlauting processes called vowel affection. The details of vowel affection are highly complicated and will not concern us here in detail. There were two basic processes in Irish: *a*-infection and *i*-infection. In *a*-infection, a high vowel (*i* or *u*) was lowered to the corresponding mid vowel (*e* or *o*) before a syllable containing a non-high vowel (*a* or *o*). Thus nomin. sing. **u̯ir-os* 'man' > **u̯ir-as* > **u̯er-as* (ultimately OIr. *fer*; contrast the nominative pl. *fir* < **u̯ir-ī*); **klut-om* 'fame' > **klut-an* > **klot-an* (ultimately OIr. *cloth*). *I*-infection produced the opposite result; a high vowel (*i* or *u*) caused an *e* or *o* in a preceding syllable to raise to *i* or *u*: *mil* 'honey' < **melit*; *bìru* 'I carry' < **berū* (earlier **berō*).

The subsequent changes of apocope and syncope were discussed above, §14.24.

Morphology of Old Irish

Verbs

14.38. The Old Irish verb is a complex subject; only a few topics pertaining to it can be treated here. There were five indicative tenses (present, imperfect, future, secondary future [also called past future or conditional], and preterite), two subjunctive tenses (present and past), and a present imperative. Active and middle endings were distinguished in the primary (non-past) tenses, and there were distinct passive endings in the third person. Special relative endings are found in the 3rd singular and plural and in the 1st plural; these were used when the verb was in a relative clause, and are historically derived from a combination of verb plus relative pronoun (§14.11 above). Instead of infinitives, each verb had a verbal noun formed from the verbal root with a suffix, somewhat like the different infinitives of Vedic (§10.44).

14.39. Present stems. There were two classes of verbs, distinguished according to their present stems: "strong" (all formed directly from verbal roots) and "weak." The strong verbs are old and continue present-stem types of PIE date: simple thematic presents, such as *berid* 'carries' (< **bhereti*); (thematized) nasal-infixed presents (e.g. *dingid* 'oppresses'); and *-na*-presents comparable to the Sanskrit ninth class (§10.42; e.g. *crenaid* 'buys', cp. Ved. *krīṇā́ti*). Weak verbs are secondarily derived presents such as causatives and denominatives, such as *móraid* 'increases' from *mór* 'great'. All original athematic verbs, except for some forms of the verb 'be', have become thematic.

14.40. Other tense-stems. There were four other stems for the other verb forms: subjunctive, future, preterite active, and preterite passive. In the strong verbs, as with the primary verbs of other IE languages like Sanskrit and Greek, the other tenses are formed directly from the root.

In contrast to most of the other older PIE languages, the present subjunctive is not formed from the present stem. The subjunctive stem is formed in two ways: with a morpheme **-ā-* that is identical to the *ā*-subjunctive of Italic (§13.19; e.g. pres. indicative *renaid* 'sells', pres. subjunctive *-ria*, cp. Lat. *attingit* 'touches', Archaic Lat. subjunctive *attigat* without nasal infix), or with an *-s-* (§14.25 above).

14.41. The future stem is formed in a variety of ways. Weak verbs take the *f*-future, whose origin has been hotly debated for over a century (e.g. pres. *léicid* 'leaves', fut. *léicfid* 'will leave'). Strong verbs generally have a reduplicated future, either with a suffix *-s-* (e.g. from *guidid* 'prays' is formed *gigis* 'will pray' < **g^{w}hi-g^{w}hedh-s-*) or without (e.g. pres. *canid* 'sings', fut. *cechnaid* < **ke-kan-a-*; *do-gní* 'knows', fut. *do-gén* < **-gi-gn-a-*; this last type is called the long-*e* future). Both of the reduplicated future types go back either directly or indirectly to the PIE reduplicated desiderative (§5.41).

14.42. The active preterite is formed with an *-s* or with reduplication (there are some other types as well which we shall not go into). All weak verbs have an *s*-preterite (§14.25). The reduplicated preterite, a continuation of the IE perfect (§14.25), is formed by many strong verbs: *canid* 'sings', perfect *cechan-*. Finally, there is a passive preterite stem, which is a continuation of the **-to*-verbal adjective (§14.25).

14.43. Absolute and conjunct verb forms. Verbs in Old Irish (and occasionally in Old Welsh) come in two different guises depending on their position in the sentence. One form appears when the verb is clause-initial, such as OIr. *berid* 'he carries'; this is the absolute form. A generally shorter form, sometimes lacking the last syllable of the absolute form, appears when the verb is preceded by certain conjunctions or a preverb, as in *ní beir* 'he does not carry', *do-beir* 'he gives'. This is called the conjunct form.

Compound verbs themselves – preverb and verb both – behave in the same way as uncompounded ones: a full form (such as *do-beir* above) occurs clause-initially, while a shorter form occurs when certain conjunctions or another preverb precedes (as in *ní tabar* 'he does not give'). The terminology is different: the full form *do-beir* is called the prototonic form, while *-tabar* is called the deuterotonic. The deuterotonic is thus sort of a conjunct of the conjunct.

14.44. The origin of the differences between absolute and conjunct forms is not altogether agreed upon, but it probably boils down to something like the following. One must first assume that in pre-Irish, clauses contained an unstressed clitic sentence particle in second position, i.e., following the first element in the clause. (This assumption is not terribly problematic since this is in one way or another true of Greek and Hittite, and frequently true in Sanskrit and elsewhere.) If the first element in the clause was an uncompounded verb, the particle attached to the verb's final syllable; when the language was hit by apocope, which got rid of most final syllables, the particle was treated as a final syllable and protected the rest of the verb in front of it. Thus a **beret(i)* + Particle became the absolute form *berid.* With compound verbs, one needs to remember that preverbs were independent adverbs originally (§8.9); therefore if a compound verb began a clause, the preverb would have been the first element in the clause and the sentence particle would have attached to it rather than to the following verb. The final syllable of the verb was therefore not protected and fell victim to apocope. Thus a **to* + Particle *beret(i)* became *do-beir*, with *-beir* the conjunct form.

If a compound verb was itself preceded by another element, such as the negative **nē*, similar principles applied. The clause would have started **nē* + Particle *to-beret(i)*. Here we must further assume that the compound **to-bereti* acted like a single word in such an environment, with stress on the first syllable like all other words in pre-Irish. The difference in stress between **to* + Particle *béreti* and **nē* + Particle *tó-beret(i)* is what mattered for the subsequent phonological developments: unstressed internal syllables were subject to syncope (§14.24) and other vowel weakenings. Thus **tó-beret(i)* became deuterotonic *-tabar.*

14.45. As these examples hint at, the effects of syncope and apocope in Irish are nowhere as apparent or as devastating as in verbal conjugations, especially those of verbs compounded with one or more preverbs. The effects are particularly widespread partly due to the fact that Old Irish had an especial fondness for piling preverbs together, giving syncope and apocope no shortage of syllabic gallows-fodder. Three preverbs in a row are quite common, e.g. *du-airngerat* 'they promise' from **do-are-in-gar-* (verbal root *gar-* 'call', literally 'call to before in' or the like; the literal translations of these compounds usually make no sense), and four or even five preverbs in a row are found as well, e.g. *fo-timmdiriut* 'I am sufficient' from **fo-to-imm-di-ret-* (verbal root **ret-* 'run'; literally 'run under to around from') and the verbal noun *contherchomracc* 'assembly' from **com-to-er-com-ro-icc-* (verbal root **icc-* 'come, reach'). Because only the first or second preverb was stressed (depending on its position in the clause), all syllables after that were unstressed and got compressed by lenition, syncope, apocope, and vowel weakening in unstressed syllables. The verbal root itself wound up leading an extremely perilous existence at or near the end of such strings, and in some cases all but entirely disappeared.

14.46. The amount of allomorphy (that is, variation in the form of a given morpheme) that these changes created was incredible, and it is worth digressing to give some examples. The Irish root *fēd-* 'say' appears in such varied guises as *fét*, *id*, and *d*, as in the following forms of the compound verb **at-fēd-* 'relate': 3rd sing. present *ad-**fét*** 'relates', perfective present *ad-cuïd* (**ad-com-fēd-*), and 2nd pl. conjunct perfective present *-éicdid*. As in this last example, sometimes the root is reduced to a single sound, particularly in the conjunct 3rd person singular *s*-subjunctive. Thus the 3rd sing. conjunct *s*-subjunctive of the verb *as-**boind*** (**oss-bond-*) 'refuses' is simply *-o**p*** (pronounced *-ob*, the regular outcome of **-óss-bod-s-t!*); and from **ret-* 'run' (present ***rethid*** 'runs') we have the compound *do-fúa**rat*** 'remains over' (**di-fó-uss-ret-*), whose conjunct 3rd sing. *s*-subjunctive is *-diúair* (< **-dí-fo-uss-ret-s-t*), with only the *-r* remaining of the original root, subjunctive suffix, and personal ending (and very little left of the preceding preverbs).

The effects of these sound changes caused absolute and conjunct forms even of relatively simple verbs to be vastly different. Thus the pre-Irish compound **di-slond-it* 'denies' becomes OIr. *do-sluindi* (absolute) but *-díltai* (conjunct); both developed by perfectly regular sound change. The absolute form comes from **di-slóndit* (accented on the verb), whereas *-díltai* comes from the same form accented on the preverb (**-dí-slondit*). The destressing of *-slondit* made all the difference: **dí-slondit* first became **di-sldi* (syncope and loss of final **-t*), then **dihlti* (weakening of **s* to **h* which devoiced the following consonant cluster), and finally *dīlti* (loss of *h* with compensatory lengthening of preceding vowel), written *-díltai*.

14.47. All of this allomorphy seems not to have posed any particular problems for Old Irish children learning the language; but as time went by the allomorphy was gradually reduced by regularization – one or another allomorph was generalized throughout the paradigm by leveling or analogy. The distinction between absolute and conjunct was lost in Middle Irish. Analogy was already a significant player in the paradigms of scores of Old Irish verbs; part of the challenge of Irish historical grammar is figuring out which forms are analogical creations and which are not.

14.48. Below are given the present, imperfect, present *ā*-subjunctive, and *t*-preterite of the verb *berid* 'carries'. The conjunct forms are illustrated with the compound verb *as-beir* 'says', whose deuterotonic forms are given in the third column (*-epur*, as would appear for instance in *ní epur* 'I do not say'):

	Present			**Imperfect**		
	Absolute	Conjunct	Deuterotonic	Absolute	Conjunct	Deuterotonic
sg. 1	*biru*	*as-biur*	*-epur*	*no berinn*	*as-berinn*	*-eprinn*
2	*biri*	*as-bir*	*-epir*	*no bertha*	*as-bertha*	*-epertha*
3	*berid*	*as-beir*	*-epir*	*no bered*	*as-bered*	*-epred*
pl. 1	*bermai*	*as-beram*	*-eprem*	*no bermis*	*as-bermis*	*-epermis*
2	*beirthe*	*as-berid*	*-eprid*	*no berthe*	*as-berthe*	*-eperthe*
3	*berait*	*as-berat*	*-epret*	*no bertis*	*as-bertis*	*-epertis*

	ā-Subjunctive			***t*-Preterite**		
	Absolute	Conjunct	Deuterotonic	Absolute	Conjunct	Deuterotonic
sg. 1	*bera*	*as-ber*	*-eper*		*as-biurt*[2]	*-epurt*[2]
2	*berae*	*as-berae*	*-epre*		*as-birt*	*-epirt*
3	*beraid*	*as-bera*	*-eprea*	*birt*	*as-bert*	*-epert*
pl. 1	*bermai*	*as-beram*	*-eprem*		*as-bertammar*	*-epertmar*[2]
2	*berthae*	*as-beraid*	*-eprid*		*as-bertid*	*-epertaid*[2]
3	*berait*	*as-berat*	*-epret*	*bertatar*[1]	*as-bertatar*	*-epertatar*[2]

[1] Late. [2] Not actually attested.

Nouns

14.49. Irish reduced the number of cases in the noun to five – nominative, vocative, accusative, genitive, and dative. Below are the paradigms of the *o*-stem *fer* 'man', the *ā*-stem *túath* 'tribe', and the consonant-stem *carae* 'friend' in the singular and plural (the superscript ^{L} means the form lenites a following word, and ^{N} means it nasalizes):

	Sing.	Pl.	Sing.	Pl.	Sing.	Pl.
nom.	*fer*	*fir*^{L}	*túath*^{L}	*túatha*	*carae*	*carait*
voc.	*á fir*^{L}	*á firu*	*á thúath*^{L}	*á thúatha*	*á charae*	*á chairtea*
acc.	*fer*^{N}	*firu*	*túaith*^{N}	*túatha*	*carait*^{N}	*cairtea*
gen.	*fir*^{L}	*fer*^{N}	*túaithe*	*túath*^{N}	*carat*	*carat*^{N}
dat.	*fiur*^{L}	*feraib*	*túaith*^{L}	*túathaib*	*carait*^{L}	*cairtib*

Forms that nasalize a following word once ended in **-m*, and forms that lenite once ended in a vowel. The vocative is always preceded by the particle *á* 'O'. Unlike any other Indo-European language, the vocative plural is distinguished from the nominative plural in the *o*-stems (and, by analogy, in the consonant stems), which happened for the following reason. The inherited nominative/vocative plural **-ōs* was replaced (as in some other branches) by the pronominal nomin. pl. **-oi* (§6.53), but interestingly only in the function of nominative plural; the old ending **-ōs* lived on in its other function as vocative plural. The replacement of a form in its main function but not in one of its secondary functions is a common process, and goes by the name of Kuryłowicz's Fourth Law of Analogy, after the Polish linguist Jerzy Kuryłowicz.

Old Irish text sample

14.50. §§17–21 of the Old Irish wisdom text *Audacht Morainn* (*Testament of Morann*), after the edition of Fergus Kelly (Dublin, 1976). The language is Archaic Old Irish. The text was written around 700, and consists of advice to a young king by a legendary judge named Morann. (The genre is called *Speculum Principum* or 'mirror of princes'.) The ethical notion of the ruler's truth is of common IE patrimony, and is found in Vedic and later India, ancient Iran, and Greece; in all these societies the verbal expression of this concept is believed to ensure prosperity and protect from harm.

§17 Is tre ḟír flathemon ad- manna mármeso márḟedo -mlasetar.
§18 Is tre ḟír flathemon ad- mlechti márbóis -moínigter.
§19 Is tre ḟír flathemon ro-bbí cech etho ardósil imbeth.
§20 Is tre ḟír flathemon to- aidble éisc i sruthaib -snáither.
§21 Is tre ḟír flathemon clanda caini cain-tussimter.

(17) It is through the justice of the ruler that abundances of great tree-fruit of the great wood are tasted. (18) It is through the justice of the ruler that milk-yields of great cattle are maintained. (19) It is through the justice of the ruler that there is abundance of every high, tall corn. (20) It is through the justice of the ruler that abundance of fish swim in streams. (21) It is through the justice of the ruler that fair children are well begotten.

14.50a. Notes. 17. Is: 'is', PIE **$h_1$esti*, pronounced [ɪʃ]. It introduces a cleft sentence ("It is . . . that . . ."), a favorite Insular Celtic sentence type used for topicalization. In the case of this particular sentiment, though, we may be dealing with a pre-Celtic pattern, since a construction beginning "by the ruler's truth" plus a sentence is structurally equivalent to truth-statements elsewhere in IE. **tre:** 'through', leniting the following sound, from the same root as Lat. *trāns* 'across'. **ḟír:** lenition of *fír* 'justice', literally 'truth', PIE **u̯eh_1-ro-* (> Lat. *uērus* 'true', German *wahr* 'true'). **flathemon:** 'ruler', genit. sing. of *fla(i)them*. The genitive shows this to be an *n*-stem, Celtic **wlati-amon-* (**wlati-* > OIr. *flaith* 'rule'), ultimately continuing the PIE suffix **-mon-* seen e.g. in Greek. *hēge-mṓn* 'leader'. **ad-mlasetar:** 'are tasted', 3rd pl. pres. passive of *ad-mlassi* (otherwise unattested), with archaic *ml-* that turned into *bl-* in Classical Old Irish. Derived from *mlas* 'a taste'. The separation (tmesis; called Bergin's Law in Irish studies, after the Irish Celticist Osborne Bergin) of preverb from verb has been seen as an archaic stylistic feature that harks back to the earlier separability of preverb from verb (§8.9); it recurs in the following lines. A growing body of evidence, however, suggests that Bergin's Law tmesis was in part or wholly a pseudo-archaism invented by monks. **manna:** 'abundances', pl. of *mann*, a borrowing from Lat. *manna* 'manna'. **mármeso:** compound of *már* 'great' (Classical OIr. *mór*; = W. *mawr*) and *meso*, genit. of *mes* 'tree-fruit', a *u*-stem cognate with W. *mes* 'acorns'. Acorns frequently symbolized a just rule. **márḟedo:** 'of great wood'; *fedo* is genit. sing. of *fed*, also a *u*-stem; Celtic **widu-* < PIE **u̯idhu-*, the source of Eng. *wood*. Note the alliteration in this and the following lines.

18. ad-moínigter: 'are treasured, are maintained', 3rd pl. pres. passive of an otherwise unattested verb *ad-moínigethar*, from *moín* 'treasure' (< **moi-ni-*, from PIE root **mei-* 'exchange', also in Lat. *mūnus* 'service done in exchange for something'). **mlechti:** 'milk-yields' (Classical *blechti*), pl. of *mlicht*, from an old *tu*-abstract noun **mleg-tu-* from PIE **$h_2$melĝ-* 'milk, to milk'. In another text, *dísce mblechta* 'dryness of milking' is mentioned as one of the proofs of a false king. **márbóis:** 'of great cattle'; PIE **g^wou-*.

19. ro-bbí: 'there is', a form of doubtful interpretation here and perhaps corrupt. **cech:** 'every', genit. sing. of *cach*, with *i*-infection from old genitive ending *-*ī*. The word comes from PIE **k^wā-k^wo-*, also seen in Russ. *kakoj* 'which?' **etho:** 'of grain', genit. sing. of *ith*. Together with its W. cognate *yd*, this continues PIE **pi-tu-* 'nourishment', seen also in Ved. *pítu-* and Av. *pitu-* 'food'. **ardósil:** 'high (and) tall', a compound of *ard* 'high' (cognate with Gk. *orthós* 'upright') and *ósal* (Archaic spelling of *úasal*) 'tall' (Gaul. *uxello-*, from PIE **up-s-*, cp. Gk. *hupsēlós* 'lofty'). Various phrases for 'tall grain' are found in traditional IE literatures. **imbeth:** 'abundance', Classical *imbed*.

20. to-snáither: 'swims'; this and the following *aidble* 'abundance' are not otherwise attested and have been restored from somewhat conflicting manuscript readings. Contains preverb *to-* (Classical *do-*) 'to' plus the Irish descendant of PIE **sneh₂-* 'swim' (also > Lat. *nā-re* 'to swim'). **éisc:** 'of fish', genit. sing. of *íasc*; PIE **peisk-* (also in Lat. *piscis*, Eng. *fish*). The manuscripts actually read *uisce éisc* 'fish in water', but modern editors assume *uisce* 'water' was added originally as a gloss and was later accidentally incorporated into the text by a copyist. **i sruthaib:** 'in streams', dat. pl. of *sruth*, originally a *tu*-abstract **sru-tu-* from **sreu-* 'flow', the source of Eng. *stream*.

21. clanda: 'children' (Classical *clanna*), pl. of *cland*, cognate with W. *plant*, both early borrowings from Lat. *planta* 'plant' at a time when *p* was heard (and adopted) by Insular Celtic speakers as k^w. **caini:** 'fair, beautiful'. **cain-tussimter:** *cain-* is 'fair' again, acting as a prefix attached to *-tussimter*, the 3rd pl. pres. passive deuterotonic form of *do-fuissim* 'I beget'. The form *-tussim-* is from **to-uss-sem-*, with two preverbs; the proterotonic form *-fuissim* has an extra preverb *fo-* inserted before *uss-*. The root **sem-* in IE meant 'draw water out of a well' (Lith. *semiù* 'I draw water').

Scottish Gaelic and Manx

14.51. Beginning around the late fourth century, immigrants from Ireland colonized what is now Scotland, establishing a colony called Dál Ríata, named after a town in northeast Ireland. The Scottish Dál Ríata became the center of a kingdom in the latter half of the fifth century, becoming more powerful than the Irish Dál Ríata; in the first half of the seventh century the connection to Ireland was severed.

The Gaelic inhabitants of Scotland expanded inland, and Scottish territory grew to about its present dimensions by around 1000. Over the ensuing centuries, however, English gradually began to replace Scottish, and the predominantly Gaelic-speaking areas are now confined to the Outer Hebrides and the islands of Skye, Tiree, and Islay. No more than 80,000 people speak Scottish Gaelic today, vanishingly few of them monolinguals.

14.52. The same group of Irish colonists that came to Scotland also settled the Isle of Man, in the Irish Sea between Ireland and England, in the fourth or fifth century.

The island's political and cultural heyday came during the period of the Viking invasion and settlement from the ninth to the thirteenth centuries, when it became the center of a Norse-Gaelic kingdom. Subsequently it was ceded to Scotland and then passed to England in the fourteenth century.

Manx is the name given to the form of Goidelic that developed on the island following the Irish colonization. Written Manx begins with a seventeenth-century translation of the Anglican *Book of Common Prayer*; however, a historical poem known as the *Manannan Ballad* is probably a hundred years older, even though its earliest manuscripts are from the eighteenth century. Most of the published literature has been religious in nature.

From the late eighteenth century on, the use of Manx declined, and the last native speaker died in December 1974. It is still in very limited use as a second language.

Brittonic

14.53. Brittonic (also Brythonic or British Celtic) was the language of the Celtic inhabitants of Britain from before the Roman conquest of the British isles beginning in AD 43. At its greatest extent, to judge by the geographical distribution of place-names and river-names, British Celtic was spoken throughout Britain except in that part of Scotland north of the Firth of Clyde and the Firth of Forth. The earliest Brittonic is in the form of some personal names on coins and in scattered Latin and Greek sources, the first being Ptolemy's *Geography* from about AD 150. No connected texts appear until the eighth century, in Old Welsh (see §14.59 below).

In northeastern Scotland lived a people called the Picts (Latin *Pictī* 'painted'), whose language, **Pictish**, has been the subject of controversy. Recent research indicates that Pictish was probably an early Brittonic language, but very little of it is preserved.

14.54. The defining phonological characteristic of Brittonic compared with Goidelic is the change of the Common Celtic labiovelar $*k^w$ to *p*, e.g. W. *pump* 'five' < Celt. $*k^w enk^w e$, cp. OIr. *cóic*. It is for this reason that Brittonic is often called "P-Celtic." Also characteristic of Brittonic is the change of initial **u̯* to *gw-*, as in W. *gwr* (OW *guir*) 'man' < **u̯iros* and *gwyn* 'white' < **u̯indos* (contrast OIr. *fer* and *finn*).

Vowel affection

14.55. In British Celtic, vowel affection happened before a syllable containing **ā* and before a syllable containing **i*, **ī*, or **i̯*. Some examples of "*ā*-infection" include W. *gwen* 'white' (feminine, < **u̯indā*; compare masc. *gwyn* < **u̯indos* above) and *Peith(-wyr)* 'Picts' < **Pixtās*. Some examples of "*i*-infection" (fronting and/or raising) are W. *meibion* 'sons' < **mabi̯on* and *bryn* 'hill' < **brunniā*.

Mutations

14.56. The initial mutations are somewhat more complicated in Brittonic than in Goidelic. By way of illustration, the Welsh system is summarized in the table below.

In Welsh orthography, *ff* represents [f], *f* represents [v], *dd* [ð], *ll* the voiceless lateral [ɬ], and *rh* a voiceless *r*, [r̥]:

Normal	Lenited	Nasalized	Spirantized
pen 'head'	*ar ben* 'on top'	*fy mhen i* 'my head'	*ei phen hi* 'her head'
tyr 'house'	*dy dyr* 'your house'	*fy nhyr i* 'my house'	*ei thyr hi* 'her house'
cath 'cat'	*y gath* 'the cat'	*fy nghath i* 'my cat'	*ei chath hi* 'her cat'
ben 'woman'	*un fen* 'a woman'	*fy men i* 'my woman'	
dyn 'man'	*dau ddyn* 'two men'	*fy nyn i* 'my man'	
glaw 'rain'	*cot law* 'raincoat'	*fy nglaw i* 'my rain'	
merch 'girl'	*un ferch* 'a girl'		
llaw 'hand'	*ei law* 'his hand'		
rhad 'cheap'	*cot rad* 'cheap coat'		

As can be seen, lenition in British Celtic is similar to Goidelic in the voiced stops, which became voiced fricatives also. (The lenition of *glaw* to *law* is due to a later development whereby [ɣ], the original lenition product of *g*, disappeared.) However, the voiceless stops became voiced stops (rather than voiceless fricatives as in Goidelic). The effect of the nasal mutation on voiced stops was also identical to Goidelic but its effect on voiceless stops was not: the latter are changed into aspirated nasals. Finally, British Celtic has a third mutation not found in Goidelic, the spirant mutation; this resulted from the geminate consonants **pp*, **tt*, and **kk*, which came about from various consonant clusters (e.g. W. *saith* 'seven' < Celtic **septam*). In Goidelic, these simply became unlenited stops, but in Brittonic they became voiceless fricatives.

Welsh

History

14.57. The early Anglo-Saxon settlers of England during the fourth and fifth centuries dubbed the indigenous Celtic tribes the 'foreigners', or *wealas*, the source of our word *Wales*, and their language as *wælisc*, the source of our word *Welsh*. At this time the British Celtic population was linguistically hardly differentiated. Following several major conflicts between them and the ever-expanding Anglo-Saxons in the sixth and seventh centuries, the Celts retreated, and after the Anglo-Saxons had advanced as far west as the river Severn (which runs roughly parallel to the present-day eastern border of Wales), they were split into two groups. One group lay to the northwest, in what is now Wales and a large area to the north; and one to the southwest, in modern Cornwall, Devon, and nearby areas. Many of the inhabitants of this second area had already migrated to northwest France, where their language would develop into Breton (see §14.62); those that stayed in Cornwall spoke what would become Cornish (§14.69). The Celtic spoken to the north of Wales, which must have resembled early Welsh, gradually died out, although traces of it survive even as far north as Cumbria (near Scotland) in the counting systems used by shepherds. One such system, for example, runs *yau tau tethera methera pimp sethera lethera nothera dothera dick*, which is strikingly similar to the Welsh numbers 1–10, *un dau tri pedwar pump chwech saith wyth naw deg*. (These rural counting systems are distantly related to the familiar *eenie meenie miney mo*.)

14.58. A few scattered short inscriptions in what is often called **Primitive Welsh** are preserved from the mid-sixth to near the end of the eighth century. While no literature is extant from this time in its original form, probably some poems by two sixth-century poets, Taliesin and Aneirin, survive in later (and modernized) twelfth- and thirteenth-century versions, most notably Aneirin's elegiac battle poem *Y Gododdin* (*The Gododdin*).

14.59. The earliest piece of connected text is the so-called *Surexit*-memorandum in **Old Welsh**, a short Welsh and Latin text concerning a lawsuit, dating probably to the end of the eighth century. Though the Old Welsh period lasted until the beginning of the twelfth century, it has left us with only a few other short texts. By contrast, we have very copious literature in **Middle Welsh**, dated from the mid-twelfth century to the end of the fourteenth. The most famous Middle Welsh prose work is the *Mabinogion*, a collection of romances; much poetry was also written, such as *Y Gododdin* mentioned above, as well as histories, grammars, translations of Latin and French literature, and legal texts (many of which drew on much older traditions). The Middle Welsh period closes with the œuvre of Dafydd ap Gwilym (c. 1325–80), a major figure in medieval European poetry, who is transitional to the modern period; his works, and those of writers through the sixteenth century, are often called Early Modern Welsh.

14.60. With the publication of the first Welsh translation of the Bible in 1588 we enter the true **Modern Welsh** era. This translation set a literary standard for generations and was instrumental in continuing the use of the language, which might well have died out otherwise. For already beginning in the Middle Welsh period the higher strata of society were becoming Anglicized, and Welsh was banned from use as an official administrative language in the mid-1500s. (This was not reversed until 1967.) The use of Welsh has slowly declined ever since; about a half-million people still speak it, with the greatest density being in the northwest Welsh county of Gwynedd.

Old Welsh text sample

14.61. The first three of the twelve anonymous "Juvencus" poems (*englynion*), written on a ninth-century manuscript containing a Latin paraphrase of the Gospels by Juvencus. The interpretation and translation below are adapted from Ifor Williams, "The Juvencus Poems" (*The Beginnings of Welsh Poetry*, Cardiff, 1980, 89–121).

niguorcosam nemheunaur henoid mitelu nit gurmaur
mi am [franc] dam ancalaur.

nicanãniguardam nicusam henoid cet iben med nouel
mi amfranc dam anpatel.

namercit mi nep leguenid henoid is discirr micoueidid
dou nam riceus unguetid.

I shall not keep watch even one hour tonight, my retinue is not very large,
I and my Frank, round our cauldron.

I shall not sing, I shall not laugh, I shall not jest tonight though we drank clear mead,
I and my Frank, round our bowl.

Let no one ask me for merriment tonight, Mean is my company,
Two lords can talk: one speaks.

14.61a. Notes. 1. niguorcosam nemheunaur: unclear; the translation above is conjectural. *Niguorcosam* is composed of *ni* 'not' and some verb in the 1st sing. present (ending *-am*) and containing the preverb *guor-* 'above, over' (= OIr. *for-*); if *nemheunaur* does mean 'even one hour', it would be segmented *nemh eun aur.* **henoid:** 'tonight', Modern W. *heno*, earlier *henoeth*; *noeth* 'night' is from PIE *$nok^{w}t$-. **mitelu:** *mi telu* 'my retinue', ModW *fy nheulu* 'my family'; the nasal mutation of the initial consonant was not indicated in the Old W. original. **gurmaur:** 'very large'; *gur-* is the same as *guor-* in *niguorcosam* above, and *maur* (ModW *mawr*) is cognate with OIr. *már, mór.* **franc:** 'Frank', also 'foreigner, mercenary soldier'. **dam:** 'around', from **do-ambi.* **ancalaur:** 'our cauldron'; *an* is 'our', and *calaur* is a loanword from Late Lat. *caldāria.*

2. **nicanã:** *nicanam*, 'I do/shall not sing' (with the common medieval notation *ã* to indicate *am*); from **kan-* 'sing' (as also in Lat. *canō* 'I sing'). **niguardam:** 'I do/shall not laugh', ModW *chwarddaf* 'I laugh'. **nicusam:** 'I shall not jest' is a conjectural translation. **iben:** 'we drank', from **pibe-* (cp. Ved. *píbati* 'drinks', Lat. *bibit*). **med:** 'mead', PIE **medhu-* 'honey, sweet drink' (cp. Gk. *méthu* 'wine', Eng. *mead*).

3. **namercit:** 'let no one ask me', containing *na-*, the negative prohibitive particle, *-m-*, infixed 1st sing. dative pronoun, and the verb *ercit*, a 3rd sing. imperative from PIE **perḱ-* 'ask' (also in OIr. *com-arc* 'he asks'). Infixed pronouns practically disappeared by Middle Welsh times; already here, *mi* 'me' is added after the verb to reinforce the infixed pronoun. **nep:** 'no one', subject, placed after the verb as usual in Celtic. **leguenid:** 'merriment', ModW *llawenydd.* **micoueidid:** 'my company, retinue'; *coueidid* (ModW *cyweithas* with a different suffix) comes from *kyueith* 'friend'. **dou:** 'two'. This last line is of uncertain meaning. **unguetid:** 'one speaks', probably *un* 'one' and *guetid* 'speaks', appearing in ModW in the compound *dyweddy* (*-g-* disappeared in composition by lenition in Welsh). The sense of the verse is that the speaker has lost all his retinue except one and is therefore in no laughing mood.

Breton

History

14.62. The encounters between the Anglo-Saxons and Britons (the native British Celtic population) were sometimes peaceful, sometimes not. A series of pitched battles between the two peoples in the sixth and seventh centuries ended in the defeat of the Britons. Even before then, the aggressive inland raids of the Anglo-Saxons struck fear into the Celts as far away as southwest England, and in the period around 450–470 a group of them, mostly from Cornwall and Devon, emigrated across the waves to northwest France, where they settled in the area now called Brittany (French *Bretagne*), named after the land of their origin. Over the course of the next century or so there were additional migrations. Their language soon developed in its own way, becoming what we now call Breton (*brezhoneg* in Breton itself, after *Breizh*, Brittany).

14.63. Breton appears to have had its greatest geographical extent in the ninth century, from about the middle of which we have our first specimens of **Old Breton** in the form of glosses. From the eleventh century we have our only continuous Old Breton text, four lines buried in a copy of a Latin charter from 821; presumably the Breton is from the time of the copy and not the original.

14.64. From the tenth to the thirteenth centuries, the area in which Breton was spoken shrank by almost one-half; since then it has shrunk slightly further. We have many literary works in **Middle Breton** (c. 1100–1659, the year of the publication of the first grammar and dictionary), most of which date to after 1450 and comprise religious texts and plays that are translations of French and Latin originals. Native literature in Breton is a relatively late creation, not appearing until the nineteenth century.

14.65. Breton never became the language of any political or cultural center, and no standardization ever developed; modern Breton is composed of the most diverse dialects of any modern Celtic language. Nowadays only the western half of the area corresponding to the erstwhile Duchy of Brittany is Breton-speaking (called Basse Bretagne, as opposed to the eastern and French-speaking Haute Bretagne), and even here the language is restricted to the countryside. Breton has also borrowed much more heavily from French throughout its history than any of the other British Celtic languages ever have from English, to the extent that two-fifths of the ordinary vocabulary is of French origin, according to some estimates.

The use of Breton was actively suppressed by the French government until 1951, when laws banning its teaching were relaxed. Since then there has been a remarkable increase in interest in the language and in materials printed in it. The current number of Breton speakers is perhaps half a million. Nevertheless, there is still barely any official recognition of the language, and its long-term survival is not certain.

14.66. Breton is similar to Welsh and Cornish in most structural respects. Syntactically, it differs by placing the subject before the verb rather than after it. One morphological feature of particular interest is the complexity of the number contrasts in the noun. Aside from the ordinary distinction of singular vs. plural, some Breton nouns can form two plurals, one of which is the ordinary one and the other of which emphasizes variety or diversity (e.g. *park* 'park' ~ *parkoù* 'parks' ~ *parkeier* 'various different parks'), while some others can form doubly marked plurals with specialized meanings (e.g. *bugel* 'child' ~ *bugale* 'children' ~ *bugaleoù* 'groups of children'). The plurals of diminutive nouns have the unusual property of being marked twice for plural, once before and once after the diminutive suffix: *bag* 'boat' and *bagig* 'little boat', plurals *bagoù* and *bagoùigoù*. Breton has a large number of collective plurals (a feature shared with Welsh), like *merien* 'ants' and *blev* 'hair', from which singulative nouns, indicating an individual member of the collective entity, are formed: *merienenn* 'an ant', *blevenn* 'a (strand of) hair'. Breton goes beyond Welsh, however, in being able to form singulatives to ordinary plurals, which then have a different shade of meaning from the ordinary singular: *pesk* 'fish' ~ *pesked* 'fishes' ~ singulative *peskedenn* 'single fish (out of a group or mass of fish)'. This singulative itself can then be pluralized: *peskedennoù* 'single fishes (out of a mass)'. Names for parts of the body can be inflected in the dual, by using a prefix etymologically derived from the number 'two', such as *lagad* 'eye' ~ *daoulagad* 'both eyes'; and, true to form, Breton can pluralize duals: *daoulagadoù* 'pairs of eyes'.

14.67. Verbs in the modern language are conjugated in a present, future, preterite, imperfect, present and past conditional, and imperative. The future is the descendant of the old present subjunctive, and occasionally still has modal usage. All these categories except for the imperative also have an impersonal form, descended from the middle, such as *karer* 'one loves'.

Middle Breton text sample

14.68. Stanza 185 from the Middle Breton poem *Tremenvan an ytron guerches Maria* (*The Journey of the Blessed Virgin Mary*), as preserved in an edition from 1530 and later re-edited in *Poèmes bretons du moyen âge* by Théodore Hersart, vicomte de la Villemarqué (Paris, 1879). The poem is ultimately derived from the medieval Latin legend *Transitus Beatae Mariae Virginis.*

Me pet Doe, Roen tir, euyt hent,	I pray to God, King of the earth, for the journey
Don miret ni hac hon holl querent.	to defend us and all our friends.
Ha nep a cret en Doe, Roe an sent,	And whoever believes in God, King of saints,
A vezo diouguel e pep hent.	will be secure on every journey.

14.68a. Notes. me: 'I'. As in the rest of Insular Celtic, the *m*-forms (originally from the oblique stem of the PIE 1st person sing. pronoun) were generalized; the nominative $*\hat{e}go h_2$ disappeared. **pet:** 'pray', a borrowing from Lat. *petere* 'to seek'. **Doe:** 'God'; cp. Old W. *diuw*. **Roen:** 'King (of) the', a contraction of *roe* 'king' (cp. Cornish *ruif*, W. *rhwyf*) plus the definite article *'n*. **tir:** 'earth', ultimately from Lat. *terra*. **euyt hent:** 'for the journey'; *hent* 'road, way' is cognate with Cornish *hins*, W. *hynt*. **don:** 'from us', contracted from *da hon*, and going with the resumptive pronoun *ni* 'us' following the verb. **miret:** 'to ward off, defend'. **ni:** 'us', also spelled *ny*; cp. W. *ni*, OIr. *sní*. **hac:** 'and'. **holl:** 'all', same in Welsh. **querent:** 'friends'; cp. W. *ceraint*, OIr. *carait*, from Celt. **karant-* 'loving, caring' (appearing in Gaulish proper names like *Carantomagus*). **nep:** 'whoever'; cp. OIr. *neb*. **a cret:** 'believes'; *a* is a particle used with verbs, and *cret* is cognate with OIr. *cretid* 'believes' and Lat. *crēdere* 'to believe'. **sent:** 'saints', pl. of *sant*. **a vezo:** 'will be', pres. subjunctive, lenited from *bezo*. **diouguel:** 'secure'; cp. W. *diogel*, from *di-* 'from, without' + *gogel* 'caution, avoidance'. **pep:** 'every'; cp. Cornish *peb* and OIr. *cach*; for etymology, see note to line 19 of the OIr. text in §14.50a.

Cornish

14.69. As noted above, Cornish is most closely related to Breton. It was spoken by the Celtic inhabitants of southwest England who remained after their neighbors migrated to Brittany in the sixth century. Our first documents in **Old Cornish** are some glosses from the late ninth or early tenth century, which are followed around the year 1100 by our largest Cornish text from this period, the *Vocabularium Cornicum* or Cornish Vocabulary, a Cornish version of a Latin–Anglo-Saxon glossary compiled a century earlier by the English monk Ælfric at Cerne in Dorset. Although the Cornish of the Vocabulary is usually called Old Cornish, linguistically it is more on a par with Middle Welsh or Middle Breton.

14.70. From the fourteenth to the sixteenth centuries are preserved close to 10,000 lines of **Middle Cornish**, largely in the form of miracle plays translated from English; these represent the bulk of our entire Cornish corpus. The **Late Cornish** period lasted until the death of the last native speaker of Cornish, traditionally said to have been one Dolly Pentreath who died in December 1777. A few other people probably remained who spoke the language, but they were surely dead by the close of the eighteenth century. A dedicated effort has been made recently to revive the language; the result cannot be called authentic, since the paucity of our documentation and the inconsistencies in spelling leave many facts about the pronunciation, grammar, and vocabulary unknown.

14.71. A characteristic phonological development of Cornish is the change of word-final dentals to *-z* (written *-s*), as in *dans* 'tooth' (cp. W. *dant*).

Middle Cornish text sample

14.72. An excerpt from the Middle Cornish religious drama *The Life of Meriasek, Bishop and Confessor*, as preserved in a manuscript from 1504 but likely copied from an earlier original. The translation is that of Whitley Stokes (*Beunans Meriasek: The Life of Meriasek, Bishop and Confessor*, London, 1872). The speaker is Nudus (the Naked Man).

3067	Mur yv sur ov galarov	Great surely are my sorrows,
	ha feynt off heb feladov	And faint am I without fail,
	mensen cafus dyweth tek	I would fain have a fair end.
3070	ny vyn mernans ov gueles	Death will not see me.
	yma orth ov goheles	It is avoiding me
	drefen ov boys anhethek	Because of my being foul.

14.72a. Notes (selective). **mur:** 'great', cp. W. *mawr*, OIr. *mór*, Gaul. *-māros* in personal names. **yv:** 'is, are'. **sur:** an English loanword, as is *feynt* in the next line. **ov:** 'my'. **ha:** 'and', the same as in Breton. **heb:** 'without', same as in Welsh. **gueles:** 'see', cp. W. *gwely*. **yma:** 'is', same as in Welsh. **goheles:** 'avoid', cp. W. *gochelyd* 'avoid, shun'. Both are compounds of *go-* 'under' (cp. Ir. *fo*; PIE **upo*) and **kel-* 'conceal' (cp. Lat. *cēlāre* 'to conceal'). **boys:** a spelling variant of *bos*, 'to be'; cp. W. *bod*. The *-y-* in the spelling indicates that the *o* is long. Note the change of the final dental to *-s* as noted above in §14.71. **anhethek:** 'foul' (originally rendered 'loathsome' by Stokes in his edition).

For Further Reading

Celtic studies is well served by reference works on most topics, many of them in English. Lewis and Pedersen 1937 is the only comprehensive comparative grammar in English and is still eminently useful; it is a shorter revised version of Pedersen 1909–13. At that time, not much Continental Celtic was yet known. A more up-to-date (but technical) treatment of various topics in Celtic historical phonology is McCone 1996, an important monograph. Of fundamental importance to the comparative study of the Celtic (especially Irish) verb is Watkins 1962. Schumacher 2004 is a very useful compendium of the Celtic primary verbs and their histories.

For Gaulish, indispensable is the handsome and just-completed four-volume critical edition of the Gaulish inscriptions, Duval 1985–2002; a useful selection is the colorful survey in Meid 1992. The longer Celtiberian texts, with illustrations and provisional translations, can be found in Meid 1994; a complete edition, together with exhaustive commentary and a glossary, is Untermann 1997. A Gaulish etymological dictionary is Delamarre 2001.

For Irish, Thurneysen 1980 is the standard comparative grammar, one of the best grammars of any IE language. A mostly complete etymological dictionary of Old Irish is Vendryes and Lambert 1959– . McManus 1991 is a thorough treatment of the Ogam inscriptions. An excellent book devoted to the early history of British Celtic up to the twelfth century is Jackson 1953. The standard reference grammar for Middle Welsh is Evans 1964. A complete historical dictionary of Welsh is *Geiriadur Prifysgol Cymru* (Cardiff: Gwasg Prifysgol Cymru, 1950–2002; in Welsh and English), which has etymologies and textual citations much like the *Oxford English Dictionary*. A recent technical book on historical Brittonic phonology is Schrijver 1995. Pictish has received an important new treatment in Forsyth 1997.

For Review

Know the meaning or significance of the following:

Hallstatt culture	"P-Celtic"	lenition	Kuryłowicz's Fourth Law of Analogy
Franz Bopp	"Q-Celtic"	nasalization	spirant mutation
Continental Celtic	infixed pronoun	vowel affection	
Insular Celtic	conjugated preposition	syncope	
Goidelic	Ogam	absolute	
Brittonic		conjunct	

Exercises

1 Give the Celtic outcomes of the following PIE sounds or sequences. Some may have more than one answer.

a	**bh*	**c**	**-dt-*	**e**	**ō*	**g**	**m̥*
b	**p*	**d**	**r̥*	**f**	**gh*	**h**	**n̥H*

2 Briefly explain the history or significance of the following forms:

a OIr. *athair*	**d** Gaul. *dugiiontiio*	**g** OIr. *á ḟiru*
b Primitive Ir. *maqi*	**e** Celtiberian *-uz*	**h** OIr. *gigis*
c Gaul. *delgu*	**f** OIr. *cath*	**i** W. *pump*

3 Words belonging to the following morphological categories cause lenition of the initial consonant of a following closely connected word in Old Irish. Assuming these categories continue the same categories in PIE, explain why these forms induce lenition.

a dative singular
b feminine nominative singular (ignore original final laryngeal)
c genitive singular of *o*-stems

4 Words belonging to the following morphological categories cause nasalization of the initial consonant of a following closely connected word in Old Irish. Assuming these categories continue the same categories in PIE, explain why these forms induce nasalization.

a genitive plural
b neuter nominative singular of *o*-stems
c accusative singular

5 Given the phonological rule discussed in §3.40, would you expect the Old Irish nominative singular *cú* 'dog' to mutate the initial consonant of a following closely connected word, and if so, what mutation would you expect to see?

6 Given a form like Gaulish *Rigomagus* 'royal field' (*magus* = 'field'), explain why the *s* in the Old Irish compound *rígṡuide* 'royal seat' is lenited.

7 **a** Based on the following data, provide an account of the development of clusters consisting of stop plus resonant in Old Irish.

muinél 'neck' < **moniklo-*
mál 'prince' < Ogam *magl-*
cenél 'kindred' < **kenetlo-*
(fo-)álagar 'is laid low' < **ad-logar*
én 'bird' < **etno-*
ár 'slaughter' < **agr-*
ám 'a moving back and forth' < **ag-mo-*

b The Old Irish verb *do-gní* 'does' has a verbal noun *dénum* 'a doing', while the verb *fo-gní* 'serves' has a verbal noun *fognam* 'service'. Which verbal noun shows the historically expected phonological outcome of the word-internal cluster **-gn-*? Provide an explanation for the other form.

8 As noted in §14.25, the Insular Celtic *t*-preterite is a special development of the *s*-preterite in resonant-final roots. Given a form like *tart* 'thirst' < **tarst-* (cp. Eng. *thirst*), and given the fact that in various languages new verbal paradigms can be created by adding personal endings to an original 3rd singular form, provide an explanation for the source of the *t*-preterite in Celtic. Hint: do not worry about the ablaut grade of the root.

PIE Vocabulary VI: Natural Environment

**$h_2$ster-* 'STAR': Hitt. *ḫašterza*, Gk. *astḗr*, Lat. *stēlla*
**seh$_2$u̯ōl*, **sh$_2$un-* 'SUN': Gk. (Homeric) *hēélios*, Lat. *sōl*
**mēn-s-*, **mēn-ōt-* 'MOON': Ved. *mā́s*, Gk. *mḗn*, Lat. *mēnsis*
**dheĝhom-* 'earth': Hitt. *tēkan*, Gk. *khthṓn*, Lat. *humus* 'ground', Toch. A *tkaṃ*
**u̯odr̥* 'WATER': Hitt. *wātar*, Gk. *húdōr*, OCS *voda*
**peh$_2$u̯r̥* 'FIRE': Hitt. *paḫḫur*, Gk. *pũr*, Umbr. *pir*, Arm. *howr*
**mori* 'body of water': Lat. *mare*, OIr. *muir*, OCS *morje*, Eng. MERE
**doru* 'wood, TREE': Ved. *dā́ru*, Gk. *dóru* 'spear'
**stenh$_2$-* 'THUNDER': Ved. *stániti* 'thunders', Lat. *tonāre* 'to thunder'
**h$_2$u̯eh$_1$n̥to-* 'WIND': Ved. *vā́ta-*, Lat. *uentus*
**nebh-* 'cloud': Ved. *nábhas-*, Gk. *néphos*, Lat. *nebula*
**sneig^{w}h-* 'SNOW': Gk. *niph-*, Lat. *nix* (*niu-*), OCS *sněgŭ*

15 Germanic

Introduction

15.1. The branch of IE to which English belongs is called Germanic (or in older literature, Teutonic). The term derives from the name of an ancient Germanic tribe rendered in Latin as *Germānī*; in spite of repeated efforts it still has no accepted etymology. The older name "Teutonic" is also derived from an ancient Germanic tribal name, that of the *Teutonī* or *Teutonēs*, 'they of the tribe, the people', from the same root as the word *Dutch* (the language 'of the people'). Archaeological and linguistic evidence suggests that speakers of Common Germanic lived in northern Europe in the first half of the first millennium BC, primarily in southern Scandinavia and along the coasts of the North and Baltic seas, in an area stretching from the Netherlands in the west to the Vistula River in the east, in what is now Poland. By the time Germanic peoples entered into history, their territory had stretched considerably farther south: the earliest accounts come from the Romans in the first century BC, with whom they would frequently come into conflict. The Roman historian Tacitus left us an important monograph on Germanic peoples and customs, in which he lists the different tribes and describes their religious practices, children's games, and various other aspects of their culture.

15.2. Contacts with prehistoric Finnic peoples were quite extensive, as evidenced by many words of early Germanic origin borrowed into the common ancestor of modern Finnic languages such as Finnish and Estonian. (These are not Germanic languages, nor even Indo-European, but belong to a separate family called Uralic.) A famous case is Finnish *kuningas* 'king', which, remarkably, is still practically identical to its source 2,000 years ago, Germanic **kuningaz* (> Old Saxon *cuning*, Old Eng. *cyning*). The almost uncanny similarity of the modern Finnish form to its ancient ancestor, so apparently frozen in time, has led researchers to mine such loanwords for evidence about the early stages of Germanic. But the degree to which Finnish has actually been a "linguistic icebox" is often overstated, and many of these loanwords are not as trustworthy in detail as they first appear.

The Germanic tribes were also in contact with Balto-Slavic peoples to the east, again as evidenced by loans, such as Slavic **kŭnęzĭ* 'prince' (> Russ. *knjaz'*) from **kuningaz*, and Slavic **xlěbŭ* 'bread' (> Russ. *xleb*) from **hlaiƀaz* (whence Eng. *loaf*).

15.3. Traditionally, the Germanic family is divided into three branches: the extinct **East Germanic**, containing Gothic and the languages of the Vandals, Burgundians, and some other tribes; **North Germanic**, containing Old Norse and its modern Scandinavian descendants; and **West Germanic**, containing English, German, Dutch, and their relatives. In addition comes **Runic** or Runic Norse, the language of the early runic inscriptions, which may tentatively be classified as North Germanic (see §15.37). The interrelationships among the three branches have been the subject of lengthy controversy. The Germanic-speaking area remained a large dialect continuum for probably all its earlier history and much of its later history too, and it can be difficult to tell if a feature shared by any two Germanic subbranches is due to early common innovation or to diffusion of a later local dialectal innovation. Today, the prevailing view is that North and West Germanic formed a subgroup, often called **Northwest Germanic**. But for most purposes the traditional threefold division of Germanic is fully satisfactory.

15.4. As is customary in Germanic philology, the voiceless fricative sound of Eng. ***thin*** will be represented by the letter thorn (þ, capital Þ; italic *þ*, *Þ*) in Germanic reconstructions and in those languages that used this letter (such as Old English and Gothic). The edh (ð) stands for the voiced *th* of Eng. ***this***.

As this textbook is written primarily for an English-speaking audience, the section on English is somewhat longer than the sections on the other Germanic languages.

From PIE to Germanic

Phonology

Consonants

15.5. Germanic is a centum branch, having merged the PIE palatal velars with the plain velars.

15.6. Grimm's Law. The sound changes that most set Germanic apart from the other IE branches are the series of changes beginning with Grimm's Law, continuing with Verner's Law, and ending with the shift from mobile pitch-accent to word-initial stress-accent. Grimm's and Verner's Laws are the most famous sound laws in historical linguistics; we shall treat the former first. It is named after the nineteenth-century scholar Johann Jacob Grimm, a lawyer turned Germanic philologist and dialectologist but nowadays most famous for the collaborative fairy-tale collecting he did with his brother Wilhelm. Grimm is one of three pioneering figures in early nineteenth-century IE studies, the others being Franz Bopp (whom we met in the previous chapter) and the Danish philologist Rasmus Kristian Rask. Rask, in fact, was the one who first figured out the sound change now named after Grimm: in 1814, at the tender age of 17, he wrote a prize-winning essay called *On the Origin of the Old Norse or Icelandic Language*, which is a very good comparative grammar of Germanic, Slavic, Lithuanian, and Greek. In it, he explained umlaut (§15.48) for the first time, and noticed the sound correspondences that form the basis for formulating Grimm's Law. Grimm had independently discovered them and was on the verge of publishing them when he chanced across Rask's work; subsequently very influenced by Rask, he published his own version in 1822 in the second edition of his *Deutsche Grammatik* (*German Grammar*).

Grimm's Law is actually not one sound change, but a series of three separate changes which had the net result of shifting all the inherited PIE stops. The first stage, which we can label Grimm I, rendered the PIE voiceless stops into voiceless fricatives; the second stage (Grimm II) changed the voiced stops into voiceless stops; and the third stage (Grimm III) changed the voiced aspirates into plain voiced stops. Thus:

Grimm I	Grimm II	Grimm III
*$p > f$	*$b > p$	*$bh > b$ (ƀ)
*$t > þ$	*$d > t$	*$dh > d$ (đ)
*$k > h$	*$g > k$	*$gh > g$ (ǥ)
*$k^w > h^w$	*$g^w > k^w$	*$g^wh > g^w$ (ǥ^w), b (ƀ)

Most handbooks actually reconstruct the velar fricatives *χ and *χ^w as the outcomes of *k and *k^w, but in all the older Germanic languages the sounds are written simply *h* or *hw*. (Early Germanic words rendered by the Romans with *ch*, such as the tribal name *Chattī*, are of uncertain phonetic interpretation.) Though we cannot be sure that this *h* did not sometimes represent a velar fricative χ, only in a few cases in the modern daughter languages is that the resultant sound. We will therefore use *h* and *hw* throughout instead of *χ and *χ^w. The outcomes of Grimm III were perhaps in the first instance voiced fricatives (represented by ƀ đ ǥ ǥ^w), but already by the end of the Common Germanic period these had hardened to stops at least word-initially and after nasals.

There seem to have been two outcomes of PIE *g^wh, the expected g^w (as in Goth. *siggwan* 'sing' < PIE *$seng^wh$-), but also *b* (as in Eng. *bid*, OE *biddan* < *g^whed-i̯e- 'pray', and *bane*, OE *bana* 'slayer' < *g^whonos) and maybe *w*, if Eng. *warm* and its relatives are from PIE *g^whor-mo- rather than from the rhyme-form *u̯or-mo- (in the first case, *warm* would be cognate with Lat. *formus* 'hot' and Gk. *thermós* 'heat'; in the second case it would be cognate with OCS *varŭ* 'heat').

The following boldfaced contrasts between English and Latin or Sanskrit consonants are direct results of Grimm's Law (forms not in the same language as the rest of a column are in brackets):

PIE	Latin	English (Grimm I)	PIE	Latin	English (Grimm II)
*$ph_2tēr$	*pater*	*father*	*leb-	*labium*	*lip*
*tenu-	*tenuis*	*thin*	*pod-	*ped-*	*foot*
*k̂mtom	*centum*	*hundred*	*gel-	*gelidus*	*cold*
*k^wod	*quod*	*what*	*g^wen-	[*gunḗ*[1]]	*queen*

PIE	Sanskrit	English (Grimm III)
*bher-	*bhar-*	*bear*
*$dheh_1$-	*dhā-*[2]	*do*

*magho-	_maghám_[3]	[_mag_[4]]
*sengʷh-	[_omphḗ_[5]]	[_siggwan_[6]]

[1] Greek, ‘woman’. [2] ‘Put’. [3] ‘Wealth’. [4] German, ‘am able’. [5] Greek, ‘voice’. [6] Gothic, ‘sing’.

15.7. Grimm I did not apply if the consonant was preceded by _s_, as in Eng. _star_ < PIE _*h$_2$ster-_ and Eng. _spew_ < PIE _*speu-_. Additionally, if the PIE form had two voiceless stops in a row, only the first one underwent Grimm’s Law, as in OE _eaht_ ‘eight’ < PIE _*ok̂tō_ and Eng. _haft_ ‘handle, hilt’ < PIE _*kapto-_ ‘seized’.

15.8. Verner’s Law. Numerous troubling exceptions to Grimm’s Law were disposed of with the discovery by the Dane Karl Verner of the sound change now known as Verner’s Law. This sound change affected only the fricatives _f þ h_ and _hʷ_ that had been produced by Grimm I: if they occurred word-internally, and were not immediately preceded by an accented syllable, they became the voiced fricatives _ƀ đ ǥ_. Some examples are given below. On the left-hand side are examples of forms that underwent Verner’s Law; on the right, for comparison, are forms that did not undergo it because the conditions were not met:

With Verner			**Without Verner**	
PIE	after Grimm	after Verner	PIE	after Grimm
*upéri	_*uféri_	_*uƀéri_ ‘over’	_*ápo_	_*áfo_ ‘off, away’
_*ph$_2$tḗr_	_*faþér_	_*fađér_ ‘father’	_*bhrā́ter-_	_*brṓþer-_ ‘brother’
*dek̂ú-	_*tehú-_	_*teǥú-_ ‘-ty (10)’	_*dék̂m̥_	_*téhm̥_ ‘ten’

15.9. Also affected by Verner’s Law was the inherited voiceless fricative _*s_, which became _*z_ if it was in the middle of a word and not preceded by the accented syllable:

With Verner			**Without Verner**	
*k̂asón-	_*hasón-_	_*hazón-_ ‘hare’	_*préusoh$_2$_	_*fréusō_ ‘I freeze’

(This _*z_ became _r_ in English and the other West Germanic languages, as we will discuss below, the -z- of Mod. Eng. _freeze_ has nothing to do with Verners Law but arose much later.) Word-final _*-s_ often also became _*-z_, as in Runic _gastiz_ ‘guest’ < PIE _*ghostis_; whether this is also part of Verner’s Law or an independent change is debated.

Sometime after Verner’s Law had run its course the mobile IE accent became fixed on initial syllables (see §15.18 below), which erased the original conditioning factor for Verner’s Law. The insight of Verner was to recover the sound change in spite of the erasure of its conditioning factor.

15.10. Final consonants. Final stops were lost in words of more than one syllable, as in the PIE optative _*u̯elih$_1$t_ > OHG _wili_ ‘he wants’, Mod. Eng. _will_. Final _*-m_ became _-n_, as exemplified below in §15.13.

15.11. Consonant clusters. In Common Germanic, _*n_ before _*h_ was lost with compensatory lengthening of the preceding vowel. This is the reason why the past tense *brought* does not have a nasal like its present, *bring*. Both forms go back to the dialectal PIE root **bhrenk-* 'bring', which became **brenh-* by Grimm's Law and, in certain forms, **breng-* by Verner's Law. The latter survives today in the present *bring*, while **brenh-* is the basis of the past-tense stem **branht-*, which underwent the loss of nasal to become **brāht-*, whence Eng. *brought*.

One more change worth mentioning is the development of clusters beginning with **z*. In **zd* and **zg*, Grimm II devoiced the stop, and the **z* became *s* by assimilation: **nizdo-* > Eng. ***nest***, **mēzg-* 'knit' > Germanic **mēsk-* > Eng. ***mesh***. Analogously, the clusters **zdh* and **zgh* became **zd* and **zg*, as in **kuzdho-* 'treasure' > Goth. *huzd*, Eng. *hoard* (showing the further West Germanic change of **z* to *r* mentioned above).

15.12. Laryngeals. Germanic has very few traces of laryngeals. Those that became vocalized in Greek, Latin, or Sanskrit were lost in most positions, such as word-initially before consonant (**h_1s-énti* 'they are' > German *sind*) and after a syllabic resonant (**ĝn̥h_3-to-* 'known' > Gmc. **kunþa-* > OE *cūþ* 'known', Mod. Eng. [*un*]*couth*, with the same outcome in Germanic as **n̥-* 'not' > Gmc. **un-* > Eng. *un-*). However, there are some examples of vocalized laryngeals, as in the word *father*, whose *-a-* continues the laryngeal of PIE **p$h_2$ter-*.

15.13. Resonants. The resonants all stayed intact: Eng. *Freeze* < **preus-*, *salt* < **sal-*, ***mind*** < **men-*. The syllabic resonants developed a *u* in front of them: e.g. PIE **mr̥-tro-* 'killing' > Gmc. **murþra-* > Eng. *murder*; PIE **pl̥$h_1$no-* 'full' > Gmc. **fulla-* > Eng. *full*; **n̥-* 'not' > Gmc. **un-* > Eng. *un-*; **nm̥(m)-ono-* 'taken' > Gmc. **numana-* > OE *numen* > Eng. *numb* and *num-skull*, literally 'taken (as to the senses).' (The *b* in *numb* is a late addition to the spelling and has no etymological significance.)

Vowels

15.14. Germanic reduced the distinctions among the short vowels from five to four by merging **a* and **o* to *a*, and there was a similar merger in the long vowels but in the opposite direction: **ā* and **ō* merged to **ō*. Thus PIE **oḱtō(u)* became German *acht* (and Eng. *eight*, with various later vowel changes), and PIE **bhreh_2tēr* (> **bhrātēr*) became Goth. *broþar* (with Gothic *o* spelling *ō*), Eng. *brother*.

15.15. Among the various conditioned changes to happen to the vowels in Common Germanic, one may be singled out here, the tendency of **e* to change to *i*. This happened in most environments in Gothic, and in certain environments in the other languages; examples from English include *mid* (cp. Lat. *medius*), *is* (cp. Lat. *est*), and *bind* (PIE **bhendh-*). Other conditioned changes, like umlaut, happened later and will be taken up below.

15.16. Long vowels were shortened in final syllables, probably after the Common Germanic period, sometimes disappearing in the individual languages: Goth. *fadar* 'father' < **ph_2tēr*, OE *giefu* 'gift' < Germanic **gibō*, Goth. *guma* 'man' < Germanic **gumē* or **gumō*. But, as noted in §3.20, long vowels that arose through contraction over a lost laryngeal (i.e. from sequences of the type **VHV*) require separate treatment. The contraction products had an extra mora of length and are called "trimoraic" in Germanic philology; they are represented with a circumflex accent. Vowels with this extra mora of length sometimes yielded different outcomes from regular long vowels. Thus in the feminine ō-stems (< PIE *-ā- < *-eh_2-) the nomin. pl. *-eh_2-*es* became *-*a'as* and ultimately *-ō̃s, while the accus. pl. *-eh_2s became simply *-ōs; the difference is reflected in the early West Saxon Old English nomin. *giefa* 'gifts' but accus. *giefe*. Interestingly, final long vowels secondarily acquired extra length as well (a feature shared with Balto-Slavic), as in *n*-stems in *-ō̃ < PIE *-ō, e.g. Goth. *namo*, OHG *namo*, OE *nama* 'name', contrasting with *-ō in e.g. the feminine nomin. sing. *-ā < *-ah_2 < *-eh_2 (recall that the laryngeal was not lost until after the breakup of PIE, §3.19), as in Goth. *giba*, OHG *geba*, OE *giefa*, *gifu* 'gift'.

15.17. Traditional historical grammars of Germanic distinguish between two long ē-vowels. One is simply the unchanged continuation of PIE *ē and is sometimes called *$\bar{e}_1$. The other, termed *$\bar{e}_2$, was a different sound having several origins, not all of them clear. The two sounds fell together in Gothic, but have divergent outcomes in North and West Germanic: *$\bar{e}_2$ became ē (as in the word for *here*, OE and OHG *hēr*, ON *hér*), whereas *$\bar{e}_1$ was lowered to *ā (as in German *Tat* and ON *dáð* 'deed' < Gmc. **dēđiz* < PIE *$dheh_1$-*ti*-). In English, interestingly, this sound was raised again (*deed*; see §15.60).

15.18. The accent shift. As alluded to above, the PIE mobile accent became fixed on the initial syllable in Germanic. Thus after *ph_2*tér*- had become **fađér*-, the accent shifted to give **fáđer*. But certain prefixes (adverbial preverbs in origin) remained unstressed, as in the English verbs *becóme, forgét, mistáke, withstánd.*

Morphology

Nouns

15.19. Germanic retained the nominative, vocative, genitive, dative, accusative, and instrumental cases, although the use of the instrumental is extremely restricted even in the oldest preserved texts. The dual was lost in nouns, but not in the personal pronouns or in the verb. The athematic noun classes of PIE are reduced in number and no longer productive except for the *s*-stems and *n*-stems. Germanic was in fact especially fond of the latter, particularly for forming animate nouns. The old *n*-stem declension is the source of such English plurals as *ox-en* and *brethr-en*, and of the so-called "weak" declension of animate German nouns such as *Hase* 'hare', oblique and plural *Hasen*. To judge by the fact that English *water* (with *r*) stands alongside ON *vatn* (with *n*), Proto-Germanic inherited the IE word for 'water' as an *r/n*-stem still (§6.31); the same is true of the word for 'fire', Eng. *fire* but Goth. *fon*.

15.20. The grammatical gender distinctions among masculine, feminine, and neuter are preserved. By the regular sound changes affecting vowels (§15.14 above), the PIE ā-stem feminines became Germanic ō-stems, while the thematic masculines and neuters with stem vowel *-*o*- became Germanic *a*-stems. Sample comparative paradigms of masculine *a*-stem and feminine ō-stem nouns from Gothic, Old High German, Old English, and Old Norse are given below. Representing the ō-stems is the noun for 'gift' (and Old Norse *skǫr* 'edge'); representing the masculine *a*-stems is the noun for 'day'.

		a-stem (masculine)				*ō*-stem (feminine)			
		Goth.	OHG	OE	ON	Goth.	OHG	OE	ON
sg.	N	*dags*	*tag*	*dæg*	*dagr*	*giba*	*geba*	*gifu*	*skǫr*
	V	*dag*	*tag*	*dæg*	*dagr*				
	A	*dag*	*tag*	*dæg*	*dag*	*giba*	*geba*	*gife*	*skǫr*
	D	*daga*	*tage*	*dæge*	*dege*	*gibai*	*gebu*	*gife*	*skǫr*
	G	*dagis*	*tages*	*dæges*	*dags*	*gibos*	*geba*	*gife*	*skarar*
	I		*tagu*	*dæge*					
pl.	NV	*dagos*	*taga*	*dagas*	*dagar*	*gibos*	*gebā*	*gifa*	*skarar*
	A	*dagans*	*taga*	*dagas*	*daga*	*gibos*	*gebā*	*gifa*	*skarar*
	D	*dagam*	*tagum*	*dagum*	*dǫgom*	*gibom*	*gebōm*	*gifum*	*skǫrom*
	G	*dage*	*tago*	*daga*	*daga*	*gibo*	*gebōno*	*gifena*	*skara*

15.21. Of all the endings represented above, Modern English preserves only two of them – the *a*-stem genitive singular, continued today as the possessive ending *-'s*, and the *a*-stem nominative plural, today our plural *-s*. The genitive, Common Germanic **-as(a)*, comes from PIE **-os(i̯)o* (§6.48), while the nominative plural, Common Germanic **-ās*, comes from PIE **-ōs* (§6.52).

Adjectives

15.22. Strong and weak adjectives. Germanic developed two different adjective declensions, called strong and weak. The so-called strong declension has endings modeled on those of the demonstrative pronouns: German *mit frisch-**em** Wasser* 'with fresh (dat.) water', with the same ending as the demonstrative pronoun *dem* 'the, this' (dat.). The weak declension has incorporated extra suffixal material in the oblique cases that comes from the PIE individualizing suffix **-on-*, which was added to adjectives to form words meaning 'the one that is X'. (It is also found in Latin names like *Catō* [stem *Catōn-*] 'the one who is *catus*, clever'.) Weak adjectives occur chiefly after a determiner or pronominal adjective, as in German *mit dem frisch-**en** Wasser* 'with the fresh water'. (Compare the similar phenomenon in Balto-Slavic of the "definite adjectives" discussed in §8.28 and §18.16.)

15.23. Comparison of adjectives. Germanic inherited the weak stem **-is-* of the IE comparative suffix **-i̯os-* (§6.78). Because the accent followed the suffix in PIE, the suffix underwent Verner to become **-iz-*, as in Goth. *manag-iza* 'more' (from *manags* 'many'). The Germanic superlative suffix was **-ista-*, as in Goth. *manag-ista* 'most'. This goes back to PIE **-is-* further suffixed with **-to-*, just like *-isto-* in Greek (§6.81).

The normal English comparative and superlative suffixes *-er* and *-est* actually do not usually go back to the suffixes above, but to related forms that were innovated within Germanic, **-ōz-* and **-ōsta-*: Gothic *frod-oza* 'wiser' and *arm-osta* 'poorest', and OE *liof-ora* 'dearer' and *liof-ost* 'dearest'. These suffixes became more common than **-iz-/-ista-* in North and West Germanic.

15.24. Pronouns. The first and second personal pronouns retain the dual in all the older Germanic languages, a category otherwise lost except in the Gothic verb:

OE *ic* 'I', *wit* 'both of us', *wē* 'we'; *þū* 'thou', *git* 'both of you', *gē* 'you (pl.)'. The PIE demonstrative pronoun **so *seh₂ *tod* 'this, the' is nicely preserved in Germanic, e.g. Goth. *sa so þata*, OE *sē sēo þæt.*

Verbs

15.25. The Germanic verbal system is much simpler than it was in PIE. Only the present and the perfect stems have remained, although some aorist inflectional endings were incorporated into the perfect. The perfect became a simple past tense called the preterite, but for the most part without reduplication. Also lost were the PIE imperfect, the subjunctive, and the future or desiderative formations. The optative survived, and became the Germanic subjunctive (the development and terminology are the same as in Italic, §13.19). The mediopassive survived as a living category to some extent in Gothic (and in the verb meaning 'be named', see §15.45). Germanic has kept the present participle in **-nt-* (§5.60, and see further below) and the verbal adjectives in **-tó-* and **-onó-* (a variant of **-nó-*, §5.61).

15.26. Strong and weak verbs. Germanic verbs belong to two broad classes, termed strong and weak, according to how they make their past-tense forms (preterite and past participle). The distinction has its origin in PIE. Germanic (or pre-Germanic) verbs that could form perfects used the perfect as their past tense; these are the strong verbs. They show ablaut of the root in the formation of the tense-stems and form their past participles with the nasal suffix **-onó-*. Strong verbs include most of the present-day "irregular" verbs like *sing sang sung* or German *singen sang gesungen.* By contrast, those verbs that did not form perfects (typically secondary verbs such as denominatives and causatives) developed an entirely new kind of past tense with an innovated suffix in **-d-*. These are the weak verbs, and they typically do not ablaut. The great bulk of verbs in any Germanic language are weak (the "regular" verbs in today's grammar), such as Eng. *settle settled settled* or its German equivalent *siedeln siedelte gesiedelt.*

15.27. Preterite of strong verbs. While all Germanic verbs have a present, preterite, and past participial stem, strong verbs further distinguish between a preterite singular and plural stem. This faithfully reflects the distinction between the singular and plural stems of the PIE perfect (§5.51). Examples of Germanic singular/plural preterite pairs include OHG ***bant*** 'he bound' ~ ***buntun*** 'they bound', ON ***greip*** 'he grasped' ~ ***gripo*** 'they grasped', and Goth. ***warþ*** 'he became' ~ ***waúrþun*** 'they became' (where *aú* represents etymologically the vowel *u*). The vowel *a* that is typical of the singular stems (*bant*, *warþ*; *greip* is from **graip*) comes from the **o* of the *o*-grade of the PIE perfect singular stem; and the zero-grade of the PIE perfect plural is reflected in *buntun, gripo*, and *waúrþun.*

15.28. In many preterites of this kind there is also a change in the stem-final consonant from the singular to the plural, as in OE sing. *wearþ* 'he became' but pl. *wurd-on* 'they became'. These consonantal changes are due to Verner's Law. Recall that the PIE perfect shifted the accent in the plural from the root to the endings (§5.51); in the plural, therefore, the accent came after the root-final consonant. If the root-final consonant was a voiceless stop, it underwent Verner's Law. Thus:

PIE perfect (without reduplication)	Grimm I	Verner	Later changes
3rd sing. **u̯órt-e* 'he turned'	**wórþe*	——	**warþ*
3rd pl. **u̯r̥t-ḗr* 'they turned'	**wr̥þḗr*	**wr̥đḗr*	**wurd-un(t)*

(The original 3rd pl. ending **-ḗr* was replaced at some point by **-un(t)* from **-n̥t*, an aorist ending.) The Vernerized form of the root in the preterite plural is also found in the past participle, since it likewise goes back to a PIE form with accent on the suffix: **u̯r̥t-onó-* '(having been) turned' > OE *worden* 'having become'.

Forms like OE *wearþ* ~ *wurdon/wurden* are called **Verner's variants**, exhibiting what the Germans call *grammatischer Wechsel* or 'grammatical change'. They are abundantly preserved in Old English, Old High German, Old Saxon, and Old Norse. Interestingly, they are quite rare in Gothic, which leveled out the consonantal differences in almost all cases. The same development eventually overtook the other Germanic languages. Modern English is the only Germanic language that still preserves one pair of Verner's variants within a single tense-paradigm: the preterites *was* (sing.) and *were* (pl.), from OE *wæs wǣron* (with *r* the English outcome of **z*, the Vernerized **s*; see §15.50).

15.29. Strong verb classes. Strong verbs are divided into seven classes, of which only the first three show the ablaut relationships inherited from PIE with perfect clarity. The modern English strong verbs have undergone so many changes that it is difficult to use them as examples of the original ablaut relationships, so the examples below are taken from Gothic. The forms given are the present infinitive, 1st sing. preterite, 1st pl. preterite, and the past participle of the verbs meaning 'bite', 'enjoy', 'bind', and 'throw'.

Class	PIE pattern	Germanic pattern	Gothic example			
I	*ei–oi–i–i*	*ī–ai–i–i*	*beitan*	*bait*	*bitum*	*bitans*
II	*eu–ou–u–u*	*eu–au–u–u*	*niutan*	*naut*	*nutum*	*nutans*
III	*eRC–oRC–R̥C–R̥C*	*eRC–aRC–uRC–uRC*	*bindan*	*band*	*bundum*	*bundans*
			wairþan	*warþ*	*waurþum*	*waurþans*

As can be seen, from the PIE point of view these all behave identically, with the present stem continuing the full grade, the preterite singular continuing the *o*-grade, and the other forms continuing the zero-grade. In Class I, PIE **ei* became **ī* in Germanic, preserved as such in Gothic but written *ei*. In Class III, Gothic *ai* and *au* represent short vowels from **e* and **u*.

The other classes do not reflect PIE ablaut as directly. Class IV, from IE roots ending with a single nasal or liquid, has replaced the zero-grade of the preterite plural with a long *ē*, e.g. Gothic *bairan bar berum baurans* 'bear' (*e* writes long *ē* in Gothic). The same is true of Class V (from IE roots ending in a stop or *s*), which has additionally changed the past participle to full grade, e.g. Gothic *giban gab gebum gibans* 'give'. Class VI is even more distant from the IE state of affairs, reflecting a Proto-Germanic pattern *a–ō–ō–a*: Gothic *faran for forum farans* 'go, fare' (*o* represents long *ō* in Gothic). This pattern may be related to that seen in Latin *scabō* 'I scrape', perfect *scābī* 'I scraped' (cf. §5.50). Finally, Class VII, substantially represented only in Gothic, contains a panoply of verbs whose preterites show reduplication, such as *haitan haihait haihaitum haitans* 'name' (where the *ai* of the root syllable *(-)hait(-)* represents a diphthong, but the *ai* of the reduplicating syllable in *haihait, haihaitum* represents a short vowel from **e*). Only traces of reduplicated preterites are found outside Gothic, e.g. OE *hehton* 'they were named', ON *rera* '(he) rowed'.

15.30. Weak verbs. Weak verbs formed their past-tense forms (preterite and past participle) by the addition of a morpheme in **-d-*, called the **dental preterite**, whose modern English descendant is the suffix spelled *-(e)d* or *-t*. The origin of the suffix is obscure, but it is usually assumed to be from the same root as the verb *do*. Weak verbs comprise mostly non-ablauting verbs, as discussed above. There were four classes of these verbs that can be established for Common Germanic. Class I contains denominatives and causatives formed with the suffix **-ja-* (< PIE suffixes **-i̯e/o-* and **-éi̯e/o-*). Examples include the Goth. denominative *andbahtjan* 'serve', pret. *andbahtida* (from the noun *andbahti* 'service, office'), and the causative *waljan* 'choose', pret. *walida*. Class II contains denominative verbs formed with a different suffix, **-ō-* (from **-ā-i̯e/o-*), e.g. Goth. *salbon* 'anoint', pret. *salboda*. Class III contains mostly stative and durative verbs like OHG *habēm* 'I have', Goth. pret. *habaida* 'had'. Finally, Class IV is formed with a nasal suffix and contains intransitive or inchoative verbs (that is, those indicating entrance into a state). It survives as a separate class only in Gothic, as in *fullnan* 'become full', *gawaknan* 'wake up'; the latter's Old English and Old Norse cognates, *wæcnan* and *vakna*, have joined Class II.

The past participle of weak verbs uses a suffix descended from the PIE verbal adjective suffix **-tó-*. In general this was Vernerized to **-da-*, as in Goth. *salbod-* 'anointed'; but the *-t-* remained in some consonant clusters, as still found e.g. in Eng. *brought* < Germanic **brāhta-*.

15.31. Other verbs. Four root athematic verbs survive, of which only one, 'be' (PIE **h₁es-*), is found in all of the family: Goth. singular paradigm *im is ist*, ON *em est es* (later *er*), and OE *eom eart is*. In West Germanic, 'do' is also athematic, as in OS *dōm dōs dōt*. Mention may also be made of the irregular verb *will*, which is historically an optative of a root present from PIE **u̯el-* 'wish' (cp. §15.10).

15.32. Preterite-presents. Several perfects/preterites have retained present-tense meaning (on this aspect of the perfect in PIE, see §5.53), and from them new preterites and participles were formed with the dental preterite suffix. In English, these primarily survive as the modal or "helping" verbs *can, shall, may*, and a few other forms. Since the present tense of these verbs is morphologically identical to a strong-verb preterite (note the lack of *-s* in the 3rd singular in Modern English), they are called preterite-presents or preterito-presents.

15.33. Subjunctive. As noted above, the Germanic subjunctive continues the PIE optative. Two tenses are distinguished, a present and a past. In Modern English, the subjunctive is formally distinguished from the indicative usually only in the third singular. Present subjunctives are found in such constructions as *Long **live** the Queen*, ***Be** that as it may*, and *(I asked) that he **go***; past subjunctives (distinguished from past indicatives only in the verb *be*) are found for instance in contrafactual statements like *If he **were** there (I would go)*. Since the IE optative had secondary endings, the 3rd sing. ended in **-t*, which disappeared in Germanic (§15.10 above); that is why

3rd singular subjunctives like *live* and *go* above seem to be "missing" the 3rd singular ending. (Analogously in German, the subjunctive *lebe* in *Es* ***lebe*** *die Königin* '[Long] live the queen' lacks the 3rd person *-t* of the indicative *leb-t* 'live-s'.)

15.34. Participles. The PIE present participle in **-nt-* survives as *-nd-*: Goth. *bairands* 'bearing', OE *berende*, OHG *beranti*, ON *berande*. Later in its history English replaced this with the unrelated suffix *-ing*, but a few traces of the old *nd*-participles can still be found in fossilized forms such as *friend* (originally a present participle **frijōnd-* 'loving') and *fiend* (Gmc. **fijand-* 'hating'). The past participles, from PIE **-tó-* and **-onó-*, have already been discussed.

Syntax

15.35. The historical and comparative syntax of both the ancient and the modern Germanic languages has been the topic of much discussion by theoretical syntacticians. One of the issues of interest has been the phenomenon often called "V2," or verb-second position. The phenomenon is most easily seen in German, which requires that all finite verbs in main clauses immediately follow the first syntactic constituent of the clause. This feature is found to some extent in Modern English, particularly with negatives: *Never* ***did*** *she look so gorgeous; Hardly* ***had*** *I entered the room when . . .* However, in the older stages of these languages, the word order tended to be freer.

It is also characteristic of several of the Germanic languages that in embedded (subordinate) clauses, the position of the finite verb is different from its position in main clauses. Thus in German one says *Ich <u>habe</u> ihm das Buch <u>gegeben</u>* 'I <u>have</u> <u>given</u> him the book', but (*Es ist wahr,*) *dass ich ihm das Buch <u>gegeben</u> <u>habe</u>* '(It is true) that I <u>have</u> <u>given</u> him the book': in the second sentence the finite verb *habe* 'have' falls at the end of the embedded clause beginning with *dass* 'that'. This was the preferred order in subordinate clauses in all the older Germanic languages.

The study of Germanic syntax is somewhat hampered by the scarcity of useful material from Gothic: Wulfila's translation of the Bible (see §15.41 below) sticks very close to the word order of the Greek original. However, Gothic does preserve an archaic feature of PIE syntax not found elsewhere in Germanic, namely the ability to place clitics between preverbs and verbs (see §15.46).

Runic

Runes

15.36. The first writing system used by Germanic peoples to record their own languages is called the runic alphabet, after the *runes*, the name for the early Germanic letters. This word has been taken over into Modern English from OE *rūn* 'secret, mystery; rune' or ON *rún* 'secret, magical sign, rune'. It is a matter of scholarly dispute just what the historical or cultural connection between 'secret, magic' and early Germanic writing was. It is often supposed that the runes were so called because writing was originally restricted to use in magic or religious rituals. Against this it has been pointed out that most of the earliest runic inscriptions are just names of the makers or possessors of objects. But since the objects in question are typically weapons and (often gold) amulets, it is certainly conceivable that they had some kind of magical use, or that writing a name on them was thought to grant them some kind of power. The connection between 'rune' and 'secret' might also reflect the fact that knowledge of writing was originally limited to a few elites.

Controversy has additionally surrounded the origin of the runes. Some scholars, especially in Scandinavia, view them as having been invented in the north and based on the Latin alphabet. However, there are more striking similarities between early runes and certain "Old Italic" alphabets in use in northern Italy, particularly a Raetic alphabet found in Bolzano in the extreme north (Tirol). These alphabets were offshoots of a northern Etruscan alphabet and developed around the mid-first century BC. Such an alphabet was used to write the Germanic name *harigasti* (also read *hariχasti*, but in this variety of the alphabet *χ* was used to represent *g*, as also in the closely related alphabet of Venetic, cf. §20.17; the name means 'army-guest') on a helmet unearthed in Negau (now Negova), a Slovenian town near the Austrian border (and not far from Tirol). The age of the inscription is disputed, but could date anywhere from the third century BC to the beginning of the first century AD; it is at any rate the earliest known inscriptional Germanic. True Germanic runes, though, are from much more northerly regions. The oldest so far discovered are inscribed on a fibula (brooch) from the town of Meldorf in western Schleswig-Holstein, Germany, from the mid-first century AD, as well as some inscriptions from around AD 200 found in the drained valley of the river Illerup near Århus in eastern Denmark. These inscriptions are all quite short, but are not without linguistic interest. More extensive inscriptions begin to appear in the fourth century.

The Germanic runic alphabet is called the *futhark* (or *futhorc* when referring to English runes), after its first six letters *f u þ a r k* (cp. the word *alphabet* after the first two letters *alpha* and *bēta* in Greek). The idiosyncratic angular shape of the runic letters, which eschew both curves and right angles, may be due to the fact that they were designed for inscribing on wood: all strokes had to run at an angle to the grain to keep the wood from splitting, straight lines are easier to carve in wood than curved ones, and strokes that cross the grain are easier to see.

15.37. Runes were used for all the Germanic languages, although by far the most numerous runic remains come from Scandinavia, particularly Denmark and Sweden. Two runic alphabets can be distinguished. The older one, often called the Elder Futhark, had twenty-four characters and is mostly attested from Denmark. An offshoot of this was modified into the futhorc of England and Friesland around 500. Beginning around the sixth century the Elder Futhark started changing, evolving into the Younger Futhark, which had only sixteen characters (the result of sound changes that allowed some older letters to be dispensed with) and became fully established by the ninth century. Inscriptions in Younger Futhark are mostly known from Sweden, and are vastly more numerous than those in Elder Futhark, reflecting the more widespread literacy of the Viking age. Christianization brought the Latin alphabet, which gradually supplanted the runes; but use of the latter continued, especially in Scandinavia, through the late medieval period and even beyond.

The language of the earliest runes, up till around AD 500, is rather uniform across a fairly wide geographical expanse, and has been named **Runic** or Runic Norse. Its position within Germanic is controversial. It is very similar to the putative ancestor of both North and West Germanic. However, the fact that it still preserves final *-z* (see next section) probably tips the balance in favor of specifically North Germanic filiation: North Germanic preserved *-z* but West Germanic lost it, and it is unlikely that West Germanic had not yet lost its **-z* by the Runic period. Nonetheless, we treat Runic separately here from the rest of North Germanic because of its age and controversial filiation.

15.38. Runic is important in preserving final *-z* before its later rhotacization to *-r* by the time it became Old Norse, as in *gastiz* 'guest' (ON *gestr*). The rune for this sound is frequently transcribed R, on the assumption that its phonetic value was between that of a *z* and an *r*; but this assumption is unnecessary. Runic also preserves short vowels before final *-s* or *-z*, as shown also by *gastiz*; these were later lost.

Most texts in Runic, before it differentiated into various local varieties that can be termed Old Swedish, Old Danish, etc., are rather short, consisting only of a name or a formulaic word. But some, such as the text below, are longer and represent our earliest native Germanic literature.

Runic text sample

15.39. Inscription on the larger of two golden horns found in Gallehus in southern Jutland, Denmark, dating to c. AD 400. (The horns unfortunately were stolen and melted down for their gold in 1802.) The first two words are written together. The inscription is poetic; like later Germanic poetic lines, it consists of two half-lines connected by alliteration (*ek h̲lewagastiz h̲oltijaz* ‖ *h̲orna tawido*).

ekhlewagastiz . holtijaz . horna . tawido .

I, Hlewagastiz Holtijaz, made (this) horn.

15.39a. Notes. ek: 'I', Runic stressed 1st person pronoun, which also appears as suffixed (unstressed) *-ka*; elsewhere in Germanic the form is *ik*. **hlewagastiz:** personal name, 'famous guest'; the elements of this name are found in many other IE personal names (cp. §§2.48, 6.82). *Hlewa-* is from **k̂leu̯-o-*, cp. Gk. *klé(w)os* 'fame'. **holtijaz:** 'of Holt(i)', meaning either 'son of Holt(i)' or 'from a place called Holt(i)'. **tawido:** 'made', 1st sing. weak preterite of a verb cognate with Goth. *tawjan*, preterite *tawida*.

East Germanic

15.40. East Germanic is the one extinct branch of Germanic and is represented principally by **Gothic**. According to the traditional history as told by the sixth-century Gothic historian Jordanes, the Goths' ancient homeland was in Scandinavia; linguistically this may be supported by the name of the island of Gotland off eastern Sweden and other place-names apparently containing *Got(h)* or a related element.

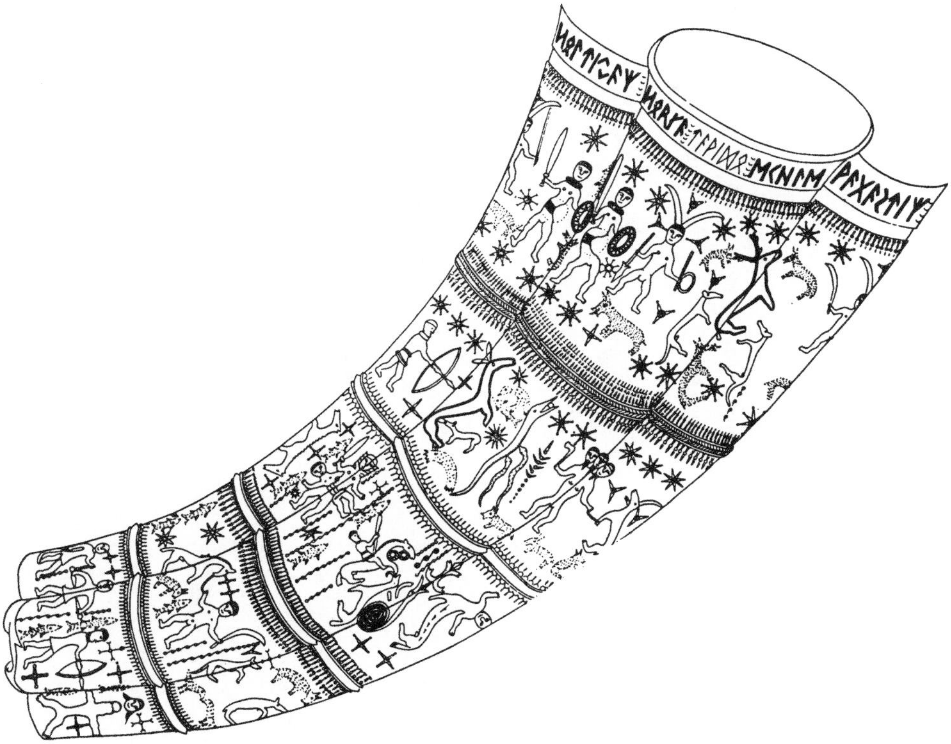

Figure 15.1 Reproduction of an eighteenth-century engraving of the Gallehus horn containing the inscription in 15.39. The engraving shows the entire decorated surface of the horn, with the rear surface peeled back. The runes encircle the top of the horn and are read rightwards, beginning with what looks like a boldfaced M (= *e*) following the non-boldfaced word in the middle (*tawido*). Most words are separated from one another by a vertical stack of four or five curved marks. From R. I. Page, *Runes* (London: British Museum Publications, 1987), p. 28. Reproduced by permission of the British Museum.

(On the speech of Gotland, called Gutnish, see §15.107.) In or slightly before the second century AD, according to Jordanes, a group of Goths migrated from Scandinavia to the Baltic coast, defeating the Vandals and other Germanic tribes who lived there, and over several generations migrated farther south and east, arriving ultimately at the Black Sea. The Goths who settled in what is now Ukraine were the East Goths or **Ostrogoths**, while their relatives to the west, in what is now Romania between the lower Danube and Dniestr Rivers, are called the West Goths or **Visigoths** (*Visi-*, also written *Vesi-* in classical sources, actually does not mean 'west', but probably 'good, noble', from PIE **u̯es-*; cp. Ved. *vásu-* 'good').

The Visigoths were attacked by Huns in the year 376, who forced them across the Danube into Roman territory. For the next half-century they wandered through various parts of Europe in search of a place to live, along the way becoming converted

Map 15.1 The Germanic peoples around AD 500

to Arian Christianity, sacking Rome in 410, and finally settling in southern Gaul and Spain, where they founded a kingdom. After reaching its height in the late sixth and early seventh centuries, it was ultimately defeated and absorbed by the Muslim invaders of Spain in 711. As for the Ostrogoths, for a time they were also defeated by the Huns, but freed themselves in the fifth century and took over the rule of Italy until the mid-sixth century, which became the western part of a large kingdom stretching as far east as the Danube River. We have a number of Ostrogothic names preserved in classical sources from this time.

One group that had settled in the Crimea retained their identity as Goths perhaps as late as the eighteenth century. Several dozen words and phrases in the language, termed **Crimean Gothic**, were collected in the early 1560s by a Flemish nobleman, Ogier Ghiselin von Busbecq, from a Greek in Constantinople. The transmission of these words seems to be inaccurate and corrupt in places, but is a precious window on a late type of Gothic different in certain ways from the dialect of the Gothic Bible (see below).

Also driven westward by the incursion of the Huns were the Vandals, whose language, **Vandalic**, was East Germanic as well. Among their various conquests, the Vandals overran part of Spain in the fourth century AD, whence probably the name of the historical region called *Andalusia*. Beginning in the early fifth century and lasting into the sixth, they took over part of northern Africa and established a kingdom there that they used as a base for plundering Italy and other parts of the Mediterranean, sacking Rome in 455. Other East Germanic languages were **Burgundian**, **Gepidic**, and **Rugian**. All of these have essentially disappeared without a trace, and are known only from scattered personal and place-names.

Gothic

15.41. Our knowledge of Gothic stems almost entirely from the remains of a translation of the New Testament by a West Gothic bishop named Wulfila or Ulfilas ('Little Wolf', c. 311–382), which he undertook for the Visigoths living along the lower Danube. In addition, we have a few fragments of the *Skeireins* ('explanation, exegesis', a commentary on the Gospel of St. John and probably not written by Wulfila), and some isolated inscriptions and words preserved in other texts.

15.42. The spelling and alphabet were invented by Wulfila but are based on Greek. In transcriptions of Gothic words, *q* stands for the labiovelar k^w and *ƕ* stands for the voiceless labiovelar glide h^w (as in some pronunciations of English *what*). The letter *g* has the value [ŋ] before another *g*, *k*, or *q* (thus *siggwan* 'sing', *sigqan* 'sink'), but *gg* can also represent a double *g* (especially when it arose by Verschärfung, see §15.44 below). The vowels are slightly complicated. Wulfila used *ai* and *au* each in two different values, as the outcomes of the diphthongs **ai* and **au* (probably [ɛː] and [ɔː]) and as the short lax vowels [ɛ] (like in Eng. *bet*) and [ɔ] (like in *bought*). (Many people distinguish these by writing *ái áu* for the diphthongs and *aí* and *aú* for the short vowels, but we shall not do that here.) The vowels *e* and *o* stand for long tense *ē* and *ō* ([eː] and [oː], as in Eng. *bare* and *bore*). The letter *u* stands for both short and long *u*, and *ei* stands for long [iː] (like Eng. *beat*).

Phonology

15.43. Although Gothic is the oldest Germanic language preserved in any abundance, it is not in every respect the most conservative or archaic; as with any language, it contains its own unique mixture of old and new. Most noteworthy in this regard is the fact that it had gotten rid of nearly all the Verner's variants (§15.28) by the time it is attested, by generalizing one or the other stem-final consonantal variant throughout any given paradigm. For example, the verb *wairþan* 'become' has singular preterite *warþ* as expected, but plural *waurþum* rather than expected **waurdum* (contrast OE *wearþ*, *wurdon*). On the other hand, Gothic preserves the Proto-Germanic vowel inventory better than any other Germanic language. For one thing, it was not affected by any of the various umlauts that spread through North and West Germanic territory some centuries later (§§15.51 and 15.94–96).

15.44. Another phonological feature of Gothic, this time shared with North Germanic, is the **Verschärfung** (or "hardening") of the Proto-Germanic geminate glides **jj* and **ww* into geminate stops plus glide. The geminate glides arose from diverse sources that need not be entered into here. In Old Norse, **ww* and **jj* became *ggv* and *ggj*, while in Gothic the outcomes were *ggw* and *ddj*. For example, from Gmc. **treww(i)a-* 'trusty, true' we have Goth. *triggws* and ON *tryggva*, and from **twajjē(n)* or **twajjō(n)* 'of the two' (genit. pl.) we have Goth. *twaddje* and ON *tveggja* (cp. OHG *zweio*). Crimean Gothic has simple *d* here, as in *ada* 'egg' from Gmc. **ajja-*; compare ON ***egg*** (from which Eng. *egg* was borrowed).

Morphology

15.45. Gothic preserves some important morphological archaisms not found in the other Germanic languages. Verbs have separate forms for the first and second persons dual, and a passive conjugation in the present tense. (The passive in Germanic is otherwise found only in the 1st singular of the verb 'to be called, named': Runic *haite* 'I am called', ON *heiti*, OE *hātte*, Mod. German *ich heisse.*) A vocative different from the nominative is preserved in some declensions (e.g. nomin. *dags* 'day', voc. *dag*). On the other hand, Gothic has lost the instrumental, which does survive in some of the other languages.

Syntax

15.46. Gothic preserves several enclitic particles that occur in the second position of a sentence by Wackernagel's Law (§§8.22ff.). These occur in chains, just as in other older IE languages (cp. Anatolian, §9.13), and preverbs count for the purposes of determining their placement – that is, second-position clitics will intervene between a preverb and its associated verb if the preverb and verb stand at the beginning of their clause. For example, the interrogative particle ***u*** appears between the preverb and verb in *ga-u-laubjats* 'Do you (both) believe . . . ?' (Matt. 9:28); the verb is *ga-laubjan* 'to believe', cognate with OHG *gilouban* (Mod. German *glauben*) and (with different prefix) Eng. *be-lieve.* An example of a chain consisting of the same particle plus the indefinite object pronoun *ƕa* 'something' is seen in the sequence *ga-u-ƕa-selvi* 'whether he saw anything' (Mark 8:23). All of this is quite foreign to North and West Germanic.

15.47. Not unexpectedly in light of these facts, Gothic is the only Germanic language to preserve a living descendant of the PIE enclitic conjunction **k^we* 'and' (§7.27), which shows up as *-h* (e.g. *ga-<u>h</u>-melida* '<u>and</u> he wrote') or *-uh* (IE **u-k^we*, e.g. *urreis nim-<u>uh</u>* 'arise <u>and</u> take!').

Gothic text sample

15.48. Mark 8:14–18. For the orthography, see §15.42 above.

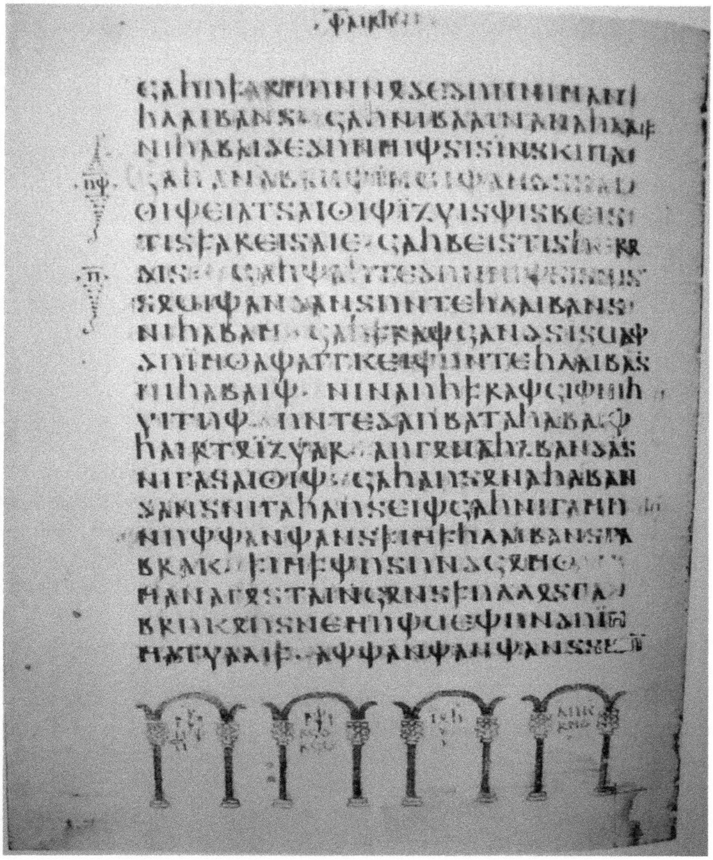

Figure 15.2 Leaf (50 v.) from the sixth-century Codex Argenteus, the only surviving manuscript containing the Gothic Bible. Mark 8:14 begins at the top and our selection runs through the first three letters of the fifth line from the bottom. Reproduced from the facsimile edition *Codex Argenteus Upsaliensis Jussu Senatus Universitatis Phototypice Editus* (Uppsala: Almqvist & Wiksell, 1927), p. 322.

14 jah ufarmunnodedun niman hlaibans jah niba ainana hlaif ni habaidedun miþ sis in skipa. 15 jah anabauþ im qiþands: saiƕiþ ei atsaiƕiþ izwis þis beistis Fareisaie jah beistis Herodis. 16 jah þāhtedun miþ sis misso qiþandans: unte hlaibans ni habam. 17 jah fraþjands Iesus qaþ du im: ƕa þaggkeiþ unte hlaibans ni habaiþ? ni nauh fraþjiþ nih wituþ, unte daubata habaiþ hairto izwar. 18 augona habandans ni gasaiƕiþ, jah ausona habandans ni gahauseiþ jah ni gamunuþ.

14 Now they had forgotten to bring bread; and they had only one loaf with them in the boat. 15 And he cautioned them, saying, "Take heed, beware of the leaven of

the Pharisees and the leaven of Herod." 16 And they discussed it with one another, saying, "We have no bread." 17 And being aware of it, Jesus said to them, "Why do you discuss the fact that you have no bread? Do you not yet perceive or understand? Are your hearts hardened? 18 Having eyes do you not see, and having ears do you not hear? And do you not remember?"

15.48a. Notes. 14. jah: 'and'; the *-h* is from PIE *k^we 'and'. **ufarmunnodedun:** 'they forgot'; *-dedun* is the 3rd pl. weak preterite ending, and *ufar-* is a preverb, lit. 'over' < **uper* (Gk. *hupér*, Lat. *s-uper*). **niman:** 'to take', German *nehmen*, OE *niman*; PIE **nem-*. The past participle of the OE verb lives on today as *numb* (§15.13). **hlaibans:** 'loaves of bread', cognate with Eng. *loaf* (OE *hlāf*); *-ans* is accus. pl., preserving the nasal (§6.55). **niba:** 'not even', combined with the following *ni* in a double negative construction. **habaidedun:** *hab-* is the root, like German *haben* 'to have'; the rest is stem plus weak dental preterite. **miþ:** 'with', cognate with German *mit* and the *mid-* of Eng. *mid-wife* (literally '[one who is] with the woman [giving birth]'). **skipa:** 'boat', cognate with both *ship* (the native English word) and *skiff* (ultimately from a Germanic language that preserved *sk-* like Gothic).

15–16. im: 'them', dat. pl. **qiþands:** 'saying'; *-ands* is the nominative of the present participle, and *qiþan* is cognate with archaic English *quoth* (past tense, equivalent to Goth. *qaþ* as in verse 17 below). **saiƕiþ ei:** 'see (2nd pl.) (to it) that . . .'. *Saiƕan*, cognate with Eng. *see*, German *sehen*, is from *sek^w-; the 2nd pl. ending *-iþ* is the same as ON *-ið*, German *-(e)t* (imperative *seht!* 'see ye!'), from PIE **-ete*. **izwis:** 'you (pl.)', dat. and accus.; the genit. is *izwar*, seen below, verse 17. **þis beistis:** 'the leaven', genit. sing. object of the verb *atsaíƕiþ* 'you look out for'. **þāhtedun:** 'thought', Gmc. **þāhtō* from earlier **þanhtō*, with loss of nasal as per §15.11; the nasal is still in the present stem (*þagkjan*, Eng. *think*). **misso:** '(each) other'. **unte:** cognate with German *und*, Eng. *and*, but here meaning 'that' after the verb of saying.

17. fraþjands: 'understanding, being aware'. **du:** 'to', with unexplained *d-*. **ƕa:** lit. 'what', here meaning 'why'; from PIE *k^wod, with regular loss of the final *-d* (preserved in the demonstrative *þata* 'that (thing)' by the addition of some enclitic particle). **nauh:** 'yet', = German *noch* 'yet, still', IE *$nu\text{-}k^we$. **nih:** 'nor, and not', IE *$ne\text{-}k^we$ (> Lat. *neque* 'nor'). **wituþ:** 'you (pl.) know'; the singular stem is *wait-*, from the old PIE perfect **u̯oid-*, **u̯id-*, see §5.52. **daubata:** 'deaf, hardened', neut. accus. of the adj. *daufs*; *-ata* is the 'strong' adjectival ending, taken over from pronominal forms like neut. accus. *þata* 'that'. **hairto:** 'heart', a neuter *n*-stem, hence its inflection in German as *Herz* (nomin.-accus.) but dat. *Herz-en*.

18. augona: 'eyes', neut. nomin.-accus. pl., also a neuter *n*-stem (German pl. *Auge-n*), from Gmc. **augōn*, ultimately from PIE *h_3ek^w- (Lat. *oc-ulus*, OCS *oko*, etc.) but influenced by Gmc. **auzōn* 'ear' (PIE *h_2eus-; the Gothic descendant, in the neut. pl., is *ausona*, a few words later in this verse). **gasaiƕiþ:** 'see', 2nd pl., with the addition of the prefix *ga-* to give it a punctual or perfective sense. The same prefix is found in *gahauseiþ* 'you hear' and *gamunuþ* 'you understand'; the Greek original has ordinary presents for all of these, so this is clearly a Gothic feature and not a literal rendition of the Greek. **gahauseiþ:** 'you hear', from the verb *hausjan* 'to hear'. In the rest of Germanic it shows the effects of Verner's Law (Eng. *hear*, ON *heyra*, all from **hauzja-*). The PIE root for 'hear' is *h_2kous-, as in Gk. *akoúō* 'I hear'.

West Germanic

15.49. Three ancient West Germanic languages are attested in meaningful quantities from before the year 1000: **Old English, Old Saxon,** and **Old High German.** Old

High German is more divergent from the other two than either of them are from each other (Old Saxon and Old English are quite similar and must have been mutually intelligible). For this reason, a division is often made between Old High German and the rest of West Germanic.

Consonants

15.50. In Common West Germanic, Germanic final **-z* was lost, as in OE *dæg* and German *Tag* 'day' from **dagaz* (cp. Goth. *dags*, ON *dagr*). Elsewhere, **z* was rhotacized to *r*, as in **luzana-* 'lost' > Eng. *lorn* (as in *love-lorn*, *for-lorn*). A consonant plus the glide **j* became a geminated consonant following a short vowel, as in many verbs with the suffix **-ja-* (see §15.30), e.g. **sitjan* 'to sit' > OE *sittan*, **bidjan* 'to ask' > OE *biddan* (cp. Goth. *bidjan*). Additionally, *h* was lost before consonants word-initially; this happened independently in all the West Germanic languages in the Middle Ages. Thus contrast Eng. *loud* and German *laut* with OE *hlūd* and OHG *hlūt*, *hlūd*. West Germanic loanwords beginning with *hl-* borrowed into early French, which had no *h*, were borrowed as *fl-* or *c(h)l-*, as in the name of the Merovingian king *Clovis* from Frankish **Hlodowīg* 'loud-battle'; a later form of the same name was borrowed as *Louis*. Finally, mention may be made of the hardening of Germanic **đ* to *d*, which happened in all positions in this branch but more limitedly in the other branches, as in OE *midd* 'mid(dle)' (vs. ON *miðr*) and OE *meodo* 'mead' (vs. ON *mjǫðr*).

Vowels

15.51. The Germanic vowels underwent more substantial changes in West Germanic than the consonants. Principal among these were the various *umlauts*, vowel shifts caused by the presence of a particular vowel or glide in a following syllable. By far the most significant, and most familiar, was ***i*-umlaut**. This sound change affected the back vowels *a*, *ā*, *ō*, *u*, and *ū* when they preceded a syllable containing *i* or *j* (the glide *i̯*). The back vowels then became fronted to vowels essentially equivalent to Modern German *ä*, *ö*, and *ü*. A tabular overview, with further remarks on other umlaut processes, is given below in the section on Old English, §15.60.

While *i*-umlaut ultimately affected most of the West Germanic-speaking area (as well as Old Norse, see §15.96 below), it did not affect all of it equally or simultaneously. It appears to have started in the northwest, as its effects are complete in Old English from the earliest documented times. It also spread to Old Norse fairly early. Farther south, however, matters are less clear: umlaut is not indicated consistently in Old High German texts, and modern southern German dialects show it less consistently too.

Old English

15.52. Around the late fourth and continuing into the fifth and sixth centuries AD, three Germanic tribes inhabiting the coastal areas of Denmark and northern Germany began migrating to England: the Angles, Saxons, and Jutes. The traditional date for their arrival is 449, but there is good evidence that their migrations had already begun by 400. The Angles, inhabiting northern Schleswig-Holstein and already mentioned by the Roman historian Tacitus in the first century AD, settled large parts of Britain in the fifth and sixth centuries, including what would become the kingdoms of Northumbria, Mercia, and East and West Anglia. Around the early fifth century, the Saxons, who had aggressively expanded into northern Germany from their homeland in eastern Schleswig-Holstein, launched pirate raids against Britain and began to colonize it, settling in areas that are now called Essex, Wessex, and Sussex (literally 'East Saxons', 'West Saxons', 'South Saxons'). The Jutes came probably from Jutland in Denmark and settled in Kent in southeast England and the Isle of Wight. The original distinctions among these closely related peoples soon disappeared; medieval writers referred to the whole population simply as *Anglī* or Angles, whence the OE name *Englaland*, 'land of the Angles, England'. In modern scholarship, they are collectively called the **Anglo-Saxons**.

15.53. The language of this new population in Britain is known as **Old English** or Anglo-Saxon. It is first known from fragmentary runic inscriptions of little linguistic value from the late fourth or early fifth century; the literary period did not start until several centuries later. The surviving corpus of Old English literature is substantial and consists of both poetry and prose. Most Old English poetry is anonymous and cannot be dated with certainty, but was probably written down between the eighth and eleventh centuries. The oldest datable poem is Caedmon's hymn (§15.69), composed around 650. The longest and most famous Old English poem is *Beowulf*, a heroic epic containing a mixture of historical and legendary material, some of it quite ancient.

The earliest Old English prose is older than the poetry. Its first known representative is the law code of King Æthelberht of Kent, written c. 600. The composition of literary prose prospered during the reign of King Alfred the Great (849–99) of Wessex, who instigated a cultural renaissance in the late ninth century and championed the use of Old English as a literary vehicle equal to Latin. Under Alfred's influence, the Wessex variety of the **West Saxon** dialect (spoken in southwestern England) became the literary standard, ushering in the period of "Classical" Old English. Literary activity in England was vigorous until the Norman Conquest (1066); many of the prose works produced during this time are in an excellent style on a par with that of any other contemporaneous literature in Europe.

15.54. Aside from West Saxon, Old English had three other major dialects: **Northumbrian**, spoken north of the Humber river, preserved in short inscriptions, poems, and glosses; **Mercian**, spoken between the Humber and the Thames, preserved in charters and glosses and the source of most Modern English native forms; and **Kentish**, spoken in a small slice of southeast England, preserved also in charters and in some literature and glosses.

15.55. Old English shares several features with Frisian, leading many scholars to posit an **Anglo-Frisian** subgroup of West Germanic. The palatalization of *k* before front vowels (see the next section) and the "brightening" of *a* to *æ* (§15.60) are among the characteristics of Anglo-Frisian.

Developments of Old English

Consonants

15.56. Palatalization. Most of the changes that Old English made to the West Germanic consonant system had to do with the velars. The voiceless velar stop **k* when neighboring front vowels (*e* and *i*) or preceding the palatal glide *j* was palatalized to the affricate [č] (written *c*, later *ch* starting in Middle English). This is the source of the *ch* in such Modern English words as *chew* (OE *cēowan*), *church* (OE *cirice*), *drench* (pre-OE **drankjan*), and *ditch* (OE *dīc*; contrast German *kauen*, *Kirche*, *tränken* 'to water', and Old Norse *díki* 'ditch', all without palatalization). The voiced velar stop **g* was weakened to the voiced velar fricative [ɣ] or the glide [j] (but still spelled *g* in Old English) in many positions, especially word-finally, between vowels, and before most front vowels. This is the source of the initial *y-* in such words as *yellow, yield*, and *yarn* (OE *geolu, geldan* 'to pay', *gearn*; compare German *gelb, gelten, Garn* with preserved *g-*); note also *day, many, saw* ('saying') from *dæg, manig*, and *sagu*. A hard *g* in these positions in a Modern English word typically marks it as a borrowing, as is the case with *get, guest, gift, egg, dreg*, and *nag*, which are all from Old Norse.

15.57. Other changes. A feature that characterizes not only Old English but all the West Germanic languages except High German is the prehistoric loss of nasals before fricatives (*f þ s*), with compensatory lengthening of the preceding vowel. Thus where OHG has *fimf* 'five', OE has *fīf* and Old Saxon has *fîf*. Similarly, the word for 'other' in Gothic is *anþar* and in OHG *ander*, while OE has *ōþer*; and contrast also OHG *uns* 'us' with OE *ūs*, and German *Gans* with OE *gōs* 'goose'. Additionally, the Germanic voiced fricative **ƀ* remained a fricative and turned into voiceless *f*, as in *hlāf* 'loaf' < **hlaiƀaz* (contrast German *Laib*).

15.58. Between vowels, the fricatives *f* and *s* were voiced to *v* and *z* in Old English, though spelled as *f* and *s*: *frēosan* 'freeze', *ofer* 'over'.

15.59. Finally, the consonant cluster **sk* became the sibilant [ʃ] in Old English (i.e. *sh*) and was spelled *sc*: *fisc* 'fish', *scip* 'ship', *wæscan* 'wash'. Words in English with the sound *sk* are borrowings, often from other Germanic languages. Thus *shirt* is native English (OE *scyrte*) but *skirt* is a borrowing of its Old Norse cognate *skyrta*. Similarly, the word *blatherskite* turns out to be a bit more colorful than its modern meaning ('foolish person') might suggest: its second element is a borrowing of the Old Norse cognate of English *shit*.

Vowels and diphthongs

15.60. The Germanic vowel system underwent more significant change than the consonants in OE. The back vowels **a* and **ā* became fronted (or "brightened") in most positions to the front vowels *æ* and *ǣ* except before nasals: thus *ræt* 'rat' (vs. German *Ratte*, which preserved the old *a*) and *hæfde* 'had' (vs. German *hatte*). (One can see with this change part of the characteristic "sound" of English shining through at an early date.) The most far-reaching change was *i*-umlaut, causing the diphthongs and most vowels to be fronted before a syllable containing _*i_ or _*j_ in pre-Old English. The following table exhibits most of the changes; the first example for each vowel or diphthong is not umlauted, while the second example is umlauted and is boldfaced:

West Germanic		Old English	Modern English
_*a_	_*drank_	_dranc_	_drank_
	*drankjan	_drencan_	_drench_
_*ō_	_*fōt_	_fōt_	_foot_
	*fōti	_fēt_	_feet_
_*u_	_*guđa_	_god_	_god_
	*guđiga-	_gydig_	_giddy_ (orig. 'possessed by god')
_*ū_	_*mūs_	_mūs_	_mouse_
	*mūsi	_mӯs_	_mice_
_*ai_	_*gaista_	_gāst_	_ghost_
	*gaist(a)līk-	_gǣstlīc_	_ghastly_
_*au_	_*staupa-_	_stēap_	_steep_
	*staupila	_stīepel_	_steeple_
_*eu_	_*þeuƀa_	_þēof_	_thief_
	*þeuƀiþō	_þīefþ_	_theft_

15.61. The new _æ_ and _ǣ_ from _*a_ and _*ā_, together with the other front vowels _e, i_, and _ī_, underwent a diphthongization in various phonetic contexts known as **breaking**. Examples include the following:

Germanic	Old English	Modern English
*lizn-	_leornian_	_learn_
*ahtau	_eahta_	_eight_
*erþō	_eorþ_	_earth_

These diphthongs reverted to single vowels later in the history of English, but spellings like _learn_ and _earth_ are orthographic remnants of the earlier diphthongal pronunciation.

There were also diphthongs inherited from Germanic, and these underwent change as well. First, _*ai_ was monophthongized to _ā_, which eventually became long _ō_ in most dialects, including the one ancestral to Modern English. This is still a diphthong in German, where it is usually written _ei_; hence English–German pairs like _bone/Bein, stone/Stein, home/Heim_, and _whole/heil_. The other two Germanic diphthongs, _*au_ and _*eu_, became _ēa_ and _ēo_: compare OE _cēap_ 'bargain' (> modern _cheap_) with German _Kauf_ 'sale', and OE _flēogan_ 'to fly' with OHG _fliogan_ (< Germanic _*fleugan_).

15.62. Recognizing ablaut and umlaut in Modern English. English contains many words or word-pairs having vowel alternations; some are due to ablaut, some to umlaut, and telling them apart usually requires some knowledge of their history. Vowel changes in the principal parts of strong or "irregular" verbs are normally vestiges of PIE ablaut; the same is true of many nouns derived from or related to them, such as *song* alongside *sing*, and *seat* alongside *sit*. Umlaut is the source of, among other things, the vowel alternations seen in irregular plurals (*mouse/mice, foot/feet, man/men*; these all go back typically to Germanic plurals with the suffix *-*iz*, which disappeared after causing umlaut), in abstract nouns ending in -*th* that are formed from adjectives (*long/length, foul/filth, whole/health*; the suffix was *-*iþō*-, with the -*i*- causing umlaut), and in the occasional irregular comparative or superlative like *elder, eldest* alongside *old* (Germanic **aldiza*- **aldista*-; recall §15.23). In some cases, a vowel alternation in Modern English is due to a combination of both ablaut and umlaut, as with *stench* alongside *stink* (Germanic **stankja*- alongside **stinkan*) and with the causative *drench* alongside *drink*.

Morphology

15.63. The morphology of Old English was little changed from that of Common Germanic, and resembles that of Modern German. There were four cases in the noun and pronoun (nominative, genitive, dative, accusative), plus traces of an instrumental case; verbs were conjugated in a present and preterite indicative and in a present and past subjunctive, with different endings for most of the persons in singular and plural.

15.64. Many Old English nominal and verbal paradigms show the effects of umlaut; virtually all of these effects were leveled out in the later development of the language, with the occasional "irregular" plurals like *man/men* being essentially the only remnants. Examples of such paradigms follow: a root noun (*fōt* 'foot'), a consonant-stem (*fēond* 'enemy'), and an *s*-stem (*lomb* 'lamb'). Also, two strong verb paradigms are given in the present and preterite, an example of Class III (*helpan* 'to help') and of Class II (*cēosan* 'to choose', this one also showing Verner's variants in the preterite):

sg.				
	N	*fōt*	*fēond*	*lomb*
	A	*fōt*	*fēond*	*lomb*
	D	*fēt*	*fīend*	*lombe*
	G	*fōtes*	*fēondes*	*lombes*
pl.				
	N	*fēt*	*fīend*	*lombru*
	A	*fēt*	*fīend*	*lombru*
	D	*fōtum*	*fēondum*	*lombrum*
	G	*fōta*	*fēonda*	*lombra*

present			
sg.	1	*helpe*	*cēose*
	2	*hilpst*	*cīest*
	3	*hilpþ*	*cīest*
pl.		*helpaþ*	*cēosaþ*
preterite			
sg.	1	*healp*	*cēas*
	2	*hulpe*	*cure*
	3	*healp*	*cēas*
pl.		*hulpon*	*curon*

It is instructive to note that Old English nouns had well over a half-dozen plural formations, of which the ancestor of the productive modern *s*-plural was merely one: *stān* 'stone' pl. *stānas*; *hēafod* 'head' pl. *hēafodu*; *word* 'word' pl. *word*; *giefu* 'gift' pl. *giefa*; *lār* 'teaching, lore' pl. *lāra*; *sāwol* 'soul' pl. *sāwla*; *eoh* 'horse' pl. *ēos*; *mǣd* 'mead, meadow' pl. *mǣdwa*; *oxa* 'ox' pl. *oxan*; and *here* 'army' pl. *herigeas*. Almost all of these have disappeared without a trace; *oxen* is a remnant of the old *n*-stem declension (note how what we think of as a plural ending *-en* was originally the stem, from the IE point of view), while *men* and *feet* go back to umlauting paradigms. The *-r-* in *children* (dialectally also *childer*) is the only remnant of the *lombru*-type plural in the paradigm above, where the *-r-* ultimately continues the *-s-* of the IE *s*-stems. The developments by which *-s* became the default plural are complex and not fully documented.

In the verb paradigms, the old 3rd plural endings have been generalized throughout the plural (*-aþ* < **-anþ* < primary **-onti*; *-on* < Germanic **-un* < secondary **-n̥t*); Old English shares this characteristic with all of West Germanic outside of High German. The 2nd singular of the preterite, with its short-vowel ending and the same ablaut grade as the plural, is characteristic of West Germanic and unusual from the PIE point of view. The ending appears to go back to Gmc. **-īz*, the 2nd sing. optative ending; what we are probably dealing with is an old perfect optative that was used for politeness. (The normal 2nd sing. perfect ending **-*th_2*e* is preserved as *-t* in the preterite presents, as in early Modern Eng. *(thou) shalt.*)

Middle and Modern English

15.65. After the Old English period, almost all the inflections seen in the previous section were lost. This loss has been frequently but erroneously attributed to the influence of Norman French (on which more shortly). In fact, changes that predated the Norman period had already set the scene for it, in particular the loss of distinctions in the vowels of final unstressed syllables. In the **Middle English** period, these syllables were lost, and with them most inflectional endings. The different classes of Old English nouns were collapsed into essentially one class which added *-es* to form the possessive singular and the plural. (This had not fully affected feminine nouns or kinship terms in *-er*, as seen by phrases like *his lady grace* and *thi brother wife.*) Grammatical gender was also lost except in a few dialects, as well as the dual inflection in pronouns. To express grammatical roles of nouns, prepositional phrases and distinctions in word order became increasingly important.

15.66. Middle English lasted from the time of the Norman Conquest (1066) to about 1500. The first century and a half of this stage is poorly documented. The Normans not only ousted the Anglo-Saxon royalty and nobility, but also replaced the native clergy and scribes with speakers of Norman French. The forced break in the scribal tradition resulted in a precipitous drop in the writing of English, and by the thirteenth century, English had absorbed hundreds of French loanwords. But after the loss of Normandy in 1204, interest in French declined and the prestige of English rose again. London was the administrative capital and attracted a steady stream of settlers who brought regional dialect features with them. London English adopted some of these features, increasing its comprehensibility far from the mouth of the Thames; gradually it assumed the role of a standard language. By the end of the fourteenth century, English was the language of instruction in schools; it had also triumphed in the originally Norse-speaking Danelaw, the area of northern England settled by the Norsemen. (But Norse had left an indelible stamp on English vocabulary; see §15.90 below.)

15.67. The bulk of surviving Middle English literature consists of anonymous religious and didactic works in verse, including romances like the brilliant late fourteenth-century poem *Sir Gawain and the Green Knight.* A linguistically valuable piece of didactic religious verse, albeit devoid of literary interest, is the *Ormulum* by a canon named Orm (fl. 1200). This poem was written in a spelling system devised by Orm himself to reflect the phonetic details of the language faithfully. Needing little introduction is the finest poet in English before Shakespeare, Geoffrey Chaucer (c. 1342–1400), who became a master of narrative poetry, especially with his unfinished *Canterbury Tales.*

15.68. The **Modern English** period includes English since 1500. Its chief linguistic development was the **Great English Vowel Shift**, a series of changes to the long vowels that had already begun in the late Middle English period and finished running their course by the eighteenth century (at least in standard English; some dialects were never affected by it, or affected only partially or in different ways). First, the long high vowels [iː] and [uː] became the diphthongs consisting of [əj, əw] (later [aj, aw]); subsequently the mid long vowels [eː] and [oː] were raised to [iː, uː] and the low vowel [aː] was fronted and raised to [eː]. In modern (standard) English pronunciation, all the resultant vowels have come to be pronounced with offglides. Compare the following examples:

Middle English		Modern English	
[iː]	*bīten*	[aj]	*bite*
[eː]	*sēen*	[ij]	*see*
[aː]	*gāte*	[ej]	*gate*
[oː]	*bōt*	[uw]	*boot*
[uː]	*lūd*	[aw]	*loud*

As can be seen from the Modern English examples, the older spelling was frequently maintained. Modern English spelling in fact typically reflects late Middle English pronunciation.

Old English text sample

15.69. Caedmon's Hymn, as preserved in the earliest Anglian (Northumbrian) version, AD 737; probably composed around 650. A *u* before a vowel represents *w*. The version on the right is in West Saxon.

Northumbrian	*West Saxon*
Nū scylun hergan hefænrīcaes Uard,	Nū wē sculon herigean heofonrīces Weard,
Metudæs maecti end his mōdgidanc,	Meotodes meahte ond his mōdgeþanc,
uerc Uuldurfadur, suē hē uundra gihuaes,	weorc Wuldorfæder, swā hē wundra gehwæs
ēci Dryctin, ōr āstelidæ.	ēce Drihten, ōr onstealde.

Hē ǣrist scōp aelda barnum
heben til hrōfe, hāleg Scepen;
thā middungeard moncynnæs Uard,
ēci Dryctin, æfter tīadæ,
fīrum foldu, Frēa allmectig.

Hē ǣrest sceōp eorðan bearnum
heofon tō hrōfe, hālig Scyppend;
þā middangeard monncynnes Weard,
ēce Drihten, æfter tēode,
fīrum foldan, Frēa ælmihtig.

Now we must praise the guardian of the heaven-kingdom,
the might of the Lord and his wisdom,
the work of the Glorious Father, how he,
eternal Lord, established the beginning of each of the miracles.
He first created for the children of men [var.: of the earth]
the heaven as a roof, the holy Creator;
then mankind's Guardian,
eternal Lord, made middle earth after that,
land for men, almighty Lord.

15.69a. Notes (selective). 1–3. hefænrīcaes: 'of the heaven-kingdom', genit. sing. Northumbrian is valuable in distinguishing *æ* (written *ae* < **a*; see §15.60) from *e* in unaccented final syllables. The noun *rīc* 'kingdom', Gmc. **rīkja-*, is a loanword from Celtic (ultimately < PIE **h_3rēǵ-* 'king', cp. Lat. *rēx* 'king', Ved. *rā́j-ān-* 'king'). **Metudæs:** 'Lord, God', genit. sing.; one of the native Germanic words adapted for use to refer to the Christian God. It originally meant 'fate' and comes from the verb *metian* 'to measure' (**med-*, cp. OIr. *midiur* 'I measure, estimate', Lat. *modus* 'measurement'). **maecti:** 'might', feminine *ti*-abstract noun (§6.42) of the verb *magan* 'be able, be powerful' (> Mod. Eng. *may*). **mōdgidanc:** 'wisdom', lit. 'mind-thought'; *mōd* (Mod. Eng. *mood*) is cognate with German *Mut* 'courage' and Goth. *moþs* 'anger', but of unclear etymology; *gidanc* is an example of a very common type of abstract noun in Germanic, made by adding the suffix **ga-* to a verbal root to form a collective. (The type survives in the noun *hand-iwork* < OE *hand-geweorc*.) **uerc:** 'work', PIE **u̯erǵ-* (Gk. *(w)érgon* and Arm. *gorc* 'work'). **uundra:** 'wonders', genit. pl.; the genit. pl. ending in OE was *-a*, from PIE **-ōm*.

4–5. ēci: 'eternal', cognate with the first part of Goth. *ajuk-dūþs* 'eternity' and ultimately derived from **$h_2$oi̯u-* 'life(time)' via Gmc. **aiw-* (which became *ā(w)* in OE; cp. German *ewig* 'forever, eternal'). **Dryctin:** 'Lord', another Germanic term appropriated to refer to God; originally just 'lord (of battle)', cp. Goth. *ga-drauht-s* 'soldier'. **ōr:** 'beginning', cognate with ON *óss* 'mouth (of a river)' and Lat. *ōs* 'mouth'. **āstelidæ:** 'established'; the preverb *ā-* is continued in Mod. Eng. *acknowledge* (from OE *ā-cnāwian* 'recognize, acknowledge'), and *stelidæ* is from *stellan* 'place, set up', cp. German *stellen*, ultimately from PIE **steh$_2$-* 'stand' with additional derivational material. **ǣrist:** 'first', derived from the superlative of Gmc. **air-* 'early, early in the day', from PIE **ai̯er-* 'morning, day' (Av. *aiiarə* 'day', Gk. *ā́riston* 'breakfast, first meal of the day'); the Germanic comparative **airiz* underlies Eng. *early*. **scōp:** 'created', preterite of *scieppan* (cp. Mod. Eng. *shape* < OE *gesceap* 'a creation', and German *schaffen* 'create, accomplish'). **aelda:** 'of ages', i.e. 'of generations, of men', genit. pl.; a *ti*-abstract from the root **$h_2$el-* 'nourish' (also seen in OE *alan* 'nourish, raise', Lat. *alumnus* 'one nourished', and Eng. *old*, lit. 'nourished, grown up' from the old *to*-participle). The West Saxon version has a different word here, *eorðan* 'earth'. **barnum:** 'children', dat. pl.; the word survives in Scots *bairn*, and literally means 'one carried (in the womb)', from **bher-* 'carry'.

6–9. **hāleg:** 'holy', a derivative of *hāl* 'whole', from Gmc. **haila-* < PIE **kai-lo-* 'whole, complete' (cp. OCS *cělŭ* 'whole', and the Old Prussian toast *Kails! Pats kails!* 'Hail! Hail yourself!', useful at parties). **middungeard:** 'middle earth', the Germanic term for the earth and humanity, and the inspiration behind J. R. R. Tolkien's fictional Middle Earth. *Middun* is ultimately from PIE **medhi̯o-* 'middle' (Lat. *medius* 'middle', Gk. *mésos* 'middle') and *geard* (*yard* nowadays) is cognate with Lat. *hortus* 'garden', from PIE **ĝher-* 'enclose'. **moncynnæs:** 'mankind', genit. sing., compound of *monn* 'man', ultimately < PIE **manu-* (cp. Ved. *mánu-* 'man'), and *cynn* 'kin' < Gmc. **kunja-* < **ĝn̥h$_1$-i̯o-*, from **ĝenh$_1$-* 'give birth'. **Frēa:** 'Lord', Gmc. **frawōn*, the feminine of which became German *Frau* 'woman'.

Old High German

15.70. The language known as High German (loosely, German; it is called "High German" after the relatively mountainous terrain of much of its early territory, to distinguish it from the "Low German" of the lowland country to the north) appears first in the form of runic inscriptions in **Old High German** dating back to 600 or so, most importantly on a spearhead found in Wurmlingen near Tübingen in southwest Germany. From the eighth century come a large number of glosses as well as the earliest literature, at first short poems and religious texts. But only in the ninth and tenth centuries does a considerable quantity of material appear on the scene, roughly contemporaneous with the flowering of Old English.

15.71. Old High German is preserved in six dialects, which often vary substantially from one another in orthography and certain grammatical features. The dialect called East Frankish, spoken in east-central Germany east of Frankfurt, is often treated by modern scholars as a kind of standard Old High German, but at the time there was no literary standard that obtained across different regions. The other dialects (Old Alemannic, Old Bavarian, South Rhine Franconian, Rhine Franconian, and West Frankish) were collectively spoken in an area stretching from Switzerland and Bavaria in the south up through Cologne and Fulda in the north.

Often considered a separate West Germanic language, but forming part of the general Old High German dialect area, was the **Frankish** spoken by the Franks, a people that progressively invaded areas of the Roman Empire, primarily eastern Gaul, beginning in the fourth century. The empire they formed, under the Merovingians and Carolingians, lasted more than 300 years, and in the west they (and their name) ultimately became part of the nationality now known as the *French*. The western variety of Frankish is not attested with certainty, but it exerted strong lexical influence on French.

Another variety of Old High German was the language of the Lombards, called **Langobardic**, about which we know very little. The Lombards came from what is now northwest Germany and migrated southward during the fifth century, eventually establishing an important kingdom in northern Italy.

15.72. The surviving corpus of Old High German literature was produced in monasteries and is almost exclusively Christian. We have only the meagerest remains of pagan Old High German literature, including the charm below in §15.81 and a solitary poem in traditional Germanic heroic verse, the incomplete, quasi-historical *Hildebrandslied*, which is intermixed with Old Saxon.

The High German Consonant Shift

15.73. The most famous hallmark of German that separates it from the other West Germanic languages to its north is the High German Consonant Shift, or as it is often called in German, the *zweite Lautverschiebung* (Second Sound Shift, that is, second after Grimm's Law). By this sound change, broadly speaking, the West Germanic voiceless stops **p *t *k* were affricated to *pf ts* (written *z* or *tz*) and *kx* in initial position, and spirantized (became fricatives) to *f s x* (written *ch*) elsewhere. A comparison of words in modern English and German will illustrate these changes in word-initial (left) and word-internal (right) positions:

English	German	English	German
pound	**Pf**und	ape	A**ff**e
tin	**Z**inn	water	Wa**ss**er
cook	**Kch**och (Swiss German)	make	ma**ch**en

As shown by the 'cook' entry, only Swiss German shifted **k* to *kx* in initial position; 'cook' in standard German is *Koch*. In fact, as one travels northward in Germany, ever fewer components of the High German Consonant Shift are met with, until one arrives in Low German territory, where none of the shift has taken place.

15.74. High German is also characterized by the shift of West Germanic **d* to *t* and **þ* to *d*: compare Eng. ***d**ee**d*** with German ***T**a**t*** and Eng. ***th**ing* with German ***D**ing*. This change also affected Dutch and spread to Low German, although the latter's ancestor, Old Saxon, does not show either change.

Changes to vowels

15.75. While Old High German vowels were affected by umlaut, they were not affected by breaking; this plus the lack of any wholesale shift later in the language's history comparable to the Great English Vowel Shift has made the German vowel system more conservative than that of English throughout its attested history. Among simple vowels, practically the only change worthy of note is that **ō* was diphthongized to *uo*, as in OHG *bluoma* 'flower', *scuoh* 'shoe' alongside OE *blōm* and *scōh*. When we turn to the original diphthongs, however, things become more interesting. Inherited ****eu*** underwent a split depending on the vowel in the following syllable: normally it became *io*, but when the following syllable contained a high vowel or *j*, the outcome was *iu*. This resulted in a number of alternations within paradigms and across related words, such as in strong verbs of Class II (infinitive ***b**io**tan*** 'offer' but 1st sing. ***b**iu**tu***, 3rd sing. ***b**iu**tit***) and in pairs like adjective ***s**io**h*** 'sick' ~ abstract noun ***s**iu**hhī*** 'sickness, plague'. (See §15.79 below for the further history of these forms.) Another important change was the monophthongization of the diphthongs **ai* and **au* to *ē* and *ō* before *h*, *r*, and *w*. The first development is seen in OHG *gēr* 'spear' (borrowed into English as a part of names like *Ger-ald* 'spear-rule', *Ro-ger* 'famous spear' from OHG *Gēr-(w)ald*, *Hrōd-gēr*) < **gair(a)* < Germanic **gaiza-*; *zēha* 'toe'

(> Modern *Zeh* or *Zehe*) < **taiha-*; and *snēo* 'snow' (Modern *Schnee*) < **snaiwa-*. (Recall from §15.61 that **ai* was monophthongized in English across the board, and to *ā* rather than *ē*: the correspondents of OHG *gēr*, *zēha*, *snēo* are OE *gār*, *tā*, *snāw*, with *gār* living on in *gar-fish* and *gar-lic*, literally 'spear-leek'.) The second development is seen in *ōra* 'ear' (> Modern *Ohr*) < **aura* < **auzō* and *hōh* 'high' (> Modern *hoch*) < **hauha-*. Otherwise the diphthongs **ai* and **au* remained unchanged to this day, where they are spelled *ei* and *au* (as in *Stein* 'stone' < **staina-*, contrast OE *stān*).

Middle and Modern High German

15.76. Around 1100 was the birth of the **Middle High German** period. For the first time, a standard German was developed, based on the Bavarian and Alemannic dialects in the south. The most important Middle High German literature is poetry, in particular courtly epic and romance, stressing chivalric virtues and refinement and exploring Christian themes. The courtly poetry also included the important genre of the *Minnesang* or song of courtly love (*minne*). Another genre, that of the national epic, is most famously represented by the anonymous *Nibelungenlied*, written in Austria c. 1200–1210; this work is rooted in the earlier Germanic warrior tradition and draws heavily upon historical and legendary material about the Danes, Saxons, Burgundians, and Huns in the fifth and sixth centuries.

15.77. Probably the most important change to affect German phonology from OHG to MHG was the weakening of unstressed syllables. Long vowels fell together with short vowels, and differences in quality were erased, with everything ultimately becoming schwa in the modern standard. The inherited *m* still retained in OHG forms like dat. pl. *tagum* 'days' and 1st pl. *habēm* 'we have' fell together with *n* (a change that was actually already underway in later OHG), whence MHG *tagen*, *haben*. These changes dramatically reduced the number and variety of different declensional and conjugational classes and brought the language much closer to its modern-day look. Another change that may be mentioned was that the OHG diphthong *io* became *ie*, as in *liebe* 'love' from OHG *lioba*.

Modern High German

15.78. For several hundred years after the height of Middle High German literature, there was no longer any standard literary language. By far the most important influence on the development of the Modern High German standard language was Martin Luther's translation of the Bible, the first edition of which appeared in 1522 (Old Testament) and 1534 (New Testament). Luther's translation was the first to be written in a direct and uncomplicated – at times even colloquial – style that strove not only to include expressions that were modern and up-and-coming, but also to incorporate linguistic features from as many regions as possible. Its impact on literary German was immense; its core was Luther's native dialect of Thuringian.

15.79. Three developments in German phonology from the medieval to the modern period may be mentioned. The first was the monophthongization of the diphthongs *uo* and *ie* to [uː] and [iː] (the latter still spelled *ie*), as in *Schuh* < MHG *schuoch* and *Liebe* < MHG *liebe*. The second is a change paralleled in English: the long high vowels *ī* and *ū* became diphthongized to [aj] and [au], as in *mîn* 'of me' > *mein* and *hûs* 'house' > *Haus*. Finally, the diphthong *iu* underwent a metathesis, becoming pronounced today as [ɔj] but spelled *eu*, as in *Seuche* 'sickness, plague' < MHG *siuche*. Continuing the thread from §15.75 concerning MHG *iu* and *ie* (< OHG *iu*, *io*), which were conditioned outcomes of the same inherited diphthong, when the difference in diphthong manifested itself in different words, the difference was preserved into the modern language: thus MHG *siech* 'sick' and *siuche* 'sickness' above are continued as Modern HG *siech* and *Seuche*. But alternations within one and the same word, such as in OHG *biotan* ~ *biutu* above, which were continued well into Middle High German, have disappeared, preserved only in rare poetic phrases like *was da kreucht und fleucht* 'what crawls and flies', where *kreucht* and *fleucht* are obsolete 3rd singulars of the verbs *kriechen* 'crawl, creep' and *fliegen* 'fly'.

In syntax, German is famous (or infamous) for the rule that the conjugated verb be the second constituent in main clauses and come at the end of subordinate clauses. Though these are statistically the most common orders already in Old High German, the real standardization of them did not happen until the modern period.

Yiddish

15.80. During the Roman Empire, Jews had settled in various places in Europe, bringing the Semitic languages Hebrew and Aramaic with them from Palestine; wherever they settled they acquired the local language but continued to use Hebrew as a religious language. By the late Middle Ages, the Jews in Germany were primarily settled in east-central and southern parts of the country, and their German was thus Bavarian or East Middle German, a variety spoken north of Bavaria. Their German contained Hebrew lexical elements mixed in with it; it is this mixture that is known as **Yiddish** ('Jewish' in its original literal meaning, German *Jüdisch*). Historically it is a form of German, not Hebrew; its sentence structure has always been German, as is about three-fourths of its vocabulary. After many of its speakers moved east into Slavic territory, it became influenced by Polish and other Slavic languages. The first documents in Yiddish date to the twelfth century; the language is usually written using the Hebrew alphabet.

Old High German text sample

15.81. The Second Merseburg Charm, from the tenth century. The two Merseburg Charms are the only surviving examples of pre-Christian pagan magic spells in German. The last two lines have numerous analogues in other IE traditions, including Anatolian, Indic, Celtic, and Tocharian; see the notes. The story of a god's horse spraining its foot and being healed by Wotan is apparently depicted also on a golden bracteate (a kind of pendant or amulet) from c. AD 500.

Phol ende Uuōdan uuorun zi holza.
Dū uuart demo Balderes uolon sīn uuoz birenkīt.
Thū biguol en Sinthgunt, Sunna era suister,

thū biguol en Frīia, Uolla era suister,
thū biguol en Uuōdan sō hē uuola conda:
sōse bēnrenkī, sōse bluotrenkī,
sōse lidirenkī:
bēn zi bēna, bluot zi bluoda,
lid zi geliden, sōse gelīmida sin.

Phol and Wodan were riding to the woods,
and the foot of Balder's foal was sprained.
So Sinthgunt, Sunna's sister, conjured it;
and Frija, Volla's sister, conjured it;
and Wodan conjured it, as he well could:
Like bone-sprain, so blood-sprain,
so joint-sprain:
Bone to bone, blood to blood,
joint to joints; so may they be glued.

15.81a. Notes. Phol: an otherwise unknown name, but probably the masculine of *Uolla* below. The names Sinthgunt and Sunna are also found only here. **ende:** 'and', PIE *$^*h_2enti$*, also in Gk. *antí* 'against', Lat. *ante* 'before'. **Uuōdan:** Wotan, the supreme Germanic god (Odin in Scandinavia). The English equivalent, *Woden*, is the source of *Wednes-day*. **uuorun:** 'rode', Mod. HG *fuhren*, from Gmc. **fōrun*, a Class VI strong verb (§15.29), from PIE **per-* 'cross over'; cognate with Eng. *fare*. **zi:** 'to', Mod. HG *zu*. In the original manuscript, *zi* and the other unstressed words (e.g. *dū/thū*, *en*, *sōse*) are often written without a break before (or after, in the case of *en*) a neighboring stressed word, a valuable indication of close connection in pronunciation (cp. Eng. *to-day*). **holza:** 'wood, forest', dat. sing. **dū:** 'then, there, so, and', often little more than a sentence-connector. **uuart:** 'became', early Mod. HG *ward*. **demo:** 'to the', dat. sing. of the definite article, modifying *uolon*. **Balderes:** 'of Balder' (or Baldur), son of Odin. **uolon:** 'foal', dat. sing. The construction is impersonal, literally 'to Balder's foal his foot was sprained'. **sīn:** 'his'. **uuoz:** 'foot', Mod. HG *Fuß*. **birenkit:** 'sprained', past participle, Mod. HG *gerenkt* (with different prefix). Cognate with Eng. *wrench*. **biguol:** 'conjured', preterite 3rd sing. **en:** 'him, it', accus.; Mod. HG *ihn*. Eng. *him* continues the dative case, cognate with OHG *im*. **era:** 'her', Mod. HG *ihre*. **suister:** 'sister', Mod. HG *Schwester*. Eng. *sister* is a borrowing from Norse; the OE form was *sweostor*. The *-t-* is epenthetic, arisen in early Germanic in the *sr*-cluster of the inherited weak stem **su̯esr-*. **Frīia:** 'Freyja', the goddess of love (ON *Frigg*). **Uolla:** perhaps the same as Fulla, a handmaid of the Norse goddess Frigg. **sō:** 'as, so'. **hē:** 'he', not the same form as Mod. HG *er*. **uuola:** 'well'. **conda:** 'could, knew how', Mod. HG *konnte*. **sōse:** 'just as'. **bēnrenkī:** 'bone-sprain'. **bluotrenkī:** 'blood-sprain'. **lidirenkī:** 'joint-sprain' or 'limb-sprain'. Note that in this and the following part of the charm, the body-parts are enumerated going from inside (bone) to outside (joint or limb), via flesh (blood), the direction for driving out the ailment. The same order of body-parts is found in spells and medical texts elsewhere in IE, and in fixed traditional descriptions of the so-called "canonical creature," and is likely inherited. The phrases *bēn zi bēna*, *bluot zi bluoda*, etc. have celebrated parallels in a magical charm in Vedic against open fractures (Atharva Veda 4.15 in the slightly less corrupt Paippalāda version but 4.12 in the more frequently cited Śaunaka version), which includes passages like "Let marrow be put together with marrow, let bone grow over with bone; we put together sinew with sinew, let skin grow with skin" (4.15.2 = 4.12.4). **geliden:** 'joints' or 'limbs'; instead of the usual plural we get a form called a collective, commonly formed in Germanic with the prefix **ga-* (> German *ge-*). The collective was eventually generalized in Mod. HG *Glied* 'joint, limb'. **gelimida sin:** 'they may be glued' or 'they are glued'. The verb is related to Mod. HG *Leim* 'lime, glue', and *sin* is a 3rd pl., either subjunctive (Mod. HG *seien*) or indicative (*sind*).

Old Saxon

15.82. Old Saxon was spoken until about the twelfth century in an area bounded by the Rhine in the west and the Elbe in the east, and from the North Sea down to Kassel and Merseburg in the south. Its most significant literary remains are the *Heliand* ('Savior'), composed about 830, which tells the life of Christ in almost 6,000 lines of alliterative Germanic verse. We also have part of an Old Saxon translation of the Book of Genesis, plus some minor fragments.

15.83. Linguistically, Old Saxon is quite close to Old English, Old Frisian, and Old Low Franconian (the ancestor of Dutch), being set apart from High German by the lack of the High German Consonant Shift (§15.73 above). It differs from the rest of West Germanic in preserving *ƀ* unchanged word-internally, as in *lioƀora* 'better, dearer' in the text sample below (contrast German *lieber*). Additionally, Old Saxon lost *h* in the cluster *hs*, as in the word for 'flax', *flas* (OE *fleax*, OHG *flahs*). Old Saxon does not show the effects of *i*-umlaut as thoroughly as Old English or Frisian, at least not in spelling; for example, the plural of *mûs* 'mouse' is also *mûs* (vs. OE *mȳs*, from **mūsiz*).

15.84. The modern-day descendants of Old Saxon are the varieties of **Low German** (*Niederdeutsch* or *Plattdeutsch*) spoken in northern Germany. They blend into Frisian and Dutch in the west and northwest. Low German reached its zenith as a literary and administrative language during the time of the Hanseatic League, a powerful commercial confederation of cities in northern Germany and along the Baltic coast whose height of power was from the thirteenth to the fifteenth centuries. The center of the Hanseatic League was Lübeck, whose variety of Low German (Eastfalian or Ostfälisch) became widely used as an administrative and literary language, and was for a time more important than Middle High German.

Old Saxon text sample

15.85. Excerpt from the story of Jesus's return to Galilee in the *Heliand* (1121–27 and 1148–50). The biblical stories contained in the *Heliand* are skilfully recast in a Germanic setting. The characters are given social roles proper to aristocratic Germanic society: Jesus, for example, is the "giver of jewels," and he is "chosen" by James and John as Lord in the same way leaders were elected in early Germanic society. Herod is similarly depicted as a "ring-giver" who holds feasts with his "ring-friends," both central Germanic images of a king. The Lord's Prayer is likened to runes or secret knowledge; in teaching it, Jesus calls to mind Woden, who knows the secrets of magical formulations.

Here Jesus is depicted like a Germanic chieftain assembling a retinue of young warriors.

Uuas im an them sinuueldi sâlig barn godes
lange huîle, untthat im thô lioƀora uuarð,
that he is craft mikil cûðien uuolda,
uueroda te uuillion. Thô forlêt he uualdes hlêo,
ênôdies ard endi sôhte im eft erlo gemang,
mâri meginthioda endi manno drôm,
geng im thô bi Iordanes staðe . . .
. . . He began im samnon thô
gumono te iungoron, gôdoro manno,
uuordspâha uueros.

(1121) The blessed son of God was in the wilderness (1122) for a long time, until it then seemed better to him (1123) that he should make known his great strength (1124) for advantage to the people. Then he left the shelter of the forest, (1125) the domicile of the wilderness, and sought a group of earls again, (1126) famous great people and the tumult of men, (1127) (and) he went then to the bank of the (River) Jordan . . . (1148) He began to gather there (1149) men for disciples, good men, (1150) word-wise men.

15.85a. **Notes** (very selective). **uualdes hlêo:** 'shelter of the forest'; *uuald* 'forest' is cognate with German *Wald*, and *hlêo* is cognate with Eng. *lee* ('sheltered side', OE *hlēo*). The desert of Judaea is transformed by the author of the *Heliand* into a more Germanic-like forested region. **gumono, manno, uueros:** three different words for 'man', all of them inherited from PIE (**dhĝhemō(n), *manu-, *u̯iH-ro-*). **uuordspâha:** 'word-wise, eloquent'; word-wise in order to convert people.

Dutch and Frisian

15.86. To the west of Old Saxon was spoken **Old Low Franconian**, the speech of a group of western Franks and closely related to Old Saxon. It is attested, very meagerly, from the ninth to the twelfth centuries in Limburg in the extreme southeast of the modern Netherlands. The particular variety of Old Low Franconian spoken in the cultural centers of Flanders and Brabant is called **Old West Low Franconian** and is the ancestor ultimately of **Dutch**. It is known only from a charming two-sentence scrap preserved in the binding of an eleventh-century Latin manuscript in England: *hebban olla vogala nestags hagunnan hinase hi*[*c e*]*nda thu w*[*at u*]*nbidan* [*w*]*e nu* "All the birds have begun nests except for you and me. What are we waiting for?"

15.87. The medieval descendant of this language was **Middle Dutch**, which is well attested starting in the late twelfth century, principally in Flanders and Brabant. The literature of this time consists of courtly romances and epics, miracle plays, and religious writings. In the seventeenth century the Dutch colonized South Africa; their descendants speak **Afrikaans**, which has diverged from Dutch significantly enough to be considered a separate language. The name of the dialect that developed around Flanders, namely **Flemish**, refers to the Dutch spoken in Belgium. Dutch, Afrikaans, and Flemish are often together called *Netherlandic*.

15.88. In northern coastal areas of the Netherlands and Germany, as well as on the North Sea islands off the coast, is spoken **Frisian**. Frisian is said to be the closest living relative of English (recall §15.55). Its first records, in Old Frisian, date only to the thirteenth century, although some scattered runic remains from the sixth through the ninth centuries have been claimed (doubtfully, at least in part) to be in an earlier form of the language.

North Germanic: Old Norse and Scandinavian

15.89. North Germanic is represented by a single ancient language, **Old Norse**, and its descendants the modern Scandinavian languages. It is probable that Runic, or Runic Norse (see §§15.36ff.), was its immediate ancestor. The homeland of the North Germanic speakers was centered in an area along the western Scandinavian coasts, especially Norway and southwest Sweden but also northern Denmark. The northern Germanic pirates known as Vikings mostly spoke varieties of Old Norse; for reasons that are still unclear, in the late eighth century these Norsemen began a series of raids that soon grew into a scourge as they ravaged and terrified any part of Europe that was reachable by boat. They had developed the best nautical technology then known and perfected the technique of the lightning raid; coastal populations were essentially defenseless against them. Raiding per se is an old Indo-European tradition; there is evidence suggesting that it was a rite of passage for young unmarried warriors to enter into a *Männerbund*, a 'band of men' or fraternity of sorts, and undertake marauding expeditions (§2.8). From the eighth through the tenth centuries and beyond, Viking bands ventured as far afield as Paris, Pisa, Newfoundland, Jerusalem, and even Baghdad. But the Norsemen were often more interested in trading than raiding, notably those that went east and settled in what is now Russia, founding and ruling Kievan Rus', the medieval East Slavic state.

For a time, Byzantine emperors employed Scandinavian mercenaries as part of their royal bodyguard, the famous axe-wielding Varangian Guard (the Varangians, ON *Væringjar*, were the Norsemen associated with the Rus'). The raids, explorations, and mercenary services of the Norsemen made Old Norse for a time the European language with the greatest geographical spread.

The Vikings that laid siege to Paris withdrew upon being granted a duchy in northern France, now called Normandy (from *Norman*, a variant of *Norseman*) in 911. The Norsemen that settled there quickly took on French ways and customs, but the restless adventurousness in their blood remained: their descendants were the Normans who seized the throne of England in 1066.

15.90. In England, the Norsemen settled along large stretches of the north and central coast, an area known as the Danelaw. The names of the cities and towns of this area are mostly of Norse origin and contain such suffixes as *-by* ('town, village', from ON *býr*, whence also Eng. *by-law* 'local or internal ordinance') and *-thorpe* ('village', ON *þorp*). Norsemen and Anglo-Saxons intermarried in this area; it is sociolinguistically significant that the word *husband* is Norse, while *wife* is Anglo-Saxon – a fact attesting to the widespread taking of Anglo-Saxon wives by

Norse settlers. Hundreds of Norse words entered English, slowly filtering through to southern England during the Middle English period, and including such basic vocabulary as *get, sister, take, both, call*, and *they*. The influence of Norse on English core vocabulary was actually greater than that of Norman French.

Old Norse literature

15.91. The Runic language of the earliest runic inscriptions, as discussed above, may be ancestral to Old Norse (see §15.37). The first inscriptions that are unambiguously Norse begin to appear around the seventh century; not much later clear dialectal differences within Norse can be detected, allowing us to distinguish among Old Icelandic, Old Norwegian, and Old Swedish.

Old Norse literature occupies a special place in the hearts of Germanic philologists because it preserves native pre-Christian Germanic mythology and folklore far better than any other old Germanic literature. Technically, most Old Norse literature is written in the dialect spoken in Iceland and called **Old Icelandic**; often the term "Old Norse" refers really to this dialect. Written literature in it dates from the mid-twelfth century, and consists of historical accounts of the travels and raids of the Norsemen, as well as mythological poetry and prose, some of it composed orally several centuries earlier. The most important of the poetry is the poetic (or Elder) Edda, a collection of mythological poems that probably represent our earliest Old Norse literature. The historian and chieftain Snorri Sturluson (1179–1241) is the source of the equally famous Prose Edda, containing prose versions of many other mythological stories compiled as part of an effort to preserve these tales for posterity. Old Norse prose is also represented famously by the sagas (*saga* 'tale'), written between the twelfth and fifteenth centuries; these represent one of the highpoints of medieval European vernacular literature. Finally, mention may be made of the poetry of the Skalds (*skáld* 'poet'), court poets in Norway who fashioned several new poetic genres and styles. Skaldic poetry is known especially for its dense and elaborate use of kennings or telescoped metaphors, which can make it quite challenging to read (e.g. *lyngfisk* 'heather fish' = 'snake', crawling in heather like a fish in the sea, or *Haka bláland* 'blue land of Haki' = 'sea' [Haki is the name of a sea king]). Kennings are in fact a characteristic feature of traditional Germanic poetry (as e.g. OE *gūþwudu* 'battle-wood' = 'shield'), but nowhere is the art of the kenning so highly developed as in skaldic poetry.

Developments of Old Norse

15.92. Old Norse looks somewhat different from the other Germanic languages of comparable age; impressionistically, the words seem shorter and the vowel inventory greater. This is due to several phonological changes that affected the language between the time of the early runes and the eighth or ninth century. As a side note, the historical phonological sketch to follow characterizes the western variety of Old Norse, chiefly Old Icelandic; but since most of the Scandinavian settlers in England spoke Old East Norse, Norse loans into English do not have all the same features. For example, not all of the assimilations of consonant clusters containing *n* (§15.99) took place in Old East Norse: thus Germanic **bankiz* 'long low seat' and **sprintan* 'jump up, sprint' became *bekkr* and *spretta* in Old Icelandic but **bænkr* and **sprinta* in Old East Norse, the sources of Eng. *bank* and *sprint.*

Vowels

15.93. Syncope. The vowels of many final syllables were syncopated (deleted), as in ON *gestr* 'guest' from **gestir* (Runic *gastiz*), and the nominative singular ending *-az*, which already in later Runic inscriptions appears as just *-z*. Before this syncope had run its course, however, the language underwent a series of vowel mutations or umlauts, described next.

15.94. *u*-Umlaut. Certain vowels were rounded preceding a syllable with a *u* in it, a change called *u*-umlaut or *u*-mutation. An *a* was rounded to a sound written *ǫ*; *e* was rounded to *ø* (pronounced like German *ö*); and long *á* was changed to long *ǫ́*. (Acute accents indicate length in standard Old Norse orthography.) So for example North Germanic **saku* became Old Norse *sǫk* 'charge, offense' (cp. OE *sacu*, Mod. Eng. *sake*); similarly, the verb *róa* 'to row' has a reduplicated 3rd pl. preterite *røru* 'they rowed' from **rerun.*

15.95. *w*-Umlaut. Closely allied with *u*-umlaut was *w*-umlaut, caused by a following *w* (later becoming *v*). In addition to the above effects, this also changed *i* to *y* (pronounced like German *ü*), as in the verb *slyngva* 'to fling, sling'.

15.96. *i*-Umlaut. Norse had *i*-umlaut just like its West Germanic cousins, whereby an *i* or *j* (the glide *i̯*) fronted a vowel in a preceding syllable. The effects of this can already be seen in later Runic. The umlauting of the back vowels *a*, *o*, and *u* and their long counterparts proceeded as in West Germanic (§15.51), with the outcomes spelled *e ø y* for the short vowels and *æ œ ý* for the long ones. Additionally, the diphthongs **au* and **eu* (which developed into *jú*) were umlauted to *ey* and *ý*, and the vowel *ǫ*, a product of *u*-umlaut, was fronted to *ø* like *o*. Examples include *framr* 'forward' ~ *fremri* 'more forward'; *áss* 'god' (nomin. sing.) ~ *æsir* 'gods' (nomin. pl.); *koma* 'to come' ~ *kømr* 'comes' (**komiz*); *fullr* 'full' ~ *fylla* 'to fill' (**fulljan*); *fljúga* 'to fly' ~ *flýgr* 'flies' (**fleugiþ*).

15.97. Breaking of *e*. Finally, we may mention the "breaking" of *e*, which was analogous but not identical to the breaking seen in Old English: *e* became *ea*, then *ja*, in a syllable followed by *a*, as in *jafn* 'even' from **ebna-* (cp. OE *efen*); and it became *eo* (later *jo* and even later *jǫ*) before a syllable containing a *u* (e.g. *jǫtunn* 'giant' < **etunaz*).

Consonants

15.98. For the consonants, a few characteristic changes may be mentioned. The most problematic for issues of Germanic subgrouping has been the "hardening" of the geminated glides **ww* and **jj* (see above, §15.44). The old *z* of Runic became *r* as in West Germanic, e.g. *vǫ́ro* 'they were' < **wāzun*. Word-initial *j* disappeared, as in *ár* 'year' (cp. German *Jahr*) and *ungr* 'young' (cp. German *jung*), which happened also to *w* word-initially before rounded vowels and resonants, as in *orð* 'word', *urðu* 'they became' (cp. German *wurden*), and *líta* 'face' (cp. OE *wlītan* 'face'). Where *w* was not lost, it became *v*, as in ON *hvat* 'what', *vatn* 'water'.

15.99. Assimilation of consonant clusters. A major source of the unusual look of Old Norse vis-à-vis the other old Germanic languages is the great number of consonant clusters that underwent assimilation. The rules are too complex to enter into here; some examples will suffice: *sótti* 'sought' (cp. OE *sōhte*); *finna* 'to find' (cp. OE *findan*); *batt* 'bound' (cp. OE *band*); *villr* 'wild' (cp. OE *wild*); *Þórr* 'Thor' (literally 'thunder' < **Þunraz*, cp. OE *Þunor*); and *drekka* 'to drink' (cp. OE *drincan*).

Morphology

15.100. Old Norse nouns and verbs show the same behavior and inflectional categories as in contemporary relatives like Old English and Old High German. Due to the massive series of umlauts, the vowel alternations in stems can be complex, even more so than in Old English (see §15.64): for example, the nominative, dative, and genitive singular of the word for 'father' was *faðir*, *feðr*, *fǫður*. Verbs do have one significant inflectional difference from the rest of Germanic in that the 3rd singular ending in the present tense was **-z*, displacing the inherited ending **-þ*. This spread from the 2nd singular. Hence *berr* (< **ber-iz*) means both 'you carry' and '(s)he carries'.

Enclitic elements

15.101. Characteristic of Old Norse is a high degree of enclisis of pronouns and adverbs that in the other Germanic languages remained separate words. The Norse definite article is ordinarily suffixed to the word it modifies: masc. *-(i)nn* (e.g. *úlfr-inn* 'the wolf'), fem. *-(i)n* (e.g. *kona-n* 'the woman'), neut. *-(i)t* (e.g. *auga-t* 'the eye'). Old Norse created a class of reflexive or middle verbs by suffixing *-mk* (1st person) and *-sk* (2nd and 3rd persons), reduced forms of the reflexive pronouns *mik* and *sik*, as in *kalla-sk* 'calls himself/herself, is called' and *kǫllu-mk* 'I am called'.

15.102. Of some historical interest are the numerous Norse negators. Originally they were not negators at all, but were used to emphasize negative words; later they acquired negative meaning of their own. A negative suffix *-gi* is found in *engi* 'no, none' (*ein* 'one' + *-gi*), *ekki* 'nothing' (neut. *eitt* of *ein* + *-gi*), *eigi* 'not' (*ei* 'ever' + *-gi*), and *hvergi* 'nowhere'. The suffix *-gi* comes ultimately from the PIE indefinite suffix **k^{w}id* (indefinites have a certain affinity for being combined with negatives and can, over time, become interpreted as negatives themselves; recall also the history of Gk. *ou* 'not' in §7.25). Of particular interest are the enclitic negative suffixes *-a* and *-at* found in early verse and attached to verbs, sometimes together with enclitic suffixed subject particles, e.g. *es-a* 'is not', *vas-k-a* 'I was not' (*-k*, enclitic form of *ek* 'I'), *hef-k-at-ek* 'I have not' (with doubled enclitic pronoun). Etymologically these are from unstressed *ein* and *eit* 'one'. The acquisition of negative meaning by words that were not negative to begin with is paralleled in numerous other languages, as with French *pas* (recall again §7.25).

The modern Scandinavian languages

15.103. Beginning about the ninth century the Runic inscriptions in Scandinavia begin to show regional differences, especially a general split into a West Nordic and an East Nordic variety, corresponding to the modern groups of West Scandinavian and East Scandinavian. Overall, the western dialects are more conservative than the eastern ones.

15.104. In the ninth century, explorers from the western Norwegian coast settled Iceland; their language developed into what is now known as **Icelandic**. The language of Iceland stayed remarkably conservative; speakers of modern Icelandic can read the Old Norse sagas and other literature without great difficulty. Modern Icelandic still retains three genders, four cases in the noun, and essentially the same pronominal and verbal system as in Old Icelandic. In pronunciation, however, there have been extensive changes. Close to Icelandic is **Faroese**, the language of the Faroe Islands between Iceland and the Shetland Islands, settled also by western Norwegians around the same time as Iceland. A handful of Faroese runic inscriptions are known from c. 1000–1500, as well as a few documents from the end of the thirteenth century. The Danes, who had become rulers of the Faroe Islands in 1380, banned the language from written use in 1536. A robust oral literature continued, however, especially in the form of satirical lays and the epic ballads called *kvæði*. Some of these were written down starting in the 1770s, but not until 1854 was a standard orthography devised for the language. The orthography is strongly traditionalist, oriented toward Old Icelandic spelling rather than the phonetics of spoken Faroese.

Closely related to Faroese was **Norn**, spoken on the Shetland and Orkney Islands until the eighteenth century. Little written evidence of the language survives, but a large number of words were borrowed into the Scots that supplanted it.

15.105. The North Germanic dialect of Norway developed into **Norwegian**, first recognizable as such (in the form of Old Norwegian) in the twelfth century. Norwegian is notable for having developed contrasting tonal contours in words of more than one syllable, called accent 1 (falling-rising; developed on words that were originally monosyllables like *kommer* 'comes' < ON *kømr*) and accent 2 (rising-falling-rising; developed on words that were originally polysyllabic, as in *gater* 'streets' < ON *gǫtur*).

15.106. To East Scandinavian belongs first of all **Danish**, arguably the least conservative Scandinavian language, which can be inscriptionally distinguished by 1000 or so (Old Danish), with the first Danish manuscripts dating to the thirteenth century. During the Middle Ages, it merged the Old Norse masculine and feminine genders into a single (common) gender, lost all the cases besides the nominative and genitive, and came under considerable influence from the neighboring Low German dialects to the south, from which it has made extensive morphological borrowings. Most Danish dialects have an unusual phonetic feature called *stød*, which is similar to a glottal stop near final consonants in monosyllables.

15.107. Around the same time as Old Danish came into existence we can also distinguish Old **Swedish**. Swedish, like Danish, lost most of the cases in the noun, merged the masculine and feminine into a single common gender, and lost the verbal personal endings. But the highly conservative **Elfdalian** in the north retains three genders and at least three cases in the noun, plus personal endings; it is sometimes considered a separate language, and has its own orthographic system. (Its syntax is also unusual for a Germanic language in several respects and has been the object of recent study.) Swedish developed accentual contrasts like those of Norwegian.

The island of Gotland off eastern Sweden, mentioned in §15.40, is home to **Gutnish.** The status of Gutnish is unclear; many consider it to be a separate East Scandinavian language primarily because of divergences in phonology and vocabulary that are already apparent in its first attestations in the mid-fourteenth century. Also having attracted attention are some correspondences with Gothic, such as the fact that the *lamb* word means 'sheep' rather than 'lamb' only in these two languages. These similarities, certain retained archaisms in the phonology of Gutnish, and the likely etymological connection of *Gotland* with *Goth* (§15.40), have led some to argue that Gutnish is closer to Gothic than to anything else; but this is far from certain. It also has the accentual contrasts of Norwegian.

Old Norse text sample

15.108. The opening of the *Þrymskvíða* or *The Lay of Thrym*, a famous tale in the Poetic Edda (given here in the linguistic form of its probable tenth-century origin rather than that of the manuscript from 1270).

1 Vreiðr vas þá Ving-Þórr   es vaknaði
ok síns hamars   of saknaði;
skegg nam at hrista,   skǫr nam at dýja,
réð Jarðar burr   um at þreifask.

2 Ok hann þat orða   alls fyrst of kvað:
'Heyrðu nú, Loki,   hvat nú mælik,
es engi veit   jarðar hvergi
né upphimins: Áss es stolinn hamri!'

1 Enraged was Ving-Thor, when he woke up
and missed his hammer;
he began to shake his beard, he began to shake his hair,
the son of Earth groped about himself.

2 And he said first of all these words:
"Hear now, Loki, what I now say,
which no one knows anywhere on earth
nor in heaven above: the god has had his hammer stolen!"

15.108a. Notes. 1. vreiðr: 'enraged', cp. Eng. *wrath*. The manuscript has just *reiðr*, showing the loss of *v-* before liquids; but when this poem was composed, the *v-* must have still been there because the word has to alliterate with *Ving-*. **Ving-Þórr:** 'Swinging Thor', referring to Thor's attribute of swinging his hammer. **vaknaði:** 'woke up, awakened', intransitive. ON has a class of verbs in *-na-* that have intransitive inchoative meaning ('become X'); exactly how they connect with other nasal presents in Germanic and IE is not fully clear. **ok:** 'and', cp. German *auch* 'also'. **hamars:** 'hammer', genitive object of the verb *sakna* 'to miss'. **nam:** lit. 'took', here more weakly 'did'; cognate with German *nahm* and used in Eddic poetry as an auxiliary for metrical convenience. **at:** 'to' with infinitives. **réð:** lit. 'counseled', also 'set about (to . . .)' or just 'did', so here 'set about to grope' or just 'did grope'. The infinitive is *ráða*, cognate with German *raten* 'counsel, advise'. **Jarðar:** 'Earth', mother of Thor; nomin. sing. *jǫrð*. **þreifask:** 'to grope'; *-a* is the infinitive ending, cognate with German *-en* (OHG *-an*), and *-sk* is a reflexive suffix; §15.101.

2. orða: 'words', genit. pl. with *þat* (lit. 'that of words'); see §15.98. **kvað:** 'spoke', cognate with Eng. *quoth*. **heyrðu:** 'Hear you', a combination of *heyr* 'hear' and the 2nd sing. pronoun *þú*. **Loki:** Loki, a god and trickster figure. **mælik:** 'I say', combination of *mæli* and suffixed clitic pronoun *-k* (cp. Runic *-ka*, the suffixed form of *ek*). **engi:** 'no one', originally 'anyone', but over time it achieved negative force by being always used with a negative, like French *personne* 'no one', lit. 'person'. **veit:** 'knows', German *weiss*, Goth. *wait*. **hvergi:** 'anywhere, nowhere', composed of *hver* '(some)where' and the negative particle *-gi*; see §15.102 above. **upphimins:** 'up-heaven, the sky above'. The word is part of a traditional formula meaning 'earth and up-heaven' that also appears in OE and OHG. **Áss:** 'god', nomin. sing., stem *ás-*; pl. *Æsir*. The word comes from PIE *$*h_2ens$-*, having derivatives pertaining to royalty and deities, such as Hitt. *ḫaššuš* 'king' and Ved. *ásu-ra-* 'lord'. The last sentence literally means 'The god is robbed as to (his) hammer'.

For Further Reading

The debate about the internal subgrouping of the Germanic branch is thoughtfully treated in Nielsen 1989 and 2000. For beginners coming at Germanic from the English point of view, see especially Robinson 1992. A good overall history of Germanic, though dated in places, is Prokosch 1939; more recently, see the linguistic and cultural overview in Green 1998. Bammesberger 1990 is a very useful overview of Germanic nominal morphology, with many comparative lists; similar but not as good is Bammesberger 1986, on the verb. An excellent exhaustive comparative listing of the Germanic strong verbs is Seebold 1970.

The standard edition of the older Runic inscriptions known by the mid-1960s is Krause and Jankuhn 1966 (see also Krause 1971 for grammar); a bit more recent, and in English, is Antonsen 1975, although some of his interpretations must be treated with caution. Antonsen's book includes a brief grammar of Runic. The complete Gothic Bible, with glossary, is in Streitberg 2000; of several good available comparative grammars of Gothic, Krause 1968 and Braune 2004 may be mentioned. The standard grammar of Old High German is Braune 1987, with an accompanying reader (Braune 1994). For Old English, consult the classic grammar of Alistair Campbell (Campbell 1959); and for Old Saxon, see Holthausen 1921. The standard introduction to Old Norse in English, with a wide selection of texts and glossary, is Gordon 1962, also with a (rather bare) grammatical sketch. In German, see also the grammar of Noreen 1923.

Many of the standard etymological dictionaries are in German. For Old English, Holthausen 1934 lists cognates in and outside Germanic but few reconstructions; for the modern language, see Watkins 2000 (discussed in chapter 2). A Gothic etymological dictionary is Lehmann 1986, although the IE reconstructions deviate somewhat from standard notation. An up-to-date and exhaustively researched Old High German dictionary, with full etymological information and contributions by several major Indo-Europeanists, is underway and has progressed through the letter E: *Althochdeutsches Wörterbuch* (Berlin: Vandenhoeck und Ruprecht, 1952–). Quite useful for German and Germanic etymology is Kluge 2002. Old Norse etymology is well served by de Vries 1962.

For Review

Know the meanings or significance of the following:

Northwest Germanic	weak verb	Wulfila	High German Consonant Shift
Grimm's Law	Verner's variant	Verschärfung	*Heliand*
Verner's Law	dental preterite	*i*-umlaut	Danelaw
Rasmus Rask	preterite-present	West Saxon	Eddas
strong adjective	"V2"	*Beowulf*	*u*-umlaut
weak adjective	rune	breaking	
strong verb	futhark	Great English Vowel Shift	
	Crimean Gothic		

Exercises

1 Give the Germanic outcomes for the following PIE sounds. Some may have more than one answer.

a	**b*	**c**	**o*	**e**	**p*	**g**	**n̥*	**i**	**dh*	**k**	**k̂*	**m**	**s*	**o**	**gh*
b	**ō*	**d**	**t*	**f**	**r̥*	**h**	**kʷ*	**j**	**u̯*	**l**	**ā*	**n**	**ei*	**p**	**gʷh*

2 Give the PIE sound from which the boldfaced sounds in the English words below are likely to have descended:

a	*lee**ch***	**c**	*see**p***	**e**	*s**t**are*	**g**	***h**ollow*
b	***qu**oth*	**d**	*ha**v**e*	**f**	*roo**t***	**h**	***b**loom*

3 Below are some slightly simplified stems in pre-Germanic and their outcomes in Modern English. (By "pre-Germanic" is meant here essentially PIE after laryngeal loss and compensatory lengthening, and the centum merger of velars.) Using §§15.6–9 and 15.18, apply the sound changes of Grimm's Law, Verner's Law, and the accent shift to each of the pre-Germanic forms. Do this step by step as in the following example:

Example: pre-Germanic **upélo-*, Modern English *evil*

answer:	**upélo-*	→	**ufélo-*	by Grimm I
	**ufélo-*	→	**uƀélo-*	by Verner
	**ubélo-*	→	**úƀelo-*	by accent shift

Not all the forms undergo change. Once a pre-Germanic sound has shifted according to one part of Grimm's Law, it will not be affected by any other part of Grimm's Law that happened earlier. A diphthong counts as a single vowel (or syllable) for the purposes of this problem.

In group **(a)**, the English gloss is at the same time the English descendant form.

	pre-Germanic	English	pre-Germanic	English
a	**ábelo-*	*apple*	**dhṓ-*	*do*
	**átalo-*	*Ethel(-red)*	**ghḗ-*	*go*
	**tréi-*	*three*	**gnṓ-*	*know*
	**triti̯ó-*	*third*	**gnéu̯o-*	*knee*
	**réise-*	*rise*	**léuse-*	*lose*
	**roisi̯é-*	*rear*	**dhrénge-*	*drink*
	**sḗdi̯o-*	*seat*	**dhrongi̯é-*	*drench*
	**sodi̯é-*	*set*	**sténge-*	*stink*
	**loiti̯é-*	*lead*	**stóngi̯o-*	*stench*
b	**péku-*	payment	**séute-*	boil
	**bhére-*	carry	**sutonó-*	boiled, soaked
	**bhr̥ronó-*	(having been) carried	**lusonó-*	lost
	**upér*	above	**altó-*	aged
	**kasó-*	rabbit		

4 For each of the forms in **3b** above, try to figure out what the Modern English descendant is.

5 Given the changes that affected vowels in the history of Germanic and Old English as detailed in §§15.14–17 and 15.60, determine which ablaut grade in IE is continued by the Old English words given below. The Modern English descendant is given when different from Old English, but do not use it to answer this question. Some of the PIE forms have been slightly simplified. Aside from the sound changes given in the text, you will need to know the following: Gmc. **u* > OE *o* except before *r* or *m*; and, for the purposes of this exercise, Gmc. **e* > OE *i*. Remember too that PIE **ē* > West Germanic **ā*.

Example: Given the root **sed-* 'sit' and OE *sadol* 'saddle', the *a* in OE must come from PIE **o*, hence *sadol* continues a PIE *o*-grade (**sod-*).

- **a** **leg-* 'to collect, gather; say': OE *lǣce* 'physician' (< *'one who speaks magic words') (early Mod. Eng. *leech*)
- **b** **lendh-* 'land': OE *land*
- **c** **u̯es-* 'to put on clothes': OE *werian* (Mod. Eng. *wear*)
- **d** **dhreibh-* 'to drive, push': OE *drift*
- **e** **reĝ-* 'to direct': OE *riht* 'right' (Mod. Eng. *right*)
- **f** **reĝ-* 'to direct': OE *gerecenian* 'to arrange in order, account' (Mod. Eng. *reckon*) (Hint: in pre-OE the word would have been **gerecinian*)

g **dhers-* 'to dare': OE 3rd sing. *durst*
h **reudh-* 'to clear land': OE *rodd* 'stick' (Mod. Eng. *rod*)
i **nem-* 'to take': OE *numen* 'seized' (Mod. Eng. *numb*)

6 Provide a historical explanation for the boldfaced consonant alternations seen in the Modern English pairs *free**z**e* ~ *fro**r**e* (archaic, 'cold, frozen') and *see**th**e* ~ *so**dd**en*.

7 The pre-Old English forms **stankja* and **drankjan* became Modern English *stench* and *drench*. Determine from this what chronological order the three sound changes of umlaut, loss of *j*, and palatalization happened in with respect to each other. More than one order is possible.

8 The form **drankjan* above literally meant 'to make drink'. What is its history, in Indo-European terms?

9 Account for the loss of the *n* in the OE 3rd pl. ending *-aþ* (§15.64), assuming the immediately preceding stage was **-āþ*.

10 Provide an explanation based in Indo-European morphology and Germanic phonology for why the preterite presents, uniquely among Germanic verbs in the indicative mood, lack an inflectional ending in the 3rd person singular.

11 Based on the Germanic word for 'daughter', **duhter-*, did Grimm's Law precede the loss of laryngeals, or vice versa? Explain your answer.

12 In the Old Norse text sample (§15.108) and notes, the forms *jarðar* and *jǫrð* were encountered. How is the difference in vocalism to be explained?

PIE Vocabulary VII: Position and Motion

*h_1*es-* 'be': Hitt. *ēšzi* 'is', Ved. *ásti* 'is', Lat. *est* 'is', Eng. IS
**sed-* 'SIT': Ved. *ásadat* 'sat', Gk. *hézomai* 'I sit', Lat. *sedeō* 'I sit', OCS *sěděti* 'to sit'
**legh-* 'LIE': Gk. *lékhetai* 'lies', OCS *ležati* 'to lie'
**k̂ei-* 'lie': Luv. *ziyari* 'lies', Ved. *śáye* 'lies', Gk. *keĩtai* 'lies'
**steh*$_2$- 'STAND': Ved. *tíṣṭhati* 'stands', Gk. (Doric) *hístāmi* 'I stand', Lat. *stāre* 'to stand'
*h_1*ei-* 'go': Hitt. *īt* 'go!', Ved. *éti* 'goes', Gk. *eĩmi* 'I (will) go', Lat. *eō* 'I go'
**g*^{w}*em-* 'COME, go': Gk. *baínō* 'I come', Lat. *ueniō* 'I come'
**sek*^{w}- 'follow': Ved. *sácate* 'follows', Gk. *hépetai* 'follows', Lat. *sequitur* 'follows'
**u̯eĝh-* 'convey': Hieroglyphic Luv. *wa-zi/a-* 'drive', Ved. *váhati* 'drives', Lat. *uehō* 'I convey', OCS *vezǫ* 'I drive'
**bher-* 'BEAR': Ved. *bhárati* 'carries', Gk. *phérō* 'I carry', Lat. *ferō* 'I carry', OCS *berǫ* 'I take'
*h_2*eĝ-* 'drive, draw': Ved. *ájati* 'drives', Gk. *ágō* 'I lead', Lat. *agō* 'I drive, do', Arm. *acem* 'I lead', Toch. AB *āk-* 'go, lead'

16 Armenian

Introduction

16.1. Little is known about the origin of the Armenians. The region in northeast Turkey that they have occupied throughout their known history is called Ḫayaša in Anatolian cuneiform texts from the mid-second millennium BC, a name that has been plausibly compared with *Hay*, the Armenian word for '(an) Armenian'. But from the available evidence it does not appear that the Armenians or their ancestors had settled this region by that early date. The Greek historian Herodotus and other ancient sources agree that they were newcomers into Anatolia; Herodotus identifies them with the Phrygians. While this identification is probably not correct per se, it is likely that they and the Phrygians belonged to the same migratory waves of Balkan immigrants that started coming into Anatolia in the late second millennium BC. The handful of Anatolian loanwords in Armenian, such as *xalam* 'skull' (cp. Hitt. *ḫalanta-* 'head'), were probably picked up during the migration eastward through Anatolia.

16.2. The region in which they settled, around Lake Van, was the home of the powerful state of Urartu in the early first millennium BC. (Its name survives, via Hebrew, as the name of Mount *Ararat*.) The Urartians were a non-Indo-European people related to the Hurrians (see §10.21); both Hurrian and Urartian furnished another set of loanwords into Armenian, such as *xnjor* 'apple' (Hurrian *ḫinzuri*). The Urartian kingdom fell to Assyria in the eighth century BC, although its culture still flourished until the Armenians took over the area in the seventh century BC. But Armenian hegemony did not last long; the region, together with all the other former Assyrian principates, were soon swallowed up by the Medes, an Iranian people to the east. Armenia became one of the vassal states of the large Iranian confederacy that formed the basis for the Persian Empire of the Achaemenids (see §11.28). It is during the Achaemenid dynasty that Armenia finally enters history as a Persian province called *Arminiya-* in the Bisotun inscription of Darius the Great.

16.3. The cultural and political domination of Armenia by Iranian civilizations continued into Middle Iranian times. The linguistic impact of this was enormous. There was a prodigious infusion of Iranian loanwords, especially from Parthian, the language of the Arsacid dynasty (247 BC–AD 224; §11.40), as well as a sizeable number from Aramaic, an important administrative language both in the Persian Empire and in Middle Iranian times. The advent of Hellenism brought many Greek words into Armenian too, but it is really the Iranian loans that typify the lexical makeup of the classical language. They are considerably more numerous than the Norman French loanwords in English, and misled two or three generations of Indo-Europeanists into thinking that Armenian was an Iranian language.

16.4. Not until 1877 was it proved that Armenian belonged to its own branch of Indo-European. The proof was furnished by a young scholar named Heinrich Hübschmann, then near the beginning of his career. His reasoning bears retelling, for it is an instructive example of good common sense. First, he pointed out that Armenian often possessed two words or morphemes for a particular concept, such as *jeṙn*, the ordinary word for 'hand', alongside *dast*, which is borrowed from Persian and appears in a number of compounds. The Iranian words were easy to recognize, but once they were weeded out the residue of words that was left had systematically different outcomes of the PIE sounds from the Iranian outcomes. These words were then recognized by Hübschmann as the native lexical core of the language. Hübschmann further showed that the Armenian inflectional endings were wholly different from those of Iranian, and since inflectional morphology is rarely borrowed, these endings must also have been inherited. As with many pioneers, Hübschmann's ideas were met at first with criticism, some of it positively outrageous in his case; but in the end he won the day.

In spite of the fundamental advances made in Armenian historical linguistics by Hübschmann and later scholars like Antoine Meillet, Armenian is still difficult for IE studies. This is primarily due to the small number of native forms left in the language by the time of its earliest attestation: no more than about 450 words are inherited. The small stock of native words has left precious few examples of many Armenian sound changes, some of which are among the most bizarre in the whole IE family (see below).

16.5. The relationship of Armenian to the other branches of IE has been much discussed. At times it has been thought to form a group with Greek, Indo-Iranian, and Phrygian (recall §10.4). Another view that has been gaining prominence regards it as part of a "Balkan Indo-European" subgroup together with Greek, Albanian, and Phrygian. The similarities are mostly in the realm of shared morphological and lexical innovations, such as the 1st sing. middle ending **-mai* and a negator descended from the phrase **(ne) $h_2$oi̯u k^wid* 'not ever at all' (discussed for Greek in §7.25), but there are also phonological similarities, such as the vocalization of word-initial laryngeals. That the branches were in contact early on seems indisputable, but it is not certain that these similarities warrant setting up a Proto-Balkan-Indo-European language ancestral to them in the same way that, for instance, Proto-Indo-Iranian was ancestral to Indic and Iranian. Given the otherwise very divergent developments of these branches, if there was a Proto-Balkan-Indo-European, it probably did not undergo much common development before disintegrating. But the issue is by no means setttled.

16.6. The writing down of Armenian was a product of Christianization. Armenia was the first country to adopt Christianity as the state religion, around the year 300, replacing the Zoroastrianism that had been taken over from the Iranians. In the early fifth century, according to tradition, a cleric and scholar named Mesrob Maštocʻ (or Mesrop Mashtots, 360?–440) devised an alphabet for writing Christian works in Armenian. The alphabet is largely based on Greek, and contains 36 letters (two additional ones were added in the twelfth century). It is excellently designed, as every sound in the language is represented by a single letter and vice versa, with only a very few exceptions. Mesrob used the alphabet to record the earliest translations into Armenian from Greek and Syriac; the Armenian translation of the Bible, which was partly due to Mesrob himself, was completed in the first half of the fifth century.

16.7. The fifth century is regarded as the golden age of Armenian literature and of the literary language called **Classical Armenian** or Grabar, which remained the standard into the nineteenth century. The best Classical Armenian is held to be that of the historian Eznik, whose *Against the Sects* (*Etc ałandoc'*), written shortly before 450, is a valuable source of information on pre-Christian Armenian religion. Also from around this time are various histories, especially those of Ełišē, P'awstos, Łazar of P'arpi, an anonymous historian known as Agat'angełos (Agathangelos), and Koriwn, who wrote a biography of Mesrob. Also very prominent is Movsēs Xorenac'i (Moses of Choren), who is important for Indo-European studies in preserving some native folklore and poetry. Although Movsēs is traditionally dated to the fifth century as well, Western scholars now think he wrote considerably later, around the ninth century. Much of early Classical Armenian literature was translated from Greek or Syriac, and its often excessive faithfulness to the syntax of those originals even led to violation of the grammatical rules of Armenian itself. Our knowledge of Classical Armenian syntax is therefore not always on a solid footing. Aside from the few tantalizing bits preserved in Movsēs, we unfortunately possess essentially no pre-Christian Armenian literature.

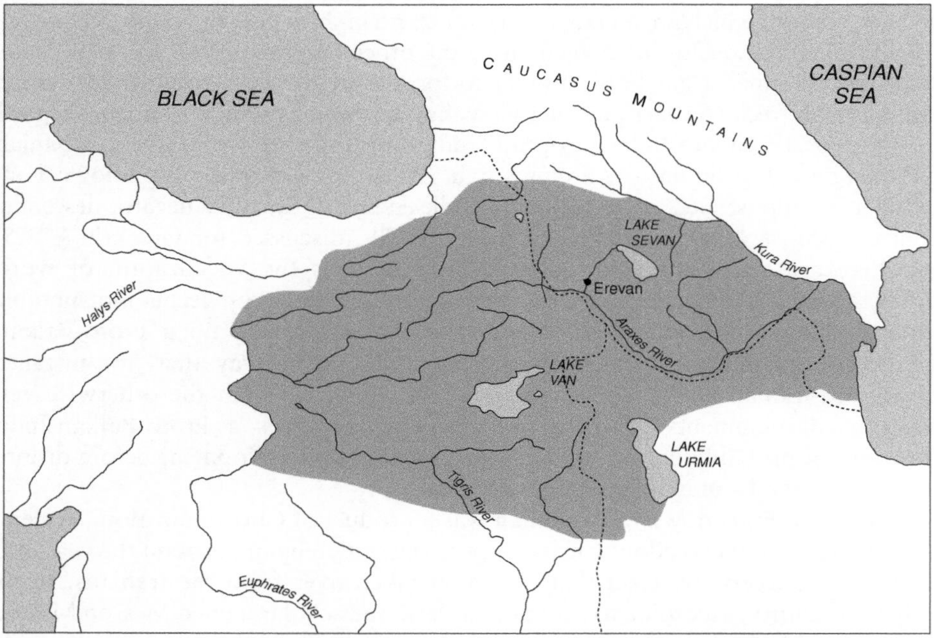

Map 16.1 Greater Armenia during the early Christian era

16.8. No manuscripts from the early centuries of Armenian literacy survive, although there are inscriptions beginning already in the fifth century. The oldest known manuscript is the so-called Moscow Gospel, which was copied in 887, but most manuscripts are from a good deal later. (Eznik, for example, is only preserved in one manuscript that dates to 1280, over 800 years after he wrote.) As is always true in such cases, many modernizations and interpolations of later material have crept in.

16.9. Classical Armenian is quite homogeneous across different authors from different areas, and may have been designed as a kind of regional standard. Supporting this hypothesis are indications of dialect mixture: the outcomes of several PIE sounds are not consistent, such as **p* and **s* (see §§16.13 and 23 below). The language had three parallel series of stops and affricates: a plain voiceless series *p t k c č* (the *c* represents the *ts*-sound of *bets*, and *č* is the *ch*-sound of *cheese*); a parallel voiced series *b d g j ǰ*; and a voiceless aspirated series transliterated as *pʿ tʿ kʿ cʿ čʿ*.

In addition to these consonants, Armenian had the fricatives *s z v* and *x* (the *ch*-sound of *Bach* in German), the nasals *m* and *n*, the glides *y* and *w*, and four liquids written *l r ł ṙ*. The two *l*'s designate "light" and "dark" (velarized) *l*, the latter becoming later a voiced uvular fricative [ʁ] (a sound similar to French *r*). The *ṙ* represented a trilled *r*, whereas ordinary *r* represented just a single tap.

16.10. There were seven vowels, transliterated as *a e ē i o ow ə*. The sequence *ow* represented the sound *u* (the Armenian convention of writing it as *ow* is borrowed from Greek, which used *ou* in its alphabet to write the same sound). Many authors transliterate *ow* as *u*, but we shall use *ow*. The schwa (*ə*) was only written at the beginning of a word (e.g. *ənd* 'with, along'), where it comes historically from a full vowel; but in the spoken language it frequently occurred preceding or breaking up consonant clusters, in which case it was not written (so *dpanem* 'I write' was pronounced *dəpanem*, and *znmanē* 'from him' was pronounced *əznəmanē*).

From PIE to Classical Armenian

Phonology

Consonants

16.11. Stops. Armenian is a satem language. The PIE labiovelars lost their labialization and became plain velars (*kʿ*, *k*, or *g*, according to §§16.13–15 below), as in *elikʿ* 'he left' < **elikʷet*. The palatals became fricatives or affricates – specifically, **k̂ > s*, **ĝ > c*, and **ĝh > j*: **dek̂m̥* 'ten' > *tasn* (with unexplained *-a-*); **ĝenh*$_1$*-o-* 'birth' > *cin*; **bhr̥ĝh-* 'high' > *barjr* (cp. Germ. *Burg* 'castle'). It is possible that *z* is another outcome of **ĝ(h)*, as in *dēz* 'heap, pile' < **dhoiĝho-* and *mēz* 'urine' < **h*$_3$*meiĝho-*, but these may also be loanwords from Iranian.

16.12. It has been claimed that Armenian has evidence of the original distinction between the plain velars and the labiovelars, in that the two series have different outcomes before a front vowel. Thus while **k* became *kʿ* in words like *kʿerem* 'I cut' (root **ker-*, cp. Gk. *keírō* 'I shear' < **ker-i̯ō*), **kʷ* became *čʿ*, as in *čʿorkʿ* 'four' < **kʷetu̯ores* (with loss of **-tu̯-*) and *ačʿ-kʿ* 'eyes' < **okʷī*; and while **ghe* remained unpalatalized as _ge_, as in _gełj-kʿ_ ‘glands’ < _*ghelĝh-_, _*g^{w}he_ became palatalized to _ǰe_, as in _ǰerm_ ‘warm’ < _*g^{w}hermo-_ and _ǰnem_ ‘I beat’ < _*g^{w}hen-_. But there are counterexamples, such as the _hinge-_ of _hinge-tasan_ ‘fifteen’ < _*penk^{w}e_, with no palatalization, and the second element of _han-geaw_ ‘rested’ from _*k^{w}iH-_ (cp. Lat. _quiētus_ ‘quiet’). (These words have voiced _g_, as opposed to voiceless _kʿ_, because of the preceding nasal.) The evidence is difficult because both the examples and the counterexamples are open to competing interpretations, and on the whole less convincing than the similar situations of Luvian and Albanian (§§9.48 and 19.10). But the matter deserves further investigation.

16.13. The three PIE series of plain voiceless, voiced, and voiced aspirated stops are kept distinct in Armenian, as also in Greek, Italic, Indic, and Germanic; but all three shifted. The shift is similar to Grimm’s Law in Germanic (see §15.6) and is often called the **Armenian Consonant Shift**. The plain voiceless stops _*t_ and _*k_ (with _*k_ representing both PIE _*k_ and _*k^w_ as per above) became the voiceless aspirates _tʿ_ and _kʿ_ (e.g. pronominal stem _*to-_ > Arm. ***tʿe*** ‘that’; _*elik^{w}et_ ‘he left’ > ***elikʿ***). Exceptional was _*p_, which usually became _h_ or completely disappeared at the beginning of a word, as in ***howr*** ‘fire’ < _*peh$_2$u̯r̥_ (cp. Gk. _pũr_ ‘fire’) and _otn_ ‘foot’ < accusative sing. _*pod-m̥_ (cp. Gk. _pod-_ and also §16.32 below); and word-internally _*p_ became _w_, as in the conjunction _ew_ ‘and’ < _*epi_ (cp. Gk. _epí_ ‘upon’). The word _pʿetowr_ ‘feather’, apparently containing “expected” _pʿ_ from _*p_ (root _*pet-_ ‘fly’), is probably a loanword. For the development of _*t_ word-internally, see §16.31.

16.14. The voiced stops _*b *d *g_ (from both _*g_ and _*g^w_) became the voiceless stops _p t k_, as in ***tam*** ‘I give’ < _*deh$_3$-_ (cp. OCS _damĭ_ ‘I will give’), and ***kov*** ‘cow’ < ****g^{w}ou-*** (cp. Eng. _cow_).

16.15. The voiced aspirates _*bh *dh *gh_ (from both _*gh_ and _*g^{w}h_) become voiced stops. Examples include ***berem*** ‘I carry’ < ****bher-e-***; ***d-nem*** ‘I place’ < ****dhh$_1$-ne-*** (from the zero-grade of _*dheh$_1$-_ ‘place, put’, cp. Skt. _dhā-_); and _mēg_ ‘cloud’ < _*h$_3$meigh-_ (cp. Ved. _meghá-_ ‘rain’). The outcome of _*gh_ (meaning both PIE _*gh_ and _*g^{w}h_) is complicated by a palatalization rule that changed it to _ǰ_ before _e_ or _i_, as for example in ***ǰerm*** ‘heat’ from ****g^{w}hermo-*** (cp. Gk. _thermós_). Word-internally, _*bh_ was weakened like _*p_ to _w_, as in the suffix _-awor_ ‘bearing, having’ discussed below in §16.41 that is ultimately from PIE _*bhoro-_.

16.16. Liquids and nasals. The liquids and nasals stayed mostly unchanged: 1st sing. present-tense ending _-m_ < _*-m(i)_; ***hing*** ‘five’ < ****penk^{w}e***; _sterǰ_ ‘sterile’ < ****ster-***; ***lizem*** ‘I lick’ < ****leiĝh-***. In some positions, especially before other consonants, the _l_ was pronounced as a “dark” or velar _ł_, as in _kałni_ ‘oak’. Nasals disappeared word-finally after vowels, hence the endingless accusative sing. of words like _get_ ‘river’ < _*u̯ed-om_ (from the same root as Eng. _wet_). For the initial _g-_ in this word, see §16.18.

16.17. The syllabic liquids and nasals developed an _a_ before them, as in ***angorc*** ‘inactive’ < _*n̥-u̯orĝ-_ and ***arbi*** ‘I drank’ < _*sr̥bh-_ (cp. Lat. _sorbēre_ ‘to soak up’). Word-finally, the syllabic nasals became _-n_, as in the numerals ***ewtʿn*** ‘seven’ and ***tasn*** ‘ten’ from ****septm̥*** and ****dekm̥***. Compare also §16.32 below.

16.18. Glides. The PIE glides are not preserved as such. PIE _*i̯_ mostly disappeared, as in ***erekʿ*** ‘three’ < ****trei̯es***, but after resonants it became _ǰ_: _ǰnǰem_ ‘I wipe, clean’ < _*g^{w}hen-i̯e-_ (root _*g^{w}hen-_ ‘beat’), _ołǰ_ ‘entire’ < _*ol-i̯o-_. The other glide, _*u̯_, became *g* word-initially, via an intermediate stage **gu̯*. This is a common, albeit strange-looking, change; compare the same development in Brittonic, §14.54, and East and North Germanic, §15.44. Examples include ***gorc*** 'work' < **u̯orĝo-* (cp. Eng. *work*) and ***gitem*** 'I know' < **u̯eid-* (cp. Ved. *véda* 'I know'). Between vowels, however, *v* is the result, as shown most dramatically by the phrase *ger i veroy* 'above and beyond', literally 'above on top', where both *ger* and *ver(-)* continue an earlier **u̯er-* (formed from ****uper*** 'above' after the **-p-* was lost).

16.19. Consonant clusters containing **u̯* show similar developments, some of them quite unusual. The cluster **su̯* became *k'*, as in ***k'oyr*** 'sister' from **su̯esor-*; presumably what happened here is that **su̯* became **hu̯* (cp. §16.23 below), which was essentially a voiceless labiovelar glide like the *wh-* in some pronunciations of Eng. *what*; this then developed into a voiceless aspirated velar stop *k'* parallel to the development of voiced **u̯* into voiced *g* above. Similarly, **u̯* developed into *k* next to the voiceless stop **k̂* in the cluster **k̂u̯*, which became *sk*, as in ***skownd*** 'little dog' < **k̂u̯on-t-* (cp. Eng. *hound*).

Especially famous (or infamous) in the annals of IE phonology is the Armenian outcome of PIE **du̯*: it became *rk*, as in the word for 'two', *erkow* (the *e-* is a later prothetic vowel). While we cannot fully reconstruct all the intermediate stages of this change, it is clear that the velar *k* is the outcome of the glide, as above, and the *r* is a rhotacized continuation of the *d*. The change is fully regular, and we have several other examples of it: ***erkar*** 'long' < ****du̯eh***$_2$***ro-*** (cp. Doric Gk. *d(w)ārós* 'long'); ***erknč'im*** 'I fear' (earlier **erki-nč'im* < ****du̯i-n-sk̂-***, cp. Gk. perfect *(dé)-d(w)i-men* 'we are afraid'); and ***erkn*** 'birth-pangs' < ****h***$_1$***du̯on-***.

16.20. Laryngeals. Laryngeals, when vocalized, turn into *a* in Armenian, as in *hayr* 'father' < **pater-* < **ph*$_2$*ter-*; this is the same development seen in Italic, Celtic, and Germanic. In longer words, sometimes they were vocalized and sometimes not: contrast *dowstr* 'daughter', without a reflex of the laryngeal (< **dhugh*$_2$*ter-*, cp. Gk. *thugátēr*), with *arawr* 'plow', which has a reflex (< **h*$_2$*erh*$_3$*tro-*, cp. Gk. *árotron*).

16.21. Armenian shares with Phrygian and Greek the phenomenon of vocalizing word-initial laryngeals before consonants, usually (but not always) as *a-*, as in ***aganim*** 'I spend the night' (ultimately from ****h***$_2$***u̯es-***, cp. Gk. *á(w)esa* 'I spent the night', Hitt. *ḫuiš-* 'live'), ***ayr*** 'man' < ****aynr-*** < ****aner-*** < ****h***$_2$***ner-***, and ***erek*** 'evening' < ****h***$_1$***reg***^{w}***os*** (cp. Gk. *érebos* 'darkness of the underworld'). But reflexes of word-initial laryngeals are not preserved as consistently as in Greek.

16.22. Some have claimed that Armenian preserves word-initial laryngeals before vowels as *h*, similar to Anatolian (see §9.5). This claim is based on a number of tantalizing forms such as *haw* 'grandfather' (PIE **h*$_2$*euh*$_2$*os*, cp. Hitt. *ḫuḫḫaš* 'grandfather'), *hanem* 'I draw out' (**h*$_2$*en-*, cp. Hitt. *ḫan-* 'scoop'), and *hot* 'odor' (**h*$_3$*ed-*). On the other hand, such an *h* is lacking in other words where one might expect it, as *ost* 'branch' (< **h*$_3$*ezd-*, cp. Hitt. *ḫašduir*) and *oror* 'gull' (if from **h*$_3$*er(o)n-*, cp. Hitt. *ḫaran-* 'eagle'). A rather grave difficulty is the fact that *h*'s were not infrequently added to vowel-initial words, leading to doublets like *ogi* 'breath' ~ *hogi* 'spirit' and *arbil* 'to drink' ~ *harbil* 'to be intoxicated'. The interpretation of forms like *haw* is therefore disputed.

16.23. Sibilant *s. PIE **s* usually disappeared word-initially and between vowels (compare the parallel developments in Greek, §12.18), as in the words *ał* 'salt'

(< **sal-*) and *k'oyr* 'sister' (< **hu̯eur* < **su̯esor-*). But sometimes it became *h* initially, as in *hin* 'old' < **seno-*. At the end of words, it appears that the outcome is (oddly) often *k'*, but as this outcome is only found in plurals, we do not know if the *-k'* comes directly from **-s* or is due to some morphological analogy. Nevertheless, the correspondences are rather striking: compare the nomin. pl. *otk'* 'feet' with Gk. *pódes*; the 1st pl. verbal ending *-mk'* with Lat. *-mus*, Ved. *-mas*; and note also the word for 'three', *erek'* < **trei̯es*. In at least one environment, final **-s* remained, namely the accusative plural from **-ns*, as in *gets* 'rivers' < earlier **u̯edons*.

Vowels

16.24. The short vowels usually stayed intact: *ac-em* 'I lead', cp. Lat. *ag-ō* 'I lead'; *cer* 'old man', cp. Gk. *gérōn* 'old man'; *elik'* 'he left', cp. Gk. *élipe* 'he left'; *hot* 'smell', cp. Lat. *odor*; *dowstr* 'daughter' (*ow* = *u*), cp. Gk. *thugátēr* 'daughter'. In unaccented syllables *i* and *u* were deleted (see §16.28 below).

16.25. The long vowels became short. The long mid vowels **ē* and **ō* were raised to *i* and *ow* (= *u*): *mi* (negative used in prohibitions), cp. Gk. *mḗ*; *towrk'* 'gift', cp. Gk. *dõron*. Long **ā* was shortened to *a*, as in *awr* 'day', cp. Gk. (Doric) *ā̃mar*. Long **ī* was shortened to *i*, as in *k'san* 'twenty' < earlier **gisan* < **u̯īk̑m̥tī*, and **ū* was probably shortened as well, as in *jowkn* 'fish' if from **dhĝhū-*.

16.26. Diphthongs. The PIE diphthongs **ai* and **au* remain unchanged, as in *ayc* 'goat' (cp. Gk. *aig-*) and *awł* 'place to spend the night' (cp. Gk. *aũlis* 'tent'). The diphthongs **eu* and **ou* both became *oy*: *loys* 'light' (**leuk-* or **louk-*). Finally, **ei* and **oi* became **ē*, as in the 3rd sing. aorist *elēz* 'he licked' (< **eleiĝhet*) and *dēz* 'heap, pile' (< **dhoiĝh-o-*, cp. Gk. *toĩkhos* 'wall').

Stress and loss of final syllables

16.27. At some point in the prehistory of Armenian, the mobile PIE accent was fixed on the penultimate syllable. After this, most vowels in final syllables were lost, and – usually but not always – final consonants. Thus for example the PIE imperfect **ebheret* 'he was carrying' became Armenian (aorist) *eber*. The loss of final syllables resulted in the stress now being word-final, since the old penultimate syllables became the new final syllables. (The same thing happened in the history of French to give the word-final accent that Modern French has; a word like *interdít* 'forbidden' comes from Latin *interdíctus*.)

16.28. The stress on final syllables resulted in weakening and syncope of certain non-final syllables, and led to a series of vowel alternations depending on the position of the stress. Underlying *i* and *ow* (*u*) disappear outright when not stressed or word-initial: thus compare *gir* 'letter' with *grem* 'I write' (< **girem*) and *k'own* 'sleep' with (genitive) *k'noy* 'of sleep' (< **k'ownoy*). Other alternations are found as well: *mēg* 'cloud' (earlier **meig*) ~ *migamac* 'foggy'; *loys* 'light' ~ *lowsawor* 'luminous'; *matean* 'book' ~ *matenagir* 'writer'. (*Migamac* and *lowsawor* show that when *i* and *ow* result from reduction of a diphthong, they remain even when unstressed.)

Morphology

16.29. Armenian has undergone moderate simplification of PIE inflectional morphology. A total of seven cases – most of the PIE inventory – are distinguished in nouns and pronouns (nominative, accusative, genitive, dative, instrumental, locative, and ablative), although no single noun or pronoun distinguishes all seven. The dual has been lost everywhere, as has grammatical gender. The verbal system of Classical Armenian is quite similar to that of PIE, but interestingly few of the actual forms are inherited. The present and aorist have survived, while the perfect has disappeared, as has the imperfect (although several individual imperfects were transferred over to the aorist category and survive as aorists, such as *eber* above). A new imperfect was created, as were a present and aorist subjunctive. Mediopassive inflection is distinguished from active inflection by a stem change, and by partially different endings in the aorist. Only one participle is found.

Nouns and pronouns

16.30. Nouns were declined in vocalic and consonantal stems. Four vocalic stems, in *o*, *a*, *i*, and *ow* (*u*), are found, exemplified below by the declensions of *get* 'river', *am* 'year', *ban* 'word', and *zgest* 'clothing':

	sg.	pl.	sg.	pl.	sg.	pl.	sg.	pl.
N	*get*	*getk'*	*am*	*amk'*	*ban*	*bank'*	*zgest*	*zgestk'*
A	*get*	*gets*	*am*	*ams*	*ban*	*bans*	*zgest*	*zgests*
GD	*getoy*	*getoc'*	*ami*	*amac'*	*bani*	*banic'*	*zgestow*	*zgestowc'*
L	*get*	*gets*	*ami*	*ams*	*bani*	*bans*	*zgestow*	*zgests*
Ab	*getoy*	*getoc'*	*amē*	*amac'*	*banē*	*banic'*	*zgestē*	*zgestowc'*
I	*getov*	*getovk'*	*amaw*	*amawk'*	*baniw*	*baniwk'*	*zgestow*	*zgestowk'*

The genitive and dative are not distinguished in nouns, only in pronouns. The plural *-k'* and the accusative plural *-s* have already been discussed (§16.23). The instrumental contains a *-v-* or *-w-* that continues the PIE instrumental ending **-bhi-*; this ending survives more clearly in such old athematic forms as *jerb-a-kal* 'taken with the hands = prisoner' < **ĝhesr̥-bhi-*. The genitive and ablative plural ending *-c'* is of uncertain origin.

16.31. The declension of consonant stems is similar, although some show unexpected alternations in the stem. For example, *hayr* 'father' has a genitive *hawr*. The difference in vocalism is due to different treatments of word-internal **t*: before a front vowel this stop became the glide *y* (**hayir* < **hatir* < **ph₂tēr*), while before back vowels and in the consonant cluster **-tr-* it became the other glide *w*, hence *hawr* < **hatros* < **ph₂tros*. Another kind of stem-alternation in a consonant stem can be exemplified by *p'ok'r* 'small', pl. *p'ok'ownk'*; it is ultimately a *u*-stem, into which an *-r* has intruded in the nominative and accusative singular and an *-n-* in the plural. This is reminiscent of the PIE *r/n*-stems, although it is not fully clear how this Armenian paradigm came to be. A true *r/n*-stem declension does not exist in

Armenian, but a trace remains in the *r/n*-alternation seen in *howr* 'fire' vs. *hn-ocʿ* 'oven' (cp. §6.31).

16.32. A small group of nouns, principally *otn* 'foot' and *jeṙn* 'hand', end in an *-n* that actually continues the old accusative singular ending **-m̥*. The loss of this ending in the productive accusative singular of consonant stems is therefore not due to sound change, but to morphological analogy with the vocalic stems, where all endings in **-Vm* were lost.

16.33. Pronouns. Of interest is the system of deictics ("pointing" words such as demonstrative pronouns, adjectives, and adverbs). Unlike English, which has only a two-fold distinction between *this* and *that* and between *here* and *there*, Armenian, like Latin and certain other ancient and modern IE languages, has a three-fold distinction corresponding to the three persons. Unlike Latin, though, the three-way distinction is systematically carried out throughout the system of demonstrative pronouns and adverbs. Armenian thus has three definite articles, the suffixes *-s*, *-d*, and *-n* (ultimately < PIE **k̂i-*, **to-*, and **eno-/ono-*), meaning roughly 'this (by me)', 'that (by you)', 'that (over by him/her/them)'. From these are formed three demonstrative pronouns *ays* 'this', *ayd* 'that', and *ayn* 'that (over there)'; three corresponding anaphoric pronouns *sa*, *da*, and *na* basically function as third person pronouns but again depending on how near to the speaker the referent stands (either physically or metaphorically). Armenian also has not one but three pronouns meaning 'the same', *soyn*, *doyn*, *noyn*; three locational adverbs for 'here' or 'there', *ast*, *aydr*, *and*; and three interjections meaning 'behold', *awasik*, *awadik*, *awanik*.

An interesting syntactic feature of the suffixed definite articles is that they can mark not only nouns and noun phrases as definite, but also relative clauses, in which case the article follows the first stressed word after the relative pronoun, regardless of its part of speech. (Compare from English the ability of the possessive suffix *-'s* to be added to any part of speech so long as it comes at the end of the noun phrase being marked for possession, as in *the woman I saw yesterday's coat*.) Thus in *zor očʿd vayel ē kʿez xawsel* 'which it is not seemly for you to relate' (Agatʿangełos 68), the article *-d* is attached to the negative *očʿ* 'not' following the relative.

Verbs

16.34. There were two verb stems, a present stem and an aorist stem, and they expressed not only an opposition in tense (non-past vs. past) but also an opposition in aspect (imperfective vs. perfective; see §5.10). While these basic categories are inherited, the personal endings have undergone significant change; and a third stem, the perfect, has been entirely lost. Some historical details of the personal endings will be taken up in the sections to follow.

The present stem is used to form the present and imperfect indicative, the present subjunctive, the prohibitive, and the infinitive. The aorist stem is used to form the aorist indicative and subjunctive, the imperative, and a passive participle.

16.35. Present classes. There are four classes of presents, with stem vowels *a*, *e*, *i*, and *ow* (*u*). The following verbs will illustrate the present and imperfect: *orsam* 'I hunt', *orsayi* 'I was hunting'; *grem* 'I write', *grei* 'I was writing'; *hayim* 'I look', *hayei* 'I was looking'; and *argelowm* 'I hinder', *argelowi* 'I was hindering'.

	Present				Imperfect			
sg. 1	*orsam*	*grem*	*hayim*	*argelowm*	*orsayi*	*grei*	*hayei*	*argelowi*
2	*orsas*	*gres*	*hayis*	*argelows*	*orsayir*	*greir*	*hayeir*	*argelowir*
3	*orsay*	*grē*	*hayi*	*argelow*	*orsayr*	*grēr*	*hayēr*	*argeloyr*
pl. 1	*orsamkʻ*	*gremkʻ*	*hayimkʻ*	*argelowmkʻ*	*orsayakʻ*	*greakʻ*	*hayeakʻ*	*argelowakʻ*
2	*orsaykʻ*	*grēkʻ*	*hayikʻ*	*argelowkʻ*	*orsayikʻ*	*greikʻ*	*hayeikʻ*	*argelowikʻ*
3	*orsan*	*gren*	*hayin*	*argelown*	*orsayin*	*grein*	*hayein*	*argelowin*

The PIE primary personal endings (sing.) *-mi *-si *-ti, (pl.) *-mes(-) *-tes(-) *-nti can be seen shining through the Armenian present-tense endings. The preservation of the *-s* in the 2nd singular is probably due to influence from the 2nd singular of the verb 'to be', which is *es* < *ess < *(h$_1$)es-si (remade from *h$_1$esi; §3.37). The 3rd singular *-y* is one of the regular developments of intervocalic *t (§16.31): thus *-ay* comes from *-a-ti, *-ē* (< *-ei) from *-e-ti, etc. The imperfect endings are modeled on the imperfect of the verb 'be', whose paradigm is *ei eir ēr* in the singular, and *eakʻ eikʻ ein* in the plural. These forms in turn have a complicated history, but the *-i-* that characterizes many of them is probably a continuation of *ēs- (*e-h$_1$es-), the old imperfect stem of *h$_1$es- 'be'. The 3rd sing. imperfect ending *-r* is an old middle ending; apparently Armenian generalized the middle ending to the 3rd singular of this tense.

16.36. Origin of the present classes. These four classes of present stems continue most of the PIE present formations; the general situation is not unlike that of Italic (see §13.13). Presents in *-em* are kind of a scrap-heap: this class includes old thematic presents like *berem* 'I carry' (*bher-e-) and *acem* 'I drive' (*h$_2$eĝ-e-); *-i̯e/o-presents like *ǰnǰem* 'I wipe, I clean' (< *g^{wh}en-i̯e-); and causative-iteratives like *owtem* 'I eat' (< *h$_1$ōd-éi̯e-) and *glem* 'I roll' (< *gowlem < *u̯ōl-ei̯e-). Very productive in Armenian is the nasal suffix *-an-*, which was often used to remake already-existing verbs: *anicanem* 'I curse' is a remodeling of *anicem, a *-i̯e/o-verb (*h$_3$neid-i̯e-, cp. Gk. *óneidos* 'blame'); *harcʻanem* 'I ask' is a remodeling of a *-sk̂e/o-verb (*pr̥(k̂)sk̂e-, cp. Lat. *poscō* 'I ask'; see §5.34); and *lkʻanem* 'I leave' is a remodeling of a nasal-infix verb (cp. Lat. *linquō* 'I leave'). The suffix *-an-* is related to the Greek suffix *-anein*, which was added to many verbs that already had a nasal infix, such as *limp-ánein* 'to leave'.

Other PIE present formations are scattered among the remaining classes, such as root athematic presents (e.g. *bam* 'I speak' < *bheh$_2$-mi) and *nu*-presents (e.g. *z-genowm* 'I get dressed' < *u̯es-nu-, exactly like Gk. *hénnūmi* 'I dress [someone]'; §5.26). The *i*-stem verbs like *hayim* are typically middles, though unlike the middles of other IE languages there is no separate set of mediopassive personal endings in the present tense. (There is in the aorist; see §16.38 below.) On the source of the *-i-*, see the next section.

16.37. The present passive. Verbs with stem vowel *-e-*, like *berem*, could form a passive in *-im* (so *berim* 'I am carried'), with endings exactly the same as those of the *i*-stem verbs like *hayim*. The origin of this conjugation has been the subject of several hypotheses. Given that middles and passives are usually constructed out of the same morphology in IE languages, the *-i-* is surely the same as of the *i*-middles just discussed. This *-i-* used to be thought to continue the intransitive suffix *-i̯e-, which came to form passives in Indo-Iranian (§5.32), but this account has phonological problems (it should have become *-ǰe-* after resonants, of which there is no trace). A more likely source is the stative suffix **-eh₁-*, further suffixed with **-i̯e/o-* to form a present; in Greek, as we have seen (§12.43), **-eh₁-* formed intransitives and passives (creating the category known as the aorist passive). And directly parallel with the Armenian situation, the Greek aorist passive has active personal endings. Here one must merely assume that the outcome of this sequence was *-i-* when not under the main word stress, since stressed **-éh₁-i̯e-* became *-ie-*, as in *diem* 'I suckle' < **dhéh₁-i̯e-*; such an assumption has many parallels. (Yet a third suggestion, that the *-i-* ultimately continues the thematic vowel *-e-*, is beset with many complications.)

16.38. The aorist. The Armenian aorist for the most part is a continuation of the PIE imperfect. There are two types of aorist stems: an unextended root (e.g. 3rd singulars *e-ber* 'carried', from an old IE imperfect **ebheret*, and *elikʿ* 'left', from an old IE thematic aorist **elikʷet*, equivalent to Gk. *élipe*); and a root extended with a suffix *-cʿ-* (e.g. 3rd sing. *gorceacʿ* 'he made' from the present *gorcem* 'I make'), usually derived from **-sḱe-*, which was used in Greek and Anatolian to form iterative past tenses (see §5.34). Unlike the present, the aorist has separate active and mediopassive personal endings. Some examples of the conjugations are provided below by the active aorists *hani* 'I drew out' and *orsacʿi* 'I hunted', and the mediopassive aorists *nstay* 'I sat' and *hayecʿay* 'I looked':

	Aorist indicative active		Aorist indicative mediopassive	
sg. 1	*hani*	*orsacʿi*	*nstay*	*hayecʿay*
2	*haner*	*orsacʿer*	*nstar*	*hayecʿar*
3	*ehan*	*orsacʿ*	*nstaw*	*hayecʿaw*
pl. 1	*hanakʿ*	*orsacʿakʿ*	*nstakʿ*	*hayecʿakʿ*
2	*hanēkʿ*	*orsacʿēkʿ*	*nstaykʿ*	*hayecʿaykʿ*
3	*hanin*	*orsacʿin*	*nstan*	*hayecʿan*

As can be seen from the form *ehan* (and *eber* cited earlier), a prefix called the augment (*e-*), identical to the augment found in Greek, Indo-Iranian, and Phrygian (§5.44), appears when the form would otherwise be a monosyllable. (Sometimes the augment is omitted; although the matter needs more study, some of the contexts in which the augment is omitted appear to match contexts in which it is omitted also in Homeric Greek.) The active aorist endings are in part a continuation of the PIE imperfect; the 3rd singular, for example, continues the imperfect thematic ending **-et*. The *-w* at the end of the 3rd singular aorist passive is a faithful descendant of the PIE past-tense middle ending **-to* (for the change of **-t-* to *-w-* recall §16.31). Similarly, the 3rd pl. *-an* is from **-n̥to*; this became **-anto* and then *-an* after the loss of final syllables, and the *-a-* in this form is thought to have spread throughout the paradigm and to be the source of the *-a-* in the other persons and numbers.

16.39. The subjunctive. The subjunctive functioned both as a future tense and as an optative and conditional. It was formed with a suffix *-icʿ-* which is usually taken to be from PIE **-isḱe-*, although this is not universally accepted. Its endings are complex, and not explained in all their particulars. One form that is generally agreed upon is the 1st singular, as in aorist subjunctive *argel-icʿ* 'I will hinder', where the ending *-icʿ* is taken to be from **-isk̂ō* (**-isk̂oh₂*), with the original ending **-ō* (< **-oh₂*) not replaced by **-m(i)* as in the present indicative.

16.40. The participle. Armenian verbs have only one participle, in *-eal*, formed typically form the aorist stem and having passive meaning, such as *greal* 'written'. This goes back ultimately to the somewhat rare PIE participial ending **-lo-* (§5.60), also found in Slavic, as in OCS *bi-lŭ* 'beaten'.

Compounding

16.41. Armenian is very fond of using compounding to form new words; interestingly, it almost never uses prefixes, a feature shared with PIE, though not necessarily inherited from it: to judge by the presence of a few archaic prefixed forms, prefixation may have once been more common. Two examples are *ənker* 'companion' (< **ənd-ker-*, literally 'with-eat(er), messmate') and *tkar* 'weak' (< **ti-kar* 'without power'; **ti* is cognate with Lat. *dē* 'from, without', as in *dē-bilis* 'without strength, incapable'). Much preferred was suffixation, and Armenian possessed a wealth of suffixes. Some examples of suffixed forms are *lows-awor* 'luminous' (*loys* 'light' + *-awor* 'bearing, having' < PIE **bhoro-*), *xałał-arar* 'peaceful' (*xałał* 'peace' + *-arar* 'doing', from *aṙnem* 'I do'), and *kʿahanay-owtʿiwn* 'priesthood' (*kʿahanay* 'priest' + *-owtʿiwn* '-hood, -ship', related to the Latin abstract nouns in *-tiōn-*). Perhaps most familiar to English speakers is the patronymic suffix *-ean* (ultimately from PIE **-i̯o-*, see §6.74) meaning 'son of', as in *Aram-ean* 'son of Aram' or *Simowneanˆ Yowda* 'Judas son of Simon' in the Armenian Bible (John 6:71). This appears transcribed from Modern Armenian into English as *-ian* in such names as *Khatchaturian*, *Hagopian*, etc.

Middle and Modern Armenian

16.42. As a result of the conquest of part of Armenia by the Seljuq Turks in the mid-eleventh century, Classical Armenian fell into disuse in that area. A group of Armenian refugees founded a new state in southern Turkey along the Mediterranean, in the historical region of Cilicia, which had been home to Armenian settlements centuries earlier. In the resultant Cilician kingdom (1080–1375, the last independent Armenian state until the twentieth century) Classical Armenian continued to be used alongside a written (and Classicizing) form of the Cilician dialect, the best-attested variety of **Middle Armenian**; it was based on the spoken language of the settlers in the region and is ancestral to Modern Western Armenian (see below). Other forms of Middle Armenian are also preserved from other areas. In 1375, the Cilician capital Sis fell to the Egyptian Mamelukes and was soon afterwards taken by the Turco-Mongol conqueror Timur (Tamerlane). This and successive struggles for power in the region, especially between the Ottoman Turks and Persians, resulted in the emigration of many Armenians (though many also stayed behind), who formed new communities in Istanbul, Europe, and elsewhere. Throughout this period, Turkish influence on the language was heavily felt.

16.43. A renaissance of Armenian literature and learning began in the seventeenth century. Cultural and economic centers were established; so that they could communicate with each other, a kind of Armenian koine grew up called **Civil Armenian,** which had dialect features from both eastern and western areas. The renaissance really flowered with the activities of the Mekhitarists, a Benedictine congregation founded by Mekhitar of Sebaste (1676–1749). They were active especially in Venice and fostered the education of Armenians and the revival of the Armenian literary past. A new written language began to be forged through efforts (continuing into the twentieth century) to purge the language of Turkish elements and replace them with features of Classical (rather than contemporary) Armenian; this language developed differently in eastern and western areas, becoming the two modern literary dialects. The official language of Armenia itself, **Modern Eastern Armenian,** is usually said to be based on the dialect around Mount Ararat and the capital Erevan, but actually contains a mixture of different dialect features (the pronunciation of the consonants, for example, hails from elsewhere). Similarly **Modern Western Armenian,** used by the diasporic communities (historically in Turkey and points west), is usually said to be based on the dialect of Istanbul, but also has many features taken from other dialects, and even some that are unique to it.

In the wake of nineteenth-century populist feelings, Classical Armenian finally ceased to be used and it was replaced by Modern Armenian.

16.44. The two literary varieties are fairly similar, but spoken Armenian does not lend itself to a simple bipartite division; there are scores of tremendously varied dialects, some of which have undergone significant phonological and syntactic transformation under the influence of neighboring Turkic and Caucasian languages. (The diaspora during and after the genocide of Turkish Armenians in 1915–23 has brought speakers of most of the Western dialects to the United States.) The modern standard language has not been free of these influences either; in many areas of syntax, such as subordinate clausal structure, it more greatly resembles a Turkic language than an Indo-European one. Morphologically, Modern Armenian has maintained essentially the same case system in the noun as the classical language, but has markedly changed verbal conjugation by introducing many periphrastic verbal constructions especially in the present and future tenses.

16.45. For Indo-European studies, the modern dialectal divergences in the stop consonant systems are the most significant. All the dialects have a series of voiceless aspirated stops that continue the PIE voiceless stops, but they differ in their outcomes of the other two series, especially the original voiced aspirates, which have no fewer than four different dialectal outcomes ([d] in Classical and Modern Eastern, [t] in dialects around Lake Van and Sasun in Turkey, [d^h] in Sebastia and Erevan, and [t^h] in Modern Western). The Classical Armenian system is more or less preserved in Modern Eastern Armenian (the one salient difference being that the Classical voiceless stops have become tense [t' p' k'] with concomitant tightening of the glottis), but Modern Western Armenian has voiced stops continuing PIE voiced stops and voiceless aspirates coming from PIE voiced aspirates. Thus PIE **t *d *dh* became Eastern [t^h t' d] and Western [t^h d t^h]. There is considerable dispute over whether the Classical system necessarily represents the oldest state of affairs within Armenian; many believe instead that Classical Armenian was just one of several dialects independently derived from Proto-Armenian. Figuring into the controversy is the fact that the oldest inscriptions, from the fifth century onward, do not yet show dialect features; they first appear around the ninth century (the Moscow Gospel, §16.8, has quite a few).

The difference between Classical orthography and Modern Western pronunciation can have, very occasionally, amusing results for the English speaker. The Anatolian storm-god Tarḫunts was picked up by the early Armenians during their migration through Anatolia and incorporated into their mythology, becoming ultimately a mythic hero called Tork'. Though Tork' does his Anatolian ancestor proud with his ability to split granite rocks with his hands and hurl hill-size boulders at enemy ships (as told in Movsēs Xorenac'i 2.8), the mighty storm-god of old might not be pleased at how his namesake has fared in the mouths of Modern Western Armenian speakers: [dork^{h}]!

Classical Armenian text sample A

16.46. The Birth of Vahagn, one of the native pre-Christian poems quoted in Movsēs Xorenac'i 1.31. Vahagn (or Vahevan), from Parthian *Varθagan*, is in origin the Iranian hero *Vərəθraγna-*, equivalent etymologically to Ved. *Vr̥tra-ghn-* 'slayer of Vr̥tra' (the serpent and monstrous adversary of the chief god Indra). This legend is not Iranian in origin, but probably Anatolian.

1	erknēr erkin erknēr erkir	Heaven was in labor, Earth was in labor,
	erknēr ew covn cirani	the purple sea was also in labor.
	erkn i covown ownēr	In the sea labor pains held
	zkarmrikn ełegnik.	the little crimson reed.
2	ənd ełegan p'oł cowx elanēr	Along the reed's stalk rose smoke;
	ənd ełegan p'oł boc' elanēr	along the reed's stalk rose flame;
	ew i boc'oyn vazēr	and from the flame leapt up
	xarteaš patanekik.	a golden-haired little boy.
3	na howr her ownēr	He had hair (of) fire;
	boc' ownēr mawrows	he had a beard (of) flame;
	ew ač'kownk'n ein aregakownk'.	and his eyes were little suns.

16.46a. Notes. 1. erknēr: 'was in labor', from *erkn* 'labor pains' (in line 3), stem *erkown-*, PIE *h_1*d-u̯on-* (for *du̯ > rk*, see §16.19), also in Gk. *odúnē* 'pain', a derivative of *h_1*ed-* 'eat' in its presumed original meaning 'bite'. A parallel suffixed form in *-u̯ol-* is represented by the Anatolian words for 'evil', Luv. *attuwal-* and Hitt. *idālu-*. **erkin:** 'heaven', etymology unclear. **erkir:** 'earth', etymology likewise unclear, but forming an obvious pair with *erkin*. **ew:** 'and, also', < *epi* 'upon'; §16.13. **covn:** 'the sea'; *-n* is the cliticized definite article (seen also below in *covown*, *zkarmrikn*, *boc'oyn*, etc.). It has been suggested that this is one of the Urartian borrowings into Armenian (§16.2), but it may also be cognate with Lydian *kofuλ* 'water'. The locative is *covow*, seen below, showing the word to be a *u*-stem. **cirani:** 'purple'. **i:** 'in' (plus locative); when followed by the ablative it means 'from', as in the second stanza. **ownēr:** 'had, held', 3rd sing., usually taken to be from a nasal present *ōp-ne-* from the same root as in Ved. *āpnóti* 'gets, takes'. **zkarmrikn:** 'the crimson', from *karmir* 'red' (cp. Hebrew *karmīl*, perhaps from Persian and ultimately related to Eng. *crimson*). The prefix *z-* marks the word as direct object; the prefix was originally a preposition but developed as a marker of definite direct objects, somewhat parallel to the development from Lat. *ad* 'to' to Spanish *a* in marking personal direct objects. **ełegnik:** 'little reed', diminutive of *ełegn* 'reed'. Note that in a definite noun phrase, either the adjective or the noun can host the definite article; in this phrase, it is the adjective.

2. ənd: 'along', from *$*h_2enti$* 'facing, against'. **ełegan:** 'reed', *n*-stem genit. sing. **p'oł:** 'stalk'. **cowx:** 'smoke'. **elanēr:** 'ascended, rose'. **boc':** 'flame'. The ablative is *boc'oy* in the next line, with a suffixed definite article *-n*. **vazēr:** 'leapt'. **xarteaš:** 'golden-haired'. **patanekik:** 'little youth', containing the same diminutive suffix *-ik* as *ełegnik* above.

3. na: 'that one, he'. **howr:** 'fire', PIE $*peh_2u\underset{\circ}{r}$ (see §§16.13 and 31). **her:** 'hair'; not related to the English word. **mawrows:** 'beard', accus. pl. (but singular in meaning), from PIE **smoḱru-*, cognate with Ved. *śmáśru-*, Lith. *smãkras* 'chin', and other forms. The Armenian word illustrates the loss of **s-* before nasals, a regular Armenian change. The cluster *-ḱr-* developed to *-wr-* just as **-tr-* did (§16.31). **ač'kownk'n:** 'the little eyes', from earlier **ač'-ikown-k'-n*, the definite (*-n*) plural (*-ownk'*, with the same intrusion of *-own-* into the plural paradigm as seen in the adjective *p'ok'r* in §16.31) of a diminutive (with suffix *-ik-*) of *akn* 'eye', PIE $*h_3ek^w$- (cp. Lat. *oc-ulus*). **ein:** 'were', 3rd pl. imperfect. **aregakownk':** 'little suns', from *aregakn*, literally 'sun-jewel', from *areg*, *arev* 'sun' (cognate with Skt. *ravis* 'sun') plus *akn* 'jewel', perhaps the same word as *akn* 'eye'.

Classical Armenian text sample B

16.47. From the Armenian Bible; Mark 14:17–21. The English translation is adapted from the *New International Version*.

17 Ew ibrew erekoy ełew gay erkotasaniwk'n handerj: 18 Ew ibrew bazmec'an ew deṙ owtein, asē Yisows. amēn asem jez, zi mi omn i jēnǰ matneloc' ē zis, or owtē isk ənd is: 19 Ew nok'a sksan trtmel ew asel mi əst misǰē. mit'e es ic'em, ew miwsn mit'e es ic'em: 20. Na patasxani et ew asē c'nosa mi yerkastasanic' ayti, or mxeac' ənd is skawaṙakd: 21. Ayl ordi mardoy ert'ay orpēs ew greal ē vasn nora. bayc' vay ic'ē mardoyn aynmik yoyr jeṙs ordi mardoy matnesc'i. law ēr nma t'ē c'ēr isk cneal mardn ayn.

17 When evening came, Jesus arrived with the Twelve. 18 While they were reclining at the table eating, he said, "I tell you the truth, one of you will betray me – one who is eating with me." 19 They were saddened, and one by one they said to him, "Surely not I?" 20 "It is one of the Twelve," he replied, "one who dips bread into the bowl with me. 21 The Son of Man will go just as it is written about him. But woe to that man by whom the Son of Man will be betrayed! It would be better for him if he had not been born."

16.47a. Notes (selective). **17–18. erekoy:** 'evening', from $*h_1reg^wo$- (cp. Gk. *érebos* 'darkness'). **gay:** 'comes', 3rd sing. of *gam* 'I come', PIE $*gheh_1$- (also the root of Eng. *go*). **erkotasaniwk'n:** 'group of twelve', instr. object of *handerj* 'together with' with suffixed definite article *-n*, from *erkow* 'two' and *tasn* 'ten'. Note that the combining form *erko-* preserves the *-o* of PIE **du̯o(-)*; similarly *hinge-tasan* 'fifteen' preserves the *-e* of **penkʷe*, over against *hing* 'five', which has lost it. **owtein:** 'were eating', 3rd pl. imperfect of *owtem* 'I eat', from PIE **h₁ōd-éi̯e-*, a lengthened-grade causative-iterative from a Narten root (see §5.23). **asē:** 'says', PIE **h₂eĝ-* 'say', the root of Gk. *ē̃* 'he said' and Lat. *ait* 'he said'. **mi:** 'one', PIE **smi-*, cp. Gk. (fem.) *mía* < **smi(i̯)h₂*. **ənd:** 'with', see the Notes to line 2 of the preceding text.

19–21. es: 'I', PIE **eĝ-*. **icʿem:** 'I will be', present subjunctive of *em* 'I am'. **patasxani et:** '(he) answered'; phrase made of the noun *patasxani* 'answer' and the aorist of the verb *tam* 'I give', PIE **deh₃-*. **cʿnosa:** 'to them', preposition *cʿ-* 'to' plus accus. pl. of *na*, 3rd person pronoun. **mardoy:** 'of man', genitive of *mard*, either an Iranian borrowing (cp. Modern Persian *mard* 'man') or directly from PIE **mr̥to-* 'mortal' (also the source of the Iranian). **greal ē:** 'it is written', periphrastic passive with the participle of *grem* 'I write' plus *ē*, 3rd sing. present of *em* 'I am'. **matnescʿi:** 'will be betrayed', 3rd sing. passive aorist subjunctive of *matnem* 'I betray', literally 'I finger, point a finger at', from *matn* 'finger'. **cneal:** 'born', participle of *cnem* 'I am born', PIE **ĝenh₁-*.

For Further Reading

Not much of any value has been written on the history of Armenian in English. The classic comparative grammar is still Meillet 1936, amazingly thorough in spite of its brevity. The grammar is partly a distillation of decades of pathbreaking scholarly work that Meillet devoted to Armenian, which can be found in the masterly articles collected in Meillet 1962–77. Newer comparative grammars are Schmitt 1981, useful for the reader with some IE background, and Lamberterie 1992. A reference grammar of Classical Armenian in English is Godel 1975. An excellent, though highly technical and not uncontroversial, study of the history of the Armenian verb is Klingenschmitt 1982. The only etymological dictionary not in Armenian dates from the nineteenth century and is badly in need of revision: Hübschmann 1895–7. The question of the relationship between Greek and Armenian has recently received a detailed investigation (if not resolution) in Clackson 1994. The Armenian noun has recently received detailed historical treatment in Olsen 1999 and Matzinger 2005.

For Review

Know the meaning or significance of the following:

Heinrich Hübschmann	Armenian Consonant Shift
Mesrob	deictic

Exercises

1 What are the Armenian outcomes of the following PIE sounds or sequences of sounds? Some may have more than one answer.

a	**bh*	**c**	**t*	**e**	**ḱ*	**g**	**u̯*	**i**	**du̯*	**k**	**kʷ*	**m**	**s*	**o**	**r̥*
b	**ī*	**d**	**p*	**f**	**i̯*	**h**	**d*	**j**	**ĝh*	**l**	**ō*	**n**	**su̯*	**p**	**eu*

2 Briefly explain the history or significance of the following Armenian forms:

a *kov*	**f** *otn*	**k** *gorc*
b *kʿoyr*	**g** *haw*	**l** *tasn*
c *ger i veroy*	**h** *erkow*	**m** *ayr*
d *-mkʿ*	**i** *jerbakal*	**n** *lowsawor*
e *hnocʿ*	**j** *bam*	**o** *acem*

3 Consider the following PIE roots and their Armenian descendants:

**ĝenh₁-*	*cin*	'birth'
**penkʷe*	*hing*	'five'
**sen-*	*hin*	'old'
**ĝer-*	*cer*	'old'
**su̯eḱs*	*vecʿ*	'six'

a Formulate a rule that accounts for the changes that affected PIE **e* in the data provided.
b Given that the verb 'to engender' derived from *cin* 'birth' is *cnel*, which happened first, your rule in (**a**) or the sound change in §16.28?

4 Among the many Iranian loanwords in Armenian are *partēz* 'paradise' (cp. Avestan *pairi.daēza-* 'enclosure') and *dast* 'hand' (cp. Middle Persian *dast*). Based on your knowledge of Armenian consonantal sound changes, which of these is the earlier borrowing into Armenian? Explain your answer.

5 How do forms like *barjr* and *dēz* (§16.11) provide evidence that Grassmann's Law was a post-PIE sound change? What other branch(es) that you have seen so far provide(s) comparable evidence? Explain your answer.

6 The preservation of the short vowels intact into the historical period (§16.24) is shared by what other branch(es) of IE that you have seen so far?

7 How does the Armenian class of verbs with stem-vowel *e* differ historically from the Italic third conjugation (also with stem-vowel *e*)?

8 What was the fate of the interdental fricative [ð] (written δ) in Parthian loanwords into Armenian, as exemplified below?

aparan-kʿ 'house, palace' < Parth. *apaδan*
awrēn 'law, right' < Parth. *aβδēn*
varagoyr 'curtain' < Parth. *barayōδ*

PIE Vocabulary VIII: Material Culture and Technology

**teks-* 'fashion, construct': Hitt. *takkešzi* 'puts together', Ved. *tā́ṣṭi* 'fashions', Gk. *téktōn* 'carpenter', Lat. *texō* 'I weave'
**k^{w}ek^{w}lo-* 'WHEEL': Ved. *cakrám*, Gk. *kúklos*
**dom-* 'house': Ved. *dámas*, Gk. *dómos*, Lat. *domus*, OCS *domŭ*
**dhu̯er-* 'DOOR': Av. *duuar-* 'gate', Gk. *thur-*, Lat. *forēs*, OCS *dvĭri*
**u̯ebh-* 'WEAVE': Ved. *ubhnā́ti* 'ties together', Gk. *huphaínō* 'I weave', Toch. B *wāp-*
**s(i̯)uH-* 'SEW': Ved. *syūtá-* 'sewn', Lat. *suō* 'I sew', Lith. *siúti* 'to sew'
**u̯es-* 'clothe, WEAR clothes': Hitt. *waššezzi* '(he) clothes', Ved. *váste* 'gets dressed', Gk. *héstai* 'gets dressed', Lat. *uestis* 'clothing'

17 Tocharian

Introduction

17.1. Tocharian, like Hittite, did not come to light until the twentieth century. For about twenty years up until the First World War, the French, Germans, and British undertook numerous archaeological expeditions to Chinese Turkestan (now the Xinjiang Uygur Autonomous Region in western China) and unearthed documents in four previously unknown languages. Two of these turned out to be Middle Iranian (Khotanese and Tumshuqese, see §§11.37 and 46), while the others were the two Tocharian languages. They were recognized as Indo-European already in 1907; their decipherment was greatly aided by the fact that most of the texts were translations (some bilingual) of familiar Buddhist works that had been widely disseminated in Central Asia. The Tocharian documents all date to between the sixth and eighth centuries AD.

17.2. From the lowland region known as the Tarim Basin in eastern Turkestan, in the area around the oases called Qārāšahr (Karashahr) and Turfan, comes **Tocharian A**, also called East Tocharian, Turfanian, or Agnean (after Agni, the Sanskrit name of Qārāšahr). From that area and farther southwest around Kučā (Kucha) comes **Tocharian B**, also called West Tocharian or Kuchean. Since Tocharian A is only known from areas where documents in Tocharian B have also been found, it has been suggested that Tocharian A was in fact an already extinct liturgical or poetic language that was kept alive by tradition, and that Tocharian B was the living administrative language. (Of the minority of texts that are not Buddhist translations – including monastic letters, caravan passes, business letters, and graffiti – almost all are in Tocharian B.) One set of Tocharian B texts, called the MQ texts (after the caves of Ming-öi Qïzïl west of Kučā, where they were found), are written in a variant dialect and may preserve some archaic distinctions in the vowel system; these have still not been adequately studied. A passage from an MQ text is given as one of the text selections at the end of this chapter.

17.3. Who the Tocharians were is still enshrouded in mystery and considerable debate. They left behind no texts about themselves, and it is unclear which of the ethnonyms preserved in contemporary Classical and Central Asian sources refers to them. The designation *Tocharian* is based on the theory, now no longer accepted, that the Tocharian languages were spoken by a Central Asian people called the *Tókharoi* in Greek sources.

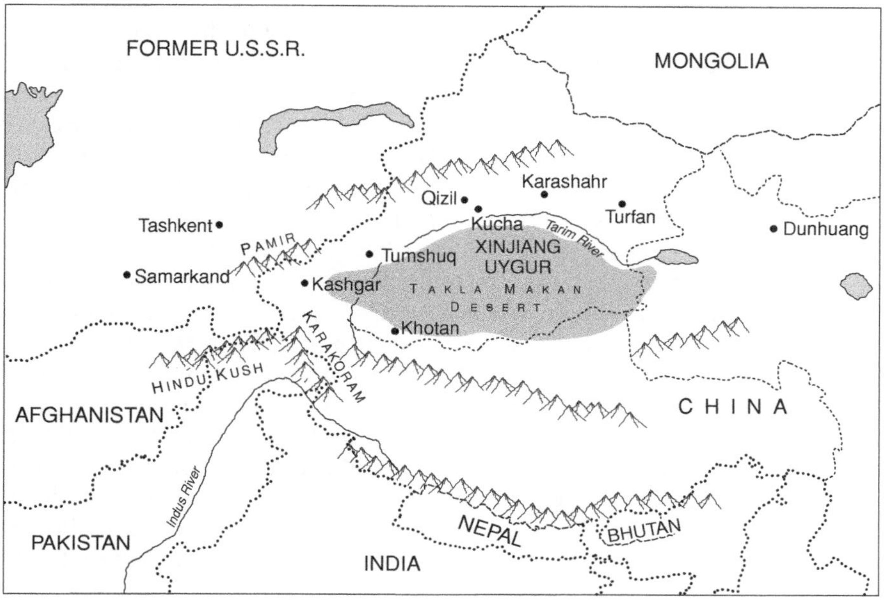

Map 17.1 The Tarim Basin

We also do not know how and when they, as Indo-Europeans from far to the west, got to such a distant corner of the world: of all the ancient IE languages, Tocharian was spoken farthest to the east. Which of the other branches of IE Tocharian is most closely related to is also an unsolved problem; a set of rather archaic features of its verbal morphology have led some researchers to claim that it, like Anatolian, split off from the rest of the family rather early. An earlier view, now abandoned, connected Tocharian with the supposed Italo-Celtic subgroup of IE (§13.5).

17.4. The vocabulary of our Tocharian texts, since they are mostly Buddhist, has been influenced by Sanskrit and Iranian, from which many religious terms were borrowed. (One of them, interestingly, may have made its way into English as the word *shaman*, if ultimately from Tocharian B *ṣamāne* 'monk', from Sanskrit *śramaṇas*.) Some structural features, such as the large number of cases in the noun (§17.23 below) and the limited stop inventory (only voiceless stops), are not typical of IE languages but are found in Uralic, Turkic, and Mongolian languages of western and central Asia. (Uralic is the language family to which Finnish and Hungarian belong.) It has been suggested that the Tocharians picked these features up from contact with those languages after they migrated eastward.

17.5. Adding to the various mysteries surrounding the Tocharians is the existence of Caucasoid populations in western China from an early date. Some old, in part controversial, Chinese sources mention tall, blonde- or red-haired, blue-eyed men, and the Roman author Pliny the Elder preserves a report by an emissary from northwest China of a people answering to the same description. Certain cave paintings in the region from later times depict warriors with red hair and other non-Asian features. These indirect sources were substantiated by the discovery of extremely well-preserved mummies in the Takla Makan Desert having Caucasoid features such as tall stature and red, blonde, or brown hair. The mummies date variously from about 1800 BC to as recent as 200 AD. Some were found with tapestries woven in plaids that are similar in weaving style and pattern to tartans from the Hallstatt culture of central Europe, which was ancestral to the Celts (§14.2). Physical and genetic evidence gathered from the mummies has revealed affinities with populations in western Eurasia, perhaps as far west as the Mediterranean. Understandably, many scholars have concluded that the mummies came from a population ancestral to or otherwise related to the Tocharians (with some claiming that the more recent mummies were instead Iranian-speaking). But there is as yet no conclusive evidence to support these views; equating physical remains or racial features with language in the absence of accompanying linguistic remains is notoriously perilous.

Most of the Tocharian that survives is found on fragments of manuscript leaves that were left in Buddhist temples and shrines in the desert as votive offerings. Once left in the shrines, the leaves were picked up by the wind; some landed in the desert sands, where they were buried and eventually dug up by archaeologists. Because of this manner of preservation, we usually have only one leaf from any given Tocharian manuscript.

17.6. With the exception of a few fragments of Tocharian B that are written in Manichean script, Tocharian was written in a modified version of the north Indian Brāhmī alphabet (see §10.57). The same version was used to write the Middle Iranian language Tumshuqese (§11.46). Among the modifications made to the script is the so-called *Fremdvokal* or 'foreign vowel', transliterated as *ä* (discussed in §17.14 below).

From PIE to Tocharian

In the ensuing discussion, forms in Tocharian A and Tocharian B will be labeled simply A and B, and AB will be used to denote a form identical in both languages.

Phonology

Consonants

17.7. Stops. As mentioned above, Tocharian has an unusual stop consonant inventory by IE standards: there were no voiced stops – only *p*, *t*, and *k*. All three manners of stop articulation in PIE – voiceless, voiced, and voiced aspirated – therefore merged into voiceless. This is most clearly seen with the labials, which all became *p*: PIE **prek̂-* 'ask' > A *prak-*, B *prek-* 'ask' (cp. Lat. *precor* 'I ask, entreat'); PIE **dhub-ro-* 'deep' > A *tpär*, B *tapre* 'high' (cp. Eng. *deep* from full-grade **dheub-*; for the semantics, cp. Lat. *altus* 'high, deep'); PIE **bhrātēr* 'brother' > A *pracar*, B *procer* (cp. Eng. *brother*).

17.8. With the dentals, things are not quite as simple. Both **t* and **dh* became *t*, but **d* became *ts*: compare PIE **k̂m̥tom* 'hundred' > A **känt**, B **kante**; PIE **$h_1$rudhro-* 'red' > A *rtär*, B *ratre* 'red'; but PIE **dak̂-* 'bite' > B *tsāk-* 'bite'. The fate of **d* is complicated in other ways as well, chiefly by its propensity to disappear under conditions that are still obscure (e.g. **doru* 'wood' > AB *or* 'wood'; **su̯eh_2d-ro-* 'sweet' > A *swār*, B *swāre* 'sweet').

17.9. This stop-consonant merger is most dramatic in the velars, where all nine of the PIE velar stops fell together as **k**. Compare the following nine examples of **k**, each from a different PIE velar:

**k̂*	A **känt**, B **kante** 'hundred' < **k̂m̥tom* (cp. Ved. *śatám* 'hundred')
**k*	AB **luk-** 'shine' < **leuk-* (cp. Lat. *lūx*, *lūc-* 'light')
**k^w*	A **ak**, B **ek** 'eye' < **h_3ek^w-* (cp. Gk. *óp-somai* 'I will see')
**ĝ*	AB **āk-** 'lead' < **h_2eĝ-* (cp. Lat. *agō* 'I lead')
**g*	A **ok-**, B **auk-** 'increase' < **$h_2$eug-* (cp. Lat. *augeō* 'I increase')
**g^w*	A **ko**, B **ke**$_u$ 'cow' < **g^wou-* (cp. Eng. *cow*)
**ĝh*	AB **ku-** 'pour' < **ĝheu-* (cp. Gk. *khé(w)ō* 'I pour')
**gh*	A **lake**, B **leki** 'bed' < **legh-* (cp. Gk. *lékhos* 'bed', German *liegen* 'lie')
**g^wh*	AB **tsäk-** 'burn' < **dheg^{w}h-* (cp. Ved. *dahanti* 'they burn')

The labiovelars may have still been labiovelars in Proto-Tocharian. Some clear examples where a labial element was still present, or rounded a following vowel, include A **kus**, B **k**$_u$**se** 'who?' < **$k^w$is*, and A **kukäl**, B **kokale** 'chariot' < **k^wek^{w}lo-* 'wheel' (cp. Gk. *kúklos* 'wheel'). The symbol *k*$_u$ in *k*$_u$*se* reflects a peculiarity of the Tocharian writing system in spelling this word: the vowel *u* was written with a subscript sign, as opposed to the other vowels which were written superscript. Tocharian B sometimes even has the sequence *kw* for a labiovelar or combination of velar plus **u̯*, as in *yakwe* 'horse' (A *yuk*) < **ek̂u̯os*.

17.10. Palatalization. The remaining obstruents found in the Tocharian sound inventory are the result of palatalization before **e* or **i* in the prehistoric period; these two vowels later changed in various ways (see below), with the result that a palatalized consonant is often our only evidence of the erstwhile presence of an **e*, **i*, or the glide **i̯*. The palatalization rules are many and complex, and will not be treated here in their entirety. The basic outlines are that *t* usually became the affricate *c* (phonetically [č]) before *e* or *i*, as in B *pācer* 'father', and *k* became the sibilant *ś*, a *sh*-like sound, as in A *śpāl* 'head' (< **ghebh-(e)l-*, cp. Gk. *kephalḗ*). There were additional changes in consonant clusters; for example, the palatalization of **st* was *śś* or *śc*, as in A *kaśśi*, B *keścye* 'hungry', the derived adjective from A *kaṣt*, B *kest* 'hunger'. Certain resonants were palatalized (see the next section below), and the glide **u̯* could be palatalized to *y* in Tocharian B, as in *yente* 'wind' < **h_2u̯e$h_1$nto-* (cp. Eng. *wind*).

17.11. Resonants. The resonants remained intact: A *läc* 'he went out' < **$h_1$ludh-et*; B *mācer* 'mother' < **mātēr*; A *want* 'wind' < **h_2u̯e$h_1$nto-*. The resonant **r* was the only consonant that was preserved word-finally. The liquid *l* and the nasal *n* could be palatalized to *ly* and *ñ*, as in A ***klyu*** 'fame' < **k̑leu-* and AB ***ñu*** 'nine' < ****neu̯n̥***.

A word on the Tocharian nasals is in order here. Besides *m*, *n*, and *ñ*, the language had a velar nasal *ṅ* (pronounced [ŋ] as in *sing*) and a letter transliterated as *ṃ* which is used to write nasals in word-final position. In the Brāhmī script this normally indicates nasalization of the preceding vowel, but in Tocharian it seems to have stood for *n*. A final **-m* became *-n* (as also in Greek and most of Celtic), which we know from the oblique stem of the word for 'earth', A *tkan-*, B *ken-* (nominative A *tkaṃ*, B *keṃ*), ultimately from PIE **dh(e)ĝhōm* (cp. §6.30). (Note incidentally that A *tkaṃ*, like its cognate Hitt. *tēkan*, preserves the original dental–velar order of the "thorn" cluster; recall §3.25.)

The **syllabic resonants** developed a prothetic **ä* in Proto-Tocharian (see §17.14 on this vowel): PIE **k̑m̥tom* 'hundred' > A *känt*, B *kante*; **dn̥ĝhu-* 'tongue' > A *käntu*, B *kantwo* (with reversal of the order of the two stops); **bhr̥ĝh-ro-* 'high' > A *pärkär*. As in Germanic, **R̥HC* (i.e., containing "long" syllabic resonants) sequences normally lost the laryngeal and developed the same as ordinary **R̥C* sequences, as in B *pällent* 'full' (of the moon) < **pl̥h$_1$no-u̯ent-* and B *pärweṣṣe* 'first' < **pr̥h$_3$u̯o-*.

17.12. Laryngeals. The laryngeals, when vocalized between consonants, became **a* in Proto-Tocharian, as in several other branches (Italic, Celtic, Germanic, Armenian); this then became *ā* in both A and B (see §17.17 below). Thus PIE **ph$_2$tēr* 'father' became A *pācar*, B *pācer*. Interestingly, at least some of the time the sequence **ih$_2$* was syllabified as **i̯h̥$_2$* and became **ya*, just as in Greek. Thus the feminine accusative singular **-ih$_2$-m* became **-yam* and ultimately *-ā* (preceded by a palatalized consonant) in the feminine oblique ending *-āṃ* (with an added particle *-ṃ*), as in A *pontsā-ṃ* 'all' < **pānt-i̯h$_2$m(-)* (cp. Gk. *pánt-* 'all'). The same was true sometimes of **uh$_2$* or **uh$_3$*, as in B *lwāsa* 'animals' from **luHs-* 'louse'. At other times, however, **iH* and **uH* became **ī* and **ū*, whose fates are treated below in §17.18.

Vowels

17.13. The development of the PIE vowels in Tocharian is very complicated, and unusual from the point of view of the other older IE languages in many respects. Not all of the details are agreed upon, but it is clear that the two Tocharian languages each went their own way in their development of the vowel system after the Common Tocharian period.

17.14. The vowel inventory. Both Tocharian languages possessed the two high vowels *i* and *u*, the mid vowels *e* and *o*, and three vowels transliterated as *a*, *ā*, and *ä*. The last of these, called the *Fremdvokal* or 'foreign vowel', is of disputed phonetic value. In the Sanskrit Devanāgarī script, derived from the same source as the Tocharian script, the vowel *a* represents schwa [ə], while *ā* represents a true long [aː], not only longer but also lower than a schwa. The Tocharian vowel *ä* is written in the Brāhmī script as an ordinary *a* with two dots over it; among other things, it is the usual epenthetic vowel in Tocharian, used for breaking up consonant clusters. The cross-linguistically most common epenthetic vowel is schwa, but on the assumption that the ordinary *a* represents schwa as just stated, the Fremdvokal must represent a different sound. It has been proposed that it represents the mid high vowel [ɨ] (found in some pronunciations of the second vowel of English *singin'* in relaxed speech).

17.15. Vowel mergers. Proto-Tocharian underwent three important mergers of the inherited vowel inventory. PIE **e*, **i*, and **u* all fell together as **ä* in Proto-Tocharian (but only after **e* and **i* had palatalized preceding consonants as per §17.10 above). This Proto-Tocharian **ä* became variously *a*, *ä*, or *ā*, depending on conditioning factors we need not go into: A *śäṃ* and B *śana* 'wife' < **g^{w}en-* 'woman' (with palatalization of the old **k* to *ś*); A *wäs*, B *wase* 'poison' < **u̯is-*; A *rtär* (< earlier **rätär*) and B *ratre* 'red' < **h$_1$rudhro-*. It could also be rounded to *u* when next to an old labiovelar, as in A *kumseñc* 'they come', with *kum-* < **k^{w}äm-* < PIE **g^{w}m̥-*.

17.16. The second vowel merger was that of PIE **o* and **ē*, which became a mid front vowel notated variously as **e* or **æ* in Proto-Tocharian; this developed to *a* in A and *e* in B. Thus **ok^w-* (earlier **h$_3$ek^w-*) became A *ak* and B *ek* 'eye', and **ph$_2$tēr* 'father' became A *pācar* and B *pācer*. Interestingly, *o* remained *o* if the following syllable contained *u*, as in AB *or* 'wood', apparently from **doru* with loss of the **d* (§17.8).

17.17. The third vowel merger is that of PIE **a* and **ō*, which, together with the vocalized laryngeals (§17.12 above), became Proto-Tocharian **a*. This then became *ā* in both A and B: AB *āk-* 'lead' (< **aĝ-* < **h$_2$eĝ-*); AB *knā-* 'know' (< **ĝnō-* < **ĝneh$_3$-*, cp. Eng. *know*). This development was not shared by PIE **ā*, which became a vowel symbolized variously as **o* or **å* in Proto-Tocharian; this turned into *a* in A and *o* in B, as in the word for 'brother' (**bhrātēr*), A *pracar* and B *procer*.

17.18. After all of these somewhat confusing developments, it will be a relief to know that PIE **ī* and **ū* (from **iH* and **uH*) simply became *i* and *u* in both languages: A *wiki* and B *ikäṃ* 'twenty' < **u̯īk̑m̥tī* (cp. Lat. *uīgintī*), B *suwo* 'pig' < **sū-* (cp. Lat. *sūs*, Eng. *sow*).

17.19. Diphthongs. The diphthongs beginning with *a* and *o* are reasonably well preserved in Tocharian B, but became monophthongs in A: B *ai-*, A *e-* 'give, take' < **ai-* < **h$_2$ei-* (cp. Gk. *aí-numai* 'I take'); B *auk-* and A *ok-* 'increase' < **aug-* (earlier **h$_2$eug-*); and B *aise* 'force' < **oiso-*.

17.20. Syncope. The Fremdvokal *ä* disappeared in unstressed open syllables in B, and in essentially any open syllable in A. This created a number of odd word-initial consonant clusters, as in B *yṣiye*, A *wṣe* 'night', AB *lkātsi* 'to see', B *wtentse* 'for a second time', A *pkänt* 'without'.

Final syllables

17.21. Final syllables were generally eliminated in Tocharian A but preserved in Tocharian B. Their elimination in A created some awkward consonant clusters at the ends of words which were then broken up by the insertion of an *ä*, as in the word for 'red', *rtär*, where originally there was no vowel between the *t* and the *r* (cp. B *ratre*; PIE **h$_1$rudhro-*).

Stress

17.22. In Tocharian B, pairs such as B *kante* 'hundred' ~ pl. *käntenma*, and *āke* 'end' ~ pl. *akenta*, where there are alternations between *a* and *ä* and between *ā* and *a*, suggest that there was a shift of the stress from the first to the second syllable in words of more than two syllables (thus *kánte* ~ *känténma*, *ā́ke* ~ *akénta*). There are similar alternations in B between *a* and zero, stemming from an original stressed **ä* and unstressed **ä* (cp. §17.20 above), as in *camel* 'birth', pl. *cmela*, and *yapoy* 'land', pl. *ypauna*.

Morphology

Nouns

17.23. Cases. Tocharian noun inflection differs significantly from that of almost all the other IE languages by actually having *more* cases than what we reconstruct for PIE. Interestingly, this did not come about by expanding the original PIE set; rather, Tocharian first drastically reduced the inherited case inventory and only later developed new case-endings of its own design. The PIE dative, instrumental, ablative, and locative were all lost; only four of the original cases survived into Proto-Tocharian, the nominative, vocative, genitive, and accusative. The accusative is continued as a case called the oblique (although not all obliques come from old accusatives), and the vocative only lives on in Tocharian B. These are often called the *primary cases*.

To express the grammatical relationships that had been expressed by the lost cases, Proto-Tocharian made use of postpositions (much as English uses prepositions for the same purpose). Over time, many of these were reanalyzed as case-endings, and at the end of the day the Tocharian languages had developed seven new cases, the so-called *secondary cases*. Although the case systems are nearly identical in the two languages and came about in the same way, most of the actual endings are not common to both languages – evidently, each language reanalyzed different postpositions. One, perhaps two, are cognate: the new locative and perhaps the perlative (expressing 'by' or 'through' someone's agency). Three others, a comitative (expressing accompaniment), allative (place towards which), and a new ablative, are found in both languages but with different endings. In addition, Tocharian A has a new instrumental case, and Tocharian B has a causal, whose function is essentially the same as the instrumental in A. The new case-endings are mostly added to the oblique, presumably once the case governed by the erstwhile postpositions. If this case system evolved under the influence of Uralic or Turkic languages, as has been suggested (see §17.4 above), the influence must have come fairly late, given that each Tocharian language developed most of the new system on its own and the endings do not usually show the expected vowel-weakenings. But the use of postpositions closely associated with their nouns was already a Common Tocharian feature.

To give an idea of the case system, paradigms of the word for 'father' in B and 'woman' in A follow. Not all the case-forms below are actually attested for these words. The vocative in B for this declension is the same as the nominative.

	B		A	
	sing.	pl.	sing.	pl.
Nom.	*pācer*	*pācera*	*k*$^{\backprime}_{u}$*li*	*k*$^{\backprime}_{u}$*lewāñ*
Obl.	*pātär*	*pācera*	*k*$^{\backprime}_{u}$*le*	*k*$^{\backprime}_{u}$*lewās*
Gen.	*pātri*	*paceraṃts*	*k*$^{\backprime}_{u}$*leyis*	*k*$^{\backprime}_{u}$*lewāśśi*
Instr.	——	——	*k*$^{\backprime}_{u}$*leyo*	*k*$^{\backprime}_{u}$*lewāsyo*
Perl.	*pātärsa*	*pacerasa*	*k*$^{\backprime}_{u}$*leyā*	*k*$^{\backprime}_{u}$*lewāsā*
Com.	*pātärmpa*	*pācerampa*	*k*$^{\backprime}_{u}$*leyaśśäl*	*k*$^{\backprime}_{u}$*lewāsaśśäl*
All.	*pātärś(c)*	*pāceraś(c)*	*k*$^{\backprime}_{u}$*leyac*	*k*$^{\backprime}_{u}$*lewāsac*
Abl.	*pātärmeṃ*	*pācerameṃ*	*k*$^{\backprime}_{u}$*leyäṣ*	*k*$^{\backprime}_{u}$*lewāsäṣ*
Loc.	*pātärne*	*pācerane*	*k*$^{\backprime}_{u}$*leyaṃ*	*k*$^{\backprime}_{u}$*lewāsaṃ*
Caus.	*pātärñ*	*pāceräñ*	——	——

17.24. "Gruppenflexion." Another feature of Tocharian that is unusual from the point of view of the rest of Indo-European is the phenomenon whereby phrases in a secondary case often exhibit a secondary case-ending on the last word only; the other words are in the oblique. This is known by its German name, *Gruppenflexion* or 'group inflection'. Thus B *kektseñ* (obl.) *reki* (obl.) *palskosa* (perlative) 'with body, word, (and) thought' ('thought' is perlative); A *yātälwātses* (obl. pl.) *tsopats-tampes* (obl. pl.) *nermitṣinäs* (obl. pl.) *wrassaśśäl* (comitative pl.) 'with the powerful, mighty, artificial beings' ('beings' is comitative).

17.25. Number. Tocharian has also innovated by adding to the inherited singular, dual, and plural numbers a paral, a kind of dual used only for naturally occurring pairs such as hands, eyes, etc., such as B *eśane*, A *aśäṃ* 'both eyes'. It was formed by suffixing a particle **-nō* to the inherited dual. Tocharian B also has a plurative in *-aiwenta* (the plural of the old word for 'one', **oi-u̯o-*), to denote 'one at a time, individually'.

17.26. Gender. The three-gender distinction of PIE is kept intact in Tocharian, although the neuter is a living category only in the pronouns. In nouns, the descendant of the PIE neuter has masculine endings in the singular and feminine endings in the plural. This also happened independently in Italian and Romanian; compare also the similar development in Albanian (§19.21).

Tocharian A has the very unusual feature of distinguishing gender in the singular of the first personal pronoun 'I': masculine nominative *näṣ*, feminine *ñuk*. It has been plausibly suggested that the feminine form ultimately descends from the PIE nominative singular **eĝoh*$_2$, while the masculine continues the accusative **me*.

Verbs

17.27. The Tocharian verbal system is built around a fundamental opposition between the ordinary verb and its associated causative, which in the present tense is usually formed with a suffix going back to PIE **-sk̂e/o-* (§5.34), a suffix which does not have causative value in the rest of IE except for a few verbs in Greek. Not all verbs have both a base form and a causative form. The causative does not always appear to have a different meaning from the base, as in B *taläṣṣäṃ* 'he raises', the "causative" of the synonymous verb *tallaṃ* 'he raises'. Sometimes the base verb is intransitive while the causative is transitive, e.g. B *tsälpetär* 'is redeemed', causative *tsälpäṣṣäṃ* 'redeems'. In a third group of verbs, the causative has real causative value: B *kärsanaṃ* 'he knows', causative *śarsäṣṣäṃ* 'he causes to know, informs'.

17.28. Verb stems. A Tocharian verb has three stems: present, preterite, and subjunctive. The present stem is used to form the present tense, the imperfect, and the present participle. In B, the imperfect is characterized by the stem-vowel *-i-* (e.g. *klyauṣim* 'I heard', imperfect of *klyauṣäṃ* 'he hears'), which comes from PIE **-ih₁-*, the zero-grade of the optative morpheme. For the semantic development, compare Eng. *he would go* in the meaning "he used to go, was going." In A, the imperfect stem vowel is *-ā-*, whose origin is uncertain.

The Tocharian present stems are divided into twelve classes, which together continue most of the PIE types of present stems, including root athematic presents (Class I, e.g. A *swiñc* 'they rain' [said of flowers] < **suh₂-énti*), nasal-infix presents in B (Class VII, e.g. *piṅkeṃ* 'they paint' < **pi-n-g-*, cp. Lat. *pingunt* 'they paint'; also Class VI, formed with the suffix *-nā-* that comes originally from **-n-H-*, that is, a nasal infix to a laryngeal-final root; e.g. AB *musnātär* 'lifts up', cp. Ved. *muṣṇā́ti* 'steals' and §10.42), thematic verbs (Class II, e.g. B *akem* 'we lead' < **h₂eĝ-o-mes*, cp. Lat. *agimus* 'we drive, lead'), denominative verbs (Class XII, e.g. B *lareññentär* 'they love' < Proto-Toch. **lāren-yä-*, cp. B *lareñ* (pl.) 'dear'), and **-sk̂e/o*-verbs (most clearly Class IX in B, e.g. *aiskau* 'I give'). Tocharian also has numerous examples of presents in **-se/o-*, which is not a common stem-formant elsewhere in IE; these form Class VIII and are especially well represented in A (e.g. *nämseñc* 'they bow down to, revere', cp. Ved. *námati* 'bows, does reverence').

Of great interest for the history of PIE verbal morphology are Classes III and IV, which contain mostly middle verbs having **-o-* as the stem vowel throughout, such as B *lipetär* 'is left over' (Class III) < **lip-o-tor* and B *osotär* 'dries' (Class IV) < **as-o-*. The stem-vowel **-o-* is originally the archaic 3rd sing. middle ending **-o* (see §5.16), which later got generalized throughout the paradigm as the thematic vowel and to which new middle endings were added.

17.29. The subjunctive stem is used to form the subjunctive and optative. The subjunctive doubles as a future tense (an inherited feature; see §5.56), while the optative is used in contrary-to-fact statements. The fact that the subjunctive stem is different from the present stem is an interesting feature shared with the *ā*-subjunctive of Italic and Celtic (though not in all details); compare Lat. present indicative *atting-it* 'touches', (archaic) subjunctive *attig-at* '(that) he touch', or OIr. present indicative *-cren* 'buys', subjunctive *-cria*. A Tocharian example is B present *kärnāstär* 'buys' (< **kʷrinh₂-sk̂-*), subjunctive *kärnātär* 'he will buy' (< **kʷrinh₂-*).

17.30. From the preterite stem are formed the preterite tense and a preterite participle. The Tocharian preterite mostly continues the PIE aorist, but a few preterite participles are from perfects.

17.31. Personal endings. The personal endings are largely the familiar ones inherited from PIE, though some of the details are not fully clear. The active and middle endings of the present tense can be illustrated from both languages with the following paradigms of B *klyausau* and A *klyosam* 'I hear':

		B	A
Active	sg. 1	*klyausau*	*klyosam*
	2	*klyauṣt(o)*	*klyoṣt*
	3	*klyauṣäṃ*	*klyoṣäṣ* (?)
	pl. 1	*klyausem(o)*	*klyosamäs*
	2	*klyauścer*	[*klyosac*]
	3	*klyauseṃ*	*klyoseñc*
Middle	sg. 1	*klyausemar*	*klyosmār*
	2	*klyauṣtar*	*klyoṣtār*
	3	*klyauṣtär*	*klyoṣtär*
	pl. 1	*klyausemt(t)är*	*klyosamtär*
	2	*klyauṣtär*	——
	3	*klyausentär*	*klyosantär*

The PIE personal endings shine through clearly in some of the forms, though by no means all. The 1st sing. active B *-au* is from **-o-mi*, that is, the thematic vowel plus the primary 1st singular ending (the **-m-* was weakened regularly to *-w-*). The *t* of the 2nd sing. active *-ṣt*(*o*) might come ultimately from the 2nd sing. pronoun **tu* added on to the ending. Both 3rd singular active endings are problematic. As for the middle voice, note that Tocharian has generalized **-r* as the middle marker, just like Italic and Celtic. The difference between 3rd pl. active A *-ñc* and B *-ṃ* is thought by some to reflect a difference between PIE primary **-nti* and secondary **-nt*, but this need not be so (there is otherwise no pattern of the A forms coming from primary verbal endings and the B forms coming from secondary endings; the 1st sing. *-au* in B is from primary **-o-mi*, for instance).

Tocharian A text sample

17.32. The poetic verses beginning the Buddhist tale known as the Puṇyavantajātaka. Each line contains 14 syllables divisible into two half-lines of seven syllables each. The last stanza consists of only one line.

1 kāsu ñom-klyu tsraṣiśśi śäk kälymentwaṃ sätkatär.
yärk ynāñmune nam poto tsraṣṣuneyā p̀ukäṣ kälpnāl;
yuknāl ymāräk yäsluñcäs, kälpnāl ymāräk yātlune.
2 tsraṣiśśi māk niṣpalntu, tsraṣiśśi māk śkaṃ ṣñaṣṣeñ.
nämseñc yäsluṣ tsraṣisac, kumseñc yärkant tsraṣisac.
tsraṣiñ waste wrasaśśi, tsraṣiśśi mā praski naṣ.
3 tämyo kāsu tsraṣṣune p̀ukaṃ pruccamo ñi pälskaṃ.

1 Good fame of the strong spreads out in ten directions.
(One) must achieve honor, worth, reverence, (and) flattery from everyone through strength.
(One) must quickly conquer enemies; (one) must quickly gain ability.

2 The strong have many riches, the strong also have many relatives.
Enemies bow down to the strong, honors come to the strong.
The strong (are) the protection of creatures; the strong have no fear.
3 Thus strength (is) good, best of all in my opinion.

17.32a. Notes. 1. kāsu: 'good'. **ñom-klyu:** 'fame', literally 'name-fame'. The corresponding word for 'name' in B is *ñem*; the two forms together must go back to a PIE **h_1nē$h_3$mn̥* with lengthened-grade. Toch. A *klyu* and B *kälywe* continue PIE **ḱleu̯os*, cp. Gk. *klé(w)os* 'fame'. For the phrase *ñom-klyu* compare Gk. *onomá-klutos* 'famous for his name'; the collocation of these two roots goes back to PIE (§2.47). **tsraṣiśśi:** 'of the strong', genit. pl. of *tsraṣi*. The source of the genit. pl. ending *-śśi* is unknown. **śäk:** 'ten', B *śak*, from PIE **deḱm̥*, with palatalization of initial dental and loss of final nasal. **kälymentwaṃ:** 'directions', loc. pl. of *kälyme*. The ten directions are the four cardinal directions, the four directions in between, plus up and down. **sätkatär:** 'spreads out', 3rd sing. Class III middle present; B *sätketär*, with *-e-* from PIE **-o-* (see §17.28). There is no convincing etymology, but the verb belongs to a group whose base ends in *-tk-* that presumably continues **ske/o*-verbs added to a root-final dental. **yärk:** 'honor', B *yarke*; PIE **erk^{w}os*, also in Ved. *árcati* 'praises' and *ŕ̥k* 'song of praise' (in *R̥g-veda*, the Rig Veda). **ynāñmune:** 'worth', a noun derived from the adjective *ynāñm* 'worth(y)'. **nam:** 'reverence', perhaps borrowed from Skt. *namas* or perhaps a native inheritance. **poto:** 'flattery'; PIE root **bheudh-* 'be aware', with derivatives meaning 'make aware, give notice'. Compare the Avestan phrase *nəmō baoδaiieiti* 'bids reverence', with the same two roots collocated as in *nam poto*. **tsraṣṣuneyā:** 'with strength', perlative of *tsraṣṣune*. **p$_u$käṣ:** 'from everyone', abl. of *puk* 'every, all'. **kälpnāl:** 'must achieve', gerundive, expressing necessity. The subject is unexpressed. **yuknāl:** 'must conquer', gerundive. **ymāräk:** 'quickly'. **yäsluñcäs:** 'enemies', oblique pl. of *yäslu*; the nomin. pl. *yäsluṣ* is in the next stanza. **yātlune:** 'ability', abstract verbal noun from *yāt-* 'be capable', cognate with Ved. *yátate* 'is in the right place'.

2. māk: 'much, many'. **niṣpalntu:** 'riches', pl. of *niṣpal* 'wealth'. **śkaṃ:** 'also, and', a postpositive (enclitic) conjunction. **ṣñaṣṣeñ:** 'relatives', a derivative of *ṣñi* '(one's) own'. **nämseñc:** 'they bow down', 3rd pl. Class VIII present; see §17.28. **tsraṣisac:** 'to the strong', allative pl. **kumseñc:** 'they come', 3rd pl. Class X present; *kum-* continues PIE **g^{w}m̥-*, zero-grade of **g^{w}em-* 'come, go' (Lat. *uen-iō* 'I come', Eng. *come*); see §17.15. **yärkant:** 'honors', pl. of *yärk* above. **tsraṣiñ:** 'the strong', nomin. pl. The repetition of this adjective in this stanza in different case-forms is a stylistic figure of IE poetry known as polyptoton. Note that the first two occurrences begin the first two half-lines, the next two end the next two half-lines, and the final two begin the last two half-lines of the stanza. **waste:** 'protection'. **wrasaśśi:** 'people', genit. pl. of *wrasom*. The paradigm is irregular, with the nominative, oblique, and perlative sing. formed to the stem *wras(o)m-*, and the other cases to the stem *wras-*. **mā:** 'not'; PIE **mē*, which in the other daughter languages is usually the negative reserved for prohibitions, but in both Tocharian languages becomes the ordinary negative (A has another negative, *mar*, used with prohibitions). **praski:** 'fear', B *proskiye*; one of a class of nouns (another being A *wṣe*, B *yṣiye* 'night') whose suffix comes from PIE **-ōi̯*, very rare elsewhere in IE. The noun is ultimately cognate with Eng. *fright*. **naṣ:** 'there is', 3rd sing. Class II present of *nas-* 'be', PIE **nes-* 'return home, be at home'; *naṣ* appears to continue an unexplained *o*-grade **nos-ti*. (Compare perhaps the *o*-grade of Gk. *nóstos* 'homecoming', as discussed in §12.65a.)

3. tämyo: 'therefore, thus', derived ultimately from the PIE demonstrative stem **to-*. **p$_u$kaṃ pruccamo:** 'the best of all'; *p$_u$kaṃ* is locative of *puk*, and *pruccamo* means 'great, wonderful'. As in Hittite and various archaic usages elsewhere in IE, Tocharian did not overtly mark the comparative or superlative degree. **ñi:** 'of me', genit. of *näṣ* 'I'. **pälskaṃ:** 'opinion', locative of *pältsäk*.

Tocharian B text sample

17.33. From Text 18 in Wolfgang Krause and Werner Thomas's *Tocharisches Elementarbuch* (Heidelberg, 1960–4); one of the MQ texts (see §17.2). The sounds *a*, *ā*, and *ä* are not always distinguished from one another in this text.

snai preṅke takoy sa kenä yke postäṃ po wars-ite, eśnesa meṅkitse tākoy kacāp ompä pärkre śāyeñca, pyorye ṣäp tākoy cew warne somo lyautai läṅktsa mā klyeñca känte pikwala epiṅkte kaccap su no tälaṣṣi aśco, rämoytär rmer ka, cpi aśce lyautaiyne tā̂ᵤ sälkoytär kewcä: tusa amāskai lwasāmeṃ onolmeṃtsä yśamna cmetsi

Suppose that the earth were continually and entirely full of water without an island, and suppose there were a tortoise there living a long time, lacking eyes; suppose furthermore that on that water there were also a yoke with one hole, buoyant and not standing still; if in the course of 100 years this tortoise should now lift up his head, and indeed should quickly bend it, and if it should happen that his head were raised up high through that hole, then this (= the following) [would be] more difficult – for beings to be [re]born from animals among (= as) men.

17.33a. Notes (selective). **snai:** 'without', cp. Lat. *sine* 'without'. **preṅke:** 'island'. **takoy:** '(as though it) were', 3rd sing. optative of the verb 'be'; usually spelled *tākoy* (as below). The Tocharian paradigm for 'be' is mostly constructed from two roots, *nes-* (B *nas-*; PIE **nes-*) and *tā-* (PIE **steh₂-* 'stand'; compare Spanish *estar* 'be' from Lat. *stāre* 'to stand' for a similar semantic development). **kenä:** 'earth, land', PIE **dhĝhem-*. **yke postäṃ:** 'continually'. **po:** 'all'. **eśnesa meṇkitse:** 'without eyes'; *eśnesa* is the dual of *eś* 'eyes' (< PIE **h₃ekʷ-*, cp. Lat. *oc-ulus*) plus the paral ending *-ne* plus the case ending *-sa*. **kacāp:** 'tortoise', borrowed from Skt. *kacchapas*. **ompä:** 'there'. **pärkre:** 'for a long time'. **śāyeñca:** 'living', present participle, from PIE **gʷi̯eh₃u̯-ont-*; the verb is cognate with Gk. *zō̃* 'I live'. **pyorye:** 'yoke'. **cew warne:** 'in that water'; *cew* is the oblique of *su* 'this, that'. The sequence *ew* is found only in the MQ texts. **somo lyautai:** 'with one hole'; *lyautai* has been connected etymologically by some with Hitt. *luttāi* 'window'. **mā:** 'not', the negator in Tocharian; cp. Gk. *mḗ*, Arm. *mi*, Ved. *mā́*. **klyeñca:** 'standing still', present participle. **känte:** 'hundred', PIE **k̂m̥tom*; normal spelling in B is *kante*. **pikwala:** 'year'; A *p̂ᵤkäl*, B *pikul*. According to an attractive recent proposal by Joshua T. Katz, this word comes from a compound **(e)pi-kʷ(e)l-o-* '(the thing) that turns around', cp. Homeric Gk. *epi-tell-oménōn eniautō̃n* 'as the years go turning round'. The word for 'year' would therefore be another example of a transferred epithet like Lat. *terra* 'earth' from 'dry (land)' (§13.31). **tälaṣṣi:** 'raises', PIE **telh₂-*; cp. Lat. *toll-ere* 'to raise'. **rämoytär:** 'should bend', optative of the Tocharian root *räm-*. **rmer:** 'quickly'; also spelled *ramer* in B (A has *ymār*). It may be related to Gk. *é-dramon* 'I ran'. **cpi:** 'his', also spelled *cwi*. **sälkoytär:** 'should be raised'. **kewcä:** 'high'; the MQ spelling of B *kauc*, A *koc*. **amāskai:** '(more) difficult'; not morphologically a comparative (Armenian also uses the positive degree to express the comparative). **lwasāmeṃ:** 'from animals'; the 'animal' word is A *lu*, B *luwo*. It has been compared with the word for 'louse' in other IE languages, probably from PIE **luHs-*. **onolmeṃtsä:** 'for beings', from *onolme* 'a being', Proto-Toch. **ān-elme*, from **ān-* 'breathe' (PIE **h₂en-*, cp. Lat. *an-ima* 'breath') plus a suffix. **yśamna:** 'among men', from **en-* 'in' plus the root for 'life', cp. *śāyeñca* above. **cmetsi:** 'to be (re)born', Tocharian root *täm-*.

For Further Reading

The number of book-length historical and comparative treatments of Tocharian is not extensive. A good recent overview of the historical phonology and morphology is Pinault 1989. In English, there is Adams 1988, which is somewhat difficult to use; the same author has also recently come out with an etymological dictionary of Tocharian B (Adams 1999), which partly supplants the older general Tocharian etymological dictionary that makes up most of van Windekens 1976–82. (This work also has comparative grammatical discussions and extensive references to earlier literature; but his own ideas sometimes need to be treated with caution.) The standard reference grammar is still Krause and Thomas 1960–4, the second volume of which contains texts and a glossary. The Tocharian A texts have been edited and published in Sieg and Siegling 1921, and the Tocharian B texts in Sieg and Siegling 1949–53. The latter has been partially supplanted by Thomas 1983. A journal called *Tocharian and Indo-European Studies*, which appears irregularly, has featured many excellent articles by prominent contemporary Tocharologists. The most recent technical work on historical Tocharian phonology is Ringe 1996. A recent thorough discussion of the Takla Makan mummies is Mallory and Mair 2000.

For Review

Know the meaning or significance of the following:

Tarim Basin   MQ texts   Fremdvokal   Gruppenflexion

Exercises

1 Briefly explain the history or significance of the following Tocharian forms:

a A *tpär*, B *tapre*	**e** B *yakwe*	**i** B *lwāsa*
b B *tsāk-*	**f** B *yente*	**j** A *aśäṃ*, B *eśane*
c AB *or*	**g** A *klyu-*	**k** B *lipetär*
d A *kukäl*, B *kokale*	**h** A *tkaṃ*	

2 In §17.11, it was stated that Toch. A *tkaṃ*, B *keṃ* 'earth', along with Hitt. *tēkan*, preserve the original order dental–velar of the word-initial "thorn" cluster; this shows that the order was reversed in *khthṓn* 'earth' in Greek. A skeptic might say that it could have been the other way around: Greek might preserve the original order, and Tocharian and Hittite might have reversed it instead. In general terms, what evidence does the Greek verb *tíktō* 'I give birth' contribute to settling the argument, assuming that this is a thematic reduplicated verb from **tek-* 'give birth'?

3 **a** PIE **dhiĝh-*, zero-grade of **dheiĝh-* 'form with the hands, shape', became Toch. B ***tsik**-ale* 'should be made', and PIE **degʷh-* 'burn' became ***tsak**-ṣtär* 'it burns'. Contrast this with PIE **dheh₁-* becoming Toch. A ***ca**-sär* 'they put', and **h₁ludh-e-t* becoming Toch. B ***lac*** '(s)he went out', which show the ordinary development of palatalized **dh*. What must have happened to the **dh* in the two first examples?

b What sound change, known also from Sanskrit and Greek, might have happened to affect **dhiĝh-* and **dhegʷh-* in Tocharian?

4 The word for 'high', A *tpär*, B *tapre* (mentioned in §17.7), has a different suffix from that seen in its Lithuanian cognate *dubùs* 'deep'. Comment on this in light of §6.87.

5 Given the history of the secondary cases, how would you explain the genesis of "Gruppenflexion" (§17.24)?

6 Briefly explain the significance of Classes III and IV of Tocharian verbs.

PIE Vocabulary IX: Form and Size

**bherĝh-* 'high': Hitt. *parku-*, Ved. *bṛhánt-*, Arm. *barjr*, OHG *burg* 'fort'
**medhi̯o-* 'middle': Ved. *mádhya-*, Gk. *mésos*, Lat. *medius*, Eng. MID
**meĝ-* 'big, great': Hitt. *mekki*, Ved. *máhi*, Gk. *méga*, Lat. *magnus*, Eng. MUCH
**mreĝhu-* 'short': Av. *mərəzu-*, Gk. *brakhús*, Lat. *breuis*, Eng. MERRY
**gʷerh₂-* 'heavy': Ved. *gurú-*, Gk. *barús*, Lat. *grauis*
**albh-* 'white': Hitt. *alpaš* 'cloud', Lat. *albus*
**h₁reudh-* 'RED': Ved. *rudhirá-*, Gk. *eruthrós*, Lat. *ruber*, Toch. B *ratre*
**dens-* 'thick': Hitt. *daššu-* 'strong', Gk. *dasús*, Lat. *dēnsus*

18 Balto-Slavic

Introduction

18.1. Balto-Slavic contains two branches, Baltic and Slavic (or Slavonic). The notion of a single Balto-Slavic speech community has been controversial in some circles, in part because of political tensions. But all major Indo-Europeanists are agreed that Baltic and Slavic deserve to be grouped together, though some dispute remains about the exact degree and nature of their affinity. Prehistorically, as discussed in more detail below, the ancestors of the Balts and Slavs were located in eastern Europe, with the Balts probably to the northwest of the Slavs. They were thus located near the Germanic tribes, and in fact there are numerous interesting features shared by Balto-Slavic and Germanic: both branches have dative and instrumental plurals with an **-m-*formant rather than the **-bh-*formant seen elsewhere in IE (cp. §6.17); both form a demonstrative pronoun with the stem **ḱi-* (e.g. Lith. *šìs* 'this, he', Goth. *himma* 'this' [dat.]; §7.10); both have merged **a* and **o*; both continue **-VHV-* sequences as long vowels that were a mora longer than inherited long vowels; and both have a distinction between ordinary and "definite" adjectives, the latter formed with the addition of a suffix (though not the same one in the two branches). There are also three striking agreements in the numeral system not found elsewhere in older IE languages: the names for the decads consist of the unit plus a collective for 'ten' (e.g. OCS *trije desęti*, Goth. *þreis tigjus* 'thirty'); the words for 'thousand' are similar (OCS *tysęštĭ*, Lith. *tū́kstantis*, Goth. *þūsundi*); and the numerals eleven and twelve in Lithuanian and Germanic are expressed with phrases meaning 'one left (over)' and 'two left (over)' (Lith. *vienúolika*, *dvýlika*, Goth. *ainlif*, *twalif*). It is unclear which of these features are shared innovations, which are areal features of north or northeast Europe, and which might be chance resemblances.

Balto-Slavic shares the "ruki" rule (§18.6 below) with Indo-Iranian, a sound change that is a far from trivial innovation. Some specialists have felt that this – together with the fact that both branches are satem – points to an early period of common development; others maintain that it was a feature that spread by diffusion from Indo-Iranian during a period of prehistoric contact. Arguing for the latter is the fact that "ruki" is far more consistently found in Slavic than in Baltic, and there is better independent evidence for early contacts between Slavic and Indo-Iranian than between the latter and Baltic.

From PIE to Balto-Slavic

Phonology overview

18.2. Balto-Slavic is defined by at least three unique phonological features in Indo-European: the development of a distinction between rising and falling pitch accents; the change of the syllabic resonants typically to resonants preceded by _i_; and the change of *_VRHC_ to *_V̄RC_. Among the basic developments that it shares with one or more other branches, Balto-Slavic is characterized by a satem development of the velars; by the merger of aspirated and unaspirated voiced stops; by the "ruki" rule; and by the merger of *_a_ and *_o_.

Consonants

18.3. Merger of aspirated and unaspirated voiced stops. The attested Balto-Slavic languages have plain voiced stops reflecting both the PIE voiced stops and the voiced aspirates. Examples include OCS **_berǫ_** 'I gather, take' < PIE **_*bher-_** 'carry', Russ. **_gorod_** 'city' < PIE **_*ghor-dho-_** 'enclosure', and Lith. **_dubùs_** 'deep' < **_*dhub-u-_**. It had been assumed that the two series merged by the time of Common Balto-Slavic until the Indo-Europeanist Werner Winter proposed in the 1970s that the distinction had persisted for longer, at least between *_dh_ and *_d_. According to his original formulation, short *_e_ was lengthened before *_d_ but not *_dh_, as in Lith. _sė́sti_ 'to sit' < *_sed-ti_ (_ė_ writes a long _e_ in Lithuanian). However, the long vowels in many of the putative examples (including this one) could also be old lengthened grades, and **Winter's Law**, as it has been dubbed, remains controversial.

18.4. Velars. Balto-Slavic is a satem branch: the PIE plain velars *_k_ *_g_ *_gh_ and the labiovelars *k^w *g^w *g^wh all became the plain velars _k_ and _g_: PIE ***k^w_os_** 'who' > Lith. **_kàs_**; *_sneig_^{w}_h-o-_ 'snow' > Russ. **_sneg_**; ***g^w_erh_$_3$_-_** 'consume' > Lith. **_geriù_** 'I drink'. The palatal velars *_k̂_ and *_ĝ_ probably became the palatal stops *_ć_ and *_ȷ́_ in the first instance, as in Indo-Iranian (§10.5), and later the palatal sibilants *_ś_ and *_ź_; these subsequently became _š/ž_ in Baltic and _s/z_ in Slavic. Thus PIE ***_k̂r̥d-_** 'heart' became OCS **_srĭd-ĭce_** and Lith. **_širdìs_**; PIE ***_ĝhl̥-to-_** 'golden' became Polish **_złoty_** 'gold piece, unit of currency'; and ***_ĝhel-to-_** 'golden' became Lith. **_žel̃tas_**.

18.5. But quite a few words do not show the expected satem development. For example, alongside Lith. **_žel̃tas_** quoted above there is also **_gel̃tas_** 'yellow' from the same PIE preform. Similarly, PIE ***_h_$_2$_ek̂-men-_** 'stone' has _k_ in most of its Balto-Slavic descendants, such as OCS **_kamy_** and Lith. **_akmuõ_**; but some Lithuanian dialects have the expected satem outcome, **_ašmuõ_**. From the extended root ***_k̂leu-s-_** 'hear', Slavic has satem _s-_ (e.g. Russian **_slušat'_** 'to hear') but not Baltic (Lith. **_klausýti_** and Latv. **_klausīt_** 'to hear'). The reverse is the case with 'goose', PIE ***_ĝhans-_**: Slavic *_gǫsĭ_ (> e.g. Russ. **_gus'_**) but Lith. **_žąsìs_**.

Various explanations have been proposed for these facts. Some of the exceptions, such as the Slavic word for 'goose', may be borrowings from a neighboring centum language like Germanic. But this explanation is difficult to maintain for many of these words. A more probable explanation is that there were early dialectal differences within Balto-Slavic with regards to the outcomes of the palatal velars, and that these differences have persisted. This hypothesis, unfortunately, cannot yet be tested.

18.6. The "ruki" rule. Like Indo-Iranian (§10.10), Balto-Slavic changed PIE **s* when it followed the sounds **r*, **u*, **k*, or **i*. The outcomes are different in Slavic and Baltic, and the change was not as consistent in Baltic. See §§18.24 and 18.62 below for more details.

18.7. Resonants and glides. The resonants and glides (except **u̯*) remained intact: PIE ***medhu-*** 'mead, honey' > Lith. ***medùs*** 'honey'; PIE ***nok*^{w}*ts*** 'night' > OCS ***noči̮***; **ghor-dho-* 'enclosure' > Russ. *gorod* 'city'; **leik*^{w}- 'leave' > Lith. *liekù* 'I remain, let'; **i̯u-n-g-* 'yoke, join' > Lith. *jùngti* 'to join'. The labiovelar glide **u̯* became *v*, as in **u̯edh-* 'lead' > OCS ***vedǫ*** and Lith. ***vedù***, both 'I lead'.

18.8. The syllabic resonants **r̥ *l̥ *m̥ *n̥* typically became **ir *il *im *in*, but also sometimes **ur *ul *um *un* under unclear conditions. The normal outcome is preserved most clearly in Baltic, as in the following Lithuanian examples: *širdìs* 'heart' < PIE **k̑r̥d-*; ***vil̃kas*** 'wolf' < **u̯l̥k*^{w}*os*; ***šim̃tas*** 'hundred' < **k̑m̥tom*; and ***giñti*** 'to drive' < **g*^{w}*hn̥-tei* 'in smiting' (or the like). Note that the form *šim̃tas* importantly preserves the *m* before the following *t*; in all the other IE languages it became *n* by assimilation, as in Lat. *centum*, Eng. *hund(red)*, and Tocharian B *kante*.

18.9. Laryngeals. Balto-Slavic does not have any reflexes of the laryngeals per se, but it does have important indirect evidence for them in the outcomes of resonants followed by laryngeal. These sequences developed into syllables with intonational contours that differ from those of similar syllables that originally did not have a laryngeal. See below, §18.12.

Vowels

18.10. In Balto-Slavic, the lower back vowels **a* and **o* merged, though with different outcomes in the two subbranches: in Slavic, they merged to *o* (perhaps via an intermediate stage **a*), whereas in Baltic they merged to *a*. The long vowels **ā* and **ō* also merged in Slavic (to *a*), but were kept distinct in Baltic. For examples and further discussion see §§18.30 and 18.65.

18.11. Rise of acute intonation. As noted in §§3.20 and 18.1 Balto-Slavic shares with Germanic a distinction in final syllables between the inherited long vowels and newer long vowels that arose from contraction where there had been an intervening laryngeal (**VHV*). The latter were characterized in the first instance by an extra mora of length (notationally **ā̃*, **ē̃*, etc.). Over time, the trimoraic **ā̃*, **ē̃*, etc. became ordinary long vowels **ā*, **ē*, while the older inherited **ā*, **ē*, etc. developed a new phonetic feature, apparently a kind of glottal or laryngeal catch or checking of the vowel (as is still the case in the "broken tone" in modern Latvian and dialectal Lithuanian; compare also the Danish *stød*, a glottal catch or creakiness of the voice that developed in certain long syllables that was mentioned at §15.106). Vowels with this feature are called *acute*; the others are called *non-acute* or *circumflex*. Importantly, these prosodic features were independent of the location of the stress-accent or ictus; there could be multiple acute or non-acute vowels in one word.

18.12. Later, the contrast between acute and non-acute/circumflex was realized intonationally, such that acute syllables had rising pitch and circumflex had falling. The combination of this system and mobility of the stress is preserved in Lithuanian and two South Slavic languages, Serbo-Croatian and dialectal Slovenian. Latvian also preserves the pitches but has fixed stress on initial syllables. Some West Slavic languages have vowel-length contrasts in place of the intonational contrasts (especially Czech and Slovak); mobility of the stress is still characteristic of all of East Slavic, but elsewhere the stress has become fixed or predictably placed. (Confusingly, the modern languages do not all use the same accent marks for writing the intonational pitches: Lithuanian _é_ and Serbo-Croatian ȅ both represent _e_ with original acute.)

18.13. Intonation and the laryngeals. Balto-Slavic is unique in IE for turning a sequence _*VRH_ before consonant into _*V̄R_. Thus for example _*ĝenh$_1$-to-_ became pre-Balto-Slavic _*źēnta-_ 'son-in-law', and _*bherHĝeh$_2$_ became pre-Balto-Slavic _*bērźā-_ 'birch'. These new long-vowel sequences arose before the advent of the acute/non-acute distinction and were treated in the same way as regular inherited long vowels, meaning that they eventually became acute. Thus _*źēnta-_ above became acute _*źḗnta-_ and _*bērźā-_ became _*bḗrźā-_. Subsequently, Osthoff's Law (§3.41) shortened all long vowels before a resonant and consonant. Balto-Slavic _*źḗnta-_ and _*bḗrźā-_ became then _*źénta-_ and _*bérźā-_, whence on the one hand Lith. _žéntas_, Serbo-Croatian _zȅt_, and on the other, Lith. _béržas_ and Serbo-Croatian _brȅza_.

18.14. The change of _*VRH_ to _*V̄R_ happened after the syllabic resonants became _*iR_ (§18.8), meaning that new sequences _*īrC *īlC *īmC *īnC_ developed from _*r̥HC *l̥HC *m̥HC *n̥HC_. These predictably became acute as well, and then shortened by Osthoff's Law. Thus _*pl̥h$_1$no-_ 'full' > _*pīlna-_ > _*pī́lna-_ > Lith. _pìlnas_ (the grave accent mark represents acute), Serbo-Croatian _pȕn_.

Since original short vowels had always been non-acute, original sequences of short vowel plus resonant now contrasted with these new, acute sequences of short vowel plus resonant. Compare the outcomes of the words for 'son-in-law' and 'full' with those for 'tooth' (in Serbo-Croatian; Lith., 'sharp edge') and 'wolf':

	PIE	Balto-Slavic	Serbo-Croatian	Lithuanian
*VRH	_*ĝenh$_1$to-_	_*źḗnta-_	_zȅt_	_žéntas_
_*R̥H_	_*pl̥h$_1$no-_	_*pī́lna-_	_pȕn_	_pìlnas_
_*VR_	_*ĝombho-_	_*źamba-_	_zȗb_	_žam̃bas_
_*R̥_	_*u̯l̥kʷo-_	_*vilka-_	_vȗk_	_vil̃kas_

An acute accent all by itself does not automatically signal the former presence of a laryngeal, since acute intonation has other sources as well. The Balto-Slavic intonational facts therefore serve primarily for confirmation of laryngeals whose existence has been deduced from other comparative evidence.

18.15. The Balto-Slavic system of accentual contrasts is one of the most complex areas of IE historical linguistics. A prodigious variety of accentual rules have been proposed over the years to account for the different patterns, and there is considerable debate about the details. Most of these are proper to the later histories of the subbranches and individual daughters, but one that affected the Common Balto-Slavic period and that had important ramifications later is **Pedersen's Law** (or more accurately **Saussure–Pedersen's Law**, as it was first recognized by Ferdinand de Saussure and later refined by the Danish Indo-Europeanist Holger Pedersen). The precise formulation of the law is debated, but in essence it appears that an original stress accent on a penultimate open syllable was retracted to the previous syllable. Thus the PIE nominative and genitive singular of the word for 'daughter', **dhugh*$_2$-*tḗr* **dhugh*$_2$-*tr-és*, retained their accent on the final syllable (> Lith. *duktė̃*, Old Lithuanian *dukterès*), while the accusative singular and nominative plural **dhugh*$_2$-*tér-m̥* **dhugh*$_2$-*tér-es* threw the accent back, yielding Lith. *dùkterį* and Old Lith. *dùkteres*. As a result of this retraction, paradigms arose that were marked only at "edges," i.e. in which the accent fell on either the initial or the final syllable but not the middle. This pattern later underwent major analogical extension.

Morphology

18.16. A characteristic innovation in Balto-Slavic morphology, found especially in verb formation, is the widespread analogical creation of so-called "neo-lengthened-grade" forms, essentially the lengthening of vowels for ablaut purposes beyond the original scope of lengthened grades in PIE. Most dramatically, inherited zero-grade forms containing the vowels **i* and **u* were often lengthened to **ī* and **ū* by analogy. For example, the zero-grade **mr̥*- 'die' (cp. Lat. *mor-t-* 'death') became **mir*- in Balto-Slavic, and from this a "neo-lengthened" root form **mīr*- was created that appears in Russ. *u-mir-at'* 'to lie dying' (see §18.30 on Slavic *i* < **ī*). Another morphological innovation of Balto-Slavic was the creation of "definite" adjectives (alongside normal adjectives), as mentioned above in §18.1. This was done by adding a suffix *-*i̯o*-: thus OCS has *dobrŭ* 'good' alongside definite *dobrŭ-jĭ* 'the good (one)', and Lithuanian has *gẽras* 'good' alongside *geràs-is* 'the good (one)'. This suffix descends from the PIE relative pronoun (recall §8.28 and compare §15.22).

In both Baltic and Slavic, the PIE verbal system was somewhat simplified (but see §18.35 on the creation of aspectual pairs in Slavic). The perfect has been lost as a category, though the perfect participial suffix survives as a past participial suffix. Of some interest is the fact that both subbranches retain one tense system formed with an *s*-suffix, but a different one in each: Baltic has an *s*-future lacking in Slavic (except for one isolated form, see §18.34), whereas Slavic has an *s*-aorist system (including secondary derivatives) lacking in Baltic. The subjunctive has been lost, but the optative survives, though only in Old Prussian as an actual optative; it otherwise got marshalled into service as the imperative in both Baltic and Slavic, and shows up in the Lithuanian permissive as well (see §18.66). Balto-Slavic is also interesting in preserving (along with Indo-Iranian and Italic) the somewhat marginal category of the supine in *-*tum* (§5.59), e.g. OCS *sŭpa-tŭ* 'to sleep', Lith.

bū́-tų 'to be'; it also became the base for the new East Baltic optative, e.g. Old Lith. 2nd sing. *butúm-bey* 'may you be'.

18.17. In both verbal and nominal morphology, Balto-Slavic importantly distinguishes between mobile and non-mobile paradigms. In the following discussion, we will concentrate on the nominal system. In slightly simplified terms, one can think of Balto-Slavic as having inherited nouns with accent on the root and others with accent on the ending. Largely as a result of the workings of Saussure–Pedersen's Law (§18.15 above) and some further changes to be discussed later (§18.70), some stresses that originally fell on endings were retracted, resulting in a new type of mobile paradigm that looked very different from the familiar mobile accent-ablaut types we have seen for PIE. In those (as will be recalled e.g. from the chart given in §6.20), the accent tended to move rightward from the strong cases to the weak in nouns and from the singular to the dual and plural in verbs; in Balto-Slavic, however, there is a *leftward* rather than a rightward movement of the accent as one goes down a paradigm. We already saw a hint of this with Lith. nomin. sg. *duktė̃*, accus. *dùkterį* (§18.15). There were also some sound changes that moved the accent forward to the end of a word, causing paradigms whose accent was originally fixed on the root to become mobile in a different way from the type just outlined. All these patterns will be discussed in more detail later in this chapter (§§18.70ff.).

18.18. Less well-understood are the changes to verbal accentual paradigms, which also differ strongly in their accentual properties from their PIE forebears. Simple thematic presents, which had fixed accent on the root in PIE, became mobile in Balto-Slavic; e.g. the PIE 1st and 3rd singular and 1st plural of 'lead', **u̯édh-oh$_2$* **u̯édh-eti* **u̯édh-ome-*, ultimately became Lith. *vedù vẽda vẽdame*. By contrast, athematic presents, which usually had mobile accent in PIE, normally have fixed accent on the stem-vowel in Balto-Slavic.

Slavic

18.19. We know little, if anything, of the Slavs before their first mention in Byzantine histories of the sixth century AD, when bands of them moved into Greece and the Balkans from the northeast. This period also saw their expansion into parts of northern Europe previously settled by Baltic and Finnic peoples. Prior to these expansions, which continued for several hundred years and probably marked the end of Proto-Slavic linguistic unity, the Slavs are believed to have occupied an area stretching from near the western Polish border eastward to the Dnieper River in Belarus'. Archaeologically this territory shows a continuum of cultural development from about 1500 BC to the period of the expansions, which may well mean that it was Slavic (or pre-Slavic) during all that time.

18.20. Some or all of the ancestors of the Slavs were once located a little further to the east, in or near Iranian territory, for a number of Iranian words were borrowed at an early date into pre-Slavic. One of these is the word for 'god', OCS *bogŭ* (Russian *bog*), which comes from Iranian **baga-* 'god'. Two others are evidenced by Russ. *sobaka* 'dog' (cp. Median *spáka*), and perhaps by OCS *sŭto* 'hundred' (if borrowed from Iranian **sata(m)*). This territory would have been to the north of the Black Sea, an area into which a number of rivers flow whose names are usually taken to be Iranian: the Dniester, Dnieper, Donets, and Don (cp. Iranian **dānu-* 'river'). As the early Slavs moved slowly westward, they came into contact with Germanic tribes; as mentioned in §16.2, from them they borrowed the word for 'bread', OCS *xlěbŭ* (Germanic **hlaiƀaz*, cp. Goth. *hlaifs*, Eng. *loaf*), 'prince', OCS *kŭnęzĭ* (Gmc. **kuningaz* 'king', cp. OE *cyning*), and several others.

18.21. The modern Slavic languages arose as the result of dialectal differentiation that only began about 1500 years ago. Even today, several of the modern languages are to some extent mutually intelligible in their spoken forms, and even more so in their written forms. A discussion of the rise of Slavic literacy is deferred until the section on Old Church Slavonic below (§§18.40ff.), the first attested Slavic language.

Slavic phonology

18.22. Consonants. As noted above, Slavic changed PIE **k̂* and **ĝ(h)* to *s* and *z*: **k̂lōu̯ā* 'fame' > OCS *slava* 'fame, glory' (cp. Gk. *klé(w)os* 'fame' < **k̂leu̯os*); **ĝneh₃-* 'know' > OCS *znati* 'know'. Aside from this change, Slavic consonants were most affected by the Law of Open Syllables and the three palatalizations discussed below.

18.23. Law of Open Syllables. A number of developments conspired to reduce the number of closed syllables in pre-Slavic, typically by deleting syllable-final consonants. This resulted in the simplification of many word-internal consonant clusters. For example, the cluster *pn* in the word **supno-* 'sleep' was syllabified *sup.no-*, with the *p* closing the first syllable; but sound changes led to the disappearance of the *p* in **sup-no-*, changing it to **su-no-* with an open first syllable. The aggregate of these changes is called the Law of Open Syllables. Two specific changes that fall under this rubric are treated below in §§18.32 and 18.33. One cluster that remained throughout all this was **st*, seen especially in the reflex of PIE dental-plus-dental clusters (§3.36), as in OCS *vesti* 'to lead' < **u̯ed-tei.*

As a result of the Law of Open Syllables, many words in Slavic exhibit some striking alternations, such as that between *sŭp-* and *sŭ-* in forms of the OCS verb meaning 'sleep': aorist *u-sŭp-e* 'fell asleep' but present infinitive *u-sŭ-nǫti* 'to fall asleep' (the latter from **u-sŭp-nǫti*; cp. Russ. *spat'* 'to sleep', *usnut'* 'to fall asleep').

18.24. The "ruki" rule. In Slavic, **s* occurring after **r*, **u*, **k*, or **i* became the voiceless velar fricative *x*: OCS *uxo* 'ear' < **h₂euso-*; 1st sing. aorist *rěxŭ* 'I spoke' < **rēk-s-om*; locative pl. *-ěxŭ* < **-oisu.* (The many Slavic words beginning with *x-* are unexplained, as ruki is the only known Slavic sound change that gave rise to *x*.)

18.25. Palatalizations. Of great importance in the history of Slavic consonants were a series of palatalizations; the changes are complex and will only be given here in outline. The **First Palatalization** caused the velars *k g x* to be palatalized to *č ž š* before **i̯* or a front vowel. Examples include OCS *služiti* 'to serve' < pre-Slav. **slug-iti* and *rǫčĭka* 'little hand, handle' < pre-Slav. **rǫk-ĭka* (diminutive of **rǫka* 'hand'). The Second and Third Palatalizations had different outcomes in different parts of Slavic-speaking territory, and happened after certain changes to the vowels had already taken place. The **Second Palatalization** affected the velars *k g x* when they stood before *ě* (the outcome of **ai* and **oi*, see §18.31 below): PIE

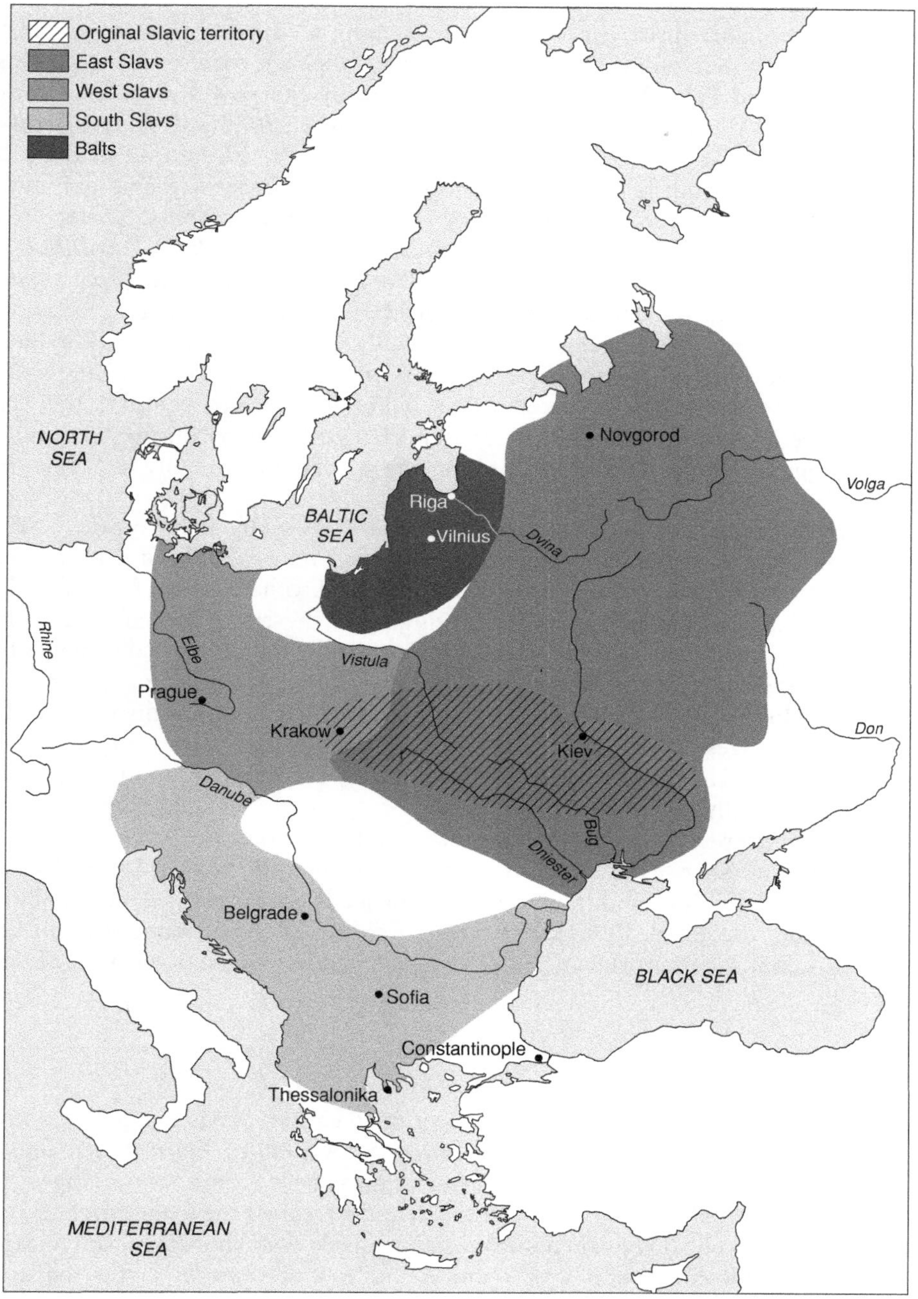

Map 18.1 The Slavs and Balts around AD 1000

k^woi-neh$_2$ 'price' > Slav. **kěna* > OCS *cěna* 'price' (*c* is [ts]; cp. Gk. *poinḗ* 'price, penalty', Lith. *káina* 'price'); pre-Slav. **xairŭ* 'grey' > **xěrŭ* > Russ. *seryj*. (These are not the only outcomes; Czech, for example, has *šerý* corresponding to Russ. *seryj*.) The **Third Palatalization** was conditioned by the vowel preceding (rather than following) the velar: *k g x* were palatalized when followed by most vowels and preceded by *ĭ*, *i*, or *ę* (on these vowels, see §§18.28, 30, and 32 below); this was a late change and its effects were more sporadic. Thus the Slavic diminutive suffix **-ĭko-* (< PIE **-iko-*) became *-ĭcĭ* or *-ĭce*: OCS *otĭcĭ* 'father' < **at-iko-* (**at-* also in Goth. *Att-ila* 'little father'); OCS *srĭdĭce* 'heart' < **srĭdĭko-* < **k̑r̥d-iko-*.

There is some dispute over when the Third Palatalization took place relative to the Second; what is clear is that it happened after various Germanic loanwords had already entered the language. Note especially OCS *pěnęzĭ* 'coin', a borrowing from OHG *pfenning* or its immediate ancestor **penning*, whose *e*-vocalism (by umlaut from **panning*) can be dated to probably the seventh century; the Slavs had to have picked up the word after that change (perhaps during the time of Charlemagne), and the Third Palatalization can be dated to roughly the same time or later.

18.26. Palatalization was not limited to the velars. In some modern Slavic languages, there is a phonemic opposition between non-palatalized ("hard") and palatalized ("soft") consonants, as in Russian *brat* 'brother' versus *brat'* 'to take'. The palatalized consonants are often distinguished by the presence of a *y*-glide after the consonant. The development of phonemically palatalized consonants had already progressed to some extent in Common Slavic. Some languages, such as Polish, developed the system to a high degree but then lost the distinction after subsequent changes.

18.27. Glides. The one surviving glide, **i̯*, mostly stayed intact in initial position and intervocalically, as in OCS *junŭ* 'young' < **i̯ou-no-*. Several Slavic languages have had the propensity to develop prothetic glides in front of certain vowels. For example, the number 'eight' began originally with *o-* (PIE **ok̑tō*); in pre-Russian this developed into **u̯o-* and then into *vo-* (whence Russ. *vosem'*, versus e.g. Polish *osiem* without the glide). Compare for this development the pronunciation of Eng. *one* with initial *w-* (the original glideless pronunciation is preserved in *on-ly* and *al-one*).

Vowels

18.28. Short vowels and the "yers". As mentioned earlier, Slavic merged **a* and **o* as *o*: **naso-* 'nose' > OCS *nosŭ*, **h$_2$ou̯i-* 'sheep' > OCS *ovĭ-ca*. Short **e* remained *e*, e.g. **g^{w}en-* 'woman' > OCS *žena*. The short high vowels **i* and **u* developed into vowels transliterated as *ĭ* and *ŭ* (in Cyrillic, ь and ъ), called the front and back **yers** (or jers), respectively. These are assumed to have been very short *i* and *u*. Examples from OCS include *čĭto* 'what' < **k^{w}i-* and *rŭžda* 'rust' < **h$_1$rudh-i̯ā* ('the red stuff', from **h$_1$reudh-* 'red').

18.29. The yers are still preserved in Old Church Slavonic, but around the end of the Common Slavic period (c. AD 800–1000), they began to be lost as a category: certain ones weakened and disappeared, while others strengthened and became full mid or low vowels. The rule was as follows: word-final yers and yers before a syllable with a full vowel (i.e., other than a yer) disappeared; these were the so-called "weak" yers. Yers before a syllable containing another yer were "strong" and later developed into full vowels. Thus in OCS *dĭnĭnica* 'morning star' and *rŭtŭ* 'mouth', the first yer was strong but the second was weak; in *vŭxodŭ* 'entrance', both were weak. The full vowels that developed from the strong yers differ from language to language; in Russian, strong *ĭ* and *ŭ* became *e* and *o*. Thus *dĭnĭnica* and *rŭtŭ* correspond to Russ. *dennica* and *rot*.

The loss of the yers had far-reaching effects. It created new consonant clusters, including complex ones word-initially, as in Russ. *čtenie* 'reading' (< *čĭt-*), *mglo* 'mist' (cp. OCS *mĭglo*), and *vzgljad* 'view' (older *vŭz-*). It also led to alternations where one form has a vowel that disappears in related forms, as in Russ. nominative *rot* 'mouth' alongside genitive *rta* 'of the mouth' (cp. the forms for 'American' in §18.38 below).

18.30. Long vowels. The long high vowels **ī* and **ū* became *i* and *y* (the latter phonetically the central high vowel [ɨ], midway between the vowels in *pit* and *put*): OCS *u-mir-ati* 'to die' < pre-Slavic **ou-mīr-atei* (< **mīr-*, neo-lengthened grade of **mir-*; see §18.16); OCS *myšĭ* 'mouse' < **mūs-*. Long **ē* became a sound transliterated as *ě*, called **yat'** (or jat') and representing phonetically the sound [æ] (as in *hat*), e.g. *děti* 'place, put' < **dhē-* < **dheh₁-*. (The apostrophe in the word *yat'* represents palatalization of the final consonant in Russian, the source of the word.) Finally, long **ā* and **ō* merged as *a* (e.g. **steh₂-* > **stā-* > OCS *sta-ti* 'to stand', **ĝneh₃-* > **ĝnō-* > OCS *zna-ti* 'to know').

18.31. Diphthongs. The diphthongs were all monophthongized: **ei* became *i* (as in PIE **steigh-* 'step, go' > OCS *stignǫ* 'I come'); **oi* became *ě* or, word-finally, often *i* (e.g. **-oisu* > OCS loc. pl. *-ěxŭ*, but masc. nomin. pl. **-oi* > OCS *-i*); **ai* also became *ě* (e.g. **laiu̯o-* 'left' > OCS *lěvŭ*); **eu* became *ju* (e.g. **bheudh-* 'be awake' > OCS *bljudǫ* 'I keep watch', with secondary *l*); and **ou* and **au* became *u* (e.g. **sūnou* 'son' [vocat. sing.] > OCS *synu*; **tauro-* 'bull' > OCS *turŭ* 'wild bull').

18.32. Rise of nasalized vowels. Common Slavic changed sequences of vowel plus nasal in closed syllables into nasalized vowels as part of the Law of Open Syllables. An original sequence **in* **en* or **im* **em* before a consonant became a front nasal vowel transliterated as *ę*: pre-Slav. **su̯ento-* 'holy' > OCS *svętŭ* 'holy'; pre-Slav. **desim-ti-* 'group of ten, decad' > OCS *desętĭ* 'ten'. Any other vowel plus nasal became a back nasalized vowel transliterated as *ǫ*: **ĝombho-* 'tooth' > OCS *zǫbŭ* 'tooth' (cp. Eng. *comb*), **ĝhans-* 'goose' > OCS *gǫsĭ*. Later, in most Slavic languages – the main exception being Polish – these were denasalized, whence e.g. Russian *svjatoj, desjat', zub*, and *gus'* for the words above (but Polish *święty, dziesięć, ząb, gęś*).

18.33. "*ToRT*" groups. One who is familiar with a bit of Russian geography may recall that some cities have names ending in *-grad* (e.g. *Lenin-grad, Kalinin-grad*), while others have names ending in *-gorod* (e.g. *Nov-gorod*). Both elements mean 'city', but one is the native Russian word (*gorod*) while the other is borrowed from OCS (*gradŭ*). Russian has many other such doublets, including *golova* 'head' vs. *glava* 'head (= leader), chief' and *moroka* 'twilight' vs. *mrak* 'gloom'. These doublets exemplify different dialectal Slavic outcomes of the Proto-Slavic sequence **oR* between two consonants, conventionally labeled "*ToRT*"; this sequence underwent various reconfigurations as part of the Law of Open Syllables. In South Slavic, this sequence became *Ra*, while in East Slavic the outcome was *oRo*. Thus Common Slavic **gord-* **golv-* **mork-* are the ancestors of OCS *gradŭ glava mrakŭ* and Russian *gorod golova morok-*. (OCS vocabulary is mined for scientific or learned words in Russian, much as Latin and Greek are mined by English for similar purposes.)

Even though East Slavic has lost the old Slavic intonations, disyllabic *-oRo-* is a useful indicator of the type of intonation that was once present. The accentual pattern *-oRó-* reflects an old acute (rising) **-óR-*, while *-óRo-* reflects an old non-acute or falling intonation. Thus Russ. *vóron* 'raven' goes back to non-acute Slavic **vornŭ* (cp. Lith. *var̃nas*), while its feminine derivative *voróna* 'crow' goes back to acute **vórna* (cp. Lith. *várna*). As we have seen, the acute here means this vowel was once long, so we reconstruct **u̯arnos* for the raven and a feminine vrddhi-derivative (§6.61) **u̯ārnā* for the crow. Thus also Russ. *koróva* 'cow' alongside Lith. acute *kárvė* 'cow', and Russ. *górod* 'city' alongside Lith. circumflex *gar̃das* 'fence'.

Morphology

Verbs

18.34. Slavic continues the PIE present, imperfect, and *s*-aorist tenses. As noted above in §18.16, the subjunctive was lost, but the optative lives on as the Slavic imperative, e.g. OCS sing. *nes-i* 'carry!', pl. *nes-ěte* (with both *-i* and *-ě-* from **-oi-*). Only one *s*-future form is found, Old Russ. (Russ. Church Slavonic) *byšęštĭ*, a participle meaning 'about to be' (< Balto-Slavic **bū-sint-j-*; cp. §5.40). Several different participles are found, most of them continuations of IE formations: a present active participle in *-ęt-* and *-ǫt-* from **-e/ont-*; a present passive in **-mo-* (see §5.60); two past active participles, one in *-vŭš-* (from the PIE perfect participle) and one (called the resultative participle) in *-l-* (see §5.60); and two past passive participles, in *-t-* and *-(e)n-*, from the old verbal adjectives in **-tó-* and **-nó-* (§5.61). Note that Baltic does not have the *l-* or the *(e)n*-participles. The Slavic infinitive in *-ti* (< **-tei*) is an old case-form, probably a locative, of a verbal abstract noun in **-ti-* (§5.58).

18.35. Perfective and imperfective aspect. The singular hallmark of the Slavic verb is its aspectual system. Almost every verb may be classified according to the category of aspect, imperfective (action that is incomplete, ongoing, repeated, or unspecified as to completion), and perfective (completed or one-time action). Some verbs may be coupled as aspectual pairs. Perfectives often continue present-tense formations in PIE, which then acquired future meaning in Slavic; thus for example PIE reduplicated (weak stem) **de-dh₃-* 'give' ultimately became the perfective OCS *damĭ* 'I will give'. However, not all PIE presents underwent this change; thus **bheroh₂* 'I carry' (extended in pre-Slavic to **bherōmi*) became the imperfective present *berǫ* 'I gather, take'. Very often a preverb marks the perfective member of the pair, as in Russ. *pro-čitaju* 'I will read (and finish reading)', perfective of *čitaju* 'I am reading'; here English offers a parallel with such pairs as *drink* vs. *drink up*, *eat* vs. *eat up*, etc. The following OCS verbs (in the 1st singular) will illustrate some of the morphological means that were pressed into service to form imperfective/perfective pairs:

Imperfective	Perfective	English meaning
dajǫ	*damĭ*	give
padajǫ	*padǫ*	fall
rasŭmatrjajǫ	*rasŭmotrjǫ*	view
byvajǫ	*bǫdǫ*	be
dvižǫ	*dvignǫ*	move

As these forms show, the compound suffix *-*ā*-*i̯e*- was often used to derive imperfectives from perfectives, sometimes in tandem with changes in ablaut (as in *rasŭmatrjajǫ* alongside *rasŭmotrjǫ*) or the use of a different stem (base *byv*- < PIE **bhū*(*u̯*)- alongside *bǫd*- < Slavic **bu*-*n*-*d*-, the latter of uncertain explanation). The last example in the chart illustrates the fairly common use of a nasal suffix to form a perfective; the corresponding imperfective in this case is from earlier **dvig*-*je*-, in IE terms a **i̯e*/*o*-present.

18.36. The situation acquires an additional layer of complexity with verbs of motion, which distinguish not only imperfectivity and perfectivity, but also iterativity. Thus Russian distinguishes ***nesu*** 'I carry' (imperfective), ***ponesu*** 'I will carry' (perfective), and ***nošu*** 'I carry (there and back), I repeatedly carry'. The *o*-grade of the last form betrays it as coming from a PIE causative-iterative **$h_1$nok̂*-*ei̯e*-, though not all the Slavic iteratives continue this type of formation.

Nouns

18.37. The rich nominal inflectional system of PIE is practically intact in Slavic. Seven cases are expressed: nominative, genitive, dative, accusative, instrumental, locative, and vocative. The genitive of *o*-stems in Slavic (and Baltic) is formally the old IE ablative in *-*āt* (a variant of the more widespread *-*ōt*; see §6.49), which took over the functions of the genitive and replaced it; this became -*a* by the change of **ō* > *a* and loss of the final stop. The functional merger of ablative and genitive is why prepositions with the meaning 'away from' take the genitive case in Slavic. (Compare Greek, where the ablative disappeared and its functions were taken over by the genitive, with the same results; recall §12.48.) Dual forms were still in use in the early periods, but have disappeared from most of the modern languages except dialectal Sorbian and Slovenian.

18.38. A striking morphosyntactic innovation of the Slavic nominal system is the distinction within the masculine gender between animate and inanimate. This began in the *o*-stems and spread to the other stem-classes gradually during the historical period. The distinction is made overt in the accusative case, which is identical to the nominative in inanimate nouns but identical to the genitive in animates (e.g. nomin. sing. *amerikanec* 'an American', accus. and genit. *amerikanca*; nomin. pl. *amerikancy*, accus. and genit. *amerikancev*). In two West Slavic languages, Polish and Sorbian, to make things even more complicated, masculine animate nouns split into human (also called personal or virile) and non-human categories, as reflected in the case-endings of the plural (and dual, in the case of Sorbian). Thus the accusative patterns with the nominative in the case of non-human masculine animates, but with the genitive in the case of personal animates, which have also gone the extra step of creating a whole new ending for the nominative. Thus 'cats' in Polish is *koty* in the nominative and accusative and *kotów* in the genitive, while 'men' is nomin. pl. *mężowie*, accus. and genit. pl. *mężów*.

Numerals

18.39. The numerals occupy a rather interesting corner of Slavic morphology. The system of numerals in almost any Slavic language is by English standards enormously complicated. In Russian, for example, the number 'one' and any compound number ending in 'one', like 21, 451 (but not 11), is an adjective agreeing with the following noun in gender and case: *odin stol* 'one table', *odno okno* 'one window', instrumental *s odnim stolom* 'along with one table'. The numbers 'two', 'three', and 'four', as well as compound numbers ending in these (such as 52, 73, 164, but not 12–14!), take the genitive singular of whatever noun follows them (e.g. *tri stola* 'three tables', where *stola* is genitive singular), and all other numbers – five through twenty and any compound number ending in five through zero – take the genitive plural of the following noun (e.g. *devjat' stolov* 'nine tables', with *stolov* genitive plural).

The historical explanation for this is an interesting example of the interrelationship of morphology and syntax. First, Common Slavic revamped the inherited cardinal numerals from five through ten by replacing them with collectives. These collectives were abstract *i*-stem nouns (e.g. OCS *pętĭ* 'five' < **penk^{w}(e)-ti-*, *osmĭ* 'eight' < **ok̑tm̥-mĭ*), and due to their literal meaning ('a group of five, a quintet', etc.) took the genitive plural of whatever noun followed. Thus OCS *pętĭ stolŭ* 'five thrones' historically meant 'a quintet/fivesome of thrones'. The number 'two' originally took the dual, and this usage spread in some Slavic dialects (including the ancestor of Russian) to the following numbers 'three' and 'four' by contamination. (Contamination frequently affects numeric systems: neighboring numerals are notorious for influencing each other phonologically, morphologically, and – as in this case – even syntactically.) The final step in the development was the formal merger of the dual with the genitive singular in some declensions, which led to a nearly complete morphological replacement of the dual by the genitive singular elsewhere in Russian and several of its relatives.

Old Church Slavonic

18.40. Slavic literacy began in 863, when two Greek brothers and missionaries, Constantine and Methodius, arrived in Moravia to teach the Christian faith in Slavic. The brothers had learned the language while growing up in Thessalonika. Constantine devised a script for it, while Methodius did the lion's share of the translation work. Constantine later went to Rome and on his deathbed became a monk, whereupon he took on the name Cyril. The script we call Cyrillic in his honor is not actually the script he invented; the latter is now called Glagolitic (OCS *glagolŭ* 'word'), with distinctive letters of uncertain origin. What we now call Cyrillic (used nowadays to write Russian, Belarusian, Ukrainian, Bulgarian, Macedonian, Serbian, and various non-Slavic languages of the former Soviet Union) was devised about thirty years later in Bulgaria and based on the Greek majuscule (capital) letters.

18.41. None of the two brothers' translations has survived. The earliest preserved Slavic comes from some of their successors in Bulgaria; this language soon spread as the liturgical language for all the Slavs, and because of its role as the language of Slavic Christendom it is usually called **Old Church Slavonic** or Old Church Slavic. OCS is very similar to the Common Slavic that has been reconstructed by linguists; but by all estimates, Common Slavic ceased to exist as a unitary language several hundred years before the time of Constantine and Methodius, and at most OCS can be regarded as one of its later dialects, albeit artificial (that is, it did not quite match the local spoken dialects of the regions in which it was used). The Old Church Slavonic of Bulgaria, regarded as something of a standard, is often called **Old Bulgarian** (or Old Macedonian).

Eastern Orthodox Christianity spread to all the East Slavs and the eastern territories of the South Slavs (inhabited by the ancestors of today's Serbs, Macedonians, and Bulgarians), and OCS spread with it; since a different dialect was spoken in each area, OCS was artificially modified to accommodate local dialect features. The term "Church Slavic" is often encountered as a general rubric for these different regional varieties of OCS. Real OCS was not spoken for terribly long before the development of the regional Church Slavic varieties, hence we do not have many documents in it – only about seven major manuscripts in the Glagolitic alphabet, and two in the Cyrillic alphabet from before the twelfth century. The oldest OCS manuscript, from the tenth century, is known as the Kiev Fragments and is written in Glagolitic.

Old Church Slavonic text sample

18.42. The Old Church Slavonic version of Luke 2:4–7, in normalized spelling.

4 vŭzide že Iosifŭ otŭ Galileję, iz grada Nazaretĭska, vĭ Ijuděǫ, vŭ gradŭ Davydovŭ
iže naricajetŭ sę Vitleemŭ, zane běaše otŭ domu i otĭčĭstvię Davydova. 5 napisati sę
sŭ Mariejǫ, obrǫčenojǫ emu ženojǫ, sǫštejǫ neprazdŭnojǫ. 6 bystŭ že, egda byste
tu, isplŭnišę sę dĭne roditi ei. 7 i rodi synŭ svoi prĭvěnĭcĭ, i povitŭ i, i položi i vĭ
ěslaxŭ, zane ne bě ima města vŭ obitěli.

4 And Joseph also went up from Galilee, from the city of Nazareth, to Judea, to the city of David, which is called Bethlehem, because he was of the house and lineage of David, 5 to be registered with Mary his betrothed, who was with child. 6 And while they were there the time came for her to be delivered. 7 And she gave birth to her first-born son and wrapped him in swaddling cloths, and laid him in a manger, because there was no place for them in the inn.

18.42a. Notes. 4. vŭzide: 'went up'; *vŭz-* means 'up', and *ide* is aorist of *iti* 'to go' < *$*h_1ei$-tei*. The stem *id-* is taken from the imperative *idi* 'go!', ultimately from the PIE imperative *$*h_1i$-dhi* (§5.54). (Compare the Greek verb *esthíō* 'I eat', formed by adding the personal endings to the original imperative **esthi* 'eat!') **že:** particle emphasizing the preceding word; PIE **ghe* (Ved. *(g)ha*). **otŭ:** 'from', perhaps related to the ablative ending *$*\text{-}(h_2)at$* (§6.49). **grada Nazaretĭska:** 'the city of Nazareth', genit. sing.; *-ĭsk-* is a common adjectival suffix added to place-names to indicate origin and related to Germanic **-iska-* (> *-ish* in Eng.; §6.75). **vĭ:** 'in', the variant of *vŭ* when before a front vowel. **Davydovŭ:** 'of David'; *-ov-* is an adjectival suffix added to proper names to indicate affiliation, and is the same suffix seen in names like *Molotov, Godunov, Chekhov*. **naricajetŭ sę:** 'calls itself' = 'is called', 3rd sing. of *naricati*, the imperfective of *narešti*, from *rešti* 'to say'. The *-c-* of *naricajetŭ* is from the Third Palatalization (§18.25); the pronoun *sę* is the old accusative of the reflexive pronoun, from PIE **su̯e-* (§7.13). **běaše:** 'was', 3rd sing. imperfect; the ending *-aše* is palatalized from *-ax-* before the front vowel *-e* (§18.25). The *-x-* is ultimately from the *s* of the *s*-aorist; this **-s-* changed to *-x-* by the "ruki" rule in certain forms, and then spread to other forms where "ruki" would not have applied, as here. **domu:** 'home, house', with *-u* < **-ou-s*, the *u*-stem genit. sing. **otĭčĭstvię:** 'lineage', genit. sing.; abstract noun from *otĭčĭ* 'father'.

5. napisati: 'to register', from *pisati* 'to write'. **sŭ:** 'with', cp. Lith. *sù*. **obrǫčenojǫ:** 'betrothed' (instr. sing.), past passive participle of *obrǫčiti* 'to betroth', from *rǫka* 'hand' (Russ. *ruka*). **emu:** 'him', dative of the masc.-neut. demonstrative pronoun, containing the oblique case-formant *-m-* (see further §18.78). **ženojǫ:** 'wife, woman', PIE *$*g^w$en-* (Gk. *gunḗ* 'woman', Eng. *queen*). **sǫštejǫ:** 'being', pres. participle < **sont-*; the *-št-* is the South Slavic development of **-tj-*. **neprazdŭnojǫ:** 'pregnant', lit. 'not idle, not empty'.

6. bystŭ: 'it was, it happened (that)', 3rd sing. perfective aorist of *byti* 'to be'. A shorter 3rd singular, *by*, is the historically older form (< **bhuH-s-t*); *bystŭ* is a blending of *by* and the present 3rd sing. *jestŭ* 'is' (< *$*h_1$esti*). **byste:** 'both of them were', 3rd dual aorist. **isplŭnišę sę dĭne:** lit. 'the days filled themselves' = 'the days became full, became complete'; *s*-aorist of *isplŭniti*, from *plŭnŭ* 'full' (PIE *$*p\underset{\circ}{l}h_1$no-*, cp. Eng. *full*). *Dĭne* is nomin. pl. of *dĭnĭ* 'day', from PIE **din-* 'day'. **roditi:** 'to give birth'; *rodi* below is the 3rd sing. aorist. **ei:** 'for her', dat. sing.

7. synŭ: 'son', accus. sing. Usually in animate nouns in Slavic the accusative and genitive singulars are identical, but not here; the genitive is *synu*. The paradigm of 'son' is archaic in this respect, for it comes from a proterokinetic *u*-stem with zero-grade of the suffix in the nominative and accusative (**-u-*, whence Slavic *-ŭ*) and full grade in the other cases (**-eu-* or **-ou-*, whence Slavic *-u*). **svoi:** '(her) own', reflexive adjective, PIE **su̯o-*, with the **-u̯-* preserved (but lost in the unstressed pronoun *sę* above). **prĭvěnĭcĭ:** 'first-born', from *prĭvŭ* 'first'. **povitŭ:** 'wrapped', 3rd sing. aorist; related to Ved. *váyati* 'weaves', Lat. *uieō* 'I twist, plait'. **i:** 'him', enclitic object pronoun. **položi:** 'lay', PIE **logh-ei̯e-* 'cause to lie', causative of **legh-*. **ěslaxŭ:** 'manger', loc. pl. (sing. in meaning). **bě:** 'was', imperfective aorist of *byti* 'be'. **ima:** 'for them', dat. pl. **města:** 'place', genit. sing.; in Slavic, negative existential arguments require the genitive, so lit. 'there was no(thing) of place'. Compare French *pas de temps* 'no time', literally 'not of time'.

Modern Slavic Languages

East Slavic

18.43. For the first two centuries or so of East Slavic literacy, which began after the early Russian state known as Rus' was Christianized in 988, there were no individually differentiated East Slavic languages, only an East Slavic dialect area – itself only a little different from the rest of Slavic. The capital of Rus' was Kiev, which is where the first East Slavic literature hails from. As part of the Slavic East Orthodox community, the East Slavs adopted Old Church Slavonic as their written liturgical language. It was modified somewhat to incorporate specifically Kievan features and is thus often called **Russian Church Slavonic.** The literary language has traditionally been called **Old Russian**, the term we use in this book, but it is a bit of a misnomer: it was ancestral not just to Russian, but also to the other East Slavic languages, Belarusian and Ukrainian. In fact, some features of the "Old Russian" of Kievan Rus' are found in modern Ukrainian but not Russian – not surprising when one recalls that Kiev is now the capital of Ukraine. More accurate terms for Russian Church Slavonic and Old Russian are *Rusian Church Slavonic* and *Old Rusian* (not a typographical error – named after Rus').

The oldest surviving dated East Slavic manuscript is the Ostromir Gospel, dating to 1056–7, but at least one work, the *Sermon on Law and Grace* of Hilarion, was composed slightly earlier in the same century. Principal original compositions of the early Kievan period were hagiographies and historical chronicles. One isolated epic in rhythmic prose, called *Slovo o polku Igoreve* (*The Song of Igor's Campaign*), is known, supposedly composed in the late twelfth century; but its authenticity has been the subject of controversy, and the sole manuscript was destroyed by fire during the War of 1812. If genuine, it would represent the literary highpoint of Kievan Rus'.

18.44. The Tatars conquered Rus' in the 1230s and were not finally overthrown until 1480, after which the northern city of Moscow became the political and literary center of the country. The term Rus' and the adjective "Russian" (Old Russian *Rusĭskyi*) now became identified in the north with the regions around Moscow and Novgorod, the old northern center of trade. As Muscovy grew stronger and gathered the territories that would eventually become known as the Russian Empire, the southern region around Kiev became referred to simply as the "border area," *U-kraina* (from *kraj* 'border'). The Old Russian literary period ended with the rule of Peter I, called the Great (sole ruler 1696–1725), although many date the beginning of Modern Russian to the work of Russia's national poet, Aleksandr Sergeyevich Pushkin (1799–1837), who fixed a number of aspects of the literary language that had been in flux.

18.45. Closely allied with Russian is **Belarusian** (Byelorussian or White Russian), whose standard form is based on the dialect of Minsk. Some old East Slavic texts (traditionally called Old Russian, as per the above) begin to show characteristic Belarusian sound changes in the first half of the thirteenth century. From the fifteenth to the seventeenth century Byelorussia belonged to the Lithuanian and Polish cultural and political world, during which time a wealth of Belarusian literature was produced. It declined as a literary language after that and was not fully resuscitated until after the Russian Revolution.

18.46. Belarusian forms a sort of bridge between Russian and the third East Slavic language, **Ukrainian** (once called Ruthenian or Little Russian; the latter term is now somewhat offensive). Like Belarusian, Ukrainian was not distinct from Russian until around the thirteenth century. With the fall of Kiev as a center of power, the language of the region practically ceased to be written, although Church Slavonic continued to be cultivated, with increasing admixture of Ukrainian features. A true native Ukrainian literary language did not emerge until the late eighteenth century. Today Ukrainian is spoken by more people than any Slavic language besides Russian.

18.47. All of East Slavic is characterized by the retention of the mobile accent inherited from Common Slavic, but the contrastive pitch has been lost. Most of the East Slavic varieties, with the exception of some northern dialects of Russian and most of Ukrainian, have undergone vowel reduction in unstressed syllables. The strong yers became *e* and *o* (for Russian examples, recall §18.29). The nasal vowels *ę* and *ǫ* were denasalized to *ja* and *u*, as in Russ. *beru* 'I take' (OCS *berǫ*) and *pjat'* 'five' (OCS *pętĭ*).

West Slavic

18.48. The Slavic language with the third-largest number of speakers is **Polish**. Texts in this language date to the fourteenth century, although isolated names and words are found going back to 1136. Since Poland was Christianized by Catholics rather than by East Orthodox missionaries, it has always used the Latin alphabet. The literary works from the fourteenth and fifteenth centuries show strong influence from Czech. In northern Poland along the Baltic coast, in the region called Pomerania, have been spoken varieties of West Slavic that are rather divergent from Polish; these are collectively called **Pomeranian**. Pomeranian is viewed by some as a dialect of Polish, by others as a separate language (the issue tends to get politicized). The only surviving variety of Pomeranian is **Kashubian**, spoken to the west and south-west of Gdańsk; **Slovincian**, apparently an old type of Kashubian, became extinct in the early twentieth century. A second extinct West Slavic language, **Polabian**, known from a very few writings in the late sixteenth and seventeenth centuries, was spoken along the Elbe River in what is now Germany. Polish, Pomeranian, and Polabian are often grouped together within West Slavic under the label **Lechitic**.

18.49. One Slavic language is still spoken in Germany, in a region called the Lausitz in the southeast not far from Dresden: **Sorbian** (also called Wendish or Lusatian in older works). Distinguished are two varieties, **Upper Sorbian** and **Lower Sorbian**. The combined total of speakers is only about 50,000, few of whom are monolingual. The Sorbs are the last remnant of the large medieval Slavic population that lived between the Elbe and the Oder rivers. A Lower Sorbian translation of the New Testament from 1548 is the first literary example of either language. Sorbian is interesting principally for preserving several archaic features that are otherwise found today only in South Slavic: the dual, the imperfect, and the aorist.

18.50. South of Sorbian territory is found **Czech**. Like Poland, the Czech-speaking historical region of Bohemia was converted to Catholicism (in the tenth century) rather than East Orthodox Christianity, and the Latin alphabet has been used for writing Czech since its first clear attestation in the fourteenth century. But there were also Slavic missionaries in the tenth century who left behind some Church Slavonic documents with a few Czech dialect characteristics. East of the Czech Republic, in Slovakia, is spoken **Slovak**, which is quite similar to Czech but much more conservative phonetically; the two languages diverged in the fifteenth century.

South Slavic

18.51. Unlike East and West Slavic, which form a continuous dialect area from Russia westwards into Germany, the South Slavs became separated from the other Slavic peoples starting in the sixth century. The early separation led to some significant differences between South Slavic and the rest of the family. South Slavic has much more faithfully preserved the Common Slavic categories of the imperfect and aorist, which were lost in all of East and West Slavic besides Sorbian (§18.49); and it is the only branch of Slavic having languages that preserve the mobile pitch-accent system.

18.52. After Old Church Slavonic, the first attested South Slavic language is **Slovenian** (or Slovene), in which are found the first Slavic documents written in the Latin alphabet, from the tenth and eleventh centuries. Nothing more is heard of the language, though, until the end of the fifteenth century. Slovenian preserves the inherited mobile pitch-accent and the dual. In spite of its relatively small number of speakers (c. two million) and the small geographic area over which it is spoken, Slovenian has an unusually large number of quite varied dialects.

18.53. To the southeast of Slovenian is spoken **Croatian**, which is closely related to **Serbian** farther to the southeast and to the recently named **Bosnian** in Bosnia and Hercegovina. Serbian and Croatian are mutually intelligible; but the differences have sometimes been exaggerated for political reasons, and they are written in different alphabets – Croatian in the Latin alphabet, Serbian in Cyrillic. Because of their mutual intelligibility, Serbian, Croatian, and Bosnian are usually thought of as constituting one language called **Serbo-Croatian**. Serbo-Croatian shares with Slovenian the preservation of the mobile pitch-accent system.

18.54. In the southeast of the former Yugoslavia is Macedonia, home of **Macedonian**. (The same name is given to the language of the ancient Macedonians, which is not connected; see §20.12.) Macedonian was not distinguished from Bulgarian for most of its history. Constantine and Methodius themselves came from Macedonian Thessalonika; their Old Bulgarian is therefore at the same time "Old Macedonian." No Macedonian literature dates from earlier than the nineteenth century, when a nationalist movement came to the fore and a literary language was established, first written with Greek letters, then in Cyrillic. From the point of view of Bulgaria, Macedonian is simply a west Bulgarian dialect.

18.55. We finally come to **Bulgarian** itself, whose earliest stage is Old Bulgarian or Old Church Slavonic, as we have already seen. Divergences from the artificial language of Church Slavonic that are due to colloquial developments in Bulgarian begin to appear in written documents in the twelfth and thirteenth centuries.

Bulgarian and Macedonian are sharply divergent from Serbo-Croatian and Slovenian in several respects. The morphology of the noun has undergone striking simplification: except for singular masculine nouns, where a nominative and an oblique case are distinguished, there are no cases in the noun anymore. A definite article has been innovated, appearing as a clitic suffixed to its noun, as in Macedonian *ezik* 'language' ~ *ezikot* 'the language', *kniga* 'book' ~ *knigata* 'the book', and *vreme* 'time' ~ *vremeto* 'the time'. In contrast to nouns, the verb is richly inflected in all the inherited Slavic tenses and moods plus two new ones, a future tense and a narrative mood. The narrative mood is used to quote material that the speaker does not know to be factual, often with a sense of mistrust; it has sometimes been called informally a "the hell you say" mood.

Some of the unusual characteristics of Bulgarian and Macedonian are shared with other languages of the Balkans, especially Greek and Albanian. These languages are usually seen as constituting the so-called Balkan speech area, which will be discussed in more detail in the next chapter (§19.5).

Baltic

18.56. In historical times, the Balts have occupied a fairly small patch of land along the Baltic Sea, but their prehistoric extent was much greater. In the late Bronze Age, they may have stretched from near the western border of Poland all the way east to the Ural Mountains, given that Baltic river names are found across a large swath of now Slavic-speaking territory in eastern Europe and present-day Russia, as far east as Moscow and as far south as Kiev. To the north the Balts were in lengthy and intimate contact with Finnic tribes, who borrowed hundreds of Baltic words, including agricultural and kinship terms, and words relating to tools and other technologies. From these loans it seems that the Balts had achieved considerable cultural prestige in the region.

Little is known about the prehistoric Balts. In the early to mid-second millennium BC, the inhabitants of the Baltic coast, perhaps but not necessarily ancestors of the Balts, began trading amber with central European tribes in exchange for metals (which the Baltic region was poor in). Amber, considered magical by many peoples, has been called the gold of the north; the Baltic coast has vast deposits of it from huge pine forests that covered the region 60 million years ago. By around 1600 BC amber was being funneled to Mycenae, Anatolia, and places even more distant deep in Asia. Archaeologists have recovered many non-Baltic Bronze Age artifacts in the Baltic regions that must have come in from the amber trade, including a thirteenth-century-BC statuette of a Hittite deity. Most of the world's best amber still comes from this region.

18.57. The first mention of Baltic peoples in ancient literature is disputed. The Greek historian Herodotus named various tribes in their general vicinity, one of which, the Neuri, he says were chased out of their homeland by an infestation of snakes. This has reminded some of the fact that snake-worship was traditional among the Balts, but the connection is tenuous. A half-millennium later, the Roman historian Tacitus mentions a tribe called the Aisti or Aistii who gathered amber and may well have been Balts; but they could also have been Germanic, since their word for 'amber', transmitted in Latin sources as *glaesum* or *glēsum*, seems most similar to *glass*, a Germanic word. Definitely Baltic are the Soudinoi and Galindai mentioned by Ptolemy the geographer (second century AD); they are known from later medieval records too. In the ninth century we hear first of a tribe called the Bruzi (in Old Bavarian) or Brūs or Burūs (in Arabic, tenth century), the source of the word *Prussia*, the historical region of the western Balts.

18.58. Baltic territory began to shrink shortly before the dawn of the Christian era due to the Gothic migrations into their southwestern territories, and shrank a good deal further as Slavic migrations started around the fifth century AD, continuing into the twelfth century. After 1225, the western Baltic lands (Prussia) became casualties of the aggressive eastward expansion of the Teutonic Order, a German religious and military organization that had been summoned to help Poland fight against the Prussians. Farther to the east, where the Lithuanians lived, the Teutonic Knights were repulsed; the Lithuanians established an empire that rapidly expanded through parts of Russia and Ukraine all the way to the Black Sea. The Grand Duchy of Lithuania lasted from 1362 to 1569 and marked the height of Baltic political might. Only toward the end of this period do the first texts in Baltic languages finally appear.

18.59. It is one of the greatest losses to Indo-European studies that the Baltic languages were written down so late, and only after the native mythologies and traditions had been all but eradicated by the Christian invaders. Luckily, some of them live on in the countless Lithuanian and Latvian folksongs or *dainos* (Lith. *daĩnos*, Latv. *dainas*) and folktales, many of which preserve Baltic cultural material of great antiquity. Comparatively little of this is known in the West, and these songs have not yet been sufficiently mined for the contributions they could make to reconstructing PIE culture.

18.60. Baltic survives today in the form of two languages, **Lithuanian** and **Latvian**, which together comprise the **East Baltic** subgroup. **West Baltic** consists of the extinct **Old Prussian**. We know the names of several other Baltic languages that were spoken in medieval Europe, but no texts have survived in them; however, a fair number of personal names are preserved from **Curonian**, a medieval East Baltic language that seems to have formed a bridge between Latvian and Old Prussian. Note in passing that Estonian, though geographically "Baltic," is not related and belongs rather to the non-IE Uralic family.

Phonology

Consonants

18.61. Like Slavic, Baltic changed the PIE palatal velars to sibilants. Outside Lithuanian, the treatment is the same as Slavic, with *s* and *z* the outcome of PIE **k̂* and **ĝ(h)*: Latv. *sirds*, OPruss. *seyr* 'heart' < **k̂r̥d-*; Latv. *zirnis*, OPruss. *syrne* 'grain' (with *s-* probably representing *z* in the German-based orthography of the language) < **ĝr̥h₂-n-* (cp. Lat. *grānum*, Eng. *corn*). In Lithuanian, however, the outcomes are *š* and *ž*: *širdìs* 'heart' and *žìrnis* 'pea'.

18.62. The "ruki" rule changed an old **s* to *š* in some words in Lithuanian: *viršùs* 'high' (cp. OCS *vrĭxŭ* 'high' < **u̯r̥s-*), *aušrà* 'dawn' < **h₂eus-r-* (cp. **h₂eus-ōs-* in Lat. *aurōra* 'dawn'). As there are many words where the change apparently did not happen, such as *klausýti* 'to hear' and *vìsas* 'all', and since the change did not affect Latvian or Old Prussian, the change appears not to have spread through the whole of Baltic territory.

Short vowels

18.63. Short $*i$ and $*u$ remained intact: Lith. *lìkti* 'to leave', Latv. *likt* < $*lik^w$- (cp. Lat. *re-lic-tus* 'left behind'); Lith. *šuñs*, Latv. *suns*, OPruss. *sunis*, all genitive singular meaning 'of (a) dog' (PIE **k̂un-os*, cp. Ved. *śúnas*, Gk. *kunós*). Short $*e$ generally stayed intact as well, as in the words for 'honey', Lith. *medùs*, Latv. *medus*, and OPruss. *meddo* < **medhu-*. But there are a number of problematic words in which $*e$ is continued by *a*, especially in word-initial position: **eĝ-* 'I' > Lith. *àš*, and **ek̂u̯o-* 'horse' > OLith. *ašva* 'mare' are two examples. These forms vary dialectally.

18.64. As in Germanic, short $*a$ and $*o$ merged as *a*: Lith. *akìs*, Latv. *acs*, OPruss. *ackis* (nomin. pl.) 'eye' < $*ok^w$- (earlier $*h_3ek^w$-); Lith. *ašìs* 'axis', Latv. *ass*, OPruss. *assis* < **aĝ-s-* (earlier $*h_2$*eĝ-s-*). Note this merger is opposite that of Slavic (§18.28).

Long vowels

18.65. Long $*\bar{a}$ and $*\bar{o}$ remained distinct in Baltic, in contrast to Slavic. The long $*\bar{a}$ remained intact in Latvian (as in *māte* 'mother' < **māter-* < $*meh_2ter$-), but became ō in Lithuanian (*mótė*). Long $*\bar{o}$ has different reflexes in the different branches of Baltic. It became the diphthong *uo* in East Baltic (Lith. *dúoti* 'to give', Latv. *duot* 'to give' < **dōti* < $*deh_3$*-tei*), but not in West Baltic (contrast OPruss. *datwei* 'to give'). The other long vowels remained intact: Lith. *bė̃gti* 'to run', Latv. *bēgt* < $*bh\bar{e}g^w$*-tei*; Lith. *gývas* 'alive', Latv. *dzīvs*, OPruss. masc. accus. pl. *gi(j)wans* or *geywans* < $*g^w\bar{\imath}$*-u̯o-* (earlier $*g^wih_3$*-u̯o-*); Lith. *bū́ti* 'to be', Latv. *būt*, OPruss. *buton* < **bhū-* (earlier **bhuH-*).

Morphology

Verbs

18.66. While Slavic preserved the aorist but lost the *s*-future, Baltic fully preserved the *s*-future but lost the aorist. Like Slavic and several other branches of IE, Baltic created a new imperfect. In the present tense of thematic verbs, the *o*-grade of the thematic vowel has been generalized in all persons: Lith. 3rd sing. *sùka*, 2nd pl. *sùkate* 'turn' from **-o *-o-te* (cp. the Tocharian verb classes III and IV, §17.28; contrast Gk. *phérei phérete*). A curious and not fully explained trait of Baltic is that in all tenses of the verb, the 3rd singular also is used for the 3rd dual and plural: thus Lith. *ẽsti* means 'is', 'both of them are', and 'they are'. This may be connected with the fact that the original 3rd plural indicative ending was reanalyzed as the nominative plural of active participles, as in Lith. *vedą̃* 'leading' < **u̯edan* < **u̯edh-ont(i)* 'they lead'. Regarding modal categories, the optative has lived on a bit more robustly than in Slavic: it not only became used as an imperative (e.g. Old Prussian 2nd pl. *īdeiti* 'eat!') but also, in the 3rd singular, gave rise to a category called the permissive in Lithuanian (*te-dirbiẽ* 'let him work', with *-ie* < **-oit*) and survived as an actual optative in Prussian, built to the *s*-future and apparently also only in the 3rd singular (e.g. *bousei* 'may it be'). (Lithuanian and Latvian also have a mood called the optative, which is partly built from the old supine, as discussed above in §18.16.)

Nouns

18.67. The Baltic noun is remarkably conservative, preserving the copious case system inherited from PIE. (See the Lithuanian paradigms given below.) Nouns with stems in *-ē-*, like Lith. *mótė* 'mother', became very prolific in Baltic; their origin is the subject of debate since PIE did not have such a class. Baltic also saw a profusion of new *i*-stems; these developed from old consonant stems by generalizing the vowel *-i-* in the accusative singular **-im*, the outcome of the old consonant-stem ending **-m̥*. One reduction worth noting is the loss of neuter gender in East Baltic.

Lithuanian

18.68. Lithuanian literature begins around 1525, when translations of the Lord's Prayer, the Creed, and the Ave Maria were composed. The language of this period is called **Old Lithuanian**, and differs from the modern language chiefly in inflection: three noun cases were in use that have since become obsolete in the standard language, the allative, illative, and adessive; and athematic verb inflection was considerably more widespread than it is today. (The extra noun cases were an invention of East Baltic; the illative is also found in older Latvian. They probably arose under the influence of neighboring Finnic languages.) The modern literary language is based on that of the author Jonas Jablonskis (1861–1930), who wrote in a variety of the highland dialect, Aukštatian, of eastern Lithuania. The lowland dialect, Žemaitian or Samogitian, is spoken in the west (albeit by an ever-dwindling number of speakers) and differs in many respects from the standard, preserving for example the additional nominal cases just mentioned, the "broken" tone, and, in some varieties, final nasals.

18.69. Lithuanian does not differ significantly from the picture drawn above for Common Baltic. The accent is mobile, with two types of intonation (rising and falling) distinguished in long syllables. A long syllable contains a long vowel, a diphthong, or a sequence of vowel plus resonant. The rising intonation is denoted by a circumflex accent (˜): *mẽdis* 'tree', *sūnaũ* 'son!', *šuñs* 'of the dog'. The falling intonation is denoted by either an acute (´) or a grave (`) accent: *výras* 'man', *pakláusti* 'to ask', *pìlnas* 'full'. The grave accent is also used over short vowels to indicate stress but without any particular pitch contrast, as in *ìki* 'until'. (Confusingly, the terminology and the accent-marks of Lithuanian are exactly backwards from the rest of Balto-Slavic since apparently Lithuanian flipped the original system: the Lithuanian "acute," though historically from the Balto-Slavic acute, is a falling intonation rather than a rising one, and the Lithuanian "circumflex," historically from the Balto-Slavic circumflex, is rising; compare §18.11.)

18.70. Having arrived at Lithuanian, we will now be able to present an overview of some typical Balto-Slavic accent classes and paradigms. For lack of space, we will present only nominal paradigms, and only a subset of them.

The original distinction was between paradigms with accent fixed on the root and those with accent on the ending. Each of these underwent some changes depending on the acuteness of the syllables involved. The simplest paradigms are those with stress on acute root syllables; in these the stress remained on the root throughout (Slavic class a, Lithuanian class 1). If, however, the root syllable was stressed non-acute, then the stress often became affected by two similar but independent sound changes in Slavic and Lithuanian that moved stresses rightward off non-acute syllables. In Lithuanian, the stress moved if the following syllable was acute; this is known as **Saussure's Law** (not to be confused with Saussure–Pedersen's Law of pre-Balto-Slavic). In Slavic, it moved regardless of the intonation of the following syllable; this is known as **Dybo's Law**, after the contemporary Russian linguist Vladimir Dybo. The result of these laws was the creation of class b in Slavic and class 2 in Lithuanian.

18.71. To illustrate these two pairs of classes, observe the paradigms below (Russ. *síto* 'sieve', Lith. *síeta* 'screen, sieve', Russ. *trubá* 'trumpet', and Lith. *rankà* 'hand'). In the boldfaced forms, the accent has been moved by Dybo's Law or Saussure's Law, whichever is applicable:

	Slav. class a	Lith. class 1	Slav. class b	Lith. class 2
Singular				
N	*sít-o*	*síet-as*	***trub-á***	***rank-à***
G	*sít-a*	*síet-o*	***trub-ý***	*rañk-os*
D	*sít-u*	*síet-ui*	***trub-é***	*rañk-ai*
A	*sít-o*	*síet-ą*	***trub-ú***	*rañk-ą*
I	*sít-om*	*síet-u*	***trub-ój***	***rank-à***
L	*sít-e*	*síet-e*	***trub-é***	*rañk-oje*
V	*sít-o*	*síet-e*	***trub-á***	*rañk-a*
Plural				
N	*sít-a*	*síet-ai*	*trúb-y*	*rañk-os*
G	*sít*	*síet-ų*	*trúb*	*rañk-ų*
D	*sít-am*	*síet-ams*	*trúb-am*	*rañk-oms*
A	*sít-a*	*síet-us*	*trúb-y*	***rank-às***
I	*sít-ami*	*síet-ais*	*trúb-ami*	*rañk-omis*
L	*sít-ax*	*síet-uose*	*trúb-ax*	*rañk-ose*
V	*sít-a*	*síet-ai*	*trúb-y*	*rañk-os*

The Slavic class b plural paradigm was stressed on the ending, but in Russian a later change moved the accent back to the root. In the Lithuanian class 2 paradigm, endings like genit. sg. *-os*, dative sg. *-ai* were non-acute because they go back to forms with contraction across a lost laryngeal (genit. **-eh$_2$-es* > **-aas* > **-ā̃s*, dat. **-eh$_2$-ei* > **-aei* > **-ā̃i*), whereas the nomin. and instr. sg. and accus. pl. had ordinary long vowels from sequences of short vowel plus laryngeal: nomin. *-a* < **-ā* < **-eh$_2$*, instr. *-a* < **-ā* < **-eh$_2$-h$_1$*, accus. *-as* < **-ās* < **-eh$_2$s*.

18.72. The other classes, where the stress was originally on the ending, present a more complicated picture because here the stress was retracted in some forms due to the workings of Saussure–Pedersen's Law. We saw that this explained the retracted accent in a form like *dùkterį*; other accusative singulars where the law did not apply nonetheless had their stress retracted analogically. To illustrate classes 3 and 4, as well as the *i*-stems, *u*-stems and consonant stems, observe the paradigms of the words for 'heart', 'son' (both class 3), and 'dog' (class 4):

	Singular			Plural		
N	*širdìs*	*sūnùs*	*šuõ*	*šìrdys*	*sū́nūs*	*šùnys, šùnes*
G	*širdiẽs*	*sūnaũs*	*šuñs*	*širdžių̃*	*sūnų̃*	*šunų̃*
D	*šìrdžiai*	*sū́nui*	*šùniui*	*širdìms*	*sūnùms*	*šunìms*
A	*šìrdį*	*sū́nų*	*šùnį*	*šìrdis*	*sū́nus*	*šunìs*
I	*širdimì*	*sūnumì*	*šunimì, šuniù*	*širdimìs*	*sūnumìs*	*šunimìs*
L	*širdyjè*	*sūnujè*	*šunyjè*	*širdysè*	*sūnuosè*	*šunysè*
V	*širdiẽ*	*sūnaũ*	*šuniẽ*	*šìrdys*	*sū́nūs*	*šùnys*

Although the accentual system is an innovation, the case-endings of the Baltic noun are remarkably conservative. The singular of the *o*-stems, for example, faithfully continues all the IE *o*-stem singular case-endings except the genitive singular. (The PIE genitive was lost, and the Baltic ending is from the ablative.) The hooked vowels in forms like *výrą* and *šùnį* were once nasal vowels that continued sequences of vowel plus nasal.

18.73. It is popularly said that Lithuanian is the oldest or most conservative Indo-European language now spoken. This impression rests largely on the high degree of faithfulness with which it has preserved the aspects of PIE phonology and nominal morphology discussed above, and is bolstered by such close equivalencies between it and Sanskrit as Lith. *kàs* 'who' and Ved. *kás* 'who'. While calling it the "oldest" IE language is a misnomer, its conservativeness in these areas cannot be gainsaid, and probably does exceed that of all the other contemporary IE languages (although such things are not easily quantified). It should be remembered, however, that the language has not been equally conservative in all domains.

Lithuanian text sample

18.74. An example of a *raudà* or traditional song of lament, in this case on the occasion of the loss of a son. From the collection by A. Juškevič, *Lëtuviszkos dainos użraszytos* (Kazan, 1881–3) III 1192. The spelling has been modernized. Virtually every word in the first stanza goes back to PIE.

Õ mãno sūnẽli, mãno dobilẽli, õ mãno artojẽli, mãno šienpiūvẽli! Išauš pavasarẽlis, visų̃ sūnẽliai põ lýgius laukeliùs sù naujomìs žagrẽlėmis, sù šėmaĩs jautẽliais; õ žmonių̃ sūnẽliai põ lýgias lankelès sù šviesaĩs dalgẽliais švytū́ja.

Õ mãno sūnẽlio búbūja šėmì jautẽliai, sãvo artojẽlio pasigeñda; õ mãno vaikẽlio rūdýja šviẽsūs dalgẽliai.

Išaus̃ pavasarė̃lis; žmonių̃ moterė̃lis põ ulytėlès sù glėbùčiais nešiójas; õ àš vienà, õ àš vienà verkiù pasižiūrė̃dama; õ àš verkiù, neturiù neĩ jokiõs patiekė̃lės, neturiù sù kūmì pasidžiaũgti.

Õ mãno sūnẽli, mãno diemedė̃li, kàd àš bū́čiau užsiaugìnus, añt kojė̃lių pastãčius. Õ mãno mažiukė̃li, ar̃ mãno rankė̃lės taĩp suñkios, ar̃ mãno žodẽliai taĩp skaũdūs?

O my little son, my little clover, o my little plowman, my little hay-mower! The springtime will grow light, everyone's sons (will be) in the flat fields with new plows, with young gray oxen; o men's dear sons make shiny motions with their gleaming scythes in the flat meadows.

O the young gray oxen of my little son bellow, they long for their little plowman; o the gleaming scythes of my little boy grow rusty.

Spring will grow light; the mother of men (will go about) in the streets carrying (her children) with her embraces; o I (am) alone, o I alone cry while looking about; o I cry, I may not take consolation in anything, may not delight in anyone.

O my little son, my little southernwood, if only I had reared (you), had placed (you) on (your) little feet. O my little one, (was) my hand too heavy, (were) my words too painful?

18.74a. Notes (to first stanza only). **mãno:** 'my', dialectal for standard *màno*. **sūnẽli:** 'little son', vocative of *sūnẽlis*, diminutive of *sūnùs*, cognate with Eng. *son* (PIE **suHnu-*). Practically every noun is turned into a diminutive in this lament, with the suffix *-ẽlis* (or *-ė̃lis* when the base has two syllables); diminutives are frequently used to express tenderness or other emotive shades of meaning. They have sometimes been rendered as 'little' or 'dear' in the translation above, and sometimes not translated in any special way. **dobilė̃li:** 'little clover', vocative diminutive of *dóbilas*. **artojė̃li:** 'little plowman', vocative diminutive of *artójis*, agent noun from *árti* 'to plow' < PIE **h_2erh_3-*, cp. Lat. *arāre* 'to plow'. **šienpiūvė̃li:** 'little hay-maker', dialectal voc. diminutive of *šienpiū̃vis*, from *šiẽnas* 'hay' (cp. OCS *sěno*) and *piáuti* 'to cut, mow' (cp. Lat. *pū-tāre* 'to cut'). **išaus̃:** 'will become daylight, will become bright day', 3rd sing. future of *iš-aũšti*; cp. *aušrà* 'dawn' < PIE **h_2eus-*. **pavasarė̃lis:** 'little springtime', from *pavãsaris* 'spring', lit. 'upon-summer' (*vãsara* 'summer'); cp. Czech *podzim* 'fall', lit. 'upon-winter' (*zima* 'winter'). **visų̃:** 'of all', genit. pl. of *vìsas*; cognate with OCS *vĭsĭ* 'all, entire', Ved. *víś-va-* 'every'. **laukeliùs:** 'little fields', accus. pl. diminutive of *laũkas*, cognate with Lat. *lūcus* 'grove' and Eng. *lea* 'meadow'. **sù:** 'with', cp. OCS *sŭ*. **naujomìs:** 'new', instr. pl. of *naũjas*, from PIE **neu-i̯o-* (also in Ved. *návya-*), a by-form of **neu̯o-* (Hitt. *newa-*, Lat. *nouus*, and Eng. *new*). **šėmaĩs:** 'blue-gray' (said of animals), instr. pl., related to Ved. *śyāmá-* 'dark'. **jautẽliais:** 'young oxen', instr. pl. diminutive of *jáutis* 'ox', cp. Ved. *yuváti* 'binds'. **žmonių̃:** 'of men', genit. pl. The paradigm is irregular; the singular is *žmogùs*, the plural is *žmónės*, which is morphologically feminine and comes from the stem of the Old Lithuanian *n*-stem singular *žmuõ*. The word is cognate with OPruss. *smuni(n)* 'person', Lat. *homō* 'man, person' (stem *homin-*), from PIE **dhĝh(e)mō(n)* (cp. §6.30). **šviesaĩs:** 'shining, gleaming', instr. pl.; from PIE **k̑u̯ei-s-*, related to *švytū́ja* at the end of the sentence. **švytū́ja:** 'flash, make a gleaming motion', dialectal 3rd pl. of *švytúoti*, from **k̑u̯īt-*, a neo-lengthened grade (§18.16) from **k̑u̯it-*, zero-grade of **k̑u̯ei-t-* (the root of OCS *svĭtiti sę* 'to shine' and Eng. *white*).

Latvian

18.75. Latvian, like Lithuanian, is first attested in a translation of a catechism, dating to 1585. The two languages are quite similar, but Latvian is less conservative and gives the impression of a Lithuanian that has been somewhat slimmed down. The accent has been fixed on the initial syllable, which has led to widespread apocope of vowels in final syllables: thus contrast Latv. *rīts* 'day' and *būt* 'to be' with Lith. *rýtas* and *bū́ti*. Unlike Lithuanian but like Old Prussian and Slavic, the PIE palatal stops **k̂* and **ĝ(h)* became *s* and *z*: *desmit* 'ten' (**dek̂m̥-t-*; cp. Lith. *dẽšimt*), *ziema* 'winter' (**ĝheim-*; cp. Lith. *žiemà*). Latvian has lost *n* before consonants, as in *ruoka* 'hand' versus Lith. *rankà*. The consonants have been widely affected by palatalization, as in *acis* 'eyes' (Lith. *ãkys*) and *dzērve* 'crane' (Lith. *gérvė*). In the native orthography, palatalization is often indicated with a comma underneath the letter (as in *ceļš* 'road' in the text passage below).

In morphology, the language is similar to Lithuanian; its most characteristic innovation is a mood known as the debitive, expressing necessity and formed by prefixing the syllable *jā-* (from the relative pronominal stem **i̯o-*) to a 3rd singular verb form: *man jālasa grāmata* 'I must read a book'. The construction is impersonal; the logical subject ('I', *man*) is in the dative case, and the logical object ('book', *grāmata*) is in the nominative.

Latvian text sample

18.76. Excerpt from the poem "Atraitnes dēls" ("The Widow's Son") by Vilis Plūdonis (1874–1940).

Es kāpt gribu kalnā visaugstākā,
Ne spēka man pietrūks, ne bail man no kā,
Lai putenis plosās, lai ziemelis elš,
Uz augšu, uz augšu tik ies man ceļš.
Es laidīšos jūras dziļumos,
Un meklēšu, pētīšu, vandīšu tos,
Līdz pērli būšu tur atradis,
Par visām skaistāk kas mirgo un viz.

I want to climb the highest mountain,
I shall neither lack any strength, nor shall I fear anything,
Although the blizzard rages, although the north wind howls,
I will climb up, I will climb up, wherever my road will go.
I shall dive into the depths of the ocean,
And I shall look for, explore, (and) rummage through them
Until I shall have found a pearl there,
Which glitters and gleams more beautifully than anything.

18.76a. Notes.1–2. es: 'I'; in contrast to Lith. *àš* it preserves the inherited **e* of PIE **eĝ-*. **kāpt:** 'to climb'; *-t* is the infinitive ending (Lith. *-ti*, Baltic **-tei*). **gribu:** 'I want', 1st sing.

present of *gribēt* 'to want'. **kalnā:** 'mountain', locative sing. **visaugstākā:** 'highest', superlative of *augsts* 'high'. **ne . . . ne:** 'neither . . . nor'. **spēka:** 'strength', genit. sing. of *spēks* 'strength', object of the impersonal verb *pietrūks*, which takes a genitive object and a dative subject (*man*, 'I'; lit. 'to me there will not be wanting of strength'). **pietrūks:** 'will lack', 3rd sing. future; *-s* is the future suffix. **bail:** 'fear'. **no kā:** 'from anything'; *kā* is genitive of *ka* 'something, anything'.

3–6. lai: 'although'. **putenis:** 'blizzard'. **plosās:** 'rages', 3rd sing. of the reflexive verb *plosīties*; in both forms the *-s* is the reflexive particle, from PIE **su̯e-*. **ziemelis:** 'north wind', from *ziema* 'winter'. **elš:** 'howls', 3rd sing. of *elsāt*. **uz:** 'up'. **augšu:** 'I will climb', 1st sing. future of *augt*. The *-š* is palatalized from *-s*, as also in the forms *ceļš*, *laidīšos*, *meklēšu*, *pētīšu*, *vandīšu*, *būšu* below. **tik:** 'thus, so', translated here 'wherever'. **ies:** 'will go', 3rd sing. fut. **ceļš:** 'road'. **laidīšos:** 'I will dive into', reflexive verb. **jūras:** 'ocean', genit. sing. of *jūra*. **dziļumos:** 'depths', accus. pl. of *dziļums*, from *dziļs* 'deep'. **meklēšu, pētīšu, vandīšu:** all 1st sing. future. **tos:** accus. pl. demonstrative pronoun.

7–8. līdz: 'until'. **būšu tur atradis:** 'I shall have found', periphrastic future perfect of *atrast* 'to find'. **par:** 'than', preposition, PIE **per* 'through'. **visām:** 'everything', cp. note on Lith. visų̄ above (§18.74a). **skaistāk:** 'more beautiful', comparative of *skaists*. Note that this whole phrase has been fronted before the relative pronoun *kas*, a syntactic feature characteristic of poetic language. **kas:** 'which'. **mirgo:** 'glitters', 3rd sing. present of *mirdzēt*. **viz:** 'gleams', 3rd sing. of *vizēt*.

Old Prussian

18.77. Old Prussian is the only known West Baltic language, and unfortunately it is not known all that well. It was spoken in the former German territory of East Prussia (now a small area of northeastern Poland along the Gulf of Gdańsk and extending to Kaliningrad), which became German when it was conquered by the knights of the Teutonic Order in 1283. We possess two vocabularies and three texts in Old Prussian. First is the Elbing Vocabulary, compiled around 1300 but existing in a copy from a century later; it contains 802 words from a southern dialect. Of poorer quality is a list of 100 Prussian words in the Prussian Chronicle of a monk named Simon Grunau from the early 1500s; these are based on northwestern Old Prussian dialects. Our only connected texts are three Lutheran catechisms from the mid-1500s that are translated from German. The translations are not of high quality, and there is much inconsistency in orthography; but they do provide us with our sole window onto the grammar and structure of the language. We also possess many Prussian personal names from German sources. By the close of the seventeenth century the language had become extinct.

18.78. Old Prussian is of great interest because it shares several traits with Slavic but not Baltic, or with other IE languages but not the rest of Balto-Slavic. For example, while the rest of Balto-Slavic replaced the *o*-stem genitive singular with the ablative, Old Prussian has a form in *-as* which can only come from PIE **-os(i̯)o* like Skt. *-asya* and Homeric Gk. *-oio*. While the rest of Balto-Slavic has a present passive participle in **-mo-*, OPruss. preserves the more familiar type in **-m(e)no-* or **-mh₁no-* (§5.60), as in the form *poklausīmanas* '(are) heard'. The pronominal oblique stem-formant **-sm-* that is found in Indo-Iranian and Italic (§7.9) also makes an appearance in Old Prussian forms like the dative *stesmu* 'to the' (cp. Ved. dat. *tásmai*, South Picene locative **esmen**), while the rest of Balto-Slavic has only *-m-* (e.g. Russ. *tomu* 'to him', Lith. *tãmui* 'to him', Latv. *tam*). Old Prussian is also the only Balto-Slavic language to preserve the original *n-* of the word for 'nine' (spelled *newints* or *newyntz*); in the rest of Balto-Slavic, the **n-* was replaced prehistorically with a *d-* that spread from the following number 'ten' (cp. OCS *devętĭ*, Lith. *devynì*, alongside OCS *desętĭ* 'ten', Lith. *dẽšimt*). One wonders what other archaic features the language boasted of which we have no knowledge.

Old Prussian text sample

18.79. The Ten Commandments from the Second Catechism of 1548.

Staey dessimpts pallapsaey
Pirmois. Tou ni tur kittans deiwans turryetwey.
Anters. Tou ni tur sten emnen twayse deywas ni enbaenden westwey.
Tirtis. Tou tur stan lankinan deynan swyntintwey.
Ketwirtz. Tou tur twayien thawan bhae mutien smunintwey.
Pyienkts. Tou ni tur gallintwey.
Usts. Tou ni tur salobisquan limtwey.
Septmas. Tou ni tur ranktwey.
Asmus. Tou ni tur reddi weydikausnan waytiaton preyken twayien tauwyschen.
Newyntz. Tou ni tur pallapsitwey twaysis tauwyschis butten.
Dessympts. Tou ni tur pallapsitwey twaysis tauwyschies gennan, waykan, mergwan, pecku, adder ka-tanaessen hest.

The Ten Commandments
First. Thou shalt not have other gods. Second. Thou shalt not take the name of thy God in vain. Third. Thou shalt keep holy the sabbath. Fourth. Thou shalt honor thy father and mother. Fifth. Thou shalt not kill. Sixth. Thou shalt not commit adultery. Seventh. Thou shalt not steal. Eighth. Thou shalt not bear false witness against thy neighbor. Ninth. Thou shalt not covet thy neighbor's house. Tenth. Thou shalt not covet thy neighbor's wife, manservant, maidservant, cattle or what is his.

18.79a. Notes (selective). **staey:** 'the', definite article, nomin. pl.; compare the accusative singulars below, *sten* and *stan*. **dessimpts:** 'ten', cp. Lith. *dẽšimt*. **pallapsaey:** 'commandments', defective spelling of *pallaipsaey*, nom. pl. of *pallaips*; cp. Lith. *liẽpti* 'to order' < **leip-*. **pirmois:** 'first', cp. Lith. *pìrmas*; see §7.19. **tou:** 'you', cp. Lith. *tù*; lengthened **tū* in OCS *ty*. **ni:** 'not'. **tur:** 'have to, must', cp. Lith. *turėti* 'have to'. **kittans:** 'other', accus. pl.; cp. Lith. *kìtas* 'other'. **deiwans:** 'gods', accus. pl., exactly continuing PIE **dei̯u-ons* (cf. §6.55). **turryetwey:** 'have', infinitive; same verb as *tur* earlier in the sentence. The infinitive ending *-twey* is similar to the infinitive ending *-ti* (< **-tei*) in the rest of Balto-Slavic, which goes back to the locative of a verbal abstract noun in **-ti-*. The OPruss. form appears to go back to an abstract in **-tu-* instead (§5.58).

anters: 'second', literally 'the other', and cognate with Eng. *other*. **emnen:** 'name', metathesized from **enmen*; Slavic has **ĭmę* from earlier **inmen-* from **$h_1\underset{\circ}{n}(h_3)$-men*; see §6.36.

westwey: literally 'to lead', from PIE **u̯eĝh-* 'convey' (> OCS *vezti* 'to convey', Lat. *uehō* 'I carry, convey', also in Eng. *wagon*). **tirtis:** 'third'. **deynan:** 'day', accus. sing. **swyntintwey:** 'keep holy', cp. Lith. *šveñtas* 'holy', OCS *svętŭ* 'holy', all cognate with Avestan *spəṇta-* 'holy'; PIE **k̂u̯ento-*. **ketwirtz:** 'fourth'. **thawan:** 'father', accus. sing.; cp. Lith. *tė̃vas*. **mutien:** 'mother', accus. sing., cp. Lith. *mótina*.

pyienkts: 'fifth'. **gallintwey:** 'to kill'. **usts:** 'sixth', written *wuschts* in the First Catechism. This would appear to come from **uk̂-to-*, with **uk̂-* being some kind of reduced form of PIE **su̯ek̂s* 'six'. Its closest relative is dialectal Lith. *ũšės* 'puerperium' (the period of six weeks of rest after giving birth). **salobisquan:** 'marital'; ultimately a borrowing from Slavic (cp. Polish *ślubić* 'to get engaged'). **limtwey:** 'to break'; cp. OCS *lomiti*. **septmas:** 'seventh', closer to PIE **sept(m̥)mo-* and OCS *sedmŭ* than Lith. *septiñtas* and Latv. *septītais*. **ranktwey:** 'to steal'. **asmus:** 'eighth'; cp. Lith. *ãšmas*, OCS *osmŭ* < **ok̂t-mo-*, probably remade from whatever the PIE form was (see §7.21) under the influence of the preceding **sept(m̥)mo-*. **reddi:** 'false'. **weydikausnan:** 'witness'. **tauwyschen:** 'neighbor'; cp. Latv. *tūvs* 'near'.

newyntz: 'ninth', important in preserving the *n-* (see §18.78). **pallapsitwey:** 'covet'. **butten:** 'house'; probably from the same root as German *bauen* 'to build'. **dessympts:** 'tenth'. **gennan:** 'wife', PIE **gʷen-* 'woman' (> Eng. *queen*). **waykan:** 'manservant', accus. sing. of *waix*. **pecku:** 'cattle', virtually unchanged from PIE **pek̂u*, but problematic in showing a centum-like treatment of the palatal *k*. See §18.5. **ka-:** 'which', relative/interrogative pronominal stem (PIE **kʷo-*), cliticized to the following word. **hest:** 'is'; the *h-* is unexplained. It is usually spelled *est* or *aest* (*ast* in the First Catechism).

For Further Reading

There is no general reference book treating historical Balto-Slavic grammar as a unit; most books treat either Baltic or Slavic, or treat just one aspect of Balto-Slavic. In the latter category may be chiefly mentioned Stang 1942, which treats the verb. Two highly technical works, Kuryłowicz 1958 and 1956 (see Bibliography, chs 3 and 4), are on general topics in IE phonology but have a wealth of material on the Slavic and Baltic vowel systems and accentology. See also more recently Petit 2003 on ablaut in Baltic, and Garde 1976 on Balto-Slavic accentology (with emphasis on Slavic).

The most thorough comparative grammar of Slavic is Vaillant 1950–77, which also treats the developments in the Slavic daughter languages. Shorter and also very useful is Meillet 1965 (with revisions and expansions by Vaillant). The history of Slavic phonology from PIE to the modern languages is given detailed and able treatment in Carlton 1990, although the few pages on PIE itself are a bit old-fashioned. On Slavic accentology, see also Stang 1965. No comprehensive Slavic etymological dictionary is yet complete; Trubachev 1974– , arranged by reconstructed Slavic form, is now up to *obsojĭnisa*. The standard etymological dictionary of Russian is Vasmer 1953–8; a revised edition appeared a few years later in Russian, and still has to do double duty as a Slavic etymological dictionary. The best grammar of Old Church Slavonic in English is Lunt 2001, although Indo-Europeanists tend to favor Leskien 1990.

The history of Baltic phonology and morphology is masterfully covered in Stang 1966, but its accessibility is lessened by the fact that quotes from scholarly literature written in various Slavic and Baltic languages are left untranslated. A supplementary volume with an index and corrections was published in 1975. Easier to use (and in English) is Endzelīns 1971. Lithuanian is well served with a good etymological dictionary, Fraenkel 1962–5; Zinkevičius 1996 has some good sections on historical grammar. Note also Senn 1957–66, a classic reference grammar whose second volume has sample texts and a glossary. For Old Prussian, useful and accessible is Schmalstieg's 1974 historical grammar; the texts are collected in Trautmann 1910. Two etymological dictionaries of Old Prussian are (in Lithuanian) Maziulis 1988–97 and (in Russian) the incomplete Toporov 1975– (through L). A Latvian etymological dictionary is Karulis 1992.

For Review

Know the meaning or significance of the following:

"ruki" rule	Pedersen's Law	Third Palatalization	Constantine and Methodius
pitch-accent	Law of Open Syllables	yer	Rus'
Winter's Law	First Palatalization	*ToRT* groups	*dainos*
acute	Second Palatalization	perfective	permissive
"neo-lengthened" grade		imperfective	Saussure's Law
		animate	Dybo's Law

Exercises

1 Explain the history or significance of each of the following Slavic forms. The forms are in OCS unless otherwise noted.

a	*tysęštĭ*	**f**	*usŭnǫtĭ*	**j**	Russ. *voróna*
b	*srĭdĭce*	**g**	*nosŭ*	**k**	*pętĭ*
c	Russ. *umirat'*	**h**	*myšĭ*	**l**	Old Russ. *byšęštĭ*
d	*bogŭ*	**i**	Russ. *gorod*	**m**	Maced. *knigata*
e	*uxo*				

2 Explain the history or significance of each of the following Baltic forms. The forms are Lithuanian unless marked otherwise.

a	*dùkterį*	**f**	*vil̃kas*	**k**	*te-dirbiẽ*
b	*sė́sti*	**g**	*viršùs*	**l**	Latv. *ziema*
c	*klausýti*	**h**	*akìs*	**m**	OPruss. *poklausīmanas*
d	*šim̃tas*	**i**	*dúoti*	**n**	OPruss. *newints*
e	*pìlnas*	**j**	*vedą̃*		

3 Give the PIE velar from which the boldfaced segments in the following forms descend. In the Slavic forms, there has been no palatalization. Some forms may have more than one answer.

a Serbo-Croatian ***zûb*** 'tooth'
b Lith. *kár**šti*** 'to age'
c Pol. ***krew*** 'blood'
d OCS ***slava*** 'fame, glory'
e Lith. ***žmogùs*** 'person'
f Latv. ***sir̃ds*** 'heart'
g Lith. ***gérvė*** 'crane'
h Lith. ***kàs*** 'who'
i Latv. ***zir̃nis*** 'grain'

4 For each of the following reconstructed proto-Slavic forms, identify whether it would later be affected by one of the Slavic palatalizations, and if so, by which one.

a **rǫkě* 'hands' (nom. pl.)
b **nogě* 'legs' (nom. pl.)
c **brěgi* 'river bank' (loc. sing.)
d **sněgĭnŭ* 'snowy'
e **starĭkĭ* 'old man' (nom. sing.)

5 Identify the yers in each of the following OCS words, and for each yer indicate whether it is weak or strong.

a *vĭsĭ* 'village'
b *dvĭrĭnikŭ* 'doorkeeper'
c *dlĭgotrĭpělivŭ* 'long-suffering'
d *zŭvati* 'to call'
e *vŭzměriti* 'to measure'
f *sŭnĭnŭ* 'relating to sleep'
g *otŭdesętĭvovati* 'pay a tithe'
h *vŭgodĭnikŭ* 'servant'

6 Explain the role that Balto-Slavic plays in the laryngeal theory.

7 Another stress shift in the prehistory of Balto-Slavic, not discussed in the text, known as Hirt's Law (after the nineteenth- and twentieth-century German Indo-Europeanist Hermann Hirt), is illustrated by the following data:

PIE	Lithuanian	gloss
**dhuHmós*	*dū́mai*	smoke
**u̯iHrós*	*výras*	man
**dhoHnéh₂*	*dúona*	bread
**pl̥h₁nós*	*pìlnas*	full

Based on these forms, state the workings of the law.

8 Below is a partial paradigm of the Lithuanian word for 'blood' and the original PIE cases. This noun was originally accented on the endings:

	sing.	PIE	plur.	PIE
nom.	*kraũjas*	**-ós*	*kraujaĩ*	**-ói*
gen.	*kraũjo*	**-óHat*	*kraujų̃*	**-óHom*
dat.	*kraũjai*	**-ṓi*		
acc.	*kraũją*	**-óm*	*kraujùs*	**-ṓns*
inst.	*kraujù*	**-óh₁*	*kraujaĩs*	**-ṓis*

As is evident, the stress has been retracted in a number of cases. In which cases is the retraction expected and in which is it analogical? Are there any cases where a stress should have been retracted but was not?

PIE Vocabulary X: Time

**nok^{w}t-* 'NIGHT': Hitt. *nekuz* 'of eventide', Gk. *núks* (*núkt-*), Lat. *nox* (*noct-*), Lith. *naktìs*
**h$_2$eusōs* 'dawn': Ved. *uṣā́s*, Gk. (Doric) *ā̄ṓs*, Lat. *aurōra*
**ĝhi̯em-*, **ĝheim-* 'winter': Gk. *kheĩma*, Lat. *hiems*, OCS *zima*
**u̯es-r̥* 'spring': Gk. *éar*, Lat. *uēr*, OCS *vesna*, Lith. *vãsara*
**u̯et-* 'year': Hitt. *witt-*, Gk. *(w)étos*, Lat. *uetus* 'old'
**i̯eh$_1$-ro-* 'YEAR': Av. *yārə*, Gk. *hṓrā* 'season'

19 Albanian

Introduction

19.1. Albanian is the official language of Albania, where it is spoken by over 3 million people. Almost as many speak it in various areas of the former Yugoslavia, and smaller but not insignificant numbers of speakers live in enclaves in Macedonia, Greece, and southern Italy (Calabria and Sicily). The speakers in northern Albania, the former Yugoslavia, Macedonia, and Turkey speak the dialect called **Geg** (or Gheg, Albanian *Gegë*), while Albanians living in southern Albania, Greece, and Italy speak **Tosk** (*Toskë*), of which the Italian variety, called *Arbëresh* (*Albanian*, etymologically), is the most archaic. In Albania, the two dialects are separated roughly by the Shkumbin River. Both dialects have a literary history (see below); the official variety of Albanian since 1952 is Tosk, but with a goodly amount of admixture from Geg. The two dialects are mutually intelligible in their standard varieties, although numerous subdialects exist that show considerable variation, especially in the north and northeast of the Geg-speaking area. The Albanian-speaking populations of Greece and Italy arose probably between the thirteenth and fifteenth centuries.

19.2. Albanian forms its own separate branch of Indo-European; it is the last branch to appear in written records. This is one of the reasons why its origins are shrouded in mystery and controversy. The widespread assertion that it is the modern-day descendant of Illyrian, spoken in much the same region during classical times (see §§20.13ff.), makes geographic and historical sense but is linguistically untestable since we know so little about Illyrian. Competing hypotheses, likewise untestable, would derive Albanian from Thracian, another lost ancient language from farther east than Illyrian, or from Daco-Mysian, a hypothetical mixture or ancestor of Thracian, Illyrian, and the nearly unknown language of Dacia (a nearby Roman province). (We will discuss these languages in more detail in the next chapter.)

The region containing modern-day Albania became Roman territory in the second century BC. The influence of Latin on the vocabulary of Albanian was tremendous. In later times, Macedonian and Bulgarian provided many loanwords, and when Albania became part of the Ottoman Empire in the fifteenth century, a phase of Turkish influence began that lasted until independence was achieved in 1912. The massive overlayering of foreign vocabulary and concomitant loss of much of the native lexicon have made the phonological and morphological history of the language unusually

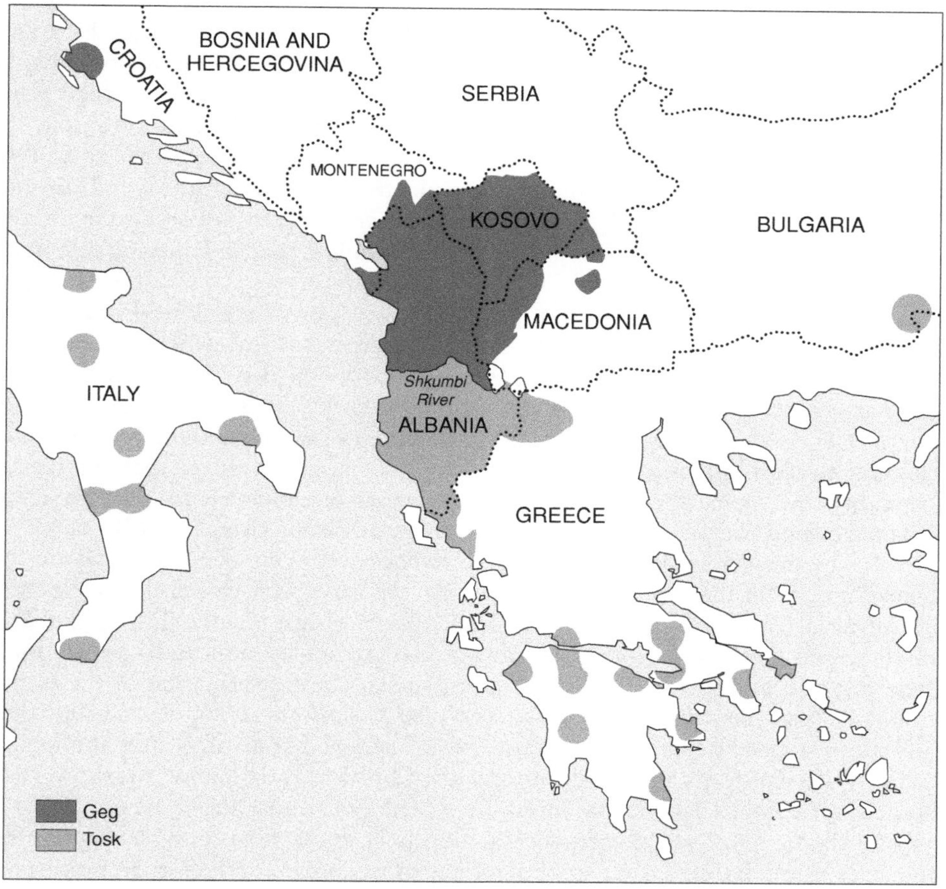

Map 19.1 Geographical distribution of Geg and Tosk

difficult to ascertain. Thanks to the many Latin loanwords, though, we are well informed about the post-Roman phonological changes; but much had already happened before then that is harder to shed light on. Albanian was in fact not universally recognized as Indo-European until the second half of the nineteenth century.

19.3. Under Turkish rule, the publication of Albanian writings was forbidden; most of the history of Albanian literature has been a history of its suppression. However, Roman Catholic missionaries working mostly in the Geg-speaking area gained permission in the fifteenth century to publish religious works. The first recorded piece of Albanian is a baptismal formula from 1462; two other fragments survive from later in the same century. A small number of Christian books were produced in the following two centuries, the earliest preserved being the *Meshari* or *Missal* of Gjon Buzuku from 1555, written in Old Geg. Tosk literature originated in Albanian-speaking regions of Sicily; the first known book in Tosk dates to 1592. But it is likely that there were earlier works which have vanished. The earliest preserved books both in Geg and in Tosk share features of spelling that point to some kind of common literary language having already developed, and a letter written by a Dominican friar named Gulielmus Adea in 1332 says that the inhabitants of Albania had a language very different from Latin but used the Latin alphabet in their writings, suggesting (if not proving) an already-existing written Albanian tradition.

The language up through the eighteenth century is often referred to as **Old Albanian.** The modern period is dated to the nineteenth century and beyond; around 1870, with the rise of nationalistic sentiment, greater numbers of works were written in Albanian, but largely by exiles. Only after Albanian independence did Albanian literature really begin to flourish.

Among the Albanian literary monuments that are of interest to Indo-Europeanists is the northern Albanian law code traditionally attributed (most likely incorrectly) to Lekë Dukagjini (1410–81), a comrade-in-arms of Gjergj Skanderbeg, the Albanian national hero who fought against the Ottoman Turks. This law code, or *kanun* ('canon'), is derived in large part from the customary law of northern Albania, and reflects many legal practices of great antiquity. The laws governing such matters as hospitality, the rights of heads of households, marriage, blood-feuds, and payment of damages find precise echoes in Vedic India and ancient Greece and Rome.

19.4. The most notable phonological differences between Geg and Tosk are the change of intervocalic *n* to *r* in Tosk (e.g. *vera* 'the wine' vs. Geg *vêna*) and the presence of nasal vowels in Geg from old sequences of vowel plus final *-n* (e.g. *shtâsë* 'animal', Old Geg *shtanse*, vs. Tosk *shtazë*; the circumflex indicates nasalization). There are also morphosyntactic differences, such as in the formation of the future tense (Geg *kam me shkue*, lit. 'I have to go', vs. Tosk *do të shkoj*, lit. 'it wants that I go'). The dialectal split into Geg and Tosk happened sometime after the region became Christianized in the fourth century AD: Christian Latin loanwords show Tosk rhotacism, such as Tosk *murgu* 'monk' (Geg *mungu*) from Lat. *monachus*.

19.5. Albanian famously shares several morphosyntactic features with neighboring languages of the Balkans – Greek, Bulgarian, Macedonian, Serbo-Croatian, eastern varieties of Romanian, and the regional variety of Romani. All four languages form what is often called the Balkan speech area or *Sprachbund* (to use the technical term that has been imported from German). Among the features common to most or all of these languages are a suffixed definite article; the loss of a true infinitive, at least in Tosk; the use of a periphrastic construction meaning 'want to . . .' to express the future tense; and the use of a particle with subjunctive verb forms. Since these features were not part of the early histories of any of these languages, how they developed and diffused throughout the region is an unsettled and interesting problem.

From PIE to Albanian

Phonology

19.6. Aside from the voiceless stops *p t k* and voiced stops *b d g*, modern Albanian has a rich complement of postalveolar and palatal consonants: the alveolar affricates *c* and *x* (roughly equal to English *ts* and *dz*), the alveopalatal affricates *ç* and *xh* (like English *ch* and *j*), and the palatal stops *q* and *gj*. It has nine fricatives, voiceless *f th s sh h* (all pronounced as in English) and voiced *v dh z zh* (where *dh* is [ð], the initial sound of English *the*). The nasals are *m*, *n*, and palatalized *nj* (like Spanish *ñ*), and the liquids *r* (a tap), *rr* (a trill), *l*, and *ll* (a "dark" *l* like the *l* in Eng. *ball*). Finally, it has the glide *j* (like Eng. *y*). The vowel system contains the ordinary *i e a o u* as well as *y* (like German *ü*) and *ë*, a schwa-like vowel.

All forms below are given in the Tosk standard unless otherwise indicated.

Consonants

19.7. Stops. PIE plain voiceless **p* and **t* are typically preserved: ***poqa*** 'I cooked' < **pēkʷ-*; ***ter*** 'I dry' (verb) < **tors-ei̯e-*; *gjalpë* 'butter' < **selpos* (cp. Gk. *élpos* 'fat', Eng. *salve*); and ***natë*** 'night' < **nokʷt-*. They were lost in some consonant clusters, as in *gjumë* 'sleep' < **supno-* and *shtatë* 'seven' < **septm̥-ti-*. Special outcomes are seen in clusters consisting of two dentals, as in the Old Geg past participle *pasë* 'had' < **pot-to-*.

19.8. The voiced aspirates lost their aspiration and fell together with the plain voiced stops, as evidenced by ***ndez*** 'I kindle' < **en-dhogʷh-ei̯e-* (root **dhegʷh-* 'burn') alongside ***di*** 'she-goat' < **deiĝh-ā* (cp. German *Ziege* 'goat'); and ***gardh*** 'hedge, fence' < **ghor-dho-* alongside ***ligë*** 'disease' < **leig-* (cp. Gk. *loigós* 'ruin, death'). The same merger is presumably also true of **bh* and **b*, though examples of the latter are hard to come by; a possible one is ***mbush*** 'fill' < **(e)n-buns-e/o-* (cf. Gk. *būnéō* 'I stuff full'). The aspirated counterpart's development to *b* is met for example in ***besë*** 'truce' from the root **bheidh-* (either **bhidh-tā* or, as recently suggested, **bhoidh-s-ā*, with **bhoidh-s-* from the same **bhoidh-es-* as Lat. *foedus* 'pact'). Word-initial **d(h)-* sometimes becomes *dh* [ð], as in ***dha*** '(s)he gave', ultimately from **deh₃-*; this development appears to have originated in certain sandhi contexts.

19.9. The Albanian reflexes of the velars present special challenges. Most specialists regard Albanian as a satem language since in the vast majority of cases the plain velars and the labiovelars fell together. But there appears to be a systematic difference in the outcomes of the plain velars and the labiovelars when they are palatalized, suggesting that the three series of velars were still kept distinct in some environments fairly late in the language's prehistory. Also unlike normal satem branches, the palatal velars lost their palatalization in certain contexts.

Albanian *k* continues **k* and **kʷ*, while *g* represents the merger of four sounds, **g*, **gʷ*, **gh*, and **gʷh*. Examples of each change include ***kohë*** 'time' < **kēsā* or **kēsk̂ā* (cp. OCS *časŭ* 'time'), ***kë*** 'whom' < **kʷom*, ***lig*** 'bad, sick' < **h₃ligo-* (cp. Gk. *olígos* 'little, few'), ***ngrënë*** 'eaten' < **on-gʷr̥h₃-* (root **gʷerh₃-* 'devour'), ***gardh*** 'fence' < **ghordho-*, and ***djeg*** 'burn' < **dhegʷh-*. The PIE palatal velars, by contrast, became dentals, a development interestingly reminiscent of Old Persian (see §11.32), as well as Castilian Spanish. The voiceless palatal **k̂* became *th*, as in ***them*** 'I say' < **k̂eHs-mi* and ***athët*** 'sour' < **h₂ek̂-* 'sharp'. The voiced palatal **ĝ(h)* became *d* or *dh*, as in ***dhëmb*** 'tooth' < **ĝombh-o-*, ***mb-ledh*** 'I gather' < **leĝ-* (*mb-* from *mbë-* 'around'), and ***dimër*** 'winter' < **ĝheimon-*. Before a following liquid, however, these sounds were depalatalized and fell together with the plain velars, as in ***gju*** 'knee' < **glu-no-* < **ĝlu-no-* (dissimilated from **ĝnu-no-*).

19.10. As stated above, a difference in the outcomes of the plain velars and labiovelars is seen before a palatalizing vowel or glide (*e*, *i*, or *j*): the original labiovelars $*k^w$ and $*g^w(h)$ become *s* and *z*, as in ***si*** 'how' < $*k^w ih_1$ (instrumental, cp. Lat. *quī* 'how') and ***zjarm*** 'fire' < $*g^w$*hermo-*; but the original plain velars **k* and **g(h)* become *q* and *gj*, as in ***pleq*** 'old' < **plak-i*, plural of ***plak*** (PIE **plh*$_2$*-ko-*), and ***ligj*** 'bad, sick' < **lig-i*, plural of ***lig***. (Greek affords a parallel in that some of the labiovelars were palatalized to dentals before front vowels, while the plain velars were not; recall §12.15.) The palatalization of *k* and *g* was later than the palatalization of the labiovelars (or whatever sounds they were at the time), since Latin loanwords underwent it as well, e.g. *qen* 'dog' < **ken* < Lat. *canis*.

The preservation of a triple reflex of the PIE velar series is accepted by most Albanologists but has never been fully embraced by general Indo-Europeanists. The reasons are understandable: aside from the near-absence of any branch that uncontroversially preserves reflexes of all three series, Albanian is not attested until very late and a great deal of its anterior history has been obscured, with often very few examples of a given sound change surviving. However, the examples in this case are not beset with too many difficulties – their etymologies and morphology are for the most part non-controversial – and the evidence for three velar series in Albanian is not much worse than the evidence in Luvian (§9.48). As with so many disputes, however, where the evidence is not absolutely overwhelming, the matter may never be definitively settled to everyone's satisfaction.

19.11. Sibilant *s. The sibilant **s* had no fewer than five outcomes: *sh*, *th*, *gj*, *h*, and loss. The factors conditioning each outcome are still not fully worked out, and many examples are problematic in one way or another. In word-initial position, it is usually thought that *gj* is the outcome before a stressed vowel and either *sh* or *h* the outcome before an unstressed vowel, depending on the vowel quality. Thus for example ***gjarpër*** 'snake' < **sérp-en-* and ***gjumë*** 'sleep' < **súp-no-* (cp. Gk. *húpnos*) have *gj-* before a stressed vowel. Before an original unstressed vowel, note ***shi*** 'rain' < **suh*$_2$*-* (with accent on the endings; cp. Gk. *hū́ei* 'it rains') and ***hurbë*** 'swallow' (probably < **sr̥bhā́*, root **serbh-*, cp. Lat. *sorbeō* 'I drink'). From such examples it appears that *sh-* was the outcome before an unstressed front vowel while *h-* was the outcome before an unstressed back vowel. A similar repartition is found word-internally, between *sh* and zero depending on the quality of the final vowel: ***vesh*** 'clothe' < *u̯os-éi̯e-* (cp. Hitt. *waššezzi* 'clothes', Eng. *wear*), the ablative plural ending *-sh* < **-si*, but ***neve*** 'of us' < **nee* (with hiatus between the two vowels; *-v-* is the consonant regularly used to break hiatus in Albanian) < **nōsōm*. The noun ***thi*** 'pig' < **suHs* has an odd outcome *th* that is usually thought to have arisen through dissimilation. Before a voiceless stop, *sh* is the usual outcome, as in ***shteg*** 'path'. But the cluster **sk̂* seems to have become *h*, as in ***hie*** 'shade' < **sk̂i-eh*$_2$ (cp. Gk. *skiā́*) and in various verbs that once had the thematic suffix **-sk̂e-*, e.g. ***ngroh*** 'make warm' < **en-g*^{w}*hr-ē-sk̂e-* (for the suffix compare Lat. *cal-ēscere* 'become warm'). Note incidentally the numeral ***gjashtë*** 'six', which has two different outcomes of **s* simultaneously, from earlier ****sesta*** < **s(u̯)ék̂s-tā-*. The sibilant disappeared word-finally, as in ***thi*** 'pig' above and in the rhyming word ***mi*** 'mouse' < **mūs*. The fate of *s* in loanwords from Greek and Latin was *sh*: ***prash*** 'leek' < Gk. *práson*, ***shkallë*** 'ladder' < Lat. *scāla or scālae*.

19.12. Resonants. The liquids and nasals remained largely intact: *gardh* 'hedge, fence' < **ghor-dho-*, ***miel*** 'milk' < **$h_2$melĝ-*, ***mi*** 'mouse' < **mūs*, ***na*** 'we' < **nos*. As noted above, Albanian has two kinds of each liquid: a tapped *r* and a trilled *rr*, as well as a light *l* and dark *ll*. Their histories are not fully clear, but trilled *rr* is typically the outcome of certain clusters, as ***rrunjë*** 'yearling lamb' < **u̯rēn-* and *ferr* 'hell' < Lat. *īnfernum*, and *ll* the outcome of single **l* between vowels, as in Geg *llânë* 'lower arm' < **ōlenā* 'elbow' and *Llezhdër* (personal name) < Gk. *Aléksandros*.

19.13. The syllabic liquids developed into liquid plus *i*, which under some conditions (§19.16) became *e*: *drekë* 'lunch' < **dr̥k^wo-* (cp. Gk. *dórpon* 'evening meal'); *drithë* 'grain' < **ĝhr̥zdo-*. The syllabic nasals became *a*, as in *shtatë* 'seven' < **s(e)ptm̥tā* and perhaps *mat* 'bank (of a river), coast' if from **mn̥ti-* (cp. Lat. *mont-* 'mountain'), though the lack of umlaut requires special explanation.

19.14. The glide **i̯* became *gj*, as in *ngjesh* 'I gird' < **en-i̯ōs-e-* (from **i̯ōs-* 'gird', cp. Gk. *zṓnē* 'belt' < **i̯ōs-nā*). The glide **u̯* became *v*, as in ***vesh*** 'I dress' < **u̯os-ei̯e-*.

19.15. Laryngeals. Albanian has few direct reflexes of the laryngeals. A proposal that some word-initial laryngeals developed into Alb. *h-* has not met with widespread approval; the putative examples all admit of other explanations. The root aorist *dha* '(s)he gave', from zero-grade **dh_3-t*, shows that syllabic laryngeals became *a*. The development of **R̥H* sequences is not entirely clear: a form like *plot* 'full', given below (§19.18) as coming from pre-Alb. **plēto-* < **pleh$_1$-to-*, could also theoretically come from pre-Albanian **plāto-*, which would continue **pl̥h$_1$-to-* and mean that **R̥H* became *Rā* as in several other branches. It has even been suggested that, like Greek and Latin, Albanian has two different reflexes of **R̥H* depending on the accent: *aRa* when accented and *Rā* when unaccented. A possible example of the accented treatment is ***parë*** 'first' < **pŕ̥h$_2$-u̯o*, cp. Ved. *pū́rva-* 'first (of two)'.

Vowels

19.16. Short vowels. The short high vowels **i* and **u* are preserved e.g. in Geg *gjî* 'bosom' < **sinos* (cp. Lat. *sinus* 'fold'), *lidh* 'I bind' < **liĝ-* (cp. Lat. *ligāre* 'to bind'), and *gjumë* 'sleep' < **sup-no-*. In contrast to these relatively straightforward developments, **e* has several different outcomes. The normal one was *je*, as in ***pjek*** 'cook' < **pek^w-* and ***jeshë*** 'I was' (imperfect) < **h$_1$esm̥*. The glide was lost if two or more consonants preceded, as in Old Geg ***kle*** 'was' < **klje* < **(e-)k^{w}l-e-t* (see §19.25 for more on this form); *e* is also the outcome before nasal, as in ***pesë*** (Geg *pêsë*) 'five' < **pense* < **penk^{w}e*. Before a following liquid, the outcome is a diphthong *íe* instead: ***bíe*** 'carry' < **bíer* < PIE **bher-*, ***míell*** 'flour' < **mel-u̯o-* (root **mel(h$_2$)-* 'grind', cp. Eng. *meal*). A different outcome *ja* is found apparently in closed syllables before an *o* or *a*, as in ***gjalpë*** 'butter' < **selpos* above (§19.7), ***gjarpër*** 'snake' < **serp-en-*, and ***zjarm*** 'fire' < **g^{w}hermo-* (cp. Gk. *thermós* 'hot'). In unstressed syllables, **e* was weakened to *i*, which often disappeared but left a trace in the umlaut of a preceding vowel, as in the examples quoted below in §19.19. Short **a* and **o* merged as *a*: *bathë* 'broad (fava) bean' < **bhakā* (cp. Gk. *phakós* 'lentil'), ***na*** 'we' < **nos*, ***natë*** 'night' < **nok^{w}t-*.

19.17. Short vowels were subject to syncope (deletion) when unstressed, as in the many verbs beginning with *n-* from the prefix **en-* 'in', e.g. *ndez*, *ngroh*, *ngrënë* above. This deletion of unstressed vowels happened after the Latin loanwords entered the language, as evidenced e.g. by *mbret* 'king' < Lat. *imperā́tor*. There was also widespread loss of final unstressed syllables. Original distinctions in stress are reflected by pairs such as *nip* 'grandson' < **népō(t)* alongside *mbesë* 'granddaughter' < **nepṓt-i̯ā* (remade from PIE **nept-ih₂*).

19.18. Long vowels. The long vowels underwent more unusual changes than their short counterparts. Long **ī* remained *ī* into the Old Albanian period at the end of monosyllables, as in *pī* 'drink' (ultimately **pih₃-*) and *dī* 'know' (< **dhiH-*, root **dheiH-*). The same development is seen for **ū*: Old Albanian *mī* 'mouse' < **mūs*, *thī* 'sow' < **sūs* (with secondary *th*, §19.11). In the modern standard language the long vowel has been shortened to *i*. The outcomes of **ū* in words of more than one syllable are complex and not fully agreed upon, especially in inherited vocabulary; in Latin loanwords, however, **ū* became *y* (pronounced like Germ. *ü*), e.g. *gjymtyrë* 'joint (of the body)' < Lat. *iūnctūra*. Long **ē* and **ā* fell together as *o* when stressed, as in *motrë* 'sister' < **māter-* < **meh₂ter-* (the 'mother' word in PIE; sense development probably via 'older sister who takes a motherly role' or the like) and *plot* 'full' < **plē-to-* (< **pleh₁-to-*). When unstressed, though, **ā* became *ë*, as in *mbesë* 'granddaughter' in the previous section. Long **ō* became *e*, as in *resh* 'rain' < **rōs-* (cp. Lat. *rōs* 'dew') and *ne* 'us' (accusative) < **nōs*.

19.19. The picture above is further muddied by a series of prehistoric umlaut processes that affected most stressed vowels before an *i* in the following syllable: *a* > *e*, *o* > *e*, *e* > *i*, and *u* > *y*. The *i* that caused the umlaut could be either an inherited *i* or an old *e* that had changed to *i*, and, being unstressed, was subject to loss. Many vowel alternations in paradigms have arisen due to this umlaut. Thus contrast *plak* 'old', nomin. pl. *pleq* < **plak-i* (also with palatalization of the *k* to *q*); *njoh* 'I know' with 2nd and 3rd sing. *njeh* < **njoh-i* (with *-i* ultimately from PIE **-esi*, **-eti*); and *shteg* 'path', nomin. pl. *shtigje* (remade from **shtigj* < **shtig-i*).

19.20. Diphthongs. The diphthongs **ei* and **oi* became *i* and *e*, respectively: *dimër* 'winter' < **ĝheimon-*, *shteg* 'path' < **stoigh-o-*. The three *u*-diphthongs appear to have fallen together ultimately as *a*, which like inherited *a* could undergo umlaut to *e*: *ag* 'dawn' < **augo-* < **h₂eugo-* (cp. Gk. *augḗ* 'sunlight'), *desh* '(s)he wanted' < **dashi* < **daushe* < perfect **(ĝe-)ĝous-e*, and perhaps Geg *nândë* 'ninth' if this continues **neunto-*, resyllabified from **neu̯n̥to-*.

Morphology and syntax

19.21. For all the change that time has wrought on Albanian phonology, it has left the language's morphology less altered. Nouns are inflected in five cases: nominative, genitive, dative, accusative, and ablative. (A sixth case, a locative, is found in some dialects and in Old Albanian.) Both numbers distinguish an indefinite from a definite form, the latter having a suffixed definite article, with or without a separate definite article before the noun. Thus contrast indefinite *mal* 'mountain' with definite *mali* 'the mountain'; indefinite *nip* 'nephew' with definite *i nipi* 'the nephew'. The definite singular frequently preserves phonetic material that was lost in the indefinite. Thus Geg *gjûni* 'the knee' preserves the second *-n-* of the preform **ĝnu-no-*, lost in the indefinite sing. *gju*. Nouns come in masculine and feminine genders, but a sizeable group are masculine in the singular but feminine in the plural, as *ujë* 'water' (masc.), pl. *ujëra* 'waters' (fem.); these are old neuters. (Compare §17.26.)

19.22. Most of the recognizable case-endings in nouns have disappeared, as can be seen from the following sample paradigm of the masculine noun *mal* 'mountain':

	indef. sing.	def. sing.	indef. pl.	def. pl.
Nom.	mal	mali	male	malet
Gen.	mali	malit	maleve	maleve(t)
Dat.	mali	malit	maleve	maleve(t)
Acc.	mal	malin	male	malet
Abl.	mali	malit	malesh	maleve(t)

The nominative plural ending *-e* is taken over from the feminine declension and is of disputed origin. Some nouns form their plurals by palatalization, e.g. Old Alb. *ujq* 'wolves', pl. of *ulk*; this palatalization is an indirect trace of what was once the ending **-oi* (> **-i*, which palatalized the preceding consonant before ultimately disappearing), the pronominal ending that replaced the original *o*-stem nominal ending in several other branches of the family (§6.53). The postposed definite article, ultimately from the demonstrative pronominal stem **to-* (§7.10), is a feature shared with other languages of the Balkans (§19.5 above). The dative and genitive have the same endings in nouns, but are distinct in pronouns. The ablative plural ending *-sh* continues the PIE locative plural **-si*, showing that Albanian innovated in the same way as Greek; §6.17.

The definite forms come from old combinations of the indefinite and a suffixed definite article in **so-* or **to-* (the latter, for example, in *mali-t*, *maleve-t*).

19.23. The Albanian verb preserves a remarkable amount of inherited material for a language first attested so late. The present and aorist have remained, the latter containing forms that are historically aorists as well as dereduplicated perfects, e.g. *dha* 'he gave' < **dh₃-t* (root aorist with generalized zero-grade), *desh* 'wanted, loved' < **(ĝe-)ĝous-* (perfect; root **ĝeus-* 'taste, enjoy'). The subjunctive and optative are alive and well, continuing the respective PIE categories; among other modern IE languages, only a small number of Iranian languages preserve this distinction (§11.52). As in PIE, the subjunctive can also be used as a future (though a separate future tense has also been developed, see below).

But there has, not surprisingly, also been considerable innovation and addition of new categories, resulting in a rather complex system. The Albanian imperfect has endings derived from both the old imperfect and the optative, and has undergone different regional remodelings to create strikingly different forms across the dialects. Five other tenses – perfect, two pluperfects, future, and future perfect – are formed periphrastically, that is, with a helping verb. Most remarkable is the complex system of moods: in addition to the familiar indicative, subjunctive, optative, and imperative, there is a separate conditional, as well as a mood called the admirative that is used to express surprise, wonder, or any action not related on the speaker's own authority (as often in indirect discourse). There is a past-tense participle, formed in part to the old IE perfect stem, which has otherwise disappeared, two infinitives (present and perfect), and two gerunds (also present and perfect). Albanian has also preserved the IE distinction in voice between active and mediopassive.

19.24. Many verbs distinguish among tenses, or among persons within a single tense, by means of vowel or consonant alternations. Thus contrast the presents *bredh* 'I run', *mbjell* 'I sow', and *vë* 'I put' with the aorists *brodha*, *mbolla*, *vura*; and contrast present 1st sing. *marr* 'I take' with 2nd sing. *merr* 'you take'. These alternations often continue PIE ablaut: thus the *-o-* of aorists like *brodha* and *mbolla* ultimately goes back to the **-ē-* of past tenses of the type seen also in e.g. Lat. *lēgī* 'I gathered, read' (a perfect in Latin). (In fact, *lēgī* is exactly cognate with the Albanian aorist *-lodha* in *mblodha* 'I gathered'; see §5.50.) Consonant alternations are of more recent vintage; examples include *pjek* 'I bake' ~ aorist *poqa* ~ present mediopassive *piqem* 'I am baked', and *djeg* ~ *dogja* ~ *digjem*, the same forms of the verb meaning 'burn'.

19.25. Only three athematic presents are found: *jam* 'I am', *kam* 'I have', and them (*thom*) 'I say', of which only *jam* and *them* are inherited athematics (from **$h_1$es-mi* and either **$\hat{k}$eh_1-mi* or **$\hat{k}$eHs-mi*). *Kam*, long thought to continue a **kap-mi* cognate with Lat. *capere* 'take', is now considered for various reasons to be a refashioning of something else; according to a recent attractive suggestion by the Austrian Indo-Europeanist Joachim Matzinger, the word is ultimately a refashioned perfect **(ku̯e-)ku̯oh_2-* to a root **ku̯eh_2-* 'achieve, get' found also in the Greek perfect *pépāmai* 'I possess' (< *'I have gotten'). The imperfect in part continues the PIE imperfect, e.g. *jeshë* 'I was' < **$h_1$es-m̥* (vs. *jam* 'I am' < **$h_1$es-mi*); but the plural endings, characterized by the vowel *-i-*, come from the optative (see below). The aorist continues several PIE formations. We have already seen the root aorist *dha* '(s)he gave' above in §19.15. Albanian also has some forms going back to thematic aorists with zero-grade of the root; since this formation was virtually absent from PIE (§5.48), these are probably innovatory. Of interest is Old Albanian *kle* (modern *qe*) '(s)he was', continuing the same **(e-)k^{w}l-e-* as Greek *é-pl-eto* '(s)he turned' and Arm. *ełew* '(s)he became'. This thematic aorist might be a common innovation of this dialect area. The *s*-aorist is traditionally seen as reflected in such forms as *dha-shë* 'I gave' and *ra-shë* 'I fell', but in Old Albanian these forms lacked the *-sh-* and in PIE these roots did not form *s*-aorists. The source of the *-sh-* in these and some other forms is not entirely clear.

19.26. To illustrate verb conjugation, below are the present, imperfect, and aorist indicative and present subjunctive of the verb *them* 'I say', plus the present optative of the verb meaning 'have' (*kam* 'I have', the present, is formed from a different stem). In the rightmost column is given a sample mediopassive present, *duhem* 'I am wanted':

	pres. ind.	impf. ind.	aor. ind.	pres. subj.	pres. opt.	pres. ind. mediopass.
sg.						
1	them	thosha	thashë	them	paça	duhem
2	thua	thoshe	the	thuash	paç	duhesh
3	thotë	thoshte	tha	thotë	pastë	duhet

pl.						
1	themi	thoshim	thamë	themi	paçim	duhemi
2	thoni	thoshit	thatë	thoni	paçi	duheni
3	thonë	thoshin	thanë	thonë	paçin	duhen

Forms like *them* and *thotë* contain recognizable reflexes of the PIE 1st and 3rd sing. personal endings **-mi* and **-ti*. Even clearer are the plural paradigms *thoshim -it -in* and *thamë -të -në*, reflecting PIE **-me- *-te- *-nt(i)*. The mediopassive is of the type seen in Greek (*-mai -sai -tai*) rather than Latin (*-mur -ris -tur*), i.e., the middle marker **-r* has been replaced by the primary active marker **-i*. The zero-grade of the PIE optative marker **-ih*$_1$- is continued by the stem vowel *-i-* in the 1st and 3rd plurals *paçim* and *paçin*, structurally *pat-shim*, *pat-shin*; the element *-shi-* continues **-s-ih*$_1$-, the optative of the *s*-aorist.

Syntax

19.27. Because of its numerous inflections, Albanian word order is relatively free. In the text below, for example, the order SVO in *qi ban farë* 'which makes seed' exists right alongside SOV in *qi farë kā* 'which has seed'. Albanian, like PIE, had both stressed and unstressed (clitic) forms of the personal pronouns; characteristic of Albanian syntax is the use of the latter to double an object noun (e.g. *Zefi e mori librin* lit. 'Joseph it took the book') and to double a stressed pronoun preceding a verb (e.g. *mua më merr malli* lit. 'me me takes longing' = 'longing takes me'). Interestingly, these enclitic pronouns, though typically not clause-initial, can appear clause-initially in commands, as *Ma ep librin* 'Give me the book'. None of the enclitic pronouns in the older IE languages can be so placed, though the phenomenon is also found in modern Slovenian.

19.28. An additional interesting detail of Albanian is the ability of the nominative case to function as the object of prepositions. Two prepositions take the nominative, *te(k)* 'to/at (the house of)' and *nga* 'from'. Normally in IE languages the nominative case cannot have this function. The situation came about through a reanalysis. *Te(k)* and *nga* were originally relative adverbs: *te* comes probably from the instrumental **toh*$_1$ of the pronominal stem **to-* and meant 'there', later (like the English demonstrative *that*) assuming relative function ('there where' > 'where'), while *nga* is shortened from **ën-ka* 'where, from where', with **ën* 'in' added to the old relative adverb *ka* 'where, from where', from **k*^{w}*or* (whence also Eng. *where*). Sentences of the type 'I went where X is', 'I went from where X is' (X being of course in the nominative case as subject of its clause) were reinterpreted as 'I went to/from X', with gapping of the verb in the relative clause.

Old Albanian (Geg) text sample

19.29. From the *Meshari (Missal)* of Gjon Buzuku, the earliest surviving Albanian book, from 1555. The language is Old Geg. The passage below is a translation of Genesis 1:29–30. The spelling has been modernized, and long vowels are indicated with macrons.

E tha Zotynë: Hinje, se u u kam dhanë gjithë bārr qi ban farë përëmbī gjithë dhēt, e gjithë pemë qi farë kā porsi e siadó farë, juve me u klenë për gjellë; (30) e gjithë shtanse të dheut e gjithë qish fluturón për qiell e gjithë shtanse qi anshtë përëmbī dhēt, qi shpirt i gjallë anshtë ëndë to, përse juve t-u jenë për gjellë.

And God said, "Behold, for I have given you every plant that makes seed (which is) upon all the earth, and every fruit which has seed as well as every seed, to be food for you; (30) and to every beast of the earth, and to everything that flies in the sky and to every beast that is upon the earth that has living breath in it, in order that they be food for you."

19.29a. Notes. E: 'and'. **tha:** 'spoke', 3rd sing. aor. < **k̂eh₁-* or **k̂eHs-* (see §19.9). **Zotynë:** 'our God', contracted from *Zoti ynë*. The word for 'god' is conjectured to come from a compound **desi̯ās-poti-* 'master of the servants in a household', and *ynë* 'our' comes from **so-nos*, where **nos* is the original old genitive 1st pl. pronoun preceded by the pronominal stem **so-*; literally 'the one (which is) ours'. **Hinje:** 'Behold'. **se:** 'that, for', conjunction. **u u kam dhanë:** 'I have given you'. The first *u* is an old (and still dialectal) short form of *unë* 'I', while the second is the 2nd pl. enclitic dative 'to you'. There follows a periphrastic perfect, formed of *kam* 'I have' (§19.25) plus the past participle *dhanë* 'given'. **gjithë:** 'every, all'. **bārr:** 'grass, plant', accus. sing. of *barnë*. **qi:** 'who', relative pronoun; Tosk *që*, from PIE **kʷi-*; cf. Lat. *quis* 'who'. **ban:** 'makes', 3rd sing. present of Geg *bâj* (Tosk *bëj*) 'make'. **farë:** 'seed', perhaps the exact cognate of Gk. *sporá* 'sowing, seed'. **përëmbī:** 'over', modern Tosk *përmbi*; consists of the prepositions *për* 'to, with' and *mbi* (older *ëmbī*) 'upon', cognate with Lat. *ambi-* 'around, both'. **dhēt:** 'earth', definite genit. sing. of *dhe* < pre-Albanian **ĝhō*, ultimately from PIE **dh(e)ĝhōm*; cp. Gk. *khthṓn*. **pemë:** 'fruit', borrowing from Lat. *pōmum*. **kā:** 'has', 3rd sing. of *kam* above. **porsi e:** lit. 'just as also'. **siadó:** 'every', modern *cilado*. **juve me u klenë:** 'to you to be'; *u* is the obligatory clitic double of *juve* 'to you' (§19.27), while *me klenë* 'to be' is the infinitive (modern standard *për të qenë*). The *-ve* of *juve* continues the PIE pronominal genit. pl. **-sōm* (§7.9); when **-s-* disappeared between vowels, a *-v-* developed as a transition. **për:** 'for', PIE **pro* or **prō*. **gjellë:** 'meal'. **shtanse:** 'animal', dat. sing., modern standard (nomin.) *shtazë*, Geg *shtâsë*. **të dheut:** 'of the earth', definite genit. sing. of *dhe* 'earth' above, with preposed article *të* as well as postposed *-t*. **gjithë qish:** 'everything (that)', modern *gjithçka*. **fluturón:** 'flies', 3rd sing. present; borrowing from Vulgar Lat. **fluctulāre*. **qiell:** 'heaven', borrowing from Lat. *caelum*. **anshtë:** 'is', modern Tosk *është*; the nasal in Geg (modern *âshtë*) betrays that the form continues not just PIE **h₁esti* but also a nasal-containing preverb. Since neighboring Greek makes wide use of *énesti* 'be in, be present', it has been suggested by the American Indo-Europeanist Eric Hamp that the Albanian form likewise continues the same preverb–verb combination. More recent research by Stefan Schumacher of Vienna indicates the preverb had *o*-grade, to account for the *a*-vocalism in this form as well as in the Old Albanian aorist *ângrë* 'ate' < **on-gʷr̥h₃-*. **shpirt:** 'breath, spirit', borrowing from Lat. *spīritus*. **i:** a connective particle used in attributive adjective constructions. **gjallë:** 'living', from PIE **sol(H)u̯o-* 'whole' (> Lat. *saluus* 'healthy'). **ëndë to:** 'in that'. **përse:** 'in order that', modern standard *që të*. **jenë:** '(they) be', 3rd pl. present subjunctive of *jam* 'I am'.

For Further Reading

Because of its marginal status in IE studies, Albanian has been chronically underserved as far as good reference works go; but that situation may be changing, as several appeared just in the 1990s. The book-length treatments in English are unfortunately problematic. Huld 1984, treats phonology and contains a 250-word etymological glossary of "core" words; it has some usefulness, but the reconstructions are idiosyncratic. The more recent Orel 2000 regrettably ignores Old Albanian for the most part, and also suffers from out-of-date PIE reconstructions. These features also mar Orel 1998, the only available etymological dictionary in English; it is more useful than the companion historical grammar, but omits loanwords from after the eleventh or twelfth century. For filling some of these gaps, Meyer 1891, though old, is still useful. An excellent historical grammar is Demiraj 1993; its treatment of the developments from PIE to Albanian is a bit spartan, but the other historical discussions are thorough and illuminating. Also very good is Sanz Ledesma 1996, a small but very informative Spanish overview of Albanian historical grammar. A much better treatment of the historical phonology than Huld's can be found in Demiraj 1997, which also has a full etymological glossary of inherited lexemes. One can profitably read the scores upon scores of short articles on Albanian by the American Indo-Europeanist Eric P. Hamp, such as Hamp 1977. The best reference grammar written in English is Newmark, Hubbard, and Prifti 1982; readers of German should also consult the masterly Buchholz and Fiedler 1987. Newmark 1998 is an excellent dictionary in English, especially useful for its inclusion of dialectal and archaic material. For Old Albanian, useful technical treatments from recent years include Fiedler 2004, essential for the study of the verb, and Matzinger 2006, which is not only a critical edition of an important Old Albanian text with linguistic commentary and analysis but also contains an up-to-date historical grammar. Fox 1989 contains the famous law code of Lekë Dukagjini with a translation and comparative notes.

Exercises

1 Provide the Albanian outcome or outcomes of the following PIE sounds:

a	**s*	**c**	**ḱ*	**e**	**gʷh*	**g**	**d*
b	**kʷ*	**d**	**bh*	**f**	**p*	**h**	**ē*

2 Explain the history or significance of the following Albanian forms. The forms are in Tosk unless otherwise noted:

a	*murgu*	**e**	*natë*	**i**	Geg *gjûni*
b	*pesë*	**f**	*mbret*	**j**	*mblodha*
c	*ngroh*	**g**	*mi*	**k**	Old Geg *kle*
d	*besë*	**h**	*ne*	**l**	*thom*

3 In the text sample, the form *juve* 'to you' (dat. pl.) was encountered. The 2nd pl. (nomin.) *ju* looks like it should continue PIE **i̯ūs*. Why is that derivation problematic?

4 In the text sample, the 1st sing. pronoun *u* 'I' was encountered. This is normally taken to be from earlier **udh*, from PIE **eĝ-* 'I', with a replacement of **e* by *u*. In light of §7.1 and Hittite *ūk* 'I', also irregularly from **eĝ-*, provide a possible explanation for the *u*. (Don't assume any early connection between Albanian and Hittite!)

5 Below is a list of some colloquial Latin loanwords (with length marks removed) that were borrowed at an early date into Albanian, with their Albanian outcomes. Describe the fate of unaccented word-initial syllables.

Latin	Albanian	gloss	Latin	Albanian	gloss
paréntis	_përind_	'parent'	_camísia_	_këmishë_	'shirt'
eríca	_riq_	'heath'	_invitáre_	_ftoj_	'invite'
Aprílis	_prill_	'April'	_amícus_	_mik_	'friend'
inférnum	_ferr_	'hell'	_aréna_	_rânë_	'sand'
Antónius	_Ndue_	'Antony'	_sanitátem_	_shëndet_	'health'
Augústus	_gusht_	'August'	_aerámen_	_rem_	'copper'

6 It was stated in §19.21 that Albanian nouns that are masculine in the singular and feminine in the plural descend from old neuters. Sketch how this development might have taken place.

PIE Vocabulary XI: Utterance

*_u̯ek_^{w}_-_ 'say': Ved. _vácas-_ 'word', Gk. _(w)épos_ 'speech', Lat. _uōx_ (_uōc-_) 'voice'
*_u̯er(h_$_1$_)-_ 'speak': Gk. _rhḗtōr_ 'public speaker', Lat. _uerbum_ 'word', Eng. WORD
*_prek̂-_ 'ask': Ved. _pr̥ccháti_ 'asks', Lat. _precor_ 'I entreat', German _fragen_, Toch. B _prek-_
*_h_$_1$_neh_$_3$_mn̥_ or *_h_$_1$_nomn̥_ 'NAME': Hitt. _lāman-_, Ved. _nāma_, Gk. _ónoma_, Lat. _nōmen_
*_kan-_ 'sing': Lat. _canō_ 'I sing', OIr. _canim_ 'I sing', Eng. HEN
*_ĝheuH-_ 'invoke (a deity)': Ved. _hávate_ 'invokes', OCS _zovǫ_ 'I call'

20 Fragmentary Languages

Introduction

20.1. There remain to be discussed over a half-dozen poorly understood IE languages whose preservation is so fragmentary that their exact position within the family tree is uncertain: Phrygian, Thracian, Macedonian, Illyrian, Venetic, Messapic, Sicel, Elymian, and Lusitanian. They are mostly known from short inscriptions, personal names, place-names, and glosses from the first millennium BC. Our survey will proceed geographically from east to west.

Since so little is known about most of these languages – especially Thracian, Macedonian, and Illyrian – the sheer variety and number of attempts at their interpretation have known no bounds. It can almost be stated as a rule in historical linguistics that the fewer the attested forms in a language and the poorer their preservation, the greater the quantity of speculative ink spilt over them. The scholarship on these languages, especially on the least well-preserved, has all too frequently thrown caution to the winds and built vast interpretive edifices with little basis in established – or establishable – fact. It is healthy to adopt a skeptical attitude with regard to much of it. Nonetheless, as we will see below, there does exist some clear (and at times valuable) IE material scattered throughout the remains of these languages.

20.2. Most of the theories concerning the interrelationships of the poorer-known languages are based on the so-called etymological method: trying to etymologize the linguistic remains that we have in light of known forms in other languages. Given that the bulk of the remains consists of personal and place-names, to which no "meaning" can be assigned in the usual sense, this method falls victim to some obvious dangers, not the least of which is circularity. Though often quite compelling on the surface, these etymologies cannot be tested against anything; they are almost always the product of seeing the morphemes that one wants to see. For example, the Thracian name *Diazenis* has been interpreted as the equivalent of Gk. *Dio-génēs* 'born of Zeus', and *Dizazenis* as the equivalent of *Theo-genēs* 'born of god' (*theo-* < Proto-Greek **theho-* < earlier **theso-*). But aside from the reasonable claim that these names contain three identifiable morphemes, *dia-*, *diza-*, and *-zenis*, we can really say nothing about their meanings or etymologies with certainty. Divine names have the same problems. A well-known interpretation of *Sabazios*, the name of the Phrygian and Thracian Bacchus, is a good example: since Bacchus's native Latin name (*Līber*) means 'free',

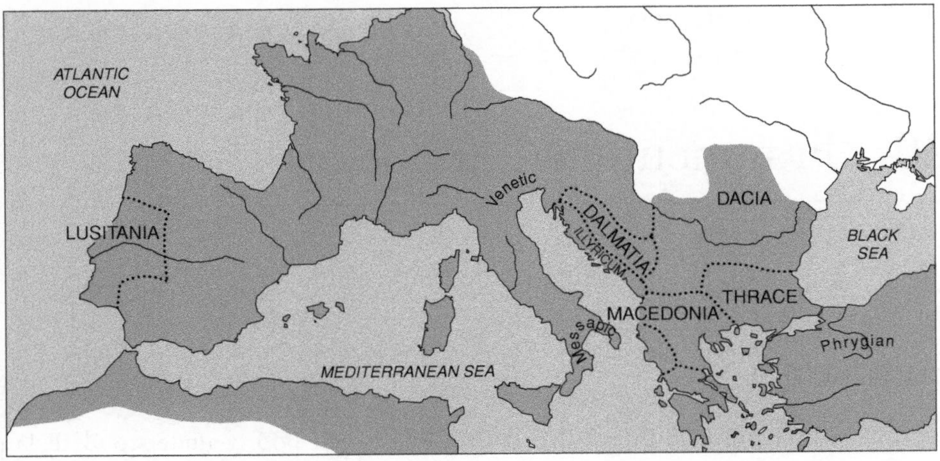

Map 20.1 The ancient Mediterranean, showing regions and languages in this chapter

it has been suggested that *Sabazios* is cognate with OCS *svobodĭ* 'free' (< **su̯o-bhodhio-*). This idea is as clever and imaginative as it is speculative and unprovable.

A truly embarrassing example of how the etymological method can backfire is the following. In the early 1900s a ring was unearthed near Shkodër in Albania with three words on it that were averred to be Illyrian; nearly identical forms were known from Messapic, and on their basis the inscription was given an interpretation: "To the goddess Oethe." But the ring later turned out to be from the Byzantine period and written in Greek – it had been read backwards.

The point of the foregoing is not to disparage speculation and imaginative thinking; any science needs both to move forward. The problem arises when such speculations harden over time into facts in people's minds and become the sole basis for further and far-reaching theories (such as the establishment of sound changes or linguistic filiation). In dealing with these fragmentary languages, it is important to distinguish at all times what is known for certain from what is only guesswork.

Phrygian

20.3. Phrygian occupies a special place in linguists' hearts because of a famous legend related by the Greek historian Herodotus. He tells how the Egyptian pharaoh Psammetichus set about to determine what the oldest language in the world was. Accordingly he isolated two newborn infants from exposure to human speech, awaiting the day that the children would say their first words. The pharaoh reasoned that whatever language they first spoke in would be mankind's original, oldest language. When that day came, the children's first utterance was *bekos*, Phrygian for 'bread'; so Psammetichus concluded that Phrygian was the world's oldest language.

The Phrygians were a people who first enter history as immigrants into northwest Anatolia sometime after the fall of the Hittite Empire in the early twelfth century BC. They emigrated probably from the Balkans; Herodotus names Macedonia as their old homeland. It has been suggested that they were related to the Thracians (see §20.10 below) as well as to the Armenians, whose ancestors most likely came into Anatolia around the same time (see §16.1). It was formerly thought that the Phrygians' entrance into Anatolia not only coincided with the demise of the Hittites but also may have been a cause of it. Recent scholarship, however, tends to date their incursion to two, perhaps three centuries later.

When they had moved farther inland, the Phrygians established a state that joined a loose confederation (called the Muški in Assyrian records) with several other peoples to the east; this confederation was the main power in Anatolia until around the early eighth century BC. Later in that century, under the legendary king Midas, the center of Phrygian power shifted westward; his kingdom fell around 700 to the Cimmerians, invaders from the north who destroyed the Phrygian capital of Gordion (Gordium). Though the Phrygians lived on for many centuries more, they never again formed a centralized state.

20.4. While the ancient accounts of the Balkan origins of the Phrygians are generally followed, the first demonstrably Phrygian artifacts, dating to the mid-eighth century BC, are from central Anatolia. About 80 inscriptions constituting **Old Phrygian** date from this time and later, until about 450 BC; they are written in an alphabet apparently derived from an early version of the Greek alphabet used in Asia Minor. Then there is a long gap before the second layer of Phrygian, called **New Phrygian**, appears; it dates from the first and second centuries AD. Over a hundred New Phrygian inscriptions are known, written in the Greek alphabet; they are mostly funerary in nature and contain curses against grave-robbers. The inscriptions typically lack word-divisions, especially in the New Phrygian period.

Ancient writers, especially the Alexandrian glossator Hesychius (fl. fifth century AD?), also preserve some Phrygian glosses (that is, Phrygian words with a definition or explanation in Greek). The glosses seem to be reliable, since several of the words are also known from Phrygian inscriptions.

Sketch of Phrygian historical grammar

20.5. Probably more is known about Phrygian than about any of the other languages in this chapter, and some outlines of its history are clear. The PIE voiced aspirates lost their aspiration: *ab-beret* 'brings to' < **ad-bher-*; *ad-daket* 'places' < **ad-dhh*$_1$-*k-* (cp. Lat. *fac-it* 'does'). For palatal **ĝh*, there are contradictory outcomes: *g* in *glouros* 'gold' (cp. Gk. *khlōrós* 'yellow-green, green') but *z* in *zemel-* 'slave' (assuming this originally meant 'man' and is cognate with Lat. *homō* and its relatives from PIE **dheĝhom-*, **dhĝhem-* 'earth'). However, the *z-* of *zemel-* could be due to a later palatalization before the *e* or to a special outcome of the original "thorn" cluster; if so, on the evidence of the more secure *glouros* Phrygian was a centum language. This word is additionally interesting because, as tantalizingly suggested by Manfred Mayrhofer, it might show the same outcome of **l̥h*$_3$ as Greek *khlōrós*, assuming (as seems likely) they both continue the zero-grade adjective **ĝhl̥h*$_3$-*ró-*. In that case,

Greek would no longer be the unique surviving IE language to have *o*-colored outcomes of sequences of the type **R̥h₃* (recall §12.25). The plain voiceless and voiced stop series remained intact, as in ***mater*** 'mother' < **mātēr* (**meh₂tēr*) and ***podas*** 'feet' (accusative) < **pod-n̥s*. The labiovelars lost their labial element, as in ***ke*** 'and' < **kʷe*. Of special interest is the fact that, as in Greek and Armenian, word-initial laryngeals before consonants were vocalized as vowels, as in ***anar*** 'man' < **h₂nēr* (cp. Gk. *anḗr*, Arm. *ayr*) and ***onoman*** 'name' (see §6.36; cp. Gk. *ónoma*, *ónuma*, Arm. *anown*).

20.6. The inscriptions allow us to tally up five cases in the noun: nominative, vocative, accusative, genitive, and dative. There may well have been others that happen not to be attested in our meager remains. We have examples of consonant stems, thematic nouns, *i*-stems, *u*-stems, and feminine *ā*-stems; in form they resemble Greek.

20.7. Phrygian verbs were conjugated in both active and middle: active *addaket* 'causes, does', middle *addaketor* (apparently with the same meaning). In the form *egeseti* 'he will do' (?) we may have an *s*-future (see §5.42), while a preterite in *-s* is attested in such forms as *edaes* '(s)he put' and *eneparkes* (sense uncertain). These last two forms show that Phrygian, like Greek, Armenian, and Indo-Iranian, prefixed finite past-tense forms with an augment *e-* (*e-daes*, *en-e-parkes*; see §5.44). Strikingly reminiscent of Greek are perfect middle participles in *-meno-* with reduplication, such as *tetikmenos* 'accursed' (?) and (with preverb) *protuss[e]stamenan* 'set up, established'. Third-person imperatives are found in such forms as sing. *eitou* 'let him be' (probably from **h₁eitōd* 'let him go', cp. Gk. *ítō* and Lat. *ītō*).

20.8. Phrygian shares more features with Greek than with any other IE language, a few of which are further shared by Armenian and Indo-Iranian. On the basis of such similarities, a subgroup of IE consisting of Greek, Phrygian, Armenian, and Indo-Iranian has been suggested (as mentioned in §10.4).

Phrygian text sample

20.9. Phrygian sepulchral curse inscribed on a doorstone from central Phrygia, second or third century AD. The text is given first in its original form without word-divisions. The first two lines are understood better than the third, and are given a provisional word-division and translation. They are formulaic, found (with minor variations) on many other New Phrygian sepulchral inscriptions. Compare the Phrygian Greek formula "Whoever will do a bad thing to this tomb, let him be cursed" (*hóstis àn tõi hērṓōi toútōi kakòn poiḗsei hupokatárātos éstō*).

iosnisemounknoumaneikakounaddaketgegreimenane
gedoutiosoutanakkeoibekosakkalostidregrouneitou
autoskeouakerokagegaritmenosasbatanteutous

ios ni semoun knoumanei kakoun addaket gegreimenan e-
gedou tios outan akke oi bekos akkalos tidregroun eitou

Whoever does evil to this grave, let him bear the . . .
curse of god, and let bread (and?) water (?) become unpalatable for him.

20.9a. Notes. ios: 'whoever, (he) who', relative pronoun, PIE **i̯os*; *ni* is apparently a particle, perhaps making the relative pronoun indefinite. **semoun:** 'this', usually taken to be a dative of **so-* 'this' with *-m-* as part of the pronominal oblique stem-formant **-sm-* (see §7.9). **knoumanei:** 'to the tomb', dat. sing.; etymology disputed. **kakoun:** 'bad, evil', some sort of accusative singular showing that **-m* became *-n* in Phrygian, as in Greek. Cp. Gk. *kakón* 'evil, an evil thing'. **addaket:** 'causes, does (to)', probably consisting of a preverb *ad-* 'to, at, upon' (cp. Lat. *ad* 'to') plus *dak-* 'do', from **dhh₁-k-*, extended zero-grade of **dheh₁-* 'place, put, do' (cp. Lat. *fa-c-ere* 'to do', Gk. aorist *(é)thē-k-e* 'he did' < full grade **e-dheh₁-k-*). **gegreimenan:** feminine accus. sing. perfect mediopassive participle, in formation like that of e.g. Gk. *lelūménēn* 'having been released'. The meaning is uncertain but apparently negative; it modifies *outan*, usually understood as 'curse'. Note the poetic word order, with the participle separated from the noun it modifies by an intervening verb and dependent genitive. **egedou:** 'let him bear' or the like, perhaps from **h₂eĝ-e-tōd*, 3rd sing. imperative; compare *eitou* at the end of the line without weakening of the *-t-* (due to being directly after the stress?). **tios:** 'of god', perhaps PIE **di̯u-os*. It could also be the name of a deity ("Tis"). **akke:** usually considered to mean 'and' and compared with Latin *atque*. **oi:** 'to him', dative, cp. Gk. dat. *hoi*. **bekos:** 'bread', see discussion in §20.3. **akkalos:** 'water' (?), cp. Lat. *aqua*. If this passage is correctly interpreted, it is reminiscent of the curse of the legendary Phrygian king Midas, who wished that everything he touched should turn to gold – the unfortunate consequence being that all the food and drink he touched he could no longer consume. **eitou:** 'let it be(come)', probably from **h₁eitōd* 'let it go' (cf. §20.7), a 3rd person imperative in **-tō(d)*. The third line of the inscription probably begins with *autos* 'he himself', a word also found in Greek. This line contains another middle participle, *gegaritmenos*, perhaps cognate with Gk. *kekharisménos* 'devoted'.

Thracian

20.10. In classical times, Thrace (Thracia) was a region in the eastern Balkans, located west of the Black Sea between the Danube River to the north and the Sea of Marmara to the south, in what is now mostly Bulgaria. Herodotus described the Thracians as the greatest and most populous people on earth after the Indians; they are mentioned in Homer as allies of the Trojans during the Trojan War. Their prowess as fighters was legendary; they were also famous for their music and poetry, none of which, regrettably, has survived.

Numerous brief coin inscriptions from as early as the sixth century BC have been found in what was once Thrace, as well as a few short inscriptions that have no agreed-upon interpretation. The coin legends and various Classical authors preserve some Thracian personal and geographic names. Personal names are attested up until the sixth century AD.

20.11. Ancient glossators, especially Hesychius, preserve about eighty or ninety words that are said to be Thracian; of these, no more than three dozen can be confidently labeled as such. Here we can identify a few that are in all likelihood Indo-European, such as *briza* 'spelt, rye' (PIE **u̯rugh-i̯ā* 'rye', cp. German *Roggen*), *br(o)utos* 'drink made from barley, beer' (PIE **bhreu-* 'bubble, ferment', the source of Eng. *brew* and *broth*), and *-para* 'ford, pass' in certain place-names (PIE **per-* 'to cross over', the source of Eng. *ford*). A Roman inscription from AD 226 has a Thracian word *midne* 'homestead' that has been plausibly compared with Latv. *mītne* 'dwelling' and Av. *maēθana-* 'dwelling'.

All attempts to relate Thracian to Phrygian, Illyrian, or Dacian (the language of the neighboring province of Dacia, preserved almost solely in some plant names in Hesychius) are likewise purely speculative. The notion of a "Thraco-Phrygian" branch of IE had currency for some time but has fallen out of favor. Our knowledge of these languages is simply too limited for claims of this kind; even the notion that what the ancients called "Thracian" was a single entity is unproven.

Macedonian

20.12. The ancient Macedonians were a group of tribes located north of Greece. They are thought to have come from the west and to have slowly migrated southeastward into lowland areas around the basin of the Haliacmon (Aliákmon) river in north-central Greece, along which they set up Aigai, their ancient capital. According to legend, they were unified under one Temenides in the seventh century BC. Their territory gradually increased to encompass Illyria, Thrace, and Phrygia. Under Philip II (382–336 BC), Macedon defeated Greece, and his son Alexander III (Alexander the Great, 356–323 BC) famously extended Macedonian conquest to much of the known world. Following his death, Macedon was riven by internal conflicts until the Antigonid dynasty (277–168 BC), after whose decline the country became a Roman province (146 BC).

Our knowledge of Macedonian is limited to glosses (again, mostly in Hesychius) and a number of personal names. The inscriptions found in former Macedonian territory are in Greek, adopted as an official language by the fifth century BC. A curse tablet in Doric Greek unearthed in 1986 in Pella, the later Macedonian capital, appears to contain some Macedonian linguistic features. Already in antiquity, Macedonian was regarded as bearing a close affinity with Greek, an impression that the glosses confirm. However, it is debated whether Macedonian was a rather deviant Greek dialect or a separate but closely allied language. Speaking for the latter is the one rather important Macedonian sound change that can be deduced from the glosses and personal names: the voiced aspirates lost their aspiration and became plain voiced stops, unlike any known Greek dialect (Macedonian *abroutes* 'eyebrow' = Gk. *ophrū̃s*; *danon* 'death' [accusative] = Gk. *thánaton*; *dōrax* 'spleen' = Gk. *thṓ̃raks* 'thorax'; personal names ***Ber(e)nika*** = Gk. ***Pherenī́kē*** 'bearing victory' and ***Bilippos*** = Gk. ***Phílippos***). Attempts to link Macedonian with Thracian and/or Illyrian in various ways are quite inconclusive.

Illyrian

20.13. The Illyrians, while not instantly familiar to most people today, were rather important in ancient history. They or their ancestors had settled in the Balkans perhaps in the early Bronze Age in the first half of the second millennium BC, and gradually expanded and founded various local kingdoms over the ensuing centuries. They came under the influence of Greek culture between the eighth and sixth centuries BC, when the Greeks set up colonies in the area, most notably Epidamnus (Dyrrhachium to the Romans, modern Durrës in Albania). After a series of conflicts with Rome, the Illyrians became Roman dependents by 165 BC; their lands constituted the new Roman province of Illyricum. Although they were to play an important role in the Roman army and even furnished later Rome with several famous emperors (including Diocletian, Constantine the Great, and Justinian I), the Illyrians never became fully assimilated Romans and kept their language.

What that language was is uncertain. The term "Illyrian" has referred to many things, until recently to any non-Celtic language in the broad area west of Thrace, north of Greece and Macedonia, and east of the Veneti (northeastern Italy). But scholarly work beginning in the 1960s has shown that the region is neither archaeologically nor onomastically uniform and that it breaks down into three distinct cultural and linguistic areas, of which only one can properly be called Illyrian. No treatment yet exists of the linguistic remains from just this region to the exclusion of the others. The remains consist of some personal and place-names and some glosses. There are no known inscriptions (and recall §20.2 above).

20.14. Two untestable hypotheses about Illyrian's connection to other languages are widely held: that Illyrian is the same as or closely related to Messapic, and that Illyrian is the ancestor of Albanian. The first hypothesis is based on the close cultural connections between the Messapians and Illyrians, and on certain similarities between some linguistic elements. The second hypothesis has very little, if any, linguistic support, but makes geographic sense; proponents also point out that the word *Albanoí* 'Albanians' is first attested (in the *Geography* of Ptolemy) as the name of an Illyrian tribe. One glossed word that has been compared with Albanian is *rhinos* 'fog' (cp. Old Geg *ren* 'cloud', modern *rê*), but this alone does not prove the case. The possible relationship to Messapic does not help, for the Messapic inscriptions evince no obvious similarities to Albanian.

A "Thraco-Illyrian" branch of Indo-European has been proposed by some who view Illyrian and Thracian as related. Others have proposed a mixture called "Daco-Mysian" or simply Dacian, a combination of Thracian, Illyrian, and the language of the neighboring Roman province of Dacia. All such proposals have very little to go on and are premature.

20.15. A few words of IE interest that are traditionally called Illyrian are: *Deipaturos*, the Illyrian name for Jupiter or Zeus that continues the PIE name 'Father Sky' (**di̯ēus ph$_2$tēr*, cp. Lat. *Iū-piter*; see §2.19); a word *teuta-* meaning 'people' in personal names from the root **teutā* found in western Europe (§2.8); the personal name *Vescleves*, usually understood to mean 'having good fame' and composed etymologically of the same elements as the Sanskrit adjective *vasu-śravas-*; and *sabaia* or *sabaium*, mentioned by the late Roman historian Ammianus Marcellinus and defined as a beer-like drink, which may be from the same root **sab-* that gives Germanic words for 'juice' (German *Saft* 'juice', Eng. *sap*). See also the notes to line 27 of the Umbrian text in §13.74a.

Venetic

20.16. Venetic was spoken in northeast Italy by the Veneti, a people famous in the Greek world for their horses. They appear to have arrived there by the end of the second millennium BC. The center of Venetic culture was the town of Este, about fifteen miles southwest of Padua; it was also the center of the cult of their main divinity, the goddess Reitia. But their territory stretched as far west as Verona and as far south as the Po valley. In the latter region they came into contact with Etruscan settlers around the sixth century BC, from whom they learned the alphabet. Venetic inscriptions, which number about 200 and date from the sixth to the first centuries BC, are written in both the Etruscan and, later, the Roman alphabet. Modern scholars sometimes divide Venetic into Archaic Venetic (550–475 BC), Old Venetic (475–300 BC), New Venetic (300–150 BC), and Veneto-Latin (150–100 BC). The inscriptions are all rather short, none being more than about ten words long; roughly half the attested words are personal names.

20.17. In view of its geographical location, it is not surprising that Venetic bears close affinities with Italic; in fact, many scholars consider it to be part of the Italic family. The similarities are both phonological and morphological. Italic and Venetic share a verb stem *fac-* 'do' (in Lat. *fac-ere* 'to do', Venetic *s*-aorist *vhag-sto* 'he did', with *vh* = *f* in the Etruscan alphabet) that represents an extension of PIE **dhh$_1$-* (zero-grade of **dheh$_1$-* 'put') with a **-k-* of unknown origin and meaning; but since the same stem is perhaps also attested in Phrygian (*addaket*, see §20.9a) and the Greek perfect *té-thē-k-a* 'I have put', this may not be a feature exclusively Italic or Italo-Venetic. More exclusive is the fact shared by Italic (specifically Latin) and Venetic that voiced aspirates developed into *f-* word-initially and into voiced stops word-internally: thus ***vhagsto*** above, and the dative plurals *louzero**ph**os* 'for the children' (with *z* and *ph* representing *d* and *b* from **loudhero-* plus **-bho-*) and *andeticobos* 'for the sons of Andetios' (?). On the other hand, some of the morphological features described in the next section, such as the pronominal forms *mego* and *sselboisselboi*, are strikingly different from Italic material. Much more evidence is needed to decide the issue.

20.18. In spite of the paucity of material, we know some outlines of the grammatical structure of the language. Five cases (nominative, accusative, genitive, dative, and instrumental) are preserved, and all three numbers – singular, dual, and plural – are found. The only known verb-forms are in the third person, such as singular present *atisteit* 'sets up (?)', past *donasto* 'gave'; plural *donasan* 'they gave'. The 3rd sing. *tolar* or *toler*, of unclear meaning, is a middle form. Unlike any of the attested Italic languages, Venetic still has a living *s*-aorist, as in *dona-s-to* and *vhag-s-to* above. The language also had active *nt*-participles (e.g. *horvionte*, a masculine nominative dual) and middle participles in *-mno-* (e.g. *alkomno* '?'). Of particular interest are some features of the pronominal system that find exact parallels in Germanic, and only there: a stem **selbh-* for the reflexive pronoun (Venetic *sselboisselboi* 'for himself', cp. the similarly doubled OHG form *selb selbo*), and a first-person accusative singular pronoun that is a rhyme formation with the nominative (Venetic *mego* 'me' rhyming with *ego* 'I'; cp. German *mich* 'me' rhyming with *ich* 'I'). Noteworthy also is an *o*-stem genitive singular in *-i*, matching Latin and Celtic.

20.19. The Venetic alphabet does not contain separate letters for the voiced stops. However, it contains a special *t*, sometimes transliterated t^2, that stands for *d*, as in the word *t^2eivos* = *deivos* 'god'. Venetic orthography generally makes use of the Etruscan system of "syllabic punctuation," treated in the Exercises below.

Venetic text sample

20.20. The inscription Es 122 found just north of Monselice (a town east of Este and south of Padua), dating from the Archaic Venetic period, before 475 BC. There are no word-divisions in the original. The interpretation follows that of Michel Lejeune, *Manuel de la langue vénète*.

ego vhontei ersiniioi
vineti karis vivoi oliialekve murtuvoi atisteit

20.20a. Notes. ego: 'I', cp. Lat. *ego*. **vhontei ersiniioi:** 'for Fons Ersinius', a personal name in the dative. *Vhont-* is an athematic noun with dative in *-ei* (§6.9), and *ersiniioi* may be a patronymic adjective in *-i̯o- ('son of Ersinus'). **vineti karis:** uncertain; perhaps a single word. Lejeune suggests 'friend of Vinetus'. **vivoi:** 'alive', dat. sing.; cp. Lat. *uīuus* 'alive'. **oliialekve:** 'and . . .'; *-kve* is from PIE *k^we; *oliiale* is not understood but is perhaps an adverb. **murtuvoi:** 'dead'; cp. Lat. *mortuus*. **atisteit:** see above, §20.18. The sense of the whole inscription is therefore something like, "I (am) for Fons Ersinius. A friend of Vinetus (?) sets up (this?) for (him), alive and . . . dead."

Messapic

20.21. Messapic is known from close to 300 inscriptions from southeast Italy in Calabria and Apulia and dating from the sixth to the first centuries BC. The language was spoken by an ancient people known both as the Messapii (or Messapians) and Iapyges. They are linked by ancient historians with Illyria, across the Adriatic Sea; the linkage is borne out archaeologically by similarities between Illyrian and Messapic metalwork and ceramics, and by personal names that appear in both locations. For this reason the Messapic language has often been connected by modern scholars to Illyrian; but, as noted above, we have too little Illyrian to be able to test this claim.

Messapic is written in an offshoot of an Ionic Greek alphabet that diffused early into southern Italy. Most of the inscriptions just contain personal names, and usually lack word-dividers, rendering interpretation of the longer inscriptions very difficult. A few things are known about its history and structure. Short **o* became *a*, as in the athematic genitive *damatras* 'of Demeter' (with genitive singular *-as* from **-os*). The *o*-stem genitive singular *-aihi* (as in *dazimaihi malohiaihi* 'of Dazimas Malohias'), earlier thought to contain the same *-ī* of Italic, Celtic, and Venetic, is now thought to be simply the continuation of **-osi̯o*. A dative-ablative plural *-bas* and instrumental plural *-bis* are found, e.g. *logetibas* 'for the *logeti*'s', *ogrebis* 'with vows' (?), as well as the *o*-stem instrumental plural *-ais* (e.g. *nomais* 'with portions' (?)). Some forms of the demonstrative pronoun **so-/to-* are found, though their grammatical determination is not certain: *toi* may be a masculine dative singular, *tai* the corresponding feminine. The latter recurs as a conjunction in *tai ma kos* . . . 'that not anyone . . . , lest anyone . . .', which also nicely preserves the PIE prohibitive **mē* and the indefinite pronoun *kos* from the stem *k^wo- or *k^wi-. A few verb forms have been tentatively identified, including the 3rd sing. present *hipakaθi* 'sets up' (?), the 3rd sing. aorist *hipades* 'set up, dedicated' (*hipa-* perhaps from *supo 'under', variant of *upo, cp. Lat. *sub-*, Gk. *hupo-*; *-des* from the *s*-aorist *dhēh$_1$-s-t or *dheh$_1$-s-t), and the 3rd pl. present optative *berain* 'they should bring'.

Probably the most valuable and interpretatively undisputed piece of Messapic is the formula *kl(a)ohi zis* found at the beginning of some inscriptions, which translates as "Listen, Zis (=Zeus)!" or "Let Zis listen." On these forms, see the Notes below.

Messapic text sample

20.22. Inscription from the second or first century BC from Basta (modern Vaste, a village in Apulia west of Otranto), copied down in the sixteenth century; the original has vanished. The division into lines below is probable but not assured; there are no word-divisions. We cannot translate the inscription, but we can provisionally divide it up analytically into words and structurally repeating units, following Hans Krahe, *Die Sprache der Illyrer*, vol. 1 (1964), pp. 27–8, with modifications.

klohizisθotoriamartapidovasteibasta
veinanaranindaranθoavastistaboos
šonedonasdaštassivaanetosinθitrigonošo
astaboosšonetθihidazimaihibeileihi
inθireššorišoakazareihišonetθihiotθeihiθi
dazohonnihiinθivastima
daštaskraθeheihiinθiardannoapoššonnihia
imarnaihi

klohi zis
θotoria marta pido vastei basta veinan aran

in daranθoa	vasti	staboos šonedonas
		daštas-si vaanetos
in-θi trigonošoa		staboos šonetθihi
		dazimaihi beileihi
in-θi reššorišoa		kazareihi šonetθihi otθeihi-θi dazohonnihi
in-θi vastima		daštas kraθeheihi
in-θi ardannoa		poššonnihi aimarnaihi

20.22a. Notes. klohi zis: 'Listen, Zis', invocation to Zis (Zeus). *Klohi*, spelled *klaohi* in older inscriptions, is probably the exact cognate of Ved. *śróṣi* 'listen', a singular *s*-aorist imperative. Others think that it is a 3rd pl. aorist optative, 'let him listen', from *k̂leu-s-ih$_1$-t. *Zis* is probably a borrowing from the Oscan of Lucania (southern Italy); a later Greek writer attests the name *Dis* from Tarentum, which may well be the same thing. **pido:** supposedly *(e)pi-dō-t 'gave, presented' or the like, with preverb *epi- (Gk. *epi-*) and a root aorist of *deh$_3$- 'give'. **in-θi:** *-θi* means 'and' and likely continues PIE *k^{w}e. It also occurs following *daštas* in line 4, assimilated to *-si*, and following *otθeihi* in line 7. Most of the words in the right-hand column are bipartite personal names in the genitive singular.

Sicel and Elymian

20.23. In Sicily were spoken at least two languages during the first millennium BC that are widely thought to have been Indo-European. The first, **Sicel** (or Siculian), was spoken by the Siculians in eastern Sicily. An inscription of moderate length, largely indecipherable, from the sixth or fifth century BC in Greek letters on a jug discovered in Centuripe in 1824 is most of what remains of the language, aside from some words preserved by Classical authors and a very few shorter inscriptions. A more recently discovered vessel contains a verb form of great interest, however: the imperative *pibe* 'drink!', exactly cognate with Sanskrit *píba* and Latin *bibe*, but without the latter's assimilation of the initial *p-* to *b-*.

Fragments of pottery and some coins from the city of Segesta in western Sicily attest a language called **Elymian** also written in the Greek alphabet from the sixth to the fourth centuries BC. In most cases the shards are so small that only a few letters survive on each. We know little aside from the verb form *emi* 'I am'. (Inscribed objects often "spoke" in the first person to indicate to whom they belonged or had been dedicated.)

In central Sicily, between the Elymians and Sicels, were the Sicanians, whose language is also only very fragmentarily preserved but does not appear to have been Indo-European.

Lusitanian

20.24. In the western Iberian peninsula, between Guadiane and Duero, three inscriptions in an IE language have been found, written in Latin letters and dating from around the time of the early Roman Empire (first century AD). This area was part of the Roman province called Lusitania, named after a people called the Lusitani; the language of these inscriptions has therefore been dubbed **Lusitanian**. The language is regarded by some to be Celtic; but this is quite uncertain. The identification of the language as IE is based on such forms as *doenti* 'they give', thematic dative singulars in *-oi* or, more commonly, *-ui* (the same as the corresponding Celtiberian ending), and accusative singulars in *-m* (e.g. *porcom* 'pig', *taurom* 'bull'). Note also the nominative plural *Veamnicori*, a name of a people, reminiscent of *Petrucorii*, the name of a Gaulish tribe.

For Further Reading

The corpora of all these languages continue to grow; the standard collections – few of them in English – contain most of the known inscriptions but lack those that have come to light more recently. For Phrygian, the most complete and recent comprehensive collection is Orel 1997, which includes both the material from the two standard collections (Haas 1966 and Brixhe and Lejeune 1984, the latter a very fine work) and the inscriptions unearthed since then. Orel's work also contains a grammar and vocabulary, but treat the interpretations with caution. An excellent comparison of Phrygian and Greek is Neumann 1988. The Thracian texts are in Detschew 1957. For Macedonian, see Kalléris 1954–76. The standard collection of Illyrian remains (but not in the narrow sense discussed in §20.13) is Krahe 1955–64; the second volume contains an edition of the Messapic inscriptions (now superseded by de Simone and Marchesini 2002) as well as a study of Illyrian personal names by Jürgen Untermann. For a good critical review of scholarship on Thracian and Illyrian, see Katičić 1976. The Venetic inscriptions known until the mid-1970s are collected in Lejeune 1974, which also contains detailed discussions of the orthography, phonology, and morphology. The Lusitanian corpus is contained in Untermann 1997.

Exercises

1 Comment on the history or significance of the following forms:

a Phryg. *addaket*	**d** Illyr. *Deipaturos*	**g** Ven. *sselboisselboi*
b Phryg. *anar*	**e** Illyr. *Vescleves*	**h** Messap. *-ihi*
c Phryg. *edaes*	**f** Ven. *vhagsto*	**i** Messap. *kl(a)ohi zis*

2 Phrygian *bekos* looks a lot like English *bake*, but what difficulty attends equating these etymologically?

3 It was mentioned in §20.8 that many scholars believe Phrygian forms a subgroup with Greek, Armenian, and Indo-Iranian. What branches of IE do the Phrygian middles in *-tor* pattern with?

4 Venetic "syllabic punctuation." Most Venetic inscriptions contain what at first appears to be a profligate fondness for interpuncts. There is, however, a fairly simple phonological principle behind their use. Interpuncts were used to frame certain kinds of sounds in certain syllabic contexts. If this framing would have led to a double interpunct, that was usually (though not always) simplified to a single one.

a Based on the following examples (whose meanings are irrelevant for the present purposes), determine the rules for interpunct placement. Recall that *vh* stands for a single consonant (the fricative *f*).

.e.kupetari.s.	vha.g.s.to	lemeto.r.na
ka.n.te.s.	.e.go	
.o.p.po.s.	ne.r.ka	

b What additional feature is reflected by the following?

.a.kuto.i.	.a.vhro.i.	ka.n.ta.i.
	votu.n.ke.a.	

c Now that you have established the basic principles, what information do the preceding examples tell us about the pronunciation of the initial *i* in *iuva.n.te.i.*?

d How many syllables does the word spelled *vo.t.te.i.iio.s.* contain? Explain.

e Now that you have established these principles, what do the following forms tell us about Venetic syllabification? State your answer as generally as possible. (Hint: compare the remarks on Latin *patre* in §1.10.) Treat *ii* as identical to *i*.

.e.kvo.n.	ve.i.gno.i.	u.r.kli
.a.vhro.i.	iiuva.n.tii.o.	mu.s.kia.l.na.i.
vhu.g.siia	.o.s.tiala.i.	

5 Imagine that you are the proud discoverer of a hitherto unknown ancient IE language belonging to a hitherto unknown branch of the family. Your task is to report your discovery to the scholarly world. Describe your language, including at least the following information:

a The date of the text(s) you have found and the place of discovery;
b The outcomes of all the PIE sounds – consonants, vowels, and diphthongs – in your language. Include at least two sound changes that are conditioned, i.e., that happened only in particular phonetic environments (some of the conditioned sound changes that we've talked about are rhotacism in Latin, umlaut in Germanic, Verner's Law, and palatalization). Be sure to specify what the phonetic environments were (beginning of a word, between vowels, before a front vowel, word-finally, etc. etc.);
c The outcomes of these PIE forms: *$ph_2t\acute{\bar{e}}r$ 'father', **mā́tēr* 'mother', **bhrā́tēr* 'brother', **su̯ésōr* 'sister', **pods, *ped-* 'foot', **mūs-* 'mouse', *k^wel- 'to turn', *h_3erbh- 'transfer to another sphere of ownership', **k̂léu̯os* 'fame', *$u̯l̥k^wos$ 'wolf', **ĝheimōn* 'winter', *$sneig^wh$- 'to snow';
d A brief description of the nominal system, including: what cases are preserved; what numbers; what genders; the general fate of athematic and thematic nouns;
e A brief description of the verbal system, including: what tenses are preserved; what numbers; the general fate of athematic and thematic verbs, of the aorist, and of the perfect;
f The paradigm in the singular and 3rd plural of the descendant of *h_1es- 'be' in the present tense, **bher-* 'carries' in the present tense, and **u̯oide* 'knows';
g A sample text in your language of a dozen words, including at least half that have an IE etymology and are different from the ones you give in (**c**) above;
h Some brief remarks about the culture, mythology, society, etc. of the people that spoke your language.

PIE Vocabulary XII: Basic Physical Acts

*$dheh_1$- 'place, put': Hitt. *dāi* 'puts', Ved. *dádhāti* 'puts', Gk. *títhēmi* 'I put', Lat. *faciō* 'I do', Eng. DO
**u̯erĝ-* 'WORK': Av. *vərəziieiti* 'works', Gk. *(w)érgon* 'work', Arm. *gorc* 'work'
**bheid-* 'split': Ved. *bhinátti* 'splits', Lat. *findō* 'I split', Eng. BITE
**sek-* 'cut': Lat. *secō* 'I cut', Eng. SAW, OCS *sěkǫ* 'I cut'
**ĝheu-* 'pour': Ved. *juhóti* 'pours', Gk. *khé(w)ō* 'I pour', Lat. *fundō* 'I pour', Eng. INGOT

Glossary

For items not listed here, see the Index.

ablative In nouns and pronouns, the case used to express source or origin and the object of certain prepositions, especially those indicating motion away from or out of. In some languages it is also used to express instrument, accompaniment, or location.

ablaut A change in the vowel of a root or word that signals a change in grammatical function or category. The change of vowels in *sing sang sung song* is an example of ablaut.

accusative In nouns and pronouns, the case used to express the direct object of a verb and the object of certain prepositions, especially those indicating motion towards, into, across, or through.

active In verbs, the voice indicating that the grammatical subject does the action.

affricate A consonant produced by stopping the flow of air completely and then releasing the stoppage gradually, resulting in a sound that begins as a stop and ends as a fricative. English *ch* and *j* are affricates. The verb to *affricate* means to change or cause to change into an affricate.

allomorph One of the variants of a morpheme. The three pronunciations of the English plural morpheme *-(e)s* (as in *bets*, *beds*, *midges*) are allomorphs of one underlying plural morpheme.

allophone One of the pronunciations of a phoneme. The aspirated *p* of English *pit* and the unaspirated *p* in *spit* are allophones of the English phoneme [p].

apocope The loss of a vowel or syllable at the end of a word.

articulation The physical production of a speech sound.

aspirate A consonant immediately followed by a puff of breath. Sanskrit *bh* was a voiced aspirate.

assimilation The change of a speech sound such that it becomes more similar to another sound, usually a neighboring one.

case A form of a noun, pronoun, or adjective that indicates a particular grammatical role.

clitic A word that has no independent word-stress and attaches to a neighboring stressed word, with which it forms a phonological unit. The *-n't* of English *didn't* is a clitic.

cognates Words in two or more languages that are descended from the same word in their common ancestor, like Latin *pater* and English *father*.

comparative method The method by which two or more languages are systematically compared to determine whether they are descended from a common ancestor.

copula The verb *be* or its equivalent in other languages in the function of identifying the predicate with a subject, as in the sentence *Humans are mortals*.

coronal Produced with the front part (blade) of the tongue, such as *t*, *s*, *r*, and *l*.

dative In nouns and pronouns, the case used to express the indirect object, the one that benefits from an action, and sometimes possession.

denominative A verb formed from a noun, such as Eng. *to book, to computerize.*

dental Produced with the tip of the tongue touching the teeth or the ridge behind the upper teeth, as *t*.

derivative A word derived from another word, typically by a productive morphological process; also, a word that is historically descended from a word or word root in an ancestral language.

derive To form a word from another word or word root, typically by a productive morphological process.

determiner A modifier that acts to select a particular referent or referents. Determiners include definite and indefinite articles, demonstratives, possessive pronouns, and indefinite pronouns.

deverbative Formed from a verb; also, a word formed in this way.

diachronic Viewed or occurring over a period of time; pertaining to a language's development through time; historical. Compare *synchronic.*

dissimilation The change of a speech sound such that it becomes less like another sound, usually a neighboring one.

dual The grammatical category indicating two in number.

enclitic A clitic, especially one that is phonologically dependent on a preceding word.

epenthesis The introduction of a vowel in pronunciation, especially between two consonants or neighboring a consonant cluster, as when *athlete* is pronounced [æθəlit].

finite Referring to a verb form that is inflected for tense, mood, voice, person, and number.

frequentative A verb form indicating repeated or habitual action.

fricative A consonant produced by partial obstruction of the vocal tract, resulting in hissing or turbulent noise, such as *s* and *f*.

gender A grammatical classificational category of nouns and some pronouns. Typical gender systems involve a three-way distinction between masculine, feminine, and neuter, or a two-way distinction between animate and inanimate. Grammatical gender sometimes overlaps with biological gender.

genitive In nouns and pronouns, the case used to indicate possession.

glide A consonant, such as *w* or *y* in English, produced with relatively little obstruction of the flow of air and resembling a vowel; also called "semivowel."

gloss A translation. Ancient glosses, such as those in Old Irish, are typically brief interlinear or marginal comments or translations.

glottis The muscular ring at the upper opening of the larynx.

guttural Produced in the back of the mouth or in the throat; also, another term for *velar*.

heavy Ending in a consonant or containing a long vowel or diphthong. Said of syllables.

high Produced with the tongue raised toward the roof of the mouth, as the vowel sounds in the words *street* and *boot*.

historical phonology (morphology, syntax) The study or account of the history and development of a language's phonology, morphology, or syntax.

imperative In verbs, the mood used to express orders and commands.

indicative In verbs, the mood used to express factual statements.

infinitive A verbal noun, especially one used as a complement of another verb. English infinitives consist of *to* plus the verb.

inflect To change form, as by the addition or change of a suffix, in order to indicate change of grammatical function.

inflection A form of a word having a particular grammatical function, such as the accusative case of a noun or the 3rd person singular of a verb.

instrumental In nouns and pronouns, the case used to indicate instrument or means.

internal reconstruction The reconstruction of an earlier stage of a language by examining alternations or other regular patterns in the phonology or morphology of a later stage of the same language. Deducing the sound change(s) whose effects created the alternations allows recovery of a stage prior to the sound chage(s).

labial Produced with the lips, such as *p*.

labiovelar A velar consonant accompanied by rounding of the lips, like Proto-Indo-European $*k^w$.

lexicon The vocabulary of a language.

light Ending in a short vowel. Said of syllables.

liquid An *r* or *l*.

loanword A word borrowed from one language into another.

locative In nouns and pronouns, the case used to express location or place at, in, or on which.

manner of articulation The way in which, and the degree to which, obstruction of the vocal tract is effected during the production of a consonant, such as stoppage or frication.

medial Occurring in the middle of a word.

mediopassive Combining middle and passive voice.

middle In verbs, the voice indicating that the grammatical subject is acting upon itself or is otherwise internal to the action of the verb.

mood A grammatical category of verbs indicating the speaker's attitude or stance taken towards the action expressed by the verb.

mora A unit of time or syllable weight, conceived as the duration of a simple syllabic speech sound. Short vowels have a length of one mora; long vowels, normally two.

morpheme The smallest unit of a language that has meaning. Two examples from English are the plural suffix *-s* and the word *word*.

morphology The system of rules for combining morphemes into words in a language, or the study thereof.

murmur The breathy voice characteristic of voiced aspirate consonants.

nasal A stop produced by letting air flow out through the nasal passages, such as *m* and *n*.

nominal Pertaining to a noun; having the function or properties of a noun.

nominalize To turn another part of speech into a noun, as in *the good and the bad*.

nominative In nouns and pronouns, the case used to express the subject of a sentence or a predicate nominative.

number The grammatical category indicating quantity, such as singular, dual, and plural.

obstruent A consonant that is not a resonant; a non-nasal stop, fricative, or affricate.

optative In verbs, the mood used to express wishes.

palatal Produced with the tongue touching or coming near the hard palate. The glide *y* and the *k* of the English word *kit* are palatal.

palatalize To change a consonant into a palatal consonant or into a consonant produced closer to the palate.

participle A verbal adjective. As an adjective it can modify a noun and be inflected in case, number, and gender; as a verb it can take an object and distinguish tense and voice.

passive In verbs, the voice indicating that the grammatical subject is acted upon by the action of the verb.

periphrastic Relating to a morphological category, such as a verb tense, that is expressed using an auxiliary rather than by a single inflected form, such as the English present perfect (*have gone*).

person A grammatical category of verbs and pronouns that indicates the person speaking (first person), person being spoken to (second person), or a third party (third person).

phoneme The smallest linguistic unit that can contrast meaning; a basic sound of a language.

phonology The system of sounds in a language, or the study thereof.

phonotactic Pertaining to the *phonotactics* of a language, the rules for combinations of sounds particular to a given language.
place of articulation The place in the vocal tract where the flow of air is obstructed during the production of a consonant.
possessive Another word for *genitive.*
postposition A word functionally equivalent to a preposition but occurring after the word it governs.
predicate nominative A noun, pronoun, or adjective that is predicated of a subject by means of a copula or copulative verb, such as *be*, *become*, or *seem*, and that stands in the nominative case.
preverb An adverbial particle that modifies the meaning of a verb and often appears attached to the verb as a prefix.
proclitic A clitic that is phonologically dependent on a following word.
productive Able to be used to form new words or inflectional forms. Said of morphemes or morphological processes, such as English *-ed*, *-ize*, *re-* (as opposed to, e.g., the *-th* of *growth*).
pronominal Pertaining to pronouns.
prosody The organization of speech sounds into rhythmic units or groups; also, the rules by which it is so organized.
proto-language A language not preserved in records that has been reconstructed on the basis of a known language or languages, of which it is the ancestor.
reflex A historical descendant or outcome of a specified ancestral sound or form. *F* is the Germanic reflex of PIE **p*, for example.
resonant A consonant capable of becoming the center of a syllable and thereby becoming syllabic, such as the liquids and nasals.
rhotacize To turn into *r.*
sandhi The process whereby one or more sounds at the juncture of two words or morphemes assimilate to one another or undergo other phonetic change.
semivowel *see* glide.
sibilant A fricative having a hissing quality, such as *s.*
spirantize To turn into a fricative, as when a *p* changes to *f* or a *b* changes to *v.*
stem The form to which grammatical endings are added; the form of a word minus its grammatical endings.
stop A consonant produced by total closure of some part of the vocal tract, whereby the flow of air is briefly stopped and then released. *P* and *d* are stops. Also called *plosive.*
subjunctive In verbs, a mood typically expressing non-factual modalities, as in clauses of purpose or result, conditions, and potentialities.
substantive A noun.
surface At the linguistic level of spoken language rather than at a deeper or more abstract (underlying) level.
syllabic Occupying the center or syllable peak of a syllable; functioning as a vowel.
synchronic Viewed at or characteristic of a particular point in time in the history of a language. Compare *diachronic.*
syncope The loss of a vowel or syllable in the interior of a word.
syntax The system of rules for combining words into phrases, clauses, and sentences in a language.
tense The grammatical category of verbs that expresses the time at which an action happens.
umlaut The partial assimilation of a vowel to a vowel in a neighboring (usually following) syllable.
underlying At a deep or abstract grammatical level rather than on the surface phonetic level.

velar Produced with the tongue touching the velum (soft palate, behind the hard palate). The *g* in English *got* is a velar stop.

vocalic Pertaining to or characteristic of vowels; also, pronounced with the addition of a vowel sound, as a vocalic laryngeal.

vocative In nouns and pronouns, the case used for direct address.

voice The verbal category expressing the role taken by the subject in the action of a verb.

voicing The vibration of the larynx during the production of a speech sound. *B* and *m* are voiced sounds; *p* and *h* are voiceless.

vowel harmony A property of some languages whereby the vowels in a given word must be alike with respect to some feature, such as height, backness, or roundness.

Bibliography

This bibliography is not intended to be even remotely exhaustive. All the titles except those marked with an asterisk are discussed in the "For Further Reading" sections at the end of the relevant chapter. Note that titles mentioned in more than one "For Further Reading" section are not listed here multiply.

Chapter 1: Introduction

Bader, Françoise, ed. 1997. *Les Langues indo-européennes.* 2nd edition. Paris: CNRS.

Beekes, Robert S. P. 1995. *Comparative Indo-European Linguistics: An Introduction.* Amsterdam: Benjamins.

Brugmann, Karl. 1897–1916. *Grundriss der vergleichenden Grammatik der indogermanischen Sprachen.* Strassburg: Trübner. (Translated as *Elements of the Comparative Grammar of the Indo-Germanic Languages* [Varanasi: Chowkhamba Sanskrit Series Office, 1972].)

Campbell, Lyle. 1999. *Historical Linguistics: An Introduction.* Cambridge, MA: MIT Press.

Clackson, James. 2007. *Indo-European Linguistics: An Introduction.* Cambridge: Cambridge University Press.

Hirt, Hermann. 1927–37. *Indogermanische Grammatik.* Heidelberg: Winter.

Mallory, J. P., and D. Q. Adams. 2006. *The Oxford Introduction to Proto-Indo-European and the Proto-Indo-European World.* Oxford: Oxford University Press.

Meier-Brügger, Michael. 2003. *Indo-European Linguistics.* Tr. Charles Gertmenian. Berlin: de Gruyter.

Meillet, Antoine. 1925. *La Méthode comparative en linguistique historique.* Paris: Champion. (Translated as *The Comparative Method in Historical Linguistics* [Paris: Champion, 1967].)

Meillet, Antoine. 1937. *Introduction à l'étude comparative des langues indo-européennes.* 8th edition. Paris: Hachette.

Pedersen, Holger. 1959. *The Discovery of Language: Linguistic Science in the 19th Century.* Bloomington: Indiana University Press.

Ramat, Anna Giacalone, and Paolo Ramat, eds. 1998. *The Indo-European Languages.* London: Routledge.

Robins, R. H. 1997. *A Short History of Linguistics.* 4th edition. New York: Longman.

Salmons, Joseph C., and Brian D. Joseph, eds. 1998. *Nostratic: Sifting the Evidence.* Amsterdam: Benjamins.

Sihler, Andrew. 2000. *Language History: An Introduction.* Philadelphia: Benjamins.

Szemerényi, Oswald. 1996. *Introduction to Indo-European Linguistics.* 4th edition. Oxford: Oxford University Press.

Tichy, Eva. 2006. *A Survey of Proto-Indo-European.* Tr. James E. Cathey. Bremen: Hempen.

Chapter 2: Culture and Archaeology

*Anthony, David. 1991. "The Archaeology of Indo-European Origins." *Journal of Indo-European Studies* 19:193–222.

Anthony, David W. 2008. *The Horse, the Wheel, and Language: How Bronze-Age Riders from the Eurasian Steppes Shaped the Modern World.* Princeton: Princeton University Press.

Benveniste, Émile. 1969. *Le Vocabulaire des institutions indo-européennes.* Paris: Minuit. (Translated as *Indo-European Language and Society* [Coral Gables: University of Miami Press, 1973].)

Buck, Carl Darling. 1949. *A Dictionary of Selected Synonyms in the Principal Indo-European Languages.* Chicago: University of Chicago Press.

Campanile, Enrico. 1977. *Ricerche di cultura poetica indoeuropea.* Pisa: Giardini.

*Campanile, Enrico. 1990. *La ricostruzione della cultura indoeuropea.* Pisa: Giardini.

*Cardona, George, Henry M. Hoenigswald, and Alfred Senn, eds. 1970. *Indo-European and Indo-Europeans: Papers Presented at the Third Indo-European Conference at the University of Pennsylvania.* Philadelphia: University of Pennsylvania Press.

Dumézil, Georges. 1952. *Les Dieux des indo-européens.* Paris: Presses Universitaires de France.

Dumézil, Georges. 1958. *L'Idéologie tripartie des indo-européennes.* Brussels: Latomus.

Gamkrelidze, Tamaz V., and Vyacheslav V. Ivanov. 1984. *Indojevropejskij jazyk i indojevropejci.* Tbilisi: Izdatel'stvo Tbilisskogo Universiteta. (Translated as *Indo-European and the Indo-Europeans* [Berlin: de Gruyter, 1995].)

Gimbutas, Marija. 1997. *The Kurgan Culture and the Indo-Europeanization of Europe: Selected Articles from 1952 to 1993.* Washington: Institute for the Study of Man.

Mallory, J. P. 1989. *In Search of the Indo-Europeans: Language, Archaeology and Myth.* London: Thames and Hudson.

Mallory, J. P., and Douglas Q. Adams, eds. 1997. *The Encyclopaedia of Indo-European Culture.* London: Fitzroy Dearborn.

Mann, Stuart E. 1984–7. *An Indo-European Comparative Dictionary.* Hamburg: Buske.

*Meid, Wolfgang. 1998. *Sprache und Kultur der Indogermanen: Akten der X. Fachtagung der Indogermanischen Gesellschaft, Innsbruck, 22.–28. September 1996.* Innsbruck: Institut für Sprachwissenschaft der Universität Innsbruck.

Pokorny, Julius. 1959–69. *Indogermanisches etymologisches Wörterbuch.* Bern: Francke.

Puhvel, Jaan. 1987. *Comparative Mythology.* Baltimore: Johns Hopkins University Press.

Renfrew, Colin. 1987. *Archaeology and Language: The Puzzle of Indo-European Origins.* London: Cape.

Schlerath, Bernfried. 1995–6. "Georges Dumézil und die Rekonstruktion der indogermanischen Kultur." *Kratylos* 40:1–48 and 41:1–67.

Schmitt, Rüdiger. 1967. *Dichtung und Dichtersprache in indogermanischer Zeit.* Wiesbaden: Harrassowitz.

*Sergent, Bernard. 1995. *Les Indo-européens: Histoire, langues, mythes.* Paris: Payot & Rivages.

*Watkins, Calvert. 1963. "Indo-European metrics and Archaic Irish Verse." *Celtica* 6:194–249.

Watkins, Calvert. 1994. *Selected Writings.* Innsbruck: Institut für Sprachwissenschaft der Universität Innsbruck.

Watkins, Calvert. 1995. *How to Kill a Dragon: Aspects of Indo-European Poetics.* Oxford: Oxford University Press.

Watkins, Calvert. 2000. *The American Heritage Dictionary of Indo-European Roots.* 2nd edition. Boston: Houghton Mifflin.

*Zimmer, Stefan. 2002–3. "Tendenzen der indogermanischen Altertumskunde 1965–2000." *Kratylos* 47:1–22 and 48:1–25.

Chapter 3: Phonology

Bammesberger, Alfred, ed. 1988. *Die Laryngaltheorie und die Rekonstruktion des indogermanischen Laut- und Formensystems*. Heidelberg: Winter.

*Beekes, Robert S. P. 1992. *Rekonstruktion und relative Chronologie. Akten der VIII. Fachtagung der Indogermanischen Gesellschaft, Leiden, 31. August–4. September 1987*. Innsbruck: Institut für Sprachwissenschaft der Universität Innsbruck.

*Collinge, N. E. 1985. *The Laws of Indo-European*. Amsterdam: Benjamins.

*Hopper, Paul J. 1973. "Glottalized and murmured occlusives in Indo-European." *Glotta* 7:141–66.

*Kuryłowicz, Jerzy. 1958. *L'Accentuation des langues indo-européennes*. Wrocław: Polska Akademia Nauk.

Lindeman, Fredrik Otto. 1987. *Introduction to the Laryngeal Theory*. Oslo: Norwegian University Press.

Mayrhofer, Manfred. 1986. *Indogermanische Grammatik*, Band I: *Lautlehre*. Heidelberg: Winter.

*Mayrhofer, Manfred, Martin Peters, and Oskar E. Pfeiffer, eds. 1980. *Lautgeschichte und Etymologie. Akten der VI. Fachtagung der Indogermanischen Gesellschaft, Wien, 24.–29. September 1978*. Wiesbaden: Reichert.

*Schindler, Jochem. 1977a. "A thorny problem." *Die Sprache* 23:25–35.

*Schindler, Jochem. 1977b. "Notizen zum Sieversschen Gesetz." *Die Sprache* 23:56–65.

Szemerényi, Oswald. 1985. "Recent developments in Indo-European linguistics." *Transactions of the Philological Society* 1985:1–71.

Winter, Werner, ed. 1965. *Evidence for Laryngeals*. The Hague: Mouton.

Chapter 4: Morphology

Anttila, Raimo. 1969. *Proto-Indo-European Schwebeablaut*. Berkeley: University of California Press.

Benveniste, Émile. 1935. *Origines de la formation des noms en indo-européen*. Paris: Maisonneuve.

Kuryłowicz, Jerzy. 1927. "ə indo-européen et ḫ hittite." In *Symbolae Grammaticae in Honorem Ioannis Rozwadowski*. Kraków: Gebethner and Wolff, pp. 1.95–104.

Kuryłowicz, Jerzy. 1956. *L'Apophonie en indo-européen*. Wrocław: Polska Akademia Nauk.

*Rix, Helmut, ed. 1975. *Flexion und Wortbildung. Akten der V. Fachtagung der Indogermanischen Gesellschaft, Regensburg, 9.–14. September 1973*. Wiesbaden: Reichert.

Saussure, Ferdinand de. 1879. *Mémoire sur le système primitif des voyelles dans les langues indo-européennes*. Leipzig: Teubner.

*Schlerath, Bernfried. 1985. *Grammatische Kategorien: Funktion und Geschichte. Akten der VII. Fachtagung der Indogermanischen Gesellschaft, Berlin, 20.–25. Februar 1983*. Wiesbaden: Reichert.

Chapter 5: Verb

Jasanoff, Jay. 1978. *Stative and Middle in Indo-European*. Innsbruck: Institut für Sprachwissenschaft der Universität Innsbruck.

Jasanoff, Jay. 2003. *Hittite and the Indo-European Verb*. Oxford: Oxford University Press.

*Kümmel, Martin. 1996. *Stativ und Passivaorist im Indoiranischen*. Göttingen: Vandenhoeck & Ruprecht.

*Narten, Johanna. 1964. *Die sigmatischen Aoriste im Veda*. Wiesbaden: Harrassowitz.

*Narten, Johanna. 1968. "Zum 'proterodynamischen' Wurzelpräsens." In J. C. Heesterman et al. (eds.), Pratidānam: *Indian, Iranian and Indo-European Studies Presented to F. B. J. Kuiper on his Sixtieth Birthday*. The Hague: Mouton, pp. 9–19.

Rix, Helmut, ed. 2001. *LIV: Lexikon der indogermanischen Verben*. 2nd edition. Wiesbaden: Reichert.

Watkins, Calvert. 1969. *Indogermanische Grammatik*, Band III, Teil 1: *Geschichte der indogermanischen Verbalflexion*. Heidelberg: Winter.

*Watkins, Calvert. 1971. "Hittite and Indo-European Studies: The denominative statives in **-ē-*." *Transactions of the Philological Society* 1971:51–93.

Chapter 6: Noun

*Benveniste, Émile. 1948. *Noms d'agent et noms d'action en indo-européen*. Paris: Maisonneuve.

*Darms, George. 1978. *Schwäher und Schwager, Hahn und Huhn: Die Vr̥ddhi-Ableitungen im Germanischen*. Munich: Kitzinger.

*Eichner, Heiner. 1973. "Die Etymologie von heth. *mehur*." *Münchener Studien zur Sprachwissenschaft* 31:53–107.

*Hoffmann, Karl. 1955. "Ein grundsprachliches Possessivsuffix." *Münchener Studien zur Sprachwissenschaft* 6:35–40.

Nussbaum, Alan. 1986. *Head and Horn in Indo-European*. Berlin: de Gruyter.

Rieken, Elisabeth. 1999. *Untersuchungen zur nominalen Stammbildung des Hethitischen*. Wiesbaden: Harrassowitz.

*Schindler, Jochem. 1972. "L'Apophonie des noms-racines." *Bulletin de la Société de Linguistique de Paris* 67:31–8.

*Schindler, Jochem. 1975a. "L'Apophonie des thèmes indo-européennes en *-r/n-*." *Bulletin de la Société de Linguistique de Paris* 70:1–10.

*Schindler, Jochem. 1975b. "Zum Ablaut der neutralen *s*-Stämme des Indogermanischen." In H. Rix (ed.), *Flexion und Wortbildung. Akten der V. Fachtagung der Indogermanischen Gesellschaft*. Wiesbaden: Reichert, pp. 259–67.

Chapter 7: Pronouns and Other Parts of Speech

Cowgill, Warren. 1960. "Greek *ou* and Armenian *oč'*." *Language* 36:347–50.

Gvozdanović, Jadranka, ed. 1992. *Indo-European Numerals*. Berlin: de Gruyter.

Katz, Joshua T. 1998. Studies in Indo-European Personal Pronouns. PhD dissertation, Harvard University.

Schmidt, Gernot. 1978. *Stammbildung und Flexion der indogermanischen Personalpronomina*. Wiesbaden: Harrassowitz.

Szemerényi, Oswald. 1960. *Studies in the Indo-European System of Numerals*. Heidelberg: Winter.

Chapter 8: Syntax

Delbrück, Berthold. 1893–1900. *Vergleichende Syntax der indogermanischen Sprachen*. Strassburg: Trübner.
Garrett, Andrew. 1990. *The Syntax of Anatolian Pronominal Clitics*. PhD dissertation, Harvard University.
Hale, Mark. 1987. "Wackernagel's Law and the language of the Rigveda." In C. Watkins (ed.), *Studies in Memory of Warren Cowgill (1929–1985)*. Berlin: de Gruyter, pp. 38–50.
Inkelas, Sharon, and Draga Zec, eds. 1990. *The Phonology–Syntax Connection*. Chicago: University of Chicago Press.
Wackernagel, Jacob. 1892. "Über ein Gesetz der indogermanischen Wortstellung." *Indogermanische Forschungen* 1:333–436.
Wackernagel, Jacob. 1920. *Vorlesungen über Syntax*. Basel: Birkhäuser.
Watkins, Calvert. 1963. "Preliminaries to a historical and comparative analysis of the syntax of the Old Irish verb." *Celtica* 6:1–49.
Watkins, Calvert. 1976. "Towards Indo-European syntax: Problems and pseudo-problems." In S. Steever et al. (eds.), *Papers from the Parasession on Diachronic Syntax*. Chicago: Chicago Linguistics Society, pp. 305–26.

Chapter 9: Anatolian

Adiego, Ignacio J. 2007. *The Carian Language*. Leiden: Brill.
Çambel, Halet. 1999. *Corpus of Hieroglyphic Luwian Inscriptions*, vol. II: *Karatepe-Aslantaş*. Berlin: de Gruyter.
Carruba, Onofrio. 1970. *Das Palaische: Texte, Grammatik, Lexikon*. Wiesbaden: Harrassowitz.
Friedrich, Johannes. 1952–66. *Kurzgefaßtes hethitisches Wörterbuch*. Heidelberg: Winter.
Friedrich, Johannes. 1974. *Hethitisches Elementarbuch*. 2nd edition. Heidelberg: Winter.
Friedrich, Johannes, and Annelies Kammenhuber. 1975– . *Hethitisches Wörterbuch*. Heidelberg: Winter.
*Garrett, Andrew. 1992. "Topics in Lycian syntax." *Historische Sprachforschung* 105:200–12.
Gusmani, Roberto. 1964. *Lydisches Wörterbuch*. Heidelberg: Winter. (Supplements: *Ergänzungsband, Lieferung 1*, 1980; *Ergänzungsband, Lieferung 2*, 1982; *Ergänzungsband, Lieferung 3*, 1986.)
Güterbock, Hans G., and Harry A. Hoffner. 1980– . *The Hittite Dictionary of the Oriental Institute of the University of Chicago*. Chicago: Oriental Institute of the University of Chicago.
Hawkins, John David. 2000. *Corpus of Hieroglyphic Luwian Inscriptions*, vol. I: *Inscriptions of the Iron Age*. Berlin: de Gruyter.
Hoffner, Harry A., Jr., and H. Craig Melchert. 2008. *A Grammar of the Hittite Language*. Winona Lake: Eisenbrauns.
Kimball, Sara E. 1999. *Hittite Historical Phonology*. Innsbruck: Institut für Sprachwissenschaft der Universität Innsbruck.
Kloekhorst, Alwin. 2008. *Etymological Dictionary of the Hittite Inherited Lexicon*. Leiden: Brill.

Laroche, Emmanuel. 1971. *Catalogue des textes hittites*. Paris: Klincksieck.
*Melchert, H. Craig. 1987. "PIE velars in Luvian." In C. Watkins (ed.), *Studies in Memory of Warren Cowgill (1929–1985)*. Berlin: de Gruyter, pp. 182–204.
Melchert, H. Craig. 1993. *Cuneiform Luvian Lexicon*. Chapel Hill: self-published.
Melchert, H. Craig. 1994. *Anatolian Historical Phonology*. Amsterdam: Rodopi.
Melchert, H. Craig, ed. 2003. *The Luwians*. Leiden: Brill.
Melchert, H. Craig. 2004. *A Dictionary of the Lycian Language*. Ann Arbor: Beech Stave.
Neumann, Günter. 1969. "Lykisch." In B. Spuler (ed.), *Handbuch der Orientalistik: Altkleinasiatische Sprachen*. Leiden: Brill, pp. 358–96.
*Otten, Heinrich, and Vladimir Souček. 1969. *Ein althethitisches Ritual für das Königspaar*. Wiesbaden: Harrassowitz.
Puhvel, Jaan. 1984– . *Hittite Etymological Dictionary*. Berlin: de Gruyter.
Starke, Frank. 1984. *Die keilschrift-luwischen Texte in Umschrift*. Wiesbaden: Harrassowitz.
Starke, Frank. 1990. *Untersuchung zur Stammbildung des keilschrift-luwischen Nomens*. Wiesbaden: Harrassowitz.
Tischler, Johann. 1977– . *Hethitisches etymologisches Glossar*. Innsbruck: Institut für Sprachwissenschaft der Universität Innsbruck.
*Yoshida, Kazuhiko. 1990. *The Hittite Mediopassive Endings in* -ri. Berlin: de Gruyter.

Chapter 10: Indic

Aufrecht, Theodor. 1877. *Die Hymnen des Rigveda*. 2nd edition. Bonn: Marcus.
Delbrück, Berthold. 1888. *Altindische Syntax*. Halle: Verlag der Waisen Hauses.
Geldner, Karl Friedrich. 1951–7. *Der Rig-Veda*. Cambridge, MA: Harvard University Press.
Grassmann, Hermann. 1873. *Wörterbuch zum Rig-Veda*. Leipzig: Brockhaus. (6th edition with revisions by M. Kozianka [Wiesbaden: Harrassowitz], 1996.)
*Hale, Mark. 1990. "Preliminaries to the study of the relationship between sandhi and syntax in the language of the Rigveda." *Münchener Studien zur Sprachwissenschaft* 51:77–96.
*Hale, Mark. 1995. Wackernagel's Law in the Language of the Rigveda. Manuscript, Concordia University, Montréal.
Hoffmann, Karl. 1975–92. *Aufsätze zur Indo-Iranistik*. Wiesbaden: Reichert.
*Jamison, Stephanie. 1991. *The Ravenous Hyenas and the Wounded Sun: Myth and Ritual in Ancient India*. Ithaca: Cornell University Press.
Macdonell, Arthur Anthony. 1910. *A Vedic Grammar*. Strassburg: Trübner.
Macdonell, Arthur Anthony. 1916. *A Vedic Grammar for Students*. Oxford: Clarendon.
Macdonell, Arthur Anthony. 1917. *A Vedic Reader for Students*. Oxford: Clarendon.
*Masica, Colin P. 1991. *The Indo-Aryan Languages*. Cambridge: Cambridge University Press.
*Mayrhofer, Manfred. 1966. *Die Indo-Arier im Alten Vorderasien*. Wiesbaden: Harrassowitz.
Mayrhofer, Manfred. 1986–2001. *Etymologisches Wörterbuch des Altindoarischen*. Heidelberg: Winter.
Oberlies, Thomas. 2001. Pāli: *A Grammar of the Language of the Theravāda* Tipiṭaka. Berlin: de Gruyter.
Renou, Louis. 1955–69. *Études védiques et pāṇinéennes*. Paris: Boccard.
*Turner, R. L. 1966–9. *A Comparative Dictionary of the Indo-Aryan Languages*. Indexes compiled by Dorothy Rivers Turner. London: Oxford University Press.
Wackernagel, Jacob, and Albert Debrunner. 1896– . *Altindische Grammatik*. Göttingen: Vandenhoeck und Ruprecht.
Whitney, William Dwight. 1896. *Sanskrit Grammar*. Leipzig: Breitkopf und Härtel.

Chapter 11: Iranian

Bartholomae, Christian. 1904. *Altiranisches Wörterbuch*. Strassburg: Trübner. (Reprint with the 1906 supplement [Berlin: de Gruyter], 1979.)

Beekes, Robert S. P. 1988. *A Grammar of Gatha-Avestan*. Leiden: Brill.

Cheung, Johnny. 2007. *Etymological Dictionary of the Iranian Verb*. Leiden: Brill.

de Vaan, Michiel. 2003. *The Avestan Vowels*. Amsterdam: Rodopi.

Geldner, Karl F. 1886–96. *Avesta: The Sacred Books of the Parsis*. Stuttgart: Kohlhammer.

Hoffmann, Karl, and Bernhard Forssman. 2004. *Avestische Laut- und Formenlehre*. 2nd edition. Innsbruck: Institut für Sprachwissenschaft der Universität Innsbruck.

Humbach, Helmut. 1991. *The Gāthās of Zarathushtra and the Other Old Avestan Texts*. Heidelberg: Winter.

Insler, Stanley. 1975. *The Gāthās of Zarathustra*. Leiden: Brill.

Kellens, Jean. 1974. *Les Noms-racines de l'Avesta*. Wiesbaden: Reichert.

Kellens, Jean. 1984. *Le Verbe avestique*. Wiesbaden: Reichert. (Supplement: *Liste du verbe avestique*, 1994.)

Kent, Roland. 1953. *Old Persian: Grammar, Texts, Lexicon*. 2nd edition. New Haven: American Oriental Society.

Reichelt, Hans. 1909. *Awestisches Elementarbuch*. Heidelberg: Winter.

Schmitt, Rüdiger, ed. 1989. *Compendium Linguarum Iranicarum*. Wiesbaden: Reichert.

Yarshater, Ehsan, ed. 1982– . *Encyclopedia Iranica*. London: Eisenbrauns.

Chapter 12: Greek

Allen, W. Sidney. 1987. *Vox Graeca: A Guide to the Pronunciation of Ancient Greek*. 3rd edition. Cambridge, UK: Cambridge University Press.

*Bartonek, Antonín. 2003. *Handbuch des mykenischen Griechisch*. Heidelberg: Winter.

Buck, Carl Darling. 1955. *The Greek Dialects: Grammar, Selected Inscriptions, Glossary*. Chicago: University of Chicago Press.

Chantraine, Pierre. 1953–8. *Grammaire homérique*. Paris: Klincksieck.

Chantraine, Pierre. 1968–80. *Dictionnaire étymologique de la langue grecque*. Paris: Klincksieck.

Devine, A. M., and Laurence D. Stephens. 1994. *The Prosody of Greek Speech*. Oxford: Oxford University Press.

Duhoux, Yves. 1984. *Introduction aux dialectes grecs anciens*. Louvain-la-Neuve: Cabay.

Frisk, Hjalmar. 1960–72. *Griechisches etymologisches Wörterbuch*. Heidelberg: Winter.

Heubeck, Alfred, et al., eds. 1988–92. *A Commentary on Homer's Odyssey*. Oxford: Oxford University Press.

*Hooker, J. T. 1980. *Linear B: An Introduction*. Bristol: Bristol Classical Press.

*Horrocks, Geoffrey. 1997. *Greek: A History of the Language and its Speakers*. London: Longman.

Kirk, G. S., ed. 1985–93. *The Iliad: A Commentary*. Cambridge, UK: Cambridge University Press.

Lejeune, Michel. 1972. *Phonétique historique du mycénien et du grec ancien*. Paris: Klincksieck.

*Meier-Brügger, Michael. 1992. *Griechische Sprachwissenschaft*. Berlin: de Gruyter.

Meillet, Antoine, and J. Vendryes. 1968. *Traité de grammaire comparée des langues classiques*. 4th edition. Paris: Champion.

Peters, Martin. 1980. *Untersuchungen zur Vertretung der indogermanischen Laryngale im Griechischen*. Vienna: Österreichische Akademie der Wissenschaften.

Risch, Ernst. 1974. *Wortbildung der homerischen Sprache*. 2nd edition. Berlin: de Gruyter.
Rix, Helmut. 1992. *Historische Grammatik des Griechischen: Laut- und Formenlehre*. 2nd edition. Darmstadt: Wissenschaftliche Buchgesellschaft.
Schmitt, Rüdiger. 1977. *Einführung in die griechischen Dialekte*. Darmstadt: Wissenschaftliche Buchgesellschaft.
Schwyzer, Eduard. 1939–71. *Griechische Grammatik*. Munich: Beck.
Sihler, Andrew. 1995. *New Comparative Grammar of Greek and Latin*. New York: Oxford University Press.
Ventris, Michael, and James Chadwick. 1973. *Documents in Mycenaean Greek*. Cambridge, UK: Cambridge University Press.

Chapter 13: Italic

*Allen, W. Sidney. 1989. *Vox Latina: A Guide to the Pronunciation of Classical Latin*. Cambridge, UK: Cambridge University Press.
Baldi, Philip. 1999. *The Foundations of Latin*. Berlin: de Gruyter.
Buck, Carl Darling. 1928. *A Grammar of Oscan and Umbrian*. Boston: Ginn.
Ernout, Alfred. 1947. *Recueil de textes latins archaïques*. 2nd edition. Paris: Klincksieck.
Ernout, Alfred, and Antoine Meillet. 1979. *Dictionnaire étymologique de la langue latine*. 4th edition revised by Jacques André. Paris: Klincksieck.
Giacomelli, Gabriella. 1963. *La lingua falisca*. Florence: Olschki.
Hartmann, Markus. 2005. *Die frühlateinischen Inschriften und ihre Datierung: Eine linguistisch-archäologisch-paläographische Untersuchung*. Bremen: Hempen.
Leumann, Manu. 1977. *Lateinische Laut- und Formenlehre*. Munich: Beck.
Marinetti, Anna. 1985. *Le iscrizioni sudpicene*. Florence: Olschki.
Meiser, Gerhard. 1986. *Lautgeschichte der umbrischen Sprache*. Innsbruck: Institut für Sprachwissenschaft der Universität Innsbruck.
Meiser, Gerhard. 1998. *Historische Laut- und Formenlehre der lateinischen Sprache*. Darmstadt: Wissenschaftliche Buchgesellschaft.
*Meyer-Lübke, Wilhelm. 1935. *Romanisches etymologisches Wörterbuch*. 3rd edition. Heidelberg: Winter.
Palmer, L. R. 1954. *The Latin Language*. London: Faber & Faber.
Poccetti, Paolo. 1979. *Nuovi documenti italici a complemento del Manuale di E. Vetter*. Pisa: Giardini.
Poultney, James. 1959. *The Bronze Tables of Iguvium*. Baltimore: American Philological Association.
Rix, Helmut. 2002. *Sabellische Texte: Die Texte des Oskischen, Umbrischen, und Südpikenischen*. Heidelberg: Winter.
Schrijver, Peter. 1991. *The Reflexes of the Proto-Indo-European Laryngeals in Latin*. Amsterdam: Rodopi.
*Sommer, Ferdinand. 1977. *Handbuch der lateinischen Laut- und Formenlehre*, vol. 1, *Lautlehre*. 4th edition, revised by Raimund Pfister. Heidelberg: Winter.
Untermann, Jürgen. 2000. *Wörterbuch des Oskisch-Umbrischen*. Heidelberg: Winter.
*Väänänen, Veikko. 1981. *Introduction au latin vulgaire*. 3rd edition. Paris: Klincksieck.
Vetter, Emil. 1953. *Handbuch der italischen Dialekte*. Heidelberg: Winter.
Vine, Brent. 1993. *Studies in Archaic Latin Inscriptions*. Innsbruck: Institut für Sprachwissenschaft der Universität Innsbruck.
Wachter, Rudolf. 1987. *Altlateinische Inschriften*. Bern: Lang.

Walde, Alois, and J. B. Hofmann. 1938–56. *Lateinisches etymologisches Wörterbuch*. Heidelberg: Winter.

Wallace, Rex E. 2007. *The Sabellic Languages of Ancient Italy*. Munich: LINCOM.

Weiss, Michael. To appear. *Outline of the Comparative Grammar of Latin*. Ann Arbor: Beech Stave.

Chapter 14: Celtic

Delamarre, Xavier. 2001. *Dictionnaire de la langue gauloise*. Paris: Errance.

Duval, Paul-Marie, ed. 1985–2002. *Recueil des inscriptions gauloises*. Paris: Centre National de la Recherche Scientifique.

Evans, D. Simon. 1964. *A Grammar of Middle Welsh*. Dublin: Institute for Advanced Studies.

Forsyth, Katherine. 1997. *Language in Pictland*. Utrecht: Keltische Draak.

Jackson, Kenneth. 1953. *Language and History in Early Britain: A Chronological Survey of the Brittonic Languages, First to Twelfth Century A.D.* Cambridge, MA: Harvard University Press.

Lewis, Henry, and Holger Pedersen. 1937. *A Concise Comparative Celtic Grammar*. Göttingen: Vandenhoeck und Ruprecht.

*McCone, Kim. 1991. *The Indo-European Origins of the Old Irish Nasal Presents, Subjunctives and Futures*. Innsbruck: Institut für Sprachwissenschaft der Universität Innsbruck.

McCone, Kim. 1996. *Towards a Relative Chronology of Ancient and Medieval Celtic Sound Change*. Maynooth: Department of Old Irish, St. Patrick's College.

McManus, Damian. 1991. *A Guide to Ogam*. Maynooth: An Sagart.

Meid, Wolfgang. 1992. *Gaulish Inscriptions*. Budapest: Archaeological Institute of the Hungarian Academy of Sciences.

Meid, Wolfgang. 1994. *Celtiberian Inscriptions*. Budapest: Archaeological Institute of the Hungarian Academy of Sciences.

Pedersen, Holger. 1909–13. *Vergleichende Grammatik der keltischen Sprachen*. Göttingen: Vandenhoeck und Ruprecht.

*Schmidt, Karl Horst, ed. 1977. *Indogermanisch und Keltisch. Kolloquium der Indogermanischen Gesellschaft am 16. und 17. Februar in Bonn*. Innsbruck: Institut für Sprachwissenschaft der Universität Innsbruck.

Schrijver, Peter. 1995. *Studies in British Celtic Historical Phonology*. Amsterdam: Rodopi.

Schumacher, Stefan. 2004. *Die keltischen Primärverben: Ein vergleichendes, etymologisches und morphologisches Lexikon*. Innsbruck: Institut für Sprachen und Literaturen der Universität Innsbruck.

*Strachan, John. 1949. *Old-Irish Paradigms and Selections from the Old-Irish Glosses*. Dublin: Royal Irish Academy.

Thurneysen, Rudolf. 1980. *A Grammar of Old Irish*. 2nd edition, translated and revised by D. A. Binchy and Osborn Bergin. Dublin: Institute for Advanced Studies.

Untermann, Jürgen. 1997. *Monumenta Linguarum Hispanicarum*. Vol. 4: *Die tartessischen, keltiberischen, und lusitanischen Inschriften*. Vol. 5: *Wörterbuch der keltiberischen Inschriften*. Wiesbaden: Reichert.

Vendryes, Jean, and P.-Y. Lambert. 1959– . *Lexique étymologique de l'irlandais ancien*. Dublin: Institute for Advanced Studies.

*Villar, F. 1995. *A New Interpretation of Celtiberian Grammar*. Innsbruck: Institut für Sprachwissenschaft der Universität Innsbruck.

Watkins, Calvert. 1962. *Indo-European Origins of the Celtic Verb I. The Sigmatic Aorist*. Dublin: Institute for Advanced Studies.

Chapter 15: Germanic

Antonsen, Elmer H. 1975. *A Concise Grammar of the Older Runic Inscriptions.* Tübingen: Niemeyer.

Bammesberger, Alfred. 1986. *Der Aufbau des urgermanischen Verbalsystems.* Heidelberg: Winter.

Bammesberger, Alfred. 1990. *Die Morphologie des urgermanischen Nomens.* Heidelberg: Winter.

*Bandle, Oskar et al., eds. 2005. *The Nordic Languages: An International Handbook of the History of the North Germanic Languages.* Berlin: de Gruyter.

Braune, Wilhelm. 1987. *Althochdeutsche Grammatik.* 14th edition, revised by H. Eggers. Tübingen: Niemeyer.

Braune, Wilhelm. 1994. *Althochdeutsches Lesebuch.* 17th edition, revised by Ernst A. Ebbinghaus. Tübingen: Niemeyer.

Braune, Wilhelm. 2004. *Gotische Grammatik.* 20th edition, revised by Frank Heidermanns. Tübingen: Niemeyer.

Campbell, Alistair. 1959. *Old English Grammar.* Oxford: Oxford University Press.

*Cathey, James E. 2002. *Heliand: Text and Commentary.* Morgantown: West Virginia University Press.

de Vries, Jan. 1962. *Altnordisches etymologisches Wörterbuch.* 2nd edition. Leiden: Brill.

Gordon, E. V. 1962. *An Introduction to Old Norse.* 2nd edition. Oxford: Oxford University Press.

Green, Dennis H. 1998. *Language and History in the Early Germanic World.* Cambridge: Cambridge University Press.

Holthausen, F. 1921. *Altsächsisches Elementarbuch.* Heidelberg: Winter.

Holthausen, F. 1934. *Altenglisches etymologisches Wörterbuch.* Heidelberg: Winter.

Kluge, Friedrich. 2002. *Etymologisches Wörterbuch der deutschen Sprache.* 24th edition, revised by Elmar Seebold. Berlin: de Gruyter.

Krause, Wolfgang. 1968. *Handbuch des Gotischen.* 3rd edition. Munich: Beck.

Krause, Wolfgang. 1971. *Die Sprache der urnordischen Runeninschriften.* Heidelberg: Winter.

Krause, Wolfgang, and Herbert Jankuhn. 1966. *Die Runeninschriften im älteren Futhark.* Göttingen: Vandenhoeck und Ruprecht.

*Kyes, Robert L. 1969. *The Old Low Franconian Psalms and Glosses.* Ann Arbor: University of Michigan Press.

Lehmann, Winfred P. 1986. *A Gothic Etymological Dictionary.* Leiden: Brill.

Nielsen, Hans Frede. 1989. *The Germanic Languages: Origins and Early Dialectal Interrelations.* Tuscaloosa: University of Alabama Press.

Nielsen, Hans Frede. 2000. *The Early Runic Language of Scandinavia.* Heidelberg: Winter.

Noreen, Adolf. 1923. *Altisländische und altnorwegische Grammatik.* 4th edition. Halle: Niemeyer.

Prokosch, Edward. 1939. *A Comparative Germanic Grammar.* Philadelphia: Linguistic Society of America.

Robinson, Orrin W. III. 1992. *Old English and Its Closest Relatives: A Survey of the Germanic Languages.* Stanford: Stanford University Press.

Seebold, Elmar. 1970. *Vergleichendes und etymologisches Wörterbuch der germanischen starken Verben.* The Hague: Mouton.

Streitberg, Wilhelm. 2000. *Die gotische Bibel.* 7th edition. Heidelberg: Winter.

Chapter 16: Armenian

Clackson, James. 1994. *The Linguistic Relationship between Armenian and Greek*. Oxford: Blackwell.

Godel, Robert. 1975. *An Introduction to the Study of Classical Armenian*. Wiesbaden: Reichert.

Hübschmann, Heinrich. 1895–7. *Armenische Grammatik*, Teil 1: *Armenische Etymologie*. Leipzig: Breitkopf und Härtel.

Klingenschmitt, Gert. 1982. *Das altarmenische Verbum*. Wiesbaden: Reichert.

Lamberterie, Charles. 1992. *Introduction à l'arménien classique*. *LALIES* 10:234–89.

Matzinger, Joachim. 2005. *Untersuchungen zum altarmenischen Nomen: Die Flexion des Substantivs*. Munich: Röll.

Meillet, Antoine. 1936. *Esquisse d'une grammaire comparée de l'arménien classique*. 2nd edition. Vienna: Mékhitharistes.

Meillet, Antoine. 1962–77. *Études de linguistique et de philologie arméniennes*. Louvain: Imprimerie Orientaliste.

Olsen, Birgit Anette. 1999. *The Noun in Biblical Armenian: Origin and Word-Formation*. Berlin: de Gruyter.

Schmitt, Rüdiger. 1981. *Grammatik des Klassisch-Armenischen mit sprachvergleichenden Erläuterungen*. Innsbruck: Institut für Sprachwissenschaft der Universität Innsbruck.

*Solta, Georg R. 1960. *Die Stellung des Armenischen im Kreise der indogermanischen Sprachen*. Vienna: Mechitharisten-Buchdruck.

*Thomson, Robert. 1989. *An Introduction to Classical Armenian*. 2nd edition. Delmar: Caravan.

Chapter 17: Tocharian

Adams, Douglas Q. 1988. *Tocharian Historical Phonology and Morphology*. New Haven: American Oriental Society.

Adams, Douglas Q. 1999. *A Dictionary of Tocharian B*. Amsterdam: Rodopi.

Krause, Wolfgang, and Werner Thomas. 1960–4. *Tocharisches Elementarbuch*. Heidelberg: Winter.

Mallory, J. P., and Victor H. Mair. 2000. *The Tarim Mummies: Ancient China and the Mystery of the Earliest Peoples from the West*. New York: Thames & Hudson.

Pinault, Georges-Jean. 1989. "Introduction au tokharien." *LALIES* 7:1–224.

Ringe, Donald. 1996. *On the Chronology of Sound Changes in Tocharian*, vol. 1: *From Proto-Indo-European to Proto-Tocharian*. New Haven: American Oriental Society.

*Schlerath, Bernfried, ed. 1994. *Tocharisch. Akten der Fachtagung der Indogermanischen Gesellschaft, Berlin, September 1990*. Reykjavík: Málvísindastofnun Háskóla Íslands.

Sieg, Emil, and Wilhelm Siegling. 1921. *Tocharische Sprachreste*. Berlin: de Gruyter.

Sieg, Emil, and Wilhelm Siegling. 1949–53. *Tocharische Sprachreste, Sprache B*. Göttingen: Vandenhoeck und Ruprecht.

Thomas, Werner. 1983. *Tocharische Sprachreste, Sprache B*. Göttingen: Vandenhoeck und Ruprecht.

van Windekens, A. J. 1976–82. *Le tokharien confronté avec les autres langues indo-européennes*. Louvain: Centre international de dialectologie générale.

Chapter 18: Balto-Slavic

Carlton, Terence R. 1990. *Introduction to the Phonological History of the Slavic Languages.* Columbus: Slavica.

Endzelīns, Jānis. 1971. *Jānis Endzelīns' Comparative Phonology and Morphology of the Baltic Languages.* Translated by William R. Schmalstieg and Benjamiņš Jēgers. The Hague: Mouton.

Fraenkel, Ernst. 1962–5. *Litauisches etymologisches Wörterbuch.* Heidelberg: Winter.

Garde, Paul. 1976. *Histoire de l'accentuation slave.* Paris: Institut d'Études Slaves.

*Illič-Svityč, V. M. 1979. *Nominal Accentuation in Baltic and Slavic.* Translated by R. L. Leed and R. F. Feldstein. Cambridge, MA: MIT Press.

Karulis, Konstantīns. 1992. *Latviešu etimoloģijas vārdnīca.* Riga: Avots.

Leskien, August. 1990. *Handbuch der altbulgarischen (altkirchenslavischen) Sprache.* 10th edition, revised by Johannes Schröpfer. Heidelberg: Winter.

Lunt, Horace. 2001. *Old Church Slavonic Grammar.* 7th edition. Berlin: de Gruyter.

Maziulis, Vytautas. 1988–97. *Prūsų kalbos etimologijos žodynas.* Vilnius: Mokslas.

Meillet, Antoine. 1965. *Le slave commun.* 2nd edition. Paris: Champion.

Petit, Daniel. 2003. *Apophonie et catégories grammaticales dans les langues baltiques.* Leuven: Peeters.

*Poljakov, Oleg. 1995. *Das Problem der balto-slavischen Sprachgemeinschaft.* Frankfurt: Lang.

Schmalstieg, William R. 1974. *An Old Prussian Grammar.* University Park: Pennsylvania State University Press.

Senn, Alfred. 1957–66. *Handbuch der litauischen Sprache.* Heidelberg: Winter.

Stang, Christian. 1942. *Das slavische und baltische Verbum.* Oslo: Dybwad.

Stang, Christian. 1965. *Slavonic Accentuation.* 2nd edition. Oslo: Universitetsforlaget.

Stang, Christian. 1966. *Vergleichende Grammatik der baltischen Sprachen.* Oslo: Universitetsforlaget. (Supplement: *Ergänzungsband*, 1975.)

Toporov, V. N. 1975– . *Prusskij jazyk.* Moscow: Nauka.

Trautmann, R. 1910. *Die altpreussischen Sprachdenkmäler.* Göttingen: Vandenhoeck und Ruprecht.

Trubachev, O. N. 1974– . *Ètimologicheskij slovar' slavjanskix jazykov.* Moscow: Nauka.

Vaillant, André. 1950–77. *Grammaire comparée des langues slaves.* Lyon: IAC.

Vasmer, Max. 1953–8. *Russisches etymologisches Wörterbuch.* Heidelberg: Winter. (Translated into Russian and revised as *Ètimologicheskij slovar' russkogo jazyka* [Moscow: Progress], 1964.)

*Winter, Werner. 1976. "The distribution of short and long vowels in stems of the type Lith. *esti* : *vèsti* : *mèsti* and OCS *jasti* : *vesti* : *mesti* in Baltic and Slavic languages." In Jacek Fisiak (ed.), *Recent Developments in Historical Phonology.* The Hague: Mouton, pp. 431–46.

Zinkevičius, Zigmas. 1996. *The History of the Lithuanian Language.* Vilnius: Mokslo ir enciklopedijų leidykla.

Chapter 19: Albanian

Buchholz, Oda, and Wilfried Fiedler. 1987. *Albanische Grammatik.* Leipzig: VEB Verlag Enzyklopädie.

Demiraj, Bardhyl. 1997. *Albanische Etymologien: Untersuchungen zum albanischen Wortschatz.* Amsterdam: Rodopi.

Demiraj, Shaban. 1993. *Historische Grammatik der albanischen Sprache.* Vienna: Österreichische Akademie der Wissenschaften.

Fiedler, Wilfried. 2004. *Das albanische Verbalsystem in der Sprache des Gjon Buzuku (1555).* Prishtina: Akademia e Shkencave dhe e Arteve e Kosovës.

Fox, Leonard. 1989. *Kanuni i Lekë Dukagjinit: The Code of Lekë Dukagjini.* New York: Gjonlekaj.

Hamp, Eric P. 1977. "A far-out equation." In Irén Hegedüs et al., eds., *Indo-European, Nostratic, and Beyond: Festschrift for Vitalij V. Shevoroshkin.* Washington: Institute for the Study of Man, pp. 94–105.

Huld, Martin E. 1984. *Basic Albanian Etymologies.* Columbus: Slavica.

Matzinger, Joachim. 2006. *Der altalbanische Text Mbsuame e krështerë (Dottrina cristiana) des Lekë Matrënga von 1592: Eine Einführung in die albanische Sprachwissenschaft.* Dettelbach: Röll.

Meyer, Gustav. 1891. *Etymologisches Wörterbuch der albanesischen Sprache.* Strassburg: Trübner.

Newmark, Leonard, ed. 1998. *Albanian–English Dictionary.* Oxford: Oxford University Press.

Newmark, Leonard, Philip Hubbard, and Peter Prifti. 1982. *Standard Albanian: A Reference Grammar for Students.* Stanford: Stanford University Press.

Orel, Vladimir. 1998. *Albanian Etymological Dictionary.* Leiden: Brill.

Orel, Vladimir. 2000. *A Concise Historical Grammar of the Albanian Language.* Leiden: Brill.

Sanz Ledesma, Manuel. 1996. *El albanés: Gramática, historia, textos.* Madrid: Ediciones Clásicas.

Chapter 20: Fragmentary Languages

Brixhe, Claude, and Michel Lejeune. 1984. *Corpus des inscriptions paléo-phrygiennes.* Paris: Recherche sur les civilisations.

de Simone, Carlo, and Simona Marchesini. 2002. *Monumenta linguae Messapicae.* Wiesbaden: Reichert.

Detschew, Dimiter. 1957. *Die thrakischen Sprachreste.* Vienna: Rohrer.

Haas, Otto. 1966. *Die phrygischen Sprachdenkmäler.* Sofia: Académie bulgare des sciences.

Kalléris, J. N. 1954–76. *Les anciens Macédoniens: Étude linguistique et historique.* Athens: Institut français d'Athènes.

Katičić, Radoslav. 1976. *Ancient Languages of the Balkans.* The Hague: Mouton.

Krahe, Hans. 1955–64. *Die Sprache der Illyrier.* Wiesbaden: Harrassowitz.

Lejeune, Michel. 1974. *Manuel de la langue vénète.* Heidelberg: Winter.

Neumann, Günter. 1988. *Phrygisch und Griechisch.* Vienna: Österreichische Akademie der Wissenschaften.

Orel, Vladimir. 1997. *The Language of the Phrygians.* Delmar: Caravan.

Untermann, Jürgen. 1997. *Monumenta Linguarum Hispanicarum*, vol. 4: *Die tartessischen, keltiberischen, und lusitanischen Inschriften.* Wiesbaden: Reichert.

Subject Index

a, roots containing, 78; ablaut of, 81
ablative, 113; in Albanian, 452, 453; in Anatolian, 172; in Armenian, 389, 390; in Avestan, 234; in Balto-Slavic, 425; in Celtiberian, 313; in Greek, 261, 313, 425; in Hittite, 182, 313; in Italic, 281; in Latin, 286; in Messapic, 467; in Old Persian, 234, 239; in PIE, 116, 118, 127–8, 129, 133; in Sanskrit, 216; in Tocharian, 406
ablaut, 79–81; origin of, 81; in thematic nouns, 131; in Albanian, 454; in Germanic verbs, 345; in Hittite, 180–1; in Modern English, 360–1; in Balto-Slavic, 418
absolute (Celtic verb), 318, 323–5
absolute constructions, 165
accent, 68, 192, 213, 216, 241, 244, 257–8, 278, 341, 343, 345–6, 376, 388, 406, 416–18, 424, 430, 431, 435–7; nature of, in PIE, 68; *see also* mobile accent; prosody; retraction of accent
accent-ablaut classes, PIE, 119–22
accent classes (Balto-Slavic), 419, 435–7
accented zero-grades, 81
Accius, 282
accusative, 113; affected by Stang's Law, 70, 121, 133; in Albanian, 452; in Armenian, 388, 389; in Baltic, 435; in Germanic, 343; in Greek, 261, 262; in Hittite, 182; in Lusitanian, 469; in Luvian, 188; in Old English, 361; in Phrygian, 462; in PIE, 115, 117, 127, 128; in Sanskrit, 216–17; in Slavic, 425–6; in Tocharian, 406; in Vulgar Latin, 288
Achaemenid dynasty, 202, 236, 238, 302, 382
Achilles, 33
acquisition, language, 5
acrostatic, 96, 120, 121, 122, 187
acrostatic presents *see* Narten presents
active voice, 89–90
acute accent: in Greek, 257; in Lithuanian, 435
acute intonation: in Balto-Slavic, 416–17, 424, 435
Adea, Gulielmus, 448
adessive, 435
adjectives: formation of, 134–5; comparison of, 135–6, 344; in Germanic, 344
admirative mood, 453
adverbs, 147
Aeolic, 249, 264–5
Aequian, 304
Aesop, 209
Æthelberht of Kent, 358
affection *see* vowel affection
Afrikaans, 371
afterlife, 28, 45
Agamemnon, 30
agent nouns, 124
Agnean *see* Tocharian
Agni, 27
agreement, subject-verb, 131, 158
agriculture, 41
Ahura Mazda, 229
a-infection, 321
ā-infection, 328
Ajax, 37
Akkadian, 177, 178, 238, 239
Akkadogram, 177–8
Aktionsart, 91, 102
Alaksandus of Wilusa, 186
Alanic, 241, 244
Albanian, 9, 11, 21, 383, 446, 448, 465; dialects, 446; law, 448; morphology, 94, 118, 245, 407, 452–5; phonology, 59, 386, 448–52; syntax, 455; *see also* Geg; Old Albanian; Tosk

Word Index

This index contains reconstructed and attested forms for which historical information or paradigms are given. The order of branches and languages is the same as the chapter order. Wherever possible, inflected forms of the same word are listed together; for PIE, inflected and derived forms are normally listed under their root. Phrases are given their own entries. Except for PIE (see below), words are listed in English alphabetical order, and diacritics and parentheses are ignored. Where they occur, β δ γ λ θ χ are alphabetized as b d g l th x, and ə þ ð ƕ ŋ as e th dh hw ng. Language abbreviations are on p. xix.

I. Proto-Indo-European

Alphabetical order: a/ā b bh d dh e/ē g ĝ gh ĝh g^w g^wh H h_1 h_2 h_3 i/ī i̯ k k̂ k^w l/l̥ m/m̥ n/n̥ o/ō p r/r̥ s t u/ū u̯ z

*abel-, 45, 79
*ag^{w}nos, 79, 129
*ai̯er-, 364
*al-i̯o-, 145
*anĝhos-, 283
*apo, 149
*at-, 422
*bel-, 57
*bhāĝos, 126
*bhak̂ā, 451
*bhe-bhru-, 125
*bheh$_2$-, 131; *bheh$_2$-mi, 391; *bheh$_2$-ti, 267
*bheidh-, 449; *bhidh-tā, 449; *bhoidh-es-, 449
*bhendh-, 342
*bher-, 58, 98, 105, 106, 364, 386, 391, 415, 451; *bher-oh$_2$, 311, 424; *bhereti, 321, 322; *bher-onti, 205; *ébherom, 254; *ebheret, 101, 254, 388, 392; *bhérete, 105; *bhér-o-ih$_1$-m̥, 107; *bhér-e, 105; *bher-ont-, 108; *bhoro-, 386, 393
*bherĝh-, 315; *bhr̥ĝh-, 385; *bhr̥ĝhent-, 204; *bhr̥ĝh-ro-, 404
*bherHĝeh$_2$, 417
*bheudh-, 410, 423; *bheudh-eti, 210; *bhudh-tó-, 211
*bhi-n-d-, 279; *bhid-to-, 277; *bhid-nó-, 109
*bhléĝh-mn̥, 122
*bhleĝh-mṓ(n), 122
*bhos-o-, 80
*bhrātēr see *bhreh$_2$tēr
*bhreh$_2$tēr (*bhrātēr), *bhreh$_2$ter-, 124, 204, 342, 402, 405
*bhreu-, 125, 463
*bhug-i̯e-, 279
*bhuH-, 80, 279, 300, 425, 434; *bhu(H)-e-, 279
*dak̂-, 403
*de, 150
*deh$_3$-, 77, 83, 91, 97, 131, 386, 397, 449; *de-deh$_3$-, *de-dh$_3$-, 83, 97, 424; *deh$_3$s, 233; *dh$_3$-t, 451; *dh$_3$-tó-, 255; *dh$_3$-to-, 278; *deh$_3$-rom, 63; *déh$_3$-tōr, 124; *dh$_3$-tḗr, 124; *dh$_3$-ti-, 62
*deiĝh-ā, 449
*dēik̂-s-, 67
*deiu̯-ó-s, 130; *deiu̯-ons, 232, 441
*dek̂m̥, 62, 125, 146, 203, 385, 386, 410; *dek̂m̥-t-, 125, 439; *dek̂m̥mo-, 147
*dem- 'build', 83
*dem- 'house', 121; *dóm-s, 121; *dem-s, 83, 121; *dm̥(m)-és, 121
*dems potis, 121, 232
*dens-, 179
*derk̂-, 254
*din-, 428
*di̯eus (*di̯ēus), *di̯eu̯-, 67, 72, 116, 121, 283; *deiu̯-, 130; *di̯ēm, 70, 121; *diu̯-os, 463
*di̯ēus ph$_2$tēr, 465
*diu̯ots, 193

II. Anatolian

Common Anatolian

Hittite

Luvian (Cuneiform unmarked)

Lycian

Palaic

Other (Lydian unmarked)

III. Indo-Iranian

Common Indo-Iranian

Indic

MITANNI INDIC

SANSKRIT

PĀLI

HINDI

Iranian

AVESTAN

OTHER (OLD PERSIAN UNMARKED)

IV. Greek (Attic unmarked)

V. Italic

Latin

Faliscan

Oscan

Umbrian

South Picene

Romance (French unmarked)

VI. Celtic

Common Celtic

Continental Celtic (Gaulish unmarked)

Insular Celtic

GOIDELIC (OLD IRISH UNMARKED)

BRITISH CELTIC

WELSH (MODERN UNMARKED)

OTHER BRITTONIC (MIDDLE BRETON UNMARKED)

VII. Germanic

Prehistoric and Inscriptional Germanic

Modern English

Old High German (and Frankish)

Middle and Modern High German (Modern unmarked)

Other West Germanic (Old Saxon unmarked)

North Germanic (Old Norse unmarked)

VIII. Armenian

IX. Tocharian

Tocharian A

Tocharian B

X. Balto-Slavic

Common Slavic

Old Church Slavonic

Russian

Other Slavic

Baltic

LITHUANIAN

LATVIAN

OLD PRUSSIAN

XI. Albanian (Tosk unmarked)

XII. Unaffiliated

Illyrian

Phrygian

Thracian

Macedonian

Venetic

Messapic

Sicel

Elymian

Lusitanian

XIII. Non-Indo-European

(Akk. Akkadian; Ass. Assyrian; Bab. Babylonian; Etr. = Etruscan; Finn. Finnish; Geor. Georgian; Heb. Hebrew; Hurr. Hurrian; Phoen. Phoenician; Sem. Semitic)